The Study of Urbanization

BOOKS BY P. M. HAUSER AND L. F. SCHNORE

The Study of Urbanization

BY P. M. HAUSER AND W. R. LEONARD

Government Statistics for Business
Use, 2nd Edition

THE STUDY OF URBANIZATION

EDITED BY

Philip M. Hauser *University of Chicago*

Leo F. Schnore *University of Wisconsin*

John Wiley & Sons, Inc., New York · London · Sydney

THIRD PRINTING, MAY, 1967

Library of Congress Catalog Card Number: 65-24223
Printed in the United States of America

PREFACE

This book originated in an interdisciplinary conference held by the Social Science Research Council on May 12, 1958, to explore the need for a committee on research on urbanization. It was the consensus of the participants that such a committee might serve a number of useful functions. Accordingly, the Council appointed a Committee on Urbanization, which first met on October 24, 1958. The original members were: Philip M. Hauser, chairman; Norton S. Ginsburg; Eric E. Lampard; Oscar Lewis; Wallace S. Sayre; Leo F. Schnore; Gideon Sjoberg; Raymond Vernon; and Beverly Duncan, secretary. In the course of the Committee's existence from 1958 to 1964, some changes in membership occurred. The pressure of other activities forced Raymond Vernon and Beverly Duncan to resign in 1961, and subsequently Edgar M. Hoover, Nathan Keyfitz, and Wilbur R. Thompson were added to the Committee.

The Committee first undertook to review the major frameworks for research on urbanization in the disciplines represented among its members, namely: economics, geography, history, political science, social anthropology, and sociology. The interdisciplinary exchanges that followed, often critical, animated, and provocative, were a stimulating educational experience for all. We learned much from one another, albeit occasionally grudgingly. We concluded that the gaps in knowledge about the antecedents and consequences of urbanization are more impressive than the available research findings; that many of the extant generalizations about urbanization either as a dependent or independent variable do not have adequate empirical justification; and that what is known is very much subject to the limitations of historicism, being based essentially on limited observations over time and space mainly in Western cultures. On the positive side, we became convinced that much was to be gained from the promotion of interdisciplinary and cross-cultural research and that there is an especially fertile field for the study of urbanization in the developing areas.

As our deliberations progressed, we became aware that it would be useful to make available to others at least part of the materials on which they were based. This book is the result, supplemented by papers prepared at the request of the Committee to fill conspicuous gaps. Charles N. Glaab accepted our commission to prepare the historical bibliographical survey that constitutes Chapter 2; Harold M. Mayer undertook the survey of urban geography contained in Chapter 3; and Brian J. L. Berry developed the essay on frontiers of geographical research on urbanism in Chapter 11. Needless to say, the Committee is grateful to these scholars who contributed so much to this overview of the status of urban study in the social sciences.

The Committee is especially indebted to Beverly Duncan (1958–1961) and Leo F. Schnore (1961–1964), who successively served as secretary. Their insightful summaries of the Committee's proceedings often made our deliberations appear possessed of greater wisdom than actually may have been the case. The Committee also is greatly appreciative of Paul Webbink's contribution, which ranged from planning Committee meetings to perceptive and sagacious participation in the discussions.

As Chairman of the Committee on Urbanization over its six years of activity, I take this opportunity to express gratitude to my Committee colleagues for their unstinted cooperation, endurance, and forbearance during our many discussions and in the preparation of their chapters. Finally, I must acknowledge my personal gratitude, as well as that of the Committee, to Leo F. Schnore who as co-editor of this book bore the major part of the time-consuming and arduous editorial task.

PHILIP M. HAUSER
Chairman, Committee on Urbanization
Social Science Research Council

Chicago, Illinois
May 1965

CONTENTS

The Study of Urbanization

1

Urbanization: An Overview

Philip M. Hauser

The Bases of Urbanization

The origin of the urban agglomeration as a form of human settlement is not precisely known. There is, however, a literature on the origin and development of cities, based in part on legend, myth, and speculation, in part on archaeology, and in part on the known origins of cities that have emerged during the period of recorded history. It seems clear that the emergence and development of the city was necessarily a function of four factors: (1) the size of the total population; (2) the control of natural environment; (3) technological development; and (4) developments in social organization.[1]

Population size is necessarily a factor in urban development because to permit any agglomeration of human beings there must be some minimum number to sustain group life; and to achieve large urban aggregations relatively large total populations are required. Similarly, the environment must be amenable to control in the sense that it meets at least minimal requirements for aggregative living. Thus, although earliest cities apparently were located in river valleys and alluvial plains, the ingenuity of man has permitted the use of a wide variety of natural environments for urban development. In any case, the natural environment, by means of relatively primitive technology, provided the necessities for survival—food, shelter, protective clothing, and, of course, an adequate water supply.

Permanent human settlement had to await technological innovation—the inventions of the neolithic revolution. It was only with the achievement of domesticated plants and animals that it became possible for man to lead a relatively settled existence. Apart from these requirements, however, other techniques were involved and certainly played a major role in determining the size that the agglomeration could reach.

1

Foremost among these was the development of agricultural technology to a point where a surplus was possible, that is, a food supply in excess of the requirements of the cultivators themselves. The emergence of the crafts and their proliferation was necessarily a function of the size of the surplus, permitting some persons to engage, at least part time, in activities other than agricultural. With improved technology, including the wheel, the road, irrigation, cultivation, stock breeding, and improvements in fishing, the surplus became large enough to support a sizable number of persons freed from the production of food. Certain it is that developments of this type were associated with the first units of settlement ten times and more the size of any known neolithic villages, as revealed in the archaeological finds in Egypt, Mesopotamia, and the Indus Basin.[2]

The development of relatively large agglomerations of population required more, however, than an increasingly efficient technology. Relatively large aggregations of population required more complex social organization, including improved communication, and social and political mechanisms permitting some form of exchange among the emergent specialists, agricultural and nonagricultural. Chief among the social organizational requirements was a working arrangement between the population agglomeration and the hinterland, its source of food and raw materials. In the history of cities there is evidence of great variation in forms of organization by means of which integration and coordination of activities was achieved between city and hinterland and within the city. The rise and fall of empires, as recorded in ancient history, may be read in large measure as a chronicle of developments in social organization by means of which the ancient cities acquired a hinterland. The Roman Legion may be interpreted as a form of social organization enabling the city to achieve effective working arrangements with a hinterland.[3] The same function centuries later was performed by emergence of the market mechanism, including money as an instrumentality of exchange.

It was not until the nineteenth century that mankind had achieved both the level of technological development and social organization that permitted the relatively widespread appearance of very large cities. On the technological side the developments included techniques that greatly increased productivity in agriculture as well as in nonagricultural commodities. A critical factor in increased productivity was, of course, the utilization of nonhuman energy in production—the emergence of the machine, powered first by water or wind, then by steam, and now by mineral fuels or electricity derived therefrom, with atomic energy in prospect.[4] Technological advance proceeded at an exponential rate under the impetus of the "scientific revolution."

Social organizational developments paralleled the technological. Strong central governments evolved, bringing relative peace and tranquility to increasingly large areas and permitting the development of local, regional, national, and international markets. Increasing division of labor and specialization were accompanied by various forms of formal and informal organization providing essential integration and coordination. New social institutions evolved or were invented to meet the needs of the increasingly complex and interdependent social and economic orders. A full account of the emergence of the large city in the context of its antecedents is yet to be achieved, if indeed it ever can be documented. But the available literature certainly provides a basis for at least pointing to the major factors associated with the emergence of the city and of relatively highly urbanized nations.[5]

In a neo-evolutionary approach, Gras has outlined with broad strokes the relationship between economic development and settlement or habitation patterns in his account of economic history.[6] He has fused historical ways of making a living with technological developments, on the one hand, and with developments in human settlement on the other. Gras writes the history of Western civilization in terms of this joint classification. He delineates five stages or periods: (1) the collectional economy; (2) the cultural-nomadic economy; (3) the settled village economy; (4) the town economy; and (5) the metropolitan economy.

The settled village economy was possible only with the development of agriculture as the dominant way of making a living. The town economy was a function of increased agricultural productivity, the proliferation of the crafts, more efficient transport, and the development of trade. The metropolitan economy was a product of the combination of technological and organizational changes associated with industrialization and the emergence of the metropolitan complex with the large city as a nucleus for an interdependent hinterland. Although Gras's five-stage scheme of urban development is open to serious question, a general neo-evolutionary interpretation of urban development has not been attempted since Gras, indicating, perhaps, a serious gap in the literature.

Economic history as seen by Gras is, in effect, an analysis of the pattern of human habitation considered as a dependent variable. Lampard approaches the problem in the same way in his treatment of urban-industrial development, following the stages, if not the language, of Geddes.[7] The antecedents of the preindustrial city may be seen in his description of cities in Europe and America toward the end of the sixteenth century: "Urban centers were court cities, cathedral cities, fortress cities, markets, ports, country towns, and mere villages. Many, of course, were composites of several types." The preindustrial European city was "limited (dominated) by the needs and capacities of the rural hinterland and a highly stratified society." The preindustrial European city was "essentially a loose-knit system of food economies centering on a few relatively large mercantile-administrative capitals, with a growing inter-regional commerce but no marked territorial division of labor."

The industrial city was the product of acceleration in agricultural productivity and industrial technology during the eighteenth century. It was "a major outlet for capital accumulated in commercialized agricultural production." Its development was facilitated by the emergence of coal and steam as sources of power and particularly by the centripetal force of the steam engine. Factories and population piled up in the industrial city as is documented in the history of English industrial cities such as Manchester and Birmingham. This history was paralleled during the first half of the nineteenth century in France, the Low Countries, and northeastern United States. Major ingredients in the very rapid development of industrial cities in Europe and the United States included the utilization of new fuels as sources of non-human energy, new materials, mechanical aids, improved transport and communication, and a closer integration of productive and managerial processes.

The twentieth century "metropolitan city" was the product of the extensive application of science to industry, the diffusion of electric power and the advent of the automobile. The metropolitan city, as compared with the industrial city, was the product of the accelerating technological revolution that permeated virtually all phases of life. Whereas the steam engine and the belt and the pulley had set centripetal forces into motion creating dense population around factory plants, the combination of electric power, the automobile, and the telephone set centrifugal forces in motion which simultaneously diffused population and industry widely over the landscape and permitted larger agglomerations of both. The metropolitan city is a nucleus or core of a metropolitan area which has become a basic economic and social unit not only in regional and national economies but also in the world economy. It is a highly complex and interdependent unit binding centralization with decentralization and specialization and differentiation of function with integration and coordinating mechanisms.

The emergence of the metropolitan community as a basic unit of economic and social organization should not obscure the relation of the metropolitan city to the larger economy and society of which it is a part. Technological and social organizational developments which have produced the metropolitan city have also produced "systems" of such cities. Recognition of a "system" in the distribution of cities is manifest in the literature, both inductively and deductively. Central-place theory points to and attempts to explain the system in the location of cities as "functions of distance, mass production, and competition." [8]

There have been at least three kinds of empirical approaches to the study of system in cities. One has been the recognition and description of the "rank-size" rule. Several investigators [9] have recognized and tried to explain the fact that cities tend to be distributed in accordance with a Pareto distribution, that is, $y = Ax^{-\alpha}$, where x is the number of inhabitants in a community, y is the number of inhabitants in a community size x or larger, and A and α are empirical parameters estimated from the size distribution. When α equals one, and $x = A/y$, x being the number of inhabitants in a given community and A being the number of inhabitants in the largest community in the system, then y is the rank of a community at x size.

The second empirical approach is represented by typological classification of centers according to different levels in a hierarchy of places.[10] The third empirical approach is represented by studies pointing to functional correlates of a city's size.[11]

Perhaps the most powerful explanation of system in the distribution of cities has been given by Simon.[12] Berry and Garrison have presented a discussion of alternative explanations of system in cities and indicated the manner in which the problem may be approached as an aspect of general systems theory.[13]

Implicit in all these approaches, it may be noted, is the treatment of the city as a dependent variable with the forces accounting for patterns of distribution of cities being treated as independent variables. Much has been learned about the urban agglomeration through these approaches—both deductive and empirical. But much remains to be done before a full understanding of the city as a dependent variable is achieved.

Historical Perspective

Despite limited data it is possible to reconstruct, generally, the growth of world and urban population. Such a reconstruction provides significant perspectives prerequisite to an understanding of contemporary urbanization and its consequences.

Among the more significant of the great changes that have characterized the modern era are the increases in the size and concentration
of world population. Man in all the millennia of his existence on this
planet had produced a population of only 500 million persons by mid-
seventeenth century. By 1962, however, world population exceeded
three billion. Within the three centuries of the modern era, world
population had increased by an amount five times that generated
throughout man's previous habitation of the globe.[14] Similarly, although man has inhabited this planet for perhaps two million years,
permanent human settlement was not achieved until relatively recently
—in the neolithic age some 10,000 years ago. Moreover, although only
2.4 per cent of the world's peoples lived in places of 20,000 or more
as recently as 1800, this proportion increased ninefold during the following century and a half.[15]

Although the first census of all of mankind has yet to be taken, it is
possible, at least in approximation, to reproduce the population history of the world. It is not known exactly when *Homo sapiens,* the
present version of man, first appeared, but he was much in evidence
in Europe 25,000–30,000 years ago. It has been estimated that for the
some 600,000 years of the paleolithic age world population growth ap-
proximated 0.02 per thousand per year.[16] By the end of the neolithic
period, world population has been estimated at ten million and may
have been as little as five million. At the beginning of the Christian
era, the population of the globe probably numbered between 200
and 300 million. It increased to about 500 million by the beginning
of the modern era (1650). By that time the rate of world population growth had increased to about four-tenths of 1 per cent per
year. At the present time it approximates 2 per cent per year. Ignoring population prior to the paleolithic period, it may be stated
that in the course of man's development since, his rate of population
growth has risen from about 2 per cent per millennium to 2 per cent
per year—a thousandfold increase.

The rate of world population increase is still accelerating. It took all
the millennia of man's existence on this planet prior to 1850 to produce a population of about one billion persons simultaneously alive.
To produce a figure of two billion simultaneously alive required only
an additional seventy-five years, for this number was achieved by about
1925. To reach a total of three billion persons required only an additional thirty-seven years—by 1962. In accordance with the trend, a
fourth billion would be attained in about fifteen years and a fifth billion in less than an additional ten years.

Over most of the millennia of his existence man was a nomad. As
has been indicated, it was not until the neolithic age that man was

able to achieve permanent settlement.[17] The neolithic village was limited by its technology and culture to a population restricted to a few hundred persons at most and was "permanent" in a relative sense. By reason of limited agricultural techniques, villages had to be shifted every twenty years or so to achieve even minimal returns from the land. It took at least 1500 years, from 5000 to 3500 B.C., for the city to develop from the neolithic peasant village, the first of which appeared in Mesopotamia and Egypt in about the middle of the fourth millennium B.C. Cities as large as 100,000 or more probably did not exist prior to the Greek or Roman period. Although it is possible that a city of a million was achieved in ancient China and in eighteenth-century Japan,[18] cities of a million or more were largely the product of eighteenth- and nineteenth-century developments.

Data on the urban population of the world as a whole are available with reasonable accuracy only since 1800.[19] Of the approximately 900 million persons on the globe in 1800, it is estimated that 1.7 per cent lived in cities of 100,000 and over; 2.4 per cent in cities of 20,000 and over; and 3 per cent in urban places of 5000 or more inhabitants.

Accelerating world population growth was accompanied by even more rapid increase in urban population since at least the beginning of the nineteenth century. Between 1800 and 1950, world population increased over two and a half times. Population in places of 5000 and over, however, increased twenty-six times; population in places of 20,000 and over twenty-three times; and population in places of 100,000 and over more than twenty times. In consequence, by mid-twentieth century almost one-third (30 per cent) of the world's people lived in urban places having 5000 and over. About 21 per cent were in places of 20,000 and over, and 13 per cent in places of 100,000 and over. Even by 1950, however, only 4 per cent of the world's people lived in places of a million or more inhabitants.

In the United States both total population growth and urban concentration far exceeded the world rates. During the three centuries of the modern era the population of the United States increased from perhaps a million Indians and a few shiploads of Europeans to about 180 million persons as reported in the eighteenth decennial census in 1960.[20] When the first census of the United States was taken in 1790, 95 per cent of the population lived in rural places of fewer than 2500 persons. There were only twenty-four urban places in the nation, only two of which had populations in excess of 25,000. By 1960, however, there were about 5400 urban places containing 70 per cent of the entire population. For the first sixty years of the present century the population of the United States increased from about 75 million to 180 million. The increase in urban population over the same period absorbed 92 per cent of the total increase of the nation. In the last decade of that period, 1950–1960, increase in the urban population accounted for more than 100 per cent of the total population growth of the country. That is, for the first time in the history of the nation, rural population actually declined during the intercensal decade. The extent to which the population of the country is becoming concentrated is even more dramatically indicated by growth of metropolitan and large metropolitan area populations. Over the first sixty years of the century, the increase in metropolitan population absorbed 85 per cent of the total growth of the nation. Although the increase in population of metropolitan areas between 1950 and 1960 (using 1960 boundaries) absorbed about the same proportion of total national growth during the decade, the increase in population classified as metropolitan (boundaries as in 1950 and 1960, respectively) absorbed 97 per cent of the total growth of the nation during the decade.

In 1900 there were only five metropolitan areas having a million or more persons in the United States. They contained about 16 per cent of the total population. By 1960 there were twenty-four such places in which over a third of the nation's population resided (34 per cent). Over the first sixty years of the century, the increase in large metropolitan area population absorbed 48 per cent of total national growth. In the decade between 1950 and 1960, population increase in large metropolitan areas accounted for 60 per cent of total national growth. Over the first sixty years of the century, then, total population increased about two and a half times, urban population increased almost fourfold, metropolitan area population increased more than fourfold, and large metropolitan area population increased fivefold.

During this same period the United States changed from a predominantly rural to a predominantly urban nation. At the turn of the century, about two-fifths of the population was urban. It was not until 1920 that more than half of the inhabitants were urban (51.2 per cent). In 1960, 70 per cent of the population was urban. It will not be until the end of this decade, 1970, that the United States will have completed its first half century as an urban nation—which is why there is still evidence that it is in transition from a preindustrial and preurban order to "urbanism as a way of life." [21]

"Urbanization" and "Urban"

The degree of urbanization of a nation for statistical purposes is generally defined as the proportion of the population resident in urban places. This demographic conception of urbanization, however, is transcended by many other uses of the term in which urbanization is recognized as a social process which has brought about great transformations in man's way of life. For purposes of convenience, especially in statistical studies, "urban" and "urbanization" are usually considered merely in a demographic sense, as agglomerations of a given size or as the proportion of a total population living in places of a given size. In the consideration of the city or the urban place either as a dependent or an independent variable, however, much more than the demographic definition is necessarily involved.

Urbanization as a process of population concentration has been systematically treated by Hope Tisdale Eldridge.[22] It involves two elements: (1) "the multiplication of points of concentration"; and (2) "the increase in the size of individual concentrations." As a result the proportion of the population living in urban places increases.

Although urban population is widely understood to include the population resident in cities, the definition of urban is, nevertheless, a complex matter. Population classified as "urban" varies greatly country by country. The delineation of areas as "urban" or "rural" is often related to administrative, political, historical, or cultural considerations as well as demographic criteria. As the United Nations *Demographic Yearbook* has indicated, definitions of "urban" fall into three major types: "(1) Classification of minor civil divisions on a chosen criterion which may include: (a) type of local government, (b) number of inhabitants, (c) proportion of population engaged in agriculture; (2) classification of administrative centers of minor rural divisions as urban and the remainder of the division as rural; and (3) classification of certain size localities (agglomerations) as urban, irrespective of administrative boundaries."[23] Even for census purposes, then, the definition of urban involves a multidimensional approach and the setting of arbitrary cutting points in differentiating "urban" from "rural."

In the United States "urban" is defined as a place having 2500 or more persons. The definition was restricted to "incorporated places" prior to the 1950 Census, but includes unincorporated as well as incorporated places since. Moreover, in the United States four different designations are used in the reporting of agglomerations of population. In addition to "urban" places, data are presented for "urbanized areas," for "Standard Metropolitan Statistical Areas," and for "Standard Consolidated Areas." The urbanized area, in brief, includes a central city plus all contiguous territory in which people live at densities of about 2000 per square mile, ignoring political boundaries. The "Standard Metropolitan Statistical Area" includes a city (or cities)

of 50,000 or more, the county in which it (or they) is located, and
such adjoining counties as by various social and economic criteria depend on the central city (or cities). The "Standard Consolidated
Areas" are contiguous Standard Metropolitan Statistical Areas. Only
two were delineated in the 1960 Census, one for "New York-Northeastern New Jersey" and the other for "Chicago-Northwestern Indiana." [24]

Increasing attention is being given to still another form of agglomeration—the coalescence of metropolitan areas more comprehensive
than those represented by the complexes recognized by the United
States government as Standard Consolidated Areas. The term "megalopolis" refers to the coalescence of a series of metropolitan areas, as
represented, for example, on the Atlantic seaboard of the United States
from Boston to Washington, D. C.[25]

An effort has been made to delineate the metropolitan areas of the
world on a comparable basis. The Institute of International Studies [26]
at the University of California has applied uniform criteria to areas
containing more than 100,000 inhabitants and delimited boundaries
for some 720 areas of a total of 1046 metropolitan areas in the world.
Limited population figures are presented for these areas for the last
census before 1954 and population estimates are given for about 1955.

By reason of the complexity of the problem, the United Nations
Population Commission has recommended that, in addition to "urban-
rural" statistics as defined by individual countries, data be presented
by size of locality or identifiable agglomeration. This makes possible
improved international comparability even though the cutting point
for "urban" population may remain an arbitrary matter. In practice,
many comparative international studies use populations in places of
20,000 or more as "urban" because the data are generally available
on that basis and because an agglomeration of this size is not likely to
retain rural characteristics.

Manifestations and Consequences of Urbanization

Although the consideration of urbanism and urbanization as a dependent variable is of major interest in the social sciences, even
greater interest, perhaps, is to be found in the consideration of the
city as an independent variable. That the city makes a difference in
the way of life was perceived by the ancients and recorded in the
earliest historical records.[27] In the nineteenth century Maine, Tönnies,
and Durkheim, and in the twentieth century Sumner, Goldenweiser,

Redfield, and Wirth grappled with various aspects of the difference that aggregative living makes.[28]

The Size-Density Model

A relatively simple size-density model provides a basis for treating the city as an independent variable in a broad and comprehensive way. The theoretical basis for the development and consideration of the model is given by Durkheim. He has stated:

> Social life rests on a substratum whose size as well as its form is determined. This substratum is constituted by the mass of individuals who make up society, the way in which they are distributed on the soil, and the nature and configuration of all sorts of things that affect collective relationships. The social substratum differs according to whether the population is large or small and more or less dense, whether it is concentrated in cities or dispersed over the countryside, how cities and houses are constructed, whether the area occupied by the society is more or less extensive, and according to the kind of boundaries that delimit it.[29]

Let us consider the implications of variation in size and density of population, confining our attention to a fixed land area. For purposes of convenience, consider a circle with a radius of 10 miles. Such a circle would have a total area of approximately 314 square miles. The size of the total population in such a circle under different density conditions is shown below: [30]

Assumed Population Density (persons per square mile)	Area with Approximate Density Assumed	Number of Persons in Circle of 10-Mile Radius
1	U. S. in 1500	314
50	World in 1960	15,700
8,000	Average central city in metropolitan area in U. S.	2,512,000
17,000	Chicago	5,338,000
25,000	New York	7,850,000
75,000	Manhattan	23,550,000

The population densities shown are not unrealistic ones. The population density of 1 may be taken as an approximation of the density of the United States prior to European occupancy. Actually, the Indian population was approximately one-third as dense as this, but 1 is a convenient figure with which to work. The density of 50 is approximately that of the United States in 1960, and approximately the population density of the world as a whole. The density of 8000 in round numbers is not too far from the density of the average central city in metropolitan areas of the United States in 1960. The density figure 17,000 is approximately that of Chicago, the figure of 25,000 approximately the density of New York, and the figure of 75,000 approximately the density of Manhattan Island.

In aboriginal America a person moving within the ten-mile circle could potentially make only 313 different contacts with other human beings. In contrast, the density of the United States as a whole today would make possible 15,699 contacts in the same land area. The density of the average central city in the United States would permit over 2.5 million contacts, the density of Chicago over 5.3 million contacts, the density of New York City over 7.8 million contacts, and the density of Manhattan over 23.5 million contacts in the same land area. The potential number of contacts, when considered as a measure of potential human interaction, provides, in a simplistic way to be sure, a basis for understandng the difference that city living makes.[31]

Since Durkheim, in his consideration of the structure of the social order, spoke of "social morphology," the multiplier effect on potential human interaction of increased population density in a fixed land area can appropriately be described as an index of the social-morphological revolution. The size-density model presented may be taken as a quantification of the social-morphological revolution and provides at least one theoretical basis for considering the city as an independent variable. More specifically, it may be stated as an hypothesis that the increase in potential human interaction produced by aggregative living has produced in the social realm a major transformation the equivalent of genetic mutation in the biological realm. Discussion of the consequences of the social-morphological revolution or social mutation is the subject matter of most of the remainder of this chapter.

The City as a Physical Construct

Permanent settlement led to fixed and relatively long-lasting shelters, evidences of which are manifest in the archaeological finds of the neolithic peasant village. Man with great ingenuity learned to make selective use of his environment. Contemporary primitive peoples provide some indication of the way in which forms of habitation must have evolved. Says Turner: "Everywhere over the earth habitations are constructed which show fine adaptation of materials to the particular needs for shelter that distinguish different environments." [32]

Architectural remains reveal well-developed patterns of construction "in which were combined tiers, columns, and walls." [33] In "the Tel el'Ubaid Phase" at Tepe Gawra in the upper Tigris Valley were "the most complete sequence of cultural strata known to archaeology —26 levels—. . . ." Finds there indicate the development of a "more or less uniform urban culture than prevailed throughout the lower Valley" just before the end of the fourth millennium B.C. During the Tel el'Ubaid Phase, Turner concludes that the "embryonic city is contrasted with the full-grown village." During the next phase, the Uruk Phase, "the full-fledged urban community is first known. A ziggurat and well-built brick temples towered over the community, which may have covered an area of about two square miles." Development of improved, more permanent forms of habitation were paralleled by other evidences of material artifacts which point to important social developments as well. The city was perforce a "man-made environment" with fixed places of habitation; places for performance of various functions—economic, administrative, religious; a network for the circulation of persons and goods—roads, means of transport, and the like.

Mumford describes the evolution of the physical plant of the city as essentially an extension of ever-more complex "containers." He notes that the neolithic period was characterized by containers: "It is an age of stone and pottery utensils, of vases, jars, vats, cisterns, bins, barns, granaries, houses, not least great collective containers, like irrigation ditches and villages." [34] He sees the most primitive dwelling yet discovered, that in Mesopotamia found by Robert Braidwood, "is a hole dug out of the soil, sun-dried to brick hardness." He is impressed by the fact that the first house seems to antedate any form of earthenware pottery. A prerequisite to the emergence of aggregative living, as has been noted, was the development of a surplus. "Wherever a surplus must be preserved and stored, containers are important," says Mumford. Increased surplus made possible larger agglomerations of people which, in turn, increased the need for containers of every variety. "Mark how much the city owes technically to the village: out of it came, directly or by elaboration, the granary, the bank, the arsenal, the library, the store. Remember, too, that the irrigation ditch, the canal, the reservoir, the moat, the aqueduct, the drain, the sewer are also containers, for automatic transport or storage. The first of these was invented long before the city; and without this whole range of inventions the ancient city could not have taken the form it finally did; for it was nothing less than a container of containers." [35]

The development of the city from the village was characterized by an increase in built-up area and population. Among the larger earlier remains Maggido in Israel covered 3½ acres. Gurnia in Crete contained about 6½ acres. Much later the walled area at Myceneae contained about 12 acres. About the same time Karkemish in Syria covered 240 acres. Ur occupied 220 acres. Nineveh, about 600 B.C., contained perhaps 1800 acres. Archaeological finds suggest that densities in ancient cities (2000 B.C.) were approximately 76,000 to 128,000 per square mile. High densities under the conditions of life of the times must have been a factor in restricting the size of the agglomeration—by reason of high morbidity and mortality. Mumford also points out that houses dating from about the middle of the third millennium B.C. are about the same size as those noted over the following 5000 years. These were primarily row houses, detached houses constituting exceptions. "Detachment and openness were originally attributes of the palace." The walled city emerged as a means of protection for the ruling group and was "one of the most prominent features of the city, in most countries, right down to the 18th century." [36]

The interrelation of physical plant and social interaction is suggested in Mumford's observation that "early cities did not grow beyond walking distance or hearing distance." Access to water supply was also an important factor in the size of the agglomeration or of "neighborhoods" within the city—the latter being to a considerable extent a function of the distance over which water could be transported by women on foot.

This restriction on the size of the early city also implies restrictions on urban life and possibly contributed to high densities. Mumford's historical treatment of the city, despite its shortcomings, permits the tracing of the development of the urban physical plant as the product of human agglomeration as well as suggesting the way in which the city as a physical entity affected the character and size of the aggregation.

Sjoberg has summarized the spatial arrangements of the preindustrial city.[37] Within the typical wall the city tended to be further divided into sections sealed off one from the other by walls, moats, and the like. The central area of the preindustrial city typically contained the prominent government and religious structures and the main market. Clustered close to these major edifices were the relatively luxurious dwellings of the elite, often facing inward and presenting an inhospitable blank wall to the streets. The distribution of the population within the city from the center was directly associated with power and wealth, the poorest living farthest from the center or outside the city walls, excluded from their protection. Within this general framework the city tended to be sectioned off on the basis of ethnic or occupational lines. There was little in the way of contemporary territorial specialization. Place of work was often identical with place of residence. The preindustrial city, with limited means of circulating peoples and goods, was highly congested and lacking in many of the amenities of contemporary urban existence with respect to environmental sanitation and hygiene.

The industrial revolution and concomitant developments greatly transformed the physical preindustrial city. Walls disappeared, sometimes changing to arteries of transportation, as they lost their defense function and as advancing technology permitted increasingly larger agglomerations of population to expand beyond established boundaries. The industrial city, characterized by the steam engine, the belt and the pulley, and the horse-drawn vehicle, was still influenced in physical pattern by centripetal forces which tended to crowd population around the factory. With improvements in transport, however, residential location near the central city lost much of its attractiveness. The newer outlying edifice and greater detachment and openness became increasingly attractive to the elite.

In the older, well-established cities, the new patterns of land use and population distribution generated by industrialization fused with and were superimposed upon the established preindustrial order. In the newer cities, as manifest in the United States, land use patterns and the distribution of population in accordance with socioeconomic status literally turned inside out—that is, the elite tended to move outward with the expansion of the city to newer and more desirable locations. In contrast with the preindustrial city, a direct relationship between status and distance from the center of the city became the dominant pattern.

With industrialization a combination of technological and social organizational changes were made possible. For one thing, a much larger agglomeration of people and economic activities emerged than was ever previously possible on an extensive scale. Urban infrastructure investment was tremendously expanded to include not only more elaborate and permanent habitations but also more complex networks of transport and communication and the multiplication of amenities including piped water, sewerage, lighting, and waste disposal.

Twentieth-century developments set new forces in motion affecting the physical structure of the city. Twentieth-century technology symbolized by electric power, the automotive complex—the automobile, the truck, and the highway—and the telephone generated centrifugal forces dispersing population and economic activities over the landscape. Moreover, twentieth-century technological developments made possible much larger agglomerations of people and economic activities than was possible with nineteenth-century or any prior technology. In Mumford's language, twentieth-century technology permitted "the removal of limits." The city, as a "container," burst with "urban sprawl and the emergence of megalopolis." [38]

In mid-twentieth century the city, spearheaded by major metropolitan complexes, such as New York, London, Tokyo, Paris, and Chicago, has become a gigantic physical entity both above and below the ground. The physical problems of the twentieth-century city have assumed tremendous proportions.

Urban physical plants in the United States, for example, residential, industrial, commercial, and governmental, were constructed hurriedly in response to rapid urbanization. Land use patterns and infrastructure development were largely the product of market forces, which produced a remarkable physical plant but which also permitted rapid obsolescence and decay. They include by prevalent standards relatively large proportions of "substandard housing" and are pockmarked by areas of slum. Air and water pollution have become increasingly critical problems, as have adequate sewerage and the removal of solid wastes. In the United States the automobile, which has been a major factor in the development of the twentieth-century metropolis, is now threatening to strangulate it with congestion and new attention is being focused on problems of the circulation within the city. In Western Europe the increase in automobiles, still far below their prevalence in the United States, threatens even worse and earlier crises in the older street patterns. The United States has only recently begun to face up to these physical problems in a major way through programs of "urban renewal," public housing, and expanded efforts at mass transit and city planning. [39]

This overview of the city as a physical structure indicates that with increasing size and density of population, the urban plant became ever a more complex, intricate physical entity assuming quite distinct patterns in accordance with the potential of the prevalent technology. New York City as a physical entity, whether considered as a monstrosity or as an elegant illustration of man's ingenuity in creating environment, is certainly a product of the size and density of population in that area and the forces that contributed to them.

There is much about the urban plant that we do not yet understand. In the Western world we have inherited urban physical works which, in predominant measure, are the product of market forces neither fully recorded nor fully understood. The size and density of population producing the physical problems of the contemporary city are forcing an increase in city planning activities. With increased city planning new forces are in motion reshaping the city as a physical construct with its various intricate layers of historical development. The future of the city as a physical entity, increasingly as a planned phenomenon, can at this stage be only a matter for speculation.[40]

The City as an Economic Mechanism

The city owes its origin to the economic advances represented by the domestication of plants and animals and the proliferation of the crafts. Once permanent human settlement was attained, however, aggregative living exerted profound influences on economic activity.

The characteristics of the city as an economic mechanism were clearly discernible in the development of the ancient Oriental urban cultures. Ever larger agglomerations of population made possible both a greater division of labor and a greater number of nonagricultural specialists. A relatively complex division of labor and specialization resulted in increased productivity permitting even greater surplus. In the matrix of ancient urban areas, a number of key economic elements became significant, including "work," "property," "economic power," "luxury," "poverty," and new forms of economic administration such as gang slavery, the ancient state system of cultivation, and an elaboration of the right to private property.[41]

Self-interest as a key economic motivation—incentive not only to secure means of subsistence but also to get as much as possible of the surplus—was manifest. Self-interest was bolstered by increasing size and density of population which tended to devalue personal and familial relationships founded on close interpersonal interaction and sentiment. Increased size and density of population produced more and more minute division of labor, specialization, and the shifting of economic relationships from "status" to "contract."

The proliferation of the crafts and increasing numbers of artisans led to an important element in the preindustrial city's economic organization—its guild system.[42] This in turn influenced the physical pattern of the city, for the guilds—craft, service, and merchant—tended to become localized into "quarters" along specific streets. Increased division of labor and specialization necessitated heightened exchange activities and generated merchants in ever larger numbers. The proliferation of specialists led also to specialization in the provision of services—the barber, the sweeper, the scavenger, and the like. Money, credit, the price system, financial institutions, all were consequences of increased division of labor and specialization. They may be regarded as mechanisms for the integration and coordination of economic activity necessitated by the increasing size and density of the population clumping. The urban economy increased the status position of the trader and manufacturer over that of the landlord and led also, in time and with organization, to a greatly increased economic power position for workers.

Increased division of labor and specialization also accelerated technological advance. It was easier to devise a machine to do a relatively simple part of a job than to produce an entire product. Technological advance, implying ever-increasing use of nonhuman energy, produced the industrial plant and the "factory system." Workers became increasingly "operatives" rather than artisans and employees rather than self-employed.

Broadened markets, partly a function of the emergence of central governments with increased jurisdiction over broader expanses of territory, encouraged "mass production." The industrial city provided increasing evidence of economies of scale, permitted external economies, operated to minimize frictions of space and communication, and led to more complex forms of economic organization. The joint stock company and corporate organization involving limited liability developed. Capital was amassed, management became professionalized and separated from ownership. Gigantic industrial combines evolved including "integrated" economic empires. To cope with large management labor unions were organized. "Big labor" evolved to deal with "big management."

With the emergence of the industrial city and the expansion of trade, the market mechanism was increasingly relied upon to order the economy—to allocate resources and to regulate the production of goods and services. This was achieved largely through the play of competition and the operation of the price mechanism. Increasing size and density of population and increasing complexity in economic organization, with ever-increasing interdependence and vulnerability, brought to the fore various problems such as abuses of labor, inequitable distribution of wealth, extreme fluctuations in the level of economic activity, increasing levels of unemployment, monopolistic practices, adulteration of products, and large-scale fraud. Despite Adam Smith's injunction that each man acting in his own interest would as "if guided by an invisible hand" act in the interests of the larger society, government increasingly intervened into the operation of the economy. Intervention took many forms including the establishment of various regulatory agencies, provision for more equitable distribution of income (for example, income tax), encouragement of labor organization, and the creation of various forms of social security such as unemployment compensation, old-age pensions, and medical care.

Increasing government intervention tended to provide greater protection for the weak and enormously to expand the services of government. Thus the public sector of the economy was greatly expanded, including the local governmental sector, in the provision of greatly expanded services for education, health, welfare, recreation, protection, transportation, and so on. This development was largely the result of greater population size and density which generated new collective needs. Because these needs were not met through the market mechanism, they became increasingly the province of government. Urbanization together with industrialization, then, by creating greater interdependence and new forms of vulnerability (for example, unemployment, industrial accident, sweat shops, contagious disease, water and air pollution), stimulated the expansion of government functions and personnel. The most extreme form of interventionism, of course, became manifest in the Soviet Union and in the Communist Bloc, in general.

In summary then, the increased size and density of population agglomerations profoundly affected the ways in which man makes a living. They generated the highly complex form of economic organization that characterizes contemporary life. Needless to say, in the process, productivity tremendously increased, producing unprecedented levels of living for mass populations. As an inevitable consequence of the increased division of labor and specialization, an ever more interdependent society has necessarily evolved new forms of coordination and integration, including increasing government interventionism. The city, itself a product of economic advance, also became a major force in economic development—the emergence of our contemporary form of complex economic organization.[43] Further consideration of urbanization and the economy may be found in Chapters 6 and 12 and on urbanization and government in the section in this chapter on "The City and Government."

The City and Human Behavior

In a small, sparsely settled population, the potential of human interaction is much below that in a large, high-density population. This is illustrated in the size-density model shown earlier. In the small community, not only are potential and actual contacts fewer, but because they are fewer, they tend also to be quite different in character. In consequence, many students have tried to show the way in which the city influences human behavior (see Chapter 13). The classical treatment of the effect of size and density and, also, heterogeneity of population on behavior is that of Louis Wirth.[44] He stated: "On the basis of the three variables, number, density of settlement, and degree of heterogeneity, of the urban population, it appears possible to explain the characteristics of urban life and to account for the differences between cities of various sizes and types."

According to this hypothesis the small community is characterized by "primary-group" contacts.[45] They tend to be face-to-face, intimate contacts of persons who meet and interact with one another in virtually all spheres of activity. In such a setting personal relations tend to be based on relatively full knowledge of the other person—on sentiment and emotion. In contrast, according to this hypothesis, in the large, high-density population situation, contacts tend to be "secondary" rather than primary, segmental rather than integral, utilitarian rather than sentimental. Moreover, in the large-size, high-density situation, populations are apt to be more heterogeneous—to include peoples of greater range and diversity in background, attitudes, and behavior. The person is subjected, therefore, to a greater variety of ways of thought and action.

The combination of heterogeneous and secondary contacts, it is held, tends greatly to modify human behavior. Thus, thought and action tend to become increasingly rational as opposed to traditional, and interpersonal relations become based on utility rather than sentiment. With increased size, density, and heterogeneity of population, the constraints of tradition—the influence of the folkways and mores—diminish. In ever larger spheres of thought and action, behavior is determined by a willful decision taken by the person, rather than automatically determined by the norms of the group. The sphere of personal decision-making is greatly extended, including areas of activity previously determined by tradition, such as kind and degree of education, occupation or profession, residential location, choice of mate, size of family, political affiliation, religiosity or even religion.

It follows, then, that increased size and density of population, especially if accompanied by heterogeneity, diminishes the power of informal social controls. Informal social control, effected largely through the play of folkways and the mores, gives way to increased formal control, the control of law, police, courts, jails, regulations, and orders. The breakdown in informal social controls is largely responsible for increased personal disorganization as manifest in juvenile delinquency, crime, prostitution, alcoholism, drug addiction, suicide, mental disease, social unrest, and political instability. Formal controls have by no means proved as efficacious as the informal in regulating human behavior.

The effect of the city on the way of life may be observed in the adjustment problems of the in-migrant.[46] The city as a recipient of migrants has played and continues to play a prominent role in the modification of thought and behavior in subjecting people with traditional and rural backgrounds to the conditions of urban living. Most of the severe physical, social, and economic problems of the city are disproportionately manifest among newcomers and are symptomatic of the difficulties of adjustment to urban life. In-migrant populations provide an opportunity for observing the impact of urbanization on the human being. In the accommodation of the rural newcomer to the city, such transformation in thought and behavior as may be effected may be traced.

In the United States, for example, the newest newcomers to urban and metropolitan areas are the Negro, the Puerto Rican, the Mexican, and the American Indian. They are now faced with accommodation to the urban milieu as were earlier immigrant groups. Each of the newcomer groups to the urban and metropolitan areas of the United States followed essentially a similar pattern with respect to location in space, the economy, and society.[47] Each of the in-migrant strains found its port of entry or areas of first settlement in the inner, older, blighted zones of the city. The longer the period of settlement, the farther out was the median location point of the newcomer group and the more dispersed was its residential pattern. The shorter the period of settlement, the closer to the center of the city was its median location and the more concentrated or segregated was its residential pattern. Similarly, the shorter the period of settlement, the lower was the occupational level and income of the newcomers. The longer the period of settlement, the higher the educational and occupational level and income. Finally, with respect to social status, a common pattern was also visible. Each of the newcomer groups was in turn greeted with hostility, suspicion, distrust, prejudice, and discriminatory practices. With the passage of time each of the newcomer groups climbed the social as well as the economic ladder to achieve access to the broader social and cultural life of the community and increased general acceptability.

The patterns by which immigrant groups became "Americanized" indicate in general the processes by which the newest newcomers— the Negro and the Puerto Rican—will make the transition from traditional behavior in their rural areas of origin to urbanism as a way of life. The process of acculturation will be similar in many respects to the process by which immigrants before them settled in American cities and metropolitan areas. This is not to say that there will not also be differences arising from their greater visibility and differences in cultural background.[48]

Such transformations in thought and behavior as are induced by increased size and density of population are, of course, greatly augmented by the increased heterogeneity of the population. Since increasing size and density of human agglomerations increase the probabilities of greater heterogeneity, the city may in a fundamental sense be regarded as the source of a whole range of problems arising from intergroup differences, whether based on language, culture, religion, or race. The problem of intergroup relations is essentially an urban problem, or at least reaches its most critical manifestations in the urban area.

The hypotheses considered have been a major factor in leading to the distinction between "folk" and "urban" societies.[49] Although the above-described impact of urbanism (size, density, and heterogenity of population) on the way of life has been widely accepted, it remains an hypothesis yet to be subjected to the test of empirical research. Similarly, the extension of the hypothesis into the differentiation of "folk" and "urban" societies is largely an ideal-type construct which empirical investigation, as yet inadequate, suggests is inapplicable to the developing areas and of questionable usefulness in the economically advanced countries.[50]

It may be that to the extent that size, density, and heterogeneity of population have changed behavior in urban places they represent necessary, rather than sufficient, conditions for such a transformation. It is clear that much behavior in urban places, both in the economically advanced and underdeveloped areas, is still traditional rather than rational, and in other respects resembles folk rather than urban characteristics. The work of Oscar Lewis, Edward M. Bruner, Douglas S. Butterworth, Theodore Caplow, William L. Kolb, O. D. Duncan and Albert Reiss, Herbert J. Gans and the Detroit Area Study at the University of Michigan indicates preurban societies that do not conform to the folk pattern or city populations that do not manifest the attitudes or behavior hypothesized as a consequence of size, density, and heterogeneity.[51] Moreover, a striking example of high urban density without the concomitants hypothesized by Wirth is afforded by Hoselitz's reference to a density of about 840,000 per square mile in a section of a ward in Bombay.[52]

The explanation for this may lie in the difference between *potential* human interaction in the city, as portrayed in the size-density model, and that *actually* achieved. That is, in large population clumpings of high density, which are essentially an agglutination of separate and distinct noninteracting communities, human behavior may still be largely the product of the primary group. In the city, although heterogeneity is present, confinement of contacts to one's own cultural group is also possible in varying degrees to almost complete isolation. In fact, large population size may actually facilitate isolation and insularity. This is evident in the history of immigration to the United States. Some immigrants have chosen to continue to live in enclaves even within metropolitan areas and thus continue traditional behavior and attitudes even with prolonged exposure to urban living. Others, in contrast, have elected to leave their enclaves, avail themselves of diversity of contacts and social world, and adopt "urbanism as a way of life."

Similarly, the patterns of accommodation and acculturation of immigrants or in-migrants may vary with differences in the cultural background of the newcomers, differences in the societies of destination, and variations in the degree to which the potential interaction possible is actually realized.

This problem is further discussed in Chapter 13. Its study may be profitably pursued in comparative and cross-cultural research which contrasts the impact of the city in the less-developed areas with that in the economically advanced ones, as well as in studies comparing behavior in urban and rural or folk settings, respectively. Certainly there is need for much research on the impact of urbanism on behavior and tasks in plenty for the joint efforts of the psychologist and anthropologist as well as the sociologist.

The City and Social Organization

Social organization has necessarily been greatly modified by reason of the increasing size and density of human agglomerations. Increased division of labor and specialization, in creating a much more complex and interdependent society, affected social as well as economic organization. It is held that the basis for social cohesion was altered in that a society became dependent on "organic" rather than "mechanical" solidarity.[53] That is, cohesion is effected organically in the urban setting through interdependence and the mechanisms of coordination and integration, rather than achieved mechanically through the operation of a homogeneous culture. In the large-size, high-density society, organization may be increasingly based on "contract" rather than "status." Relationships among persons or groups are made explicit in terms of reciprocal obligations and duties, on the one hand, and rights or powers on the other. Needless to say, utility rather than sentiment enters into the definition of the relationships.

As a microcosm of the social whole, the family is a convenient unit through which to trace many of the influences of the city on social institutions. The family in most societies is regarded as the primary social unit. The colonial family in early America, predominantly resident in rural areas, was the keystone of social organization. For example, it was a basic and largely self-sufficient economic unit; it had primary responsibility for the socialization and education of the young; it was a focal point for religious training and practices; it provided for the security and protection of its members; and it was the center for their affectional and recreational life.[54]

The family in contemporary urban United States, however, has certainly been transformed. Compared with the colonial family the urban family today is smaller; it is more often childless and has few children, if fertile. The urban family, collectively and individually, is much more mobile; it is not rooted to the soil or even to a home in the manner of its rural counterpart. It possesses comparatively little economic or social unity; it is more frequently broken by separation or divorce and, as William F. Ogburn demonstrated some time ago, has long since lost or shared many of its various historic functions with new, specialized urban institutions.[55] Examples of these new institutions include, on the one hand, the clothing store, the grocery, and the restaurant, and on the other, the school, the library, and social security system.

Accompanying these changes in the family have been redefinitions in the roles of its members—in the relationships of spouses and in parent-child and sibling interrelationships. Especially important in this regard is the changed role of the woman in the family and in society at large, a phenomenon certainly not unrelated to the changed conditions of urban life.

Finally, in respect of the family, it may be noted that in the urban milieu the "nuclear" family, the two-generation family, tends to replace the "extended," the three or more generation family as the model household unit.[56] This, however, does not necessarily mean that the larger family unit disappears as a system of interaction and as an important element of social organization. More study is needed on the role of the extended family in an urban area even when it no longer occupies a single household.[57]

In the city, social institutions tend to be "enacted" rather than "crescive," that is, spontaneous.[58] In the mass society social institutions are frequently invented, are the product of administrative edict or legislation, rather than the result of slow development representing the crystallization of patterns of thought and action as a product of group life. New institutions arise in great number partly as the result of the breakdown of traditional ones that do not meet the requirements of urban living, and partly through the need to invent new institutions by reason of unprecedented situations and problems for which tradition has no answers. Examples of the multiplication of new institutions in response to new and unprecedented needs is represented by the proliferation of such institutions associated with urban living as the police and fire departments, the welfare agency, and public housing.

In the city, "bureaucracy" becomes a ubiquitous form of organization. It is a rational-formal-legal organization which is an inevitable and indispensable concomitant of populations of large size and density and high levels of interaction. It is a form of complex organization involving (1) the distribution in a fixed way of regular activities, (2) the distribution in a fixed way of authority in accordance with rules, (3) the methodical provision for fulfillment of duties and execution of rights, and (4) the selection of personnel on the basis of qualifications rather than of birth or status.[59] Bureaucracy in this sense is found not only in government but also in business enterprise, in labor unions, in religious organizations, in educational institutions, in fraternal organizations—in brief, in all aspects of the mass society in which collective activity is required on a continuing basis. Bureaucracy is necessarily impersonal and requires the subordination of the individual to the organization. It produces "organization man," [60] despite the fact that it also produces greater individual freedom. City life makes man relatively free from the constraints of tradition and opens wide avenues of choice in many realms, even while it may require conformity in some facets of existence as exemplified in "organization man." This is more an apparent than a real contradiction —for conformity in an organization touches only a single segment of the total human experience. Though conformity in some realms is stifling and may incite rebellion, it is nonetheless a necessary aspect of life in a mass society.

The development of the city has altered and produced forms of social stratification, both on a power and a prestige basis. The surplus making cities possible was at first controlled by the king and the priest or, as in Egypt, the two fused into one.[61] The military, an adjunct of the top administration, was closely associated with the elite and enjoyed the distinction of being part of the upper class. Workers, merchants, peasants, craftsmen, or slaves were subordinate and lower classes.

The rise of the commercial city greatly increased the importance of the merchants, who became an ever more powerful group. With the increasing size and power of the city, merchants displaced landlords not only in the power structure of the cities but increasingly in the power structure of larger entities, including nations as a whole. With the ascendancy of the industrial city, the industrialist, the financier, and the manager achieved positions of power arising from wealth and strategic location in the economy. Older sources of social stratification also persisted and the "upper" social strata, in varying degrees, included persons whose position was based on status, that is, birth or "social" honor, as well as on economic power.[62] The development of intellectual traditions, bolstered by the scientific revolution, provided high status to persons in intellectual and professional pursuits.

Contemporary Western society, therefore, tends to be stratified on three axes, power as achieved through wealth, status as achieved through birth, and prestige as achieved largely through intellectual and professional pursuits. The tremendous increase in mass levels of living, however, and the emergence of a large middle class which increasingly becomes a predominant proportion of the population tends, of course, to undermine existing systems of social stratification.

The City and Government [63]

We have noted that government in its earliest form in the city performed primarily the function of distributing the agricultural surplus which made aggregative living possible. Early government also embodied defense and police functions and, in collaboration with the religious hierarchy, played some role in respect to the welfare and spiritual life of the people.

The increasing size and density of population, the increasing interdependence of the social order, the breakdown of traditional social controls, and the inability of inherited social institutions to cope with the new problems of urban life have led inexorably to the manifold expansion of government functions and powers. This process is by no means yet completed. A few concrete examples may serve to clarify this point. There is certainly some relationship between the inability of the family as an inherited social institution to cope with the security problems posed by urban health hazards, industrial accidents, and unemployment and the development of government programs throughout the Western world such as the various public health services, workmen's compensation laws, and unemployment insurance benefits. Similarly, the creation of government agencies to regulate public utilities, stock exchanges, and the manufacture and distribution of food and drugs; and the provision by government of various services such as transportation, recreation, education, public housing, urban renewal, sewerage, water, solid waste disposal, and fire and police protection are additional examples of the expanded functions of government necessitated by increasing urbanization and industrialization.

The complex of technological, economic, and social changes which have been both antecedent to, and consequent upon, increasing urbanization not only profoundly affected the role of government but also political ideology. Significant changes in such ideology, dependent upon increasing size and density of population, are apparent in the history of the Western world. For example, the Constitution of the United States, which established the framework of the federal government, and, in the main, the constitutions of the individual states, which in turn created the local governments, were drawn in a preindustrial, rural setting. The political thought that dominated the minds of Americans in the critical period during which the federal government and many of the state and local governments were established was composed of many strains reflecting the transition of the political order from a feudal-autocratic to a liberal-democratic state. The great alterations which have occurred in the original governmental system established by the founding fathers, and which are still in process in the United States, may be interpreted as a consequence of the changes which have occurred in the size, distribution, and composition of the population.

At the risk of oversimplification it may be said that foremost in the concept of the role of government in the American political heritage, the product of a preurban world, is emphasis on the tenet that "that government is best which governs least." This doctrine, coupled with the liberal tradition in economic thinking, that each man acting in his own interest automatically acts in the interest of the larger whole, constitutes fundamentally the inherited framework of principles on the basis of which the founding fathers laid out American government. Yet, despite the dominance of these principles in the political philosophy of the United States, the record, reflecting the power of forces of social change, shows that the functions of American government on all levels have tremendously expanded and multiplied in the course of history; and that the expansion has been continuous without regard to the complexion of the political party in power.

Similar changes in the role of government, and ideology in respect to it, are evident in the history of the West, in general.[64] The issue of "big" versus "little" government is by no means yet resolved and constitutes a major source of cleavage in the world political scene as evident in the postures of the "communist" nations, on the one hand, and the "capitalist" nations, on the other. Moreover, there is, of course, considerable variation in practice both among capitalist and communist nations on the extent to which government actually regulates or operates economic and social affairs.[65]

Increasing size and density of population have also brought about great changes in the nature of representative government. Representative government in the Western world was, in general, an adaptation of the "democracy" of the Greek city-state. It is one thing, however, for a representative to speak for a small, homogeneous, rural, agricultural constituency, and quite another thing to "represent" a large heterogeneous population with diverse and often conflicting interests. The contemporary representative must determine for himself just whom he represents in his votes on specific issues, and he is almost mercilessly subjected to conflicting pressures and influences. The emergence of the public opinion poll may be regarded as an invention in the urban setting for the measurement of "the will" of the people. It may play an increasingly important role in representative government in the years to come.

Increasing urbanization has generated some of the foremost political issues of the time. First, the very role of government itself has become a major political issue. It constitutes undoubtedly the major point of cleavage between "conservatives" and "liberals" throughout the world. Then, too, specific issues, especially those involving increasing provision of welfare and security measures and increasing regulation of economic and social affairs, arise from conditions of urban living.

The complex and often technical character of urban problems has changed the requirements of "governing." In the urban setting, governmental problems grow increasingly technical and require professional attention. The "expert" has emerged as a new and powerful element in government, and "public administration" has become a profession. With the proliferation of government functions, government has become increasingly "bureaucratized," and because of its conspicuous role in mass society, government bureaucracy is frequently misinterpreted as the only form of bureaucracy in the contemporary order. Government bureaucracy, like other forms of bureaucracy, has become an indispensable tool in the functioning of the mass society.

Urban growth accompanied by increasing regional, national, and international interdependence has exerted new forces affecting the interrelations of central, regional, and local governments. In greatly decentralized systems such as in the United States, there has been a growing tendency to increase direct central-municipal governmental relationships. In greatly centralized systems such as in Latin America, there has been a tendency, however, for municipalities to seek greater autonomy.[66] It may be that increasing urbanization may produce convergence in present centralized and decentralized systems, respectively, in the interrelationship of central and local governments. Robson states that "the general tendency seems to be for the higher authorities to exercise, or at least to acquire, increasing powers of control over the great city." [67]

Accelerating urban growth has also placed great strains on local governmental structures throughout the world. The emergence of the twentieth-century metropolis has made obsolete many inherited forms of municipal government. The metropolitan area characterized by governmental fragmentation is experiencing increasing strain and conflict of various types.[68]

The combined trends of population concentration into metropolitan areas and decentralization within them have greatly altered intra-metropolitan-area relationships. Population and community changes, along with economic and technological changes, have jurisdictionally separated place of residence and political responsibility, on the one hand, and place of work and economic responsibility, on the other. Moreover, they have also sometimes jurisdictionally separated both place of work and place of residence from place of shopping, place of recreation, or place of schooling. In consequence, great disparities have arisen among local jurisdictions within metropolitan areas between the need for urban services and the utilization of such services, and ability adequately to plan for, administer, and finance them.[69] The common explanation for these afflictions is to be found in the outmoded assumption, valid in the premetropolitan world, that the area of local governmental jurisdiction was simultaneously the area of residence, work, consumer expenditure, schooling, religious observance, and living in general. The differentiation of function and urbanism as a way of life exacerbate the frictions produced by the disparity between twentieth-century clumpings of people and economic activities and inherited local governmental structure.

One specific and serious source of difficulty arises from the pattern of intrametropolitan-area population distribution described above. The tendency for higher socioeconomic elements of the population to move outward in many Western cities has left central cities with increasingly larger proportions of population with relatively low socioeconomic status. Thus, central cities find they are confronted with a shrinking tax base even as their problems—physical, human, and governmental—become more severe, and even though they continue to provide indispensable services to the entire metropolitan complex.

Moreover, in many metropolitan areas throughout the world, municipal governments without suburban jurisdiction face acute problems in respect to the control of outlying land uses that affect the welfare and destiny of the central city.[70] Basic deficiencies of present metropolitan governmental organization are becoming ever more apparent, and proposals for changes in local governmental structure may be expected to increase.[71] This in manifested in increasing movements toward consolidation of local governments, in the creation of metropolitan-area agencies to perform specific functions, in the creation of metropolitan-area planning agencies and in the creation in Canada of the Toronto metropolitan governmental structure, which may serve as a prototype for other metropolitan areas.

Finally, rapid urbanization may create strains in the relative political power position of urban and rural population groupings. In some countries, as in the United States, urban populations may be underrepresented in government by reason of the failure of those political institutions to reflect the rapidly changing urban-rural population composition.[72] In other areas, as in parts of Asia and Latin America, rapidly growing urban centers, especially the capital cities, may exert disproportionate control over the entire nation by reason of their strategic location in the economy and government.[73]

Urbanization, then, has profoundly affected government as one form of social organization. It has greatly increased government interventionism, challenged traditional ideologies with respect to the role of government, modified the nature of representative government, introduced new substantive political issues, changed the character of public administration, altered central, regional, and local intergovernmental relationships, and made obsolete many local governmental structures. Rapid urbanization has also increasingly affected the political power position of urban and rural population groupings, respectively.

Finally, the impact of urbanization on the role of government is by no means restricted to national boundaries. Worldwide urbanization has produced increasing international interdependence which in turn is modifying the traditional concepts of "sovereignty" and "nationalism." The role of individual nations as members of the United Nations, and its specialized agencies, has certainly profoundly altered inherited concepts of both. The ever-shrinking world and manifestations of international order may also be viewed as constituting, in some measure, a consequence of world urbanization.

The City and Population Growth

Increases in urban population are affected through three sources—natural increase, net migration, and reclassification. Natural increase is the excess of births over deaths. Net migration is the excess of in-migration over out-migration. Reclassification is the allocation of populations of places previously defined as "rural" to "urban" at that point at which the criterion for becoming "urban" is achieved. That is, in the statistics relating to rural-urban population, an appreciable proportion of the increase in urban population from census to census is the result of reclassification of population from rural to urban.

Adequate data are not available to trace the growth of the cities in terms of each of these components over long periods of time. It is probably true that the early neolithic village grew primarily as a result of natural increase up to the relatively low population ceiling imposed by its limited technology and social organization. The evidence indicates that the neolithic village, when it attained its population limit, generated another village through a process of fission.[74] That is, some considerable part of the original village migrated as a group to a favorable site for a new village.

As advancing technology and social organization permitted larger population agglomerations, in-migration must have increased in importance as a source of urban population growth. Certain it is that with the emergence of the large industrial and commercial city, the conditions of life producing relatively high mortality and relatively low fertility, in part as a result of selective male in-migration, must have made natural increase a relatively minor factor in urban growth. In contemporary developing nations, available data indicate that net migration is a very important source and, perhaps, for most nations the most important source of urban growth.[75] Under contemporary conditions, net migration, although consisting largely of rural to urban movement, includes for some nations relatively important components of net immigration, that is, migration from abroad. In six of ten Latin American countries for which estimates are available, for example, migration accounted for more than half of total urban growth over periods ranging roughly from 1930 to 1950 (Venezuela, Colombia, the Dominican Republic, Nicaragua, Paraguay, and El Salvador). In three additional countries, migration accounted for more than 40 per cent of total urban growth (Brazil, Chile, and Mexico).

In the history of the economically advanced countries, urban-rural differences in fertility and mortality have apparently been the rule, at least since the emergence of the industrial city.[76] Early industrial cities tended to have relatively high mortality induced by conditions of congestion, poor environmental sanitation and personal hygiene, and abysmally poor working conditions. In the United States the recorded mortality of urban population was much higher than that of the rural population throughout the nineteenth century.[77] Despite the limitations of the data, this urban-rural differential was probably real, for even in nineteenth-century America poor living conditions, lack of sanitation, and the high incidence of infectious diseases generated relatively high death rates.

In contrast with mortality, fertility apparently was lower in urban than in rural areas in the early city.[78] Selective migration brought disproportionately large numbers of men into the cities, contributing to low urban fertility. Infectious and debilitating diseases contributing to high mortality also played some role in restricting the birth rate. In the United States differences in urban and rural fertility have been evident throughout the history of the nation.

The unsatisfactory character of the data does not permit accurate evaluation of the roles of net migration and natural increase, respectively, to urban growth over the years. In the United States vital statistics do not permit satisfactory allocation of urban and rural births and deaths. It is possible, however, to evaluate the respective roles of natural increase and net migration in the recent growth of metropolitan areas in the United States. Between 1950 and 1960, the Bureau of the Census has estimated that of the total increase of 23.2 million persons in "metropolitan state economic areas," 15.1 million was the result of natural increase and 8.1 million the result of net migration.[79] It is to be borne in mind, however, that between 1950 and 1960 the birth rate of the United States was still relatively high as a result of the postwar boom in marriages and babies. In contrast, the increase of 4.7 million in "non-metropolitan state economic areas" was made up of the natural increase of 10.2 million persons and a net out-migration of 5.5 million persons.

In contemporary underdeveloped areas, fertility in both rural and urban communities is generally high with indications that there is no uniformity in such differentials that can be measured. Robinson found in his analyses of selected non-Western countries that urban fertility was below rural in about half the cases, whereas in the remaining countries there was no apparent difference or urban fertility appeared to be higher than rural.[80] Moreover, he demonstrates that the apparent urban-rural differences in fertility as measured by fertility ratios (a ratio of children under five to women of childbearing age as reported in a census) are mainly the result of differences in infant mortality.

In underdeveloped areas in Asia and the Far East, evidence indicates that the death rates of the population in general, and particularly of infants, appears to be higher in cities than in rural areas, but the evidence is neither clear nor consistent. In the five countries in Latin America for which mortality data are reasonably good, infant mortality is lower in urban than in the rural areas. It is difficult to draw a firm conclusion about urban-rural differences in general mortality in the developing regions.[81]

The experience of the economically advanced nations does permit some firm conclusions with respect to the impact of their urbanization on fertility and mortality trends. With respect to mortality it is clear that in the Western nations a combination of factors, including improved environmental sanitation, personal hygiene and modern medicine, including the antibiotics and the insecticides, is operating to effect convergence in urban and rural mortality rates at low levels.

It is also clear in the experience of the West that great declines in fertility were first evident in urban areas.[82] With the emergence of urbanism as a way of life, rational decision-making was extended to size of family, and fertility was deliberately controlled by urban populations. Within urban areas, family planning originated among the elite, better-educated, and higher-income groups, and then diffused to the remainder of the population. This process is by no means yet completed. The poor and uneducated even in urban areas are not yet controlling their fertility. Although it is true that birth rates have gone up in urban even more than in rural areas with fluctuations in fertility, the general pattern of lower urban than rural fertility is ubiquitous and persistent. It is also clear in the more economically advanced nations that family planning has spread from urban to rural areas and that rural fertility is now also experiencing a great decline. There is some evidence, at least in the United States, of convergence in urban and rural fertility, although the data are far from adequate and conclusive.

The emergence of the city was, in some measure, a function of rapid population growth to which it in turn also contributed. In the West, the city in due course has become the point of origin and diffusion of fertility control. The city in the advanced areas increasingly holds forth the prospect of deliberate control of population growth.

Up to the present time, however, the city in the underdeveloped areas has given little evidence of playing a similar role. But the concerted efforts under way on an ever greater scale to induce fertility control may eventually achieve their objective. It may be anticipated that major successes in regulation of family size will first occur in the urban rather than the rural population in the developing areas.

Urbanization in Advanced and Developing Nations

The foregoing consideration of the consequences of urbanization necessarily is based primarily on the observed and hypothesized experience of the economically advanced nations. Although there are many similarities with respect to urbanization in the advanced nations and the present developing areas, there are also important differences.[83] The differences merit attention for at least two reasons. First, they demonstrate that it may be hazardous to assume that all of the patterns of urbanization observed in the past in the advanced areas will necessarily apply in the future to the developing regions; second, critical examination of the process and impact of urbanization in the developing areas may provide a basis for testing the generalizations and the hypotheses in respect of urbanization derived from the experience of the West. Urbanization in the developing regions of the world provides an opportunity for significant research which not only may help to explain the process and its consequences in specific underdeveloped regions but also may shed light on the antecedents and consequences of urbanization in the West.

Among the differences between urbanization in the advanced areas and in the developing regions are: (1) differences in the world political situation at the present time as compared with that prevalent when the advanced nations first experienced rapid urbanization; (2) differences in the forces making for urbanization; (3) differences in the ratio of population to resources and levels of living; (4) differences in basic outlook and value systems.

The World Political Situation

There can be little doubt that the differences in the world political situation today, as contrasted with that in the eighteenth and nineteenth centuries, are influencing the course of urbanization in the developing regions. The world since the Second World War is characterized by an unprecedented degree of international organization. The presence of the United Nations, its international agencies and various forms of regional organization, is providing the developing areas with stimulation and assistance in economic growth and urbanization. The international organizations have contributed materially to the "revolution of rising expectations" which has led virtually all peoples on the face of the earth to aspire to higher levels of living and political independence if not yet achieved. A number of the international organizations have specific programs designed to deal with problems of urbanization as well as economic development in general.[84] Moreover, technical assistance is also being provided bilaterally by governments and various private organizations. Such technical assistance through bilateral arrangements is stimulated by the polarization of world politics. As a result of these influences it seems reasonable to anticipate that the pace of urbanization may be accelerated for the underdeveloped areas and that both the antecedents and the consequences of urbanization may differ from those observed in the past.

Forces of Urbanization

Several other forces also are operating to effect differences in urbanization among the present developing nations from that observed in the past in the economically advanced areas. For one thing, partly as a result of the changed world political framework, it may be anticipated that central planning will play a much more prominent role in urbanization than it previously did. In the present advanced nations industrialization, urbanization, and economic development in general are largely the product of market forces through which differentiation of function, spatial arrangement, resource allocation, and economic growth were largely achieved. It may be argued that rapid industrialization and urbanization and attendant higher levels of living were experienced by the economically advanced nations despite the fact that the interplay of factors most conducive to efficient and balanced development and orderly urbanization were far from fully understood. In increasing the mix of government interventionism and central planning in the urbanization of the present developing areas, it is possible that many of the problems of Western urbanization may be avoided or ameliorated. But it is also possible that new and equally difficult types of problems will be encountered. In the developing nations there is a great need for a full understanding of the forces making for economic growth and urbanization to provide a sound basis for policy and action. That is, there is greater need for knowledge among the underdeveloped areas today than there ever was in the early stages of urbanization in the present advanced nations. In the absence of such knowledge there is danger of effecting serious diseconomies in planning urbanization. Certainly, what little is known of the experience of countries which have employed central planning indicates that it is by no means free of serious economic, social, and political problems.[85] In any case, although planning was definitely a factor in development in many parts of the West, the increased use of central planning in the developing areas is also likely to contribute to different patterns of urbanization than that observed in the West.

Differences in the urbanization of the present developing areas may arise also from their colonial heritage. In many of the countries in Asia, Latin America, and Africa, cities are more the product of colonial experience—that is, the result of exogenous factors—than indigenous economic development. Many of the underdeveloped nations have but one major city, "the primate city," which dominates the urban situation. The "great city" is often five to ten times as large as the next largest city, and the urban population in general does not portray the same "system" as observed in Western development.

The primate city generally owes its origin and growth largely to its function as an *entrepôt* between the colony and the imperial country. It owed its growth and development to its role in an imperial system rather than to indigenous national economic growth. With the disruption of empire many of the cities in the economically underdeveloped areas experienced some loss of basic economic function. To the extent that this has occurred, such cities must await further national economic growth adequately to support their present size. As a result, many of the underdeveloped countries may have larger urban populations than is justified by their degree of industrialization and economic development by the standards observed in the development of cities in the West.

The position that underdeveloped areas are in this sense "overurbanized" has been challenged, among others by N. V. Sovani.[86] He also marshals data which tend to refute the contention that rural "push" is a major factor in urban growth in developing areas. It is clear, nevertheless, that urbanization in the developing areas has not been associated with dramatic increases in levels of living as in the West, where the city was a consequent of, and antecedent to, increased productivity.

Another force making for differences in urbanization between the present advanced and economically developing areas is found in the fact that the developing regions now have available to them twentieth-century technology. In the developing regions, the entire complex of twentieth-century technology, including electric power, the automobile, and the telephone, is available for effecting and influencing urban growth. In consequence, developing cities today, by diffusion from the West simultaneously, rather than sequentially, can experience the centrifugal and centripetal forces, respectively, generated by changing technology. Both general and specific forms of spatial arrangements of plant and population, therefore, may vary considerably from that observed in the past. A technological factor that may impede urban development in present developing areas is to be found in their relatively primitive state of agricultural technology. Agricultural technology in the West at the beginning of its rapid industrial development was in a more advanced state than in the underdeveloped areas today, and improving agricultural technology along with more plentiful land undoubtedly contributed to industrialization in the West by providing increased income and, therefore, savings for industrial investment.[87]

The accelerated growth of many of the cities in the underdeveloped areas since the end of the Second World War may also be regarded, in part, as the result of their colonial heritage. Disorganization occasioned by the war and postwar developments generated social unrest and political instability which have contributed to large refugee populations flooding the cities. Accelerating urban growth in many of the underdeveloped areas therefore is not so much the product of economic development and the pull of population into cities from rural areas but rather is the result of the push of population from troubled and insecure rural areas. The push is further augmented by accelerating total population growth, discussed further below.

Population and Resources

The third factor which may account for differences in urbanization in the developing areas from that observed in the past is to be found in differences in the ratio of population to resources. In most of the developing areas today the ratio of population to resources is much higher than that which prevailed at the beginning of the industrialization and urbanization of the West. Population was relatively sparse in relation to resources at the outset of Western industrialization and urbanization. Moreover, as the demographic revolution advanced with increased industrialization and urbanization in the West, such surplus populations as were generated were free to migrate to the vast unexploited and relatively uninhabited continents of the Western Hemisphere and Oceania. In contrast, many of the developing areas today are already characterized by a very high ratio of population to land and other resources. Moreover, they are experiencing a more rapid decline in mortality than was ever experienced in the Western world and consequently more rapid rates of population increase.[88]

Much of urban growth in the developing areas today is in fact the result of the push of population from the already overpopulated rural countryside. Moreover, in the contemporary world there are no un-inhabited lands to which overpopulated nations may send their surplus peoples. The problem of effecting economic exchange between urban and rural populations is therefore more difficult and poses serious political as well as economic problems.[89]

Basic Outlook

Finally, a fourth factor which may differentially affect patterns of urbanization is to be found in the differences between the West and the developing areas in basic outlook and value system. The differences in outlook and values are exemplified in the differences between the "Protestant ethic," on one hand, and Hindu, Buddhist, and Islamic traditions on the other. Some scholars have taken the position that a prerequisite to Western economic development producing urbanization was the value system of the West as exemplified in the Protestant ethic.[90] This outlook has been characterized as rational rather than traditional and as involving a willingness and ability to defer immediate gratifications for more desirable later ones. It places emphasis on achievement and success as distinguished from status and prestige, the cosmopolitan as distinguished from the parochial, and the material as distinguished from the spiritual. It embraces interrelationships that are impersonal and utilitarian as distinguished from personal and sentimental. It is a moot question, however, whether the Western outlook so characterized is an antecedent or consequent of urbanization or something of both. It is also a moot question as to whether this outlook or elements of it really are essential ingredients of economic development and urbanization.[91] Conceivably, the differences between outlook in the advanced and developing areas may produce different types of urbanization. It is also conceivable that much of what has been written on the subject is a product of generalizations based solely on Western experience and is therefore subject to the limitations of historicism.

Some Differences in Consequences

Perhaps, by reason of the types of differences indicated, both the processes and consequences of urbanization in the developing areas may differ from those in the advanced areas of the world. For example, the physical patterning of the large city in the underdeveloped areas tends to differ appreciably from that of cities in the economically advanced nations. Although many of the cities in the developing areas have central cores resembling the structure of Western cities (as part of the colonial heritage), such cores are usually surrounded by vast populations living in "native quarters." Thus cities in the underdeveloped areas tend to have a dual form of structure. There is some tendency for lower-income groups to live toward the central area with higher-income groups living toward the periphery within their Westernized cores. But surrounding the entire central core are the native quarters containing the poorest and newest in-migrants. Thus the large city in the developing area may portray a pattern of population distribution within its central core of a type similar to that found in the United States; but it may also resemble the structure of the medieval and ancient city in that the poorest and newest in-migrants are likely to be found on the periphery of the total agglomeration.[92] Similarly, the differences in levels of living between cities in the developed and developing areas may be traced to the differences between them in the forces making for urbanization. Kuznets has demonstrated that the levels of living in the economically advanced areas were higher at their point of take-off in economic development than is prevalent in the underdeveloped regions today.[93] This situation, coupled with the fact that urban growth in the developing areas may be more the result of the push of population from the impoverished countryside than the pull of population to urban areas by reason of greater economic opportunity and productivity,[94] may help to account for the relatively low level of living found in urban places in the underdeveloped nations.

Similarly, the differences in economic organization and the extent to which urbanism as a way of life prevails may be traced to differences in forces making for urbanization in the developed as contrasted with the developing areas. In the developing areas, large population agglomerations are largely the product of agglutination, that is, the compressing into physical proximity of what remain essentially discrete population groupings. Under such circumstances, large population size does not necessarily lead to greatly increased division of labor, specialization, and its concomitants leading to increased productivity per capita and more complex economic organization. Similarly, the agglutinated character of the population agglomeration in developing areas may account for the absence of more manifestations of urbanism as a way of life. Although the cities in the developing areas have large size, high density, and often heterogeneous populations, they do not portray the consequences of urbanization in the transformation of human nature, social organization, and government as observed in the West. The explanation for this phenomenon may lie in Durkheim's consideration of "moral density," that is, in the absence of interaction and intercommunication between the diverse elements of the urban population.[95]

Purpose and Organization of This Book

The preceding overview is subject to many limitations. It is drawn in part from the available literature and in part from impression and hypothesis. In both respects it is disproportionately based on the experience of the West, and such generalizations as are contained therein are subject, therefore, to the limitations of historicism. Moreover, in the attempt to present a comprehensive perspective, the treatment is necessarily uneven and contains many gaps.

Both the processes and consequences of urbanization are complex, and there are many ramifications that have by no means yet been subjected to adequate research. The deficiencies of this overview help to explain the purpose of this book and of the Committee on Urbanization of the Social Science Research Council which has produced it. It is, in brief, to set forth extant assumptions and generalizations in respect of urbanization as available in the social sciences, to subject them to critical review, and to point to the need for further research on this extremely important phenomenon.

Although the Committee included representatives of the social sciences in which various aspects of urbanization have been investigated —history, geography, political science, sociology, economics, and anthropology—the collection of papers by no means includes all the aspects of urbanization that might have been treated. Some of the disciplines or subdisciplines which have much to contribute to a fuller understanding of the antecedents or consequences of urbanization are not represented at all, for example, archaeology, psychology, and education. Moreover, the rapidly expanding areas of social engineering concerned with urban problems are entirely omitted, such as city planning, urban transport, and public administration. Such materials as are included in this symposium are necessarily restricted to the social sciences and to subjects on which the individual members of the Committee have worked.

The book is organized into three parts: The Study of Urbanization in the Social Sciences, Comparative Urban Research, and Selected Research Problems. In Part 1, five chapters review the literature and point to the basic problems of urbanization as considered in history, geography, political science, sociology, and economics, respectively. In Part 2, comparative urban research is stressed, with special attention to the need for studies of urbanization in the developing countries. Part 3 contains papers dealing with selected specific areas of research. Examples are drawn from geography, economics, anthropology, sociology, and history.

In its deliberations the Committee on Urbanization identified four main needs in urban research:

1. There is need to differentiate the study of the city as a dependent variable and as an independent variable. Much of the apparent conflict in the literature on urbanization lies in the failure to make the distinction clear.

2. Consideration should be given to the advancement of multidisciplinary research on the problems of urbanization.

3. More comparative and historical studies, both of the processes and consequences of urbanization, should be undertaken.

4. There is great opportunity in the underdeveloped areas of the world for comparative urban studies. Through such studies better perspective could be achieved on the generalizations that have been made about urbanization, most of which have been derived from consideration of a relatively small number of Western cities over relatively limited periods of time.

It is hoped that this volume of essays will contribute to an enhanced understanding of urban phenomena and to a more adequate view of the city by directing attention to gaps in existing knowledge and stimulating research designed to fill these gaps.

NOTES

1. Otis Dudley Duncan, "Human Ecology and Population Studies," in Philip M. Hauser and Otis Dudley Duncan (Eds.), *The Study of Population: An Inventory and Appraisal* (Chicago: University of Chicago Press, 1959), pp. 681ff.

2. Ralph Turner, *The Great Cultural Traditions*, Vol. I, *The Ancient Cities* (New York: McGraw-Hill, 1941), pp. 126ff.

3. *Ibid.*, Vol. II, *The Classical Empires*, pp. 856ff.

4. Fred Cottrell, *Energy and Society* (New York: McGraw-Hill, 1955).

5. For example, Ralph Turner, *op. cit.*, Vols. I, II; V. Gordon Childe, *Man Makes Himself* (London: Watts, 1941), Chaps. 5–6; *What Happened in History* (London: Penguin Books, 1946), Chaps. 3–4; Robert J. Braidwood and Gordon R. Willey (Eds.), *Courses Toward Urban Life* (Chicago: Aldine, 1962); N. S. B. Gras, *An Introduction to Economic History* (New York: Harper, 1922); Lewis Mumford, *The City in History* (New York: Harcourt, Brace & World, 1961).

6. N. S. B. Gras, *op. cit.*

7. Eric E. Lampard, "The History of Cities in the Economically Advanced Areas," *Economic Development and Cultural Change,* 3 (January 1955), pp. 103–104.

8. August Lösch, *The Economics of Location* (New Haven: Yale University Press, 1954). Cited in O. D. Duncan et al., *Metropolis and Region* (Baltimore: Johns Hopkins Press, 1960), p. 25.

9. O. D. Duncan, et al., *ibid.,* Chap. 2.

10. For example, George K. Zipf, *Human Behavior and the Principle of Least Effort* (Cambridge: Addison-Wesley, 1949); Rutledge Vining, "A Description of Certain Spatial Aspects of an Economic System," *Economic Development and Cultural Change,* 3 (January 1955), pp. 147–195; Herbert A. Simon, *Models of Man* (New York: Wiley, 1957), Chap. 9; Brian J. L. Berry and William L. Garrison, "Alternate Explanations of Urban Rank-Size Relationships," *Annals of the Association of American Geographers,* 48 (March 1958), pp. 83–91.

11. William F. Ogburn, *Social Characteristics of Cities* (Chicago: International City Manager's Association, 1937); Otis Dudley Duncan and Albert J. Reiss, Jr., *Social Characteristics of Urban and Rural Communities, 1950* (New York: Wiley, 1956).

12. Herbert A. Simon, *loc. cit.* Simon, utilizing stochastic processes and probability concepts and using the "Yule distribution" as a point of departure, has provided a basis for quite accurate prediction of actual distributions of cities by size.

13. Brian J. L. Berry and William L. Garrison, *op. cit.,* p. 90.

14. United Nations, *Determinants and Consequences of Population Trends* (New York: United Nations, 1953), Chap. 2.

15. Kingsley Davis, "The Origin and Growth of Urbanization in the World," *American Journal of Sociology* (special issue on "World Urbanism" edited by Philip M. Hauser), 60 (March 1955), p. 433.

16. J. Fletcher Wellemeyer (in consultation with Frank Lorimer), "Appendix," *Population Bulletin,* 18 (February 1962), p. 19.

17. Ralph Turner, *op. cit.,* Vol. I, pp. 51ff.

18. Gideon Sjoberg, *The Pre-Industrial City* (Glencoe, Ill.: Free Press, 1960), pp. 80–81.

19. Kingsley Davis, *op. cit.,* pp. 429–437.

20. Statistics related to the United States are drawn from publications of the U. S. Bureau of the Census unless otherwise indicated. The historical data are drawn largely from: U. S. Bureau of the Census, *Historical Statistics of the United States, Colonial Times to 1957* (Washington, D. C.: U. S. Government Printing Office, 1960); and U. S. Bureau of the Census, *Statistical Abstract of the United States,* issued annually. Other data are drawn mainly from decennial census volumes. To save space and repetition, specific references to the census publications are not given.

21. Louis Wirth, *Community Life and Social Policy* (Chicago: University of Chicago Press, 1956), pp. 110–132.

22. Hope Tisdale Eldridge, "The Process of Urbanization," in J. J. Spengler and O. D. Duncan (Eds.), *Demographic Analysis* (Glencoe, Ill.: Free Press, 1956), pp. 338–343.

23. United Nations, *Demographic Yearbook* (New York: United Nations, 1955), p. 16.

24. U. S. Bureau of the Census, *U. S. Census of Population: 1960*, Vol. I, *Characteristics of the Population*, Part A, "Number of Inhabitants" (Washington: U. S. Government Printing Office), pp. xiv–xxvii.

25. Jean Gottmann, *Virginia at Mid-Century* (New York: Holt, 1955), pp. 41, 174, 472–479; also, *Megalopolis—The Urbanized Northeastern Seaboard of the United States* (New York: Twentieth Century Fund, 1961).

26. International Urban Research, *The World's Metropolitan Areas* (Berkeley: University of California Press, 1959), pp. 6–33.

27. Joyce O. Hertzler, *The Social Thought of the Ancient Civilizations* (New York: McGraw-Hill, 1936), pp. 298ff., 350.

28. See Chapter 13B.

29. Emile Durkheim, *L'annee Sociologique*, Vol. II, 1897–1898.

30. Adapted from Amos H. Hawley, *Human Ecology* (New York: Ronald Press, 1950), pp. 100ff.

31. For qualification of this simplistic model, see pages 39 and 40.

32. Ralph Turner, *op. cit.*, Vol. I, p. 73.

33. *Ibid.*, pp. 128ff.

34. Lewis Mumford, *op. cit.*, p. 16.

35. *Ibid.*

36. *Ibid.*, pp. 61ff.

37. Gideon Sjoberg, *op. cit.*, pp. 91ff.

38. Lewis Mumford, *op. cit.*, pp. 540ff.

39. Philip M. Hauser, *On the Impact of Population and Community Changes on Local Government*, Seventh Annual Wherrett Lecture on Local Government (Pittsburgh: Institute of Local Government, University of Pittsburgh, 1961), pp. 19ff.

40. Coleman Woodbury (Ed.), *The Future of Cities and Urban Redevelopment* (Chicago: University of Chicago Press, 1953); U. S. Department of Health, Education and Welfare, Public Health Service, *Report of the Committee on Environmental Health Problems* (Washington: U. S. Government Printing Office, 1962); "Metropolis in Ferment," *Annals of the American Academy of Political and Social Science*, 314 (November 1957); John C. Bollens, *Exploring the Metropolitan Community* (Berkeley: University of California Press, 1961); Raymond Vernon, *Metropolis 1985* (Cambridge: Harvard University Press, 1960); Pittsburgh Regional Planning Association, *Region With a Future* (Pittsburgh: University of Pittsburgh Press, 1963).

41. Ralph Turner, *op. cit*, Vol. I, pp. 277ff.

42. Gideon Sjoberg, *op. cit.*, pp. 187ff.

43. N. S. B. Gras, *op. cit.*; Edgar M. Hoover and Raymond Vernon, *Anatomy of a Metropolis* (Cambridge: Harvard University Press, 1959).

44. Louis Wirth, *op. cit.*, pp. 117ff.

45. Charles Horton Cooley, *Social Organization* (New York: Scribner, 1925), Chap. 3; Louis Wirth, *op. cit.*, pp. 118ff.

46. For example, Bureau of Social Affairs, United Nations, "Urbanization and Crime and Delinquency in Asia and the Far East," in Philip M. Hauser (Ed.), *Urbanization in Asia and the Far East* (Calcutta: UNESCO, 1957), Chap. 9; Philip M. Hauser (Ed.), *Urbanization in Latin America* (Paris: UNESCO, 1961), especially "Migration and Urbanization—The Barriadas of Lima: An Example of Integration into Urban Life," Chap. 6; Andrew Pearse, "Some Characteristics of Urbanization in the City of Rio

de Janeiro," Chap. 7; Gino Germani, "Inquiry into the Social Effects of Urbanization in a Working Class Sector of Greater Buenos Aires," Chap. 8; J. R. B. Lopes, "Aspects of the Adjustment of Rural Migrants to Urban-Industrial Conditions in Sao Paulo, Brazil," Chap. 9; H. Rotando, "Psychological and Mental Health Problems of Urbanization Based on Case Studies in Peru," Chap. 10; UNESCO, *The Social Implications of Industrialization and Urbanization—Five Studies in Asia* (Calcutta: UNESCO, 1956); UNESCO, *Social Implications of Industrialization and Urbanization in Africa South of the Sahara* (Paris: UNESCO, 1956).

47. Philip M. Hauser, *Population Perspectives* (New Brunswick, N. J.: Rutgers University Press, 1960), pp. 120ff.; Oscar Handlin, *The Uprooted* (Boston: Little, Brown, 1951), and *The Newcomers* (Cambridge: Harvard University Press, 1959); Otis Dudley Duncan and Beverly Duncan, *The Negro Population of Chicago* (Chicago: University of Chicago Press, 1957).

48. Philip M. Hauser, *op. cit.*, pp. 149ff.

49. Robert Redfield, "The Folk Society," *American Journal of Sociology,* 52 (January 1947), pp. 293–308; Louis Wirth, *op. cit.*, pp. 110–132.

50. See Chapter 13 (A by Oscar Lewis; B by Philip M. Hauser).

51. Oscar Lewis, *Life in a Mexican Village: Tepotzlan Restudied* (Urbana: University of Illinois Press, 1951); Edward M. Bruner, "Urbanization and Culture Change: Indonesia" (paper read at the 58th Annual Meeting of the American Anthropological Association, Mexico City, December 28, 1959); Douglas S. Butterworth, "A Study of the Urbanization Process Among Mixtec Migrants from Tilantongo in Mexico City," *America Indigena,* 22 (July 1962), pp. 257–274; Theodore Caplow, "The Social Ecology of Guatemala City," *Social Forces,* 28 (December 1949), pp. 113–135; William L. Kolb, "The Social Structure and Function of Cities," *Economic Development and Cultural Change,* 3 (October 1954), pp. 30–46; O. D. Duncan and Albert J. Reiss, Jr., *Social Characteristics of Urban and Rural Communities, 1950* (New York: Wiley, 1956); Herbert J. Gans, *The Urban Villagers: Group and Class in the Life of Italian-Americans* (Glencoe, Ill.: Free Press, 1962); *A Social Profile of Detroit, 1955* (Ann Arbor: Department of Sociology and Survey Research Center, University of Michigan, 1956).

52. Bert F. Hoselitz, "A Survey of the Literature on Urbanization in India," in Roy Turner (Ed.), *India's Urban Future* (Berkeley: University of California Press, 1962), p. 427.

53. Emile Durkheim, *On the Division of Labor in Society,* trans. by George Simpson (New York: Macmillan, 1933), Book I, Chaps. 2 and 3.

54. William F. Ogburn (with the assistance of Clark Tibbitts), "The Family and Its Functions," Report of the President's Research Committee on Social Trends, *Recent Social Trends* (New York: McGraw-Hill, 1933), Vol. I, pp. 661–708.

55. *Ibid.*, pp. 662ff.

56. Arthur W. Calhoun, *A Social History of the American Family* (Cleveland: Clark, 1919), Vol. III, pp. 169ff.; William J. Goode, *World Revolution and Family Patterns* (New York: Free Press of Glencoe, 1963), pp. 128–129.

57. *A Social Profile of Detroit, 1955, op. cit.*; Herbert J. Gans, *op. cit.*, Chap. 3.

58. William Graham Sumner, *Folkways* (Boston: Ginn, 1907), p. 54.

59. *From Max Weber: Essays in Sociology,* trans. and ed. by H. H. Gerth and C. Wright Mills (New York: Oxford University Press, 1946), pp. 196ff.
60. William H. Whyte, *The Organization Man* (New York: Doubleday, 1957).
61. Ralph Turner, *op. cit.,* Vol. I, p. 182.
62. Max Weber, *op. cit.,* pp. 180ff.
63. Adapted from Philip M. Hauser, *On the Impact of Population and Community Changes on Local Government,* Seventh Annual Wherrett Lecture on Local Government (Pittsburgh: Institute of Local Government, University of Pittsburgh, 1961), pp. 19ff. See also Chapter 4 by Wallace S. Sayre and Nelson W. Polsby on "American Political Science and the Study of Urbanization." A major treatment of problems of government in great cities in the world is given in William A. Robson (Ed.), *Great Cities of the World, Their Government, Politics and Planning,* 2nd ed. (New York: Macmillan, 1957).
64. Karl Polanyi, *The Great Transformation* (New York: Farrar and Rinehart, 1944); Gunnar Myrdal, *Beyond the Welfare State* (New Haven: Yale University Press, 1960).
65. In general, political science and comparative government textbooks and treatises have treated this problem only tangentially. For a discussion bearing directly on this point, see D. W. Brogan and Douglas V. Verney, *Political Patterns in Today's World* (New York: Harcourt, Brace & World, 1963), Chaps. 4 and 9. Also useful: Taylor Cole, *European Political Systems* (New York: Knopf, 1959), Chaps. 5 and 6.
66. Morton Grodzins, "The Federal System," *Goals for Americans* (President's Commission on National Goals), 1960, pp. 265–284. Wallace S. Sayre, "Cities and the State" and "State-City Government Relations," *Final Report* (New York State-New York City Fiscal Relations Committee, November 1956), pp. 55–65, 281–288. J. Medina Echavarria and Philip M. Hauser, "Rapporteurs' Report," in Philip M. Hauser (Ed.), *Urbanization in Latin America* (Paris: UNESCO, 1961), pp. 70ff.
67. William A. Robson, *op. cit.,* p. 79.
68. *Ibid.,* pp. 55–71.
69. *Ibid.,* pp. 83–87; C. E. Merriam, A. Lepawsky, and S. Parratt, *The Government of Metropolitan Chicago* (Chicago: University of Chicago Press, 1933); Victor Jones, *Metropolitan Government* (Chicago: University of Chicago Press, 1942); Douglas Price, *The Metropolis and Its Problems* (Syracuse: Syracuse University Press, 1960); Paul Studenski, *The Government of Metropolitan Areas in the United States* (New York: National Municipal League, 1930).
70. J. Medina Echavarria and Philip M. Hauser, *op. cit.,* p. 60; Bureau of Social Affairs, United Nations, "Some Policy Implications of Urbanization," *op. cit.,* pp. 319ff.
71. William A. Robson, *op. cit.,* pp. 98–105.
72. *Ibid.,* p. 78; Paul T. David and Ralph Eisenberg, *Devaluation of the Urban and Suburban Vote* (Charlottesville: University of Virginia Press, 1961), p. 9; Andrew Hacker, *Congressional Districting* (Washington, D. C.: The Brookings Institution, 1963), p. 84; Gordon Baker, *Rural vs. Urban Political Power* (New York: Doubleday, 1955); The

Commission on Intergovernmental Relations, *A Report to the President for Transmittal to Congress* (June 1955), pp. 40, 102–103.

73. Bureau of Social Affairs, United Nations, *op. cit.*, p. 305; see also Nathan Keyfitz, Chapter 8, "Political-Economic Aspects of Urbanization in South and Southeast Asia."

74. V. Gordon Childe, "The Urban Revolution," *Town Planning Review,* 21 (April 1950), p. 5.

75. Population Branch, United Nations, "Demographic Aspects of Urbanization in Latin America," in Philip M. Hauser (Ed.), *Urbanization in Latin America* (Paris: UNESCO, 1961), p. 110.

76. John Graunt, *Natural and Political Observations . . . Made Upon the Bills of Mortality* (American edition: Baltimore: Johns Hopkins Press, 1939), pp. 41–42; Frank Lorimer, "The Development of Demography," in Philip M. Hauser and Otis Dudley Duncan (Eds.), *The Study of Population* (Chicago: University of Chicago Press, 1959), pp. 155ff.

77. Conrad Taeuber and Irene B. Taeuber, *The Changing Population of the United States* (New York: Wiley, 1958), pp. 269ff.

78. John Graunt, *op. cit.*, pp. 52ff.; Louis I. Dublin, Alfred J. Lotka, and Mortimer Spiegelman, *Length of Life* (New York: Ronald Press, 1949), Chap. 4.

79. U. S. Bureau of the Census, "Components of Population Change, 1950 to 1960, for Counties, Standard Metropolitan Statistical Areas, State Economic Areas and Economic Subregions," *Current Population Reports,* Series P23-7 (November 1962), p. 85.

80. Warren G. Robinson, "Urbanization and Fertility: The Non-Western Experience," *The Milbank Memorial Fund Quarterly,* 41 (July 1963), pp. 291–308.

81. Population Branch, United Nations, "Demographic Aspects of Urbanization in the ECAFE Region," in Philip M. Hauser (Ed.), *Urbanization in Asia and the Far East* (Calcutta: UNESCO, 1957), pp. 116ff., 111ff.; "Demographic Aspects of Urbanization in Latin America," in Philip M. Hauser (Ed.), *Urbanization in Latin America* (Paris: UNESCO, 1961), pp. 102ff., 106–107.

82. United Nations, *Determinants and Consequences of Population Trends* (New York: United Nations, 1953), pp. 78ff.

83. Adapted and elaborated from Philip M. Hauser, "World and Asian Urbanization in Relation to Economic Development and Social Change," in Philip M. Hauser (Ed.), *Urbanization in Asia and the Far East* (Calcutta: UNESCO, 1957, pp. 86ff.

84. They include the United Nations, UNESCO, ILO, and WHO. The seminars on urbanization in Latin America, Asia, and the Far East and other activities have been cooperative enterprises by these agencies.

85. United Nations, *Processes and Problems of Industrialization in Underdeveloped Countries* (New York: United Nations, 1955), pp. 71ff.; ECAFE, "Economic Development Policies in Relation to Types, Scale and Location of Industries, as a Factor Likely to Influence Urbanization Trends in ECAFE Countries, Joint UN/UNESCO Seminar on Urbanization in the ECAFE Region," in Philip M. Hauser (Ed.), *Urbanization in Asia and the Far East* (Calcutta: UNESCO, 1957), pp. 163–178.

86. N. V. Sovani, "The Analysis of 'Over-Urbanization,'" *Economic Development and Cultural Change,* 12 (January 1964), pp. 113–122.

87. Simon Kuznets, "Quantitative Aspects of the Economic Growth of Nations—II, Industrial Distribution of National Product and Labor Force," *Economic Development and Cultural Change,* Supp. to Vol. 5 (July 1957), pp. 52ff.

88. Harold Dorn, "World Population Growth," in Philip M. Hauser (Ed.), *The Population Dilemma* (Englewood Cliffs, N. J.: Prentice-Hall, 1963), pp. 8ff.

89. Nathan Keyfitz, *loc. cit.*

90. Max Weber, *The Protestant Ethic and the Spirit of Capitalism* (London: Allen and Unwin, 1930).

91. Philip M. Hauser, "World and Asian Urbanization . . . ," *op. cit.,* pp. 91–92.

92. Richard W. Redick, "A Demographic and Ecological Study of Rangoon, Burma: 1953" (unpublished Ph.D. dissertation, Department of Sociology, University of Chicago, 1961); Paul Cressey, "The Ecological Organization of Rangoon, Burma," *Sociology and Social Research,* 40 (January 1956), pp. 166–169).

93. Simon Kuznets, *Six Lectures on Economic Growth* (Glencoe, Ill.: Free Press, 1959), pp. 23–28.

94. Philip M. Hauser, "Summary Report of the General Rapporteur," *Urbanization in Asia and the Far East, op. cit.,* pp. 6–10; J. Medina Echavarria and Philip M. Hauser, "Rapporteurs' Report," *Urbanization in Latin America, op. cit.,* pp. 55–56.

95. Emile Durkheim, *op. cit.,* Book II, Chap. 2.

PART ONE

The Study of Urbanization
in the Social Sciences

The study of urbanization is clearly not an enterprise that is being pursued by only one or two academic disciplines. Contributions to the urban literature have been and are being made by scholars working in many fields. From its inception in 1958, the Committee on Urbanization of the Social Science Research Council has had multidisciplinary representation. Members have been drawn from the fields of economics, geography, history, political science, social anthropology, and sociology.

As with any complex phenomenon, different aspects of urbanization can be seen from different perspectives. It seemed proper, therefore, to begin the assessment of the present status and prospects of the study of urbanization with a series of "disciplinary" statements dealing with the main lines of effort in each field, past and present. In this

49

way, it is hoped, the student of urbanization—whether a veteran scholar or a neophyte—will gain not only an overview of developments in his own particular specialty but also a sense of the main points of articulation with other approaches.

The first two chapters are devoted to the most general and descriptive approaches to urbanization as it manifests itself through time and space. Chapter 2, by Charles N. Glaab, deals with "The Historian and the American City," and Chapter 3, by Harold M. Mayer, offers "A Survey of Urban Geography." As Glaab clearly shows, "urban history" is a relatively new specialty within American history; it can be roughly dated from 1933, when Arthur M. Schlesinger, Sr., published his highly influential treatment of *The Rise of the City*. In the wake of this work appeared a great number of "city biographies," or detailed historical case studies of particular places. There were also three significant short essays that appeared just before the Second World War and helped shape the major outlines of the new specialty— "The City in American History," by Arthur M. Schlesinger, Sr., "The Industrial City: Center of Cultural Change," by Ralph E. Turner, and "On the Dangers of an Urban Interpretation of History," by William Diamond. Aside from continuing empirical efforts, mainly oriented toward particular places and particular periods, the only discernible shifts in recent years appear to be (*a*) in the direction of a larger conception of urbanization as a societywide process and (*b*) in a greater willingness on the part of historians to draw upon the theoretical insights and research techniques of the allied social sciences.

Compared to urban history, urban geography is a somewhat older and more established specialty. Mayer's survey shows that contributions to urban geography were being made as early as the 1920's. The most significant recent change is in the direction of more sophisticated and increasingly quantitative empirical effort. Mayer's survey ranges over quite a wide array of topics covered in the urban geographical literature, including studies of the urban "economic base" and the related problems of the "central-place" functions of cities and the relations among cities and their hinterlands. Complementing this interest in the "external" relations of the urban place is the detailed attention given to urban internal organization and morphology.

Chapter 4, "American Political Science and the Study of Urbanization," by Wallace S. Sayre and Nelson W. Polsby, conveys quite a different impression. An interest in the city and its institutions on the part of this discipline antedates the twentieth century. Urbanization is clearly not a new topic; what is new is the recent change of perspective by political scientists. From the beginning—roughly dated from the first edition of *The American Commonwealth* in 1888—the American political scientist was inclined to view the city with alarm. The mission was reform and prescription was the keynote. According to Sayre and Polsby, the zeal of the reformer set the tone until after the Second World War, when a descriptive approach began to displace the prescriptive. The last decade, in particular, has been marked by an increasingly eclectic approach that draws upon the methods and techniques of other disciplines (for example, sociology) in the reexamination of certain "classical" questions concerning the locus and disposition of political power in the urban environment.

"Theory and Research in Urban Sociology" is the subject of Chapter 5 by Gideon Sjoberg. In this chapter, circumstances dictated that quite a different approach be taken. Rather than setting out a bibliographic survey, as in the chapters on history, geography, and political science, this chapter provides an introduction to various "theoretical orientations" that have emerged within urban sociology over the years. (Two comprehensive bibliographic surveys of urban sociology were recently published,[1] and it was the Committee's judgment that no useful purpose would be served by a mere updating of these surveys.) Sjoberg identifies some eight schools of thought that he perceives as operative in the field. It is doubtful that any two urban sociologists would agree on the composition of such a list of schools; the editors happen to be sociologists, for example, but their lists would probably be much shorter and differently organized had they been faced with the challenge that Sjoberg set for himself in this chapter. In any case, his views will undoubtedly serve to stimulate thought and discussion among those who are interested in this particular specialty.

The last chapter in this section is "Economic Aspects of Urban Research," by Raymond Vernon and Edgar M. Hoover. Again, the format differs from that employed in earlier chapters, and for good reason. For one thing, "urban economics" is probably the least well established of the specialties considered here, even though the prior existence of urban land economics, real estate research, and locational economics might suggest otherwise. Actually, this chapter constitutes one of the very first efforts to delineate the field in an explicit way, and becomes therefore more an evaluation of the potential of the field

---

[1] Albert J. Reiss, Jr., "Urban Sociology, 1945–55," in Hans L. Zetterberg (Ed.), *Sociology in the United States of America* (Paris: UNESCO, 1956), pp. 107–113; Noel P. Gist, "The Urban Community," in Joseph B. Gittler (Ed.), *Review of Sociology: Analysis of a Decade* (New York: Wiley, 1957), pp. 159–185.

than a review of a fragmentary literature. It begins with an effort at identifying just what is distinctive about the economist's approach to the urban scene. It goes on to comment on some broad methodological issues that are only now being subjected to serious debate. Finally, it establishes some priorities for research in different settings.

2

The Historian and the American City:
A Bibliographic Survey

Charles N. Glaab

American historians came late to the study of cities, the forces that created them, and their part in the development of the United States. Turn-of-the-century scholars who led the revolt against the rigid, formalistic history of the nineteenth century, which was often little more than a narrative of past politics and diplomacy, captured the study of the American past from the gentleman-amateur chronicler and introduced a variety of new subjects and approaches into their chosen discipline. But interest in cities and the way they had developed was not a part of the new outlook. The leaders of the movement toward a "New History" (among them James Harvey Robinson, Charles A. Beard, and Frederick Jackson Turner) focused attention on history as an instrument of social reform, on a broad kind of cultural history from which stemmed an interest in social and intellectual history, on the clash of economic interests in the past, and particularly on the creative force of the Great West—Turner's "frontier"—in shaping the unique qualities of American civilization. As the study of history penetrated graduate instruction in American universities, conflict between classes, between interest groups, or between geographic sections became fundamental dichotomies absorbed by students as readily as they acquired a respect for evidence and the exact procedures of the German seminar method. Owing in part to his enormous success as a teacher of graduate students, Turner was particularly influential. His "frontier thesis," which emphasized the continuing development of the free land of the west as the vital force in our nation's history, erected a scaffolding within which a generation of professional historians could construct craftsmanlike monographs devoted to examination of heuristic themes in the master's essays. Eventually there was reaction against his theories, but the Turnerian scheme determined the character of the dialectic. Refutation, defense, modification, or amplification of Turner is still considered a valid historical exercise.

Although Turner to some extent had always recognized the importance of the city and late in his life had even suggested the need for "an urban reinterpretation of our history," it was not until the 1930's—as an outgrowth of interest in an essentially descriptive social history concerned with the "life of the people"—that historians began to pay attention to the city. To the extent that urbanization thereafter began to work its way into general interpretations of American history, it was as part of a dramatic post-Civil War "rise of the city." This development was interpreted as an aspect of the triumph of industrialism or as part of the growth of a commercial-urban East threatening an agrarian-rural West, which represented much that was best in the American tradition. The city had created a number of new social and political problems—the slum, the machine, the political boss, the downtrodden immigrant—that were to be dealt with in future years by a new generation of Progressive reformers. Economically, the "rise of the city" exemplified the growing power of a class of exploitative capitalists, dealing in traction franchises, corrupting city governments, and oppressing workers and immigrants, but who were soon to face an aroused populace willing to enact a variety of desirable social and regulatory legislation. The Progressive Movement thus assured that under new conditions old values would be preserved with new methods; particularly in cities, as it was frequently stated, Hamiltonian means were necessary to maintain Jeffersonian ends. Although, as Eric E. Lampard has observed, an "urban-industrial transformation" has now become "part of the furniture displayed in every up-to-date textbook of United States history," there is little evidence that the substantial body of writing in urban history has influenced in any significant way general interpretations of the American past or the approaches employed by practicing American historians.[1]

In large part, this is the result of urban history's lack of academic respectability. Unlike many urban fields in the social sciences, neither the method nor the subject matter of urban history has been well defined. There are no textbooks providing a framework for inquiry, and only very recently has urban history acquired a small measure of recognition in an occasional major graduate school in American history. Only a handful of courses are taught under a variety of names, "The History of the American City," "American Urban History," or

"The History of Urban Society in the United States." The content of these courses varies much more than the titles. Is urban history the history of cities, the history of urbanization, or the history of anything that takes place in an urban setting? The question has not been answered. Many studies seem customarily to be classified as urban history simply because they deal with events that have something to do with cities and cannot conveniently be fitted into one of the more formally established categories of American history. Nevertheless, there are a number of urban historians, *soi-disant*, who feel they are working within a worthwhile—and distinct enough—framework. Their scholarship is often impressive. Some of them—rather casually to be sure, but this is the fashion of the historian—have even begun to try to formulate definitions of the subject and to suggest general approaches by which more systematic future work can be conducted.[2]

The Development of Urban History

American historians, of course, have never ignored the city altogether. Among the great nineteenth-century historians, even James Ford Rhodes, for all his allegiance to the traditions of conventional political history, considered some aspects of urban development in the years after the Civil War, and John Bach McMaster in his multivolume account of the life of the people in the antebellum period occasionally provided descriptions of the growth of individual towns and cities. The fifth volume of Edward Channing's *History of the United States,* published in 1921, contained an excellent assessment of "The Urban Migration" of the years 1815–1848.[3] A formal interest in the history of American cities really dates, however, from the early 1930's with the start of publication of volumes in the famous *History of American Life* series. This series represented an ambitious attempt to write the social history of the United States. Although the volumes were generally descriptive rather than interpretative, many of them have not been superseded by anything better. In shaping the design of the study, the editors fixed on urban life as one of the important dimensions of the American social experience, and opened a new area of historical inquiry. Arthur M. Schlesinger, Sr., one of the editors, entitled his own volume on the period 1878–1898, *The Rise of the City.* Although only a portion of his work was actually devoted to the subject, Schlesinger found the growth of cities to be the unifying theme of the period. From a variety of original sources, he provided an account of population movement during the twenty-year period and described in rich detail the pattern of life in the rapidly growing

American cities. His volume proved the most influential in the series in generating further research.[4]

In a bibliographical essay in *The Rise of the City*, Schlesinger noted explicitly the lack of historical urban studies. "The American city has not yet been studied generically," he wrote, "nor do there exist any adequate social histories of particular cities."[5] In the next few years, scholars began to fill this gap. By the late 1930's, a number of studies of individual cities had appeared: Holyoke, Memphis, portions of New York's history, and the beginnings of Bessie L. Pierce's multi-volume history of Chicago. In an introduction to his study of early Memphis, Gerald M. Capers provided a defense of the new line of inquiry. The city, he argued, because of its relationship to an economic hinterland represented a much better unit for the study of sectional economic interests than did the state, which was merely an artificial political division. Pointing to the problems of trying to write American history in terms of a broad East-West division, he found that study of a city such as Memphis illuminated an important lower and upper Mississippi Valley sectional division. Capers also ringingly endorsed the principle of urban biography:

> After a year's study [of Memphis], I became convinced that an adequate biography of our key cities—New York, Chicago, New Orleans, San Francisco, Kansas City, and a dozen more—would be more significant to the national epic than the biography of even so prominent a figure as Theodore Roosevelt. A large proportion of our citizens live in cities; yet how much do we actually know about the natural history of the institutional development of that political and social amoeba, the American city. This all-important task, though it interests the sociologist, the economist, the genealogist, and the literatus, is primarily and fundamentally the job of the historian—a job that he has so far neglected.[6]

As a result of this interest, Blake McKelvey in a 1952 bibliographical essay, which still provides the only general survey of scholarly writing in urban history, could cite the publication after 1930 of forty volumes of urban biography and another "dozen good books of urban history on a broader scope."[7]

The Conceptual Framework of Urban History

In 1940 Arthur M. Schlesinger, whose *Rise of the City* had stimulated much of the scholarship in urban history, published his significant essay, "The City in American History," which launched the debate on the nature of this new field.[8] Schlesinger's approach had been vaguely foreshadowed the year before when Ralph E. Turner at a meeting of the American Historical Association devoted to cultural history had presented an important paper which had turned the thesis of his more famous namesake inside out to show that the industrial city could constitute a distinct cultural environment in the same fashion as had the frontier.[9] He argued that three fundamental forces—the labor market, machine technology, and urban association —had reshaped the cultural milieu and altered the circumstances of human life. Ralph Turner was concerned with the general effect of the rise of the industrial city in the Western world. Schlesinger in his essay found a similar urban factor at work throughout the course of American history. He pointed to the growing concern of American historians with the city and called on them to devote even more attention to the subject. Without attempting to define precisely either "urbanization" or the "city," he suggested the importance of these at various stages in our history. His examples were numerous: a sense of collective responsibility and a growing spirit of nationalism had developed in the colonial towns; the framing and ratification of the Constitution represented in part a triumph of urban business and creditor classes over the small farmers of the countryside; in the nineteenth century, the breach between North and South was due in no small measure to the "urban spirit of progress animating the one section and the static, rural life of the other"; the farmers' protest movements of the late nineteenth century could be considered an agrarian reaction against urban imperialism.

Schlesinger apparently hoped that his essay might stimulate a fundamental reassessment of our history in the same fashion as had Turner's statement of "The Significance of the Frontier in American History." He made Turner his starting point, and the two essays have many organizational parallels. But in spite of its influence in focusing attention on urban themes, "The City in American History" did not cause historians to try to shape an "urban reinterpretation" of American history. A year later, William Diamond, in an excellent article which summarized the history of urban sociology and related urban studies in the United States, warned of the dangers in so doing.[10] Diamond charged that Schlesinger had failed to define his concept of the "city" and carefully showed that Schlesinger had used it in a variety of senses at different points in the essay. Diamond also argued that much that Schlesinger had attributed to urbanization could as well be the result of industrialization or of technological development. Demonstrating the influence of the Beardian school, he strongly urged that historians continue to concentrate their attention on the conflict of economic interests in our past. This in effect ended debate on method for at least a decade. In reprinting his essay in 1949, Schlesinger summarized Diamond's critique. Aside from commenting that he did not consider urban and class interpretations mutually exclusive, he suggested only that the reader judge the issues for himself.[11] Historians continued to write about cities as they had before, unconcerned for the most part about any weaknesses in their method. It is perhaps significant that most general essays on the city in American history have tended to follow the Schlesinger model.[12]

Recent theoretical pieces on urban history have emphasized two themes: (1) If urban history is to become a viable field of inquiry, historians will have to employ the more exact methods of the social sciences. (2) In writing about cities in the past, historians should take into account the findings of social sciences concerned with the present-day city. In a 1953 essay, W. Stull Holt, who had directed studies in urban history at Johns Hopkins University and who has had a long-standing interest in historical patterns of population movement, charged historians who wrote about city development with ignoring the forest for the trees, with failing to use "urbanization as the basis for a new synthesis." Holt summarized a variety of material from the social sciences and suggested the value to historians of such topics as the sources of urban population, trends in the urban birth rate, and urban migration.[13]

R. Richard Wohl, a historian trained also in economics and sociology who in 1954 launched an ambitious project to write a multivolume history of Kansas City using new techniques, speculated a year later that historians ought to join social science teams in examining the history of a single city. The "full discovery of what has passed in a city's history," he wrote, "can only be called forth by cooperative, interdisciplinary inquiry." On the basis of the Kansas City example, Wohl suggested six themes that might enable historians to broaden their narrowly antiquarian inquiries into the history of a single city: (1) the cultural definition of environment; (2) the establishment of permanent communities; (3) the city's range of influence; (4) the changing shape of the culture of the city; (5) the flow of urban institutionalization; (6) targets for urbanization (that is, an examination of fits and starts in the pattern of urban development which are often shaped by a progressive redirection of the city's purposes).[14] A. Theodore Brown, who assumed direction of the History of Kansas City Project after Wohl's premature death, in a commentary on urban history expressed similar sentiments.

The history of American urbanization . . . calls for a good bit of illumination from sociology and social psychology, as well as economics. Also one could wish for more time to read nineteenth and twentieth century novels and short stories for their insights into the nature and quality of urban life. The point is that there is no sense in which I can pursue studies in city history as a practitioner of a self-sustaining "discipline" called history. If this approach is worth anything at all, it needs a great deal of re-inforcing from other so-called disciplines.[15]

The British urban historian, Asa Briggs, who has pointed out the similarity of British and American practices in his field, argued in a 1958 article that historians had not kept up with social scientists in their method. It was true that sociologists had been lacking in imagination in their approach to the city, but more recently demographers had "suggested that all studies of cities and of urbanization should begin with an analysis of population trends, and so valuable has been that contribution that none of the other specialists have been able to neglect either their methods or their conclusions."[16]

The most fully developed argument in this vein is contained in Eric E. Lampard's recent searching and detailed critique of urban history. Lampard urged historians to begin "the study of urbanization as a societal process and the comparative study of communities in a framework of human ecology" in order to provide "a more certain and systematic foundation for the writing of American social history." Lampard argued that if urban history were to have any importance, more exact approaches were critical.

If the urban historian is to be more than a historian who happens to do his research and writing on the subject of cities, it will be necessary to show that the term "urban" explains something in history that cannot be better explained by recourse to other frames of reference. In short, "urban" must signify not subject matter alone but a scheme of conceptualization, in much the same way as "economic" or "culture" history.[17]

How much effect has this kind of exhortation had on the actual procedures of urban historians? Probably very little. At the 1961 meeting of the American Historical Association, most of the active scholars writing in the field gathered to discuss Lampard's article. The questioning revealed limited understanding of his position and less sympathy for it.[18] The role of precise definition and logically constructed theory in historical work has traditionally been minor, and so it is likely to remain. In spite of claims to objectivity, history—particularly history centering on one national state—is affected by the need of a society to maintain unifying social traditions. As long as the "agrarian myth" influences our cultural attitudes, historians are likely to continue to write about the rise of the city in the United States as a deviation from a natural agrarian order and to pose a dichotomy in the past between city and country, between rural and urban. Wohl and Brown, in a provocative case study of local historiography, have demonstrated how changing community circumstances within a framework of changing national circumstances affect the fundamental interpretations embodied in city histories written during different periods of time.[19] Their conception has larger applications and could profitably be utilized to explore other aspects of urban history. Before further instructions are issued as to what urban history ought to be, it would perhaps be profitable for critics to examine its organic relationship to the whole tradition of American historiography rather than to try to continue to delimit the extent of its divergence from the canons of the more rigorous branches of social science.

In this connection, theoretical examination to this point has perhaps not sufficiently emphasized the fact that urban history at least in its ordinary forms is as much related to the long standing tradition of local history written by amateurs with an interest in their own communities as it is to the tradition of scholarly academic history. The special research problems involved, for example, in trying to construct a city history from masses of unconventional sources and unorganized materials may interest the fox but seldom the hedgehog. In the best urban histories, minor themes are thoughtfully developed but seldom does the whole work offer an interpretative framework that could be applied to another subject. It is impossible to establish any satisfactory criteria that would distinguish the "scholarly" urban biography from the best works produced by the amateur local historian. The urban biography does not always escape altogether tones of "sentimentality, antiquarianism, and chamber of commerce advertising." It seldom does much to illuminate the general process of urbanization. There is little concern with what the city is and little indication that the problem has been more than casually considered. The history is written around the legal unit with only limited attention to relationships with regions and hinterlands. Often the work seems to degenerate into a narrative of virtually anything going on within a city's limits which seems of interest.

But this line of criticism can be carried too far, and it often has been. An intensively localistic approach can yield rich rewards in modifying the easy generalizations that permeate the textbooks in American history. The urban biography or the comparative city history often represents the tradition of local history at its best.[20] Reviewers in the social sciences have sometimes criticized urban biographies for the very feature that many historians take to be a virtue—presentation of masses of carefully assembled facts about such matters as land speculation, town promotion, business development, and internal improvements.[21] If carefully read, these studies provide significant insights into general themes of American development. Politically, for example, the city provides a setting for political action and leadership seldom comparable to the national setting, one in which national party concerns are quite irrelevant. If the findings of a large number of urban biographies were absorbed, the ancient ideological party synthesis, which still casts its shadow over treatments of national history, would undoubtedly be seriously modified. Within another conventional division of American history, urban biographies, by enabling historians more accurately to relate ideas to typical group experience, can supply a needed perspective for intellectual history. Much of the exuberance and the rhetoric of mid-nineteenth century "manifest destiny"—to cite one example unnoted in our general histories—clearly stemmed from the projects of promoters in the towns and cities of the West. In a recent study of nineteenth-century cholera epidemics, Charles Rosenberg has imaginatively demonstrated the possibilities in relating ideology to the urban milieu.[22]

Illumination of themes in national history, however, should perhaps be considered an incidental contribution of urban history. Asa Briggs has pointed to a fundamental confusion of purpose in the historical study of individual cities. The urban historian, he writes, "has often not been sure whether he is fitting local history into a stock national framework or whether he is helping to construct a new scaffolding." [23] Briggs, among others, has suggested that urban history can perhaps make a more distinct contribution in providing new ways of looking at the nature of periodization in national history.

The stages of an individual city's history do not really reflect the received divisions of national history. Periods in community history derive from critical turning points within the community itself; it is often useful for limited purposes to regard urban communities as organic entities—developing objective needs and characteristics at different periods of their growth. A variety of examples are available from the existing histories of American cities. In the development of Kansas City, for example, there was a premetropolitan epoch lasting from around 1850 to 1870, defined by bitter competition for predominance among several river towns. Then there was a period of rapid growth from the late 1860's into the early twentieth century with the appearance of a standard set of urban problems and strong tendencies toward social and political disorganization. There followed a period from the 1890's coming down perhaps to 1940 or later, during which bosses, transit monopoly, and some impressive city planning imposed a degree of control and regularity upon the city. Although such familiar divisions of our national history as the Civil War and the Progressive Movement marked Kansas City's history, they did not define its contours.[24] The urban biographies of Chicago, Milwaukee, and Rochester exhibit sequences of growth peculiar to those communities. A series of entrepreneurial decisions in New York City in 1817 clearly marked what its historian has called the *annus mirabilis* of the city. Similarly, the competition offered by New York's unsuccessful rivals— Baltimore, Philadelphia, and Boston—defined important stages in their histories.[25]

Turns in the course of events which change the characteristic problems a community faces change also the range of choices open to its leadership. Moreover, the age of a community and the character of its economic activities and social structure can shape its fate in rivalry with other communities. Philadelphia, an old securely established city under conservative Quaker leadership, seemed at one time unable to shift strategies rapidly enough to keep up with the much younger, more dynamic Baltimore. A prosperous and conservative group of St. Louis leaders, whose ties to the river trade were both cultural and economic, failed to match Chicago's aggressive railroad promotions and consequently lost much of the city's hinterland to the younger rival. Kansas City, in the 1850's and 1860's, was the right age to win a struggle among several towns contending for urban supremacy at the great bend of the Missouri River. St. Joseph and Independence, each a generation older, had developed specialized interest groups which opposed the community programs necessary in an age of railroad expansion. Leavenworth, Kansas City's most formidable rival, became disrupted internally as the result of the rapidity of its growth during the same period, and no unified railroad program could crystallize.[26]

Numerous other examples that point up the importance of urban history as a means of refining our understanding of social process in national development could be constructed from existing urban biographies and studies in urban rivalry. Asa Briggs, on the basis of examination of the early history of the industrial cities of Great Britain, has emphasized the same point about a different national history: "The more that one can develop these comparative studies, even within the framework of one culture, the clearer one will be, I think, about the economic and social structural differences in the rhythm and pattern of early industrial society." Briggs went on to argue that the history of the relationship between Birmingham and Manchester offered a synthesizing theme by which a history of England in the nineteenth century could be written.[27] On the basis of the published materials then available, Blake McKelvey, in his 1952 bibliographical essay, suggested a broad period scheme within which further work on the history of the city might be conducted: (1) the era of the colonial city, a period which at that date had received the most detailed scrutiny; (2) the era of the boom town as part of the westward movement of population, extending from the early part of the nineteenth century to around 1835; (3) the era of the Yankee City, 1835–1870, during which time the "enterprise and ingenuity and capital of old Americans developed more efficient trade facilities, transformed earlier handicrafts into factory industries and exploited the labor of hundreds of thousands of newcomers from across the Atlantic"; (4) the era of cosmopolitan cities from 1870 to 1915; (5) the era of emergence of metropolitan area and core cities, which had not then been examined by historians.[28]

There is little evidence that McKelvey's suggestions had much influence on subsequent writing in urban history. Injunctions to break loose from the restrictions of the national synthesis, to develop period schemes on the basis of the subject studied in terms of a broad pattern of social development and population movement have been little heeded by urban historians. It is a rare work in urban biography that does not overemphasize the impact of Civil War, First or Second World War, Progressive Movement, or New Deal on the community under consideration. The only general scholarly work available on the history of American cities, Constance Green, *American Cities in the Growth of the Nation,* though pleasantly written and valuable, is weakened by a tendency to treat individual cities as locales in which the events of national history can be examined.[29] Asa Briggs has found the same tendency in English academic urban histories and has warned of the dangers:

> The historian often starts with a picture of national history, and tends to illustrate it from local information. . . . Such an approach can be stultifying. It possesses exactly the opposite dangers to those of the antiquarian. Too few facts are given value,

and the opportunity to rearrange national history is missed. Urban histories which fit too easily into the conventional national framework may well mislead rather than illuminate.[30]

Urban Histories

Reading only the critiques of urban history, one might reasonably conclude that the field is so chaotic as to defy classification. Still, the body of scholarship produced in terms of a loose definition of urban history, if examined on its own merits, is often impressive. McKelvey, in his bibliographic essay, suggested the broad limits within which inquiry has taken place. "The task of urban historians," he wrote, "is to chart the interrelated streams of life active in a specific community at a given period, or to weigh the cumulative effect in time of the problems and achievements of many cities within a given society, and in both cases to measure the extent to which the ideals and aspirations of that society found expression, growth, or rebirth in urban centers." [31] The following review of writings is not based on any reasoned scheme of classification as to what should or should not be called urban history. It includes representative works which most American historians—who seldom concern themselves with these matters of definition—would probably agree belonged to the field.

The Process of Urbanization

Lampard has pointed to the major deficiency in American urban history—the lack of studies of urbanization as a process. The only general work available is still Adna F. Weber, *The Growth of Cities in the Nineteenth Century,* a comparative study first published in 1899. Its continuing value is attested by its reprinting in a new edition, which includes a biographical sketch of Weber and a bibliography of his writings.[32] There are numerous neglected nineteenth-century works which examine the movement of population toward cities. These have little statistical sophistication, but they are important historical sources reflecting contemporary attitudes toward urbanization. The force of agrarian traditions in nineteenth-century America has undoubtedly been exaggerated owing to the simple fact that historians, because of their long preoccupation with the agricultural frontier, seldom examined documents that related to the growth of cities.[33]

General Works on American Cities

The best scholarly work available on the history of American cities is Constance McLaughlin Green, *American Cities in the Growth of the*

Nation.[34] Originally presented as a series of lectures in London, the study illuminates aspects of United States national history through case studies of sixteen individual cities in various periods. Christopher Tunnard and Henry Hope Reed, *American Skyline,* is an ambitious attempt to survey the development of American cities largely in terms of the urban landscape.[35] The work contains much historical background, but it is often superficial. Lewis Mumford, *The City in History,* relates the American city to the world city, but knowledge of American history is not one of Mumford's strengths.[36] Works that deal with the history of urban architecture or city planning sometimes furnish valuable general material.[37] Charles N. Glaab, *The American City: A Documentary History,* is a collection that emphasizes nineteenth-century historical documents.[38]

Urban Biography

The history of the individual city has been the most productive single area of urban history. In the last two decades, support from private foundations has led to ambitious attempts to produce definitive multivolume histories of Chicago, Kansas City, and Washington, D. C.[39] These projects have provided training for a substantial number of younger historians, who have continued to maintain a scholarly interest in urban history. Urban biography has perhaps even won a measure of popular acceptance, as evidenced by Constance Green's receipt of the Pulitzer Prize in history for the first volume of her history of Washington. This is a fitting tribute, for Mrs. Green has been the most vigorous defender of the notion that an individual city has a "personality" which can be delineated through historical techniques.

In terms of this conception, the range of "personality types" represented in existing studies tends to be limited. A major proportion of the studies deal with cities in the East and in the more eastern parts of the Midwest and with cities not quite of first rank in size and importance. In addition to Pierce's *Chicago,* Blake McKelvey's recently completed *Rochester* and Bayrd Still's *Milwaukee* are outstanding examples of the genre.[40] New England cities, particularly those with an economic base in manufacturing, have received considerable attention.[41] Thomas J. Wertenbaker, *Norfolk,* is important, for it develops the history of a city with unusual natural advantages which lost to more aggressive rivals in the struggle for urban supremacy.[42] Ordinarily, the urban biography recounts a success story; a few studies of aspiring communities that failed would enlarge our understanding of the processes of city growth. Aside from an occasional isolated study such as Edgar B. Wesley's distinctive history of Owatonna,

Minnesota, little work has been done on the individual histories of small American cities.[43] There are numerous scholarly studies dealing with limited periods of a city's development in the fashion of the urban biography—two studies of Memphis, one of Nashville, portions of New York's history, examinations of economic development in early Detroit and Pittsburgh, and others.[44] Through the inclusion of numerous nonacademic histories of earlier eras and works that are of popular character, many of these quite able, a bibliography of worthwhile studies of individual cities of formidable length could be compiled.[45]

Nevertheless, there are numerous cities whose histories remain almost unexamined in any serious fashion. Among eastern cities, there are no satisfactory general histories of Philadelphia or Baltimore. There is no scholarly examination of an easterly lake port, such as Toledo or Cleveland; no adequate history of St. Louis, the key city in the westward movement; no histories of a Deep South city or of New Orleans. West of the ninety-eighth meridian urban history remains all but unwritten. Aside from a recent economic history of the Latter-Day Saints, which develops the early history of Salt Lake City, there is no good example of a history of a high plains or Rocky Mountain city.[46] The Southwest and the West Coast, areas which illustrate special aspects of the historical development of American cities, are unrepresented by any scholarly urban biography.[47] The comment of a recent bibliographical guide to American studies has considerable validity:

> The greatest tide in recent America, which has run for over a century but seems only to grow in strength, is the tide of urbanization. It can hardly be said that historians and geographers, as distinct from the sociologists who view it as material for abstractions, have kept abreast of it. In America there are many great urban universities whose graduate schools produce learned monographs on ancient Greek pottery or the foreign policy of Bismarck, but never dream of searching for order and significance in the prodigious developments which have been going on under their noses. And there are many great cities unrepresented here by any history or even any title, because there is no up-to-date and comprehensive history to be had.[48]

Period Studies

Owing largely to the extraordinary labors of one historian, Carl Bridenbaugh, the development of cities during the colonial period has received thorough treatment. In two monumental pieces of scholarship, Bridenbaugh has applied the techniques of urban biography to a comparative study of Boston, New York, Charleston, Philadelphia, and Newport.[49] Although critics have questioned his loose definitions of "city" and "urban," all have paid tribute to the massive task he performed in developing an unknown aspect of American history and in doing it thoroughly. Thomas J. Wertenbaker, *The Golden Age of Colonial Culture* examines Boston, New York, Philadelphia, Annapolis, Williamsburg, and Charleston as "crucibles of culture" in colonial America.[50] A major study, Richard C. Wade, *The Urban Frontier, 1790–1830,* demonstrates the importance of the Ohio Valley cities in the westward movement and supplies a needed corrective to the overemphasis in American historiography on the development of an agricultural frontier.[51]

A major deficiency among existing urban histories is the lack of any systematic study of the years from 1830 to 1860, a period of extremely rapid urbanization.[52] Although the historian is theoretically most concerned with origins, the rise of cities in the United States is ordinarily treated in general accounts as if it were almost exclusively a post-Civil War phenomenon. A thorough study of urban development in the earlier part of the century would do much to correct this faulty emphasis. Blake McKelvey's recently published *The Urbanization of America, 1860–1915* supplies a detailed treatment of the period of the growth of the modern city.[53] The work carefully synthesizes the findings of a vast amount of scholarly material dealing with this period produced in the last twenty years. The years covered by McKelvey—during which the rise of the city came to be looked upon as one of the gravest American social problems—is of course a period that is particularly rich in significant contemporary works. The Census Bureau's *Social Statistics of Cities* (1880) marked official recognition of the importance of urbanization and was the first of a number of important government documents on aspects of city life.[54] The growth of scholarly interest in the city around the turn of the century represented by the work of the economist Richard Ely at Johns Hopkins, the founding of the Chicago school of urban sociology, and the development of the social survey technique of examining community life produced a rich urban literature of great value to historians.[55] No historian has yet attempted a general assessment of urban developments in the recent period although the writing in other urban fields, of course, has been enormous.

Urban Rivalry and Transportation

Rivalry among aspiring nineteenth-century towns and cities for trade and transportation has been the subject of a number of urban histories. "Studies in urban rivalry" could be said, in fact, to constitute a principal division of the field. Although these studies are important, they are confined largely to the discussion of economic developments in the middle part of the century. Edward C. Kirkland, *Men, Cities and Transportation: A Study in New England History, 1820–1900*, is a thorough study, which emphasizes transportation more than urban development.[56] The efforts of Boston, Baltimore, and Philadelphia to compete with the urban success of New York in the years before the Civil War have received considerable attention, notably in the previously cited works of Albion, Krout and Fox, and in the recent study by Julius Rubin.[57] Rubin demonstrates on the basis of detailed examination that local factors rather than differences in the technological or economic positions of the three communities shaped their varied responses to the Erie Canal. His emphasis that "the understanding of the historical process depends as much upon the analysis of the subjective traits of groups as it does upon the analysis of the pressure of objective circumstances" suggests a fruitful line of inquiry in urban history, which has long been affected by doctrines of objective necessity in considering the location and growth of American cities. James W. Livingood, *The Philadelphia-Baltimore Trade Rivalry, 1780–1860*, is a detailed monograph.[58] Rivalry between two smaller cities is discussed in David M. Ellis, "Albany and Troy—Commercial Rivals." [59] Wyatt W. Belcher, *The Economic Rivalry Between St. Louis and Chicago, 1850–1880*, is an excellent study of the most significant midwestern rivalry of the nineteenth century.[60] A larger study examining the relationship between the interior river and lake cities of the nineteenth century would be particularly useful. Whether the future metropolises of America would be located on lakes or rivers was a principal consideration shaping the nature of the rationales and justifications that were a part of nineteenth-century interior urban rivalries. Rivalry in Ohio and the surrounding region is examined in an article by Harry N. Scheiber, in Wisconsin by Herbert W. Rice, and in Indiana by Francis P. Weisenberger.[61] Transportation and urban rivalry in the region farther west is examined in Charles N. Glaab, *Kansas City and the Railroads*.[62] Glenn C. Quiett, *They Built the West: An Epic of Rails and Cities*, is a colorful but often inadequate popular treatment of transportation and the growth of Denver, San Francisco, Los Angeles, San Diego, Spokane, and Tacoma.[63] Historical relationships between cities, between metropolises and hinterland communities, particularly in the late nineteenth and early twentieth centuries, would seem to offer a promising subject for further attention by urban historians. The late Charles M. Gates in an unpublished paper entitled "Concept of the Metropolis in the American Westward Movement" enlarged on themes in the classic work of the economic historian N. S. B. Gras and suggested a number of ways along which such an inquiry might proceed.[64]

Special Themes in American Urban History

Histories dealing with a number of aspects of life in an urban setting are conventionally, though not necessarily logically, fitted into the field of urban history. These include studies that consider such subjects as the urban immigrant and the history of ethnic groups in American cities; histories of municipal services; urban politics and especially the urban aspects of Progressivism and twentieth-century reform movements; housing and the slum; the development of the public health movement; and the city in American thought. A great portion of these studies fall into the traditional 1860–1915 "rise-of-the-city" period. Many of them deal not with urban developments as such but with national topics considered in an urban setting. The extensive recent literature on the urban Progressive, for example, is more concerned with throwing light on the nature of Progressivism as a general political movement than in showing the part played by Progressivism in shaping the nature and direction of American urban life. One of the critical needs in urban history is for new approaches to this kind of topic that do more than merely echo the themes of national history.

Among the more important studies of the urban immigrant are Robert Ernst, *Immigrant Life in New York City, 1825–1863;* [65] Oscar Handlin, *Boston's Immigrants, 1790–1865;* [66] and Ralph Weld, *Brooklyn Is America.*[67] Other works not directly concerned with the subject but which contain considerable material are Marcus L. Hansen, *The Atlantic Migration, 1607–1860;* [68] Carl Wittke, *We Who Built America;* [69] Rowland T. Berthoff, *British Immigrants in Industrial America, 1790–1950;* [70] and E. P. Hutchinson, *Immigrants and Their Children, 1850–1950,*[71] which contains illuminating data on immigrant occupational patterns. The role of Jews in cities is considered in Frank Rosenthal, *The Jews of Des Moines: The First Century;* [72] Stuart E. Rosenberg, *The Jewish Community in Rochester, 1843–1925;* [73] Selig Adler and Thomas E. Connolly, *From Ararat to Suburbia: The History of the Jewish Community of Buffalo;* [74] and Moses Rischin, *The Promised City: New York's Jews, 1870–1914.*[75] Immigrant life in an industrial city is examined in Donald B. Cole, *Immigrant City: Lawrence, Massachusetts, 1845–1921.*[76] Documentary material on the urban immigrant can be found in two works by Edith Abbott (editor), *Immigration: Select Documents and Case Records* [77] and *Historical Aspects of the Immigration Problem: Select Documents.*[78]

Studies of tenements, the slum problem, and housing reform include the older works: Edith Abbott, *Tenements of Chicago, 1908–1935;* [79] R. W. De Forest and Lawrence Veiller, *The Tenement House Problem;* [80] and James Ford, et al., *Slums and Housing: With Special Reference to New York City.*[81] Roy Lubove, *The Progressive and the Slums: Tenement House Reform in New York City, 1890–1917* [82] provides a recent scholarly assessment of the subject. A significant lithographed dissertation is Gordon Atkins, *Health, Housing and Poverty in New York City, 1865–1898.*[83] A broader related study has been done by Robert H. Bremner, *From the Depths: The Discovery of Poverty in the United States.*[84]

The problem of the health of the city is treated in M. P. Ravenel (editor), *A Half Century of Public Health* [85] and in James H. Cassedy, *Charles V. Chapin and the Public Health Movement.*[86] For an earlier period the relationship between science, disease, public health, and conceptions of the urban environment is treated in Charles E. Rosenberg, *The Cholera Years.*[87]

The municipal reform movement and urban aspects of national reform are discussed in Clifford W. Patton, *The Battle for Municipal Reform, 1875–1900;* [88] Frank M. Stewart, *A Half Century of Municipal Reform: The History of the National Municipal League;* [89] Ray Ginger, *Altgeld's America,* which deals with Chicago reformers; [90] and Arthur Mann, *Yankee Reformers in the Urban Age.*[91] Richard Hofstadter, *The Age of Reform,*[92] is a convenient synthetic account which stimulated much of the current historical reevaluation of the urban bases of Progressivism. The attempt to supply an urban interpretation of twentieth-century American reform is demonstrated in J. Joseph Huthmacher, "Urban Liberalism and the Age of Reform." [93] Louis G. Geiger, "Joseph W. Folk V. Edward Butler," [94] is a significant demur to current interpretations. A. Theodore Brown, *The Politics of Reform,*[95] provides an important case study of urban reform in a more recent period.

The place of the city in American thought has recently been assessed in Morton White and Lucia White, *The Intellectual Versus the City: From Thomas Jefferson to Frank Lloyd Wright.*[96] The Whites argue that generally the American intellectual has been opposed to the city. Although their definition of anti-urbanism sometimes becomes rather tortured and their concentration is on a limited, highly selective group of thinkers, the work is an important one. Anselm L. Strauss, *Images of the American City,*[97] attempts to develop the historical evolution of American reactions to the city through the application of techniques of social psychology. The work is original in conception, but marred in sections by inadequate research in historical documents. Older documentary collections of travelers' reactions are also concerned with delimiting changing reactions to the American city.[98] The impact of the city on American literature is surveyed in George A. Dunlap, *The City in the American Novel, 1789–1900,*[99] which deals exclusively with the Eastern city, and in Blanche H. Gelfant, *The American City Novel, 1900–1940,*[100] which too rigorously applies sociological theses to the writings of Dreiser, Dos Passos, Farrell, and other novelists who have dealt with the urban scene. Robert H. Walker, "The Poet and the Rise of the City," [101] surveys a wide variety of late nineteenth-century verse and finds that the bulk of it is critical of the place of the city in American life. Catholic thought about the city is discussed in Robert D. Cross, "The Changing Image of the City Among American Catholics." [102]

Important miscellaneous studies in urban history include the following: William Haller, Jr., *The Puritan Frontier: Town Planning in New England Colonial Development, 1630–1660;* [103] Nelson M. Blake, *Water for the Cities: A History of the Urban Water Supply Problem in the United States,*[104] an original, thoroughly researched study which should be duplicated for other municipal functions; E. Digby Baltzell, *Philadelphia Gentlemen: The Making of a National Upper Class,*[105] which traces the development of a power and class structure in Philadelphia; Lewis E. Atherton, *Main Street on the Middle Border,*[106] which thoroughly examines the midwestern small city and its cultural relationships to the metropolis; Powell A. Moore, *The Calumet Region: Indiana's Last Frontier,*[107] a somewhat pedestrian history of a significant urban-industrial area. Aaron Abell, *The Urban Impact on American Protestantism, 1865–1900,*[108] and Henry F. May, *Protestant Churches and Industrial America,*[109] are important for the impact of the rise of the city on American churches. Paul F. Conkin, *Tomorrow a New World: The New Deal Community Program,*[110] discusses the Greenbelt towns and other New Deal experiments in community planning. Sam B. Warner, Jr., *Streetcar Suburbs: The Process of Growth in Boston, 1870–1890,*[111] is based on an unusual amount of carefully collected data, but his findings are rather unincisively presented. His appendix on the use of social statistics is an important discussion of research problems in urban history.[112]

In recent years, as the historian has turned his attention to urban themes, general series in American history have taken more account of the importance of the growth of cities. In some cases, these sections are based on original research and hence have importance as sources. The *Economic History of the United States* series might logically be expected to contain more material on urbanization than it does, but two volumes are significant: George R. Taylor, *The Transportation Revolution, 1815–1860*,[113] which considers the pre-civil War development of cities in relation to transportation, and Edward C. Kirkland, *Industry Comes of Age: Business, Labor, and Public Policy, 1860–1897*,[114] which contains an important essay on "Building American Cities." Kirkland develops the thesis that city building was a factor stimulating continued economic growth in a period in which railroad building had been substantially completed. Among volumes in the "New American Nation" series, Clemont Eaton, *The Growth of Southern Civilization*,[115] contains a chapter on "Town Life," Harold U. Faulkner, *Politics, Reform and Expansion, 1890–1900*,[116] considers "The Revolt of the Cities," and George E. Mowry, *The Era of Theodore Roosevelt, 1900–1912*,[117] discusses the politics of "The Cities and the States" and indicates the role of the city in the Progressive Movement. Among older single volume general studies, Roger Burlingame, *Engines of Democracy: Inventions and Society in Mature America*,[118] provides a necessary starting point for the study of urban technology and Thomas C. Cochran and William Miller, *The Age of Enterprise: A Social History of Industrial America*,[119] contains a thoughtful chapter on "Industry and the City."

Conclusions

Urban history is a relatively new and unestablished division of American history. Reflecting the long-standing interest of academic historians in sectional and economic forces and their tendency to write within the framework of an agrarian tradition, the field has only recently gained a measure of academic recognition. It is characterized by its lack of precise definition both in subject matter and method; much of the scholarship that falls within its vague limits cannot easily be disassociated from antiquarian local history. It has been attacked by social scientists, who recognize its potential value but who are revolted by its seeming chaos; it has often been dismissed by the ordinary academic historian as a gaudy frill which may desecrate an old-fashioned, humanistic discipline.

Still the United States has become an urban nation. The writing of national history reflects cultural imperatives, and urban history will become more important. In fact, a rather dramatic academic breakthrough seems imminent as a number of universities move rapidly to establish programs in urban history and as a number of textbooks are in preparation. Scholars who style themselves urban historians have made important contributions to historical knowledge; and certainly much more useful work could be done within the past framework of inquiry.[120] But there are indications that a number of younger scholars have taken some of the exhortatory analysis to heart, and as the field develops it well may move—slowly, to be sure—into closer partnership with the urban divisions of the related social sciences.

NOTES

1. Eric E. Lampard, "American Historians and the Study of Urbanization," *American Historical Review*, 67 (October 1961), p. 52.

2. The Urban History Group *Newsletter* (1954 to present) contains descriptions of courses taught in American Urban History and occasional reflections on the nature of the field.

3. (New York, 1921), pp. 70–93.

4. Arthur M. Schlesinger, Sr., and Dixon Ryan Fox (Eds.), *A History of American Life*, 13 vols. (New York, 1927–1948). Significant sections of Schlesinger's volume (New York, 1933) include "The Lure of the City," pp. 53–77 and "The Urban World," pp. 78–120. For examples of urban themes in other volumes of the series, see John A. Krout and Dixon Ryan Fox, *The Completion of Independence, 1790–1830* (New York, 1944), "The Atlantic Ports," pp. 1–27, "The Day of the Merchant," pp. 212–245, and "Urban Influences," pp. 370–401; Arthur C. Cole, *The Irrepressible Conflict, 1850–1865* (New York, 1934), "Prosperity and Panic," pp. 1–33, and "Health and Happiness," pp. 179–204; Allan Nevins, *The Emergence of Modern America, 1865–1878* (New York, 1927), "Urban Living and Routes of Travel," pp. 75–100; Harold U. Faulkner, *The Quest for Social Justice, 1898–1914* (New York, 1931), "The New Democracy," pp. 81–109, and "The Decline of Laissez Faire," pp. 110–129.

5. Schlesinger, *Rise*, p. 448.

6. Gerald M. Capers, *The Biography of a River Town: Memphis, Its Heroic Age* (Chapel Hill, 1939), pp. viii–ix.

7. Blake McKelvey, "American Urban History Today," *American Historical Review*, 57 (July 1952), pp. 919–929. A more recent bibliographical essay surveying political science materials concerned with urban development also contains numerous works that are historical in nature: R. T. Daland, "Political Science and the Study of Urbanism," *American Political Science Review*, 51 (June 1957), pp. 491–509. The Urban History Group *Newsletter* (1954 to present), an irregular, mimeographed publication, surveys current bibliography in urban history and related fields. For late nineteenth-century works consult the magnificent Robert C. Brooks, "A Bibliography of Municipal Problems and City Conditions," *Municipal Affairs*, 1 (March 1897), pp. 1–234; and its revised version *Municipal Affairs*, 5 (March 1901), pp. 1–346. This work includes both American and European studies. Seemingly definitive for the period after 1880, its value diminishes as one moves further back into the nineteenth century.

8. Arthur M. Schlesinger, Sr., "The City in American History," *Missis-*

sippi Valley Historical Review, 27 (June 1940), pp. 43–66, reprinted in revised form as "The City in American Civilization," *Paths to the Present* (New York, 1949), pp. 210–233.

9. Ralph E. Turner, "The Industrial City: Center of Cultural Change," in Caroline F. Ware (Ed.), *The Cultural Approach to History* (New York, 1940), pp. 228–242. For an earlier article which suggests some of Turner's themes, see Leon S. Marshall, "The English and American Industrial City of the Nineteenth Century," *Western Pennsylvania Historical Magazine*, 20 (September 1937), pp. 169–180.

10. William Diamond, "On the Dangers of an Urban Interpretation of History," in Eric F. Goldman (Ed.), *Historiography and Urbanization: Essays in American History in Honor of W. Stull Holt* (Baltimore, 1941), pp. 67–108.

11. Schlesinger, *Paths*, p. 297.

12. See, for example, Bayrd Still, "The History of the City in American Life," *The American Review*, 2 (May 1962), pp. 20–34; and Richard C. Wade, "The City in History—Some American Perspectives," in Werner Z. Hirsch (Ed.), *Urban Life and Form* (New York, 1963), pp. 59–77. Wade in particular emphasizes the relationship of the growth of cities to such general political developments as the struggle over slavery, Populism, and Progressivism. Other recent essays by urban historians include Blake Mc-Kelvey, "Urban Social and Economic Institutions in North America," Chap. 24 in *La Ville*, Recueils de la Societe Jean Bodic, Vol. 7 (Brussels, 1955), and Mark D. Hirsch, "Reflections on Urban History and Urban Reform 1865–1915," in D. H. Sheehan and H. C. Syrett (Eds.), *Essays in American Historiography: Papers Presented in Honor of Allan Nevins* (New York, 1960). John D. Hicks, "The Third American Revolution," *Nebraska History*, 36 (December 1955), pp. 227–245, stresses the importance of urbanization as part of a twentieth-century urban-industrial revolution.

13. W. Stull Holt, "Some Consequences of the Urban Movement," *Pacific Historical Review*, 22 (November 1953), pp. 337–352.

14. R. Richard Wohl, "Urbanism, Urbanity, and the Historian," *University of Kansas City Review*, 22 (Autumn 1955), pp. 53–61.

15. Urban History Group *Newsletter*, No. 13 (December 1960).

16. Asa Briggs, "The Study of Cities," *Confluence*, 7 (Summer 1958), p. 107; see also p. 112.

17. Lampard, "American Historians," p. 61.

18. The meeting is reported in the Urban History Group *Newsletter*, No. 15 (April 1962).

19. R. Richard Wohl and A. Theodore Brown, "The Usable Past: A Study of Historical Traditions in Kansas City," *Huntington Library Quarterly*, 23 (May 1960), pp. 237–259.

20. For examinations of the relationship between local and urban history, see Constance McL. Green, "The Value of Local History," in Caroline F. Ware (Ed.), *The Cultural Approach to History* (New York, 1940), pp. 275–286, and Bayrd Still, "Local History Contributions and Techniques in the Study of Two Colonial Cities," *Bulletin of the American Association for State and Local History*, 2 (April 1960), pp. 495–514.

21. See, for example, review of Blake McKelvey, *Rochester: The Water Power City* in *American Journal of Sociology*, 52 (March 1947), p. 466;

review of Constance McL. Green, *Naugatuck*, by C. Wendell King in *American Sociological Review*, 15 (February 1950), p. 155; review of Gerald M. Capers, Jr., *The Biography of a River Town*, by Albert Blumenthal in *American Sociological Review*, 5 (December 1940), pp. 980–981.

22. Charles E. Rosenberg, *The Cholera Years* (Chicago, 1962). The value of traditional urban history is developed more fully in an unpublished paper by A. Theodore Brown and Charles N. Glaab, "Antiquarianism Revisited: A Note on Urban History."

23. Asa Briggs, "The Study of Cities," p. 112.

24. A. Theodore Brown, "The History of Kansas City, Vol. II," unpublished manuscript.

25. Robert G. Albion, *The Rise of New York Port* (New York, 1939), p. 1; Julius Rubin, *Canal or Railroad? Imitation and Innovation in the Response to the Erie Canal in Philadelphia, Baltimore, and Boston* (Philadelphia, 1961), *passim*.

26. James W. Livingood, *The Philadelphia-Baltimore Trade Rivalry, 1780–1860* (Harrisburg, Penn., 1947), pp. 1–3, *passim*; Wyatt W. Belcher, *The Economic Rivalry Between St. Louis and Chicago, 1850–1880* (New York, 1947), pp. 72–75; Charles N. Glaab, *Kansas City and the Railroads* (Madison, 1962), *passim*.

27. Asa Briggs, "The Historian and the Study of Cities," mimeographed lecture delivered at the University of Chicago, April 6, 1956.

28. McKelvey, "American Urban History Today," pp. 921–927.

29. (New York, 1957).

30. Briggs, "The Historian and the Study of Cities."

31. McKelvey, "American Urban History Today," p. 920.

32. (New York, 1899), reprint (Ithaca, 1963).

33. Adam Seybert, *Statistical Annals . . . of the United States of America . . .* (Philadelphia, 1818) is one of the earliest attempts to assess the importance of the development of towns and cities. George Tucker, *The Progress of the United States in Population and Wealth in Fifty Years* (Boston, 1843), contains an interesting chapter analyzing the growth of cities and evaluating the weaknesses of census returns as an index to measure this development. The most systematic nineteenth-century student of urbanization was probably Jesup W. Scott (1799–1873), a Toledo newspaperman who wrote approximately fifteen articles examining the growth of cities, particularly those in the West. See, for example, his "Internal Trade of the United States," *Hunt's Merchants' Magazine*, 31 (October 1854), pp. 403–413; and "Westward the Star of Empire," *DeBow's Review*, 27 (August 1859), pp. 123–136. In general the files of the business publication, *Hunt's Merchants' Magazine*, 1839–1870, are an excellent source for the study of urban development in the first half of the nineteenth century. To a lesser extent, this is true also of the New Orleans commercial magazine, *DeBow's Review*, 1846–1864. For contemporary material on urbanization in the latter part of the nineteenth century, see the bibliographical essays in Nevins, *Emergence*, Schlesinger, *Rise*, and the Brooks bibliography.

34. (New York, 1957).

35. (Boston, 1955).

36. (New York, 1961). See also his earlier *The Culture of Cities* (New York, 1938).

37. Christopher Tunnard, *The City of Man* (New York, 1953) develops city planning and civic art in historical terms. John Burchard and Albert Bush-Brown, *The Architecture of America: A Social and Cultural History* (Boston, 1961), considers urban architecture in relation to the historical development of American cities.

38. (Homewood, Ill., 1963).

39. Bessie L. Pierce, *A History of Chicago*, in progress, I. *The Beginning of a City, 1673–1848*, II. *From Town to City, 1848–1871*, III. *The Rise of a Modern City, 1871–1893* (New York, 1937–1957); A. Theodore Brown, *The History of Kansas City*, in progress, I. *Frontier Community: Kansas City to 1870* (Columbia, Mo., 1963); Constance McL. Green, *Washington, Village and Capital, 1800–1878; Washington, Capital City, 1879–1950* (Princeton, 1962–1963).

40. Blake McKelvey, *Rochester*, 4 vols., I. *The Water-Power City, 1812–1854*, II. *The Flower City, 1855–1890*, III. *The Quest for Quality, 1890–1925*, IV. *Rochester: An Emerging Metropolis, 1925–1961* (Cambridge and Rochester, 1945–1961); Still (Madison, 1948).

41. Constance McL. Green, *Holyoke, Massachusetts* (New Haven, 1939), and *History of Naugatuck, Connecticut* (New Haven, 1948); Vera Shlakman, *Economic History of a Factory Town* (Northampton, Mass., 1935); Rollin G. Osterweis, *Three Centuries of New Haven, 1638–1938* (New Haven, 1953).

42. Revised edition by Marvin W. Schlegel (Durham, 1962).

43. *Owatonna, The Social Development of a Minnesota Community* (Minneapolis, 1938).

44. Capers, *Biography of a River Town;* William Miller, *Memphis During the Progressive Era: 1900–1917* (Madison, 1957); Francis G. Davenport, *Cultural Life in Nashville on the Eve of the Civil War* (Chapel Hill, 1941); Albion, *Rise of New York Port;* Ralph Weld, *Brooklyn Village, 1816–1834* (New York, 1938); Harold C. Syrett, *The City of Brooklyn, 1865–1898* (New York, 1944); Sidney I. Pomerantz, *New York: An American City, 1783–1803* (New York, 1938); Allan Nevins and J. A. Krout (Eds.), *The Greater City: New York, 1898–1948* (New York, 1948); Floyd R. Dain, *Every House a Frontier: Detroit's Economic Progress, 1815–1825* (Detroit, 1956); Catherine E. Reiser, *Pittsburgh's Commercial Development, 1800–1850* (Harrisburg, 1951).

45. Works in local history of unusual value include Isaac N. P. Stokes, *The Iconography of Manhattan Island, 1498–1909*, 6 vols. (New York, 1916–1925) and Justin Winsor, *Memorial History of Boston, 1630–1880*, 4 vols. (Boston, 1880–1881). Popular works of value include Leland A. Baldwin, *Pittsburgh: The Story of a City* (Pittsburgh, 1937); Robert Molloy, *Charleston, A Gracious Heritage* (New York, 1947); Harold Sinclair, *Port of New Orleans* (New York, 1942); C. L. de Chambrun, *Cincinnati, Story of the Queen City* (New York, 1939); William G. Rose, *Cleveland, The Making of a City* (Cleveland, 1950). Detailed examination of the history of American cities requires consultation of a variety of diverse sources such as the Federal Writers' Project and the Writers' Program, *American Guide* series, 153 vols. (1935–1943), new editions and reprints (1939–1956); or of the regional studies *American Folkways*, 26 vols. (New York, 1941–

1955). Volumes in these series are of such sharply varying value that it is easy to overlook the occasional worthwhile study. In the latter series, for example, see Carey McWilliams, *Southern California Country* (New York, 1946).

46. Leonard J. Arrington, *Great Basin Kingdom* (Cambridge, 1958). For popular but interesting interpretative sketches see Ray B. West (Ed.), *Rocky Mountain Cities* (New York, 1949).

47. Oscar O. Winther, "The Rise of Metropolitan Los Angeles: 1870–1910," *Huntington Library Quarterly,* 10 (August 1947), pp. 391–398, is an important article. For a popular account of the early days of the city, see Remi A. Nadeau, *City Makers* (Garden City, 1948).

48. *A Guide to the Study of the United States of America* (Washington, 1960), p. 467.

49. *Cities in the Wilderness* (New York, 1938, 1960) and *Cities in Revolt* (New York, 1955). See also Carl Bridenbaugh and Jessica Bridenbaugh, *Rebels and Gentlemen: Philadelphia in the Age of Franklin* (New York, 1942).

50. (Ithaca, 1942).

51. (Cambridge, 1959). See also his article, "Urban Life in Western America, 1790–1830," *American Historical Review,* 64 (October 1958), pp. 14–30.

52. See, however, two important articles: Bessie L. Pierce, "Changing Urban Patterns in the Mississippi Valley," *Journal* of the Illinois Historical Society, 43 (Spring 1950), pp. 46–57; and Bayrd Still, "Patterns of Mid-Nineteenth Century Urbanization in the Middle West," *Mississippi Valley Historical Review,* 28 (September 1941), pp. 187–206. Still shows the adoption by Midwestern cities of the established practices and procedures of the older urban centers of the East.

53. (New Brunswick, N. J., 1963).

54. See, for example, U. S. Bureau of the Census, *Telephones and Telegraphs* (1902), *Statistics of Cities* (1906), and *Street and Electric Railways* (1907); U. S. Senate, *Cost of Living in American Towns* (62nd Congress, 1st Session, Senate Document 22, 1911).

55. For a good short account of the history of the scholarship of American cities, see Diamond, "The Urban Interpretation," in Goldman (Ed.), *Historiography and Urbanization,* pp. 67–89. The following are important representative contemporary studies. Religiously oriented analyses of the meaning of urban life include A. D. Mayo, *The Symbols of the Capital; or Civilization in New York* (1859); E. H. Chapin, *Moral Aspects of City Life* (1853) and *Humanity in the City* (1854); Charles L. Brace, *The Dangerous Classes of New York* (1880); Josiah Strong, *Our Country* (1885), which has been called the *Uncle Tom's Cabin* of the urban reform movement, and his *The Twentieth Century City* (New York, 1898), and *The Challenge of the City* (1907); Samuel L. Loomis, *Modern Cities and Their Religious Problems* (1887); B. O. Flower, *Civilization's Inferno* (1893); William A. Stead, *If Christ Came to Chicago* (1894) and his *Satan's Invisible World Displayed* (1897). For developing conceptions of city planning and lines of defense of the city, see Frederick Law Olmsted, "Public Parks and the Enlargement of Towns," *Journal of Social Science,* 3 (November 1871); F. J. Kingsbury, "The Tendency of Men to Live in

Cities," *Journal of Social Science*, 33 (November 1895); Charles M. Robinson, *The Improvement of Towns and Cities* (1901) and his *The Call of the City* (1908). For the problems of the slums, urban philanthropy and city youth, see C. D. Randall (Ed.), *History of Child Saving in the United States* (1893); C. R. Henderson, *Social Spirit in America* (1897) and his *Social Settlements* (1899); Robert A. Woods et al., *The Poor in Great Cities* (1895) and Robert A. Woods (Ed.), *Americans in Process: A Settlement Study* (1902); Jacob A. Riis, *How the Other Half Lives* (1890) and his *The Children of the Poor* (1892), *Ten Years' War* (1900), *The Making of an American* (1901), and *The Battle with Slums* (1902); Jane Addams et al., *Philanthropy and Social Progress* (1893); Jane Addams, *Twenty Years at Hull House* (1910) and her *The Spirit of Youth and the City Streets* (1914); and Lillian D. Wald, *The House on Henry Street* (1915). For a statement of the rural protest against the city, see John W. Bookwalter, *Rural Versus Urban: Their Conflict and Its Cause* (1911). For consideration of the city in political and governmental terms, see Frederick C. Howe, *The City: The Hope of Democracy* (1905) and his *The Modern City and Its Problems* (1915); Richard T. Ely, *The Coming City* (1902); Delos F. Wilcox, *The American City: A Problem in Democracy* (1904) and his *Great Cities in America* (1910). For municipal functions see J. A. Fairlie, *Municipal Administration* (1901), a particularly useful study that compares the history of American and European practices; George E. Waring, *Sanitary Drainage* (1876) and his *Street-Cleaning* (1897), and *Modern Methods of Sewage Disposal* (1894); Charles Zueblin, *American Municipal Progress* (1902, 1916), both editions should be consulted as a reflection of changing attitudes toward the city; Delos F. Wilcox, *Municipal Franchises*, 2 vols. (1910); E. W. Bemis (Ed.), *Municipal Monopolies* (1899); and James B. Walker, *Fifty Years of Rapid Transit* (New York, 1917). For an important study which considers the significance of geography in the location and growth of cities, see Ellen C. Semple, *American History and Its Geographic Conditions* (1903). For two early studies of twentieth-century suburbanization, see Graham R. Taylor, *Satellite Cities* (1915) and H. Paul Douglass, *The Suburban Trend* (1925).

56. 2 vols. (Cambridge, 1948).

57. Albion, *Rise of New York Port;* Krout and Fox, *The Completion of Independence;* Rubin, *Canal or Railroad?*, all previously cited.

58. Previously cited.

59. *New York History*, 24 (October 1943), pp. 484–511.

60. Previously cited.

61. Harry N. Scheiber, "Urban Rivalry and Internal Improvements in the Old Northwest, 1820–1860," *Ohio History*, 71 (October 1962), pp. 227–239; Herbert W. Rice, "Early Rivalry Among Wisconsin Cities for Railroads," *Wisconsin Magazine of History*, 35 (Autumn 1951), pp. 10–15; Francis P. Weisenburger, "The Urbanization of the Middle West: Town and Village in the Pioneer Period," *Indiana Magazine of History*, 41 (March 1954), pp. 19–30.

62. Previously cited.

63. (New York, 1934).

64. A precis of the paper along with commentaries is printed in the Urban History Group *Newsletter* No. 16 (October 1962).

65. (New York, 1949).
66. (Cambridge, 1941).
67. (New York, 1950).
68. (Cambridge, 1940).
69. (New York, 1939).
70. (Cambridge, 1953).
71. (New York, 1956).
72. (Des Moines, 1957).
73. (New York, 1953).
74. (Philadelphia, 1960).
75. (Cambridge, 1962).
76. (Chapel Hill, 1963).
77. (Chicago, 1924).
78. (Chicago, 1926).
79. (Chicago, 1936).
80. (New York, 1903).
81. (Cambridge, 1936).
82. (Pittsburgh, 1963). See also his "Lawrence Veiller and the New York State Tenement House Commission of 1900," *Mississippi Valley Historical Review*, 47 (March 1961), pp. 659–667, and "New Cities for Old: The Urban Reconstruction Program of the 1930's," *The Social Studies*, 53 (November 1962), pp. 203–212, and Robert H. Bremner, "The Big Flat: History of a New York Tenement House," *American Historical Review*, 63 (October 1958), pp. 54–62.
83. (Ann Arbor, 1947).
84. (New York, 1956).
85. (New York, 1921).
86. (Cambridge, 1962).
87. Previously cited.
88. (Washington, 1940).
89. (Berkeley, 1950).
90. (New York, 1958).
91. (Cambridge, 1954).
92. (New York, 1955).
93. *Mississippi Valley Historical Review*, 49 (September 1962), pp. 231–241.
94. *Journal of Southern History*, 28 (November 1962), pp. 438–449.
95. (Kansas City, 1958).
96. (Cambridge, 1962).
97. (New York, 1961).
98. Bessie L. Pierce (Ed.), *As Others See Chicago: Impressions of Visitors, 1673–1933* (Chicago, 1933); Bayrd Still, "The Growth of Milwaukee As Recorded by Contemporaries," *Wisconsin Magazine of History*, 21 (March 1938), pp. 262–293; Bayrd Still, *Mirror for Gotham: New York as Seen by Contemporaries from Dutch Days to the Present* (New York, 1956).
99. (Philadelphia, 1934).
100. (Norman, 1954).
101. *Mississippi Valley Historical Review*, 49 (June 1962), pp. 85–89.
102. *Catholic Historical Review*, 48 (April 1962), pp. 33–52.
103. (New York, 1951).

104. (Syracuse, 1956).

105. (Glencoe, 1958).

106. (Bloomington, 1954).

107. (Indianapolis, 1959).

108. (Cambridge, 1943).

109. (New York, 1949).

110. (Ithaca, 1959).

111. (Cambridge, 1962).

112. Reprinted as "Technical Leaflet 7, Social Studies: A Local Historian's Guide," *History News*, 18 (March 1963), pp. 67–70.

113. (New York, 1951), pp. 3–14, 348–398.

114. (New York, 1961), pp. 237–261.

115. (New York, 1961), pp. 247–260.

116. (New York, 1959), pp. 23–47.

117. (New York, 1958), pp. 59–84.

118. (New York, 1940), pp. 73–94.

119. (New York, 1942), pp. 249–272.

120. Important recent studies in urban history include Oscar Handlin and John Burchard (Eds.), *The Historian and the City* (Cambridge, Mass., 1963), a symposium which contains important theoretical material and excellent bibliographies; Lawrence L. Graves (Ed.), *A History of Lubbock* (Lubbock, Tex., 1962), a solid urban biography of a High Plains city; Richard C. Wade, *Slavery in the Cities: The South 1820–1860* (New York, 1964), broader in its treatment of Southern cities than the title might suggest; and John W. Reps, *The Making of Urban America: A History of City Planning in the United States* (Princeton, N. J., 1965), a magnificent piece of scholarship. Two important monographs on aspects of planning are Roy Lubove, *Community Planning in the 1920's: The Contribution of the Regional Planning Association of America* (Pittsburgh, 1963), and William H. Wilson, *The City Beautiful Movement in Kansas City* (Columbia, Mo., 1964).

3

A Survey of Urban Geography

Harold M. Mayer

The literature of urban geography has been rather neglected by workers in many of the other social sciences, but it has been expanding in recent years at an accelerating rate. Many of the contributions of geographers to understanding of the nature, characteristics, and problems of cities transcend the boundaries of the discipline. This chapter constitutes an annotated bibliography of this literature, with special emphasis on the contributions of American urban geographers to understanding of American, and by extension, "Western" cities.

In general, geographers are concerned with cities as elements in the fabric of settlement of regions. They are thus interested in the mapping, interpretation, and projection of distributions of urban population, employment, social and economic characteristics, traffic movements, and physical facilities, which together constitute the urban pattern. These variables are indicative of the functional relationships within and among cities. Form follows function, in geography as in architecture. Until relatively recently most urban geographic investigations were predominantly empirical and inductive, concerned with building up a body of substantive knowledge from which generalizations could be made. More recently, they have included modern techniques of model building, followed by testing of hypotheses in concrete situations, but both approaches usually involve field investigations in the absence of adequate censuses or other survey data. Urban geographic investigations are concerned primarily with the areal variations within and among cities, including the relationships between urban and nonurban areas, and the forces of development and change that are shaping the urban landscape.[1] They comprehend not only the contemporary city and its historical development, but also, insofar as it can be dealt with, the future of cities, which may in part be subject to some degree of control and direction by intelligent use of knowledge of the forces underlying urban growth and decline.

Although much of the research in urban geography has concentrated on the functions and morphology of individual cities or classes of cities, increasingly it has dealt with the measurement, interpretation, and understanding of the reciprocal relationships between cities and their complementary regions, as well as among cities, and with the complex of relationships among the functional areas that characterize urban internal structure. These relationships, both internal and external, are basically expressed in two forms, one static and one kinetic: (1) as *land uses and structures,* each of which occupies area and which together constitute the urban landscape, and (2) as *traffic flows* along routes between areas or zones of origin and destination, constituting part of what Edward L. Ullman calls "spatial interaction." Thus, in a spatial sense, the field is concerned both with the more-or-less static aspects of the distribution and areal variations of land use, population, and the location of activities, and with the kinetic aspects, as represented by movement from place to place. Without such movement or spatial interaction, areal specialization—and hence cities—would be impossible.

Since intercity comparisons can be made only on the basis of comparably delimited areas, however, one major aspect of urban geographic activity has been the areal delimitation and definition of cities, urbanized areas,[2] metropolitan areas,[3] and suprametropolitan agglomerations or conurbations,[4] internationally as well as within individual nations. The concept of the "urbanized area," as developed and used by the United States Bureau of the Census, has been evolved and subjected to precise measurement by the Geography Division of that bureau. It is essentially a delimitation of the physical—as distinguished from the administrative—boundaries of the city, in terms of a *density threshold.* Other criteria demand consideration of connectivity between and among activities and areas. Many of the measures of the population, functions, economic base, and physical character of cities depend on the application of uniform criteria for urban delimitation; for the inclusion or exclusion, as the case may be, of people, structures, land uses, traffic flows, and social, cultural, political, and economic phenomena.

Urban Functions

Like other social scientists, geographers ask: Why do cities exist? What functions do they perform? How are urban functions related to city and metropolitan growth and development?

The Economic Base [5]

Cities provide goods and services, both for the residents of the city and for the populations of areas outside of them. These urban functions have certain characteristics that serve to differentiate them from non-urban functions. Rarely do the urban functions involve "primary" production in the classical economic sense. Jean Brunhes has called such features as houses and roads "unproductive occupation of the soil." [6] On the other hand, as Chauncy D. Harris points out, a surplus of agricultural production exists in many areas, and land therefore can be converted from rural to urban uses without creating serious problems of shortages of primary produce, because the net economic return per acre from urban occupance may be many times greater than the return from nonurban use of the same land.[7] Urban functions also are generally characterized by *nodality* or *centrality* and by mutual proximity of related functions.[8]

Basic urban functions involve the processing or trading of goods or the furnishing of goods and services for residents or establishments located outside of the urban area. The classic cliché is that cities do not thrive where people merely take in each others' washing. Some goods and services must be "exported" from the urban area, in return for goods, services, or income coming into the urban area from outside. Thus, there is an interchange, or interaction, between the city and the outside world, varying in extent for each of the multitude of urban functions associated with each city, for which the city serves as a node. There are also interactions between cities forming regional, national, or international *systems* of cities, depending on the scale of observation.

Interactions between cities and their hinterlands can be studied through the actual flows of goods and services, as well as the related flows of money and credit. Over the years a body of general concepts, based on the empirical studies of geographers and others, has appeared, relating to the spatial interaction between cities and between cities and their respective hinterlands or service areas.[9] From an increasing number of studies of city-region relations has emerged a greater understanding of the nature and areal variations of the roles of cities, as well as of the causes of and conditions relating to the generation of traffic to, from, and within cities and regions.[10]

If it were feasible, the measurement of the actual flows of goods and services, of people, and of money and credit, across the boundaries of the urban area would be the best method of studying the economic base of a city or metropolitan area. In practice, however, there are great difficulties. Urban areas do not have definite boundaries, as do nations, and even if they did, it would not usually be possible to account for all of the flows in and out of them. There is nothing available for most cities or metropolitan areas analogous to the statistics on national foreign trade or international migration. In practice, moreover, studies of urban balance of payments are of less direct interest than some other types of studies which involve physical phenomena, such as flows of goods, or which involve direct measurements of variables such as employment, which is a partial determinant of population and hence of size of city.

Techniques for Studying Urban Economic Functions

A city's income may be divided into two major components. One component consists of the income that circulates entirely within the city or urban area and is analogous to the portion of a nation's income that circulates within the national boundaries. Just as a nation produces goods for export which are roughly balanced by payments coming into it, so do varying proportions of a city's total activity result in the production of goods and services that are for consumers outside of it. They may be termed "urban-area exports," and they are balanced by flows of materials, money, and credit into the urban area. Of course, cities are not nearly as self-contained economically as are nations, particularly large ones, so that a higher proportion of a city's trade crosses its boundaries than the proportion of a nation's trade that crosses national boundaries. These "export" activities of the city or metropolitan area constitute its sources of "basic" or "city-forming" income, as contrasted with the income derived from internal circulation of goods, money, and credit, which is termed "nonbasic" or "city-serving." [11]

The so-called "basic-nonbasic" approach has been extensively employed in the analysis of urban and metropolitan economies.[12] From such analysis is derived the "basic-nonbasic (B/N) ratio," the ratio of all basic to all nonbasic employment in the area. However, several characteristics of the B/N ratio require that it be used with caution. These are its variability with respect to (a) the size of the urban or metropolitan area, and (b) the extent to which activities within and without the area are integrated. As size of city increases, the diversity of types of establishments within it also increases. With increased diversity, there is an increase in ability of the city to provide for its multitude of diverse needs from establishments within its own area. Roterus and Calef, for example, have noted that the basic-nonbasic ratio is a function of the size of the area for which the ratio is computed, and that therefore comparative studies of the ratio for areas of variable delimitation are invalid.[13]

The basic-nonbasic approach has been subjected to criticism on other grounds as well. Blumenfeld, for example, points out that the so-called "nonbasic" or internal activities serving the urban populations are increasingly important, and the "external economies" resulting from large concentrations of activities in urban areas become major considerations in assessing the economic base of such areas.[14] Stewart has remarked also that the basic-nonbasic approach assumes a constant B/N ratio independent of urban growth, that the most volatile components of urban growth cannot be predicted easily, that the method does not involve consideration of changes in level and distribution of income or of tastes, and that significant changes may result from changes in the localization of "sporadic" or nonubiquitous industries that are basic to the specialized economic character of many urban agglomerations.[15]

Another approach to the study of the functions of cities in terms of their economic base is the "minimum requirements" technique. This is essentially a comparative method in which a series of individual cities is compared with respect to the "mix" of activities that produce employment for the respective urban populations. By measurement of the amount of employment in each category of activity of *all* the cities or metropolitan areas within a region or country, such as the United States, the minimum percentage of employment in each category in *any* of the cities is determined. This is presumed to be the "minimum requirement" of all cities in the series for that type of employment.

Gunnar Alexandersson, in his well-known study of the industrial structure of American cities, used the "minimum requirements" approach.[16] First, he differentiated "ubiquitous" industries (those found in all or nearly all cities in significant amounts) from "sporadic" industries (those highly concentrated in a limited number of cities). He then asked: "What ratios in different industries are a necessary minimum to supply a city's own population with goods and services of the type which are produced in every normal city?" On a series of cumulative distribution diagrams for each category of industrial activity, he took a point below which 5 per cent of the cities were represented (his k ratio), in order to eliminate distortions due to highly atypical cities. At the 5 per cent ratio, the proportion of the various activities for all cities was taken as representing the minimum requirement of employment in each category of activity for all cities except the most atypical. Any employment in a given city within a given industry above that amount was taken to represent "city-forming" or basic employment, whereas the per cent of total employment in the given city represented by the k ratio for the remaining 95 per cent of the cities was taken as the presumed minimum proportion of the city's total employment to meet its own needs, or, in other words, the "city-serving" or "nonbasic" employment.

The minimum requirements approach to the urban economic base also has been used by Morrissett[17] and by Ullman and Dacey, who studied the economic base of a number of American cities including San Francisco and St. Louis.[18] In order to estimate the amount of employment required for a city's internal needs, they selected a group of American cities, and calculated for each the percentage of the labor force employed in each of fourteen census categories of activity. For each category, the minimum percentage of employment in each activity was found. This was done for a group of cities in each population size class. These minima were then summed for all activity categories in cities of each size class, and that percentage figure was taken to be the minimum requirement for "city-serving" or "nonbasic" employment for cities of a given size class. For any city within that size class, the excess employment was considered to be the "export," "city-forming," or "basic" employment, both in total and specifically for each category of employment. As expected, it was found that the larger the city the larger the sum of the minima, thus indicating that the larger cities have a larger number of specialized activities and hence are more nearly self-contained.

A significant application to practical planning problems of a modification of this method was made by Linge. In order to make recommendations relative to a development policy for Canberra, he assumed that a diversified economic base would be desirable, and in order to determine the future composition of the economy of the city, he took the median percentage of total employment represented by various categories of employment in Australian cities of various size groups corresponding to the anticipated future sizes of Canberra. The median for each group was taken as representing the typical pattern, relatively uninfluenced by the extremes.[19]

Functional Classification of Cities

Many studies have been concerned with the functional classification of cities. Harris and Ullman divided cities into three categories, depending on the predominant types of functions: (1) "central-place cities," which perform centralized services, such as retail trade and political administration, for the adjacent areas, variously called "service areas," "hinterlands," "umlands," or "urban fields"; (2) "transport cities," which owe their economic base primarily to their situation with respect to the transport network and include railroad centers, ports, and so on; and (3) "specialized function cities," such as resort and retirement cities, mining and other resource-extraction centers, and military bases.[20] The central-place cities tend to be homogeneously distributed; the transport centers tend to be aligned along transport routes, such as railroads, or along coastlines; and the specialized function cities usually cluster in areas having special conditions favoring their development.

The methods of economic base analysis described above, if applied to a number of cities, also can lead to a functional classification of cities in terms of the relative importance of the specializations, and the kinds of specializations, which constitute the "basic," "export" or "city-forming" functions of the respective cities.[21]

Among the significant studies relating to the functional classification of cities outside of the United States are those of Harris on the Soviet Union,[22] Pownall on New Zealand,[23] and Steigenga on the Netherlands.[24] The latter classified cities on the basis of the "mix" of activities which affects their vulnerability to economic fluctuations.

A more sophisticated technique for classifying cities, made possible by modern electronic computers which can handle masses of data, is factor analysis or "components analysis," in which a large number of variables can be grouped into a smaller number of related or similar components, and the cities classified in accordance with these similarities. A recent study of 157 towns in England and Wales involved analysis of 57 socioeconomic characteristics. These characteristics were found to "group" into four components, which were then used to classify the towns.[25]

Urban Sites and Situations

In considering the spatial interrelationships within and among cities, as well as the interactions between cities and their respective external areas, which affect the sizes, spacings, and inherent characteristics of cities, geographers have traditionally emphasized, as well as differentiated between, site and situation. *Site* refers to the area occupied by the city. Among the site characteristics of particular importance are the relief, slope, and configuration of land and water areas, shorelines, vulnerability to earthquakes, landslides, floods, and other catastrophic conditions, the supporting capacity of the bedrock and overburden, drainage, and microclimatological conditions. *Situation*, on the other hand, refers to the relative location of a city and its inter-actions, with respect to external areas, as affected by location.

The first doctoral dissertation in urban geography submitted to an American university, for example, examined the relations of site to the development of New York city.[26] Many studies of the site char-acteristics of individual cities followed, and causal connections were assumed between site factors and the course of urban development on given sites.[27] A few early studies also introduced man as a decision-maker with respect to urban adjustments to site factors. Among them was Thomas's study of the pattern of industrial and commercial ac-tivities in metropolitan St. Louis, in which the basic theme was the dominant effect of the division of the area by the Mississippi River and the consequent adaptations of land uses and functional organiza-tion to the river barrier.[28]

More recent studies have dealt primarily with policies concerning the development of land uses and structures on sites subject to various adverse conditions, such as floods. A series of recent studies made at the University of Chicago has had considerable effect in stimulating review of previous ideas regarding the effects of engineer-ing structures, land-use controls such as zoning, and stream-regulation policies upon the vulnerability of urban areas to floods.[29] As a result of these studies, it was found that past and current governmental policies with respect to emphasis on engineering structures to reduce vulnerability of flood plains to flooding actually has increased the dam-age potential by producing a false sense of security and thereby stim-ulating intensive urban occupance of flood-prone areas. Other studies have dealt with site conditions and their relation to urban water supply,[30] and particularly to water supply for industries, as a major consideration in industrial location.[31]

Another site characteristic which is beginning to receive the atten-tion it deserves is microclimate. It is well known that within small distances, as within a city, there may be significant differences in cli-mate, affected by relief, configuration of shorelines, and the extent of ground coverage by structures and pavements.[32] These differences are often reflected in the intra-urban patterns of land uses and land values. The problems of fog in the San Francisco Bay Area,[33] smog in Los Angeles,[34] and air pollution in many areas,[35] are among the types of studies of geographic significance completed.

On a quite different scale, geographic research has focused on the rapid urbanization of the Pacific Coast, the southwestern desert areas of the United States, and Florida—in part the result of a combination of increased leisure and attraction of climatic amenities, the higher proportion of retired persons in the American population, and the use of inducements of those amenities by business and governmental organizations in the recruitment of professional and other personnel.[36] Site relationships of urban areas which heretofore had been considered as not favoring urbanization constitute a series of relationships in which some geographers, returning in part to more-or-less traditional approaches to the man-environment concepts, but with greater sophistication than in the past, can potentially make contributions to the understanding of both theoretical and practical problems of urban development.

Cities as Central Places [37]

With some exceptions, tertiary activities involving the distribution of goods and services, including transfer of title (wholesale and retail trade) and administrative, financial, and other services, though almost entirely urban phenomena, do not depend on the unique attributes of particular urban sites or situations, but rather on a condition of centrality with regard to service establishments and their hinterlands. Probably in no aspect of urban geography has theory been advanced as rapidly in recent years as in the study of these so-called "central-place" activities or functions. Significant regularities have been discovered between them and the number, size, and spacing of cities, and a body of theory has been developed to explain these relationships. Central-place types of functions are generally ubiquitous, in contrast to the "sporadic" or nonubiquitous functions, such as resort or manufacturing activities which represent deviations from central-place regularities.

A "central place" consists in part of a cluster of service functions located at the point most accessible to the maximum "profit area" which can be commanded. Each type of central place tends to have a hinterland coterminous with this profit area, although such hinterlands vary in areal extent because certain localities are more intensively used than others and thus yield more profits. Trade areas for community facilities *within* cities are much smaller than rural trade areas for the community-type facilities that smaller towns provide. Centers of "lower order" tend to "nest" within the hinterlands of centers of the next "higher order." They depend on these centers of higher order for the functions of greater complexity which they cannot provide profitably for their more restricted hinterlands. This symbiotic nesting relationship of higher- and lower-order centers defines the so-called "hierarchy of central places." [38] Each higher-order center performs all the functions that lower-order centers perform for lower-order hinterlands, plus a group of more complex functions for a larger hinterland that encompasses several lower-order centers and their immediate hinterlands. Related to the hierarchic arrangement of centers is a characteristic spatial pattern of centers, hinterlands, and transportation routes by which they are interconnected. Also, when central-place types of function constitute the major economic bases of cities, discrete population levels characterize the centers of each order or level, modified only where noncentral-place types of functions are significant.

Central-place theory also appears to be applicable to the distribution of retail and service business location *within* cities. More specifically, it applies to nucleated shopping centers within cities and postulates that hamlets, villages, towns, and cities are paralleled by street intersection, neighborhood, community, and regional shopping centers.[39]

Central-place theory has two key concepts: threshold and range. *Threshold* defines the "condition of entry" of a business, that is, the minimum sales volume required to support the establishment. *Range* relates to the area occupied by this threshold sales volume. The group of functions which, for example, sets cities at a level above towns is that group of functions with thresholds too large to be performed by towns because of their more restricted hinterlands, yet not so large that cities cannot perform them so that they must be relinquished to regional metropoli of higher order with still larger trade areas. As the amount of purchasing power available per unit area decreases, the range (or size of hinterland) needed to encompass a given threshold increases, and centers of a given class therefore become more widely spaced.

The first modern theoretical statement concerned with the sizes, spacings, functions, and grouping of functions of the central-place type was by Walter Christaller in 1933.[40] A few years later, an interpretation by Ullman was significant in arousing interest among English-speaking geographers in Christaller's concepts,[41] and the literature thereafter expanded rapidly.[42] Christaller pointed out that the "complementary region" or trade area of a center should take the form of a hexagon, since that is the shape which, with a minimum perimeter, blankets an area without overlap and without gaps. In practice, the boundary between adjacent trade areas or hinterlands of centers of comparable order could be located in accordance with Reilly's Law of Retail Gravitation, which states that the "pull" of a center is proportional to mass (purchasing power, or disposable income per capita multiplied by population), and inversely proportional to distance from another center.[43] Christaller, in his extensive studies in southern Germany, found that trade centers tended to cluster in size-groups which were closely related to the nature of the functions present in each center, but in areas where modern transportation has extended the trade areas, the lowest-order centers have tended to atrophy in favor of fewer but larger centers where higher thresholds can be served. Thus in the United States, small hamlets and villages, based upon pre-automobile transportation, tend to decline, and small subneighborhood shopping concentrations in cities cannot compete with the larger nucleations of higher order, which also contain higher-order establishments serving more extensive trade areas. The "supermarket" has a higher threshold requirement than the "ma-and-pa" grocery store, which is tending to disappear.

A special problem of the urban hierarchy concerns the great cities and their relations to smaller urban concentrations. In 1939 Mark Jefferson formulated what he called "The Law of the Primate City," in which he pointed out that in many regions there is a cumulative tendency for the largest city in a region or country to attract, by the multitude of its opportunities, the greatest proportion of the region's or country's population.[44] A more general statement of the relationships among city sizes is that of Zipf and Stewart, who formulated the "Rank-Size Rule," which states that within a country or region there is a tendency for a city of any given rank among the group of cities in that country or region to have a population which is in inverse proportion to its rank. Thus, the second city would have half the population of the largest, and the nth city would have $1/n$th the population of the largest city.[45] Recent studies by Berry, Ginsburg, and others indicate that the primate-city pattern and the rank-size pattern may actually represent two ends of a continuum, in which the various regions and countries are characterized by one or the other, or by intermediate patterns of city-size distribution in terms of population.[46]

A special case of primacy involves the *Weltstadt*, or world metropolis, a distinctive urban unit characterized by functions and facilities that require an extremely high threshold, and hence are the least ubiquitous of all urban functions.[47] A metropolis with a population of ten million would have a number of functions that are not found, for example, in any of ten cities with population of one million each.[48] For these distinctive functions, the range, or areal extent of the territory and population served, must be very great, and in some instances it is worldwide. The multitudinous functions of the extremely large urban agglomeration combine economies of scale and external economies in a complex series of linkages which, in turn, produce tendencies toward further agglomeration. The result is a relatively more rapid growth of the great metropolitan areas than of smaller cities, which tend to grow more rapidly than do the rural areas, where the continuing rationalization of agriculture is producing labor surpluses.

Urban Internal Structure and Pattern

Great size is accompanied by great complexity, and the very large metropolitan cities are increasingly subject to internal diseconomies—congestion, increasing separation of residential areas from working areas with consequent time and expense of commuting, and urban "sprawl," or the haphazard arrangement of land uses and functional areas with little regard for the overall efficiency of the metropolitan organism. These problems are of concern to geographers, as well as other social scientists and planners, who are concerned with the total urban pattern—its form, the areal organization of its functional components, the circulation patterns and facilities that make internal functional differentiation possible, and the interrelationships among the specialized areas that constitute the urban anatomy and physiology.

There exist a number of formulations, none of which by itself can explain or describe the internal organization of any particular city, but all of which, in combination or individually, have proved to be useful in interpreting urban growth and existing physical and functional patterns within cities. Among the generalized descriptive models, each based on concepts of process developed by sociologists and land economists, the ones that have gained most widespread acceptance are (1) the concentric-circle or zonal model, (2) the wedge or sector model, and (3) the multiple-nuclei model. These are so well known among social scientists that they require no description here. Concern with these formulations has been reflected in literally hundreds of studies of individual cities which have been described in great detail with regard to their internal structures and functional organization of land uses, buildings, and circulation patterns.

Recent research has focused more on the development of generalizations from these descriptive efforts. Many of these were anticipated in a classic statement by Charles C. Colby in 1933, in which it was pointed out that a city pattern is the resultant of two opposing forces, centripetal and centrifugal.[49] Contemporary studies, however, are making use of quantitative methods, greatly facilitated by the use of computers and advanced data-processing equipment. Nevertheless, since no study is better than the quality of data on which it is based, survey techniques in urban areas also must be improved. There is a considerable literature on field methods in urban geography.[50] An extremely useful tool is the air photograph, and sophisticated techniques of air-photo interpretation are being developed.[51]

In Europe, cultural-historical studies of urban internal patterns, particularly as evidenced in the "townscape," constitute a considerable literature. Smailes expressed this approach in the following terms:

> . . . [T]he strongest appeal of the study of urban morphology to the geographer's attention and interest must surely lie in the scope that exists for generalization, for the recognition among townscapes of recurrent associations of important constituent elements that may afford a basis for the recognition of types. Elucidation of the complexes of features pertaining to some or all the related aspects of setting, function, form, and tone is the key to a more deeply significant and satisfactory generic classification and terminology.[52]

In America, however, cities are the products of a relatively homogeneous cultural history, and most of their features are of recent growth. American scholars, therefore, have been less concerned with the effects of cultural changes upon urban structure and form than have their European colleagues, although a number of historical studies of urban structure appear in the American literature.[53] They have been actively concerned, however, with the decision-making processes, both public and private, in the location of urban activities and facilities, and, as consultants and staff members of public planning agencies, they have developed close affinities with city, regional, and metropolitan planners.[54]

In his consideration of urban form, structure, and internal functional organization, the geographer shares a common core of theory with the urban land economist. Both regard urban land as a scarce resource, with a multitude of uses, and a multitude of establishments within each category of use, in competition for each of the sites within and near the urban mass. Forces of agglomeration come into play, producing high land values at the most accessible locations. Commonly, the highest land values are in the central business district of the city, where accessibility is greatest, and where the greatest number of establishments seek locations. Since all users of urban land, whether commercial, industrial, residential, or other, cannot locate on the same sites, there is a sorting out of establishments and functions in relative order of their ability to benefit from, and hence pay site costs for, the most accessible locations with relation to other establishments with which they have linkages.

Some establishments, such as "heavy" industries which require large-scale bulk transportation, proximity to suppliers, to water, to fuel, or to other resources, have much more specialized site requirements than others, and commonly form nuclei around which symbiotically related land uses tend to cluster. These specialized site requirements can be met only by a limited number of sites, which therefore carry land values for the specialized uses higher than the general level of land values in their vicinities.

On the other hand, many types of activities and establishments have less specialized site requirements, and can therefore locate in a greater variety of areas within the urban complex. For example, for residences and, in many instances, "light" industries, accessibility can be in the form of transportation routes and services rather than mutual proximity. There thus can be a substitution of transport costs for site costs, and each such establishment, in an ideal model, would locate at a point which represents optimum balance between transport and site costs. (These instances exemplify Weber's "agglomerating" and "deglomerating" forces, and Colby's "centrifugal" and "centripetal" forces.) In such a model, where transport is assumed to be available equally in all directions from the urban center, the characteristic land uses sort themselves out in descending order of intensity from the center, as in the concentric zonal models of Von Thünen and Burgess. In fact, however, since transport follows a limited number of routes, usually radial from the center, urban forms tend to be stellate or lobate and *not* ring-shaped, with the most intensive development and the maximum radial extent along the radial transport routes. Before the advent of the automobile, these routes were railroads with commuter services, urban street railways, and, later in a few cities, rapid transit lines with multiple-unit electrified operation; and these shaped most American cities well before the advent of the automobile. Now, new areas are being opened up by expressways which commonly radiate from the city center through the interstitial and relatively low-density areas between the older radial prongs of urbanization. The express highway interchange is somewhat analogous to the suburban railroad station of an earlier generation as a locus of outlying retail and service business. The effects of improved transport technology and availability have been most marked in reduction of average density of the urban built-up areas and rapid increase in their extent.[55] Recent "highway-impact" studies have been especially important in illuminating trends and suggesting hypotheses of high predictive value.[56]

In addition to research on the overall areal structure and internal functional organization of cities, many studies of individual component areas have appeared as well, some emphasizing method; others, under the auspices of planning agencies and other public bodies or of commercial or industrial organizations, are concerned with the practical application of findings. Among these types of functional areas are: (1) central business districts; (2) outlying commercial areas; (3) industrial areas; (4) residential areas, including those which have become blighted and which may be subject to renewal; and (5) suburban areas and the rural-urban fringe.

Central Business District Studies

The core of most Western cities is the central business district (CBD). Here is the focus of internal urban transportation, the area of maximum accessibility, of both vehicular and pedestrian traffic volume, of highest land values, and, of course, therefore, of maximum intensity of business activity. In the numerous studies of central business districts, many similarities with major outlying business concentrations have been documented, so that the principles which are emerging relative to the structure, organization, patterns, and growth of central business districts also seem applicable to other concentrations of retail and service businesses within the urban area. One of the earliest studies, however, concerned the vertical differentiation of activities in CBD's, and a method was developed for studying the complexities of three-dimensional business areas.[57]

Some studies have been directed toward developing uniform criteria of CBD boundary delimitation, a necessary first step in comparative studies, and have indicated the existence of similarities and analogies among a number of cities of roughly comparable size. Noteworthy are the comparative studies of Murphy and his colleagues, who compared the central business districts of nine moderate-sized American cities.[58] The methods and criteria developed in these studies have been applied to a number of cities outside the United States, with results indicating that the techniques, with modifications, are generally applicable to the study of central business districts of all Western-type cities of moderate size.[59] Still remaining, however, is the testing of the methods developed by Murphy and his associates in cities of much larger size and in small urban concentrations.[60] Other studies concerned with the changing functions of the CBD have been made for a number of cities in the United States,[61] and many comparable studies have been made of the central areas of Western-type cities in other countries.[62] Several recent studies also have pointed out the distinctive differences in functions and character of the "hard core" of the central

business district in contrast with those of the "core frame," characterized by less intensive uses such as warehouses, light manufacturing
establishments, automobile parking for CBD destinations, and transportation terminals, together with surviving remnants, in some instances, of earlier residential occupance of the areas.[63]

General Business Structure Studies

The central business district is, of course, only one part of the business structure of cities and metropolitan areas. Malcolm Proudfoot
pioneered in the study of general patterns of retail and service business
within urban areas.[64] He identified the principal concentrations of
urban retail and service business establishments, among which the
CBD was recognized as the major focus, with a descending hierarchical order of business nucleations, including the major outlying (regional) center, the community business center, the neighborhood
center, the isolated shop, and the ribbons along the major arterial
routes. The familiar pattern of ribbons, with intensification approaching the major intersections, together with a gradient of intensity along
the ribbons, was recognized. Empirical studies by Mayer and others
confirmed his findings.[65]

Several factors have stimulated more sophisticated research on urban
business structure, among them the rapid postwar growth of planned
shopping centers of newer types, the recognition of the importance
of retail and service business concentrations as major elements in comprehensive planning of cities and metropolitan regions, and the changes
being made in the business structures of urban areas by the construction of the new express highways concomitant with the general decline in use of mass transportation, which formerly constituted a major
localizing force. From these studies is emerging a theoretical predictive model of urban structure,[66] and empirical studies in many cities, both in America and elsewhere, show that the patterns are similar
wherever Western culture is dominant.[67]

Of course, not all retail and service business is nucleated. Many
establishments are aligned along arterial routes and depend upon access by automobile, rather than upon a contiguous service area. Thus,
business location can only partly be explained in terms of central-
place theory; traffic flows generate locational patterns of business
along their routes of movement both rural [68] and urban.[69] Many types
of service business, furthermore, are not compatible with the type
characteristically associated with nucleations, whether of the older
intersectionally localized type or the newer planned type. Such service
and retail establishments constitute a problem to the city planners,

and analysis of their locational patterns and requirements is proving to be helpful.[70]

Industrial Locations and Land Uses [71]

At the regional and interregional scale, location of industry involves considerations of access to resources, labor, fuels and power, and markets. Optimal location of industrial establishments involves consideration of minimal transport costs. An extensive body of theory relating to location is familiar to nearly all urban specialists, most of it contributed by nongeographers, including Weber,[72] Hoover,[73] Lösch,[74] and Isard.[75]

At the scale of the individual metropolitan area, however, there is a considerable literature concerned with industrial location and problems of individual urban areas. Some works are concerned with the historical development of urban industry.[76] Others reflect interest in individual types of industries; the iron-and-steel industry, for example, has been the subject of many studies, since it is basic to the economy of many cities.[77] Other industries treated include textiles,[78] automobiles,[79] aircraft,[80] and printing.[81] In addition, there are numerous empirical studies of the patterns and trends of industry and industrial land use in individual cities and metropolitan areas.[82]

Much information is also available about the processes of growth and decline of older industrial districts.[83] Many of these, favored by central locations, are being rehabilitated either as more modern industrial areas or for other uses.[84] On the other hand, industry also is deconcentrating and seeking new and expansive locations on and beyond the urban periphery.[85] Location of industry in many areas has been associated with the creation of organized industrial districts, in which the individual plants, in a community of industrial plants, share many advantages of mutual proximity in a planned environment.[86] The effects of technological change in stimulating shifts in the locational patterns of industry also have been the subjects of research.[87] In this connection, one of the potentially most significant factors affecting the pattern of location of industry is power, particularly the technological changes occurring in the utilization of fuels and techniques of power production.[88]

Residential Areas and Housing

Residence constitutes the most extensive form of urban land use in most cities, except for streets, most of which function primarily for residential access. The typical city has from 30 to 40 per cent of its land area in residential parcels. The distribution and functional interrelationships of residential areas, of housing types, of variations in housing quality, and of residential areas to other urban functional areas have long attracted the attention of geographers. Techniques for the mapping of these spatial distributions, widely used by planners and developers as well as by official statistical agencies, were in part developed by geographers. During the 1930's, the United States government became greatly concerned with the implementation of new housing policies, and in connection therewith encouraged and participated in the financing of a series of comprehensive land use surveys or "real-property inventories" in many cities, using, for comparative purposes, more-or-less standard techniques of mapping, classification, and statistical analysis. Techniques of classification and mapping were important geographic contributions to the research base used in the formulation of public policy at both national and local levels.[89] Contributing to the body of techniques used in these surveys were the backgrounds of techniques earlier developed both in rural and urban areas for land-use classification, including mapping of urban residential types by Wellington Jones,[90] fractional-code mapping, developed originally by geographers in the Tennessee Valley and elsewhere, and isopleth mapping of ratios, including population densities.[91] One very useful source is the Sanborn map, available for most built-up areas in American cities.[92]

In the United States, studies of the structure, characteristics, growth, and population distributions within urban areas have been greatly facilitated by the widespread tracting of cities and suburban areas in recent years, making statistics available, especially on population and residential characteristics, for areas smaller than incorporated municipalities. The Geography Division of the United States Bureau of the Census has set uniform criteria for census tracts throughout the nation, and has coordinated the tracting done by local committees in each metropolitan area.

The development of techniques of mapping and analysis relative to urban renewal—the rebuilding and rehabilitation of the older and more obsolete, deteriorated areas of cities—presents outflow problems. The measurement of blight, for example, involves determination of the areal extent of those qualitative conditions which are associated with physical, social, and economic deterioration.[93]

Suburban Areas and the Rural-Urban Fringe

The rapid increase in urban population, particularly during the past two decades, has been accompanied by an even more spectacular increase in the demand for urban land. Not only has the population of metropolitan areas increased substantially in the face of general declines in the older areas of the central cities, but the demands of residential lands have been augmented by spectacular increases in the standards of housing in the urban areas, with much lower densities prevalent than formerly. Types of urban land uses other than residential have also produced augmented demands for land as deconcentration toward the suburban areas has taken place.

The processes by which cities expand their areas have been intensively studied in the fringe areas of many cities.[94] The popular concept of the suburb as a high-grade dormitory area for the population employed in the central cities was effectively destroyed by an article by Chauncy Harris, in which he demonstrated that a substantial proportion of the American suburbs are of types other than upper-income commuting areas, and that, indeed, many suburbs are predominantly of nonresidential character.[95]

The lags in the political and administrative organization of the rapidly expanding urban areas have been clearly set forth in a number of studies of the problems of providing the requisite public services in metropolitan areas despite their organizational fragmentation.[96] Another kind of lag—the time lag between the subdivision of land, which makes it no longer available for rural types of uses, and its final absorption into urban use—has also received attention. Fellman, for example, in studies of the sequence of subdivision activity in the area now included within the City of Chicago, demonstrated that subdivision often has taken place under the stimulus of improved transportation far in advance of the actual absorption of the land for urban use.[97]

Two other problems associated with peripheral expansion of cities into the rural-urban fringe areas also are of major research interest: (1) the competition of urban with rural land uses, and (2) the preservation of open space in the vicinities of the large urban populations. As cities expand, the demand for conversion of land from low-density rural uses to higher-density suburban and urban uses is almost invariably resolved in favor of the higher densities. Agricultural and other lower-density uses thus disappear. There is no general shortage of agricultural land in the United States, as there is in some smaller but highly urbanized nations such as Great Britain, but locally the problem of disappearance of agriculture and other low-density land uses in the face of urbanization is of considerable importance.[98]

Geographers emphasize a continuum of urban-rural gradation, which is not necessarily circular, but which reflects variations in site conditions, building and zoning codes, taxation rates and policies, and particularly in the availability of public utilities and transportation.

The effects of areal differentials in transport accessibility on the peripheral expansion of cities and the resultant stellate or lobate form of the city, with tentacles along the major transportation routes, have been described in detail.[99] With the universal use of the automobile, the stellate form of the urban outline is being modified by the filling in of the interstitial areas between the radiating prongs of earlier growth.[100] As a result, the disappearance of remaining open areas in the vicinities of cities is causing much concern.[101] Individual types of urban and suburban land uses having an "open" character have also been studied. Among those that have been examined systematically are cemeteries,[102] local airports,[103] market gardens, and other urban fringe types of agricultural land uses.[104] In addition, there are many studies of recreational land use [105] and several of the locations and service areas of educational facilities [106] and of churches.[107]

Transportation Facilities and Land Uses

Without transportation, cities could not exist, since transportation makes areal specialization possible, and hence the growth and existence of cities. Apart from studies of the internal circulation of cities and metropolitan areas, there exists a considerable literature on the roles of cities as transportation foci. Although some literature overlaps the field of transportation, and therefore is not discussed here, much is closely related to an understanding, on the one hand, of the urban economic base and, on the other, of the internal structure and functional organization of cities and metropolitan areas.

Studies of cities as ports constitute probably the most extensive portion of the literature on cities as transportation centers. There are several reasons for this. First, data are usually more readily available for movements through ports than through cities that are not ports. Second, ports epitomize the economic geography of the regions that they serve, for at the ports are concentrated most of the external movements connecting the region with other regions. Third, port development has practical significance for economic and urban geographers, many of whom have participated in the planning and development of ports.[108]

Many of the port studies have anticipated subsequent concepts which have become widely accepted principles of urban geography. For example, the delimitation of port hinterlands preceded by some years the extension of the concept to the delimitation of urban "fields," and the relations of ports of various sizes to each other and to entrepôts anticipated the later development of the concepts of an urban hierarchy. The effects of ports on industrial developments in their respective metropolitan areas and cities, and the relations to the changing demands for land uses in waterfront and interior locations have been the subjects of several studies. Moreover, the reciprocal relations of waterfront development and other aspects of the physical and functional structure of the city have received considerable attention in numerous reports, many of which were made with the sponsorship of planning and port development agencies.[109]

Research on the relations between railroads and urban development is neither as extensive nor as sophisticated as that on ports, since in the United States data by area rather than corporation are relatively scarce. At the interregional scale, a series of studies by Ullman constitute a geographic portrayal of the significance of the United States railroad system. These resulted in the development of the concept of "spatial interaction," involving gravity analogues, considerations of complementarity of regions, and independence due to intervening opportunities.[110] Moreover, there have been a number of studies of the evolution of the railroad patterns of cities and metropolitan areas, as well as of the railroads' significance to the development of the city.[111] The nodality of cities in regional development, emphasized by their roles as railroad centers, also has been emphasized.[112]

Research on the relations between highway transportation and city patterns and development has recently been stimulated by research funds available in connection with the federal interstate highway system, although studies by American geographers of the patterns of highway carrier operations are few.[113] On the other hand, in Great Britain and in Sweden, where local bus services connecting towns are much more common than in the United States, these services have been extensively used in the delimitation of service areas of towns and in the identification of the urban hierarchy.[114]

The major urban centers are greatly affected by the growth of air transportation and the intensification of competition for hinterland connections among the larger cities. Edward J. Taaffe has developed techniques for measuring the relationships between air traffic and urban hinterlands.[115] On a world scale, the significance of air transportation in the transmission of culture, and hence in reinforcing the role of large cities as centers of cultural diffusion, was recognized in a classic paper by Robert S. Platt.[116]

Conclusion

The significant contributions that geography is making to urban studies are defined by its emphasis on the spatial organization of cities on the one hand, and on city-external relations on the other.

In recent years, the major advances in urban geography have been: (1) in the development of concepts of the hierarchy of central places and the clustering or association of urban functions and facilities; (2) in applications of geographic method and techniques relative to spatial organization of urban land uses to practical problems of city and metropolitan planning; (3) in the identification of significant relationships between land uses and densities and the generation of traffic interconnecting the specialized functional areas both within and outside cities; and (4) in the development of general hypotheses regarding the numbers, sizes, and spacings of urban places.

Increasingly, these hypotheses are proving of value as predictive devices and are finding application in many types of planning—in government, in manufacturing and merchandising organizations, and in such fields as urban renewal and transportation planning.

NOTES

1. Peter Schöller, "Aufgaben und Probleme der Stadtgeographie," *Erdkunde*, 7 (1953), p. 161.

2. Robert L. Wrigley, Jr., "Urbanized Areas and the 1950 Census," *Journal of the American Institute of Planners*, 16 (1950), pp. 66–70.

3. Robert C. Klove, "The Definition of Standard Metropolitan Areas," *Economic Geography*, 28 (1952), pp. 95–104.

4. Jean Gottmann, *Megalopolis, the Urbanized Northeastern Seaboard of the United States* (New York: The Twentieth Century Fund, 1961).

5. For an economist's review of economic base studies, analysis, and local structure, see C. M. Tiebout, *The Community Economic Base Study*, Supp. Paper No. 16 (New York: Committee for Economic Development, 1962).

6. Jean Brunhes, *Human Geography* (Chicago: Rand McNally, 1920), pp. 74–229.

7. Chauncy D. Harris, "The Pressure of Residential-Industrial Land Use," in William L. Thomas, Jr. (Ed.), *Man's Role in Changing the Face of the Earth* (Chicago: University of Chicago Press, 1956), pp. 881–890.

8. Harold M. Mayer, "Urban Nodality and the Economic Base," *Journal of the American Institute of Planners*, 20 (1954), pp. 117–121.

9. Many of the concepts were well known a decade or two ago. For example, a comprehensive statement is Robert L. Dickinson, *City, Region and Regionalism* (London: Kegan Paul, Trench, Trubner, 1947).

10. Edward L. Ullman, *American Commodity Flow* (Seattle: University of Washington Press, 1957).

11. Gunnar Alexandersson, *The Industrial Structure of American Cities* (Lincoln: University of Nebraska Press, 1956).

12. For a review of the history of the concept with special reference to geographical contributions, see John W. Alexander, "The Basic-Nonbasic Concept of Urban Economic Functions," *Economic Geography*, 30 (1954),

pp. 246–261. M. Aurousseau, "The Distribution of Population: A Constructive Problem," *The Geographical Review*, 11 (1921), p. 574; Robert S. Platt, "An Urban Field Study: Marquette, Michigan," *Annals of the Association of American Geographers*, 21 (1931), p. 72; Richard Hartshorne, "The Twin City District, A Unique Form of Urban Landscape," *The Geographical Review*, 22 (1932), pp. 431–442; Cincinnati City Planning Commission, *The Economy of the Cincinnati Metropolitan Area* (Cincinnati, 1946); John W. Alexander, "Oshkosh, Wisconsin, An Economic Base Study," *Wisconsin Commerce Papers*, 1 (1951); John W. Alexander, "An Economic Base Study of Madison, Wisconsin," *ibid.*, 1 (1953).

13. Victor Roterus and Wesley C. Calef, "Notes on the Basic-Nonbasic Employment Ratio," *Economic Geography*, 31 (1955), pp. 17–20.

14. Hans Blumenfeld, "The Economic Base of the Metropolis," *Journal of the American Institute of Planners*, 21 (1955), pp. 114–132.

15. Charles T. Stewart, Jr., "Economic Base Dynamics," *Land Economics*, 35 (1959), pp. 327–336.

16. Alexandersson, *op. cit.*

17. Irving Morrissett, "The Economic Structure of American Cities," *Papers and Proceedings of the Regional Science Association*, 4 (1958), pp. 239–256.

18. Edward L. Ullman and Michael F. Dacey, "The Minimum Requirements Approach to the Urban Economic Base," *Papers and Proceedings of the Regional Science Association*, 6 (1960), pp. 175–194.

19. G. J. R. Linge, *The Future Work Force of Canberra*, a report for the National Capital Development Commission (Canberra, 1960).

20. Chauncy D. Harris and Edward L. Ullman, "The Nature of Cities," *Annals of the American Academy of Political and Social Science*, 242 (1945), pp. 7–17.

21. Among the functional classifications of United States cities by geographers are Chauncy D. Harris, "A Functional Classification of Cities in the United States," *The Geographical Review*, 33 (1943), pp. 86–99; Howard J. Nelson, "A Service Classification of American Cities," *Economic Geography*, 31 (1955), pp. 189–210; John Fraser Hart, "Functions and Occupational Structures of Cities of the American South," *Annals of the Association of American Geographers*, 45 (1955), pp. 269–286; and Robert A. Harper, "Economic Functions of Downstate Illinois Cities," *Transactions of the Illinois State Academy of Science*, 47 (1955), pp. 99–103.

22. Chauncy D. Harris, "Cities of the Soviet Union," *The Geographical Review*, 35 (1945), pp. 107–121.

23. L. L. Pownall, "The Functions of New Zealand Towns," *Annals of the Association of American Geographers*, 43 (1953), pp. 232–250.

24. William Steigenga, "A Comparative Analysis and a Classification of Netherlands Towns," *Tijdschrift voor Economische en Sociale Geografie*, 44 (1955), pp. 105–119.

25. C. A. Moser and Wolf Scott, *British Towns: A Statistical Study of their Social and Economic Differences* (Edinburgh and London: Oliver and Boyd, 1961).

26. V. F. Emerson, "A Geographic Interpretation of New York City," *Bulletin of the American Geographical Society*, 40 (1908), pp. 587–612, 726–738; 41 (1909), pp. 3–20.

27. See, for example, R. D. Salisbury and W. C. Alden, *The Geography of Chicago and its Environs*, Geographical Society of Chicago, Bulletin No. 1 (Chicago: University of Chicago Press, 1920).

28. Lewis F. Thomas, *Localization of Business Activities in Metropolitan St. Louis* (St. Louis: Washington University Press, 1927).

29. Gilbert F. White et al., *Changes in Urban Occupance of Flood Plains in the United States;* Gilbert F. White (Ed.), *Papers on Flood Problems;* John R. Sheaffer, *Flood Proofing;* Robert W. Kates, *Hazard and Choice Perception in Flood Plain Management.* University of Chicago, Department of Geography, Research Papers Nos. 57 (1958), 65 (1960), 70 (1961), and 78 (1962).

30. For example, John R. Borchert, "The Surface Water Supply of American Municipalities," *Annals of the Association of American Geographers,* 44 (1954), pp. 15–32; A. Van Burkalow, "The Geography of New York City's Water Supply, A Study of Interactions," *The Geographical Review,* 49 (1959), pp. 369–386; Carol Y. Mason, "Municipal Water Supplies of New England," *Economic Geography,* 13 (1937), pp. 347–364; Minnie E. Lemaire, "Wachusett Reservoir, A Metropolitan Water Supply," *Economic Geography,* 13 (1937), pp. 181–186.

31. Gilbert F. White, discussion in *Water for Industry,* edited by Jack B. Graham for the American Association for the Advancement of Science, 1956, pp. 121–124; C. Langdon White, "Water—A Neglected Factor in the Geographical Literature of Iron and Steel," *The Geographical Review,* 47 (1957), pp. 463–489.

32. Among the studies of urban microclimatology are M. Parry, "The Climate of Towns," *Weather* (1950), pp. 351–356; Helmut Landsberg, "The Weather in the Streets," *Landscape,* 9 (1959), pp. 26–28; Helmut Landsberg, "The Climate of Towns," in William L. Thomas, Jr. (Ed.), *Man's Role in Changing the Face of the Earth* (Chicago: University of Chicago Press, 1956), pp. 584–606; Fowler S. Duckworth and James S. Sandberg, "The Effects of Cities upon Horizontal and Vertical Temperature Gradients," *Bulletin of the American Meteorological Society,* 35 (1954), pp. 198–207; Charles E. P. Brooks, "Selected Annotated Bibliography on Urban Climates," *Meteorological Abstracts and Bibliography,* 3 (1952), pp. 734–773.

33. Clyde P. Patton, "Climatology of Summer Fogs in the San Francisco Bay Area," *University of California Publications in Geography,* 10 (1956), pp. 113–200.

34. F. N. Frenkel, "Atmospheric Pollution and Zoning in an Urban Area," *The Scientific Monthly,* 82 (1956), pp. 194–203.

35. *The Air over Louisville,* Joint Report by the Special Air Pollution Study of Louisville and Jefferson County, Kentucky (1956–1957); *Pollution of the Atmosphere in the Detroit River Area, Report of the International Joint Commission* (Washington and Ottawa, 1960); *Air Pollution in the National Capital Area,* U. S. Public Health Service (Washington, 1962).

36. Edward L. Ullman, "Amenities as a Factor in Regional Growth," *The Geographical Review,* 44 (1954), pp. 119–132; Margaret T. Parker, "Tucson, City of Sunshine," *Economic Geography,* 24 (1948), pp. 79–113; Howard J. Nelson, "The Spread of an Artificial Landscape over Southern California," *Annals of the Association of American Geographers,* 49, Part 2,

pp. 80–99; Andrew W. Wilson, "Urbanization of the Arid Lands," *The Professional Geographer,* 12 (1960), pp. 4–7.

37. This section should be regarded as an introduction to Berry's discussion of central-place research in Chapter 11 in this book. See also Brian J. L. Berry and Allen Pred, *Central Place Studies: A Bibliography of Theory and Applications* (Philadelphia: Regional Science Research Institute, 1961).

38. Allen K. Philbrick, "Principles of Areal Functional Organization in Regional Human Geography," *Economic Geography,* 33 (1957), pp. 299–336; R. H. Brown, *Political Areal Functional Organization,* University of Chicago, Department of Geography, Research Paper No. 51 (1957); A. E. Larimore, *The Alien Town,* University of Chicago, Department of Geography, Research Paper No. 55 (1958).

39. H. Carol, "The Hierarchy of Central Place Functions within the City," *Annals of the Association of American Geographers,* 50 (1960), pp. 419–438; M. J. Proudfoot, "The Outlying Business Centers of Chicago," *Journal of Land and Public Utility Economics,* 13 (1937), pp. 57–70.

40. Walter Christaller, *Die zentralen Orte in Süddeutschland* (Jena: Gustav Fischer Verlag, 1933).

41. Edward Ullman, "A Theory of Location for Cities," *American Journal of Sociology,* 46 (1941), pp. 853–864.

42. A few representative studies from various regions include J. B. Fleming and F. H. W. Green, "Some Relations between Country and Town in Scotland," *The Scottish Geographical Magazine,* 68 (1952), pp. 2–12; John E. Brush, "The Hierarchy of Central Places in Southwestern Wisconsin," *The Geographical Review,* 43 (1953), pp. 380–404; H. E. Bracey, "Towns as Rural Service Centers, An Index of Centrality with Special Reference to Somerset," *Institute of British Geographers, Transactions and Papers, 1953* (1954), pp. 95–106; John E. Brush and Howard F. Bracey, "Rural Service Centers in Southwestern Wisconsin and Southern England," *Geographical Review,* 45 (1955), pp. 559–569; J. S. Duncan, "New Zealand Towns as Service Centers," *New Zealand Geographer,* 11 (1955), pp. 119–138; Marvin W. Mikesell, "Market Centers of Northeastern Spain: A Review," *Geographical Review,* 50 (1960), pp. 247–251; Edward L. Ullman, "Trade Centers and Tributary Areas of the Philippines," *Geographical Review,* 50 (1960), pp. 203–218; J. S. Whitelaw, "The Measurement of Urban Influence in the Waikato," *New Zealand Geographer,* 18 (1962), pp. 72–92.

43. William J. Reilly, *The Law of Retail Gravitation* (New York: William J. Reilly, 1931). Reilly, on the other hand, was not concerned with developing a hypothetical spatial model of tertiary activity as was Christaller.

44. Mark Jefferson, "The Law of the Primate City," *The Geographical Review,* 29 (1939), pp. 226–232.

45. G. K. Zipf, "The Hypothesis of the Minimum Equation as a Unifying Social Principle," *American Sociological Review,* 22 (1947), pp. 627–650; J. Q. Stewart, "Empirical Mathematical Rules Concerning the Distribution and Equilibrium of Population," *The Geographical Review,* 38 (1947), pp. 461–485.

46. See pp. 34–37 in N. S. Ginsburg, *Atlas of Economic Development* (Chicago: University of Chicago Press, 1961) and B. J. L. Berry, "City Size

Distributions and Economic Development," *Economic Development and Cultural Change,* 9 (1961), pp. 573–587.

47. For example, Joachim H. Schultze (Ed.), *Zum Problem der Weltstadt* (Berlin: Verlag Walter de Gruyter, 1959). This volume contains interpretive articles on selected large cities of world importance, stressing their special functions and characteristics.

48. See the reference to K. Tange's Tokyo plan in Ginsburg's chapter in this book.

49. Charles C. Colby, "Centrifugal and Centripetal Forces in Urban Geography," *Annals of the Association of American Geographers,* 23 (1933), pp. 1–20.

50. For example, Charles M. Davis, "Field Techniques," in P. E. James and C. F. Jones (Eds.), *American Geography: Inventory and Prospect* (Syracuse: Syracuse University Press, 1954), pp. 496–529; W. D. Jones, "Field Mapping of Residential Areas in Metropolitan Chicago," *Annals of the Association of American Geographers,* 21 (1931), pp. 129–130; William Applebaum, "A Technique of Constructing a Population and Urban Land Use Map," *Economic Geography,* 31 (1955), pp. 364–371; Allen K. Philbrick, "A Unit Area Method of Mapping Gross Land-Use Associations in Urban Regions," in *Proceedings, 8th General Assembly and 17th International Geographical Congress* (Washington: International Geographical Union, 1952), pp. 758–764. Many examples prior to the contemporary period are given in Robert S. Platt, *Field Study in American Geography,* University of Chicago, Department of Geography Research Paper No. 61 (1959).

51. James R. Wray et al., "Photo Interpretation in Urban Area Analysis," Chap. 12 of *Manual of Photographic Interpretation* (Washington: American Society of Photogrammetry, 1960), pp. 667–716; H. V. B. Kline, Jr., "The Interpretation of Air Photographs," Chap. 25 of P. E. James and C. E. Jones (Eds.), *American Geography, Inventory and Prospect* (Syracuse: Syracuse University Press, 1954), pp. 530–552.

52. A. E. Smailes, "Some Reflections on the Geographical Description and Analysis of Townscapes," *The Institute of British Geographers, Transactions and Papers,* 21 (1955), pp. 99–115.

53. Among the historical, geographic studies of the evolution of American urban structure are the following: Preston E. James, "Vicksburg: A Study in Urban Geography," *Geographical Review,* 21 (1931), pp. 234–243; Howard J. Nelson, "The Spread of an Artificial Landscape over Southern California," *Annals of the Association of American Geographers,* 49, 3, Part 2 (1959), pp. 80–99; John R. Borchert, "The Twin Cities Urbanized Area: Past, Present, Future," *Geographical Review,* 51 (1961), pp. 47–70; Jerome D. Fellman, "Pre-Building Growth Patterns in Chicago," *Annals of the Association of American Geographers,* 47 (1957), pp. 59–82; Dan Stanislawski, "The Origin and Spread of the Grid-Pattern Town," *Geographical Review,* 36 (1946), pp. 105–120; Howard J. Nelson, "The Walled City in America," *Annals of the Association of American Geographers,* 51 (1961), pp. 1–22. The technique of "sequent occupance" as developed by Whittlesey also has been applied to urban landscapes by Ackerman and Murphey.

54. Harold M. Mayer, "Geography in City and Regional Planning," *The Professional Geographer*, Vol. 6, No. 3 (1954), pp. 7–12; Gary M. Cooper, "Geography as a Foundation for City Planning," *Journal of Geography*, 58 (1959), pp. 434–441; W. T. Freeman, *Geography and Planning* (London: Hutchinson, 1958); "Status and Trends in Geography in Planning" in *Status and Trends of Geography in the United States, 1957–1960*, published by Association of American Geographers in collaboration with the National Academy of Sciences-National Research Council (1961), pp. 27–32.

55. There is a considerable planning literature on urban growth and structure, some of which is the result of studies by geographers. For example, see the *Master Plan of Residential Land Use of Chicago* (Chicago Plan Commission, 1943); John R. Borchert, "The Twin Cities . . . ," *op. cit.*

56. William L. Garrison et al., *Influence of Highway Improvements on Urban Land: A Graphic Summary* (Seattle: University of Washington, Department of Geography and Department of Civil Engineering, 1958); Garrison et al., *Studies of Highway Development and Geographic Change* (Seattle: University of Washington Press, 1959).

57. A. E. Parkins, "Profiles of the Retail Business Section of Nashville, Tennessee, and Their Interpretation," *Annals of the Association of American Geographers*, 20 (1930), pp. 164–175.

58. Raymond E. Murphy and J. E. Vance, Jr., "Delimiting the CBD," *Economic Geography*, 30 (1954), pp. 189–222; Raymond E. Murphy and J. E. Vance, Jr., "A Comparative Study of Nine Central Business Districts," *ibid.*, 30 (1954), pp. 301–336; Raymond E. Murphy, J. E. Vance, Jr., and Bart J. Epstein, "Internal Structure of the CBD," *ibid.*, 31 (1955), pp. 21–46.

59. For example: D. Hywel Davies, "Boundary Study as a Tool in CBD Analysis: An Interpretation of Certain Aspects of the Boundary of Cape Town's Central Business District," *Economic Geography*, 35 (1959), pp. 322–345; Peter Scott, "The Australian CBD," *ibid.*, 35 (1959), pp. 290–314; Harm J. de Blij, "The Functional Structure and Central Business District of Lourenco Marques, Mocambique," *Economic Geography*, 38 (1962), pp. 56–77.

60. These methods, along with others, were applied to the study of the central business districts of two special-function cities of relatively small size, in Dickinson Weber, *A Comparison of Two Oil City Business Centers* (Odessa-Midland, Texas), University of Chicago, Department of Geography, Research Paper No. 60 (Chicago, 1958).

61. Edgar M. Horwood and Ronald R. Boyce, *Studies of the Central Business District and Urban Freeway Development* (Seattle: University of Washington Press, 1959).

62. For example, Thomas R. Weir, "Land Use and Population Characteristics of Central Winnipeg," *Geographical Bulletin*, Department of Mines and Technical Surveys (Ottawa, 1956), pp. 5–21; A. E. Smailes, "The City Core: Hobart, Tasmania," *Geographical Review*, 46 (1956), pp. 420–421; Harm J. de Blij, "The Functional Structure and Central Business District of Lourenco Marques, Mocambique," *Economic Geography*, 38 (1962), pp. 56–77.

63. Cincinnati City Planning Commission, *The Cincinnati Central Busi-

ness District Space Use Study: A Summary (Cincinnati, 1956); Horwood and Boyce, *op cit.*

64. Malcolm J. Proudfoot, "City Retail Structure," *Economic Geography,* 13 (1937), pp. 425–428; Malcolm J. Proudfoot, "The Selection of a Business Site," *Journal of Land and Public Utility Economics,* 14 (1938), pp. 373ff.; Malcolm J. Proudfoot, "The Major Outlying Business Centers of Chicago," (Ph.D. Dissertation, University of Chicago, Department of Geography, 1938).

65. Harold M. Mayer, "Patterns and Recent Trends of Chicago's Outlying Business Centers," *Journal of Land and Public Utility Economics,* 17 (1942), pp. 4–16.

66. Brian J. L. Berry and William L. Garrison, "The Functional Bases of the Central-Place Hierarchy," *Economic Geography,* 34 (1958), pp. 145–154; Brian J. L. Berry and William L. Garrison, "The Spatial Organization of Business Land Uses," Chap. 3 of *Studies of Highway Development and Geographic Change* (Seattle: University of Washington Press, 1959), pp. 39–66.

67. Examples include Charles N. Forward, "Distribution of Commercial Establishments in St. John's, Newfoundland," *The Canadian Geographer,* 9 (1957), pp. 30–48; William Applebaum and Bernard L. Schapker, *A Quarter Century of Change in Cincinnati Business Centers* (Cincinnati: The Cincinnati Enquirer, 1956); Wallace E. McIntyre, "The Retail Pattern of Manila," *Geographical Review,* 45 (1955), pp. 66–80; Paul H. Sisco, *The Retail Function of Memphis,* University of Chicago, Department of Geography, Research Paper No. 37 (1954).

68. J. M. Roberts, R. M. Kozelka, M. L. Kiell, and T. M. Newman, "The Small Highway Business on U. S. 30 in Nebraska," *Economic Geography,* 32 (1956), pp. 139–152.

69. Brian J. L. Berry, "Ribbon Developments in the Urban Business Pattern," *Annals of the Association of American Geographers,* 49 (1959), pp. 145–155.

70. Paul H. Sisco, "Geographic Training and Method Applied to Trade Area Analysis of Local Shopping Centers," *Journal of Geography,* 56 (1957), pp. 201–212; Saul B. Cohen and William Applebaum, "Evaluating Store Sites and Determining Store Rents," *Economic Geography,* 36 (1960), pp. 1–35.

71. Particularly significant for industrial location, both at the national and regional scales and within given urban and metropolitan areas, is the availability and cost of transportation. Transportation geography, which is concerned with costs, flow patterns, and physical facilities, overlaps urban geography, but the literature of that field is enormous, and space limits prohibit a discussion of it. For a convenient summary of the field, see Edward L. Ullman and Harold M. Mayer, "Transportation Geography," Chap. 13 of P. E. James and C. L. Jones (Eds.), *American Geography, Inventory and Prospect* (Syracuse: Syracuse University Press, 1954), pp. 310–331.

72. Alfred Weber, *Theory of the Location of Industry* (Chicago: University of Chicago Press, 1929).

73. Edgar M. Hoover, *Location of Economic Activity* (New York: McGraw-Hill, 1948).

74. August Lösch, *The Economics of Location* (New Haven: Yale University Press, 1954).

75. Walter Isard, *Location and Space-Economy: A General Theory Relating to Industrial Location, Market Areas, Land Use, Trade, and Urban Structure* (Cambridge: M. I. T. Press, 1956); Walter Isard, *Methods of Regional Analysis: An Introduction to Regional Science* (Cambridge: M. I. T. Press, 1960).

76. B. H. Schockel, *Manufacturing Evansville, 1830–1933* (Chicago: University of Chicago, Department of Geography, 1947).

77. Richard Hartshorne, "Location Factors in the Iron and Steel Industry," *Economic Geography*, 4 (1928), pp. 241–252; C. Langdon White, "Geography's Part in the Plant Cost of Iron and Steel Production at Pittsburgh, Chicago and Birmingham," *ibid.*, 5 (1929), pp. 327–334; C. Langdon White and G. Primmer, "The Iron and Steel Industry of Duluth: A Study in Locational Maladjustment," *Geographical Review*, 27 (1937), pp. 82–91; John B. Appleton, "The Iron and Steel Industry of the Calumet District," *University of Illinois Studies in the Social Sciences*, 13, No. 2 (1925); Gunnar Alexandersson, "Changes in the Location Pattern of the Anglo-American Steel Industry, 1948–1959," *Economic Geography*, 37 (1961), pp. 95–114.

78. J. H. Burgy, *The New England Cotton Textile Industry* (Baltimore: Johns Hopkins Press, 1932); B. F. Lamert, *The Cotton Textile Industry of the Southern Appalachian Piedmont* (Chapel Hill: University of North Carolina Press, 1933).

79. *Study of Expansion Trends in the Automobile Industry with Special Reference to the Detroit Region* (Detroit Metropolitan Area Regional Planning Commission, 1956).

80. W. G. Cunningham, *The Aircraft Industry: A Study in Industrial Location* (Los Angeles, 1951).

81. Meredith F. Burrill, "The Printing Industry: A Study in Zonal Agglomeration" (abstract), *Annals of the Association of American Geographers*, 30 (1940), p. 50.

82. Margaret T. Parker, *Lowell, A Study of Industrial Development* (New York: Macmillan, 1940); Robert N. Gold, *Manufacturing Structure and Pattern of the South Bend-Mishawaka Area*, University of Chicago, Department of Geography, Research Paper No. 36 (1954); John W. Alexander, "Rockford, Illinois, A Medium-Sized Manufacturing City," *Annals of the Association of American Geographers*, 42 (1952), pp. 1–23; Raymond E. Murphy, "Johnstown and York: A Comparative Study of Two Industrial Cities," *ibid.*, 25 (1935), pp. 175–196; L. W. Davis, "Economic Development of the Great Kanawah Valley," *Economic Geography*, 19 (1943), pp. 388–404; P. Blood, "Factors in the Economic Development of Baltimore, Md.," *Economic Geography*, 13 (1937), pp. 187–208; Clifford M. Zierer, "Scranton as an Urban Community," *Geographical Review*, 17 (1927), pp. 415–428; Harold V. Miller, "Industrial Development of New Albany, Indiana," *Economic Geography*, 14 (1938), pp. 47–54; Tom Lee McKnight, *Manufacturing in Dallas: A Study of Effects* (Austin: University of Texas, Bureau of Business Research, 1956); Edward B. Espenshade, *Urban Development at the Upper Rapids of the Mississippi* (University of Chicago, Department of Geography, 1944); Lewis F. Thomas, *The Local-*

ization of Business Activities in Metropolitan St. Louis (St. Louis: Washington University, 1927), and many others.

83. Marcel J. DeMeirleir, *Manufacturing Occupance in the West Central Area of Chicago,* University of Chicago, Department of Geography, Research Paper No. 11 (1950); Robert E. Cramer, *Manufacturing Structure of the Cicero District,* University of Chicago, Department of Geography, Research Paper No. 27 (1952); James B. Kenyon, *Industrial Localization and Metropolitan Growth: The Paterson-Passaic District,* University of Chicago, Department of Geography, Research Paper No. 67 (1960).

84. K. S. Hall, H. M. Mayer, and R. L. Wrigley, Jr., "Mapping Chicago's Industrial and Commercial Land Use," *Journal of Land and Public Utility Economics,* 20 (1944), pp. 365–370; *Chicago Industrial Study, Summary Report* (Chicago Plan Commission, 1952); *The Calumet Area of Metropolitan Chicago* (Chicago Plan Commission, 1956); *Industrial Renewal* (Detroit City Plan Commission, 1956); Herbert D. Smith, *Manufacturing and Commuting in Metropolitan Indianapolis* (Indianapolis: The Metropolitan Planning Department of Marion County, 1957); Harold M. Mayer, "Procedure in Preparation of an Industrial 'Sketch Plan' for Metropolitan Philadelphia" (abstract), *Annals of the Association of American Geographers,* 37 (1947), pp. 29–30; Arthur F. Loeben, "Philadelphia Waterfront Industry," *Geographical Review,* 47 (1957), pp. 272–273.

85. James B. Kenyon, *The Industrialization of the Skokie Area,* University of Chicago, Department of Geography, Research Paper No. 33 (1954); Alfred H. Meyer and Paul F. Miller, "Manufacturing Geography of Chicago Heights, Illinois," *Proceedings of the Indiana Academy of Sciences,* 66 (1957), pp. 209–229.

86. Robert L. Wrigley, Jr., "Organized Industrial Districts with Special Reference to the Chicago Area," *Journal of Land and Public Utility Economics,* 23 (1947), pp. 180–198; T. K. Pasma, *Organized Industrial Districts: A Tool for Community Development,* U. S. Department of Commerce, Area Development Division (Washington: Government Printing Office, 1954).

87. David G. Osborn, *Geographical Features of the Automation of Industry,* University of Chicago, Department of Geography, Research Paper No. 30 (1953); David G. Osborn, "Automation of Industry—A Geographical Consideration," *Journal of the American Institute of Planners,* 19 (1953), pp. 203–213.

88. For example, See Martha Church, *Spatial Organization of Electric Power Territories in Massachusetts,* University of Chicago, Department of Geography, Research Paper No. 69 (1960), and Chauncy D. Harris, "Electricity Generation in London, England," *Geographical Review,* 31 (1941), pp. 127–134.

89. See, for example, *Residential Chicago* and *Land Use in Chicago,* Vols. I and II of the Chicago Land Use Survey (Chicago Plan Commission, 1941 and 1942); *Land Use Handbook, A Guide to Undertaking Land Use Surveys* (Chicago: Northeastern Illinois Metropolitan Area Planning Commission, 1961).

90. Wellington D. Jones, "Field Mapping of Residential Areas in Metropolitan Chicago" (abstract), *Annals of the Association of American Geographers,* 21 (1931), pp. 129–130.

91. W. D. Jones and H. M. Leppard, "Population Map of Metropolitan Chicago" (abstract), *Annals of the Association of American Geographers,* 24 (1934), pp. 58–59.

92. Robert L. Wrigley, Jr., "The Sanborn Map as a Source of Land Use Information for City Planning," *Land Economics,* 25 (1949), pp. 216–219.

93. Robert C. Klove, "A Technique for Delimiting Chicago's Blighted Areas," *Journal of Land and Public Utility Economics,* 17 (1941), pp. 483–484; Harold M. Mayer, "Applications of Residential Data from the Chicago Land Use Survey," *ibid.,* 19 (1943), pp. 85–87. A typical additional example is *Master Plan of Residential Land Use of Chicago* (Chicago Plan Commission, 1943). For an evaluation see Robert C. Klove, "City Planning in Chicago, A Review," *Geographical Review,* 38 (1948), pp. 127–131; George W. Hartman and John C. Hook, "Substandard Urban Housing in the United States: A Quantitative Analysis," *Economic Geography,* 32 (1956), pp. 95–114.

94. Robert C. Klove, *The Park Ridge-Barrington Area* (University of Chicago, 1943); Helen L. Smith, "White Bluff, A Community of Commuters," *Economic Geography,* 19 (1943), pp. 143–147; Helen H. Balk, "Rurbanization of Worcester's Environs," *Economic Geography,* 21 (1945), pp. 104–116; Charles B. Hitchcock, "Westchester-Fairfield Proposed Site for the Permanent Seat of the United Nations," *Geographical Review,* 36 (1946), pp. 351–397; Vincent M. Throop, "The Suburban Zone of Metropolitan Portland, Oregon" (University of Chicago, 1948); George Langdon, "Delimiting the Main Line District of Philadelphia," *Economic Geography,* 28 (1952), pp. 57–65; Edwin N. Thomas, "Areal Associations Between Population Growth and Selected Factors in the Chicago Urbanized Area," *Economic Geography,* 36 (1960), pp. 158–170. A comprehensive sociological analysis is that of Donald J. Bogue, *Metropolitan Growth and the Conversion of Land to Non-Agricultural Uses,* Studies in Population Distribution No. 11 (Oxford, Ohio: Scripps Foundation, 1956).

95. Chauncy D. Harris, "Suburbs," *American Journal of Sociology,* 49 (1943), pp. 1–13.

96. Malcolm J. Proudfoot, "Chicago's Fragmented Political Structure," *Geographical Review,* 47 (1957), pp. 106–117.

97. Jerome D. Fellman, "Pre-Building Growth Patterns in Chicago," *Annals of the Association of American Geographers,* 47 (1957), pp. 59–82.

98. For example, Paul F. Griffin and Ronald L. Chatham, "Urban Impact on Agriculture in Santa Clara County, California," *Annals of the Association of American Geographers,* 48 (1958), pp. 195–208.

99. Fellman, *op. cit.;* Klove, *op. cit.;* Pierre de Visé, *A Social Geography of Metropolitan Chicago* (Chicago: Northeastern Illinois Metropolitan Area Planning Commission, 1960); Charles R. Hayes, "Suburban Residential Land Values along the C. B. & Q. Railroad," *Land Economics,* 33 (1957), pp. 177–181.

100. William L. Garrison and Marion E. Marts, *Influence of Highway Improvements on Urban Land, A Graphic Summary* (Seattle: University of Washington, 1958).

101. For example, John J. B. Miller, *Open Land in Metropolitan Chicago* (Midwest Open Land Association, 1962).

102. William D. Pattison, "The Cemeteries of Chicago: A Phase of Land

Utilization," *Annals of the Association of American Geographers*, 45 (1955), pp. 245–257.

103. Eugene C. Kirchherr, "Changing Pattern of Airport Land Use in the Chicago Metropolitan Area," *Annals of the Association of American Geographers*, 50 (1960), p. 331.

104. Ivor Davies, "Urban Farming: A Study of the Agriculture of the City of Birmingham," *Geography*, 38 (1953), pp. 296–303; Donald T. Hunt, "Market Gardening in Metropolitan Auckland," *The New Zealand Geographer*, 15 (1959), pp. 130–155; John H. Thompson, "Urban Agriculture in Southern Japan," *Economic Geography*, 33 (1957), pp. 224–237.

105. Marion Clawson, *The Dynamics of Park Demand* (New York: Regional Plan Association, 1960); Arthur Glikson, "Recreational Land Use," in William L. Thomas, Jr. (Ed.), *Man's Role in Changing the Face of the Earth* (Chicago: University of Chicago Press, 1956), pp. 896–914; R. L. Stevens, "The Mexico City Picnic Area: A Study in Recreational Geography," *Annals of the Association of American Geographers*, 46 (1956), p. 274; Gordon D. Taylor, "Non-Urban Recreation as an Element of Urban Geography," *The Canadian Geographer*, 10 (1957), p. 72; Robert A. Harper, *Recreational Occupance of the Moraine Lake Region of Northeastern Illinois and Southeastern Wisconsin*, University of Chicago, Department of Geography, Research Paper No. 14 (1950).

106. Edna B. Eisen, *Educational Land Use in Lake County, Ohio*, University of Chicago, Department of Geography, Research Paper No. 2 (1948); Allen K. Philbrick, *The Geography of Education in the Winnetka and Bridgeport Communities of Metropolitan Chicago*, University of Chicago, Department of Geography, Research Paper No. 8 (1949).

107. Wesley A. Hotchkiss, *Areal Pattern of Religious Institutions in Cincinnati*, University of Chicago, Department of Geography, Research Paper No. 13 (1950).

108. Among general treatments of port subjects by geographers are: Guido G. Weigend, "Some Elements in the Study of Port Geography," *Geographical Review*, 48 (1958), pp. 185–200; Pierre Camu, "Notes on Port Studies," *The Canadian Geographer*, 6 (1955), pp. 51–59; Harold M. Mayer, "Port Operation, United States," *Encyclopaedia Britannica*, 1958 ed., Vol. 18, pp. 264–265; Donald S. Patton, "General Cargo Hinterlands of New York, Philadelphia, Baltimore and New Orleans," *Annals of the Association of American Geographers*, 48 (1958), pp. 436–455; F. W. Morgan, *Ports and Harbours* (London: Hutchinson House, 1952). There are hundreds of studies of specific ports by geographers, among them Edward L. Ullman, *Mobile, Industrial Seaport and Trade Center* (University of Chicago, 1943); Edward Hamming, *The Port of Milwaukee*, University of Chicago, Department of Geography, Research Paper No. 26 (1952); Harold M. Mayer, "Development Problems of the Port of Delaware," *Annals of the Association of American Geographers*, 38 (1948), pp. 99–100; W. T. Chambers, "The Gulf Port City Region of Texas," *Economic Geography*, 7 (1931), pp. 69–83; Allan L. Rodgers, *The Industrial Geography of the Port of Genoa*, University of Chicago, Department of Geography, Research Paper No. 66 (1960); Harold M. Mayer, *The Port of Chicago and the St. Lawrence Seaway* (Chicago: University of Chicago Press, 1957).

109. W. A. Douglas Jackson, *Philadelphia Waterfront Industry: Indus-*

trial Land and its Potentials on the Delaware River (Philadelphia Department of Commerce, 1955); Arthur F. Loeben, "Philadelphia Waterfront Industry," *Geographical Review,* 47 (1957), pp. 272–273; *Where Two Great Waterways Meet: The First Biennial Report of the Chicago Regional Port District Board* (Chicago, 1953); *The Calumet Region of Metropolitan Chicago* (Chicago Plan Commission, 1956).

110. Edward L. Ullman, "The Railroad Pattern of the United States," *Geographical Review,* 39 (1949), pp. 242–256; Edward L. Ullman, "Geography as Spatial Interaction," *Annals of the Association of American Geographers,* 44 (1954), pp. 283–284; Edward L. Ullman, *American Commodity Flow* (Seattle: University of Washington Press, 1957).

111. S. H. Beaver, "The Railways of Great Cities," *Geography,* 22, Part 2 (1937), pp. 116–120; Harold M. Mayer, "Localization of Railway Facilities in Metropolitan Centers as Typified by Chicago," *Journal of Land and Public Utilities Economics,* 20 (1944), pp. 299–315; Harold M. Mayer, "The Railway Terminal Problem of Central Chicago," *Economic Geography,* 21 (1945), pp. 62–76; *Philadelphia Railroads* (Philadelphia City Planning Commission, 2 vols., 1959).

112. Richard L. Day, "An Analysis of Through Freight Traffic in the East St. Louis Gateway," *Annals of the Association of American Geographers,* 50 (1960), pp. 313–314; Chauncy D. Harris, *Salt Lake City, A Regional Capital* (University of Chicago, 1940); Robert L. Wrigley, Jr., "Pocatello, Idaho, as a Railroad Center," *Economic Geography,* 21 (1943), pp. 325–336; H. F. Roup, "San Bernardino, California: Settlement and Growth of a Pass-site City," *University of California Publications in Geography,* 8 (1940), pp. 1–64.

113. Jerome D. Fellman, *Truck Transportation Patterns of Chicago,* University of Chicago, Department of Geography, Research Paper No. 12 (1950).

114. F. W. H. Green, "Urban Hinterlands in England and Wales: An Analysis of Bus Services," *The Geographical Journal,* 116 (1950), pp. 64–88; F. W. H. Green, "Community of Interest Areas in Western Europe—Some Geographical Aspects of Local Passenger Traffic," *Economic Geography,* 29 (1953), pp. 283–298; Sven Godlund, "The Function and Growth of Bus Traffic Within the Sphere of Urban Influence," *Lund Studies in Geography, Series B, Human Geography,* No. 18 (1956); John E. Brush, "Bus Service Hinterlands in Great Britain," *Geographical Review,* 46 (1956), pp. 267–269.

115. Edward J. Taaffe, *The Air Passenger Hinterland of Chicago,* University of Chicago, Department of Geography, Research Paper No. 24 (1952); Edward J. Taaffe, "Air Transportation and United States Urban Distribution," *Geographical Review,* 46 (1956), pp. 219–238; Edward J. Taaffe, "The Urban Hierarchy: An Air Passenger Definition," *Economic Geography,* 38 (1962), pp. 1–14.

116. Robert S. Platt, "Problems of Our Times," *Annals of the Association of American Geographers,* 36 (1946), pp. 1–43.

American Political Science
and the Study of Urbanization

Wallace S. Sayre and Nelson W. Polsby

Prescription before Description

The initial approach of American political science to its subject matter of government and politics shared the strong prescriptive tendencies of the nineteenth-century social sciences. Especially did the political scientists have a sharp sense of mission when they confronted the political and governmental institutions of urban America. In their view the urban condition was pathological, and they saw it as the proper task of the political scientists to prescribe the required remedies. This they did with vigor and eloquence, and their prescriptive mood was to endure among urban political scientists for at least a half century.

From Bryce to the Doctrines of 1915

When James Bryce in 1888 prepared the first edition of *The American Commonwealth,* there were no general systematic treatises to aid him. If one may judge from his bibliographical references, he was compelled to rely for his data concerning American cities, their government and politics, upon a few studies that had been published at Johns Hopkins University concerning individual American cities (studies that were largely historical and legalistic in content) and upon scattered articles in magazines of the decade. He also found occasionally helpful the reports of some official commissions and of several reform groups in the cities. With these materials in hand, Bryce wrote two general chapters—"The Government of Cities" and "The Working of City Governments." To these he added a chapter on "The Philadelphia Gas Ring," a chapter by Seth Low entitled "An American View of Municipal Government in the United States," and a chapter by Frank J. Goodnow on "The Tweed Ring in New York City."

These five chapters not only set the stage but also determined the approach and tone for a long generation of American political scientists in looking at the government and politics of urban centers. It is therefore worth noting what Bryce and his colleagues in 1888 assumed and concluded about city government and politics.

Bryce began by declaring: "The growth of great cities has been among the most significant and least fortunate changes in the character of the population of the United States during the century since 1787." (There were thirty cities in the United States in 1888 with populations exceeding 100,000.) Bryce noted that "the history of American cities, though striking and instructive, has been short," and that although their governments

> . . . have a general resemblance to those English municipalities which were their first model, their present structure shows them to have been much influenced by that of the State governments. We find in all the larger cities:
>
> A mayor, head of the executive, and elected directly by the voters within the city
>
> Certain executive officers or boards, some directly elected by the city voters, others nominated by the mayor or chosen by the city legislature
>
> A legislature, consisting usually of two, but sometimes of one chamber, directly elected by the city voters
>
> Judges, usually elected by the city voters, but sometimes appointed by the State.
>
> What is this but the frame of a State government applied to the smaller area of the city?

After examining these arrangements in some detail, including special attention to the government of Boston (1880 population, 360,000), and after noting with disapproval the preeminent role of political parties in city elections, Bryce concluded his first chapter with the observation that

> . . . The European reader . . . will contrast what may be called the political character of the whole city constitution with the somewhat simpler and less ambitious, though also less democratic arrangements, which have been found sufficient for the management of European cities.

Bryce then turned, in his second chapter, to more concrete matters.

> Two questions may be applied to the government of a city: What does it provide for the people, and what does it cost the

people? Space fails me to apply in detail the former of these tests, by showing what each city does or omits to do for its inhabitants; so I must be content with observing that in the United States generally constant complaints are directed against the bad paving and cleansing of the streets, the non-enforcement of the laws forbidding gambling and illicit drinking, and in some places against the sanitary arrangements and management of public buildings and parks. It would appear that in the greatest cities there is far more dissatisfaction than exists with the municipal administration in such cities as Glasgow, Liverpool, Manchester, Leeds, Dublin. . . .

The other test, that of expense, is easily applied. Both the debt and the taxation of American cities have risen with unprecedented rapidity, and now stand at an alarming figure.

Then came Bryce's famous indictment:

There is no denying that the government of cities is the one conspicuous failure of the United States. The deficiencies of the National government tell but little for evil on the welfare of the people. The faults of the State governments are insignificant compared with the extravagance, corruption, and mismanagement which mark the administration of most of the great cities . . . there is not a city with a population exceeding 200,000 where the poison germs have not sprung into a vigorous life; and in some of the smaller ones, down to 70,000 it needs no microscope to note the results of their growth. Even in the cities of the third rank similar phenomena may occasionally be discerned, though there, as some one has said, the jet black of New York and San Francisco dies away into a harmless gray.

Bryce was anxious to find an explanation:

For evils which appear wherever a large population is densely aggregated, there must be some general and widespread causes. What are these causes? . . . [The] party system . . . has, not perhaps created, but certainly enormously aggravated them, and impressed on them their specific type.

For more specific explanations, Bryce then turned to the report of the New York State Commission on Cities (1877), which had enumerated the following causes:

1. Incompetent and unfaithful governing boards and officials. . . .

2. The introduction of State and National politics into municipal affairs. . . .

3. The assumption by the legislature of the direct control of local affairs. . . .

Bryce added his own more pointed interpretation: the spoils system and the defects of the urban electorate were the central cause.

> Now the Spoils system, with the party machinery which keeps it oiled and greased and always working at high pressure, is far more potent and pernicious in great cities than in country districts. For in great cities we find an ignorant multitude, largely composed of recent immigrants, untrained in self-government; we find a great proportion of the voters paying no direct taxes, and therefore feeling no interest in moderate taxation and economical administration; we find able citizens absorbed in their private businesses, cultivated citizens unusually sensitive to the vulgarities of practical politics, and both sets unwilling to sacrifice their time and tastes and comfort in the struggle with sordid wire-pullers and noisy demagogues. In great cities the forces that attack and pervert democratic government are exceptionally numerous, the defensive forces that protect it, exceptionally ill-placed for resistance. Satan has turned his heaviest batteries on the weakest part of the ramparts.

The remedies? Bryce adopted the recommendations of the New York Commission: (1) restrict the power of the state legislature to intervene by special legislation in the affairs of cities (the "home rule" doctrine); (2) hold municipal elections at a different period of the year from state and national elections; (3) vest the legislative powers of municipalities in two bodies—a board of aldermen, elected by the ordinary suffrage, and a smaller board of finance, elected by a limited, propertied suffrage, to have primary control over taxes, debt, expenditures; (4) limit the borrowing power of municipalities; (5) extend the powers of the mayor.

In summing up, Bryce was mildly hopeful:

> City government . . . is admittedly the weak point of the country. . . . Yet no one who studies the municipal history of the last decades will doubt that things are better than they were twenty years ago. The newer frames of government are an improvement upon the older. Rogues are less audacious. Good citizens are more active. Party spirit is less and less permitted to dominate and pervert municipal politics.

Bryce's American colleagues joined him in the general terms of his diagnosis and therapy. Seth Low wanted the European reader especially to understand some important differences between American and European cities:

> (1) In the United States . . . no distinction is recognized between governing and governed classes, and the problem of government is conceived to be this, that the whole body of society should learn and apply to itself the art of government. Bearing this in mind, it becomes apparent that the tide of immigration into the United States is a continually disturbing factor. . . . In many of the cities of the United States, indeed in almost all of them, the population not only is largely untrained in the art of self-government, but it is not even homogeneous. (2) American cities as a rule have grown with a rapidity to which the Old World presents few parallels. . . . [This] has compelled very lavish expenditure under great pressure for quick results. . . . American cities have laboured under . . . inability to provide adequately for their needs, while discounting the future so freely in order to provide their permament plant. (3) Charters were framed as though cities were little states. Americans are only now learning, after many years of bitter experience, that they are not so much little states as large corporations.

He pointed to the rise of the "strong mayor" in several cities (including Brooklyn, where Low had recently been mayor under a new charter) as evidence of the acceptance of the corporation model.

> (4) The one organic problem in connection with the charters of cities, which apparently remains as far from solution as ever in America, is that which concerns the legislative branch of city government. . . . [T]hat it is so, illustrates with vividness the justice of the American view that it is a dangerous thing, in wholly democratic communities, to make the legislative body supreme over the executive.

Low concluded, echoing but going beyond Bryce:

> The average American city is not going from bad to worse. . . . The general tendency, even in the larger cities, is toward improvement. . . . It may be claimed for American institutions, even in cities, that they lend themselves with wonderfully little friction to growth and development and to the peaceful assimilation of new and strange populations.

Frank Goodnow, with his more restricted focus on Tammany Hall, supported Bryce also.

> The year 1857 [he noted] marks an important epoch in the history of the city of New York. It may be taken as the date of a great change in the character of the population of the city —a change which has vastly increased the difficulties of municipal government, and presented problems whose solution has unfortunately not yet been attained. The middle classes, which had thus far controlled the municipal government, were displaced by an ignorant proletariat, mostly of foreign birth, which came under the sway of ambitious political leaders and was made to subserve schemes of political corruption such as had not before been concocted on American soil.
>
> The year 1857 is also [he continued] the date of a great change in the legal status of the city. Down to this time all charters, and almost all laws affecting the government of the city, were either framed or suggested by the municipal authorities or made to depend for their validity on the approval of the people. But in 1857, the legislature committed itself finally and definitely to the doctrine that it might change at will the city institutions, framing the municipal government and distributing the municipal powers as it saw fit.

The story of the Tweed Ring (1870–1871), Goodnow believed, was a natural consequence of these two factors. Looking back on that episode, Goodnow in 1888 concluded:

> . . . [T]he old party system still remains and must, in a large city like New York with its great masses of ignorant voters, ever offer a great obstacle to the selection of the best men for office. The radical changes now advocated in the methods of elections, and the reform of the civil service by the extension of competitive examinations, can only serve as palliatives. Many of the evils which the city has experienced in the past may be expected to recur, until such time as its electors are more intelligent, their allegiance to party less strong, and their political leaders more pure.

These initial analyses by Bryce, Goodnow, and Low provided the main assumptions and conclusions that guided American political scientists for a half century and are still influential in the textbooks. The posture of these three early analysts may be summarized in the following attitudes:

1. Pessimism concerning urbanism and the institutions of urban society, a pessimism ranging from Low's moderation to the sharp dislike of Bryce and Goodnow.

2. Hostility toward political parties as instruments for the governing of cities.

3. Indictment of the immigrant groups in the urban electorate as a central cause of urban political and governmental pathology.

4. Hostility toward the state legislatures as alleged violators of urban rights to self-government.

If Bryce and his colleagues had been writing their summaries a generation later (in 1919, let us say) they would have been able to use an enormously larger literature, but they would not have needed, on the basis of that literature, to change very much their posture of 1888. The optimism of the Progressive Movement, reflected in some degree in the literature on city politics and government, might have made them somewhat more moderate in their attitudes toward urban society, but their remaining assumptions would not have been directly challenged.

The 1890's and the early 1900's produced a flood of literature and action on the urban front. The 1894 Philadelphia Conference for Good City Government, a joint meeting of New York City and Philadelphia urban reformers held in January, led directly to the organization of the National Municipal League in May. In that same year Alfred R. Conkling published his *City Government in the United States,* a reformer's tract. In 1895 Albert Shaw introduced a broader dimension with his two volumes: *Municipal Government in Great Britain* and *Municipal Government in Continental Europe,* each of which seemed to buttress the reformers. In 1895 also, Frank J. Goodnow, who was to become the dominant intellectual figure for more than a decade in the field of urban government, brought out his *Municipal Home Rule: A Study in Administration,* and in 1897 his *Municipal Problems,* the first approach to a systematic textbook. These important beginnings were added to by William H. Tolman's *Municipal Reform Movements: The Textbook of the New Reformation* (1895), Delos F. Wilcox, *Study of City Government* (1897), and Dorman B. Eaton's, *Government of Municipalities* (1899).[1]

These urban political and governmental studies of the 1890's were crowned by the publication in 1900 of the doctrinal bible of municipal reform: the National Municipal League's *A Municipal Program.* Presenting its first Model Charter and Model General Charter Act, the League specified the goals of urban reform, urged on and supported generally by the political scientists of the day. These prescriptions, fully consistent with the assumptions of Bryce, Goodnow, and Low a decade earlier, may be paraphrased as follows:

1. Put no faith in political parties
   a. Separate city elections from state and national elections
   b. Shorten the ballot (elect mayor and council only)
   c. Nominate by petition in a system of "free nominations" (not more than fifty signatures required)
   d. Make the ballot nonpartisan (list all candidates alphabetically under each office)
   e. Make appointive officials' terms indefinite: establish a "merit system" for all employees
2. Grant "home rule" to city governments of limited power
   a. Restrict powers of state legislatures to enact special legislation affecting cities
   b. But restrain city governments by general legislation—for example, by debt and tax ceilings
   c. Empower cities to frame and adopt their own charters
3. Concentrate power and responsibility in the city's chief executive, thus adopting for cities the model of the business corporation
   a. The League spelled out this goal in terms of the "strong mayor" elected by the voters
   b. But Eaton and some others preferred a chief executive chosen by the council

These doctrinal prescriptions for the governing of cities in the United States were sustained and elaborated in the literature produced by the reformers and by the political scientists during the two decades following 1900. The most eventful episode of the period was provided by the National Municipal League's *New Municipal Program,* issued in 1915. In this revision of the bible of 1900, the council-manager plan (the council to be elected by proportional representation, the manager to be a professional executive) replaced the "strong-mayor" plan as a key item of structural doctrine. This modification gave to both the reformers and the political scientists a coherent program which represented, they believed, the optimum expression of their central values for urban politics and government: *separation of city government from state and national parties, nonpartisanship in elections and appointments to office, minority representation in the city council, the business corporation as a model for the conduct of the city government, and the "merit system" in city employment.*[2]

The 1915 revision virtually completed the doctrinal evolution of municipal reform. Political scientists and urban reformers were to work in a close partnership based on the 1915 premises for more than three decades thereafter, with only a few of the former inclined to dissent. In this partnership the political scientists were primarily cast in the role of "social engineers," consultants to the reformers and to officialdom in achieving the goals prescribed in the *New Municipal Program*. In this respect they were not unlike their colleagues who were then and later prescribing national and state constitutional reform, executive and administrative reform, and political party reform. The difference was to turn out to be in the long duration of their role as "social engineer" in urban government and politics, and in their continuing and almost literal fidelity to the doctrines of 1915.

1915–1950: Doctrine and Dissent

The era of "social engineering" by urban political scientists in the United States was accompanied by the appearance of a large body of literature codifying and elaborating the prevailing prescriptive doctrines. The municipal government textbooks, which burgeoned in the 1920's and the 1930's especially, carried the main task of codification. All of them reflected rather uniformly the earlier attitudes and premises of Bryce and Goodnow, and presented with mild variation the prescriptions of the 1915 *New Municipal Program*. None of them dissented sharply from that platform of premises and remedies.[3]

As a key item of the established doctrine, the council-manager plan, with election of the council by proportional representation as an approved refinement, received the needed elaboration and support in the literature. The enduring popularity of the city manager idea and the steady rate of its adoption by additional cities each year provided eloquent testimony for the tracts and monographs which celebrated its virtues. The urban "social engineers" recognized the plan as their most saleable product. The National Municipal League was thus regularly reinforced in its inherently strong inclinations to retain the council-manager plan as the central feature in the successive revisions of its Model Charter, the continuing embodiment of the bible of 1915.[4]

But the shape of urban America was changing. The relatively self-contained cities of earlier decades were becoming, especially by the 1920's, surrounded by populous satellite cities and suburbs. Complex metropolitan regions were developing distinctive stresses and strains. At first the metropolitan region was perceived as simply another problem in "social engineering"; if annexation, city-county consolidation, intermunicipal cooperation, or special districts were not feasible "solutions," then the more drastic remedy of a fully integrated metropolitan government was required. As political scientists looked more closely at metropolitan regions, however, complexity and uncertainty became more apparent. For example, one of the prescriptions of 1915—home rule—was now seen as an ideological and strategic barrier to metropolitan integration. And each metropolitan region seemed to present some markedly unique conditions, resisting any single universal formula for governmental structure. Consequently, although the "social engineers" who surveyed and recommended solutions for metropolitan reform in the four decades after 1920 tended to follow a common pattern of prescriptions, no comprehensive, codified "Model Metropolitan Charter" achieved acceptance among urban political scientists.[5]

Other questions had also emerged by this time in urban political science in the United States. Political scientists interested in the study of political parties and political behavior had begun to turn their attention to urban politics, viewing urban party institutions and political processes more as clinical data for description and analysis than as opportunities for their indictment or for the prescription of remedies. This effort was especially centered (from 1925 to 1940) among the political scientists at the University of Chicago, where the sociologists also were attempting a broad analysis of urban life. The consequence was a new stream of political science literature about American cities which was, in due time, to play an important part in the reevaluation of the premises and methods of urban political science. In their day, however, these studies did not shake the doctrines of the textbooks.[6]

1950–1965: New Emphases on Description and Diagnosis

The municipal government textbooks remain largely inviolate even in the 1960's, despite some direct criticism by political scientists and occasional revisionist gestures.[7] All save a handful of the textbooks continue to carry forward the "social engineering" tradition of political science, defining the postwar urban problems of Negro in-migration, population explosion and dispersion, deterioration of physical plant, water and air pollution, and so forth, as difficulties to be dealt with by adjusting legal and governmental machinery. The problem, says one distinguished exponent of this approach to the study of urbanization, is not one of sheer size of cities:

> [T]he problem is adjustment of management devices to the size which is forced upon us by events. . . . We have the organ-

izational and managerial knowledge and tools. There is no reason for running away from scale. . . . The underlying problems become impossible of rational attack unless there is a single center for coordinated analysis, planning, and action.[8]

Questioning Established Doctrine

There is little argument among political scientists that the scale of urban problems has increased with the increasing concentration of people in and near great central cities. But a growing number of political scientists are becoming impressed with the moral ambiguity of "engineering" solutions to municipal problems. Is the council-manager system the best form of city government? Should cities and suburbs combine under a unified metropolitan government? Are the nonpartisan ballot, the merit system, and zoning "good things"? The answers to these and other such questions, at one time an almost automatic "yes" among political scientists, are now much less obvious, especially when applied to communities with racially, ethnically, and economically diverse populations, which of course means at least all the larger ones.

Research on "nonpartisan" election systems, for example, has indicated that this "reform" tends to bring "better people" of high prestige into politics, to increase the influence of allegedly neutral organs of publicity, such as newspapers, and in some (perhaps most) cases to diminish the influence of the local political party organizations. Other consequences of depoliticizing urban electoral decisions appear to be the attenuation of the links between city officialdom and the low-income, low-status groups in the population, and the substitution of doctrinaire solutions for solutions resulting from continuous bargaining among visible subgroups in the city's politics.[9]

The council-manager plan has also confronted some explicit reappraisal. Why, it has been asked, do some state political systems seem to be more hospitable to the plan than others? Other questions center on the attractions of the plan for some types of groups in urban politics, the hostility which other groups display toward it. It has even been suggested that whether one prefers the council-manager plan to some other form depends on whose ox one wants gored.[10]

And home-rule doctrine, in its turn, has undergone some reexamination. The parallels between the strategic uses, frequently antigovernmental, of "states' rights" ideology and of "home-rule" ideology have been noted; the fictitious quality of proposals to seal off the governments of cities from those of the state and nation, in an era of increasing mutual involvement and interdependence of all three levels of government, has also been underscored. The simple myth of city virtue frustrated by rural villainy in unrepresentative state legislatures, it is suggested, is in need of revision in order to reveal the more complex reality of urban-state relationships.[11]

Some unanticipated consequences of merit-system doctrines, which aimed at depoliticizing the bureaucracies, have also begun to attract the attention of urban political scientists. The municipal bureaucracies, once they were emancipated from party organization control, became more and more active politically in their external environments. Especially when organized as interest groups, they have often become autonomous and potent actors in urban politics. As such, they have the same intrinsic interest for political scientists as do political parties, candidates, and officials, or other urban interest groups.[12]

The claim for the virtues of metropolitan integration has evoked questions, too. "Social engineers" have pointed to the proliferation of metropolitan "governments": counties, towns, cities, villages, police, fire, school and other special districts, independent boards and commissions, intermunicipal compacts, and so on. This "outmoded" array of governments should be replaced, it is argued, with an integrated metropolitan government which could not only take advantage of economies of scale in administration but which would also command the interest and involvement of citizens who are now thoroughly confused and frustrated by the multiplicity of governments having a claim on their attention.

But the uncertainties attending purely formal solutions to political problems in a metropolitan society have begun to impress political scientists. Why should central-city party leaders want to "unify" with suburban party leaders? Presumably because they feel confident of controlling the resulting consolidated government. But in that case, why should suburban leaders assent to this arrangement? On the other hand, if suburban leaders seem likely to win out, why should central-city leaders agree to consolidation? What are the inducements for collaboration between central-city and suburban interest groups? A few observers see the problem primarily as one of race. As Negroes increase in numbers in large cities and whites in the suburbs, the question of metropolitan centralization can be rephrased: will central-city Negroes choose to forfeit the election of their own political leaders to high public office by supporting proposals to consolidate with white suburban populations large enough to outnumber them? To these observers, the "solution" of metropolitan government, when exposed to the values and practices of the real world, creates "problems." [13]

Who Rules? A Return to Politics and Political Theory

One of the dilemmas confronting the urban political scientists in the 1960's is revealed by the tensions between the political scientist as adviser or consultant to reformers or officials—the role of "social engineer"—and the political scientist as clinical observer and analyst of urban political and governmental systems. Some find the two roles reasonably compatible and interchangeable, and mutually reinforcing. Others are impressed by the conflicts between the roles, and suggest a division of labor between political scientists and political engineers; they point also to indications that the professional journals of political science increasingly reflect one orientation, whereas the journals of activist groups (for example, the *National Civic Review*) reflect the other. The gap, it is suggested, is growing and will continue to widen. For the texts and the reformist literature have remained almost untouched by the work of political scientists who in recent years have begun to view urban communities as political systems capable of yielding answers to some of the enduring problems of political science as a discipline.[14] To a considerable extent, and notably since the mid-1950's, political scientists have turned from what Hugh Douglas Price has called " 'actor-defined problems' (actual subjects of metropolitan complaint, such as housing and transportation)" to " 'observer-defined problems' (such as the social scientists' interest in the abstract question of power structure)"; that is, to the study of cities and metropolitan areas because of their intrinsic interest as political systems and not primarily because they need a doctor's attention.[15]

This transition began, as we have noted, in the urban studies at the University of Chicago, especially in the 1930's. The influence of these studies was intensified and extended by the works of V. O. Key on political parties as national and state systems, and by the many studies inspired by his work.[16] Another contribution to the transition came from those political scientists interested in "case studies" for the teaching of public administration. Taking a "decision" by an administrator as their focus of attention, these political scientists sought to discover the actual conditions and influences present in the exercise of official power in explicitly identified situations. Decisions by city officials were included among their studies; the result was a new kind of urban political science literature.[17] To these eventually were added case studies of urban political party decisions.[18]

More recently, in this trend toward matters of description rather than prescription, urban political scientists have placed themselves in the debt of sociologists, with whom they have fallen into dialogue on the significant general question of "who rules" in American communities. The sociologist's answer typically has been couched in the vocabulary of the analyst of social stratification. In a series of field researches dating from the influential Middletown studies by Robert and Helen Lynd, forward into the present, sociologists have elaborated five key propositions about local community life, in American cities both large and small.[19] These propositions, stated baldly, hold that (1) an upper-class power elite rules, (2) politicians and civic leaders are subordinate to this elite, (3) there is only one elite in each community, exerting dominance on substantially all nontrivial community issues, (4) the elite rules in its own interests exclusively, and largely to the detriment of the lower classes, and (5) as a consequence, social conflict takes place primarily between the elite and the non-elite.

This pattern of community power has generally been held to exist whenever the social structure of the community is well formed and relatively stable. Deviations from the pattern have been accounted for by referring to apparent malformations, immaturities, or situations of flux in the community social structure, but that this was the "normal" pattern of power distribution, few sociologists seriously doubted. Many political scientists shared in the general satisfaction with these largely sociological findings; understandably, since the propositions were apparently buttressed and reconfirmed by considerable field experience—experience of which political scientists then keenly felt a lack.[20] But as political scientists began to move into field research, dissatisfaction began to take hold. The literature shows a growing sense of skepticism toward both the methods and the findings of studies on community power.[21]

As James Thurber has said, "Skepticism is a useful tool of the inquisitive mind, but it is scarcely a method of investigation." As political scientists began to come in contact with American communities in their new role as field researchers (rather than as consultants or reformers), they were forced to develop methods for viewing community politics and decision-making. In contrast with the sociological approach, political scientists recently concerned with the topics of power and influence in American communities have emphasized the examination of decisions and policies rather than the identification of alleged "influentials," of political decision-makers rather than economic or social elites, of observed behavior rather than reputations for influence.[22]

One consequence of these changes in methodological emphasis has been the rather persistent rejection of the five key propositions set forth in the sociological studies of community power. Political scientists have been compelled by this situation to state rather carefully the theoretical rationale for conducting research in the way they did, and to demonstrate its superior scientific utility to the approaches taken by sociologists. This has been necessary in order to establish grounds for rejection of the key propositions about community power asserted by sociologists.

Thus present-day political science literature on urbanism is increasingly concerned with two major problems: (1) stating the conditions and consequences of decision-making in various concrete situations, and (2) defending the methods used in arriving at conclusions about community policy-making patterns.

The rationale for conducting research in the way political scientists generally have proceeded has been developed principally in a series of papers growing out of an intensive study of New Haven by Robert A. Dahl and his associates.[23] Major points made in these papers have been: (1) that the concept "power," in order to have empirical meaning, should refer to observable changes in behavior brought about by the actions of one person upon another. In order to compare the power of actors, it seems necessary to refer to concrete decisions in the community where research observers have the opportunity to examine the changes in the probabilities of various outcomes taking place that follow from the initiatives, vetoes, and successes and failures of participants in policy-making. (2) The methods used by sociologists in studying community power bypassed the examination of behavior and of outcomes, relying instead upon samples of *belief about* power distributions. (3) Proffered confirmations of the five key propositions were often unconvincing because of (*a*) methods that did not adequately test the key propositions, (*b*) unexplained evidence that contradicted the propositions, and (*c*) repeated and varied attempts to save the propositions from contrary evidence by resort to *ad hoc, post-factum* explanations.

Although the research strategies of political scientists have been described and defended in a fairly comprehensive manner, the actual findings of research on community power and influence are just beginning to appear in the literature.[24] It is possible at this time only to sketch in some of the conclusions of these studies. A few such findings are outlined in the following paragraphs.

One of the most common patterns of behavior observed in American cities is that participation in the making of specific decisions is normally concentrated in the hands of a small proportion of the population. But this does not mean that the cities are ruled by a single, all-purpose elite, after the fashion suggested by stratification theory in sociology. At least three significant modifications of the finding of limited participation in decision-making must be made. First, different small groups normally make decisions on different community problems, and, likewise, the personnel of decision-making groups often change, even over the short run.[25] Second, the decisions made by small groups are most often considered routine or are otherwise ignored by most other members of the community. Third, when small groups undertake innovation, or decision-making, in cases salient or likely to become salient to many others in the community, they must achieve special kinds of legitimacy, and the strength acquired by competitive bargaining and meaningful accommodations among themselves, or risk the likelihood of failure.

The finding that participants in decision-making are largely specialized to certain *issue areas* has been confirmed by data gathered using a variety of methods prevalent in community power research. Thus, when citizens, or "experts," were asked to nominate leaders in specific issue areas, different leaders emerged in different issue areas.[26] This was also the finding when students used research techniques approximating a "total immersion" in the community. This latter method involved a combination of approaches, including such data-gathering devices as the examination of specific decisions and events in the life of the community, accompanied by lengthy, relatively nondirective interviews, participant observation, and the inspection of newspapers and other appropriate documents.[27]

One such study, by Norton Long in Boston, suggested the conclusion that important decisions in the community were made in a process which was largely decentralized. Insofar as different decision-making processes could be summarized by the observer seeking to characterize the total community, Long suggested the metaphor of "an ecology of games." This was defined as a territorial system in which a variety of "games"—banking, manufacturing, administering municipal government agencies, and many others—give structures, goals, roles, strategies, and publics to the players, the players in each game making use of players in the others for their own particular purposes. Long suggested:

> At the local level [it is feasible] to look at the municipal government, its departments, and the agencies of state and national government as so many institutions, resembling banks, newspapers, trade unions, chambers of commerce, churches, etc., occupying a territorial field and interacting with one another.

This interaction can be conceptualized as a system without reducing the interacting institutions and individuals to membership in any single comprehensive group.[28]

The first full-scale documentation of similar conclusions was provided in Wallace S. Sayre and Herbert Kaufman, *Governing New York City: Politics in the Metropolis* (1960). In this study political outcomes were viewed as a product of a contest in which there are stakes and prizes, contestants, and rules governing the strategies of the contestants. As Hugh Douglas Price describes its conclusions:

> . . . [The contest] may have very high stakes, including ideological goals, public office and jobs, economic gains and losses, and provision of desired services. There are a variety of participants seeking various of these stakes, including party leaders, public officials, organized municipal bureaucracies, nongovernmental interest groups, officials of other governments, and ordinary voters. The contest is carried on by certain generally understood "rules of the game," some formal and some informal. . . . There are many varieties of strategies open to the various participants. They may seek to influence the nominations made, or the electoral outcome, or the appointments of nonelective officials, or the policies adopted by various officials, or the execution of policies after their adoption.[29]

The volume concludes that the governance of New York City takes place within a multicentered system, in which no single ruling elite can be identified; instead, the system is open, competitive, and fluid. Herbert Kaufman has summarized the conclusions of the New York City study bearing on the propositions of the stratification theory in these words:

> Decisions of the municipal government emanate from no single source, but from many centers; conflicts and clashes are referred to no single authority, but are settled at many levels and at many points in the system: no single group can guarantee the success of any proposal it supports, the defeat of every idea it objects to.[30]

Beyond issue specialization, other patterns of interaction also modify and constrain the rule of the few. One such pattern has to do with the grant of legitimacy made to these small groups, entitling them to make decisions. Careful examination of the evidence at hand seems to indicate that elites are freest in their power to commit the resources of the community when these decisions are relatively routine and innocuous; when any elite attempts other kinds of decision-making, of a nonroutine, unbureaucratized, or innovative variety, it seems to require special consent by other elites and citizens who fall outside the small decision-making group.

If this pattern is correctly identified, certain propositions might be seen to follow from it. We might reasonably expect, for example, that (1) a dominant "general elite," if one were found to exist, would place great emphasis on maintenance of sociability and contact with a wide range of citizens in the community, and less emphasis on "doing things," or innovation—in fact any such general elite would prudently seek to restrict its own activities in various ways; (2) an elite group wanting innovations in public policy would seek systematically to acquire consent from other elites and from nonelite members of the community; (3) an attempt by any one elite to put a program into effect without achieving in the community a legitimacy wider than its own sponsorship would fail; and (4) nonelite members of the community would seek to bring elites under control in areas of concern to them.

The evidence which has begun to accumulate on each of these points indicates that, in general, these propositions are all correct,[31] and hence we can say that in a wide range of community situations, participation in decision-making is limited to a relatively few members of the community, but only within the constraints of a bargaining process among competing elites and of an underlying consensus supplied by a much larger percentage of the local population, whose approval is often costly to secure.

At least three devices are available to nonelites in seeking to bring elites under control. Nonelites can withhold support at critical junctures in the decision-making process, by failing to support necessary referenda, for example. Or they can promote the creation of counter-elites, as has happened, for example, in many communities with large unionized populations. A third device is simply to promulgate controversy, to "make an issue." As James Coleman has shown, this technique usually activates new participants in community decisions, and not uncommonly changes the decision outcomes drastically.[32]

Another area of interest to urban political science concerns the paths people travel in order to become involved in decision-making. Information concerning leadership recruitment is fragmentary in many community studies, but enough data exist for us to infer that few if any authoritative community decision-making groups are made up of participants whose backgrounds are entirely homogeneous. Contrary to the assumption in stratification theory to the effect that leadership recruitment is a process whereby the top leaders "pull" into their midst congenial new blood like themselves,[33] there is a good deal of evidence indicating that decision-makers become so by *self*-selection, "pushing" themselves into the leadership group by showing interest, willingness to work, and competence.[34]

Success in community decision-making evidently does not come automatically to possessors of great amounts of any one of the many possible resources available to actors in community life. Many resources in combination—time, knowledge, energy, esteem, wealth, legitimacy, and so on—must be applied with skill and diligence for actors to succeed in influencing community decisions in desired directions. This suggests that community power cannot be sensibly measured by noting the sheer amount and distribution of resources available in the community; rather, we have to know something about the rate and efficiency with which they are employed.[35]

Resources, skill, and diligence in exploiting them are three conditions that make for success in influencing community decisions. A fourth may often be the ability to choose goals that do not strain the compliance of others in the system. A fifth condition of successful participation is closely related to the fourth: capacity to form coalitions with other participants in order to achieve one's goals. This entails choosing goals which do not preclude the possibility of joining with others, and hence, like the fourth factor, implies that certain limits on the preferences of actors may be required for success. Another limitation this condition for success imposes is on the strategies available to actors for achieving their goals. In order to form coalitions with others successfully, it is necessary to pursue courses of action which do not conflict with potential allies.

Thus political science research over the last few years has vastly complicated our view of power distribution in American cities. As one observer has noted:

> What began with Floyd Hunter and C. Wright Mills as a simple search for *the* power elite deepens into a study of a variety of powerful actors with different scopes of influence; but even this dissolves into a complex system where each actor is operating at partial capacity and can always muster more resources either by becoming more heavily involved or by diverting them from other enterprises. The simple logical model of how much A can influence B becomes largely irrelevant, for the outcome will depend on how far A goes in mustering his resources, and how

far B goes in replying in kind. And since both A and B are usually involved with a wide range of other actors, we are inevitably pulled away from the relatively simple problem of partial equilibrium and faced with the necessity for explaining the general equilibrium among *all* the actors. Worse yet, this cannot be successfully done as a static analysis, but must be essayed in terms of dynamics. . . . If A is able to pyramid power over time then the whole system will change, but if A diverts resources under conditions of diminishing returns the change in power will be in the opposite direction.[36]

A Research Agenda

The research priorities for urban political science in the next decade no doubt will include projects designed to test accepted doctrines, projects intended to be cumulative in relation to earlier research, and projects attempting to break new ground entirely. The central theme of all these endeavors will be the search for the political correlates of urbanization. The program of research suggested in the following pages is both eclectic and ambitious; its authors are aware, too, that the political scientists interested in the politics of the cities are autonomous and self-willed—to them an agenda is properly something to be departed from as often as it is followed. The intended function of this agenda, in a sense simply a list of preferences held by its two authors, is to stimulate urban research by political scientists. We have nominated our own somewhat subjective items as illustrating apparent opportunities, but they are set out in no firm order of priority and with no claim for inclusiveness.

Comparative Analysis of Community Power

The sheer number of case studies in depth describing power and decision-making in individual urban communities has begun to pose a formidable storage problem for the seeker of a more general view. Hence, high on the agenda would rank the comparative analysis of cities. The purpose of such a comparative analysis would be to aggregate findings so as to lay bare, if possible, the underlying conditions, processes and activities common to city life and politics. This may sound suspiciously like a counsel of perfection, for it does not answer a prior question: what is it about cities that we can profitably compare so as to arrive at general propositions—for example, about patterns of power and decision-making within them?

This question is more complicated than it appears. One source of complication is the fact that most descriptions of urban decision-making patterns attempt to demonstrate either that a ruling elite exists, or that it does not. Evidence arguing that the typical American community is run by a small, unified, multipurpose elite has now been discredited for the most part, and so we are left in the position of having to explain the existence virtually everywhere of "pluralistic" systems of decision-making. A clearly necessary first step, then, is the reexamination of urban pluralism, in order to sort out some characteristic types. Coalitions of elites are built on different sources of strength in different urban centers; the prevailing ideology or ethos differs from city to city, some being innovative, others static; the institutional patterns, formal and informal, range widely; the scope, frequency, and intensity of elite and nonelite participation in urban decisions differ widely among cities—criteria such as these might be used to construct a number of typical urban patterns of pluralistic decision-making, a typology of urban political orders.

Only after differentiating among different forms of urban pluralism can the next step be taken, a step that involves inspecting underlying social, demographic, economic, legal, institutional, and cultural patterns in search of determinants of the different forms of pluralism. This second step is what usually comes immediately to mind when one thinks of comparative analysis: the aggregation of cities by size, geographic location, economic diversification, age, and so forth, on the assumption that similarities in these basic characteristics will produce similarities in the prevailing political order, and differences in the independent variables will likewise produce differences in the dependent variable of politics.

This may turn out to be true, but at present our categories describing types of urban political orders are so insensitive as to make any such conclusion premature. If we are to pursue a broadly comparative analysis, we must first refine our categories and, second, actually compare the political orders of cities, on the one hand, and the possible determinants of these types of political life, on the other.[37]

Political Parties in Urban America

Although the macroanalysis of political systems is currently the most fashionable way for political scientists to study urban communities, there are other attractive opportunities. There is, for example, the nature of the political party in urban America. The urban political party is perhaps our most maligned single political institution, and probably the least understood.

Many political scientists suspect that urban parties have been quite drastically transformed in the last three decades. But most of the literature is distressingly vague about how local parties are now organized and led, how electorates are won or lost. In fact, the picture appears to be quite complex. Within recent memory, for example, City Hall has changed hands, and parties, in a number of large cities—New York, Philadelphia, Detroit, and Los Angeles come immediately to mind. In some cities—Baltimore, Chicago, and Boston are three recent and notable examples—reform mayors coming from "out" factions of the dominant political party have been elected. This evidence suggests that urban party organizations are somewhat more vulnerable than we are accustomed to admitting. And though Northern cities may be more likely than rural areas to be governed by Democrats, the major inroads made by Republicans in the Solid South have been almost exclusively among voters in the urban areas. The rulers of the large Northern cities are not all one kind of Democrat; nor, for that matter, do urbanism and one-party rule invariably go hand in hand. Different states have conflicting stories to tell on this subject.[38]

One hypothesis which deserves elaboration and documentation suggests that local parties have been "nationalized." [39] The melting pot has done its work, and internal migration and the public school system have sautéed the distinctiveness out of our urban neighborhoods—so runs the logical extension of this hypothesis. Nowadays city folk no longer congregate at various meeting places in the neighborhood, but rather stay indoors and get their political gossip from the television or the newspapers. The superior visibility of national news in these media depresses the saliency of local issues, and, come election day, voters respond to city elections by voting the ticket they agree with nationally. Administrative types have taken City Hall over from the great charismatic ethnic leaders of yore—so this argument concludes.

There is a great deal of plausibility to the "nationalization" hypothesis, but a casual examination of the urban political scene suggests caution lest it be pushed too far. The examples of Mayors Lawrence of Pittsburgh, Daley of Chicago, Tucker of St. Louis, Clark and Dilworth of Philadelphia, and Lee of New Haven may represent administrative adroitness of a high order, but they are political leaders as well. In what ways, then, are their skills and situations different from those of the men who presided over City Hall in earlier days? Assuredly the times have changed: now mayors must glue together local parties in ways more difficult and complex than in the days before social security, state unemployment compensation, and the merit system. But city governments still have indulgences and deprivations to distribute, assessments and taxes to levy or to vary, licenses to hand out or to lift, inspections to perform, rules to enforce, construction, snow removal, and insurance contracts to let, prestige to dispense or withhold, and so forth. One major change may be the extent to which new resources are available in the form of federal funds, for those cities mobilizing the technical know-how to claim their share. "Nationalization" of urban parties is a provocative hypothesis which invites testing.

Other questions about urban political parties present comparable research opportunities. Do urban party organizations share the tendencies toward "atrophy" which V. O. Key finds for state party organizations? What incentives, what sources of sustenance, leadership, and electoral followings, support the minority party or parties in the cities? [40] What strategies distinguish the minority party from the majority party? What conditions, incentives, resources, and strategies characterize insurgency within urban parties? [41]

Some urban political systems are greatly affected by the pivotal role their electorates have in statewide electoral contests for governor, senator, and president; in turn, they greatly affect their state political systems. Boston, New York City, Detroit, and Chicago represent examples of one such category. In other states a pair of cities share this role: Philadelphia and Pittsburgh, Cincinnati and Cleveland, Kansas City and St. Louis, Dallas and Houston, Los Angeles and San Francisco are illustrations. What are the dimensions of accommodation and competition, within and between the parties, in these situations? What are the consequences, for party organization, for electoral behavior, for public policy?

Groups within Cities

For a long time we have relied on rather crude designations of city political groups—as businessmen, or labor, or Negroes, or immigrants, or the professions, or rich, or poor, and so forth. It is now necessary to expand and enrich our view of these groups. For example, there are apparently several kinds of effective Negro political leadership in urban America.[42] Likewise, the term "businessmen" lumps together politically vulnerable retail merchants with insulated and apolitical managers of branch plants of large corporations, neighborhood merchants with downtown bankers, slum landlords with "civic" leaders, department store owners with real-estate men.[43] But the differences among these groups and among other large categories—in their political styles, their political interests, activities, and so on—are profound, and worth exploring.

Even a popular stereotype such as the monolithic qualities of the Roman Catholic Church must be set aside as an obstacle to straight thinking in research. Rather, factions representing parish and hierarchy, different orders, and diverse social philosophies within the Catholic Church, have their impact in political affairs.[44] So, of course, do national origins among communicants of the Catholic Church. In the industrial towns and cities of New England, Irishmen, arriving in the first wave of Catholic immigration, took over the Democratic Party. When their coreligionists from Italy arrived, the Irish did not voluntarily relinquish their grip, but rather drove the Italians into the wide-open spaces of the Republican Party, which, after years out of office, was in most cities glad to see them. To this day, working-class Italian Catholics tend to be Republicans in local politics in many New England cities.[45]

The smaller decision-making arenas often provide the research setting within which to discover the competition, the accommodations, and the alliances among the groups most relevant to urban politics. School boards are a pertinent example.[46] Despite the status similarities of school boards across the nation, the degrees of doctrinal division, of capture by superintendents, of susceptibility to party or business or other pressure, vary tremendously from case to case.

It would also be useful to capture and catalogue the various roles in the urban political systems played by information agencies, such as the newspapers. The communications media have significant multiple roles in urban politics: as reporters of the behavior of the other actors, as partisans of some actors and critics of others, and as "kingmakers." The structure of competition among news media has for too long been allowed to dominate the discussion of their political behavior.[47] This is an understandable response in terms of democratic theory, but it does not exhaust our problems or our questions.

The urban bureaucracies, too, are worthy of additional attention as actors in the urban political systems. Their role in "routine administrative decisions" is now widely recognized in political science literature. Their electoral activities, their participation in crucial policy decisions, their alliances and competition with elected officials, high administrative officials, and other interest groups are as yet only beginning to be explored. Both their competition with each other and their tendencies to form alliances make urban bureaucracies significant urban political forces about which we know but little.[48]

Numerous groups are active in urban political systems. Political scientists are just beginning to learn their precise identity, their internal dynamics and governance, their resources and incentives, their individual strategies, and their capacities in building and rebuilding alliances. Their political roles are still more a matter of legend than knowledge.

External Political Forces

So far we have suggested research dealing primarily with trends and patterns of urban life as they affect the internal political workings and institutions of cities. Equally important is the web of relations tying cities to external political bodies. One persistent question concerns the sore point of equal representation in state politics. Despite the much-decried overrepresentation of rural areas, many state legislatures contain at least one house apportioned rather strictly according to population. This means that almost everywhere cities have some leverage in state politics even when they are not instrumental—as after all they usually are—in electing the governor. Rotten boroughs in one house are merely a predictable and rather stable element in what is in fact often an extremely complicated equation. Very little empirical consideration has been given to variables such as the numbers of different cities within the state and the extent to which they compete against one another, rather than against rural "interests," and the existence of coalitions involving the triad of rural, urban, and *sub*urban factions.[49]

The state legislature is only one of a series of external political bodies significantly linked to urban political systems. State constitutions provide a balance sheet and a battleground of urban political relations with state political systems, as do the offices of the governors, the state administrative agencies, the state court systems, the state government bureaucracies. County governments and special districts provide another important category. The federal government institutions dealing with cities represent similarly significant foci for urban political research.[50]

One angle of approach to the external political forces which affect urban politics is to regard the city as a subsystem within the state political system, with some capacity and tendency to deal directly with the national political system and with other subsystems in the state. The relevant questions then include: what resources does the city system possess in its external relations; in what strategies and counterstrategies does it engage; how do resources and strategies vary over time and from one decision arena to another (for example, in the constitutional arena, the electoral, party, gubernatorial, legislative, judicial, administrative arenas)?

Conditions of Urban Life

Another aspect of urban political life which beckons the researcher must be approached with great circumspection. Much popular criticism in books and magazines holds that cities are becoming unfit habitations for mankind.[51] The responsible political science researcher, heeding the clarion call, might well ask himself: "What are the political prerequisites for making our cities more livable?"

The problem Coleman Woodbury describes as "the paradox of urban public finance" will serve as an example. The paradox, as Woodbury puts it, is this:

> Although our urban localities today are the greatest aggregations of income-producing power the world has ever seen, the overwhelming majority of urban governments, from those of the new, lower and middle income suburbs and fringe areas to the mightiest central cities of metropolitan areas, are in financial stringencies that apparently are becoming more and more severe.[52]

At least some aspects of this situation can be assigned to the behavior of state legislatures gerrymandered so as to appear to be, from the standpoint of the cities, excessively sensitive to the preferences of "rural" constituencies. One result, as the President's Commission on Intergovernmental Relations has pointed out, "is that urban governments have bypassed the States and made direct cooperative arrangements with the National Government in such fields as housing and urban development, airports and community defense facilities." [53] But increasing demands on services traditionally provided by cities have on the whole far outrun municipal ingenuity in finding new ways of paying for these services.

To the extent that outside agencies cannot be depended on for relief, the problem becomes a classical political one of calculation and control—of deciding who is to pay, of determining which demands should and should not be met. As Woodbury says, researchers have already supplied information about the effects of some kinds of taxation on industrial and commercial location, but this hardly exhausts the possibilities. What are the factors predisposing communities to give different priorities to similar "needs" and demands? What governs who pays how much? What determines how much a city takes on in order to provide for its residents? The standard problem of politics in our cities—of heavy demands on scarce resources, and the resulting patterns of choice—remains largely unchronicled and unanalyzed.[54]

Who is entitled to define what the problems are? The researcher must be prepared to defend the legitimacy of the people whose problems he accepts as his own, or, if he prefers, should be prepared to grind his own axes cheerfully, but without disguising the boundaries of his own "objectivity."

Although it is possible to define some of these "problems" in a way that avoids the necessity for taking sides among interested parties, some of the most compelling social criticisms of city life do not permit political scientists this luxury. Without arguing the merits of the social critics' positions, it seems manifest to us that political scientists, if they chose to do so, could describe some of the political prerequisites of abolishing the "tyranny" of motor cars, of curing the blight of obsolete physical plants, of controlling increases in densities of land use, and so on. The catalogue of critic-defined problems is a long one. So is the array of possible "solutions": subsidy of mass transit, urban redevelopment, zoning laws, and enforcement of certain kinds. The political scientist perhaps can contribute best not by formulating the particular panaceas to be applied locally, but rather by examining and discussing the political preconditions of getting various panaceas suggested by the social critics to work, and the political consequences of their success and failure.

Political scientists perhaps can make a valuable contribution to utopian criticisms of the qualities of urban life beyond the task of pulling utopians down to earth, beyond helping them to assess the social, economic, and political costs of achieving what they hope to achieve in cities. One of the major functions of political science has always been to formulate rationales for the prevailing social order. In some ways, the democratic "ideologies" of present-day America are more expressive of utopian ideals than are planned utopian cities themselves on the drawing board or in three-dimensional life.[55] Frank Lloyd Wright's Broadacres is an expression of a nostalgia for an agrarian social order which, as Louis Hartz has cogently argued, never was.[56] The various planned "new towns" here and abroad have often even in middle age retained the barrackslike qualities which proclaim them the work of hierarchical forces. To the casual reader of the news, Brasilia, the newest and most audacious hierarchically created combine-for-living, gives every indication of providing monotony where unity was sought, of having expunged variety in search of harmony.

We suggest the possibility that the failure in human terms of utopian city building (and the same possibly goes for gigantic "projects" *within* cities) is a failure to appreciate the qualities of social and political life which bind men together in peace yet do not efface their diversity. Utopian planners have often failed to mirror accurately the societies they were attempting to symbolize in their buildings, for lack of an adequate political theory. Clearly, the creators of Stalinist plaster castles in Eastern Europe are exempt from this criticism: in terms of symbolic values they doubtless built better than they knew. It is rather the large-scale planners of pluralistic societies who stand in greatest need of an appropriately pluralistic political theory, so that they may better look to the recently neglected values of variety and human scale in their attempts to symbolize and give a steel and concrete framework to the social order.[57]

Other problems, perhaps easier to keep within manageable focus and more overtly useful to scholars if not to citizens of most cities, can be posed as "scientific" questions. Answers to these kinds of questions can be used by all parties to disputes over the distributions of costs and benefits in cities. One series of "scientific" questions might be asked of urban renewal programs: Who initiates urban renewal programs? Who mobilizes for and against them? What techniques are used to mobilize the various sides? Who legitimizes renewal programs? Who vetoes them? Who prevails in cases of conflict? Which techniques and resources seem to be associated with winning and which with losing?[58] Fluoridation programs could be discussed using the same kinds of questions. The pertinacity and utility of questions of this kind seem obvious.[59]

Nor does this end the list of programs which might be similarly examined: air pollution control, water supply and sanitation, master plans, open-space programs, in fact the whole list of critic-defined or actor-defined "problems" of urban public policy are candidates for the useful application of such questions.

The Judicial Process in Cities

An area long neglected by political scientists is the judicial process in the urban setting. The tradition has been to envelop this process in studies of public law, and to treat it as a task in analyzing rulings of judges to test hypotheses about wise substantive rules of law, or as a problem in "depoliticizing" the judiciary. The courts, the judges, the police, the prosecutors, the bar associations, and closely related groups have seldom been studied as actors in the urban political system.

Several types of inquiry press for attention in this segment of urban politics. Judicial behavior in trial courts is one example. Studies applying quantitative techniques to decisions in discretionary, small-docket appellate courts have recently interested a number of political scientists; the method might also be productive at trial-court levels. Using the records in criminal courts for a time period, the pleas made by defendants, the appearances of various types of character witnesses, the ethnic, racial, and religious characteristics of defendants, and the types of sentences imposed might be studied to test relations between "discretionary justice" and the political system. Similarly, the disposition of civil suits, or the assignment of receiverships and bankruptcies, might be probed.

Another line of research is represented by possible comparative studies of the relation between "legal" issues and "political" issues. In some cities declaratory judgment procedures to test the validity of official actions are relatively easy to use; in other cities, tighter restrictions on test cases prevail. In the former, does this difference make more "political questions" into "legal questions"? What are the consequences for the judiciary's role in the urban political system? What groups in the city derive advantages, or disadvantages, under the alternative procedures?

The special role of lawyers in urban politics is a matter of general note by political scientists. But what are the politics of bar associations? How is their leadership recruited, what are their resources and strategies in the political process—for example, in the selection and advancement of judges, prosecutors, and the staffs of both; in the development of the formal and informal rules which guide judicial behavior? The roles of law schools, leading law firms, and other specialized groups in the legal profession in the political-judicial processes of cities are also worthy of research attention.[60]

Emerging Metropolitan Systems—and Suburbia

Political scientists, as we have seen, have so far confronted the "metropolitan problem" mainly as consultants required to prescribe remedies. Enough has been discovered, and sufficient disenchantment encountered, to support the suggestion that the most pertinent research efforts by political scientists might now be directed at discovering the political preconditions for various stages of metropolitan political integration. One set of questions for this purpose might inquire into the present perceptions of, and dispositions toward or against, metropolitan integration held by party leaders, elected officials, urban bureaucracies, interest group leaders, and the communications media in a particular metropolitan region. Another set of questions might ask: Who initiates proposals for metropolitan integration? Who supports and who opposes? With what resources and strategies? Which conditions produce acceptance, which rejection?

Still another series of questions might seek to relate the prospects of each of the standard metropolitan proposals—annexation, consolidation, multipurpose or special districts, federation, and so on—to the variations in the political and governmental environment of metropolitan regions—one-party, two-party; one-county, multicounty; one-state, multistate; international.

From such a program of research urban political scientists could develop not only a base of knowledge which would enhance their value as metropolitan consultants but, even more importantly, they would add appreciably to the understandings which political scientists have about the rudimentary or emerging metropolitan political systems.

Suburbia in the political process is a related but more neglected phenomenon. The numerous jurisdictional subsystems which flourish in the suburban counties have not been subjected to the kind of case analysis we now have for city political systems. As a consequence, knowledge about suburban politics is at best highly generalized, for the most part unabashedly impressionistic. There are quite obviously many different kinds of suburbs—old, new, homogeneous, heterogeneous, Republican, Democratic, residential, industrial, populous, sparsely settled, upper class, middle class, restricted, unrestricted and others. Most current generalizations ignore or blur these variations. More valid generalizations about suburbia and its politics will clearly have to wait upon studies in depth of a sufficient number of the several types of suburbs and their political systems.[61] A few illustrative questions may serve to suggest points of entry for political science research in the world of suburbia: Is nonpartisanship a distinctive political style for local governments in suburbia generally, or only for certain types of suburbs? What conditions determine its incidence and distribution? Are the number and activities of interest groups in suburban politics proportionately greater or lesser than in central cities, or are the differences a function of visibility? Are suburban bureaucracies dependent on party leaders, or is their role relatively autonomous?

Urbanization and Democracy in Emergent Nations

American political science has reflected insufficiently the growing pains of cities in the United States. As we have attempted to show, much of the political history of urbanization in this country failed to capture the attention of the reformers and social engineers who dominated the early development of urban political science. Journalists and novelists took up some of the slack through the latter half of the nineteenth century and into the twentieth, during the violent expansion

of industry and mass employment which underlay modern urbanization in America. But the political growth of cities is still only a partly
told story.

Today throughout the world new nations are simultaneously restructuring their political, economic, and social systems. The relationship
in these nations between urbanization and politics is intimate and
difficult to describe. Gigantic political decisions have in modern times
led to drastic redistributions of populations within nations—redistributions which formerly occurred by a concatenation of individual independent decisions by workers seeking employment and shelter, and
employers seeking laborers. Nowadays, politics enters not only into
the consequences of urbanization, but into its causes as well. But
though political decisions can vastly promote and retard the process
of urbanization, the internal political consequences of urbanization
are seldom counted so heavily by new governments as are consequences relating to capital formation, economic development, and international prestige.

The newly emerging nations are unanimously seeking economic development; they are less unanimous and less energetic, on the whole,
in their pursuit of democratic politics. American political scientists
can generally agree on many of the attributes of political systems
which would tend to promote human dignity, in the terms of Western
civilization. They may well be doing their country and the free world
a considerable service by attacking with energy and diligence the
knotty problem of identifying and encouraging conditions necessary
for democratic politics in the midst of economic development and accelerated urbanization.[62]

Certain hypotheses can be constructed outlining relations among
independent variables such as literacy and education, income distribution and gross national income, ethnic homogeneity and variety,
geographic mobility and stability, and other economic and social characteristics of populations, on the one hand—and the dependent variable of democratic politics on the other.[63] Rates and types of urbanization could function in such hypotheses as critical intervening variables. Marx long ago suggested, for example, that urban workers, because of their economic distress and spatial concentration, would be
fertile soil for revolutionary activity. Today urban mobs in North
Africa, the Middle East, and East Asia erupt into violence from time
to time, on various pretexts.

The characteristics of urban groups in developing countries, and
most particularly their links with the political system, are topics of research having obvious political significance. The foreign, economic,

and domestic political policies of many countries depend greatly upon factual premises about the strengths and dispositions of these urban groups, but many of these premises—and the policies based on them— may be drastically if not disastrously out of date.

Political science is perhaps ready now to meet both the scientific and policy challenges posed by urbanization in the developing areas in ways it was not when America, West and Central Europe, Japan, and even Soviet Russia became urbanized. It is curious to reflect that the areas now emerging into political independence and economic ambition will in all probability be the last in history to undergo the massive changes in family structure, occupational and income patterns, and social organization associated with urbanization. How these changes affect and are affected by the pattern of politics and decision-making, the distribution of controls among leaders and nonleaders, the rights and privileges of citizens, and in some sense the dignity of men are topics which could easily and perhaps should imperatively engage the attention of the political scientist.

Urbanization is a process which continues long after cities replace villages and citizens replace tribe and clansmen. As people are drawn into cities and as cities grow into metropolitan areas, their political problems proliferate and intensify. As these problems increase and deepen, more resources are distributed intentionally and inadvertently, and more and more actors involve themselves in the political processes which affect the restriction and diffusion of valued outcomes. As the political problems of urbanization expand beyond state lines and leap beyond national borders, the scientific problems of *urban* political scientists merge with those of political scientists generally. These tendencies combine to discourage parochialism among political scientists and underscore the significance of urbanization as a focal point for research, for in many ways cities and urbanizing areas are the most dynamic elements in our political life.

NOTES

1. See, especially for this early period, Robert C. Brooks, "Bibliography of Municipal Problems and Conditions of City Life," *Municipal Affairs*, 5 (1903), a 300-page bibliography. For a recent and perceptive commentary and bibliography, see Robert T. Daland, "Political Science and the Study of Urbanism, A Bibliographical Essay," *American Political Science Review*, 51 (June 1957), pp. 491–509.

2. Goodnow provided the center of gravity for political scientists with two texts: *City Government in the United States* (1904), and *Municipal*

Government (1909), which added comparative material on Great Britain and Western Europe. James A. Fairlie, *Municipal Administration* (1901); William B. Munro, *Principles and Methods of Municipal Administration* (1916); and Herman G. James, *Municipal Functions* (1917), extended the Goodnow and League premises into the discussion of city administrative agencies. Charles Zueblin, *American Municipal Progress* (1902); Delos F. Wilcox, *The American City: A Problem in Democracy* (1904); Lincoln Steffens, *The Shame of the Cities* (1904); L. S. Rowe, *Problems of City Government* (1908); Horace C. Deming, *The Government of American Cities* (1909); Charles A. Beard, *American City Government* (1912); Walter T. Arndt, *The Emancipation of the American City* (1917), all added confirmation.

Lincoln Steffens was enormously influential in this period as an essayist on urban politics. While confirming the image of urban life then held by reformers and most political scientists (he produced the classic literature on urban bosses and machines), and while anticipating the model of an ultimately controlling economic elite in the cities which some sociologists were to rediscover much later, he also expressed profound skepticism about the nostrums of the urban reformers. His indictment of misgovernment was accepted; his pessimism about reform doctrines was ignored. See R. V. Sampson, "Lincoln Steffens: An Interpretation," *Western Political Quarterly*, 8 (1955), pp. 58–67.

One deviant enthusiasm, the commission form of government, claiming for itself the maximum use of the business corporation as model, brought its spate of advocates: John J. Hamilton, *The Dethronement of the City Boss* (1910); Ernest R. Bradford, *Commission Government in American Cities* (1911); Clinton R. Woodruff, *City Government by Commission* (1911); Henry Bruère, *The New City Government* (1912); Oswald Ryan, *Municipal Freedom: A Study of Commission Government* (1915).

Two volumes in the period reflect hopeful premises about urban society. Richard T. Ely, *The Coming City* (1902), and Frederick C. Howe, *The City: The Hope of Democracy* (1906), welcomed the arrival of urbanization. Frank Parsons, *The City for the People* (1901), advocated municipal ownership of utilities. In other respects, none of these three studies departed greatly from the conventional reform prescriptions. Three relatively detached examinations of the urban scene, with minimum emphasis on prescription, also appeared during the period: Howard Lee McBain, *The Law and Practice of Municipal Home Rule* (1916); Tso-Shuen Chang, *Commission and City Manager Plans* (1918); Russell M. Story, *The American Municipal Executive* (1918). Less detached was Harry A. Toulmin's *The City Manager: A New Profession* (1915).

3. Munro (1923), Maxey (1924), Anderson (1925), Reed, Hanford, Upson (all in 1926), MacDonald (1929), Kneier (1934), Hodges, Zink (both in 1939), Pfiffner (1940), MacCorkle (1942), Schulz (1949), Bromage (1950) indicate their growth in number; several appeared during the period in revisions or modifications.

4. Leonard White's *The City Manager* (1927) testified to the emergence of a profession. The International City Managers' Association was established, began the publication of its own journal, and in 1935 issued the first of its series of handbooks on municipal management. Charles P. Taft

published *City Management: The Cincinnati Experiment* in 1933, and C. E. Ridley and O. F. Nolting, *The City Manager Profession* in 1934. In 1940, Harold Stone, Kathryn Stone, and Don K. Price issued their definitive and patristic document: *City Manager Government: A Review After Twenty-Five Years.*

5. Although Goodnow had devoted a chapter to "The Metropolitan City" in his text of 1897, and others (including Reed, as well as the authors of the *Regional Plan of New York*) had been concerned with metropolitan phenomena in the 1920's, the first systematic reconnaissance did not appear until Paul Studenski and others, under National Municipal League sponsorship, produced *Government of Metropolitan Areas* in 1930. This was followed by R. D. McKenzie, *The Metropolitan Community* (1933); C. E. Merriam, A. Lepawsky, and S. Parratt, *The Government of Metropolitan Chicago* (1933); John A. Rusk, *The City-County Consolidated* (1941); and Victor Jones, *Metropolitan Government* (1942). Jones raised some searching questions about the causes and sources of resistance to metropolitan integration.

6. Robert E. Park, Ernest W. Burgess, and R. D. McKenzie, *The City* (1925); Charles E. Merriam, *Chicago: A More Intimate View of Urban Politics* (1929); Robert and Helen Lynd, *Middletown* (1929) and *Middletown in Transition* (1937); Harold Zink, *City Bosses* (1930); Harold Gosnell, *Negro Politicians: The Rise of Negro Politics in Chicago* (1933); Roy V. Peel, *The Political Clubs of New York City* (1935); J. T. Salter, *Boss Rule: Portraits in City Politics* (1935); David H. Kurtzman, *Methods of Controlling Votes in Philadelphia* (1935); Harold Gosnell, *Machine Politics: Chicago Model* (1937); National Resources Committee, *Our Cities: Their Role in the National Economy* (1937) and *Urban Government* (1939); Dayton McKean, *Machine Politics: The Hague Machine in Action* (1940); Robert A. Walker, *The Planning Function in Urban Government* (1941); Arthur N. Holcombe, *The Political Parties of Today* (1924) and *The New Party Politics* (1933); Charles E. Merriam and Harold F. Gosnell, *The American Party System* (1923).

7. See Lawrence J. R. Herson, "The Lost World of Municipal Government," *American Political Science Review,* 51 (1957), pp. 330–345; Robert T. Daland, *op. cit.;* Hugh Douglas Price, *The Metropolis and Its Problems* (1960); Charles R. Adrian, *Governing Urban America* (1955; revised, 1961). Finally, in 1963, major revision of the texts had begun to take hold. See Edward C. Banfield and James Q. Wilson, *City Politics* (1963); Herbert Kaufman, *Politics and Policies in State and Local Governments* (1963); and Duane Lockard, *The Politics of State and Local Government* (1963).

8. Luther Gulick, "Metropolitan Organization," *The Annals,* 314 (1957), pp. 57–59. See also, for example, Arthur W. Bromage, "Political Representation in Metropolitan Areas," *American Political Science Review,* 52 (1958), pp. 406–418.

9. Duane Lockard summarizes much relevant material in Lockard, *op. cit.,* pp. 226–238. See also Oliver P. Williams and Charles R. Adrian, "The Insulation of Local Politics Under the Non-Partisan Ballot," *American Political Science Review,* 53 (1959), pp. 1052–1063; Charles R. Adrian, "A Typology of Non-Partisan Elections," *Western Political Quarterly,* 12 (1959), pp. 449–458; J. Leiper Freeman, "Local Party Systems: Theoretical Con-

siderations and a Case Analysis," *American Journal of Sociology*, 64 (1958), pp. 282–289; Eugene C. Lee, *The Politics of Nonpartisanship: A Study of California Cities* (1960); Charles E. Gilbert and Christopher Clague, "Electoral Competition and Electoral Systems in Large Cities," *Journal of Politics*, 24 (1962), pp. 323–349.

10. "Leadership and Decision-Making in Manager Cities" (a symposium), *Public Administration Review*, 19 (1958), pp. 208–222; C. E. Ridley, *The Role of the City Manager in Policy Formulation* (1958); C. A. Harrell and D. G. Weidford, "The City Manager and the Policy Process," *Public Administration Review*, 2 (1959), pp. 101–107; Kent Mathewson, "Democracy in Council Manager Government," *ibid.*, pp. 183–185; Wallace S. Sayre, "The General Manager Idea for Large Cities," *Public Administration Review*, 4 (1954), pp. 253–258.

11. Morton Grodzins, "The Federal System" in President's Commission on National Goals, *Goals for Americans* (1960), pp. 265–284; Wallace S. Sayre, "Cities and the State" and "State-City Government Relations," in New York State-New York City Fiscal Relations Committee, *Final Report* (November 1956), pp. 55–65 and 281–288. See also Wallace S. Sayre and Herbert Kaufman, *Governing New York City: Politics in the Metropolis* (1960), Chap. 15.

12. William C. Thomas, Jr., *The Bureau Chiefs in New York City Government* (1962), unpublished Columbia University doctoral dissertation; Sayre and Kaufman, *op. cit.*, Chap. 11; Theodore J. Lowi, *At the Pleasure of the Mayor* (1964).

13. On the race factor, see especially Edward C. Banfield, "The Politics of Metropolitan Area Organization," *Midwest Journal of Political Science*, 1 (1957), pp. 77–91; Edward C. Banfield and Morton Grodzins, *Government and Housing in Metropolitan Areas* (1958); Morton Grodzins, *The Metropolitan Area as a Racial Problem* (1958); James Q. Wilson, *Negro Politics: The Search for Leadership* (1960).

14. See Herson, *op. cit.;* and Herbert Kaufman, "Emerging Conflicts in the Doctrines of Public Administration," *American Political Science Review*, 50 (1956), pp. 1057–1073.

15. Hugh Douglas Price, *op. cit.*, p. 25.

16. V. O. Key, *Southern Politics* (1949), *American State Politics* (1956); Allan P. Sindler, *Huey Long's Louisiana* (1956); Duane Lockard, *New England State Politics* (1958); Leon D. Epstein, *Politics in Wisconsin* (1958); John H. Fenton, *Politics in the Border States* (1958).

17. Harold Stein (Ed.), *Public Administration and Policy Development* (1952): "The Cambridge City Manager" by Frank Abbott, and "Gotham in the Air Age" by Herbert Kaufman. These were followed (1953–1955) by the case studies of the Inter-University Case Program: for example, "The Gainesville School Problem" by Frank Adams; "The New York City Health Centers" by Herbert Kaufman; "The Promotion of Lem Merrill" by Chester and Valerie Earl; "Defending 'the Hill' against Metal Houses" by William Muir; "Closing Newark Airport" by Paul Tillett and Myron Weiner. The ICP published in 1964 a *Casebook in State and Local Government*, a collection of cases already published individually plus a number published for the first time. See also Richard T. Frost (Ed.), *Cases in State and Local Government* (1961). Solon T. Kimball and M. Pearsall, *The Talledega*

Story (1953), examining public health decisions in a Southern city, represented a more fully developed case study of the same genre, as did Martin Meyerson and Edward C. Banfield, *Politics, Planning, and The Public Interest* (1955), and Harold Kaplan, *Urban Renewal Politics: Slum Clearance in Newark* (1963).

18. See the Eagleton Foundation Series, *Case Studies in Practical Politics* (1958), and especially Paul Tillett (Ed.), *Cases on Party Organization* (1963).

19. Much of the discussion in the following pages of this section is treated more fully in Nelson W. Polsby, *Community Power and Political Theory* (1963). See also, for example, E. Digby Baltzell, *Philadelphia Gentlemen* (1958); Ernest A. T. Barth and Baha Abu-Laban, "Power Structure and the Negro Sub-Community," *American Sociological Review*, 24 (1959), pp. 69–76; William H. Form and William V. D'Antonio, "Integration and Cleavage Among Community Influentials in Two Border Cities," *American Sociological Review*, 24 (1959), pp. 804–814; August B. Hollingshead, *Elmtown's Youth* (1949); Floyd Hunter, *Community Power Structure* (1953); Floyd Hunter, Cecil B. Sheps, and Ruth C. Shaffer, *Community Organization: Action and Inaction* (1958); Morris Janowitz (Ed.), *Community Political Systems* (1961); Orrin E. Klapp and L. Vincent Padgett, "Power Structure and Decision-Making in a Mexican Border City," *American Journal of Sociology*, 65 (1960), pp. 400–406; Delbert C. Miller, "Decision-Making Cliques in Community Power Structures: A Comparative Study of an American and an English City, "*American Journal of Sociology*, 64 (1958), pp. 299–310; Delbert C. Miller, "Industry and Community Power Structure: A Comparative Study of an American and an English City," *American Sociological Review*, 23 (1958), pp. 9–15; C. Wright Mills, "The Middle Classes in Middle-Sized Cities," *American Sociological Review*, 11 (1946), pp. 520–529; Roland J. Pellegrin and Charles H. Coates, "Absentee-Owned Corporations and Community Power Structure," *American Journal of Sociology*, 61 (1956), pp. 413–419; Robert O. Schulze, "The Role of Economic Dominants in Community Power Structure," *American Sociological Review*, 23 (1958), pp. 3–9; W. Lloyd Warner et al., *Democracy in Jonesville* (1949); W. Lloyd Warner, *The Living and the Dead* (1947); W. Lloyd Warner and Paul S. Lunt, *The Social Life of a Modern Community* (1941); W. Lloyd Warner and Paul S. Lunt, *The Status System of a Modern Community* (1942); W. Lloyd Warner and Leo Srole, *The Social Systems of American Ethnic Groups* (1945); and especially, Robert S. Lynd and Helen Merrill Lynd, *Middletown* (1929) and *Middletown in Transition* (1937).

20. Kaufman and Jones, although sharply critical of findings in the field, have noted this lack among political scientists. Herbert Kaufman and Victor Jones, "The Mystery of Power," *Public Administration Review*, 14 (1954), pp. 205–212; see also Lawrence J. R. Herson, *op. cit.;* Robert T. Daland, *Dixie City: A Portrait of Political Leadership* (1956); William J. Gore and Fred S. Silander, "A Bibliographical Essay on Decision-Making," *Administrative Science Quarterly*, 4 (1959), p. 106–121; Robert E. Lane, *Political Life* (1959); and Edwin Hoffman Rhyne, "Political Parties and Decision-Making in Three Southern Counties," *American Political Science Review*, 52 (1958), pp. 1091–1107.

21. Sociologists as well as political scientists have joined in this current reevaluation. See C. Arnold Anderson, "The Need for a Functional Theory of Social Class," *Rural Sociology*, 19 (1954), pp. 152–160; C. Arnold Anderson and Harry L. Gracey, "A Review of C. Wright Mills' 'The Power Elite,'" *Kentucky Law Journal*, 46 (1958), pp. 301–317; George M. Belknap, "A Plan for Research on the Socio-Political Dynamics of Metropolitan Areas," presented before a Seminar on Urban Leadership of the Social Science Research Council, New York, August 1957.

See also Robert A. Dahl, *Who Governs? Democracy and Power in an American City* (1961); Robert A. Dahl, "A Critique of the Ruling Elite Model," *American Political Science Review*, 52 (1958), pp. 463–469; Robert A. Dahl, "Hierarchy, Democracy and Bargaining in Politics and Economics," in Stephen K. Bailey et al., *Research Frontiers in Politics and Government* (1955), pp. 45–69; Robert A. Dahl, "Leadership in a Fragmented Political System: Notes for a Theory," presented to the Conference on Metropolitan Leadership of the Social Science Research Council, Evanston, April 1–3, 1960; Robert A. Dahl, "The New Haven Community Leadership Study," Working Paper No. 1, December 12, 1957 (mimeographed); Robert A. Dahl, "Organization for Decision in New Haven," presented before the meetings of the American Political Science Association, 1958; Robert A. Dahl, "Some Notes and Models for Political Systems," presented before a Seminar on Urban Leadership of the Social Science Research Council, New York, August 1957.

Morris Janowitz, *op. cit.;* Herbert Kaufman and Victor Jones, *op. cit.;* Reinhard Bendix and Seymour Martin Lipset, "Political Sociology," *Current Sociology*, 6 (1957), pp. 79–99; James B. McKee, "Status and Power in the Industrial Community: A Comment on Drucker's Thesis," *American Journal of Sociology*, 58 (1953), pp. 364–370; Nelson W. Polsby, "Power in Middletown: Fact and Value in Community Research," *Canadian Journal of Economics and Political Science*, 26 (1960), pp. 592–602; Nelson W. Polsby, "The Sociology of Community Power: A Reassessment," *Social Forces*, 37 (1959), pp. 232–236; Nelson W. Polsby, "Three Problems in the Analysis of Community Power," *American Sociological Review*, 24 (1959), pp. 796–803; Peter H. Rossi, "Community Decision-Making," *Administrative Science Quarterly*, 1 (1957), pp. 415–443 (but see Peter H. Rossi, "Theory and Method in the Study of Power in the Local Community," presented to the Social Science Research Council's Conference on Metropolitan Leadership, Evanston, April 1–3, 1960, where he reexamines his reexamination); Harry M. Scoble, "Yankeetown: Leadership in Three Decision-Making Processes," in Janowitz, *op. cit.;* Benjamin Walter, "Political Decision-Making in North Carolina Cities," *Prod*, 3 (1960), pp. 18–21; Raymond E. Wolfinger, "Reputation and Reality in the Study of 'Community Power,'" *American Sociological Review*, 25 (1960), pp. 636–644.

22. See, for example, Edward C. Banfield, *Political Influence* (1961); George M. Belknap and John H. Bunzel, "The Trade Union in the Political Community," *Prod*, 2 (1958), pp. 3–6; Peter B. Clark, *The Chicago Big Businessman as a Civic Leader* (New Haven, September 1959), mimeographed; Robert A. Dahl, "The New Haven Community Leadership Study," *op. cit.;* Robert A. Dahl, "Organization for Decision in New Haven," *op. cit.;*

Robert A. Dahl, "A Proposed Inquiry into Political Influences in an American Community" (New Haven, April 1956), mimeographed; Robert A. Dahl, *Who Governs?*, *op. cit.;* Herbert Kaufman, "Metropolitan Leadership: The Snark of the Social Sciences," presented at a conference on Metropolitan Leadership of the Social Science Research Council, Evanston, April 1–3, 1960; Norton S. Long and George M. Belknap, *op. cit.;* Murray Levin, *The Compleat Politician* (1962); James B. McKee, *op. cit.;* Martin Meyerson and Edward Banfield, *op. cit.;* Nelson W. Polsby, "Three Problems in the Analysis of Community Power," *op. cit.;* Hugh Douglas Price, "Research on Metropolitanism: Economics, Welfare, and Politics" (Columbia University, Summer 1959), mimeographed; James Reichley, *The Art of Government: Reform and Organization Politics in Philadelphia* (1959); Peter H. Rossi and Robert A. Dentler, *The Politics of Urban Renewal* (1961); Harry M. Scoble, *op. cit.;* James Q. Wilson, *Negro Politics, op. cit.;* James Q. Wilson, *The Amateur Democrat: Club Politics in Three Cities* (1962); Raymond E. Wolfinger, *The Politics of Progress* (1961), unpublished Yale University doctoral dissertation.

23. See the works by Dahl, Polsby, and Wolfinger cited above, and also Robert A. Dahl, "The Concept of Power," *Behavioral Science*, 2 (1957), pp. 201–215; Nelson W. Polsby, "How to Study Community Power: The Pluralist Alternative," *Journal of Politics*, 22 (1960), pp. 474–484.

24. See the works cited in note 22 above.

25. On this last point, see Donald Olmsted, "Organizational Leadership and Social Structure in a Small City," *American Sociological Review*, 19 (1954), pp. 273–281.

26. See Robert E. Agger, "Power Attributions in the Local Community," *Social Forces*, 34 (1960), pp. 322–331; Robert E. Agger and Daniel Goldrich, "Community Power Structures and Partisanship," *American Sociological Review*, 23 (1958), pp. 383–392; Robert E. Agger and Vincent Ostrom, "The Political Structure of a Small Community," *Public Opinion Quarterly*, 20 (1956), pp. 81–89; Robert E. Agger and Vincent Ostrom, "Political Participation in a Small Community," in Heinz Eulau, Samuel Eldersveld, and Morris Janowitz (Eds.), *Political Behavior* (1957), pp. 138–148; George M. Belknap and Ralph Smuckler, "Political Power Relations in a Midwest City," *Public Opinion Quarterly*, 20 (1956), pp. 73–91; Ralph Smuckler and George M. Belknap, *Leadership and Participation in Urban Political Affairs* (1956); Harry M. Scoble, *op. cit.;* Robert K. Merton, "Patterns of Influence: A Study of Interpersonal Influence and of Communications Behavior in a Local Community," in Paul F. Lazarsfeld and Frank N. Stanton (Eds.), *Communications Research, 1948–1949* (1949), pp. 180–219; A. Alexander Fanelli, "Extensiveness of Communication Contacts and Perceptions of the Community," *American Sociological Review*, 21 (1956), pp. 439–446; A. Alexander Fanelli, "A Typology of Community Leadership Based on Influence Within the Leader Sub-System," *Social Forces*, 34 (1956), pp. 332–338; and V. O. Key, Jr., *Southern Politics, op. cit.,* pp. 99–100.

27. See William B. McKee, *op. cit.;* Herbert Kaufman, "Metropolitan Leadership . . . ," *op. cit.;* Wallace S. Sayre and Herbert Kaufman, *op. cit.;* Nelson W. Polsby, "Three Problems . . . ," *op. cit.;* Robert A. Dahl, *Who Governs?* and "Organization for Decision . . . ," *op. cit.,* and "Lead-

ership in a Fragmented Political System . . . ," *op. cit.;* C. W. M. Hart, "Industrial Relations Research and Social Theory," *Canadian Journal of Economics and Political Science,* 15 (1949), pp. 53–73.

28. Norton E. Long, "The Local Community As an Ecology of Games," *American Journal of Sociology,* 64 (1958), pp. 251–252. See also Norton E. Long, "Aristotle and the Study of Local Government," *Social Research* (Fall 1957); Norton E. Long, "The Corporation, Its Satellites and the Local Community," in E. S. Mason (Ed.), *The Corporation and Modern Society* (1960); and Norton E. Long, "An Institutional Framework for Responsible Citizenship," in *Nomos,* 3 (Annual of the Society for Legal and Political Philosophy), 1960. All of these, and other stimulating essays by Long, are reprinted in Charles Press (Ed.), *The Polity* (1962).

29. Hugh Douglas Price, *The Metropolis . . . , op. cit.,* pp. 25–26.

30. Herbert Kaufman, "Metropolitan Leadership . . . ," *op. cit.,* p. 5. More fully in Sayre and Kaufman, *op. cit.,* pp. 710 ff.

31. See Harry M. Scoble, *op. cit.,* p. 39; Robert K. Merton, *op. cit.;* Arthur J. Vidich and Joseph Bensman, *Small Town in Mass Society* (1958), pp. 98–99; Paul A. Miller, "The Process of Decision-Making Within the Context of Community Organization," *Rural Sociology,* 16 (1952), pp. 153–161.

32. James S. Coleman, *Community Conflict* (1957). See also W. Lloyd Warner and J. O. Low, *op. cit., passim;* James B. McKee, *op. cit.;* and Morris Janowitz, *op. cit.*

33. See C. Wright Mills, *The Power Elite* (1956), for the clearest statement of this position.

34. See Peter H. Rossi and Robert A. Dentler, *op. cit.;* Martin Meyerson and Edward C. Banfield, *op. cit.;* Edward C. Banfield, *Political Influence, op. cit.;* Wallace S. Sayre and Herbert Kaufman, *op. cit.;* Robert A. Dahl, *Who Governs?, op. cit.;* Raymond Wolfinger, *op. cit.;* and on New York City, the dissertations by Lowi and Thomas, previously cited.

35. See Robert A. Dahl, "Leadership in a Fragmented Political System," *op. cit.,* for the first and most elaborate statement of this point.

36. Hugh Douglas Price, *The Metropolis . . . , op. cit.,* pp. 27–28.

37. See David B. Truman, "Theory and Research on Metropolitan Political Leadership: Report on a Conference," Social Science Research Council *Items,* 15 (March 1961).

38. See David Gold and John R. Schmidhauser, "Urbanization and Party Competition: The Case of Iowa," *Midwest Journal of Political Science,* 4 (1960), pp. 62–75; Heinz Eulau, "The Ecological Basis of Party Systems: The Case of Ohio," *Midwest Journal of Political Science,* 1 (1957), pp. 125–135; Leon D. Epstein, *op. cit.,* pp. 151, 177; Robert T. Golembiewski, "A Taxonomic Approach to State Political Strength," *Western Political Quarterly,* 12 (1958), pp. 494–513; Donald S. Strong, *Urban Republicanism in the South* (1960).

39. An eloquent presentation of the basic hypothesis, emphasizing the consequences of "nationalization" for national party structure, is E. E. Schattschneider, "United States: The Functional Approach to Party Government," in Sigmund Neumann (Ed.), *Modern Political Parties* (1956), pp. 194–215. See also E. E. Schattschneider, *The Semi-Sovereign People* (1960).

40. V. O. Key, Jr., *American State Politics* (1956); Marvin Weinbaum, *op. cit.*; Houston Fluornoy, *The Liberal Party in New York* (1960), unpublished doctoral dissertation, Princeton University.

41. For somewhat different questions, see Murray Levin, *The Alienated Voter: Politics in Boston* (1960); Scott Greer, "Urbanism Reconsidered," *American Sociological Review*, 21 (1956), pp. 19–25.

42. See James Q. Wilson, *Negro Politics, op. cit.*; Wilson, "Two Negro Politicians: An Interpretation," *Midwest Journal of Political Science*, 4 (1960), pp. 346–369; Hugh Douglas Price, *The Negro and Southern Politics* (1957); Oscar Handlin, *The Newcomers* (1959); Oscar Glants, "The Negro Voter in Northern Industrial Cities," *Western Political Quarterly*, 13 (1960), pp. 999ff.

43. The case for differentiation among these groups is variously put in Robert O. Schulze, *op. cit.*; Warner and Low, *op. cit.*; Long and Belknap, *op. cit.*; Sayre and Kaufman, *op. cit.*, Chap. 13; Clark, *op. cit.*; Kenneth Wilson Underwood, *Protestant and Catholic* (1957); Rossi and Dentler, *op. cit.*; Meyerson and Banfield, *op. cit.*; Arnold Bornfriend, *Business Leadership in a Metropolis: The Commerce and Industry Association of New York*, doctoral dissertation in preparation, Columbia University.

44. See Rossi and Dentler, *op. cit.*; Underwood, *op. cit.*; and, for a fictional presentation of the theme, the stories of J. F. Powers.

45. See Dahl, *Who Governs?, op. cit.*, Chap. 4; Elmer E. Cornwell, Jr., "Party Absorption of Ethnic Groups," *Social Forces*, 38 (1960), pp. 205–210; Nelson W. Polsby, "Three Problems . . . ," *op. cit.* See also Will Herberg, *Protestant-Catholic-Jew* (1960); Samuel Lubell, *The Future of American Politics* (1951).

46. See August B. Hollingshead, *op. cit.*; Robert A. Dahl, "Organization for Decision in New Haven . . . ," *loc. cit.*; Neal Gross, *Who Runs Our Schools* (1959); Thomas H. Eliot, "Toward an Understanding of Public School Politics," *American Political Science Review*, 53 (1959), pp. 1032–1051; W. W. Charters, "Social Class Analysis and the Control of Education," *Harvard Educational Review*, 23 (1953), 268–283; Sayre and Kaufman, *op. cit.*, Chaps. 8 and 11. Theodore Powell, *The School Bus Law, A Case Study in Education, Religion and Politics* (1960). See also the Syracuse University Press series on *The Economics and Politics of Public Education* (12 vols., paperback, 1962–1963), especially the studies by Bailey, Wood, Frost and Marsh, Martin, Munger and Fenno, Bloomberg and Sunshine.

47. As in, for example, A. J. Liebling, *The Press* (1961). Cf. Bernard C. Cohen, *The Press and Foreign Policy* (1963).

48. See Sayre and Kaufman, *op. cit.*, Chap. 11; and dissertations by Lowi, *op. cit.*, and Thomas, *op. cit.*

49. See especially Banfield, *Political Influence*, Chap. 6.

50. Paul T. David and R. Eisenberg, *Devaluation of the Urban and Suburban Vote* (1961); Gordon E. Baker, *Rural versus Urban Political Power* (1955); David R. Derge, "Metropolitan and Outstate Alignments in Illinois and Missouri Legislative Delegations," *American Political Science Review*, 52 (1958), pp. 1051–1065; Gilbert Y. Steiner and Samuel K. Gove, *Legislative Politics in Illinois* (1960); Vernon A. O'Rourke and Douglas Campbell, *Constitution-Making in a Democracy: Theory and Prac-*

tice in New York State (1943); Sayre and Kaufman, *op. cit.*, Chap. 15; Wallace S. Sayre, "A Rejoinder . . . ," *The Annals*, 314 (1957), pp. 82–85; Robert C. Wood, "The Case for a Department of Urban Affairs," a paper delivered at 1960 Annual Meeting of the American Political Science Association.

51. Distinguished examples of this kind of criticism are contained in Percival and Paul Goodman, *Communitas* (1960); and Lewis Mumford, *The City in History* (1961).

52. Coleman Woodbury, *Urban Studies: Some Questions of Outlook and Selection*, Sixth Annual Wherrett Lecture on Local Government of the University of Pittsburgh (1960), p. 15.

53. The Commission on Intergovernmental Relations, *A Report to the President for Transmittal to Congress* (June 1955), p. 40. See also pp. 102–**103.**

54. Woodbury, *op. cit., passim;* see also Robert C. Wood, *1400 Governments* (1961); Lloyd Rodwin and Kevin Lynch (Eds.), "The Future Metropolis," *Daedalus* (Winter 1961); Hugh Douglas Price, "Research on Metropolitanism: Economics, Welfare, and Politics," Columbia University (1959) mimeographed; Anthony Downs, *An Economic Theory of Democracy* (1957); Robert A. Dahl and Charles E. Lindblom, *Politics, Economics and Welfare* (1953).

55. The terms "ideology" and "utopia" are used here in a manner similar to the usage presented in Harold D. Lasswell and Abraham Kaplan, *Power and Society* (1950), pp. 123–133.

56. See Louis Hartz, "Democracy: Image and Reality," in W. N. Chambers and R. H. Salisbury (Eds.), *Democracy in the Mid-Twentieth Century* (1960), pp. 13–29.

57. We do not mean to carry the argument as far as Jane Jacobs seems to do in *The Death and Life of Great American Cities* (1961), but see Herbert Gans, *The Urban Villagers* (1962).

58. The Institute of Government and Public Affairs at the University of Illinois is currently collecting information from a variety of sources under headings approximately like these questions. See also Rossi and Dentler, *op. cit.;* Harold Kaplan, *op. cit.;* Raymond Vernon, "The Myth and Reality of Our Urban Problems," Stafford Little Lectures of Princeton University, Spring 1961 (unpublished); and Wolfinger, *op. cit.*

59. See James Coleman, *op. cit.* The Harvard School of Public Health has a research commitment in this area, which thus far has resulted in a number of mimeographed research papers. See also Thomas F. A. Plaut, "Analysis of Voting Behavior on a Fluoridation Referendum," *Public Opinion Quarterly*, 23 (1959), pp. 213–222.

60. For an early study of urban judicial processes, see Roscoe Pound and Felix Frankfurter (Eds.), *Criminal Justice in Cleveland* (1922). See also: Walter F. Murphy and C. Herman Pritchett, *Courts, Judges and Politics* (1961); Jack W. Peltason, *Federal Courts in the Political Process* (1955); Sayre and Kaufman, *op. cit.*, Chap. 14; Clement Vose, *Caucasians Only* (1959).

61. See Robert C. Wood, *Suburbia: Its People and Their Politics* (1959); Edward Sofen, *The Miami Metropolitan Experiment* (1963); Forbes Hays, *The New York Regional Plan Association* (1965); Roscoe Martin et al.,

Decisions in Syracuse (1961); Henry J. Schmandt, P. G. Steinbicker, and G. D. Wendel, *Metropolitan Reform in St. Louis: A Case Study* (1961); Leo F. Schnore and Robert R. Alford, "Forms of Government and Socio-economic Characteristics of 300 Suburbs," *Administrative Science Quarterly,* 8 (1963), pp. 1–17; Charles S. Liebman, "Functional Differentiation and Political Characteristics of Suburbs," *American Journal of Sociology,* 66 (1961), pp. 485–490; Henry J. Schmandt, "The City and the Ring," *The American Behavioral Scientist* (November 1960), pp. 17–19; York Willbern, "Case Studies of Metropolitan Action Programs," *Western Political Quarterly,* 12 (1959), pp. 580–581; Frederick M. Wirt, "Suburban Patterns in American Politics," paper delivered at 1960 Annual Meeting of the American Political Science Association; Robert C. Wood, *1400 Governments, op. cit.*

62. See, for suggestive leads, William A. Kornhauser, *The Politics of Mass Society* (1959); Daniel Lerner, *The Passing of Traditional Society* (1958); Seymour Martin Lipset, "Some Social Requisites of Democracy," *American Political Science Review,* 53 (1959), pp. 69–105.

63. For an interesting attempt, see Phillips Cutright, "National Political Development: Social and Economic Correlates," in Nelson W. Polsby, Robert A. Dentler, and P. A. Smith (Eds.), *Politics and Social Life* (1963). See also Russell H. Fitzgibbon, "A Statistical Evaluation of Latin American Democracy," *Western Political Quarterly,* 9 (1956), pp. 607–619, and Phillips Cutright, "National Political Development: Measurement and Analysis," *American Sociological Review,* 28 (1963), pp. 253–264.

Theory and Research
in Urban Sociology

Gideon Sjoberg

A critical appraisal of urban sociological theory, especially in its relation to cross-cultural studies, is the primary goal of this chapter.[1] In
the process we strive to clarify certain theoretical controversies in the
urban field, and we briefly consider some of the methodological issues
the comparativist encounters as he collects his data on cities and seeks
to test hypotheses. Ours is not a bibliographic survey, however, because such surveys are available elsewhere.[2]

The Need for More Adequate Theories

The data on cities over the world, though uneven in quality and
inadequate on many counts, are nonetheless increasing by leaps and
bounds. New materials are constantly being amassed by social scientists of many hues. Unfortunately, these data tend to be ignored by
American urban sociologists.[3] Still more likely to be overlooked is the
information collected by non-social scientists ranging from newspaper
reporters to bureaucratic officials. Persons who occupy governmental
posts must draw upon a profusion of materials if they are to engage
in rational planning in the industrial-urban or industrializing society.
In the Soviet Union, for example, the managerial and political elite
increasingly require reliable data on the operation of the industrial-
urban complex. Consequently, considerable data are accumulating on
the familial, economic, educational, governmental, and other structures, although these materials are frequently published outside the
mainstream of social science literature. As new societies enter the industrial-urban orbit, the data on urban centers can be expected to
multiply still more rapidly.

157

Admittedly, use of material gathered by non-social scientists poses special problems for the sociologist; yet for many societies, such as the U. S. S. R. and China, recourse to such information is mandatory. The reports of government officials are prime sources of data on life in urban centers in these countries.

This is not to deny the need for sociologically oriented descriptive materials on cities, particularly for research projects that are designed to test specific hypotheses. In a real sense, "the more we know, the more we need to know." But to order the ever-accumulating mountains of data and make sense out of seemingly contradictory findings, we must formulate more adequate theories. Indeed this should be our chief goal. Besides facilitating the analysis of existing materials, better theories expose the significant gaps in our knowledge and pave the way for more strategic research.

As Reiss has observed,[4] sociologists have been more interested in studying and theorizing about segments of urban social and ecological structure than in dealing with the totality; and they have tended to use the city as a laboratory for testing theories and hypotheses not specifically related to urban sociology. With increased specialization these trends are likely to persist. Nevertheless, a gestalt perspective—one that views the urbanization process or the urban community in its totality—has much to offer.

Anyone who theorizes about worldwide urban forms faces the task of clarifying and refining some basic concepts, including the community, urbanism, the city, urban society, and ecology. These often are loosely employed in the literature, and many fruitless debates result from the failure of the antagonists to understand each other's definitions of these concepts. Some of the tensions that result from this confusion over definitions will be treated within the context of our discussion.

Types of Theoretical Orientation
and Their Respective Schools of Thought

No classification of urban theory can be fully satisfactory. Adherence to any particular system inevitably excludes from consideration certain salient issues. This, however, is not peculiar to urban sociology; it occurs in all theorizing.

The very nature of urban sociology poses certain problems for our analysis. First, most urban sociologists in the United States apparently subscribe to the view that their field must evince a distinctive theoretical or methodological orientation in order to justify its existence. The opposing position, toward which I lean, takes the urban community as the substantive area of study; thus the prime purpose of urban sociology is to understand and predict, by whatever theoretical or methodological tools are available, the social and ecological structure of cities or the actions of their inhabitants.

Another difficulty stems from an "historical accident"—from the fact that in the United States the early students of the city were heavily committed to ecology. Consequently, some writers equate urban sociology with ecology. As the field of ecology has expanded and proliferated in several directions, the boundaries of urban theory have extended accordingly. Nowadays certain of the theoretical orientations associated with urban sociology have been designed to explain the ecological dimension of cities; others are intended to cope specifically with the social sphere. Still other theories seek to account for both the ecology and the social organization of the city.

Some theoretical dilemmas afford the urban sociologist with a unique opportunity to contribute to social theory more generally. For one thing, the urban field is a major battleground for those who stress the impact on urban life of "objective conditions"—the external environment, population structure, and the like—and those who emphasize, for instance, the role of social or cultural values as a key determinant of the so-called objective conditions and of human action in general. Urban sociologists could make a major contribution if they would clarify, perhaps even resolve, some of the issues that separate the antagonists: the "materialists" and "nonmaterialists." [5] At the very least one should seek to be more explicit concerning the assumptions that underlie the selection of one's problems, the collection of data, and the analysis thereof.

Our classification of the major schools of thought in urban sociology is based on the particular variable or variables to which each gives priority. As we shall observe, some schools stress the "external conditions" as determinants of a city's development and social organization, whereas others give priority to values or social power. At the same time, some of these schools of thought include subgroupings that diverge perceptibly from one another because of their differing theoretical or methodological assumptions. We shall at least suggest the range of these disagreements.

The Urbanization School

A number of sociologists have examined the impact of the city upon human ecology and social structure. Park and Burgess and their colleagues and students, most notably Wirth and Redfield, have been instrumental in developing and popularizing this theoretical perspective.[6] They drew heavily upon the writings of such European sociologists as Simmel, Maine, Tönnies, Durkheim, and Max Weber.[7] The "urbanization school" has addressed itself, in its own fashion, to an issue of central concern to most leading sociologists—namely, "What are the patterns and processes involved in the transition from a preindustrial, or agrarian, or feudal way of life to an industrial, or urban, or capitalistic order?"

Within modern urban sociology, Wirth's "Urbanism as a Way of Life"[8] is perhaps the most widely cited theoretical orientation. Wirth takes the city—characterized by size, density, and heterogeneity—as the key determinant of many kinds of social action. Redfield, too, in his *Folk Culture of Yucatán*, utilizes the city as a key variable; however, he considers heterogeneity and lack of isolation to be the city's chief characteristics.[9]

To Wirth, and to a degree Redfield, urbanism as a way of life is typified by secularization, secondary-group relationships, voluntary associations, increased segmentation of roles, and poorly defined social norms. The city is, then, a focal point of fluidity and of tenuous social relationships. Implicitly or explicitly the urban center is contrasted with the rural community or, more frequently, with the folk society. The aforementioned characteristics of the urban milieu are regarded as inevitable concomitants of the rise of cities. Significantly, Wirth viewed the effects of urban development as distinctive and independent of those stemming from cultural values or from industrialization; these latter are "held constant." According to this reasoning, all cities, historical and contemporary, share certain key characteristics.

The Wirth-Redfield perspective, though sharply scored in recent years, continues to claim some staunch adherents among students of the city. Recent research, such as that by Smith on preindustrial Tokyo, lends support to Wirth's position.[10] Furthermore, the theorizing of Wirth and Redfield is being perpetuated in introductory textbooks in sociology. But what is more important, many of the ideas of Wirth and Redfield are today being analyzed and researched not by urban sociologists but by those sociologists who speak in terms of "loss of identity," "alienation," or "anomie," in mass societies.[11]

On the other hand, the researches of Babchuk and Gordon, Whyte, Gans,[12] and others on the American scene pinpoint some serious weaknesses of the Wirth perspective. Even for the United States, Wirth exaggerated the amount of secularization and "disorganization" that supposedly typifies the urban setting. We know now that the city is more highly organized than the early Chicago group presumed. Over-

looked or deemphasized by writers such as Zorbaugh [13] are certain
complex networks of interaction. Slum areas display intricate patterns
that often go unobserved by social scientists who come from "the
right side of the tracks." [14] And not to be minimized are the bureaucratic organizations that play an increasingly significant role in the
lives of American city-dwellers. A mounting body of literature, including the recent studies of Miller and Swanson, documents this
trend.[15]

In retrospect it is easy to recognize that Wirth's writings reflect the
ethos of the 1920's and 1930's, a period when many American "intellectuals," sociologists among them, were seeking to account for and
cope with the stresses and strains of urban life arising from forces
such as the First World War, the ingress of large numbers of immigrants from diverse cultures, and the Great Depression. During this
era the metropolis was a veritable "seething cauldron."

The limitations of a preoccupation with "disorganization" loom even
larger when the Wirth frame of reference is applied to other societies. Oscar Lewis's data support the proposition that in Mexico City
urbanization is not necessarily accompanied by a destruction of the
social and moral order.[16] And studies of African cities today demonstrate that although the urban milieu is experiencing greatly accelerated change, certain traditional patterns persist alongside the new
organizational forms that have emerged.[17] Furthermore, traditional
preindustrial cities—including Le Tourneau's Fez and Miner's Timbuctoo [18]—are living testimonials to the fact that cities may evince a
quite rigid normative order.

Another shortcoming of the Wirth approach, one that is dramatized
particularly in Redfield's early writings, concerns the logical structure of the folk-urban comparison. Redfield saw the folk, or preliterate, society as a closed system. Yet the urban community with which
the folk order is contrasted is but a partial system; it survives only
because of a hinterland that supplies it with food and raw materials.
In effect, Redfield and his followers have been comparing a whole
with a part, which is certainly a questionable procedure. Logically,
and empirically, the social units to be contrasted are folk versus urban
societies and rural versus urban communities. Redfield subsequently
modified his position, recognizing that a major distinction obtains
between peasants, who form part of a broader society, and preliter-
ates, or folk, who constitute a self-sufficient system that functions apart
from any "great tradition." [19]

As for rural-urban differences per se, a number of the generalizations
that have emerged from research within the Wirth-Redfield tradition,

and are reflected still in sociology textbooks, are badly in need of revision. Numerous patterns that typify the American industrial-urban society are erroneously thought to hold for other social orders as well. By way of illustration, the rural-urban differences that prevail in industrial orders are quite distinct from those that typify preindustrial civilized (or feudal) societies. In the latter, the family organization in its most highly developed form—the large extended family functioning under a single roof—is characteristic of the urban elite rather than of the inhabitants of small villages (where in fact the elite rarely reside). Census materials, though admittedly inadequate in many respects, point to the persistence of these patterns in India today.[20] Then, too, new kinds of rural-urban relationships, depending on the society's level of industrialization, seem to be emerging. In mature industrial orders such as the United States, rural-urban differences are not nearly as marked as those in, say, Southeast Asia. We need to determine just what rural-urban differences hold for all societies and, where this is not possible, we need to define the precise limits of the generalizations concerning these differences by identifying the conditions under which specific patterns obtain.

Implicit in the foregoing discussion is another criticism of Wirth and sociologists of like mind: they fail to recognize that the city is shaped along certain lines by the broader, embracing society. Thus, for some problems, the sociologist must consider the city a dependent rather than an independent variable, for much of its ecological and social structure is determined by social forces external to it. Sociologists have perhaps been overly influenced by writers such as Pirenne,[21] who sought to dramatize the social and political independence of the medieval European city. But this thesis is unrealistic for that period, even in Western Europe. True, some cities of the past achieved political autonomy, but, in general, cities—certainly contemporary ones—have been mere subsystems subject to societal controls. (We elaborate upon this argument later, especially in our analysis of social power as an independent variable.)

We have been rather critical of the formulations that take the city as an independent variable. At the same time such an orientation is not without some value for the comparative study of cities. In their eagerness to establish the specific "correlates" of urban life, sociologists have generalized all too freely from the American scene, but their emphasis upon the city as a variable cannot be ignored. Urban and rural communities have always diverged and will continue to do so for some time to come.[22]

The city, as the focal point of communication, has always facilitated significant kinds of social change, not the least of which are those stemming from creative intellectual endeavor. Intellectuals have functioned most effectively where the interaction of ideas has been intensive. The city, too, is the repository of the libraries that perpetuate knowledge. Not only does the city provide the necessary conditions for many kinds of social change, including acculturation,[23] but it seems to foster certain varieties of collective behavior, mob action included. Wirth and Redfield rightly gave prominence to the city as a positive force in social change, although often it is more of a "necessary" than a "sufficient" condition. The urban community's precise role in this process, however, awaits clearer theoretical and empirical documentation.

To counterbalance the overemphasis on disorganization, urban sociologists must pay greater heed to social organization, especially to the "differential organization" found among subgroupings within an urban setting, or among different types of cities. Then, too, in societies over the world the city, not the rural area, is the fulcrum of the political, educational, religious, and other organizations (or bureaucracies) that control and support urban life. We must strive to isolate the structural correlates, or functional prerequisites, or imperatives, that hold not only for cities in general but also for specific types of cities. To achieve this a drastic overhaul of the Wirth-Redfield formulation seems mandatory.

Emerging out of the Wirth-Redfield [24] tradition is a group of sociologists [25] who have defined "urbanization" solely in demographic terms.[26] In many instances these writers developed their orientations within the context of other, more elaborate theoretical perspectives (discussed later), and they differ among themselves in some of their methodological and theoretical premises. Thus some approach the study of cities with an eye to discovering patterns or formulating hypotheses, whereas others begin with existing hypotheses and use these as a basis for constructing deductive (axiomatic) theories of a sort.[27]

The primary advantage of the demographic approach to the study of urbanization is that it so readily lends itself to measurement. Now that the metropolitan areas of the world have been roughly delineated, one can more easily formulate and test hypotheses about cities in divergent cultural settings. Certainly, descriptive data on the distribution of urbanites over the world cannot be ignored. Moreover, in contrast to Wirth and Redfield, those sociologists who have adopted the demographic orientation have studied urbanization from the viewpoint of the broader society, which gives them a definite advantage for understanding urban social organization.

Yet special difficulties plague those who define urbanization in demographic terms. In some instances it is unclear whether urbanization is defined in terms of size or whether size is taken as the index of what is urban. Both approaches are legitimate, but the failure to make one's analytical scheme explicit can hardly be defended. In practice it is difficult, if not impossible, in cross-cultural research to take size as the sole criterion of what is urban. It is evident, for instance, that communities of, say, 5000 differ considerably in India, Mexico, and the United States, and any analysis predicated on size alone is a poor one. Even communities in the 100,000 category differ so strikingly in preindustrial and industrial orders that the researcher, to make his analysis meaningful, is likely to introduce criteria other than size into his definition of what is urban. In other words, it is often essential to specify the social conditions under which size is taken as the criterion for urban centers. Actually, Hope Tisdale's article,[28] which gave such impetus to the study of urbanization in demographic terms, has an implicit, and often overlooked, assumption built into her theorizing: she recognized that urbanization is a dependent variable, for it is technology that makes urbanization possible.

The Subsocial School

This school, developed by Park and Burgess and often identified as "the Chicago School," has been intent upon studying man in his temporal and spatial dimensions and explaining the resulting patterns in terms of subsocial variables. For upholders of this view the fundamental subsocial variable has been impersonal competition.

In large part, the theorizing of the Chicago ecologists can be said to represent the confluence of two streams of thought—Social Darwinism and Classical Economics—that swept into prominence during the nineteenth century. Both explain human action in terms of impersonal competition, though the Classical Economists, by casting their theories in terms of a laissez-faire doctrine and focusing primarily on the operation of the marketplace, have functioned within narrower boundaries than the Social Darwinists.

The members of the Chicago School of ecology differ in a number of respects. Burgess, for example, gave more attention to the economic dimension than did Park, who seems to have relied more heavily upon Social Darwinist thinking, though he did not always make this explicit.[29] Consequently, interpretations of the thinking of the Chicago group diverge from one another considerably. Firey,[30] for instance, gives far more attention to the economic facets of the subsocial theory than do certain other critics who play up the Darwinian features.

As to the theorizing and research emanating from this school of thought, Firey,[31] among others, has shown that the resulting generalizations are not fully applicable to American cities. Certain urban patterns cannot be explained in terms of the city's economic organization alone; for example, the factor of sentiment must be recognized. On the basis of research in Austin, Texas, Willhelm and Sjoberg suggest that certain subgroups in American cities, notably businessmen, have incorporated so-called impersonal or subsocial forces into their value system.[32] Thus impersonal forces, as values, are used to justify certain actions in zoning the community.

Although the Chicago School has been sharply criticized, it continues to exert influence. Many of the early studies are still widely cited. Also, certain sociologists (discussed later) have sought to reformulate the Chicago School's theory of ecology, in the process divesting it of many of its Social Darwinistic features.

The Ecological Complex (or Sustenance) School

A bridge between the older Chicago School and a highly active group of younger ecologists, prominent among whom are Duncan and Schnore and Gibbs and Martin, was provided first by McKenzie and later by Hawley.[33] These present-day writers have been influenced not only by the earlier Chicago ecologists but also by Durkheim (especially his *Division of Labor*), Classical Economists (including location economists like von Thünen and Lösch), and to some extent the materialist orientation of Marx and his followers. However, among the leaders of this school, Duncan and Schnore diverge perceptibly from Gibbs and Martin, not just in some of their theoretical premises but in their methodology as well. The first two employ the concept of the "ecological complex" and are committed to "induction" or, more accurately, "discovery," whereas the latter stress the notion of "sustenance" and tend to employ a "neo-deductive" approach.[34]

The "ecological complex" of Duncan and Schnore has four basic components: environment, population, social organization, and technology.[35] These variables are seen as functionally interrelated: a change in one leads to modifications in the others. Duncan and Schnore argue that their approach differs significantly from the perspectives of the two other major schools in sociology—the cultural and the social-psychological.

The ecological complex obviously encompasses more than just the urban field, but its chief proponents have focused their attention mainly on the study of cities and urbanization. The major advantage of this framework is its utility for organizing large masses of numerical data, most notably those collected via censuses. Certainly this orientation facilitates the use of measurement.

Metropolis and Region,[36] the major work of Duncan and his associates, enhances our knowledge of the urban hierarchy, or the dominance pattern of cities in American society; in the process it presents an "industrial profile" of some fifty of the largest Standard Metropolitan Areas. Schnore's work also has contributed substantially to the study of metropolitan communities, particularly in the United States.[37]

The shortcomings of the Duncan-Schnore orientation are several. First, the authors have failed to explicate the assumptions underlying their theory—assumptions that affect their interpretation of the empirical data. A clear account of the materialist view they espouse is definitely in order; [38] more crucial still is the need to enumerate those premises apparently adapted from Classical Economics. In addition, the four dimensions of environment, population, social organization, and technology require further refinements. The concept of "social organization," which Duncan and Schnore tend to equate with "the division of labor," is particularly spongy. And in my judgment these four dimensions are not of the same order, that is, on the same level of analysis. For example, the nature of man's "environment" continues to be redefined as a result of changing technology and social organization; the opposite direction of influence is not likely to be encountered, though the environment presents barriers as well as resources, and it contains other human populations as well as "physical" elements.

Another point of contention in Duncan and Schnore's theorizing is their apparent belief that a value-orientation approach is by nature individualistic (or reductionist). This is doubtful. Values, to be meaningful, must be shared; value systems of necessity are more than individualistic. To study values one must deal with "aggregates." As to the application of the "ecological complex" in actual research, Willhelm contends that both Duncan and Schnore seem to introduce values and other cultural criteria without formally acknowledging this deviation from their theoretical model.[39]

Further comments on the Duncan-Schnore perspective can be introduced in the context of our discussion of the Gibbs-Martin orientation —one that emphasizes sustenance activities rather than the ecological complex. Illustrative of the work of Gibbs and Martin is their study, "Urbanization, Technology, and the Division of Labor." [40] In this they set forth the following propositions:

IA   The degree of urbanization in a society varies directly with the division of labor;

IB   The division of labor in a society varies directly with the dispersion of objects of consumption. . . .

IIA   The degree of urbanization in a society varies directly with technological development;

IIB   Technological development in a society varies directly with the dispersion of objects of consumption.

Another proposition tested in an earlier study—namely, "the degree of urbanization in a society varies directly with the dispersion of objects of consumption"—can then be considered as a theorem "derived" from the preceding postulates. Gibbs and Martin advance one other corollary proposition. They then proceed to test the first four propositions rather than any theorems.

Gibbs and Martin, like Duncan and Schnore, have used their so-called ecological approach to organize an impressive amount of empirical data into some meaningful whole. But they falter when they attempt to theorize concerning their framework, especially in the matter of values. Gibbs and Martin write: [41]

> . . . It may even be true that, *within* certain limits, socio-cultural values and ideologies influence urbanization. But we do reject these phenomena as possible explanations of the particular relationships observed in this study. This would be the case even if a spatial association between urbanization and certain types of values could be demonstrated. It is entirely possible that as urbanization occurs certain values will come to prevail. Unfortunately, this opens the door to future confusion by making it possible at some later date for observers to conclude that the presence of these values explains urbanization.

But the relationship of values to the division of labor (explored by Gibbs and Martin as well as by Duncan and Schnore) merits far more analytical attention than it has received. The argument that values do not enter into the division of labor prompts the question: how can goods and services be exchanged among elements of a labor force unless certain values are shared by the groups involved? In general, people must agree on a "fair price" if an exchange is to be effected; such an agreement often precedes rather than follows the exchange. The assumption that the division of labor can be entirely dissociated from values has not been demonstrated either theoretically or empirically.

Then, too, the theory of Gibbs and Martin, perhaps more than that of Duncan and Schnore, includes a number of implicit assumptions about "economic man" taken over from Classical Economics—for example, the notion that men strive to maximize "profits" or "economic gain" seems to underlie much of the analysis of the division of labor. The relationship between economic theory and the sustenance organization (or the ecological complex) must be elaborated if this theory is to be extended beyond its present quite descriptive state.

In the end, these modern ecologists have confused the study of a substantive problem (for example, the spatial aspect of human action or of social systems) with a particular theoretical perspective.[42] This is likely to stifle interest in alternative approaches to explanation of the spatial dimension of urban activities.

The Economic School

Although the economic orientation is frequently confused with the technological one, and does in fact overlap with it in the works of various social scientists, we treat the proponents of this approach as a separate group.

An important segment of this school, and one to which American sociologists pay little heed, are the Marxists. Social historians in the U. S. S. R. classify cities in terms of Marxian categories: they speak of the slave-owning city, the feudal city, the capitalist city, and the socialist city.[43] Some extensive historical studies of cities have been carried out within this evolutionary framework.[44] It should be informative to observe how neo-Marxist sociologists of the future will modify this orientation to make it more realistic and useful for the analysis of city life.

Another subgroup within the Economic School includes sociologists such as Shevky and Bell and Lacoste who take Colin Clark as their point d'appui.[45] Although Shevky and Bell are known almost solely for their methodology, they have adopted Clark's classification of economies into primary, secondary, and tertiary types under the assumption that these are associated with different kinds of urban ecological and social structures. Shevky and Bell avow that:

> . . . *it is not the city which is an underlying "prime mover" in the recent transformation of Western society, but the necessities of economic expansion itself.* Size, density, and heterogeneity, important in describing the urban ambit, are not the significant *structural* aspects of urbanization—for urbanization is a state of a total society, as well as of its cities.[46]

They speak of an increase in the "scale of society," in the scope of social interaction and dependency, as one moves from primary to tertiary forms of production. The structural indicators of this "increasing scale" are (1) changes in the distribution of skills, (2) changes in the structure of productive activity, and (3) changes in the composition of population.

Applying Colin Clark's formulation to the study of urban phenomena helps us see the city in relation to its broader society. And the distinction between secondary and tertiary kinds of economic activity seems useful for distinguishing between two types of "industrial" cities. But the "social area analysis" of Shevky and Bell has to be employed with caution. We must not assume, for instance, that services (tertiary industries) are unique to advanced industrial cities. There may be proportionately more service occupations in preindustrial than in industrial centers, but the *kinds* of services offered differ markedly in these cities. At the moment, "social area analysis" is little more than a method for manipulating census tract data.

Unfortunately, the proponents of this framework have failed to explicate their theory, and some of their research is only indirectly related to their frame of reference.[47] Greer, who makes much of the increase in the scale of society, neglects to study the impact of the broader societal structure (especially the national political structure) upon the local urban community.[48] Until we possess more satisfactory applications of this theoretical perspective, we must reserve judgment as to its potential utility.

The Environmental School

This school of thought has had little impact in urban sociology; yet its leading exponent is avidly read by social scientists, including some sociologists. We are referring to Lewis Mumford, a product of the Patrick Geddes tradition.

Although Mumford is more a moralizer than a scientist, his primary theme is of interest here. He seems to believe that men must somehow come to terms with "nature." To be sure, Mumford discusses technology from time to time, but his chief preoccupation is with the "natural environment." In his view the city (and its inhabitants), to function effectively, must adjust to or even blend into the world of nature. As such, the natural environment is a determinant, with man necessarily accommodating his technology and social organization to it. For Mumford the crucial problems facing society today are products of an imbalance between nature and human culture, including the city as an artifact. In his recent book, *The City in History,* Mumford looks back on Athens as the ideal community that modern cities should emulate.[49]

Our reservations concerning this thesis are many. Mumford seems to suggest that modern man cannot hope to shape his own destiny and must therefore adjust to the environment rather than strive to control the forces of nature. We disagree with this thesis. And we contend that the major problems facing modern urbanites—above all the possibility of an atomic holocaust—are essentially struggles not of man against nature but of man against man.

The Technological School

Among those sociologists who give primacy to the technological variable, a line can be drawn between those like Hawley and Ogburn who define technology strictly in terms of tools or energy (the "material conditions") and those who incorporate the concept of "know-how." [50] We espouse the latter view: that the knowledge of how to make and utilize tools is as much a part of technology as the tools themselves. From this perspective science can be considered as part of technology.

The empirical research of Ogburn, Hawley, and scholars of like mind has advanced our knowledge of the effect of technology upon the spatial ordering of elements within cities and of cities themselves. Yet some of these writers' generalizations concerning the impact of technology upon the spatial and organizational patterning of cities are not as universal as is often assumed. We would certainly not go as far as Ogburn in stating that ". . . the placement of city populations, residences, and places is singularly a function of local transportation as cities themselves are the creation of long-distance transportation. . . ." [51] So too, Hawley's assertion that "the scatter of population about urban centers is a *direct* response to the increased ease of movement" [52] demands careful qualification.

Considerable data have accumulated suggesting that cultural values and power factors, for example, may induce major distortions in the ideal or actual patterns that supposedly result from technological change. The Dotsons' study of Mexican cities, various works on European cities, and Gist's survey of Bangalore suggest that in these industrializing communities, sociocultural factors have slowed the suburbanization process.[53] The patterns found in American cities certainly are not duplicated in all respects. And observe how the Wall in Berlin, a creation of the political structure, has overridden technological factors in determining migration and residence patterns.

These remarks are not intended to minimize the role of technology, least of all industrial technology, in urban ecology and social organization. Certainly its salience is apparent in any comparison of preindustrial and industrial cities.

The implications of technology for urban life can be studied from several vantage points. Besides contrasting cities in preindustrial civilized (or feudal) societies with those in industrial orders, we might compare the differential impact of industrial urbanization on folk and on preindustrial civilized societies. Primitive orders—whether in Africa or New Guinea or parts of Latin America—lack a written tradition and a well-defined literate elite, traits that characterize feudal societies; consequently they appear to have relatively little potential for resisting the impact of industrial urbanization upon their social structure. A literate elite could be a potent force in conserving the traditional way of life.[54]

Another tack might be to examine the impact of various kinds of technology upon the social patterning of cities. We have already indicated that preindustrial and industrial cities, functioning as they do upon distinctive technological bases, diverge perceptibly in many areas of social organization. We must also seek to determine the differential effects of various stages of industrialization upon urban social structure. A pressing need is to compare the present patterns in developing countries of Asia, Africa, and Latin America with earlier forms in Europe. An examination of the variations in the industrial-urban process over the course of European history would also be a profitable venture.[55] The impact of the industrial-urban complex itself upon the rural hinterland is a research area that must not be ignored. The indications are that advanced industrialization obliterates most of the traditional distinctions between city and country. But which, if any, differences will persist?

A necessary goal, but one that is difficult to achieve, is further clarification of certain pertinent theoretical constructs. Technology should be defined in such a manner as to make it operationally researchable, yet theoretically meaningful. The danger lies in defining technology either too narrowly or so broadly as to make analysis meaningless. (Other issues relating to the use of technology as an independent variable are considered in Chapter 7 of this book.)

The Value-Orientation School

A perspective that is at odds with most of the aforementioned schools stresses values, social or cultural, as the key determinant in the study of urban land use and urban social structure. The writings of Max Weber fall within this tradition.[56] In essence, Weber took the values of sociocultural systems as his explanatory variable and the social structure of the city as his dependent variable. This view was perhaps first elaborated, at least with respect to ecology, in a hitherto obscure and unappreciated article by Znaniecki.[57] More recently

Kolb,[58] applying Parsons' pattern-variable approach, has argued that values are the most significant variable for explaining urban ecological and social organization.

More than any other sociologist, Firey has constructed a sound empirical base for those who would take values as a key determinant of a city's ecology.[59] Drawing upon empirical data from Boston, he contrasted the influence of sentiments (that is, values) with that arising from economic factors. Recently, Willhelm extended and revised Firey's position, arguing that economic factors in themselves are values, and that cultural values alone determine man's adaptation to space. Willhelm clearly details the impact of man's concept of time upon his spatial arrangements.[60]

Although the value-orientation approach has been much criticized, social scientists have amassed impressive if rather unsystematic amounts of data demonstrating that values cannot be ignored. Dickinson's *The West European City*, Jones's *A Social Geography of Belfast*, and von Grunebaum's impressionistic essay on Muslim cities all reinforce elements of Firey's theory.[61]

Indeed, it is when we compare cities in highly divergent cultures that we perceive most clearly how values affect urban ecology. Thus in traditional Muslim cities religious values order temporal activities to a high degree. In each part of the city the muezzin's call to prayer at given times of the day sets the pace for numerous activities. And during the month-long festival of Ramadan, people adjust most of their activities to the religious strictures that impose fasting from dawn to sunset. Many daily pursuits take place at night, whereas other activities, especially in the commercial and manufacturing spheres, necessarily undergo some curtailment. Any approach that ignores values cannot explain ecological patterns of this sort.

Values also influence a city's size, density, and heterogeneity—the very characteristics Wirth used to define the city. In the matter of urban expansion some societies' value systems are more permissive than others. In southern Europe, for instance, certain groups have attempted to slow the advance of industrialization. Weber's observations on the function of religious values in the development of economic enterprise have relevance also for the study of urbanization.[62]

Values affect the development not just of cities in general but of specific kinds of cities. Those like Mecca, Benares, Jerusalem, or Rome largely owe their prominence and persistence over many centuries to the positive religious values assigned to them.[63] And today some nations are building capital cities (for example, Brasilia) as showplaces intended to symbolize the country's progress and independence.

The nexus, however, between values and the internal ecology of cities demands more careful exploration even in the United States, to say nothing of the rest of the world. A study by Whyte,[64] though moralistic, is provocative for its discussion of the relationships between values and the influx of a small but significant number of Americans from the suburbs to the central city. A definite association exists between suburban *versus* central-city living and the values people hold. More important still, Whyte and especially Meadows [65] have explored the interconnection between the ideology of city planners and their proposals for remaking the central city. Certainly the early planning programs such as the Garden City movement in England were motivated by strong negative values toward the industrial city. Purposive city planning (whether locally or nationally inspired) is increasingly shaping urban life in the United States and in Europe, including the Communist bloc. As a result we need many more studies like Orlans' on a planned city in England,[66] and that by Marris on Lagos, Nigeria,[67] detailing how values (along with social power) influence the planning process. Conversely, situations exist where certain values seem to have relatively little effect upon urban land-use patterns.[68]

Many sociologists have proceeded on the assumption that values shape many facets of social structure and social action within the urban context.[69] The notion that the value system is responsible for many of the differences among cities in distinctive cultural settings is explicit in Weber's writings on the city, and in recent decades it has come to dominate the thinking of researchers studying social organization in cross-cultural perspective. But certain drawbacks of this approach call for comment.

First, the precise relationships between values and social structure (or values and ecology) in complex urban communities are difficult to assess. In industrial-urban orders the number of shared values may be few. Drawing upon his own research, Shils observes only tenuous connections between the action patterns of many individuals and subgroups and the more abstract value systems.[70] Certainly it is questionable procedure to assume any one-to-one correspondence between values and the social and ecological organization of urban centers in the United States or any other society.

Second, members of the Value-Orientation School often fail to distinguish among values, ideas, knowledge, beliefs, and the like. To refer to all these varied components of culture as "values," as some writers do, undermines the utility of this frame of reference. Actually, values are those concepts, distinctive of an individual or characteristic of a group, that specify the desirability or undesirability of social phenomena.

Third, an excessive concern with values can lead one to emphasize the differences among cities in various cultures rather than the similarities. Some social scientists assert that special value systems make for unique urban patterns. But my own research on preindustrial cities indicates that for many societies, so-called "unique" cultural patterns in the realms of the family, social class, education, and the like actually have their counterparts in other social orders. This is not to say that the unique should not be sought, but, ultimately, it can be correctly identified only in light of the general.

Sociologists need more satisfactory invariant points of reference by which to assess the impact of values. Parsons' [71] pattern-variable schema—an elaborate effort to isolate a limited number of universal reference points that will hold for all societies—has considerable relevance for the comparative study of urban social structures despite its many evident limitations. Ideally, this approach should enable one to demonstrate that different value systems result in distinctive combinations of pattern variables.

But sociologists can, and must, pursue still other tacks when seeking to isolate universal categories, that is, those that hold for all cities or, more narrowly, for special types such as industrial cities. They can then determine how differing value systems induce deviations from the ideal patterns. This procedure has been followed, at least implicitly, in some ecological studies that have sought to demonstrate that certain "ideal" arrangements wherein complete dominance of the technological or economic variable has been presumed have in fact been distorted by cultural values. The point is that the perspective which gives prominence to cultural values is not necessarily at odds with the Wirth-Redfield schema or with the technological orientation, to cite only two examples; ideally, these latter perspectives should provide us with reference points by which we can measure, in given types of societies, the effects of values upon urban ecology and social organization.

The Social Power School

This group's theoretical schema is the "special interest" approach wherein power becomes the critical independent variable. This was explicitly introduced into urban sociology by Form [72] as a means of explaining urban land-use patterns. Although Form refers to this orientation as a "structural" one, the main variable employed is "social power" as wielded by various groups in the community or nation.

Unfortunately, Form fails to pursue many of the implications of his theory. He focuses upon local community patterns, overlooking the utility of his schema for analyzing the effects of national and international power struggles upon the development of the city, not just in its internal land-use patterns but in its growth and its social organization as well. In fact, a good case can be made for interpreting the entire realm of social planning within the "special interest" frame of reference. With this orientation, and drawing upon existing theories pertaining to competitive group life—for example, the theory of games—one might develop certain general principles about urban life. And though we focus here upon political power, this approach can be extended to cover the effects of social power as wielded by religious or economic or other organizations.

We shall now sketch some of the implications for urban ecology and social organization of political power factors operating on three levels—the local, the national, and the international. Concerning the first of these, Form has discussed the impact of local power decisions upon a city's ecology. This matter has been treated more fully by Meyerson and Banfield, and by Banfield alone.[73] These authors describe how certain land-use patterns are the products of compromise among competing interest groups. Such patterns are prevalent in American cities and undoubtedly find their counterparts in urban centers in other societies. The task that confronts us is that of working out some principles in this sphere that will hold cross-culturally, not just with respect to urban land use but in the area of social organization as well.

A city's ecological structure can be strongly influenced by power decisions on the national level. Recent patterns in the Union of South Africa provide an especially dramatic instance.[74] Here the impact of national power struggles upon the internal spatial and temporal patterns of cities is clearly evident. The national "pass" laws sharply curtail the movement of Natives into, and within, urban centers. Moreover, in recent years large numbers of Natives have been forcibly removed from tracts in and near the centers of cities such as Johannesburg and relocated in newly created communities on the outskirts. In Johannesburg these new sites are miles from the central city, forcing many Natives to travel long distances to their places of employment. Purposive land use changes such as these, seeking as they do to implement the policy of apartheid, demonstrate the futility of interpreting *all* land-use change within frames of reference solely devoted to value orientations or technology. Still less appropriate would be a materialistic or biotic framework. By global standards the cities of South Africa are highly industrialized, but a sizable portion of the urban labor force has been transplanted to residential areas well removed from their occupational situses. This is not a "rational" deployment of workers from the standpoint of furthering industrialization. Nor can values fully account for this large-scale population movement. Although the Afrikaners highly value spatial, and social, apartheid, the Natives have not always relinquished their urban residence voluntarily. Already leading a marginal existence, they have suffered further hardships as a result of their removal to outlying areas. Unquestionably the decisive "intervening variable" permitting these new arrangements has been the social power of the Afrikaners, who wield control of the society's governmental (including military) organization and economic structure. As a result, they are able to put some of their values into practice despite the protests of the Natives, some Britishers, and the governments of other countries.

Power factors on the national level influence not only the city's internal ecology but its growth as well. Historical evidence indicates that the rise and fall of cities has been closely associated and even determined by the rise and fall of empires.[75] More narrowly, many cities today owe their existence to purposive social planning by the national government. In the U. S. S. R. the Communist leadership has sought to promote industrial urbanization in part by obliterating, via the exercise of police powers, the traditional peasant way of life.[76] Although the peasantry resisted for a time, ultimately they had to capitulate. For one thing, the collectivization of farms, by implementing the industrialization of agriculture, made many agriculturists redundant and thus drove them into the urban labor force. In the process the central government gained further control over the agricultural surplus and was thereby enabled to sustain the expanding urban population.

Another facet of this problem is observable in modernizing societies. In India, for example, disagreement exists between certain elements who desire heavy industry and large cities and those who advocate light industries and smaller cities. The course of urban development in India will rest in high degree upon which faction emerges the victor in this struggle.

Power decisions on the national level also affect the urban community's social organization. In the United States the Supreme Court's rulings on desegregation, reinforced by the power of the federal government, have left their clear impress upon the social structure of cities from Little Rock to New Orleans, to Birmingham and beyond. So too, the world over, most notably in countries undergoing purposive social change, the impact of national governmental decisions on the activities of the local urban community's inhabitants can be dramatic. Russia since the Revolution has experienced a vast upheaval in its urban social structure, and the reports filtering out of Communist China indicate that its central government has effected radical transformations in almost every sphere of urban life, but particularly in the intellectual, the political, and the economic realms. The sheer weight of the social power wielded by the Communist oligarchy is obiliterating patterns that were fixed over millennia. No analysis of urban social organization can be deemed adequate unless it considers the impact of the changes initiated and/or reinforced by the vast powers of modern national governments. Nor can we overlook the conflicts between local and national power groups that this process engenders.

The implications for cities of international power struggles have been almost totally ignored by sociologists. But the struggle for dominance among nations has given strong impetus to industrialization and urbanization in many parts of the world. Thus in many developing countries external considerations are forcing modifications in the traditional social organization. In many cases the elite itself is encouraging this process, for if this group is to maintain social status and power on the international level, and if it is to escape subjugation to some new kind of colonialism, it must advance its country's industrial urbanization, even though in the end this elite will undoubtedly suffer some diminution in its power and status within the society. Japan's industrial urbanization, for instance, was stimulated, in part at least, by the ruling group's concern with external status and power considerations.

But what about those power struggles on the international scene that culminate in war? These leave a still firmer impress upon urban centers, as has been amply demonstrated in preindustrial and industrial communities throughout history. The Second World War was certainly no exception. The German occupation of Polish cities, for example, had profound repercussions for their spatial and temporal patterns and their social organization and above all for the ghettos and the very existence of the Jewish population.[77] The procedures and techniques devised by the Nazis to obliterate the Jews (a largely urban population) point to the complexities of the organizational apparatuses that can arise in industrial-urban centers in time of crisis, as well as to the almost insuperable difficulties an urban subgroup may experience. (As a brief aside, we observe that few urban sociologists concerned with social organization in rapidly changing urban communities, particularly organization of the informal sort, have examined the functioning of the underground movements in European cities occupied by the Germans.)

International conflicts have other kinds of repercussions for cities. Berlin, after its division into the Western and Eastern sectors, has developed two quite different ecological and social organizations. Or consider the impact of bombing on cities in Europe and Japan. The possible effects of nuclear weapons upon urban life over the world staggers the imagination. Overall, the implications of social power for urban centers may be implicit in sociological writings, but their fuller theoretical significance awaits exploration.

Interrelationships among the Schools: Special Problems

We have surveyed the dominant theoretical orientations in the field of urban sociology. What can we conclude from this discussion? First, each of these perspectives has certain strengths and weaknesses. None of them, in their present form, can be viewed as adequate. Even researchers who strive toward formal deductive models have failed to explicate some of their key assumptions.

Second, these theoretical orientations can be refined only if urban sociologists pay greater heed to certain problems that inhere in sociological theory. American urban sociology is still primarily intent upon data gathering, not upon building theoretical systems. This preoccupation with particulars, though for many purposes a desideratum, is partly responsible for the reluctance of many sociologists to examine some of the more general issues implied in comparative research. Cross-cultural research demands more abstract categories and analytical techniques than does the study of cities within a single cultural setting. Only at higher levels of abstraction do many of the significant similarities among cities emerge, and, as indicated later, comparative study forces one into the kind of abstract conceptualization that the empiricist might hesitate to undertake.

Third, the interrelationships among the variables employed by the different schools demand careful attention.[78] We have already suggested some of these. Thus the expansion of technology, notably industrialization, not only gives impetus to urbanization but is itself spurred by the growth of cities. Also, definite ties exist between technological advance and the dominant ideology and power structure. A society's value orientation, or ideology, determines to a marked degree the manner in which social power is applied.

Moreover, although certain structural arrangements, with their particular supporting values, appear in all cities at a given level of technology, these configurations may readily be distorted by special constellations of power or values in given societies. But only an awareness of the universal patterns among cities enables us to discern the impact of these "unique" value systems or power arrangements. The unique, after all, is demonstrable only in terms of some general standard. An urgent need is for more careful attention to the social conditions under which particular generalizations seem to hold.

We should also seek to resolve the disagreements between those who stress values and those who emphasize "external conditions" as factors in the spatial and social structure of cities.[79] A necessary step in this direction is the recognition by sociologists that their theoretical assumptions shape their choices of project, their methods, and their analyses; but they must do more. We would like to suggest one possible approach.

A vast amount of evidence has accumulated demonstrating that material objects or artifacts are interpreted differently in divergent cultural settings. Indeed, as Sorokin argues, material objects form part of culture only when they become "vehicles," that is, when they become meaningful to the actor. Yet Sorokin also contends that one's "conceptual system"—for example, his ideas, values, and beliefs—must be objectified in terms of certain vehicles. Although he believes that meanings affect these vehicles and play havoc with their "natural" properties, such vehicles as artifacts and tools simultaneously impose limitations and modifications upon meanings.[80] Indirectly at least, Sorokin suggests that the "external world" sets limits to the kinds of concepts, including values, that can arise and persist.

In line with this reasoning, we offer the following neo-evolutionary hypothesis: *as industrial urbanization proceeds and as the technological environment becomes increasingly complex, the possibility of evaluating one's external environment in a variety of ways is concomitantly lessened.* Thus preliterate societies display a very wide variety of values in, for example, the familial, political, and religious spheres. In contrast to this, values, ideas and beliefs in industrial-urban systems are more circumscribed. After all, the "vehicles" in this setting are highly complex. If a society is to sustain atomic research facilities, mass transportation and communication, and a host of other advanced technologies, certain cultural values seem mandatory. One must positively value not only the complex tools but the scientific knowledge which is an integral part of this technology. Consequently, it is in the scientific-technological-economic sphere that specific values are most frequently shared across sociocultural systems. As one enters the realm of religion and the cultural arts, one can expect to find a greater variety of values among industrial-urban systems.[81]

Formulating and Testing Hypotheses in a Comparative Setting

The logical query is: what next? Because sociologists still have so much to learn about comparative analysis, it is likely that their energies in the years to come will be devoted primarily to formulating more adequate propositions, to engaging in discovery rather than in the formal testing of well-defined hypotheses. But this last must not be neglected; especially do we need to test those hypotheses that form part of some logico-deductive model.

As we observed earlier, however, the impediments to effective comparative research are such that a rigorous testing of many hypotheses will probably not be accomplished to the satisfaction of the more rigorous empiricists. A harsh fact is that a number of research techniques currently in favor among urban sociologists are not readily exportable to other cultural settings; they have been formulated to fit a constellation of traits that are rather unique to American cities. Warner's Index of Status Characteristics is a case in point.[82] Here the occupational category can be applied cross-culturally to evaluate social status or class position, but those relating to house type and dwelling area and, by implication, housing seem to be poor indices of social status in, say, contemporary Russian cities.[83] A realistic portrayal of the status or class configuration of cities in other societies (assuming that comparable data are available in the first instance) would require drastic revision of Warner's method. Similarly, the various segregation indices, the Shevky-Williams-Bell technique, perhaps even the Queen and Carpenter urbanism index [84]—all of which have gained acceptance among sociologists in many quarters—must be substantially altered before they can be utilized in certain social orders, and in some societies they appear not to be applicable at all. For one thing, these devices presuppose methods of data collection that are realized in relatively few societies. The Shevky-Williams-Bell technique, for example, has been criticized by sociologists on several counts, but its most glaring defect is its culture-boundedness.[85] Its effectiveness rests upon the availability of certain types of data assembled in a specified manner, particularly in terms of census tracts or similar areal units. To reiterate, these techniques have proved their general usefulness for certain research purposes in societies like the United States, but their utility in cross-cultural study appears to be sharply limited at the present time.

Urban sociologists also face problems when they must rely upon data gathered by non-social scientists, notably government functionaries. As we stressed earlier, industrial-urban societies must amass prodigious bodies of information in order to plan rationally and function efficiently. Even in the United States, where untold numbers of questionnaires are distributed by public and private agencies, the demand for data still seems to exceed the supply. Because of their limited numbers and scanty resources, social scientists must rely upon these materials when studying certain problems.

Government bureaucrats, however, are rarely interested in collecting information specifically directed to scientific generalization on a worldwide basis. They are more often concerned with data bearing on the industrialization and urbanization of their own societies. Even in the United States and other advanced industrial countries, a great deal of social-scientific research is geared to the requirements of governmental and other bureaucracies as these seek to resolve specific problems. Pertinent in this regard is Shryock's discussion of the pressures exerted on the United States Bureau of the Census as it has devised classificatory schemes such as the Standard Metropolitan Area (SMA). For reasons of prestige, Chambers of Commerce all over the country vie to have their particular communities included in the classification, and many exert pressures for greater elasticity in the classification scheme—pressures that threaten to undermine the "scientific validity" of the SMA concept.[86]

The problems of gaining adequate standardized data are greatly magnified, of course, in comparative study. The cross-cultural consistency that does exist in such matters as census categories is mainly attributable to the efforts of United Nations agencies. Perhaps more significant is the fact that industrial-urban communities and societies around the world must deal with similar social problems.

Another quite formidable barrier to research in many societies is the resistance of the leaders to the activities of social scientists. The use of rigorous research procedures within and among societies thereby becomes circumscribed. For our knowledge of Chinese cities today, to cite an instance, we must often resort to indirect sources such as the comments of foreign visitors to China, interviews with refugees, the observations of newspapermen, and the writings of Chinese laymen. All nations restrict, in varying degrees, the dissemination of official governmental data, including census materials. Even in the United States sociologists can hardly probe with impunity into any and all facets of urban life. In certain instances indirect evidence is the best that can be obtained. But a source of optimism lies in the fact that the range of freedom for social research in industrial-urban orders seems to be expanding rather than contracting. One reason for this is that a great deal of data on the operation of the industrial order must be diffused if modern cities are to function effectively.

What is mandatory is a realistic appraisal of the methodology of scientific inquiry as it relates to cross-cultural research. Through ingenious use of census materials obtained from numerous societies, Jack Gibbs [87] has been able to examine certain aspects of world urbanization, and by piecing together scattered materials, Inkeles and Rossi [88] have advanced our knowledge of the comparative ranking of occupations in industrial-urban societies. Cross-cultural studies of this kind, however, treat only a relatively narrow range of problems, and the empirical categories employed generally permit only gross comparisons.

The methodology of comparative inquiry needs rethinking, and urban sociologists must prepare to assist in this task. Although Max Weber's ideal type and Howard Becker's constructed type [89] have been much criticized, we must not minimize the utility of typologies in comparative study. Plainly, we need some conceptual tools to bridge the gaps between data that are not strictly comparable on an empirical plane. Moreover, sociologists should make greater use of the "negative case" method. We agree with Karl Popper that one can disprove a scientific hypothesis but can never prove one with finality.[90] In light of this, we need more research aimed at refuting or setting limits to existing propositions. Moreover, we can use the negative case approach to set up careful research designs that can be duplicated by social scientists in other societies. In essence we must use some modification of Florian Znaniecki's "method of analytical induction." [91] Possessing only limited time and resources and facing the special difficulties of comparative research, sociologists should seek out strategic negative cases with an eye to refuting existing notions and replacing them with more tenable generalizations. At the very least, this procedure should reduce considerably our area of ignorance.

NOTES

1. For a related but distinct discussion, see Gideon Sjoberg, "Comparative Urban Sociology," in Robert K. Merton et al. (Eds.), *Sociology Today* (New York: Basic Books, 1959), pp. 334–359.

2. See Albert J. Reiss, Jr., "The Sociology of Urban Life: 1946–1956," in Paul K. Hatt and Albert J. Reiss, Jr. (Eds.), *Cities and Society: The Revised Reader in Urban Sociology* (New York: Free Press of Glencoe, 1957),

pp. 3–11; Noel P. Gist, "The Urban Community," in Joseph B. Gittler (Ed.), *Review of Sociology: Analysis of a Decade* (New York: Wiley, 1957), Chap. 6; Ruth Glass, "Urban Sociology in Great Britain: A Trend Report," *Current Sociology*, 4 (1955), pp. 5–19; Philip M. Hauser, "Ecological Aspects of Urban Research," in Leonard D. White (Ed.), *The State of the Social Sciences* (Chicago: University of Chicago Press, 1956), pp. 229–254.

3. We have only to read Scott Greer's theoretical effort, *The Emerging City* (New York: Free Press of Glencoe, 1962), to observe how little attention some writers give to cities in other societies.

4. Reiss, *op. cit.*, pp. 10–11.

5. The cleavage between the "materialists" and the "nonmaterialists" in sociology is generally ignored in survey studies dealing with social theory; see, for example, Don Martindale, *The Nature and Types of Sociological Theory* (Boston: Houghton Mifflin, 1960). But this neglect is not an index of its importance, for the differing assumptions about reality influence one's choice of research problem and explanatory variables. The "materialists," who differ to some degree among themselves, reject the study of values, attitudes, ideas, or beliefs or else seek to predict these by studying objective conditions. Moreover, they tend to examine the social order in highly mechanistic terms. A comparison of "materialists" and "nonmaterialists" is complicated by the heterogeneity of the latter. Included within this category are those who study values and ideas within a mechanistic framework and those who employ a more voluntaristic orientation. Although a detailed examination of these issues lies beyond the scope of this essay, our comparison of the Subsocial or the Ecological Complex (or Sustenance) School with the Value-Orientation School suggests some of the divergencies between the "materialists" and "nonmaterialists" in urban sociology.

6. See Robert E. Park, *Human Communities* (New York: Free Press of Glencoe, 1952).

7. Georg Simmel, "The Metropolis and Mental Life," in Hatt and Reiss, *op. cit.*, pp. 635–646; Henry Sumner Maine, *Ancient Law* (London: J. Murray, 1930); Emile Durkheim, *The Division of Labor in Society*, trans. and ed. by George Simpson (Glencoe, Ill.: Free Press, 1947); Max Weber, *The City*, trans. and ed. by Don Martindale and Gertrud Neuwirth (New York: Free Press of Glencoe, 1958); Ferdinand Tönnies, *Fundamental Concepts of Sociology*, trans. and supplemented by Charles P. Loomis (New York: American Book Co., 1940).

8. Louis Wirth, "Urbanism as a Way of Life," in Hatt and Reiss, *op. cit.*, pp. 46–63.

9. Robert Redfield, *The Folk Culture of Yucatán* (Chicago: University of Chicago Press, 1941). In some respects Redfield's definition of the "city" makes him less "materialistic" than Wirth.

10. Robert J. Smith, "Pre-Industrial Urbanism in Japan: A Consideration of Multiple Traditions in a Feudal Society," in Thomas C. Smith (Ed.), *City and Village in Japan*, Part II of *Economic Development and Cultural Change*, 9 (October 1960), pp. 241–257. It should be stressed that Smith does qualify the Wirth position in terms of recent research findings. Some scholars continue to adhere quite closely to the traditional Wirth framework; see, for example, Marshall B. Clinard, "A Cross-Cultural Replication of the

Relation of Urbanism to Criminal Behavior," *American Sociological Review,* 25 (1960), pp. 253–257.

11. Joseph Bensman and Bernard Rosenberg, *Mass, Class, and Bureaucracy* (Englewood Cliffs, N. J.: Prentice-Hall, 1963); Maurice R. Stein, *The Eclipse of Community* (Princeton: Princeton University Press, 1960).

12. Nicholas Babchuk and C. Wayne Gordon, *The Voluntary Association in the Slum,* University of Nebraska Studies, No. 27 (Lincoln: University of Nebraska, 1962); William F. Whyte, *Street Corner Society* (Chicago: University of Chicago Press, 1943); Herbert J. Gans, *The Urban Villagers* (New York: Free Press of Glencoe, 1962).

13. Harvey W. Zorbaugh, *The Gold Coast and the Slum* (Chicago: University of Chicago Press, 1929).

14. In fairness to the early Chicago sociologists, we must recognize that certain researchers did perceive recurrent social patterns within the urban slum; see, for example, Nels Anderson, *The Hobo* (Chicago: University of Chicago Press, 1923).

15. Daniel R. Miller and Guy E. Swanson, *The Changing American Parent* (New York: Wiley, 1958).

16. Oscar Lewis, "Urbanization Without Breakdown: A Case Study," *Scientific Monthly,* 75 (1952), pp. 31–41. At the same time, life in the urban slum in Mexico City may exhibit considerable instability; see Oscar Lewis, *The Children of Sánchez* (New York: Random House, 1961).

17. A. L. Epstein, *Politics in an Urban African Community* (Manchester: Manchester University Press, 1958); Aidan Southall (Ed.), *Social Change in Modern Africa* (London: Oxford University Press, 1961); Peter Marris, *Family and Social Change in an African City* (Evanston: Northwestern University Press, 1962).

18. Roger Le Tourneau, *Fès: Avant le Protectorat* (Casablanca: Société Marocaine de Librairie et d'Edition, 1949); Horace Miner, *The Primitive City of Timbuctoo* (Princeton: Princeton University Press, 1953).

19. See Robert Redfield, *Peasant Society and Culture* (Chicago: University of Chicago Press, 1956). Actually, in one of his articles, written with Milton Singer, "The Cultural Role of Cities," *Economic Development and Cultural Change,* 3 (1954), pp. 53–73, Redfield implicitly abandons the notion that the city is the key independent variable.

20. K. M. Kapadia, "Rural Family Patterns: A Study of Urban-Rural Relations," *Sociological Bulletin,* 5 (1956), p. 119; S. C. Dube, *Indian Village* (Ithaca: Cornell University Press, 1955), p. 133. Other deviations from American urban-rural differences occur in family patterns in India. There appear to be rather insignificant urban-rural differentials in the total number of children born to women who were married during 1930–1939; see Philip M. Hauser (Ed.), *Urbanization in Asia and the Far East* (Calcutta: UNESCO, 1957), pp. 117–118.

21. Henri Pirenne, *Medieval Cities* (Princeton: Princeton University Press, 1925).

22. The study of rural-urban differences has generated a vast literature, and much research will no doubt be carried out along these lines in modernizing societies. See Michael Kenny, *A Spanish Tapestry* (Bloomington: Indiana University Press, 1962), and R. D. Lambert, "The Impact of Urban Society Upon Village Life," in Roy Turner (Ed.), *India's Urban Future*

(Berkeley: University of California Press, 1962), pp. 117–140. In fact, such studies still have significance: consider the rural-urban differences in industrial societies, as exemplified in Otis Dudley Duncan and Albert J. Reiss, Jr., *Social Characteristics of Urban and Rural Communities, 1950* (New York: Wiley, 1956).

23. Ralph Beals, "Urbanism, Urbanization and Acculturation," *American Anthropologist,* 53 (1951), pp. 1–10.

24. Wirth, *op. cit.*; Redfield, *op. cit.*

25. See Hope Tisdale, "The Process of Urbanization," *Social Forces,* 20 (1942), pp. 311–316; Harley L. Browning, "Urbanization in Mexico," unpublished Ph.D. dissertation, University of California (Berkeley), 1962; Duncan and Reiss, *op. cit.*

26. "Urbanization is a process of population concentration. It proceeds in two ways: the multiplication of points of concentration and the increase in size of individual concentrations." This is the definition set forth by Tisdale, *op. cit.*, p. 311.

27. Kent P. Schwirian and John W. Prehn, "An Axiomatic Theory of Urbanization," *American Sociological Review,* 27 (1962), pp. 812–825.

28. Tisdale, *op. cit.*

29. Robert Ezra Park, "Human Ecology," and Ernest W. Burgess, "The Growth of the City: An Introduction to a Research Project," in George A. Theodorson (Ed.), *Studies in Human Ecology* (Evanston: Row Peterson, 1961), pp. 22–29 and 37–44.

30. Walter Firey, *Land Use in Central Boston* (Cambridge: Harvard University Press, 1947).

31. *Ibid.*

32. Sidney M. Willhelm and Gideon Sjoberg, "Economic vs. Protective Values in Urban Land Use Change," *American Journal of Economics and Sociology,* 19 (1960), pp. 151–160.

33. For example, Amos H. Hawley, *Human Ecology* (New York: Ronald Press, 1950).

34. In oversimplified terms, the researcher who stresses "discovery" analyzes data with an eye to formulating or generating hypotheses. The patterns emerge out of the analysis. See Norwood Hanson, *Patterns of Discovery* (Cambridge: Cambridge University Press, 1958). In "deduction," ideally we have a set of logically interrelated postulates from which hypotheses are derived. We proceed to test the hypotheses, and this automatically involves a test of the postulates. See Karl Popper, *The Logic of Scientific Discovery* (New York: Science Editions, 1961). I refer to Gibbs and Martin's approach as "neo-deductive" because they seem to test their "postulates" directly.

35. Otis Dudley Duncan and Leo F. Schnore, "Cultural, Behavioral, and Ecological Perspectives in the Study of Social Organization," *American Journal of Sociology,* 65 (1959), pp. 132–146; Otis Dudley Duncan, "Human Ecology and Population Studies," in Philip M. Hauser and Otis Dudley Duncan (Eds.), *The Study of Population* (Chicago: University of Chicago Press, 1959), pp. 678–716; Leo F. Schnore, "Social Morphology and Human Ecology," *American Journal of Sociology,* 63 (1958), pp. 620–634. The most explicit criticism of the Duncan-Schnore position is Sidney

M. Willhelm, "The Concept of the 'Ecological Complex': A Critique," *American Journal of Economics and Sociology*, 23 (1964), pp. 241–248.

36. Otis Dudley Duncan et al., *Metropolis and Region* (Baltimore: Johns Hopkins University Press, 1960).

37. Leo F. Schnore, "Urban Form: The Case of the Metropolitan Community," in Werner Z. Hirsch (Ed.), *Urban Life and Form* (New York: Holt, Rinehart and Winston, 1963), pp. 167–197; Leo F. Schnore, "Social Problems in the Underdeveloped Areas," *Social Problems*, 8 (1961), pp. 182–201; Leo F. Schnore, "The Statistical Measurement of Urbanization and Economic Development," *Land Economics*, 37 (1961), pp. 229–245.

38. Some of the assumptions underlying the materialist view of society can be found in A. K. Saran, "The Marxian Theory of Social Change," *Inquiry*, 6 (1963), pp. 70–128.

39. Sidney M. Willhelm, *Urban Zoning and Land-Use Theory* (New York: Free Press of Glencoe, 1962), pp. 25–26.

40. Jack P. Gibbs and Walter T. Martin, "Urbanization, Technology, and the Division of Labor: International Patterns," *American Sociological Review*, 27 (1962), pp. 667–677. Also, Jack P. Gibbs and Walter T. Martin, "Toward a Theoretical System of Human Ecology," *Pacific Sociological Review*, 2 (1959), pp. 29–36.

41. Gibbs and Martin, "Urbanization, Technology, and the Division of Labor," *op. cit.*, p. 677. In light of this general comment, it is interesting that Gibbs and Martin include certain knowledge and *beliefs* in their definition of technology (p. 672). Would not a belief system regarding technology be an ideology?

42. Materialism as a theory should be openly represented in sociology, but to equate it with ecology is likely only to confuse the issues involved.

43. "Gorod," *Bol'shaya Sovetskaya Entsiklopediya*, XII, 2nd ed. (Moskva: Gosudarstvennoe nauchnoe izdatel'stvo, 1952), pp. 172ff.

44. SH.A. Meskhia, *Goroda i Gorodskoĭ Stroĭ Feodal'noĭ Gruzii: XVII–XVIII vv.* (Tbilisi, U. S. S. R.: Izdatel'stvo Tbilisskogo Gosudarstvennogo Universiteta Imeni Stalina, 1959).

45. Eshref Shevky and Wendell Bell, *Social Area Analysis: Theory, Illustrative Application, and Computational Procedures* (Stanford: Stanford University Press, 1955); Norbert Lacoste, *Les Caractéristiques Sociales de la Population du Grand Montréal* (Montréal: Université de Montréal, 1958); Surinder K. Mehta, "A Comparative Analysis of the Industrial Structure of the Urban Labor Force of Burma and the United States," *Economic Development and Cultural Change*, 9 (1961), pp. 164–179.

46. Shevky and Bell, *op. cit.*, p. 8.

47. See Amos H. Hawley and Otis Dudley Duncan, "Social Area Analysis: A Critical Appraisal," *Land Economics*, 33 (1957), pp. 337–344, and the *Pacific Sociological Review*, 5 (1962), with the debate among Bell and Greer, Van Arsdol et al., and Schnore.

48. Greer, *op. cit.*

49. Lewis Mumford, *The City in History* (New York: Harcourt, Brace & World, 1961).

50. Hawley, *op. cit.*; William F. Ogburn, "Inventions of Local Transportation and the Patterns of Cities," in Hatt and Reiss, *op. cit.*, pp. 274–

282; Fred Cottrell, *Energy and Society* (New York: McGraw-Hill, 1955).

51. Ogburn, *op. cit.*, p. 281.

52. Hawley, *op. cit.*, p. 421, italics added.

53. For example, Noel P. Gist, "The Ecology of Bangalore, India: An East-West Comparison," *Social Forces*, 35 (1957), pp. 356–365; Floyd Dotson and Lillian Ota Dotson, "Urban Centralization and Decentralization in Mexico," *Rural Sociology*, 21 (1956), pp. 41–49; Emrys Jones, *A Social Geography of Belfast* (London: Oxford University Press, 1960).

54. The difficulties that nonliterate groups face in coping with modern changes can be inferred from the data in Melville J. Herskovits, *The Human Factor in Changing Africa* (New York: Knopf, 1962).

55. Some of these variations can be inferred from David S. Landes, "The Structure of Enterprise in the Nineteenth Century: The Cases of Britain and Germany," Reprint No. 152, Institute of Industrial Relations, Berkeley, University of California, 1960.

56. Weber, *op. cit.*

57. Florian Znaniecki, "The Sociological Approach to Rural and Urban Ecology," *Arbeiten des XIV. Internationalen Soziologen Kongresses.* Bucuresti, Mitteilungen, Abteilung D.—Stadt und Land, I (1939?), pp. 147–166.

58. William L. Kolb, "The Social Structure and Function of Cities," *Economic Development and Cultural Change*, 3 (1954), pp. 3–46.

59. Firey, *op. cit.*

60. Willhelm, *Urban Zoning and Land-Use Theory, op. cit., passim.*

61. Robert E. Dickinson, *The West European City* (London: Routledge and Kegan Paul, 1951); G. E. von Grunebaum, *Islam* (Menasha: American Anthropological Association, Memoir No. 81, 1955), Chap. 8; Jones, *op. cit.* Also, Jack C. Fisher, "The Continuity of Urban Patterns Under Socialism," Ann Arbor: University Microfilms, 1962. Fisher clearly demonstrates the importance of tradition in determining land-use patterns in Yugoslavian cities.

62. Max Weber, *The Protestant Ethic and the Spirit of Capitalism* (London: George Allen and Unwin, 1930). Cf. Robert N. Bellah, *Tokugawa Religion* (New York: Free Press of Glencoe, 1957).

63. See C. Snouck Hurgronje, *Mekka in the Latter Part of the Nineteenth Century*, trans. by J. H. Monahan (London: Luzac, 1931).

64. Editors of Fortune, *The Exploding Metropolis* (Garden City: Doubleday, 1958).

65. Paul Meadows, "The Urbanists: Profiles of Professional Ideologies," *1963 Yearbook, School of Architecture* (Syracuse: Syracuse University, forthcoming). Also see Jane Jacobs, *The Death and Life of Great American Cities* (New York: Random House, 1961), and the controversies surrounding this work.

66. Harold Orlans, *Stevenage* (London: Routledge & Kegan Paul, 1952).

67. Marris, *op. cit.* For example, Marris observes that one argument for slum clearance was that "Central Lagos was the heart of the Federal capital, and its development was urgent for the sake of national pride" (p. 90).

68. See Fisher's discussion, *op. cit.*, of the impact of the Communist ideology and value system upon the older cities of Yugoslavia.

69. Values have constituted the key independent variable in the works of Weber, Parsons, Sorokin, and many others.

70. Edward Shils, "Primordial, Personal, Sacred and Civil Ties," *British Journal of Sociology*, 8 (1957), pp. 130–145.

71. Talcott Parsons, *The Social System* (New York: Free Press of Glencoe, 1951).

72. William H. Form, "The Place of Social Structure in the Determination of Land Use: Some Implications for a Theory of Urban Ecology," *Social Forces*, 32 (1954), pp. 317–323.

73. Martin Meyerson and Edward C. Banfield, *Politics, Planning and the Public Interest* (New York: Free Press of Glencoe, 1955); Edward C. Banfield, *Political Influence* (New York: Free Press of Glencoe, 1961). In general, the idea of a monolithic power structure, as propounded by Floyd Hunter and others, is of little value for interpreting or analyzing the social structure and ecology of most industrial cities. See Floyd Hunter, *Community Power Structure* (Chapel Hill: University of North Carolina Press, 1953).

74. For example, Leo Kuper et al., *Durban: A Study in Racial Ecology* (New York: Columbia University Press, 1958); "Johannesburg Pushes Apartheid Evacuations," *Christian Science Monitor*, August 29, 1956, p. 6; Colin Legum, "South Africa: The West at Bay," *The Nation*, 197 (August 10, 1963), pp. 70–73.

75. Gideon Sjoberg, "The Rise and Fall of Cities: A Theoretical Perspective," *International Journal of Comparative Sociology*, 4 (1963), pp. 107–120.

76. Barrington Moore, Jr., *Terror and Progress: USSR* (Cambridge: Harvard University Press, 1954), Chaps. 2 and 3.

77. Emmanuel Ringelblum, *Notes from the Warsaw Ghetto*, trans. and ed. by Jacob Sloan (New York: McGraw-Hill, 1958); Raul Hilberg, *The Destruction of the European Jews* (Chicago: Quadrangle Books, 1961).

78. For a somewhat different perspective on these matters, see Leonard Reissman, "Class, the City, and Social Cohesion," *International Review of Community Development*, No. 7 (1961), pp. 39–51. Also, William M. Dobriner, *Class in Suburbia* (Englewood Cliffs, N. J.: Prentice-Hall, 1963).

79. More generally, the "phenomenological" orientation of Alfred Schutz may well offer one avenue of escape from the "idealist" vs. "materialist" dilemma. See Alfred Schutz, *Collected Papers, I, The Problem of Social Reality* (The Hague: Martinus Nijhoff, 1962). To Schutz, the "fundamental reality" resides neither in material objects nor in ideas or concepts (including values) but in the interrelationships between the two.

80. Pitirim Sorokin, *Social and Cultural Dynamics*, Vol. IV (New York: American Book Co., 1941), pp. 165–167.

81. The fact that science and technology are highly cumulative would seem to account in part for some of these patterns. It is interesting that Sorokin, who has attacked the "material-nonmaterial" dichotomy, is forced to admit, in the face of criticism, this special feature of the scientific-technological sphere. P. J. Allen (Ed.), *Pitirim A. Sorokin in Review* (Durham: Duke University Press, 1963), p. 427.

82. W. Lloyd Warner et al., *Social Class in America: A Manual of Procedure for the Measurement of Social Status* (Chicago: Science Research Associates, 1949).

83. Robert A. Feldmesser, "Social Status and Access to Higher Educa-

tion: A Comparison of the United States and the Soviet Union," *Harvard Educational Review*, 27 (1957), p. 98. Cf. Ellen Hellmann, *Racial Laws versus Economic and Social Forces* (Johannesburg: South African Institute of Race Relations, 1955), p. 20.

84. Shevky and Bell, *op. cit.;* Stuart A. Queen and David B. Carpenter, *The American City* (New York: McGraw-Hill, 1953).

85. The Shevky-Bell procedure can be used in studying cities with appropriate data in other societies. See Dennis C. McElrath, "The Social Areas of Rome: A Comparative Analysis," *American Sociological Review*, 27 (1962), pp. 376–391.

86. Henry S. Shryock, Jr., "The Natural History of Standard Metropolitan Areas," *American Journal of Sociology*, 63 (1957), pp. 163–170.

87. Jack P. Gibbs (Ed.), *Urban Research Methods* (Princeton: Van Nostrand, 1961).

88. Alex Inkeles and Peter H. Rossi, "National Comparisons of Occupational Prestige," *American Journal of Sociology*, 61 (1956), pp. 329–339.

89. For a discussion of typologies, see John C. McKinney, "Constructive Typology and Social Research," in John T. Doby (Ed.), *An Introduction to Social Research* (Harrisburg: Stackpole, 1954), Chap. 7.

90. Popper, *op. cit.*

91. Florian Znaniecki, *The Method of Sociology* (New York: Farrar and Rinehart, 1934).

Economic Aspects of Urban Research*

Raymond Vernon and Edgar M. Hoover

Some Distinctive Characteristics of Urban Economics

Anyone examining current work on spatial patterns within urban areas is likely to be struck by the interdisciplinary nature of the attack. On the basis of perusing a specific analysis it is often impossible to determine whether the author is nominally an urban economist, an urban geographer, an urban ecologist, an "urban regional scientist," or even just an "urbanist." All have jumped into a common pool, though from different spots on the bank. For this reason, it would be redundant to catalogue here the kinds of work that economists are doing on spatial patterns within urban areas, or the ways in which economic analysis is being applied in such areas by urban social scientists of various disciplinary origins. Indeed, the greater part of that effort has already been described in other chapters of this book, particularly those by Mayer, Berry, and Schnore.

There are, however, some specific emphases that characterize the "economic" approach, tending to be more prominent in the work of those who call themselves urban economists. Comparing the "economic" approach with the usual "geographic" approach, the former is less content to rest upon "explanations" that are essentially statistical measures of observed relations among spatial patterns, such as "gravity models," the "minimum-requirements" method for estimating community economic bases, the "rank-size" rule, and much of the empirical work involving central-place patterns.[1] As a discipline, economics characteristically looks for explanations in terms of the behavior of actual decision units. The decision units may be individuals or households, business firms or municipal governments, or even labor unions and business associations.

Economists assume that decisions made by these units reflect certain economic aims of the decision-making parties. They also assume that there are broader collective aims that do guide or should guide the economic behavior of particular interest groups and of the urban community as a whole. This assumption implies not merely that alternative urban spatial patterns can be described, explained, and (within limits) forecast; it also implies that such patterns can and should be evaluated in terms of their relative efficiency in meeting such postulated economic aims as higher output per unit of labor employed, fuller employment, greater economic stability and security, or higher average levels of per capita real income. This kind of evaluation is seen in the chapter by Thompson.[2]

An economic analytical model of urban spatial structure or growth ideally incorporates "optimization" on the part of the individual decision units involved; and an economic normative model introduces optimization for the community or other group whose economic welfare is the concern of those public policies for which guidance is sought. Among present alternatives, linear programming is perhaps the most mathematically elegant way of applying such normative criteria, and economists are attempting to use it operationally in urban studies that seek to guide policies on land use and transportation planning in particular.[3] Less elegant but more flexible techniques assessing "costs and benefits" of specific changes in urban patterns are more widely used.[4]

Another concept basic to the economic approach is that of prices and markets for goods and services, including land. Concentric-ring patterns of land use and hierarchies of central places are explained in terms of a price mechanism in the writings of von Thünen, Lösch, and Isard, and similar explanations of these and other patterns occur in the work of land economists and housing market analysts. It would obviously be impossible to apply any principles of economic motivation, or to evaluate the efficiency of an urban development project, pattern, or plan, without specifically examining the prices at which goods and services are exchanged and the ways in which supply and demand interact with those prices.

The peculiarly economic approach to urban analysis, then, considers the economy of the urban community as a complex of markets for land, labor, housing, and goods and services. Moreover, it views the economic "pathology" of urban areas in terms of malfunctioning of some of those markets. A wealth of analysis already exists on the positive and inertial forces operating in markets for urban real estate, particularly housing.[5] Labor economists have devoted much effort to analyzing the determination of wages in urban "labor market areas."[6]

Until very recently, however, not much attention has been paid by economists to the market for urban internal transportation, which has come to the fore as perhaps the most vexing urban problem. Economists have begun to ask why that market works so badly, and what new kinds of policy might produce more acceptable solutions. William H. Vickrey and others have tended to stress the economic rule that prices produce socially efficient utilization of resources only if these prices reflect the principal social costs and benefits entailed; some of these writers argue that a major part of the costs involved in the use of private automobile transport in congested urban areas are not presently assessed upon the drivers involved in such a way as to restrain adequately their use of scarce and expensive space and public facilities. These economists have concluded that the economic efficiency of urban areas would be improved by various devices to rectify the allocation of costs, especially (1) between public-transit users and users of private automobiles, (2) between travelers in more congested versus less congested parts of the urban area, and (3) between peak-hour and off-peak travelers and parkers.[7]

Thus economic tools of analysis are peculiarly adapted (1) to exploring causal factors as distinct from empirical relationships in space, (2) to evaluating the merits of alternatives on at least a rough cost-benefit basis, and (3) to suggesting ways of letting a semiautomatic market mechanism help to provide acceptable allocations of resources. These strengths of economic analysis have encouraged its use in applied research designed to project future regional growth and development patterns under various policy alternatives and to guide public policy. It is already clear that economists can produce something more adequate than the more usual types of "economic base studies" and "transportation studies." The former have been largely descriptive in character, and have rested on the relatively primitive analytical basis of "export" earnings and an extension of the "foreign-trade multiplier" concept.[8] The latter have been addressed essentially to the problem of minimum-cost provision of facilities for postulated patterns of residences and trip destinations.[9] The narrowly conceived transportation study has two grave deficiencies. First, it fails to take into account the fact that spatial development patterns themselves are determined to a large extent by the availability of transport facilities. Second, it often (though not always) relies on mechanical projection of historical trends in travel habits, including choice of mode and distance of journey, thus assuming away the question of whether these trends might be modified by altered allocation of the private and social costs of urban transport, as alluded to earlier.

Elements of what we have characterized here as the distinctively economic approach to intra-urban spatial analysis have played a role in a number of recent and current studies of major metropolitan areas in the United States—of which those in the New York, Philadelphia, and Pittsburgh areas can be cited as leading examples.[10] In these studies, the internal spatial pattern is viewed in terms of a limited number of categories of residential and nonresidential occupance which have more or less interdependent locational patterns. Types of occupance with similar locational preferences are lumped together for practical reasons. As a result, there tends to emerge a simple breakdown of residence occupance on the basis of income, occupational status, race, and household size, and a breakdown of nonresidential activities on the basis of the relative importance of various intra-urban locational factors such as need for close contact, access to terminals for transport to the outside world, proximity to a diversified or to a specialized labor pool, or cheap land. The costs of space and of certain services are examined as part of the pricing mechanism that allocates various types of land occupance in relation to the central business district and other focal points. Conceptually, this approach is in the direct line of descent from von Thünen, though it is complicated by such realistic considerations as structural inertia and obsolescence, multiple foci of movement, and the locational interdependence of related activities.

Such studies as those cited show significant progress in the formulation of economic models of intra-urban spatial structure and change. As yet, however, no "optimizing" model incorporating linear programming has been brought to an operational stage. Nevertheless, the Penn-Jersey Transportation Study in the Philadelphia area is working in that direction, and work in the Pittsburgh area is likewise developing a fairly sophisticated mechanism.[11] In any case, formal quantitative models are being employed with increasing frequency.

Economic studies of urban regions are employing economic analysis to increasing effect in developing projections of future change and in evaluating the impact of alternative developments and policies. This effort includes explicit allowance for the local effects of foreseeable national economic trends of growth, together with changes in technology and location. Another noteworthy feature is more discerning analysis of the operations of regional real estate, transportation, and labor markets. There is also greater appreciation of the relation between regional development and local public finance. Finally, new applications of locational economics are being made to activities in which local communication and contact needs play a primary role. Some of these matters are taken up in more detail in the next section of this chapter.

Some Comments on Methodology

The techniques for conceptualizing and measuring the process of urban development and urban change run the gamut of statistical method, from the crudest time-series analysis to the most sophisticated applications of factor analysis and input-output matrices. This is not the place for an exhaustive analysis of the strengths and weaknesses of all these techniques, but there are some observations worth making which have special application to urban studies.[12]

Models and Systems

Since the beginnings of modern research on the character and causes of urban agglomerations, a major thread of effort has been devoted to trying to find some generalized formula expressing the size of the urban clusters likely to be found in any economy. Professor Berry's chapter in this book provides an admirable summary of the recent work done along these lines.[13]

One wonders, however, whether the preoccupation with systems of this sort, so ingeniously pursued by so many researchers in the urban field, has not come to represent a misallocation of scarce ingenuity. Some of the reasons for the attraction to such systems are clear enough. To the mind that insists on clarity and rigor, the pursuit of research in the social sciences is not a wholly satisfying activity. The results of such research tend to be spongy, qualified, and equivocal; independent variables rarely prove altogether independent either of one another or of the dependent phenomena on which they are presumed to act; residual variance proves more important than what has been "explained." The "true" model lies very deep, indeed, if it exists at all. But the thirst for a simple order proves hard to quench; the adumbrations that the order may exist exert an overwhelming pull upon the researcher.

When this era of urban research has been fully appraised, models of the sort described by Berry will no doubt be awarded a considerable measure of well-deserved credit. But such models may also be appropriate target of some equally justified blame if they should come to be regarded as providing a reliable predictive device. There is little reason to expect, for instance, that the newly developed countries should develop a hierarchy of cities on the spatial patterns of the older ones. The circumstances prevailing at the birth of new cities in these newly developing countries differ from anything observed in the prior history of man. Swift transportation by air, rail, or automobile is available almost from the developmental birth of many such countries, accelerating travel to a degree which could not even be imagined in the nineteenth century. Face-to-face communication seems to play a critical role in the affairs of government, commerce, and industry in these new countries to a degree that may be quite different from the role it played seventy-five or a hundred years ago; and external economies of scale, in the form of power, repair specialists, and skilled labor, appear more critical to industry than formerly. Hence there is no reason to suppose that the clusters of habitation toward which man is driven by the political and social circumstances of his existence will necessarily follow their past patterns. And of course such observed regularities as the rank-size rule are of little help to those who would project the population of any particular place.

We should be wary of the rank-size regularity and similar empirically determined relationships for an even more important reason. It is the fate of many who claim to observe regularities in man's behavior that they begin not only to predict the future on the basis of these regularities, but also to insist that such regularities "ought to be." An observed relationship soon becomes a restraining law which should order the environment of society. These observed relationships were responses to a given set of economic, social, and psychic factors in their time. The object of one's research may well be—indeed it typically is—to find the means for satisfying some articulated set of goals quite different from the sum of the goals of the individuals who happen to have produced these relationships. For instance, few individuals who choose a home site make the choice with due regard for the need to preserve land for open space or for factory sites, or with regard for the need to protect an unpolluted water supply. The researcher's end may be to find the means of achieving those results. To achieve them, he may be obliged to recommend distributions of population and jobs quite at variance with the observed patterns of existing settlements. There is no basis, so far, for his assuming that there are invariant laws of nature which will defeat his alternative proposals. Such a basis might emerge once we understand the underlying forces that produced the observed patterns of urban agglomeration. It might turn out, for instance, that the desire to minimize communication or transportation costs and time were bringing about the observed patterns of urban agglomeration; and it might be apparent that this need was so compelling that only the strongest and most costly forms of intervention could alter the size of the clusters.[14] In that case, it might be necessary and desirable to accept the observed regularities as fixed parameters of our universe. But it is clear that we have not yet reached this state of knowledge and understanding in our research.

The points that have been made regarding the rank-size phenomenon apply as well to a wide range of other empirical relationships which many researchers have discovered about the internal structure of urban areas. For instance, the population and employment density gradients for urban areas, described by Berry, often represent admirably consistent patterns, provided the urban areas to which the measures are applied are carefully selected by the researcher. But the discovery of these gradients must not be confused with the existence of an immutable rule or an effective predictive device. The relevance of the urban "center" from which gradients of this sort are usually measured will change as transport and communications change; we are already dealing with gradients in some cities which slope upward from the center for several miles before they begin to move downward. In addition, the appropriate classification of a given urban area ought to change as its function is altered; for instance, if the functions of cities like St. Louis and Philadelphia are changing under the impact of changing transport technology, as impressionistic evidence suggests, there would be no reason to anticipate that the old gradients will persist. What is wanted, once more, is some understanding of the forces producing the results—forces more explicit than those cloaked by such phrases as "tendency to agglomerate," "linkage propensities," and other nonteleological and nonanalytical expressions of this sort.[15]

The search for causal links accounts in part for the recent extensive efforts of scholars to develop a system of "regional accounts," which would describe the income and expenditure structure of each region and its relations with the outside world. When data of this kind are at hand for major urban regions, no one can doubt that they will add to our understanding of the growth process of such areas. But a word of caution is needed. When in the 1950's problems of growth took over from problems of cycles as the first preoccupation of politicians, the economists did what they could to apply their hard-learned Keynesian concepts to the new preoccupation. Various *simpliste* growth models were devised, many of them being first cousins to the regional analyst's basic-nonbasic concept generated a little earlier. Today, after a period of ferment, economists take a more qualified view of the analytical usefulness of these national aggregates. Observing the simultaneous creation of capital and output in an economy, for instance, they are not altogether certain whether it is more useful to observe that capital begets output or that output begets capital. Although economics will never be the same as it was before these tools were created, we still seem far from an adequate understanding of the key variables in the growth of the national economy.

All these points are bound to prove true regarding the utility of regional accounts—only more so. One reason is the easy movement of capital and labor across a region's borders, a problem that is far less difficult in the national context than in the study of a region. A second reason—perhaps a more general version of the first reason—is the fact that intersectoral and interindustry relationships inside any region are so much less stable than those within a nation as a whole.

The importance of this second point is illustrated by the problems of using input-output techniques in explaining and predicting a region's performance. Tomes have been written on the strengths and limitations of input-output matrices as a device for describing and predicting the performance of any economy. A number of rather formidable efforts have been made to apply the technique to an understanding of urban economies.[16]

The input-output technique, of course, is one that begins from a description of the interindustry flows operating in the economy—from a table that describes how much of the output of the economy's steel industry goes to each other industry in the economy and to the outside world, how much of the chemical industry's output goes to each other industry and to the outside world, and so on. With these relationships known, a number of useful possibilities develop. If one can specify, for instance, the bundle of products that will be wanted as final outputs from the particular economy, one can presumably estimate all the things which the economy will have to produce to make possible the filling of that demand. One can then proceed to evaluate the impact upon various parts of the economy that would result from any specified change in either the amounts of final output or the interindustry relations.

In addition to all the usual difficulties that exist in the application of input-output analysis, there are some difficulties that are particularly important when the approach is applied to an urban area. One of these has already been observed—the fact that an urban area is even less a closed economy than a nation is. This openness of the urban economy is particularly significant in respect to movements of factors of production. A region can rapidly lose a significant part of its labor force by emigration or augment it by immigration; and it can lose or gain capital resources with even greater ease. So the analyst who is concerned to understand a particular urban area soon finds that he is obliged to study all other competing areas before he can be sure that he knows what is likely to go on in the region on which his interest is centered. It is true, of course, that this problem applies conceptually to every attempt at understanding a given urban area. But the problem is not one that is most readily solved by the use of input-output techniques.

A second difficulty that applies with special force to urban analysis is the problem of developing an input-output matrix that can be said to be "representative" in any enduring way. The interrelationships among industries in a nation may have enduring qualities; or if they change, they may change sluggishly over time in accordance with some visible trend. But the relationships inside an urban area are bound to be more haphazard, varying sharply from time to time in accordance with shifts in relative prices, product mix, and sources of supply. Accordingly, any "representative" input-output matrix developed for a given area out of the performance of a given time period will be subject to considerably larger margins of error than would be the case for a nation.

Finally, there is the problem of the unsubtlety and inflexibility of the input-output technique. As one works with these models, one constantly finds oneself wishing to introduce complicating assumptions about the interrelationships among industries and constantly discovering that the cost of introducing these complications is so great that as a practical matter they cannot be introduced.

The extent to which it may be appropriate to use the interindustry approach, in the light of its limitations and difficulties, depends on the kind of question that must be answered. For broad projections of the growth of an economy, as has been indicated, simpler and easier methods are available. But explicit recognition of interindustry relationships is needed for the assessing of impacts upon the structure of an economy if those effects are either (1) to be evaluated in terms of specific industries or (2) viewed as the outcome of initial changes in specific industries.

One approach that has produced useful results in empirical studies has been to separate the urban economy into two parts: to study as one kind of problem the location and production of the urban economy's establishments that compete with other regions; then to study as a separate problem the implications that the growth of these "national-market" industries may have for the "local-market" industries of the urban area. The first problem is dealt with through industry studies along the lines suggested later, whereas the latter problem is dealt with as an input-output exercise in which the activities of the "national-market" industries are given. The virtue of this approach is that it confines the use of input-output analysis to industries in which the technical coefficients tend to be relatively stable, partly because of the character of the local industries and partly because such industries by definition are bound to be located within the areas they serve.[17]

The Problem of Meaningful Classification in Locational Analysis

Anyone concerned about understanding the forces that are shaping an urban area will soon find himself speculating on the factors responsible for the location of business enterprises and residences. His next stage, almost surely, will be to try to look at various categories of enterprises or residences and to try to make some generalizations about their locational behavior. And if he is alert to his problems, he will find himself asking, "What is a useful system of classification?"

In this regard, the economist has more enlightening things to say with regard to business establishments than with respect to residences. Every locational decision is the outcome of a complex of interacting forces—principally of transport costs and time, labor costs and availability, communication means and time, space costs and availability, site needs, and "inertial" or sunk costs. To complicate the problem even more for the analyst, there is a two-way causal flow. It is true that a given firm may make its calculations and select its location on the basis of the calculated outcome; but it is also true that the available locations may affect the technology and alter the character of the enterprises concerned.

Apart from the complexity of the problem, it should also be evident that we are not speaking of any unique system of classification. The usefulness of any system of classification depends on its purpose. A classification intended to shed light on the locational responses of establishments inside an urban area—their propensity to locate in the central city, for instance, versus their attraction to the suburbs—would be somewhat different from a classification intended to analyze locational preferences as among different parts of the country. In the first setting, categories like "waste-generating" or "nuisance" industries might prove exceedingly useful, whereas in the second setting such categories might be irrelevant.

Nonetheless, despite the complexity of the phenomenon, there have been some efforts to try to explain or evaluate the distribution of industry by the use of some single variable, particularly through models that try to minimize transportation costs.[18] As exercises in the application of mathematical techniques, these are extremely sophisticated efforts. As reflections of the locational process in the real world, however, they are unsatisfyingly naive.

Another technique has been to attempt a classification of industries on the basis of their dominant locational force, distinguishing those industries that find it important to minimize transport costs from those that are principally moved by labor considerations, external economy factors, problems of sunk costs, or some other factor.[19] The analysis then proceeds to try to find locational propositions that stand up in each separate category. There are, of course, obvious problems with this approach. There is the fact that one is obliged to impose an oversimplified version of the decision-making process in setting up one's categories, and the fact that the empirical evidence for classifying any industry is so spotty.

Also involved is the question of the level of industry classification needed before the approach can be justified. It does no good to try to classify so gross and heterogeneous an industry as "food and kindred products" by its dominant locational characteristic. One has to get down into such fine components as "poultry dressing plants," "rice milling plants," and the like; even then one cannot be sure that one's units of analysis are adequately homogeneous. Or if one is satisfied on that score, one runs at least two other risks: the risk that one's universe is so small that its behavior will be determined by unique factors, and the risk that one will be unable to extract the requisite data for one's narrowly defined groups from the stubborn and unsatisfying statistical sources.

The classification of business establishments that are part of the extremely heterogeneous "office industry" presents especially difficult problems on all these points. The locational imperatives of the executive offices of a national cosmetics company are almost as different from those of a life insurance office as they are from the needs of a textile plant. Yet with respect to office activities, the data are even more gross and more fragmentary than they are for manufacturing.

Nonetheless, despite these difficulties, seemingly adequate classifications of all types of enterprises—manufacturing, office, and all the rest—have been developed in some empirical studies and have proved extremely useful in explaining and predicting locational shifts.[20] The next step in locational analysis is one which would add still another dimension. This would be an effort to explain the locational behavior of each of the various "homogeneous" groups of enterprises by acknowledging that any such group—even if labeled "transport-sensitive," for instance—actually responds to a *complex* of locational factors, including not only transport but also labor costs, communication time factors, and other forces. For each such group, there might be an effort to generalize the relationship that reflects the whole complex of forces affecting the locational decision-making process.

Some Priorities in the Economic Aspects of Urban Research

Our final task is to suggest a system of priorities in urban economic research. Some of the implications of the priorities concept should be explored. A system of priorities implies the prior existence of a set of objectives. The objectives might be broadly stated as the improvement of knowledge, and success might be measured in terms of the explanatory power of tested hypotheses; but that does not necessarily provide an adequate basis for establishment of priorities in research areas or projects. Priorities can be suggested, however, in terms that reflect some system of normative values, such as an effort to find the means to affect the urban environment in directions taken to be desirable. The discussion that follows is cast in such terms.

It often falls to the lot of the economist engaged in urban research that he is asked to provide the analytical work that society needs in order to achieve some preconceived normative goal. In comparison to the sociologist, for example, he is more often concerned with what society may be able to do to urban areas than with what the urban environment may be doing to society. For the long run, the latter question may be the more important; but the economist's particular set of tools is probably not too helpful in trying to probe this issue.

What are the objectives, then, for which society seems to be pressing hardest and in which it enlists the economist's help?

The Underdeveloped Areas

In the underdeveloped areas, the acceleration of economic growth ranks high. In the aims of governments in most of these areas, statistical growth takes precedence over many welfare aims that sometimes conflict with it. Questions about the extent to which the nation's resources should be used for housing, health, education, and welfare will tend to be tested in the first instance against the criterion of their contribution to such growth.

On the assumption that he wishes to be responsive to such demands, the economist concerned with underdeveloped areas should be placing high priority on studies of the "pull factors" in urban population increases in underdeveloped areas. Much more needs to be known concerning the nature and magnitude of the changes in the economic activities performed in urban areas of developing countries, accompanying the growth of manufacturing, business services, and government. An effort is needed to isolate the critical forces behind the obvious facts: an analysis of economic factors behind the clustering of manufacturing, business services, and government in urban areas; an appraisal of the growth implications of the clustering, with inquiry into the role of transport and communication cost and time and the use and development of external economies. And some imaginative comparative analysis is wanted to suggest more firmly the relative cost and the growth possibilities for dispersed versus clustered development, that is, a totaling of the economies and diseconomies of dispersal.[21]

The Developed Countries

In the developed countries of the world—those principally in North America and Western Europe plus Japan—the urban economist confronts a different kind of objective. Here we are no longer so sure what more "growth" means. Having provided for the basic needs of most of the population, the objectives of society have become diffused and fragmented. As far as the urban economist is concerned, he is involved in at least five such objectives: (1) the provision of residences for the minority that still does not have decent shelter; (2) the achievement of an esthetically pleasing environment; (3) the provision of opportunities for cultural growth; (4) the maintenance of fiscal solvency for local government; and (5) the maintenance of a living environment that is at least moderately efficient as a producer of goods and services. (On this final point, the priority seems a little lower than the others.)

These diffused objectives present frequent internal contradictions. None is allowed totally to dominate the others. The typical problem is to satisfy each a little, without wholly neglecting any of them. A list of priorities for urban research in the developed nations, therefore, seems almost like a series of familiar clichés; it roams over all the old fields of inquiry.

Simple background data constitute a critical need. Data showing the present breakdown of total economic activity in individual metropolitan areas, by employment or any other measure, do not exist except for a very few areas; historical data of this sort are almost entirely nonexistent; and data, historical or current, breaking such figures down further by subareas of metropolitan areas are even more rare. Filling these *lacunae* should have high priority.

For different reasons and with different kinds of qualifications, data describing the residents of metropolitan areas and subareas are also incomplete, and in fact they are generally lacking between the decennial censuses of population. Income data, data identifying the economic activity of residents, and data tying the resident to some place of work are particularly poor, despite recent advances.[22]

Changes in the spatial distribution of enterprises in urban areas require further attention. In an analysis of the basic forces that have been changing the locational distribution of business establishments and residences within the urban areas, it is hard to draw the line between the contribution to be made by the economist and that to be made by the sociologist, the political scientist, the geographer, and so on. From an economist's viewpoint, more data are needed on changes in national economic activity, by fairly fine sectors. The classification should be sufficiently fine as to have some significant ability to discriminate in terms of locational needs. Changes in the *composition* of enterprises demanding an urban location also must be examined. Presumably some types of enterprise are being added to the list while others disappear. We must also study changes in the space and physical housing needs of such enterprises and changes in their locational preferences based on such factors as transportation, communication, labor force, and space needs. Finally, we have to consider the implications of the obsolescence and possible reuse of existing structures and land sites for future location.

Change in the distribution of residences in urban areas in the advanced countries constitutes an area of research in its own right. Here, of course, the caution about the interdisciplinary nature of urban problems is even more compelling. The economist's contribution would be especially important in studies of changes in currents of migration to and from urban areas, and changes in the patterns of consumption of urban households also deserve more study. However, even intra-urban residential spatial patterns are fair game for the economist to the extent that they reflect urban land prices that are below the full private and social costs of sprawl. In addition, intra-urban movement (especially by private vehicle) usually is priced too low to ration scarce urban lot and street space efficiently.

Internal transportation is another field of study in which the economist can help. An analysis is needed of the prospective burden to be borne by mass-transit facilities, the adequacy of those facilities to bear the burden, and the implications for growth of various lines of policy regarding mass transit, such as increasing the price of alternative transport modes, letting mass transit die gradually, letting it die suddenly, subsidizing mass transit to keep it alive indefinitely, or investing in radical mass-transit improvement.

The fiscal implications of urban change also need more exploring. The economist is especially well equipped to deal with much of this problem, though he may require the assistance of the political scientist at many points in a concrete analysis. Efforts should be made to determine how income and outgo are likely to be balanced, on various assumptions about the future growth of cities and suburbs; and to determine what the implications of alternative paths to balance are likely to be for added city and urban renewal projects, absorbing write-downs of industrial land sites, and so on.[23]

Finally, housing research requires more effort. In the United States, "slum clearance" and urban renewal have revived interest in this topic. But much more work needs to be done on the prospective supply of housing for low-income groups; the increment likely to be downgraded to that purpose in the decades just ahead and the reductions likely to develop out of razing, conversions, and so on. The information developed on these lines has to be compared with the prospective locus in urban areas of jobs for low-income groups, to determine if supply and needs are developing compatibly.

Even some modest progress along the lines just described would be sufficient to engage a generation of economic researchers in the urban field.

NOTES

* Chapter 12, by Wilbur R. Thompson, is addressed essentially to the analysis of entire urban areas in their external economic contexts. The discussion in the opening section of this chapter, which was written by Hoover, is accordingly focused mainly on the question of the internal spatial organization of activities within urban areas. The remainder of the chapter was written by Vernon.

1. See Walter Isard, *Location and Space-Economy* (Cambridge, 1956), Chap. 3, for a summary view of "empirical regularities of the space-economy." The subsequent literature is discussed in the Mayer and Berry chapters of the present volume, and in Brian J. L. Berry, "Cities as Systems Within Systems of Cities," in John Friedmann and William Alonso (Eds.), *Regional Development and Planning* (Cambridge, 1964), pp. 116–137. The complementarity of the inductive and deductive approaches to urban spatial analysis is discussed in Otis Dudley Duncan et al., *Metropolis and Region* (Baltimore, 1960), a work dedicated primarily to the inductive approach.

2. Wilbur R. Thompson, "Urban Economic Growth and Development in a National System of Cities," Chapter 12 in the present volume.

3. The most ambitious effort to incorporate linear programming in an operational land use model has been in the Penn-Jersey Transportation Study in the Philadelphia area. See *PJ Papers* (Philadelphia, various dates,

mimeographed), especially John D. Herbert and Benjamin H. Stevens, "A Model for the Distribution of Residential Activity in Urban Areas" (*PJ Paper* No. 2), and Britton Harris, "Linear Programming and the Projection of Land Uses" (*PJ Paper* No. 20). See also Benjamin H. Stevens, "A Review of the Literature on Linear Methods and Models for Spatial Analysis," *Journal of the American Institute of Planners*, 26 (1960), pp. 253–259.

4. See Nathaniel Lichfield and Julius Margolis, "Benefit-Cost Analysis as a Tool in Urban Government Decision Making," in Howard G. Schaller (Ed.), *Public Expenditure Decisions in the Urban Economy* (Washington, 1963), pp. 118–146.

5. See, for example, Edgar M. Hoover and Raymond Vernon, *Anatomy of a Metropolis* (Cambridge, 1959); Louis Winnick, *American Housing and Its Use* (New York, 1957); and Beverly Duncan and Philip M. Hauser, *Housing a Metropolis—Chicago* (Glencoe, 1960).

6. See, for example, Martin Segal, *Wages in the Metropolis* (Cambridge, 1960).

7. See *Transportation Plan for the National Capital Region,* Hearings before the Joint Committee on Washington Metropolitan Problems, 86th Congress, 1st Session, on the Report of the Washington Mass Transportation Survey, November 9–14, 1959, especially the statements and exhibits by William H. Vickrey, pp. 454–513. Two somewhat more recent and accessible statements by Vickrey are in his "General and Specific Financing of Urban Services," in Schaller (Ed.), *op. cit.,* pp. 62–90, and "Pricing in Urban and Suburban Transportation," *Papers and Proceedings of the American Economic Association* (1963), pp. 452–465. See also Richard B. Andrews, *Urban Growth and Development* (New York, 1962), Chap. 4.

8. See Charles M. Tiebout, *The Community Economic Base Study* (New York, 1962).

9. See, for example, the reports of the Detroit Metropolitan Area Traffic Study, the Chicago Area Transportation Study, and the Pittsburgh Area Transportation Study, all of which employed an analytical approach developed by J. Douglas Carroll, Jr., and his associates.

10. See the various reports of the New York Metropolitan Region Study, the Penn-Jersey Transportation Study (the *PJ Papers* already cited), and the reports of the Economic Study of the Pittsburgh Region: *Region in Transition, Portrait of a Region,* and *Region with a Future* (Pittsburgh, 1964).

11. As the present volume goes to press, this work is being done for the Planning Department of the City of Pittsburgh by the Center for Regional Economic Studies at the University of Pittsburgh and by the Consad Research Corporation. The ultimate form of publication has not yet been determined.

12. Much of this section is based on the writer's (Vernon's) experience as Director of the New York Metropolitan Region Study. For a more extended treatment of the techniques mentioned here, see the following volumes of that Study's reports: Raymond Vernon, *Metropolis 1985* (Cambridge, 1960); Barbara Berman, Benjamin Chinitz, and Edgar M. Hoover, *Projection of a Metropolis* (Cambridge, 1960); and Robert H. Lichtenberg, *One-Tenth of a Nation* (Cambridge, 1960), especially Chap. 11.

13. See also Brian J. L. Berry, "Cities as Systems Within Systems of Cities," *op. cit.*, and Herbert A. Simon, *Models of Man* (New York, 1957), Chap. 9.

14. London and Paris are leading examples of metropolitan areas in which policies designed to curb growth have been pursued for a considerable period without signal success. See Lloyd Rodwin, "Planned Decentralization and Regional Development with Special Reference to the British New Towns," *Papers and Proceedings of the Regional Science Association*, 1 (1955), pp. 1–8.

15. On the construction and uses of systems of regional accounts, see Charles L. Leven, *Theory and Method of Income and Product Accounts for Metropolitan Areas, Including the Elgin-Dundee Area as a Case Study* (Ames, 1958); Werner Hochwald (Ed.), *Design of Regional Accounts* (Baltimore, 1961); Werner Z. Hirsch (Ed.), *Elements of Regional Accounts* (Baltimore, 1964).

16. Werner Hochwald, Herbert E. Striner, and Sidney Sonenblum, *Local Impact of Foreign Trade* (Washington, 1960), especially the Appendix, pp. 108ff.; Walter Isard et al., *Methods of Regional Analysis* (New York, 1960), especially Chap. 8 and the bibliography to that chapter, pp. 372–374; Werner Z. Hirsch, "Interindustry Relations of a Metropolitan Area," *The Review of Economics and Statistics*, 41 (1959), pp. 360–369; Roland Artle, *The Structure of the Stockholm Economy* (Ithaca, N. Y., 1965).

17. Barbara Berman, Benjamin Chinitz, and Edgar M. Hoover, *op. cit.*; Raymond Vernon, *op. cit.*; Walter Isard et al., *Methods of Regional Analysis*, *op. cit.*

18. For illustrations, see Isard, *op. cit.*, Chap. 10.

19. *Ibid.*, pp. 233–234 and the references listed on pp. 305–308. See also Edgar M. Hoover, *The Location of Economic Activity* (New York, 1948), and Melvin L. Greenhut, *Plant Location in Theory and Practice* (Chapel Hill, 1956).

20. Robert H. Lichtenberg, *op. cit.*; Raymond Vernon, *op. cit.*

21. For suggestive leads, see Kingsley Davis, "Urbanization in India: Past and Future," in Roy Turner (Ed.), *India's Urban Future* (Berkeley, 1962), pp. 3–26, and John P. Lewis, *Quiet Crisis in India* (Washington, 1963).

22. In 1960, the U. S. Census of Population collected for the first time (on a sample basis) information on place of work and means of transportation to work. For residents of Standard Metropolitan Statistical Areas (SMSA's), work places are tabulated as in the central city of the SMSA, in the remainder of the SMSA, or outside the SMSA. For those persons living outside SMSA's, work places are tabulated as in the state of residence, in specified contiguous states, or elsewhere.

23. At present we have only the cross-sectional analyses of Margolis and Brazer. See Julius Margolis, "Municipal Fiscal Structure in a Metropolitan Region," *The Journal of Political Economy*, 65 (1957), pp. 225–236, and Harvey E. Brazer, "Some Fiscal Implications of Metropolitanism," in *Metropolitan Issues: Social, Governmental, Fiscal* (Syracuse, 1962). See also Wilbur R. Thompson, *A Preface to Urban Economics* (Washington, 1963), Chap. 7.

PART TWO

Comparative Urban Research

Part 1 has presented five disciplinary statements outlining diverse perspectives and approaches to the study of urbanization. In the four chapters that follow, stress is placed by general orientation or by consideration of specific aspects of urbanization on the comparative study of urbanism and its concomitants.

Much of the early work in the study of the city and the process of urbanization was descriptive and focused largely on Western cities. There was, on the whole, little concern with the history of urbanization and more with urban biography and with the consideration and treatment of urban problems. Moreover, urbanization was often equated with industrialization. Earlier work is therefore subject to the criticism of historicism and, in retrospect, early research findings were mostly overgeneralized, especially in text-

209

books in urban sociology and related literature. Relatively early in its deliberations, the Committee on Urbanization of the Social Science Research Council agreed that greatly increased cross-cultural and comparative study was essential to obtaining a fuller understanding of the process of urbanization and its consequences.

Indeed, as Western scholars have had increasing opportunity to live in and to observe urban areas in other parts of the world, they have become increasingly aware that the process of urbanization is far from a unitary one; on the contrary, there are various types of urbanization, in respect to origin, process, and consequences. Much remains to be done in the historical study of urbanization both in the Western and non-Western world, with special emphasis on comparative study. In such comparative research multidisciplinary or interdisciplinary efforts can be particularly fruitful.

The first two chapters in Part 2 are comprehensive and general in orientation, scope, and substantive considerations.

In Chapter 7, Sjoberg considers "Cities in Developing and in Industrial Societies: A Cross-cultural Analysis," building on his monograph *The Preindustrial City*.[1] He attempts to isolate the structural correlates of industrial cities and the societies in which they are found. A sketch of the preindustrial city serves as a backdrop against which we can view (1) "cities in transition," or those urban communities now undergoing industrialization around the world, and (2) true industrial cities. Sjoberg's objective is not to summarize existing research but to focus on certain critical theoretical issues and to delineate problem areas that require intensive study. Special attention is devoted to the matter of social integration and the division of labor and to the role of "mediators" in modern urban-industrial systems. Comparative analysis, he declares, "must advance on both theoretical and empirical fronts" and the city must be examined "in its broader societal context."

In Chapter 8, Keyfitz presents an essay on the "Political-Economic Aspects of Urbanization in South and Southeast Asia." He examines the political-economic relationship between the city and rural area. His central hypothesis is that an imbalance in the exchange of goods between city and countryside is made up by the exercise of power on the part of the city, and that the decline in the food surplus available in the countryside (owing to the rapid growth of population) attenuates the base which the city had in colonial and precolonial times. Moreover, increasing population in the city means increased pressure

[1] Glencoe, Ill.: Free Press, 1960.

on the countryside for food. In exchange the city offers the promise of better things to come—by means of economic development. Taxes have been and still are the principal means by which the peasant was induced to produce more in order to meet the needs of the urban population. The autonomy of cities depends on the efficiency of their production for exchange or on the physical control of the sources of their foodstuffs. In South and Southeast Asia the latter tends to be the rule. The central problem on which Keyfitz focuses "concerns ecology in the fundamental, indeed primitive, sense of relating concentrations of populations to the sources of their food; how will the city people eat as their numbers and the numbers of those in the countryside increase?" The attempt to answer this question constitutes a framework for comparative studies that can be extended, of course, beyond South and Southeast Asia.

Chapters 9 and 10 by Ginsburg and Schnore, respectively, focus on more specific comparative problems—the former with the variety of urban forms and functions and the latter with the distribution of social classes in the urban community.

Ginsburg in "Urban Geography and 'Non-Western' Areas" is concerned with the city in Africa and Asia and, especially, the city in India and Japan. He examines the questions "whether the urbanization process is unidimensional or multidimensional" and "whether it is culturally, as well as temporally, differentiated." "To what extent," he asks, "are basic differences in culture, even given the spread of 'modern Western' technology and values, likely to give rise to different urbanization processes and the creation of cities as artifacts that differ from culture to culture?" Although Ginsburg is modest in his conclusions he demonstrates, by presenting some convincing evidence on the variety of urban forms and functions, that the narrowly "Western" view of the city is incomplete.

In Chapter 10, "On the Spatial Structure of Cities in the Two Americas," Schnore examines the residential distribution of social classes in Anglo and Latin American cities. A number of scholars have observed that the pattern so familiar to us—with the lower socioeconomic strata heavily concentrated near the center of the city and the higher classes at the periphery and in the suburbs—was exactly reversed in the "classical" Latin American city. There the elites were clustered near the central plaza and the lower classes resided at the edge of the city. Schnore systematically searches for the factors that account for these differences, and for the fact that cities south of the Rio Grande are now straining toward similarity to those in the United States and Canada.

Part 2, then, not only discusses the need for more cross-cultural and comparative research but also delineates some important problems in comparative study and illustrates how such studies may be pursued.

7

Cities in Developing and in Industrial Societies: A Cross-cultural Analysis *

Gideon Sjoberg

We shall examine the industrial-urban order on the world scene. More narrowly we strive to isolate the structural correlates of industrial cities and their societies. First we consider briefly our particular theoretical commitment. Then we present an adumbrated sketch of the preindustrial city. This serves as a backdrop against which we can contrast those urban communities now undergoing industrialization— that is, cities in transition—and industrial cities, which are the end product and our chief concern.

Our primary aim is not to summarize existing research but rather to focus on certain crucial theoretical issues and to delineate problem areas that merit intensive study.[1] In addition to our effort to isolate the structural correlates of industrial cities, we devote special attention to the matter of social integration and the division of labor and the role of mediators in modern industrial-urban systems. This general problem—central to much of sociological analysis—is too frequently ignored.

Theoretical Background

If we are to understand the city in both its historical and its current social settings, our scope must be broad. A wide perspective is essential, for social systems do not arrange themselves into neat compartments that conform with arbitrary disciplinary boundaries or the divisions sociologists establish for teaching purposes. We believe that

213

the search for structural correlates of industrial cities is of sufficient theoretical and practical import to warrant acceptance of the risks that inhere in any macroscopic cross-cultural investigation.

Although the obstacles to cross-cultural research and analysis loom discouragingly large, there is cause for optimism, for by limiting ourselves to isolating the *shared* characteristics of industrial cities our task is simplified. We are spared concern with a host of niggling traits peculiar to one or a few systems at most.

The macroscopic orientation, in contradistinction to the microscopic one, maximizes synthesis and minimizes analysis.[2] Sociologists who adhere to a macroscopic perspective, as we do, are often accused of removing themselves from social reality. However, generalizing across cultures usually demands a relatively high level of abstraction. Patterns that appear to diverge perceptibly on a concrete, empirical plane frequently seem quite similar on a more abstract level. Moreover, the macroscopic orientation brings to the fore relationships that scholars who concentrate upon particular organizations are apt to ignore.

Earlier (in Chapter 5) we observed that urban sociologists may employ a variety of theoretical orientations. Ours takes technology as the key variable for explaining the nature of the industrial city. As we define technology, it involves the tools, the sources of energy, and the know-how connected with the use of both tools and energy that a social system employs. Industrialization is that kind of technology that relies on inanimate energy sources, highly complex tools, and the specialized know-how required to tap these power sources and utilize these advanced tools.

Sociologists tend to use the concept "technology" uncritically. Our conceptualization diverges from most in that it incorporates the notion of "know-how"—thereby making science, or the scientific method, an essential ingredient of modern industrial technology. Such a viewpoint sidesteps the pitfalls of a stark materialism and articulates with the current conceptual drift in social science. Unlike researchers of a few decades ago who spoke mainly of the impact of the factory system on modern society, scholars nowadays are much more concerned with the effects of the "scientific revolution."[3] Viewed in these terms, a city with a highly specialized labor force—say, a university community harboring a large number of scientists—is highly industrialized along at least one of its dimensions.[4]

Although technology is our primary variable, we do not reject out of hand other orientations but rather use these to supplement our analysis. Certainly we cannot ignore the role of cultural values. For one thing, industrial cities, even in divergent cultural settings, share certain values.[5] But each may also display certain "unique" values that in turn are associated with differing structures. These structural differences, however, are meaningful from a scientific viewpoint only if we contrast them with the structural similarities. We must isolate, therefore, the structural similarities before we can hope to establish the cultural or stylistic differences among industrial cities.

Nor do we disregard the impact of the city on social organization, for some rural-urban differences persist even in industrial orders. So, too, if we are to explain the rise and proliferation of industrial centers, we must pay heed to the impact of social power. Because of the interplay between a society's power structure (on both the national and the international planes) and its value system, different nations follow somewhat different paths to industrial urbanization—a point stressed by Kerr and others as well as by Moore and Feldman.[6]

Still, the impact of technology on urban social structure is our main point of departure. For purposes of analysis we distinguish among three "constructed types" of cities: the preindustrial, the transitional, and the industrial. Actually these are subsystems within broader social orders: the preindustrial civilized (or feudal), the modernizing (or developing), and the industrial, respectively. And one of our primary assumptions is that the city cannot be understood except in its relationships to the broader society of which it is a part.

Still another facet of our theoretical orientation requires clarification: in our examination of the key structural arrangements of industrial cities we adhere to a structural-functional frame of reference—with significant modifications.[7] We recognize that alternative structures may serve given "imperatives."[8] However, the number of such alternatives is far from infinite; there are some limits to the kinds of structural arrangements that can obtain. At times we can more easily assess these limits than determine the particular structure a system requires for its operation. The negative case approach is especially useful for establishing these structural limits. Nor can we ignore the dilemma posed by structural-functional theorizing. For though a given structure may be "imperative" for the functioning of an industrial city, this same structure may depend on industrialization for its existence. This is true of advanced or specialized education, for example.[9]

Above all, we incorporate into our theoretical framework the concepts of "contradictory structures" and "contradictory functional requirements."[10] By and large, structural-functionalists have stressed the matter of internal integration in social orders; some see it as essential for a society's maintenance or "survival." But to us, recognition of the coexistence of antagonistic structures, and even their essentiality for the maintenance of the system, is empirically more realistic.

The Preindustrial City [11]

Until barely two centuries ago all cities were of the preindustrial type. From the time they arose approximately five and a half millennia ago in the Mesopotamian riverine area, they spread outward until they spanned much of the globe, forming the nuclei of preindustrial civilized societies.

Of the cities that flourished before the spread of industrialization, few attained populations of over 100,000, and many sheltered fewer than 10,000 persons. Moreover, subjected as they have been to the vagaries of nature and the instabilities of the political systems supporting them, preindustrial cities have fluctuated considerably in size over time. Yet, over broad regions and in diverse social orders their *structural* characteristics have remained more or less the same, whereas their specific cultural content has varied widely.

Preindustrial cities have always functioned primarily as governmental and religious centers, and only secondarily as commercial establishments. As to the internal spatial structure, the elite typically has resided in or near the center, with the lower class and outcaste groups fanning out toward the periphery. Added to this ecological differentiation in terms of class are land-use patterns reflecting occupational and ethnic distinctions. Typically, each occupational group lives and works in a particular street or quarter, one that frequently bears the name of the trade in question. And ethnic groups form relatively self-contained subsystems that frequently are spatially isolated from one another. Yet despite the high degree of socioeconomic differentiation, a minimum of specialization in land use is the rule: a single site frequently serves multiple functions.

With respect to the preindustrial city's social structure, the effects of social class tend to be all-pervasive. The small upper class, readily identifiable by its distinctive garb, speech, and personal mannerisms, controls the key organizational units of government, religion, and education. This privileged group—whose locus is mainly urban rather than rural—dominates not just the cityscape but the entire preindustrial civilized society. In striking contrast to the elite is the vast bulk of the populace. Though these two broad groups evince internal gradations of status, the wide gap between the elite and the lower class is the most obvious feature of the stratification system. The lower class includes both the urban commoners and the rural peasantry. Standing apart from and below this lower class are the outcastes, whose locus is primarily urban, and whose chief function is carrying out activities that are essential to the continuance of the system yet clearly outside the pale of respectability. Some mobility occurs among the several strata, including some movement between the lower class and the elite, as a result of shifting political fortunes, contradictory structural arrangements, and the like, but from the purview of the individual actor this mobility seems slight indeed.

The revered societal forms in feudal orders reach their fullest flowering within the urban upper class. This group sets the standards for the entire society. For example, the preindustrial urbanite functions within a family system to which he must subordinate his own interests. Consequently marriages are familial rather than individual arrangements. The large, extended family, with numerous relatives residing within a single "household" and functioning more or less as a social and economic unit, is the urban ideal. But preserving close ties among family members and keeping the entire unit under a single "roof" is generally possible only for the elite. Economic circumstances prevent the urban poor and the peasantry alike from maintaining such households; for them the *famille souche* is the more usual form. Families in the lower strata, existing within a "culture of poverty" and having higher morbidity and mortality rates, are more unstable and fragile than upper-class families.

Within the urban elite family the men lord it over their womenfolk. "Respectable" women are isolated from many facets of community life, whereas women of the urban lower class play a far more salient role in the family and the community. But almost everywhere in feudal societies it is the rural woman who enjoys the most freedom.

The family is the primary socializing agency in the community and serves for women and children, and to a lesser degree for men, as the focus of leisure-time activity. More significantly, given the relatively limited social mobility, one's family becomes the chief determinant of one's occupational position. The society's leaders, bureaucratic personnel, and most craftsmen are recruited primarily on the basis of kinship and other particularistic ties.

By industrial standards the technology and the economic organization of the preindustrial city are simple. Commercial activities, manual labor, or "practical pursuits" in general are depreciated and shunned by the elite. Except for a few large-scale merchants, persons engaged in commerce or the crafts belong to the lower class or the outcaste group.

Within the economic realm the main unit is the guild, typically a community-bound organization. Through the guilds, handicraftsmen, merchants, and members of various service occupations seek to minimize competition, determine standards and prices, and control the recruitment and training of personnel in their particular economic activity.

From the viewpoint of the industrial-urban order, the production of goods and services depends on a division of labor that involves little specialization of knowledge. The craftsman performs all or most of the steps in the fashioning of an article and often also markets it himself. Thus we find relatively little standardization of process in manufacturing; rather, specialization is according to product.

So too in commerce a modicum of standardization exists in prices, currency, weights and measures, and in the grading of commodities. In the main the price of an item is fixed through haggling between individual buyers and sellers. Different systems of currency may be in use at a given moment, even in a single community or region; similarly, weights and measures frequently vary among crafts and markets within a city. On top of this, the widespread adulteration of goods impedes standarization in production and marketing.

Economic development is inhibited by the educated stratum's negation of business activity and work with the hands, the paucity of standardization, and the meager facilities for credit and capital formation. All of these tend to slow technological innovation and, conversely, the inadequacies of the technology hinder advance in the broader economic realm.

As for the political system, we find the upper class in command of the key governmental posts. The political apparatus tends to be strongly centralized, with the chief provincial and local administrators (some of whom share kinship ties with the societal ruler) being personally accountable to the leaders in the capital. Although the sovereign exercises autocratic powers, countervailing forces mean that the "absolute despotism" posited by Wittfogel is never really attained.[12]

The authority of the ruling group and the bureaucracies it commands rests upon appeals to tradition and to absolutes. As in the educational and religious spheres, the political bureaucracy is characterized by rigid hierarchical arrangements. However, the lines of authority tend to be imprecise. As a result, decisions are arrived at more in terms of the incumbent's personal prestige than in accordance with any set of impersonal rules. The office, in other words, is largely a function of the "person." This pattern is reinforced because bureaucracies usually select their key personnel and serve their clientele according to particularistic criteria. These norms, combined with the lack of a fixed salary system, provide a favorable climate for "graft" and similar activities whereby bureaucrats supplement their earnings by extracting gratuities for the services they perform. This pattern is an accepted and legitimate part of the normative order.

Like the political structure, the bureaucracy supporting religious values is a potent integrative and stabilizing mechanism. The highly prescriptive norms control numerous facets of the urbanite's everyday existence. The religious personnel and their functions and beliefs exhibit the same tripartite (elite, lower class, outcaste) division that is so apparent in other realms of activity in the preindustrial-urban order. Members of the upper class command the key posts in the religious hierarchy and are the most faithful adherents to the ideal religious norms. Consequently, the preindustrial city, though it is in one sense a focus of change, is also the chief bastion of orthodoxy.

Magic also plays a vital role in the preindustrial city, for in this setting man seeks not to remake the natural and social order but rather to adjust to it, and to do so he resorts to a variety of magical practices. Protective magic serves to maintain the world on an even keel; restorative magic attempts to right it when it goes awry; and through predictive magic one seeks to determine how to avoid disturbing the natural equilibrium in the future.

The formal educational structure, serving primarily the elite and usually only males, does much to perpetuate this magico-religious heritage. The traditional learning is overwhelmingly of the religious-philosophical variety and tends to be standardized over time and space. It is because the upper class acquires this common body of ideas and knowledge that it is far more homogeneous than the lower class. This pattern reinforces and sustains the elite's privileged position in the social order.

Experimental science, wherein abstract thought is coherent with practical knowledge, and through which man endeavors to manipulate the natural order (both physical and social), is almost absent in the traditional society. The existent technology is perpetuated primarily by the lower class and is only slowly enhanced. The educated minds that could fertilize these seeds of knowledge have been narrowly attuned to the traditional learning, which must not be questioned and revised. The elite's avoidance of practical pursuits and work with the hands has further sundered the theoretical aspects of knowledge from the practical. It was only in the centuries just prior to the Industrial Revolution in Europe that the two coexisting traditions merged, giving birth to modern science and the industrial-urban order.

The foregoing typology is offered not as an end in itself but rather as a basis for deriving hypotheses about existing cities that are still largely preindustrial. And our constructed type provides a reference point for analyzing modernizing and industrial cities. Obviously its utility can be tested only within the crucible of research experience.

The Industrializing City

Cities in traditional civilized orders do not undergo any sudden and complete transformation into the industrial form. As transitional cities, they are partly industrial, partly preindustrial in character. (We could obviously distinguish among types of transitional cities—for example, those that are largely the products of Western colonial rule, such as Calcutta or Shanghai, and those that are indigenous to the preindustrial civilized order. Although such types are worthy of detailed consideration, we cannot examine them here.)

In our analysis of the industrializing city, we are obliged to stress social *processes* rather than form or structure, which is the focus of our attention in sections devoted to preindustrial and industrial cities.

Reasons for, and Patterning of, Industrial Urbanization

Sociologists who study transitional cities in such areas as Africa and Asia soon encounter two major questions: (1) Why is the society to which these cities belong so anxious to industrialize? (2) How does it seek to attain this goal?

Nowadays most nations, large and small, are striving to achieve a higher degree of industrial urbanization. Indeed, some countries are taxing all their resources to achieve this goal. A prime motivation is the desire to attain "the good life," with freedom and plenty for all, but apparently more compelling is the struggle among nations for power and status. The societies that enjoy high prestige, and are emulated by others, are usually those that wield political and military advantage, and this depends on an advanced industrial-urban base in today's world. Social orders farther down the scale that have recently thrown off the colonial yoke have set their sights on imitating the powerful nations. Most significant of all is the fact that societal rulers are implementing such policies even at the expense of the traditional authority structure that supports their own power position. They recognize that unless the society industrializes and urbanizes, it may revert to its former colonial status, a possibility that is so repugnant that industrial urbanization becomes the lesser of the evils.

Social scientists' knowledge of the power structure in the traditional society and its effects upon industrial-urban development is all too meager. We must learn more about the relationships among a country's resource base, its political organization, and industrial urbanization.[13] A common research focus for students of the city—sociologists, anthropologists, economists, historians, and political scientists—is the differential impact upon industrial urbanization of various power structures and ideologies.[14] The rate of industrial-urban growth and the social structure of transitional cities appear to differ in "totalitarian" and in "democratic" societies. Those modernizing nations that adopt the Communist model are more prone, or so it seems, to stress heavy industry than are nations that seek inspiration from the democratic model. The latter are likely to emphasize light industry—attempting even to salvage or sustain the earlier handicraft orientation—and are much less intent upon revising the traditional social structure.[15]

Nations committed to some variant on the democratic model also tend to differ markedly from totalitarian ones in their ideology concerning which groups are to bear the "human cost" of industrial urbanization. The Communists, certainly in the U. S. S. R., have called upon the traditional elite and the peasantry to assume a disproportionately heavy share of the burden.[16] They have also sought, via political controls, to suppress the wants of urban consumers, whose expectations would otherwise rise very rapidly.[17] The leaders believe that capital should be channeled toward large-scale industrial enterprises and used to advance scientific know-how. In contrast, the democratic model ideally seeks to equalize the cost of industrial urbanization among the various classes, and it gives greater attention to rising consumer demands, but this in turn fosters a "revolution of rising expectations"; and when these expectations cannot be met political turmoil is likely to result.

The contrast we describe between the totalitarian and the democratic models is admittedly somewhat overdrawn. Some totalitarian regimes (for example, that of Peron in Argentina) have sought to further industrial urbanization while catering to the rising expectations of the urban working class. Even granting this limitation, however, the democratic and totalitarian models are a convenient basis from which to initiate research.

Urban sociologists should not overlook the forces that impede the industrial city's development. In most preindustrial civilized orders now in the throes of industrialization, considerable hostility, latent and manifest, toward the introduction of the newer urban forms is apparent on both the community and the national levels. The incipient industrial forms in the cities become targets of resentment for those who would preserve the traditional, "sacred" order. Knowledge of the sources of this anti-industrial urbanism is an urgent need, because present evidence indicates that under certain conditions they effectively slow the industrial-urban process. This is especially likely, we hypothesize, where traditional values are reinforced by a long-standing and deeply entrenched bureaucratic apparatus. The historical role of the Catholic Church in southern Europe is a case in point. The manner in which the Church has resisted, adapted to, and disseminated industrial-urban lifeways deserves intensive study. In some countries it has effectively opposed industrial urbanization; in others it has sought to mold the social structure of emergent industrial cities in conformance with its own ideology.[18] Of course, any such research would have to take into account the sharp disagreements within the Church itself over policy vis-à-vis the industrial-urban order.

More generally, a comparison of the Nazi movement in Germany, the Poujade movement in France, and the conservative reaction in Turkey after the Second World War supports the proposition that the inhabitants of small towns and villages (those most closely linked to the feudal past) have been the backbone of movements with strong anti-industrial-urban sentiments.[19] Usually these are the groups who have profited least from the industrial-urbanizing efforts of the new order; in effect, they are reacting against the new order from which they are "alienated."

Unfortunately, the attempts at analysis of industrial urbanization in modernizing societies have been riddled with unstated ideological premises. Whether consciously or not, American social scientists tend to reject industrial urbanization as an ideal for these transitional societies; instead they favor the development of moderate-size towns with handicraft industries and the preservation of many rural traditions. The fact that social scientists who hold to "democratic" ideals should implicitly oppose extensive industrial urbanization is somewhat ironical,[20] for recent research supports the hypothesis that democracy flourishes most vigorously within advanced industrial-urban societies.[21] Some constructive self-criticism by social scientists regarding their own implicit or explicit assumptions is in order.

This ideological stance, moreover, involves a question: are people better off in large metropolises or should they stay in the smaller centers, or even in the villages, making a living following the ox and the plow? The answer depends partly upon one's conception of "the good life." But of more immediate significance for us is the concept of "over-urbanization" used generally by social scientists who view the burgeoning of large cities as an impediment to optimum economic development. Some of these writers feel that large metropolises are not only inefficient but that they also inevitably breed slums, disease, and poverty. That these conditions do exist in cities in many modernizing countries can hardly be denied.[22]

However, these fundamentally anti-urban views are deserving of searching criticism, for city dwellers in most modernizing countries enjoy many economic, educational, and other social advantages over ruralites. Consider the economic dimension. Urbanites are the greatest beneficiaries of the few welfare programs that exist in these societies. The fact that ruralites continue to flock to the large cities—in India, Egypt, Greece, Mexico, and elsewhere—suggests that the urban communities are providing these people with certain advantages not found in the villages.[23]

American social scientists are perhaps misled by the greater concentration and higher visibility of poverty in the city; the misery of the countryside, though often greater, is inevitably more diffuse and less transparent. Actually, the high visibility of urban problems encourages the formulation of programs to cope with the "ills" that beset transitional societies, thereby intensifying the industrial-urbanization process. And from a long-run perspective, the inhabitants of large cities are more likely to acquire the skills and values of the emerging industrial system than are people who live in small towns or villages.

Barring nuclear warfare, industrial-urban forms are likely to proliferate at an increasing rate. If sociologists persist in their anti-urban tendencies they will be ill-equipped to generalize concerning the vast urban agglomerations of the future that Davis predicts will encompass tens of millions of people.[24] They must admit the possibility of the emergence in these metropolises of novel social and ecological patterns.

Urban Patterns and Differential Change

Whether industrial urbanization has resulted in a broadening rather than a narrowing of the gap between rural and urban subsystems is a question open to research. Rural-urban contrasts seem to differ in Communist and in non-Communist societies, and the divergency between rural and urban communities may be greater today in some countries of Asia than it was in Western Europe in the nineteenth century. Yet, while the transitional city is importing from abroad much advanced industrial-urban know-how that is intensifying its differentiation from the village, the latter is more than ever before being influenced by mass media, thereby reducing to a degree the gap between city and country. In any event, marked differences between villages and cities persist in developing societies. Consequently, one urgent research need is to examine the means by which ruralites, and preindustrial urbanites, adjust to the modernizing city. To appreciate this process we must understand the changing structure of this kind of city.

We might begin with the general proposition that different elements of the transitional city's social structure change at different rates: those traditional arrangements most closely associated with the economic-technological order seem to buckle first under the impact of industrial urbanization. More specifically, we observe the following processes occurring more or less simultaneously: (1) the persistence of traditional forms, (2) revision or modification of traditional forms, (3) disappearance of traditional forms, and (4) emergence of new structures.

Although much has been written of the tenacity of traditional patterns in modernizing cities, surprisingly few cross-cultural generalizations have been formulated. We are unable to state with confidence which traditional structures are most likely to persist in cities in divergent cultural settings; we sorely need this information.

The most obvious pattern is the reshaping of preindustrial forms—familial, economic, political, and so on—to accord with the needs of the emerging industrial-urban system.[25] Many of these structures are tending toward the industrial model discussed later. Even special types of organizations evince patterns of this sort. In India some facets of the traditional caste system are dying out, whereas others are being remolded along extracommunity lines and are acquiring new and novel functions. The castes, for example, serve as special interest groups in the political arena on both the regional and the national levels.[26] Vogel contends that the marriage broker in Japan plays a more critical role in the transitional order than he did in the preindustrial setting, for his is a key accommodative mechanism between the older patterns and the new.[27]

Some of these changes may generate "ruptures" in segments of the urban social structure and, from the actor's perspective, his social environment may lack integration. It is not uncommon for hiatuses to develop between the newer urban ideals and the institutionalized means available for their achievement. This occurs in marriage patterns in many transitional societies. On the basis of his research in a Tokyo ward, Dore contends that young people consider romantic love as an ideal in courtship and marriage; yet no satisfactory structural means has developed to make this goal attainable.[28] Similar patterns appear in the economic realm. People in industrializing cities are being socialized into certain ideals, especially a high standard of living, that are still unattainable. The result is political and social unrest.

Another dimension of social change in transitional cities is the matter of class. Though it exhibits considerable fluidity and ambiguity, the class structure is typified by a yawning gap between the upper and lower socioeconomic levels.[29] The elite's close involvement with the formal educational structure, which disseminates the knowledge emanating from science and the new technology, means that this class is usually the first to assimilate the new industrial-urban forms. Some of its members have been educated abroad, in advanced industrial-urban settings. Nevertheless, many of them cling to traditional ways that are not easily obliterated. A vexing dilemma for many modernizing countries is how to socialize educated persons into accepting "work with the hands" as a dignified rather than degrading activity. The leaders in China have made intensive efforts to induce "intellectuals" to share in tasks demanding physical labor; one method is insistence upon physical exercise sessions for scientists, students, and the like to rid them of so-called "archaic" values.[30] Government planners in India, too, are distressed by the educated man's aversion to practical pursuits, work with the hands, and entrepreneurship, all of which are essential for industrial urbanization.[31] Indeed, in many societies certain elements of the traditional elite have been the most fervent opponents of industrial urbanization. The bases for the upper socioeconomic group's acceptance or rejection of industrial-urban forms merit detailed investigation.

The adaptation of the lower strata to the emerging industrial-urban milieu is an even more complex matter. Some studies suggest that lower-class persons in the cities and in the villages are striving to attain traditional ideals at the very time that the higher groups are rejecting them and are moving toward the industrial-urban forms. Thanks to the indirect subsidy of industrialization, the common man is now able to realize certain traditional ideals that he could not achieve in the past. From this perspective, industrial urbanization may well breed conservatism. While many Indians in the upper strata are discarding features of the traditional Sanskritized culture, various disadvantaged groups, their lot improved somewhat by industrial progress, are bent on acquiring at long last some of the traditional ideals; this is especially true of certain older family and religious values, and even those relating to caste.[32] As Friedl has observed, contemporary Greek villagers still take the preindustrial city model as their reference point; in the meantime the cities of Greece are modernizing and industrializing.[33]

Yet certain forces contravene this pattern. Modern mass media can directly and rapidly socialize the common man into the industrial-urban way of life. Communist regimes purposively utilize movies, the theater, newspapers, and so on to this end.[34] In nations having close contacts with highly industrial-urban orders such as Mexico vis-à-vis the United States, some lower-class urbanites are bypassing the traditional forms, moving directly toward the industrial-urban ideals.[35]

Minority groups in many transitional cities present a special problem; the traditional outcaste groups are the most notable example. On the other hand, the emerging values generally call for greater equality of opportunity, thus setting in motion forces that undermine the long-perpetuated segregation of minority or outcaste elements. On the other hand, it is often easier for members of minorities to climb within the broader society by identifying with their respective groups than by functioning as lone individuals. In some modernizing societies minorities are given preferential treatment in the political and educational spheres as a means of advancing the ideals of democracy. Thus, the Harijans, or Outcastes, in India are nowadays accorded special advantages to assist them in overcoming their lowly status.[36]

Ultimately we are led back to an examination of the formal and informal organizations through which persons are enabled to adapt to the industrializing urban milieu. Sociologists and anthropologists have come to recognize that newcomers to the city do not function as isolated individuals; rather, they identify with earlier in-migrants from their own village or region and/or persons of the same class, ethnic, or occupational grouping.[37] The enclaves that arise as a result of these similar interests or cultural backgrounds are analogous to the immigrant communities that were typical of American cities some decades ago.[38]

These subsystems in transitional cities perform at least three major functions: (1) Through them the migrant from the village or from another city is oriented to the new and complex urban milieu. Often composed of relatives or acquaintances of the newcomer, the members of these subsystems indoctrinate him into the unfamiliar lifeways and provide him with at least a modicum of knowledge concerning such essentials as how to secure employment and how to avoid arrest. Moreover, it is through these informal subsystems that the newcomer gains access to formal organizations such as schools and unions, which assist him in adapting to the demands of the industrializing city. (2) These informal subsystems are the prime means by which the urbanite sustains ties with the rural traditions. Frequently these groupings sponsor ceremonies whereby the past is recreated and thus perpetuated. (3) It is through these urban groupings that elements of industrial-urban lifeways are carried back to the villages. Some of this knowledge is diffused via the visiting patterns that arise between the rural villagers and out-migrants who have moved to the city.

The Role of Tradition

Analysis of the aforementioned patterns leads us to a strategic question: are these internally integrated subcommunities functional or dysfunctional to the industrial-urban process? Generalizing from his findings in Turkey, Suzuki argues that these kinds of subsystems perform a positive function in furthering industrialization.[39] He argues that the social stability that derives from membership in them makes for a more efficient and effective labor force. On the other hand, some scholars contend that integrated subcommunities which sustain ties with the rural past are an impediment to industrial urbanization.[40] Thus, in many cases the in-migrant's prime loyalty is to his village; so too, the lifelong urbanite may be firmly attached to traditional groupings whose structural links are with the preindustrial way of life. In either case, the members of these subgroups are oriented more to the past than to the future; as such, they tend to resist the goals and values of the emergent industrial-urban order.

The aforementioned controversy results in part from the divergent frames of reference employed by social researchers. Some sociologists study industrial urbanization from the standpoint of the individual and his subgroup, whereas others view this process from the perspective of the total society. Suzuki belongs in the first category, for he neglected to place his subcommunity in the context of the broader Turkish society. He also failed to state explicitly that the community in which he did his research was semi-industrial in nature.

The kinds of subcommunities about which Suzuki wrote have a role to play, but they cannot possibly train and socialize the labor force required to build and sustain a complex industrial city. For this purpose complex, large-scale organizations—for example, formal education media supported by the state—become imperative. Moreover, a society bent on constructing an advanced industrial-urban order must sever most of its ties with the feudal past, although some links with tradition may be essential.

We cannot possibly understand or predict the future course of transitional cities if we do not examine them in their broader societal context. Organizations are being created in many of today's societies for the purpose of rupturing the urbanite's past allegiances and hastening the adoption of industrial-urban forms. In Russia, the Communist

Party and the labor unions have been prime vehicles for instilling in workers the norms of discipline, punctuality, and efficiency. In China, the Party as well as the urban communes have been employed to socialize native urbanites *and* newcomers to the city into the desired norms, including those of health and sanitation.[41] One can picture the Party leaders regularly haranguing the workers with speeches and slogans calling for greater and greater effort. Even in India the labor unions are an important channel through which the urban factory worker is indoctrinated into his role.[42] In all modernizing societies, of course, the formal educational structure is the prime medium for socializing urbanites into the new industrial way of life.

Just as some societal structures foster change, so others help the urbanite sustain some ties with the past. We have already indicated how certain local community organizations may serve this end. The role of the national government in maintaining continuity is easier to overlook. Here charismatic leaders are especially vital. If sociologists are to interpret correctly the transformation of preindustrial cities, they cannot ignore the function of nationalism.[43] For this ideology calls for a glorification of the society's heritage, its history and traditions.[44] Such idealization of the past provides people with a sense of belonging and a feeling of continuity, making it easier for them to shed much of the preindustrial organization and to adopt new structural forms. The Russian leaders, in particular, have purposively encouraged resuscitation of the art, literature, and music of the Turkic peoples of Soviet Central Asia at the very time they have been striving to destroy these groups' traditional economic, political, familial, and religious organizations. In Communist China, too, the leaders are encouraging the revival of the folk arts. Even in India, folk art, music, and literature are gaining in prestige and favor as the preindustrial structure undergoes fundamental change. One consequence of this pattern is the resurgence of traditional ceremonies that have lost their former functions and "content" and thus can readily be adapted to new ideologies.

This search for stability and continuity—the fact that during rapid industrialization urbanites require some link with the past—points up certain contradictory functional imperatives whose theoretical and empirical ramifications have not been explored by sociologists, urban or otherwise. To further revolutionary change, a social order must sustain or revive certain traditions. But just where the balance lies between rapid change and continuity is exceedingly difficult to determine, except in extreme instances.

The Industrial City

In our treatment of the transitional city, we have discussed the main problems relating to research on the processes of change from the preindustrial to the industrial type. We can now delineate the key issues concerning investigation of the social structure of the industrial city, the form toward which the transitional city is moving.

Ecology

Systematic efforts to examine cross-culturally the spatial organization of industrial cities are virtually nonexistent. This holds for the relationship of cities to their hinterland (including other cities) and for their internal arrangements as well. Without a doubt, the efforts to rectify this situation in urban sociology deserve high priority, for an impressive body of research materials on the subject has accumulated. Although the data on cities in Germany, England, France, Japan, the United States, and so on, are not strictly comparable since the levels of industrialization differ, they can provide the basis for some major advances in urban sociology.

The existing propositions concerning urban dominance must be examined cross-culturally.[45] Those who study the industrial city and its relationships to its hinterland must come to grips with the proposition that advanced industrial-urban systems require some all-encompassing political superstructure if they are to achieve economic and social stability and attain the goals implicit in industrial urbanization. The Common Market is one such superstructure.

On the matter of spatial arrangements *within* industrial cities, we can offer certain generalizations that can serve as a guide for research.[46] Industrial cities, in contrast to preindustrial ones, are more likely to revolve about a commercial and/or industrial focus than around a religious-governmental complex. (The larger political capitals in industrial orders tend to be exceptions to this pattern.) Symbolically as well as physically, the typical industrial city's commercial and industrial edifices tower over those of government and religion.

Industrial cities exhibit a high degree of specialization in land use. Unlike the situation in preindustrial centers, residential and occupational sites in the industrial milieu tend to be separated. The continual outward expansion of suburbs in the modern metropolis is one expression of this trend. In marked contrast to the privileged class in preindustrial and modernizing societies, the upper and middle socioeconomic groups in the industrial city tend to reside beyond the city's core, leaving the central area to various low-status groups, and elements of the elite as well.

In many European cities, including those in the U. S. S. R., the persistence of the feudal tradition has inhibited suburbanization because high status has attached to residence in the central city. Contrast this with the pattern in American cities, which lack a feudal heritage. Still, suburbanization in Europe is proceeding relentlessly, hand-in-hand with the diffusion of the "automobile culture." As new residential suburbs arise, a variety of shops and services springs up in the area. Specific types of businesses no longer concentrate in a narrowly defined sector of the city.

The residence patterns of the industrial city's status groups are not so clearly distinguishable as those in the preindustrial context. Just as the lines between classes, ethnic minorities, and occupations are less clearly drawn in the industrial-urban milieu, so too they are much less obvious spatially. But what about the many studies pointing to "islands of segregation" in highly industrialized cities? [47] These cases dramatize the fact that complete residential equality for all urbanites has not been attained; nor is there unlimited social and spatial mobility. With some exceptions, such as the Negroes in America, these enclaves are fewer and less isolated today than in the past, for advancing industrialization has drawn various "minority groups" increasingly into the mainstream of community activity. Looking to the future, we can expect some forces for neighborliness and exclusiveness to persist in the industrial city. While some kinds of spatial segregation are declining others are likely to emerge. Beyond this we cannot safely make any predictions about these new strains toward exclusiveness.

The spatial distribution of the industrial city's people and institutions is also tied to a distinctive set of values. In contrast to preindustrialites, industrial urbanites adhere far more to secular than to sacred or traditional values. Where people do hold sacred conceptions of space (for example, with respect to some historical sites), and the power structure reinforces these views, land-use change and even industrialization itself may be inhibited. Conversely, the values associated with industrialization—punctuality, efficiency, and so on—find expression in particular kinds of spatial arrangements such as newer, more effective transportation routes.

When we move beyond these limited generalizations, we encounter serious difficulties. Recent studies of industrial cities in Europe suggest that a number of common features are discernible despite certain differences among these cities. By way of illustration, consider the city's central core. As people abandon it for the suburbs, the central area is taken over by such units as specialty shops and the managerial and administrative offices of large-scale organizations.[48] By locating in the downtown area, the managers of key enterprises maximize the possibility of personal contacts with one another; such contacts are essential if they are to carry out their functions effectively. Meanwhile, industries are fanning out toward the periphery. This is true of the United States, but whether similar kinds of industrial enterprise exhibit similar spatial patterns in cities in different societies is a question that needs to be answered.

Delineation of urban land use patterns in modern cities is complicated by various current trends: automation, the rapid rise in the proportion of white-collar workers, the increasing amount of leisure time, and the burgeoning of urban agglomerations.[49] While some pressures push the city's boundaries ever outward, contrary forces are at work. For example, we might hypothesize that the automobile will in time "choke itself off" and thus greatly slow, or perhaps even reverse, the trend toward suburbanization.

An industrial technology both demands and makes possible new urban land-use forms. However, at the present state of our knowledge it is exceedingly difficult to determine how particular land-use patterns sustain the industrial complex. Which land-use arrangements provide "optimum" gains for the industrial city as a whole? More specifically, how much separation of work and residence is required for an industrial city to function effectively, and what are the limits of this separation? [50]

Social Differentiation and Stratification

Two facets of the stratification system in industrial cities require detailed cross-cultural study: (1) differences in the nature of the organization of various status groupings within the city, and (2) basic trends in the overall class structure.

On the first point, the evidence suggests that members of the upper socioeconomic strata are the leaders and main participants in the activities of formal organizations on both the community and the societal levels. Although persons in the upper strata also engage in informal activities, the lower status groups fall back upon them almost to the exclusion of formal associational ties. Of course, we can expect this differential to decrease with the advance of automation and education.

As for the permanency and stability of the bonds among persons in the different status groupings, the early Chicago sociologists made much of the disorganization of the lower class and immigrant groups in the city; this was the pattern dramatized by Zorbaugh in his study of *The Gold Coast and the Slum.*[51] But Whyte and others have shown that the slum is organized in its own way.[52] Still, some sectors of the urban community are more loosely organized than others, displaying less cohesion and stability. The lower strata, in particular, enjoy much more fragile personal relationships than do persons who belong to the middle and upper classes. Poverty in itself generates uncertainty and instability. Consider the "beats" in Greenwich Village, described in a sensitive essay by Ned Polsky.[53] As a result of their withdrawal from the formal structures of industrial-urban life, they evince relatively little social integration and stability. Mention of the "beats" brings to mind the role of the rebel in industrial cities in diverse cultures. Are there standardized patterns in this realm? Although the *stilyagi* in Russian cities differ in significant respects from the "beats" in America,[54] the similar actions of youth in various industrial societies suggest the presence of some standardized patterns in the realm of deviant behavior.

Of special significance to the student of differential organization in industrial cities are numerous "mediators"—social workers, teachers, social scientists, among others. These functionaries stand between the lower class and deviant groups on the one hand and the middle- and upper-class groups on the other. These go-betweens diffuse information to the disadvantaged elements and also seek to socialize the latter into the views of the dominant groups within the city and the broader society.

As to the overall patterning of the class structure, many social scientists posit a close association between industrial urbanization and class fluidity, whereas others detect an opposite trend—a firming up of class barriers in such highly industrialized societies as the United States and the Soviet Union.[55]

One reason for this divergency in current theorizing is that social scientists are examining the empirical data through different conceptual lenses. Those who claim to observe trends toward greater rigidity in industrial cities often contrast observed reality with the model of a classless society, with the result that these cities appear to be class-ridden. On the other hand, social scientists who compare the class system of industrial cities with that in preindustrial centers arrive at quite different conclusions: from this perspective the industrial-urban community seems quite fluid. Further confusion arises when sociologists who are seeking to assess the changes in a society's class structure take different time periods as their reference points.[56] Add to this the fact that contradictory forces are at work within the industrial city, some encouraging greater rigidity and some discouraging it,

Yet it is clear that the industrial city's poor are neither so stiflingly poor, nor the elite so far removed from the common man, as their counterparts in preindustrial or transitional cities.[57] Nor are ethnic minorities so clearly distinguishable in the industrial-urban milieu. Although pressures to preserve ethnic ties persist, as members of minorities search for identity or use their minority group connections to ascend the social ladder, the overall structural change, as well as the value system that calls for status by achievement rather than ascription, serves to override many of the traditional patterns.

There are several dimensions to the industrial city's class system that require special attention. One significant pattern concerns the standardization of personal attributes—speech, personal mannerisms, and dress. In contrast to the preindustrial setting, these attributes are vague and amorphous. Yet urban sociologists have given little attention to the implications arising from the loss of personal attributes within the secondary-group setting of large metropolitan areas. The ambiguity of these personal markers facilitates a person's escape from his class or other status identities, with multiple consequences for the social control patterns within modern cities.

Occupation is another dimension of class, or stratification more generally, that is of special interest to sociologists. Clearly, there is much more upward mobility within industrial than preindustrial cities. Moreover, the mobility patterns in the urban sector of industrial societies—at least as measured by the movement of urbanites from manual to nonmanual occupations—appear to be rather similar across national boundaries.[58] Without this individual mobility the many new occupational positions being created by the advancing technology could not be staffed. In addition, entire occupational groups continue to experience major shifts in their relative power, prestige, and monetary rewards. And automation will likely heighten this type of mobility in ways that urban sociologists must explore.[59] For example: Will the cybernetics revolution, which is eliminating many blue-collar and white-collar workers, lead, as some writers suggest, to a few intellectuals, scientists, and managers working long hours in contrast to the mass urban population, who will live in relative leisure? Or will service occupations proliferate so as to absorb those occupational groups now being eliminated from the labor force by automation, with a consequent restructuring of the class system?

But one must analyze not only the movement of individuals and groups but the supposed cross-cultural similarities of social rankings in industrial cities and societies. Some unexplained anomalies exist. The work of Inkeles and Rossi,[60] among others, indicates that in diverse industrial cities and societies leading governmental officials, professional persons (notably doctors, lawyers, and teachers), and industrial managers all enjoy elevated social standing. The industrial-urban structure supports, and is apparently sustained by, a common core of values with respect to the ranking of occupational groups. Still, the imperatives of the industrial-urban order do not account for all the similarities, for certain high-status pursuits in industrial cities have traditionally carried high prestige in preindustrial orders as well. Apparently all large-scale social systems require that certain occupations, such as key governmental roles, enjoy elevated status. However, a number of occupational groups having low prestige in the preindustrial city—physicians, managers of manufacturing or commercial enterprises, and entertainers—have risen considerably in status under the aegis of industrialism. At the same time, some traditionally high-status occupations like the clergy and certain categories of intellectuals seem to have declined.

The patterning of the power dimension of social class is of utmost significance. The intensive specialization of occupational roles that characterizes the industrial city tends to delimit the effective dominance of ruling elites on both the local and the societal levels. The complexity of the industrial-urban order makes it impossible for those in positions of power to keep before them all pertinent facts concerning the system's manifold activities. Although he is not a manager or administrator, the highly trained specialist can exercise a degree of authority because of his monopoly of strategic information. Indeed, the acknowledged leaders in political or other spheres may become "captives" of the experts below them. Concentration of vital technical information in the hands of these specialists is furthered also by the nature of authority in a democracy; here the leaders derive their authority from "the consent of the governed."

Along with the greatly increased fluidity in the class system, certain requirements of the industrial-urban order call for some kind of stratification.[61] Sociologists in the Durkheimian tradition reason that stratification is intensified by the industrial society's complex division of labor, a feature which many sociologists believe minimizes class distinctions and reduces the ruling group's authority. Thus managers, or persons of superior prestige and power, are needed to coordinate or synchronize the activities of specialists who operate, with only a minimal understanding of one another's roles, on both the community and the societal levels. Extrapolating from this fact, some social scientists doubt that democracy can survive the onslaught of advanced industrialization with its demands for a managerial elite.[62]

Significantly, however, most students of ruling elites overlook the distinctive nature of leadership in industrial-urban systems. Whereas the preindustrial-urban elite rationalizes its dominance by appeal to absolutes and to tradition, the elite in industrial-urban orders depends for its self-justification upon the popular largesse. This is true of the political realm as well as the economic and cultural spheres. Since popular opinion is more capricious than are tradition and absolutes, the new elite's power and authority in various spheres of activity is far more tenuous than that enjoyed by the preindustrial system's leaders. The emergence of an elite based upon mass support, on either the community or the national levels, is deserving of more attention than it has received. Overall, sociologists have made only meager efforts to examine the contradictory structural arrangements that obtain in the class and power structure in the industrial city.

Family

Most sociologists assume that the ideal and the usual family form in mature industrial cities is the conjugal unit, as opposed to the large, extended type with members of three or more generations living under a single "roof." However, some dissenting voices have recently been heard. As noted earlier, the urban lower class and the peasantry in feudal orders have typically been unable to sustain the society's ideal of a large extended family residing within a single "household." It is this esteemed form, achievable mainly by the upper class in the cities, that is dysfunctional in the industrial-urban context.

The conjugal unit, as the ideal family type, has perhaps reached its most striking development in American cities, though it is becoming increasingly dominant in industrial cities in Great Britain, Germany, the U. S. S. R., and apparently even Japan. The industrial city's conjugal family is closely associated with heightened status and freedom for women and adolescents within the family and the community at large. In turn these patterns are functionally linked to other trends. One is the formation of a "youth culture" and the accompanying "social problem" of juvenile delinquency. The Russian leaders are distressed by the young "hooligans" in the cities who clearly lack dedication to Soviet ideals; Japan worries over its youthful beatniks and revolutionaries; and so on.[63] The high standard of living in industrial cities frees young people from the need to seek employment in order to eke out a livelihood and contribute to the family's earnings. Then, too, few positions can be filled by adolescents; the industrial-urban order demands of its workers more and more formal education or specialized training. Consequently, adolescents with considerable time on their hands are thrown together and left to their own devices. The mass media further sever them from the adult world and help to loosen family ties by emphasizing certain lifeways to which young people aspire.

This unfolding of a "youth culture" sets the stage for "romantic love" as a legitimized basis for marriage. Contrary to the allegations of some social scientists, romantic love as a foundation for marriage and family life is a relatively recent and unique phenomenon. Where parents no longer select mates for their offspring according to strictly social considerations, romantic love serves as the chief medium in the development of mutual understanding, particularly where the couple have quite different social backgrounds.

One of the most striking features of the industrial city concerns the role and status of women.[64] As industrialization has advanced, "respectable" women have sallied forth from the home to carve a niche for themselves in the world outside. One index of their heightened status is the extensive formal education they have been acquiring, and their role as wage-earners, decision-makers, and so on outside the home has sharply elevated their status within the family. Both in the labor market and in the home, the formerly clear-cut division of labor has largely disappeared. As a result, industrial cities evince a wide range of possible adaptations in husband-wife roles, about which we have only a modicum of information.[65]

Although women have invaded almost every occupational field, sex discrimination survives in industrial cities. Full equality in the labor market has not been achieved, and perhaps it never will be. One factor is the periodic withdrawal of many women from the labor force for the bearing and rearing of children. Another is the stress given to femininity, or to woman as a "sex symbol." [66] These emphases contravene some of the egalitarian tendencies. Sociologists have paid surprisingly little attention to the contradictions that inhere in the roles played by women in modern cities.

We can now return to the conjugal family and pose two questions. (1) Why is this the prevailing form in industrial-urban centers? (2) What are some of the countertendencies? One reason for the prominence of the relatively small, flexible family system is that it seems to accord best with a highly trained mobile labor force. Mass education and the opening up of countless new occupations demand loose family ties; without this freedom, urbanites could not take advantage of the new opportunities and adjust to the ever-changing scientific technology. Simultaneously the conjugal family has come to serve as a prime source of emotional security for the individual. Yet this tendency also acts to loosen family bonds, for the notion of "emotional well-being" is a highly individualistic matter and, as such, is difficult to institutionalize as part of a normative order. One result has been the proliferation of counselors, lawyers, psychiatrists, and other mediators who can arbitrate differences among family members.

Some groups in the industrial city profit economically and politically from maintaining extensive kinship ties. The recent studies by Townsend [67] and others on London's lower class have created quite a stir; some sociologists assume these findings refute the proposition that the conjugal family is a necessary adjunct of the industrial city. But this is hardly the case. The data do seem to refute the notion that the conjugal family unit lacks extensive kinship ties. But they do not point to a resuscitation of the preindustrial-urban ideal, namely a large, extended family gathered under a single "roof." Rather, Townsend found that even where old people reside with the family of a son or daughter many would prefer to live alone, albeit near at hand.[68]

In practice, family forms in industrial-urban centers differ according to social class. On the basis of an extensive survey of the literature, Goode contends that

> . . . the contacts of upper-strata families with their kin form a smaller proportion of their total social interactions, since the higher strata belong to more voluntary organizations, clubs, and formal groups than the lower strata. On the other hand, they have more resources with which to maintain their ties with kin, and because of these means, mutual exchanges are also more frequent than in the lower strata.[69]

As cities industrialize, especially in the context of a feudal past, the lower strata may well adopt the preindustrial-urban family model, for as their income rises they come closer than ever to achieving the ideal that has long been held before them. This may account for some of Townsend's findings.

Looking ahead, we discern still other changes under way in familial organization. We know little about how lengthening life expectancy or the expanding leisure time will modify family patterns, but we can expect the relationships among generations to become more complex. We should also explore the interconnections between the broader kinship system and the actions of individuals and bureaucratic structures in the industrial-urban setting.[70]

Economic Structure

Industrial cities diverge dramatically from preindustrial cities in their economic organization. Within the industrial city, extended leisure, a product of new production methods and a shorter work week, is increasingly the prerogative of the common man.[71] Today many high-status persons work longer hours than do those in low-status occupations, a situation quite the reverse of that in the preindustrial-urban setting.

Within affluent industrial cities the ordinary man lives far above the survival threshold. The economic rewards for his labor, as well as his overall health standards, have improved markedly. Industrialization has also made possible and imperative the development of a host of services, many of them totally unknown to the preindustrial urbanite. These range from special welfare benefits to provisions in the cultural arts and include facilities that cater to industrial man's self-perpetuating appetite for consumption goods of various kinds.

In the process the composition of the labor force (as suggested earlier) is undergoing marked change. Industrial technology demands more and more professional persons, scientific specialists, and skilled technicians who are committed to the ideals of efficiency and rationality as well as to "the good life" in the material realm. Actually, automation has progressed to the point where the question of how to integrate the little-educated person into the city's economic system has become a major social problem in some industrial orders.

The proliferation of specialists has been associated with the evolution of a highly complex educational apparatus. Formal educational systems are found side by side with a bevy of special institutes, seminars, and on-the-job training programs whose task is to socialize workers into the demands of the industrial order. And this educational system shares with the mass media the responsibility for keeping the populace informed about technological innovations and their social implications.

Sociologists are in general agreement concerning the patterning of these features of the economy, but the theoretical implications are another matter. Considerable argumentation revolves about one question in particular: Does the heightened division of labor in the urban community foster integration or disunity? The followers of Durkheim have long contended that it leads to greater interdependency among segments of the social order and, therefore, to integration. In general the data support this view of the industrial city as compared to the preindustrial, but certain qualifications must be interjected.

First, an intensive division of labor can breed disunity. In industrial-urban systems it fosters the vested interest groups that crystallize about specialized occupations and vie for the social rewards that derive from industrialization. Second, a vast extension of education and mass communication has accompanied further division of labor;

this has fostered greater homogeneity along ethnic, class, and regional dimensions.[72] Perhaps it is the broader commonality of values, added to the complex division of labor, that lends cohesion to the industrial-urban order.

While recognizing these qualifications, we believe that the industrial city's division of labor plays a strategic role in social integration, though an empirical test is difficult. The division of labor in the contemporary city involves a set of *social norms* that demand interdependency among workers having special technical knowledge. Such a pattern is quite different from that in the preindustrial city, where the division of labor involves specialization according to product rather than process, and where the technical information possessed by any one person is quite limited. Here only a modicum of cooperation among workers is required for the system to function. Udy and other sociologists fail to differentiate between the kind of division of labor in industrial cities and that found in preindustrial centers; as a result, they cannot adequately interpret modern urban social and economic patterns.[73]

A corollary of this intensive specialization is the demand on both the local and the national levels for large-scale bureaucracies to direct and integrate the operations of manifold segments of the labor force. The industrial order's bureaucratic structure, unlike that in the feudal system, tends to gigantism. Essentially interurban in character, it encourages linkages of an extracommunity sort. Moreover, the industrial-urban bureaucracy requires an echelon of managers to prod the system toward achievement of its objectives. As a result of their training, these functionaries stress innovation and entrepreneurship. Certainly, there appear to be a number of common features in the industrial manager's role across sociocultural boundaries.[74] In addition to the managers, another highly significant group of functionaries has emerged in industrial-urban orders. It includes such mediators as labor negotiators and members of grievance committees. Almost no attention has been given to the function these mediators play in harmonizing the many complex, and often contradictory, roles that exist within various sectors of the occupational structure, and in integrating them with those in the broader social order.[75]

Overall, industrial-urban bureaucracies display many of the characteristics Weber assigned to rational, capitalistic structures. Weber's theory, of course, has been seriously questioned in recent years. If we take the preindustrial-urban order as our point of comparison, however, modern bureaucracies appear highly rational and efficient. The industrial city's economic structure is characterized by intensive planning and by numerous reports, audits, and investigations by experts, all of which are lacking or rudimentary in the preindustrial city, where they are unnecessary for the functioning of the economic system. The present-day budgeting and auditing procedures, the maintenance of personnel files, the recruitment of workers according to universalistic criteria so as to obtain the most highly qualified persons—all these presuppose social and technological innovations that are unquestionably more industrial than preindustrial in form.

The advance of social science itself is inextricably associated with the striving for rationality. We may consider only one example. Although social science activity in the Soviet Union is sharply restricted, the demands for empirical data are incessant, and the barriers surrounding social research must be lowered for reasons of political expediency.

The achievement of greater rationality and efficiency in the industrial city presumes a fairly high level of technical knowledge, and it also requires considerable standardization in the production and distribution processes. This is possible only if the economic and political organizations formalize their rules and procedures. Regularization of coinage, weights and measures, prices, and the quality of goods and services far exceeds that in the preindustrial city.

Counterpressures obviously act to reduce standardization. Even in the Soviet Union different styles in radios, clothing, and so on are produced for different consumer levels. Furthermore, even a small degree of competition among producers helps to sustain the quality of consumer goods; theoretically, the consumer will buy the "best" and thus will weed out the producers of inferior goods.[76] Thus advertising, though decried as sheer capitalistic wastage, plays a role in the Soviet Union. It stimulates a degree of competition among producers, and it is a means of educating consumers to accept the new products that result from technological innovation.

Another question arises: "How much centralization of decision-making in the economic and/or political orbits is feasible in industrial-urban societies?" There do seem to be functional limits to both centralization and decentralization.[77] According to some observers, the Soviets are retreating from their commitment to extreme centralization, whereas in the United States the heightened demands for national planning have been nibbling away at the local community's autonomy.

A critical issue in industrial-urban orders concerns the amount of autonomy the local community can wield in an industrial-urban society. We hypothesize that the range within which urban communities can function effectively is rather wide, although it may be narrower than in the preindustrial, civilized society. It is difficult to specify with precision what is the optimum "balance," or point of equilibrium, between the opposing structural requirements. Given our present state of knowledge, we may have to be satisfied with delineating, through the use of "negative cases," the boundaries to feasible centralization and decentralization.

Political Structure

A comparison of the political organization of the preindustrial or the modernizing city and society with that found in advanced industrial-urban orders suggests some significant hypotheses. For example, there seems to be a close association between democracy and an industrial-urban way of life, though it is by no means a perfect one. But just what is meant by "democracy"? A "democratic" political system is characterized by (1) an institutionalized opposition vis-à-vis the group in command, and (2) the consent of the governed as the ultimate basis of authority. The two criteria are obviously interrelated. Only as the existence of an opposition becomes institutionalized can one governing element effectively transfer authority to another without detriment to the system's stability.

Lipset contends that certain traits we associate with highly industrialized orders—an open class system, mass literacy, and so on—are factors that favor the rise and effective functioning of a democratic political system.[78] Restating this hypothesis we advance the proposition that democracy is a necessary, though perhaps not a sufficient, condition for the maintenance of a relatively stable industrial-urban system on both the local *and* the national levels.

The rise of democracy is also related to the division of labor within the industrial-urban order. The vast proliferation of experts has diffused both knowledge and authority over a broad spectrum of the social system. It is through the democratic process that the industrial-urban system harmonizes and integrates the conflicting views of experts and of the various interest groups that form about them.

Earlier we mentioned that specialists in the economic, political, and educational bureaucracies tend to carve out niches for themselves— little islands of localized power and authority. Whether in the white-collar or the blue-collar category, many individuals are organized into special interest groups, including professional associations, unions, and the like. These associations not only cut across bureaucratic structures but tend to be extracommunity oriented. Kerr and his co-authors believe that the cleavages among various special interest groups will eventually supplant the schisms along class lines that have so long prevailed in civilized societies.[79] This is an hypothesis that requires intensive investigation.

Moreover, political and other leaders in industrial cities seek vital information from experts—the "trustees of scientific knowledge." Indeed, recourse to these specialists is deemed the only rational mode of decision-making. Thus politicians in various societies argue for military or economic progress in terms of the knowledge provided them by military or economic experts.[80] At the same time, experts often fail to perceive the broader community or societal implications of their own actions, and as a group they are frequently incapable of reaching consensus on many vital issues. Indeed, social scientists cluster at opposite poles on questions of how to cope with economic recessions, while physical scientists are at odds over the long-run effects of radiation. More often than not it is the politician who must mediate the opposing viewpoints and keep the system on a relatively even keel. At times the politician must balance the opinions of the experts against the views of the mass populace upon whose votes he depends for his continuance in office. Ultimately, the politician serves as a strategic mediator among various interest groups, who reflect the internal contradictions within the industrial-urban system.[81]

Questions may arise concerning our argument to the effect that democracy is a product of and is functionally essential to the maintenance of an industrial-urban order. What about the industrial-urban societies that have deviated from this pattern? Germany under Hitler comes to mind. One could argue, however, that in large degree the basis of Hitler's power lay in the support he received from proponents of the older feudal structure and its values.[82] The Soviet Union is another case in point. It is especially strategic for either disproving or confirming the hypothesis regarding the relationship of democracy and industrial urbanization. Some fragmentation in the power and authority structure of the Soviet system is quite apparent nowadays, and there is a concomitant enhancement of the status of the scientific expert. In addition, leaders are more and more concerned with "feedback" from below, with the public's reactions to various programs the government initiates. The emergence of public opinion polls, though they are limited in scope, is a development of significance. For some years the Russian leadership has permitted and even encouraged the public to use the letters-to-the-editor columns in newspapers to upbraid lesser officials who deviate from the system's ideals. These partial ruptures with the authoritarian past demand attention from students of urban life.[83]

More generally, the dictatorships we associate with industrial-urban systems are of a different kind than those in the preindustrial context, at least in their mode of rationalizing their power. The modern dictator gives at least lip service to the notion of "the consent of the governed"; he does not appeal to absolutes such as "divine right" to justify his rule.

Still, industrial urbanization will not lead to any utopia. Many urbanites are said to experience a sense of alienation as a result of the complexity of modern life. Even in a democracy the individual may feel powerless to influence the political course of events. Then, too, an industrial-urban order is beset by instabilities that emerge from contradictions within the system as well as strains between external and internal imperatives. The external requirements, in particular, lead to deviations from the democratic ideal. Thus secrecy in many areas of international relations is the accepted mode of action. Leaders strive to seal themselves off from the conflicting and sometimes uninformed opinions of the populace in order to cope with certain external problems.

Another dilemma confronting the democratic industrial-urban order can be phrased as a question: How much "pluralism" and how much "homogeneity" are required for the system's effective functioning? Many American social scientists assume that pluralism of some sort is essential to offset the mass society's inherent instability, as well as to curb the authoritarian tendencies of any ruling element.[84] In this context, "pluralism" refers to heterogeneity in terms of power and authority. But it appears to be highly fragile and little understood. It is not the political pluralism, as in France, that tends to stultify the democratic process. Nor is it the pluralism of language and caste characteristic of cities in India.[85] Democratic pluralism signifies the erasing of ethnic and religious barriers and an end to the kind of fragmentation that characterizes the feudal society and its cities. It implies commonality in the overall goals of the society; any divergencies of opinion are confined to the selection of the proper means to these ends. It implies a spirit of trust and compromise and tolerance of rather divergent values. But such tolerance may make this system vulnerable to extremist movements.[86]

This reasoning leads us back to our earlier discussion concerning the heightened specialization of the labor force in industrial cities. The close integration of diverse elements of the social order, which some sociologists attribute to the complex division of labor, may be partially a result of the cultural homogeneity that obtains in industrial centers. In the end, the question of how much homogeneity and how much heterogeneity are feasible in an industrial-urban order can best be determined by specifying the limits within which democracy can function rather than by seeking to establish some optimum balance point.

In our consideration of the political structure and the integration of modern industrial cities, we cannot ignore the legal system. Like politicians, those who occupy roles in the legal structure are often called upon to compromise the differences among vested interest groups or among occupational specialists. They must also deal with the fundamental conflict between the rights of the individual and those of the collectivity. The individual versus collectivity dilemma has attracted little attention in urban sociology.[87]

Unlike the politician, who typically seeks accommodation through negotiation, mainly by probing for areas of common interest, the legal functionary employs highly formalized procedures. Moreover, the administration of these legal norms differs markedly from one system to another. The modes of ascertaining guilt or innocence are quite distinct in industrial and preindustrial cities. In the latter, one is assumed to be guilty until proved innocent, and magico-religious rites are common means of determining the result. The law offers little protection for the accused. In the industrial city, however, the trend is toward universalism and a deepening rationalization of the legal structure, a pattern that seems to be developing even in the U. S. S. R., albeit slowly and painfully.[88] These changes result in part from the greater authority of the common man today, and in part from the need for some standardized rules so that differences among scientific experts can be more satisfactorily adjudicated.

Mass Communication and Education

Industrialization fosters the rapid proliferation of communication media—including magazines, newspapers, radio, television, and movies. In turn, the industrial-urban order depends for its very existence upon the functioning of these media; the complex body of knowledge that must continually be disseminated cannot be diffused simply by word of mouth.

In addition to transmitting technical information vital for the city's operation, the mass media keep the populace informed about the many technological innovations that lead to revisions in the economic, political, and educational realms. Education is an ongoing, day-by-day process. Moreover, it is through the mass media that much purposive control is exerted, whether by leaders bent on influencing popular thinking or by elements of the citizenry who seek to prod the leaders into initiating particular reforms.[89]

We have also witnessed the rise of "popular culture" in the industrial-urban system as a byproduct of the mass media. The proliferation of this culture reflects not only the common man's growing importance but also the expanding leisure time he enjoys. Today urbanites of divergent social backgrounds and residing in widely separate communities can share in many popular leisure-time pursuits. This pattern also seems to integrate elements of the urban community in ways that sociologists have not examined. Actually some elements of popular culture such as jazz thrive so well in the individualized urban milieu that they have diffused even to societies whose leaders actively oppose such influences.

Intellectuals in Europe and America have commented on the so-called deleterious effects of the mass media on urban man.[90] But the results are actually rather contradictory. Although the mass media may foster certain kinds of disintegration, they also exert a standardizing influence on the thinking, beliefs, and tastes of the ordinary urbanite, and this fosters social integration. The mass media also open up to societal leaders possibilities of manipulating the average urbanite to a degree unimagined in the preindustrial city. Yet these same channels provide the ordinary man with the sophistication he needs to protect himself against the machinations of leaders who would exploit the mass media for questionable ends.

Still more significant for diffusing information in the industrial-urban order is the formal educational system. Advanced industrialization, having freed man from the incessant struggle for bread, provides him with the leisure necessary for formal study. But just as imperative, the industrial city (and the broader society) demands assiduously trained experts for its advancement and very continuance. As automation hurries its pace, the demands upon the educational structure increase accordingly. Thus, many industrial-urban orders in Europe are in the throes of an educational revolution that bids fair to revise fundamentally the social structure of their cities.[91] Not only are more persons gaining advanced education, but most of the newly educated are specialists steeped in scientific know-how rather than in the humanities, which so long dominated European education. The resultant proliferation of scientific specialists generates even more rapid change. And scientific research becomes a major economic enterprise into which vast funds are channeled.

The impact upon the city of an educational system committed to the scientific method has been largely ignored. But if one views science as part of technology, as we do, analysis of this problem area is central to an understanding of the social and cultural patterns within industrial communities.

While on the matter of the relationship of education and scientific learning, it seems appropriate to raise a critical question: What are the essential ingredients and consequences of this new kind of knowledge for the industrial-urban order? Given our own theoretical commitment—one that views science as part of technology—the answer to this question is central to our analysis. Our thesis is that many of the values and beliefs of the industrial-urban system have their origin in the scientific method. In science, positive values attach to "negation" and to the notion of "institutionalized opposition." Quite unlike the knowledge that typifies the preindustrial city, modern science thrives on a degree of scepticism; it advances by negating existing interpretations of the physical and social systems and by substituting more adequate ones. The industrial technology is constantly undergoing revision; indeed it involves a "permanent revolution." [92] Not surprisingly, a degree of secularization results from application of the scientific method.

Furthermore, science fosters institutionalized opposition in other realms of human activity. The period since the Industrial Revolution gives evidence of a causal connection between the advancement of science and the rise of political democracy. Yet the association is by no means perfect. Industrial urbanites—and scientists are no exception —display a remarkable capacity for playing multiple roles, for compartmentalizing their thought and action patterns. Thus Nazi scientists found themselves faithfully pursuing their labors amid the horrors of concentration camps, all the while gaining security and satisfaction from performance of their technical duties. All the same, we hypothesize that such an extreme divergency in one's roles cannot be sustained over a long period of time.

Another facet of the scientific method, and one that shapes the industrial urbanite's "world view," consists in explaining physical and social phenomena (including disasters such as earthquakes, disease, and economic depressions) in natural rather than divine terms. One who is committed to the scientific method sees the physical and social worlds as manipulable and controllable. In contrast, the preindustrial urbanite attributes disasters, physical and social, to divine will or the caprices of hostile supernatural forces; he does not ordinarily attempt to revise the existing order. Rather he assumes that it is not to be tampered with by mere human beings. This fundamental divergency in the interpretation of reality lies at the heart of many of the structural and ideological disparities between preindustrial-urban and industrial-urban societies.

Furthermore, science must stress universalism over particularism if it is to be successful. One cannot hope to falsify or confirm hypotheses on particularistic grounds So, too, scientific personnel must be recruited primarily on the basis of achievement rather than in terms of ascription. This gives rise to the following proposition: the more closely social organizations depend for their operation upon modern science, the more likely they are to emphasize norms like universalism and achievement when dealing with their employees and their clientele. We would expect a religious order to deviate from these ideal norms to a greater degree than would a scientific institute. Even in the latter, however, the existence of contradictory requirements prevents the full realization of these norms.

Still another effect of the scientific method upon the industrial-urban system derives from the fact that science flourishes when scientists can identify with a loosely organized professional group and effectively exchange data and thus cross-fertilize budding ideas. From this perspective, scientists are committed to maintaining an "open society." As a result, they seek to sustain contacts with colleagues in other communities and beyond national boundaries. The local community is clearly unable to hold these persons in its grip, and even the nation must compete with these transcultural, multinational professional ties for the scientist's allegiance.

Finally, the idea of "ethical neutrality," intrinsic in the scientific method, serves the cause of science in that it challenges the efforts of politicians who would confine the scientist to some narrow ideology. The very notion of neutral, objective knowledge facilitates compromise among competing individuals or interest groups in modern society. Mediators, including politicians, may appeal to the "facts" as the basis for achieving consensus among conflicting parties.

Yet the principle of ethical neutrality generates problems of its own. Consider the educational realm. An industrial-urban system, which must educate its members into accepting the principle of ethical neutrality, has to train certain persons to make sound "extrascientific" judgments. Scientists seem to have grasped the issues here more clearly than sociologists, as witness the writings of C. P. Snow.[93] Nor is this dilemma confined to industrial-urban systems in the democratic West; the Soviet Union also is groping for a more effective means of balancing the demands for technicians with those for persons educated in the humanities. Training party functionaries to be the primary "moralizers" in the society leaves much to be desired.[94] It allows little room for such intellectuals as social philosophers and novelists to probe for meaning in the industrial-urban setting apart from the immediate concerns of practical politics.

Once more we encounter the question that troubled Durkheim and has plagued other sociologists since his time: Is a complex division of labor sufficient to sustain an industrial-urban order? The demand for persons who moralize, who make extrascientific judgments, indicates that an industrial-urban system requires more than just skilled technicians.

Religious Structure and the Value System

Although much is still to be learned by sociologists about certain facets of industrial-urban life, our ignorance of the religious structure and its related value system is particularly glaring. One proposition, however, seems well documented in the literature: a heightened secularization of religion occurs in the industrial city, particularly as opposed to the preindustrial city type. Religious values no longer permeate the entire social fabric. Indeed, large sectors of activity have become exempt from religious injunctions in the industrial city. The existing religious norms tend to be permissive rather than prescriptive. Inasmuch as industrial urbanites often are called upon to play multiple and even contradictory roles, any rigid moralization would subject people to incessant conflict and indecision.

True, some industrial-urban orders are less secular than others, and considerable variation with respect to religious ties persists within and among societies.[95] Even the Soviet Union, which has pursued a vigorous antireligious policy and envisages no place for religion in the social system, is experiencing efforts to revive religion.[96] Some observers claim that the United States has undergone a religious revival in urban centers during recent decades. Other sociologists doubt the validity of the statistics cited. Actually it is highly unlikely that religion is having a greater impact upon the daily life of urbanites now than a few generations ago.[97]

Overall, the following working hypothesis seems in order: religion continues to shape the lives of many urbanites, but less so than in past decades, and certainly to a far lesser degree than in preindustrial cities.[98] In the process religion has become more a private than a public matter.[99] Even many devoutly religious persons are applying their religious ideals to only limited spheres of daily life.

Concerning the organization of the church itself, we can offer only the most tentative of hypotheses. Close on the heels of industrial urbanization have sprung up numerous sectarian groupings that seem in many ways to meet the needs of certain lower-class urbanites.[100] Yet given the generalized weakness of the religious commitment, these fragmented ecclesiastical bodies tend to be unstable; they eventually disappear or merge with others of their kind.

Still unanswered is the following question: Can urbanites function effectively over a long period without the stabilizing influence of some traditional religious ideology, particularly one that seeks to provide a meaning for life after death? [101] Most sociologists would probably respond in the affirmative. Nevertheless, the problem of meaning for the individual continues to trouble social philosophers and social scientists in industrial-urban orders. By and large, this problem has been the province of religion throughout history.

Some industrial urbanites seek meaning in life by embracing such secular religions as nationalism and scientism. We know little about the function of either of these ideologies. Although nationalism in industrial cities is not as potent a force as it is in transitional ones, it still provides a rationale for living and for dying and, like religion, it demands sacrifices. And it is highly significant that in the U. S. S. R. the intellectuals have taken the "scientific socialism" of the nineteenth century as the basis for their utopian model for industrial-urban living.[102]

Other industrial urbanites have found meaning in a kind of secular ceremonialism or "ritualism." In a city oriented to consumption and leisure-time pursuits, parties, sports, and vacations—associated with a "fun morality" that is highly stylized and ritualized—become a way of life for many people. Those who engage in these activities feel they are "in the swing of things" and thereby gain a sense of personal direction. Such a pattern of existence—dramatized effectively in the movie *La Dolce Vita*—stresses only the present and minimizes any concept of the past or of the future. A major research problem is to understand how large segments of the urban populace are able to maintain a sense of direction when work or traditional religion are no longer dominant forces in their lives.

The End Product: A Reassessment of Some Basic Issues

That industrial cities over the world are becoming alike in many aspects of their social structure is our main thesis. Implicit in our analysis is another hypothesis: as technology becomes increasingly complex, a significant number of structural imperatives become more narrowly defined. Thus preliterate societies with their simple technology display greater diversity in their economic and familial organization than do preindustrial civilized societies, and the latter in turn display greater diversity in these realms than do industrial ones.

Yet we cannot ignore the potential objections to our primary thesis. A Marxist, for one, would insist upon the fundamental dissimilarities between cities in communist and in capitalist societies, for he is committed to the thesis that these divergent types of economic systems lead to basically different kinds of social organization within a community or a society as a whole. It is of some ideological consequence that West European and American social scientists have generally abandoned the capitalist-socialist dichotomy for the industrial-nonindustrial one; by so doing, they recognize many more similarities among industrial systems than do the Soviet theorists. This is true even of writers like Parsons, who were nurtured in the Weberian heritage.

Another constellation of scholars who challenge the notion of an increasing similarity among industrial-urban orders are those who insist upon the preeminence of cultural values.[103] We also believe that cultural values induce stylistic differences among industrial cities that cannot be ignored. However, a value system cannot modify structural arrangements in an infinite variety of ways. Industrial cities share certain values because of their dependence on the scientific method and modern technology. Overemphasis of cultural values as an independent variable leads to historicism and a denial of the possibility of making cross-cultural generalizations.

A third source of opposition to our theoretical perspective finds its reference in the French Revolution. Writers steeped in this tradition emphasize the impact of different political values and institutions upon industrial-urban systems. They stress the differences between the social structures of democratic and of totalitarian systems. It cannot be denied that some divergencies exist in urban forms as a result of differing political structures, but this should not allow one to disregard the similarities.

Sociologists like ourselves, who champion the notion of the "convergence" of industrial societies and their cities, clearly focus on the similarities. Our antagonists have recourse to variables other than technology and on this basis they stress the differences among industrial-urban systems. Add to this the emphasis given to selected features of industrial cities and the dissensus becomes even more pronounced.

These disagreements affect the social scientist's analysis of industrial-urban systems in specific societies. It has been argued that Japan's industrial organization, and many other features of its urban life, diverges sharply from those in the West because of the unique cultural milieu within which it has been shaped. Abegglen stresses those patterns in Japanese factories that diverge from the factory organization in Western cities.[104] But his reasoning is not persuasive. As Drucker indicates, some recently emergent sectors of the Japanese industrial complex are quite unlike the traditional forms of which Abegglen speaks; they resemble their Western counterparts far more closely.[105] Odaka supports Drucker's thesis and goes on to criticize Abegglen for overemphasis on the positive contribution of tradition to industrial-urban development in Japan.[106] Approaching the problem from another perspective, Dore also concludes that Japanese urban life is moving toward some approximation of the Western model.[107] Significantly, Dore has been concerned with comparing the present with the past within a Tokyo ward. From this vantage point, the present structure is closer to Western urban-industrial forms than to Tokyo's preindustrial past.

So it is with scholars who contrast the United States and the Soviet Union. Those who stress the structural similarities see much in common between the two, especially in contrast to modernizing or preindustrial civilized societies.[108] The more intrepid thinkers assume some kind of convergence in the development of these industrial giants. Even those who underline the differences recognize that in matters of education and literacy, the structure of the labor force, and so on, cities in the United States and in the Soviet Union resemble one another more closely than they do the cities of, say, India or Iran.[109] Of course, not even the most committed of the writers who perceive marked similarities would claim that the Soviet Union and the United States are alike in all major respects. Obviously, important differences exist. Yet for the scientist these differences acquire significance only in terms of the similarities.[110]

We should recognize, of course, that many structural imperatives are not absolute. The industrial-urban society is often free—within certain limits—to work out alternative solutions. It is because of the presence of these alternatives that sociologists need to pay special heed to the negative cases that demarcate the limits within which the economic, political, and educational structures must function.

Furthermore, industrial technology is ever changing or evolving. On several occasions we have indicated that automation and the cybernetics revolution are remaking many facets of the industrial city's social structure. Although this structure obviously will not revert to the preindustrial form, merely projecting from current industrial-urban patterns seems inadequate as a method for predicting the future.

Conclusions

The comparative analysis of cities must advance on both the theoretical and the empirical fronts. To this end we have employed a modified form of structural-functional analysis, one that incorporates the idea of contradictory functional requirements. Moreover, we have rejected a "city-limit" kind of sociology in favor of study of the city in relation to the broader societal context.

The preindustrial city's social structure has served as the basis for our interpretation of both industrializing and advanced industrial cities. When we considered the transitional city we focused on those processes that accompany the shift from a preindustrial to an industrial-urban form. Especially significant are the differential changes in the social structure and in the role of tradition in the industrializing or transitional city, matters that have been little studied.

Our main emphasis has been upon the industrial city. Here are the primary conclusions we draw from our analysis of this kind of urban center:

1. Although sociologists generally agree on the broad outlines of the structural correlates of industrial cities, there are significant areas of disagreement. Some of the confusion stems from differing frames of reference, some from apparently contradictory data. But one reason for the supposedly contradictory findings is the existence of contradictory functional requirements, and consequently contradictory structures, within industrial cities and societies. For example, some writers see the class system as becoming more rigid, whereas others view it as becoming more flexible. We contend that the empirical data run counter to the assumption of Parsons, Weber, and many other sociologists that structures or social systems are rather neatly and consistently arranged. Because of structural contradictions, sociologists must make explicit their bases of comparison if we are ever to achieve a modicum of consensus as to the nature of industrial-urban systems. The preindustrial city is our basic reference point.

2. We believe that the structural arrangements of the industrial city are functionally related to the nature of modern technology—a technology that encompasses scientific know-how. In turn, the scientific method seems to support and is itself sustained by an ideology that gives rise to and promotes the democratic process, and such norms as universalism and emphasis on achievement in modern bureaucracies.

3. Cutting across our analysis of the common structural correlates of the industrial city is the problem of the division of labor, a major

concern to students of industrialization and urbanization since Durkheim. We have noted some of the neglected theoretical aspects of the division of labor for the industrial-urban system. For example, a clear distinction must be drawn between the division of labor that characterizes the preindustrial city and that which typifies the industrial center if we are to answer such questions as the following: What is the function of the division of labor as an integrative mechanism, and as a divisive force, in the industrial-urban setting? And how is the division of labor related to the emergence of a "society of mediators"? Family counselors, welfare workers, labor arbitrators, politicians, and legal functionaries, including lawyers, come to mediate differences (1) among individuals, (2) between individuals and the broader society, and (3) among special interest and occupational groups that may support contradictory structures within the society. Some mediators, such as family counselors, function quite informally as they search out areas of value consensus among disputants; others, such as legal functionaries, employ rather formalized procedures when they seek to resolve disagreements.

Admittedly, the existing knowledge on the nature of integration and consensus in the industrial city is limited. We need to know much more about the interrelationships of the value system, the division of labor, and the role of mediators. This is an area of research to which urban sociologists could make a particularly significant contribution.

NOTES

* The author acknowledges with thanks the assistance of his wife, Andrée F. Sjoberg, in examining various materials in foreign languages.

1. At this stage of cross-cultural research, we believe that the emphasis must be upon "discovery" or "asking questions" rather than upon the formal testing of well-defined hypotheses. We are oriented to the procedure set forth in Norwood Hanson, *Patterns of Discovery* (Cambridge: Cambridge University Press, 1958).

2. Roger Nett, "System Building in Sociology—a Methodological Analysis," *Social Forces*, 31 (1952), pp. 25–30.

3. Robert A. Brady, *Organization, Automation, and Society* (Berkeley: University of California Press, 1961).

4. As employed in this essay, "technology" has several dimensions. We could perhaps simplify our analysis by using only "energy" as a variable. For such an approach, see Fred Cottrell, *Energy and Society* (New York: McGraw-Hill, 1955). Even so, we could not ignore the dimension of "know-how."

5. See Alex Inkeles, "Industrial Man: The Relation of Status to Experi-

ence, Perception, and Value," *American Journal of Sociology,* 66 (1960), pp. 1–31.

6. Clark Kerr, John T. Dunlop, Frederick Harbison, and Charles Myers, *Industrialism and Industrial Man* (Cambridge: Harvard University Press, 1960); Wilbert E. Moore and Arnold S. Feldman (Eds.), *Labor Commitment and Social Change in Developing Areas* (New York: Social Science Research Council, 1960).

7. Structural-functional analysis has been subjected to sharp attack in recent years for its "teleological bias." See Carl G. Hempel, "The Logic of Functional Analysis," in Llewellyn Gross (Ed.), *Symposium on Sociological Theory* (Evanston: Row, Peterson, 1959), pp. 271–310. But Hempel takes a reductionist position, denying that the "collectivity" is more than the sum of its parts. But such actors as key decision-makers in modern societies think and act *as if* a social system were teleologically oriented.

8. Although some writers draw the fine distinctions among the terms "imperatives," "requisites," and "prerequisites," these concepts are employed synonymously herein.

9. For a critical analysis of the idea of "prerequisites of modern industrialization," see Alexander Gerschenkron, *Economic Backwardness in Historical Perspective* (Cambridge: Belknap Press, 1962), Chap. 2.

10. Gideon Sjoberg, "Contradictory Functional Requirements and Social Systems," *Journal of Conflict Resolution,* 4 (1960), pp. 198–208.

11. For a detailed analysis, see Gideon Sjoberg, *The Preindustrial City: Past and Present* (New York: Free Press of Glencoe, 1960).

12. Karl A. Wittfogel, *Oriental Despotism* (New Haven: Yale University Press, 1957).

13. One proposition in particular needs to be tested: If a nation cannot draw upon a varied and complex resource base, it must resort to some kind of "colonialism" to further its industrial urbanization. For suggestive leads on this problem, see George W. Barclay, *Colonial Development and Population in Taiwan* (Princeton: Princeton University Press, 1954), and K. Berrill, "International Trade and the Rate of Economic Growth," *Economic History Review,* 12 (1960), pp. 351–359.

14. See Francis Seton, "Planning and Economic Growth," *Soviet Survey,* No. 31 (1960), pp. 38–44; John Kenneth Galbraith, "The Poverty of Nations," *Atlantic Monthly,* 210 (1962), pp. 47–53; Gerschenkron, *op. cit.;* Morton A. Kaplan (Ed.), *The Revolution in World Politics* (New York: Wiley, 1962).

15. Galbraith, *op. cit.*

16. Barrington Moore, Jr., *Terror and Progress: USSR* (Cambridge: Harvard University Press, 1954).

17. Naum Jasny, *Soviet Industrialization, 1928–1952* (Chicago: University of Chicago Press, 1961), especially Chap. 5.

18. Although the Catholic Church has generally aligned itself with anti-industrial forces, it has also made certain adjustments to this trend. Some have been successful, some unsuccessful. See William Bosworth, *Catholicism and Crisis in Modern France* (Princeton: Princeton University Press, 1962); Emile Poulat, "La découverte de la ville par le catholicisme français contemporain," *Annales,* 15 (1960), pp. 1168–1179; Alfred Dia-

mont, *Austrian Catholics and the First Republic* (Princeton: Princeton University Press, 1960).

19. See Dankwart A. Rustow, "Politics and Islam in Turkey 1920–1955," in Richard N. Frye (Ed.), *Islam and the West* (The Hague: Mouton, 1956), p. 92; S. M. Lipset, *Political Man* (Garden City: Doubleday, 1960), pp. 145–146; Jacques Fauvet and Henri Mendras, *Les Paysans et la Politique*, Cahiers de la Fondation Nationale des Sciences Politiques, No. 94 (Paris: Armand Colin, 1958).

20. There are exceptions to this pattern. See W. W. Rostow, *The Stages of Economic Growth: A Non-Communist Manifesto* (New York: Cambridge University Press, 1960).

21. Lipset, *op. cit.*, Chap. 2.

22. A convenient summary of some of the data on Indian cities can be found in Bert F. Hoselitz, "Indian Cities: The Surveys of Calcutta, Kanpur and Jamshedpur," *Economic Weekly*, 13 (1961), pp. 1071–1078.

23. See Vasant P. Pethe, "Congestion and Over-Crowding in Cities and Towns: A Scrutiny of Some Popular Beliefs," *Asian Economic Review*, 3 (1960), pp. 1–11; Doris G. Phillips, "Rural-to-Urban Migration in Iraq," *Economic Development and Cultural Change*, 7 (1959), pp. 405–421; Dimas Maulit, "Income Ratio Between Rural and Urban Workers in the Philippines," *Economic Research Journal*, 6 (1959), pp. 83–95.

24. Kingsley Davis, "Urbanization in India: Past and Future," in Roy Turner (Ed.), *India's Urban Future* (Berkeley: University of California Press, 1962), pp. 3–26.

25. See Bertram Hutchinson et al., *Mobilidade e Trabalho: Um Estudo na Cidade de São Paulo* (Rio de Janeiro: Centro Brasileiro do Pesquisas Educacionais, 1960); Donald Willmott, *The Chinese of Semarang: A Changing Minority Community in Indonesia* (Ithaca: Cornell University Press, 1960); Aileen D. Ross, *The Hindu Family in its Urban Setting* (Toronto: University of Toronto Press, 1961). Although much research on transitional cities is still to be carried out, we have reached the point where a systematic evaluation of current data is mandatory.

26. See Selig Harrison, *India: The Most Dangerous Decades* (Princeton: Princeton University Press, 1960); M. N. Srinivas, *Caste in Modern India* (London: Asia Publishing House, 1962), Chaps. 1 and 6; and various articles in the special issue of the *Sociological Bulletin*, 11 (1961), on the "Nature and Extent of Social Change in India."

27. Ezra Vogel, "The Go-Between in a Developing Society: The Case of the Japanese Marriage Arranger," *Human Organization*, 20 (1961), pp. 112–120.

28. Ronald P. Dore, *City Life in Japan* (Berkeley: University of California Press, 1958), p. 170.

29. For data that bear upon this argument, see Hutchinson, *op. cit.*, and J. C. Olivé Negrete and B. Barba de Piña Chán, "Estudio de las clases sociales en la Ciudad de México," *Anales del Instituto Nacional de Antropología e Historia*, 14 (1962), pp. 219–262.

30. Tuzo Wilson, *One Chinese Moon* (New York: Hill and Wang, 1959), p. 80.

31. See K. M. Munshi, *The Gospel of the Dirty Hand* (Delhi: Government of India, 1952).

32. See Bernard S. Cohn, "Changing Traditions of a Low Caste," *Journal of American Folklore,* 71 (1958), pp. 413–421; A. P. Barnabas, "Sanskritisation," *Economic Weekly,* 13 (1961), pp. 613–618.

33. Ernestine Friedl, "Lagging Emulation in Post-Peasant Society: A Greek Case," *American Anthropologist,* 66 (1964), pp. 569–586.

34. See Frederick T. C. Yu, "Communications and Politics in Communist China," in Lucian W. Pye (Ed.), *Communications and Political Development* (Princeton: Princeton University Press, 1963), Chap. 16.

35. Oscar Lewis, *The Children of Sánchez* (New York: Random House, 1961). Some data on the impact of the mass media on lower socioeconomic groups can be found in Daniel Lerner, *The Passing of Traditional Society* (New York: Free Press of Glencoe, 1958).

36. Harrison, *op. cit.*

37. See Janet Abu-Lughod, "Migrant Adjustment to City Life: The Egyptian Case," *American Journal of Sociology,* 67 (1961), pp. 22–32; Peter Suzuki, "Village Solidarity Among Turkish Peasants Undergoing Urbanization," *Science,* 132 (1960), pp. 891–892; Donald Petesch, "Mexican Urban Ecology," unpublished M. A. thesis, University of Texas, 1960, pp. 200ff.; Edward M. Bruner, "Medan: The Role of Kinship in an Indonesian City," to be published in Alexander Spoehr (Ed.), *Pacific Port Towns and Cities;* Robert B. Textor, *From Peasant to Pedicab Driver,* Cultural Report Series No. 9 (New Haven: Yale University, Southeast Asia Studies, 1961). Textor, in particular, points up the fragile nature of the organization among some of the urban in-migrants.

38. See John MacDonald and Beatrice D. MacDonald, "Urbanization, Ethnic Groups, and Social Relationships," *Social Research,* 29 (1962), pp. 433–448.

39. Suzuki, *op. cit.*

40. Galbraith, *op. cit.;* Bert Hoselitz, "Urbanization in India," *Kyklos,* 13 (1960), p. 369; Scarlett Epstein, "Industrial Employment for Landless Labourers Only," *Economic Weekly,* 11 (1959), pp. 967–974; Srinivas, *op. cit.;* Arthur Niehoff, *Factory Workers in India,* Publications in Anthropology, No. 5 (Milwaukee: Milwaukee Public Museum, 1959).

41. Shih Ch'eng-chih, *Urban Commune Experiments in Communist China* (Hong Kong: Union Research Institute, 1962).

42. Morris David Morris, "Labor Discipline, Trade-Unions, and the State in India," *Journal of Political Economy,* 63 (1955), pp. 293–308; Karl de Schweinitz, Jr., "Industrialization, Labor Controls, and Democracy," *Economic Development and Cultural Change,* 7 (1959), pp. 385–404.

43. See Gideon Sjoberg, "Political Structure, Ideology, and Economic Development," The Carnegie Faculty Seminar on Political and Administrative Development (Bloomington: Department of Government, Indiana University, 1963), for an argument to the effect that the charismatic leader and his ideology are necessary conditions for *rapid* industrial urbanization.

44. See "Folk Dances," *The Hindu,* January 31, 1957, p. 10; Felix Greene, *China* (New York: Ballantine Books, 1962), pp. 231ff.

45. Some of these can be found in Otis Dudley Duncan et al., *Metropolis and Region* (Baltimore: Johns Hopkins Press, 1960).

46. The following items illustrate the range of data available: André

Cornette, "Arras et sa banlieue," *Revue du Nord*, 42 (1960), pp. 9–137; Jean Daric, "La localisation de quelques professions liberales dans Paris et le Departement de la Seine," *Population*, 8 (1953), pp. 555–578; P. H. Chombart de Lauwe et al., *Paris et l'Agglomération Parisienne* (Paris: Presses Universitaires de France, 1952); P. Gourou, "L'agglomération bruxelloise," *Bulletin de la Société Royale Belge de Géographie*, 82 (1958), pp. 3–83; René Lebeau, "Zurich, métropole de la Suisse," *Revue de Géographie de Lyon*, 35 (1960), pp. 7–47; Rainer Mackensen et al., *Daseinsformen der Grosstadt* (Tubingen: Mohr, 1959); L. P. Green, *Provincial Metropolis* (London: George Allen and Unwin, 1959); T. W. Freeman, *The Conurbations of Great Britain* (Manchester: Manchester University Press, 1959); Emrys Jones, *A Social Geography of Belfast* (London: Oxford University Press, 1960); W. William-Olsson, *Stockholm: Structure and Development* (Stockholm: Almqvist and Wiksell, 1961); *The Paper Metropolis* (London: Town and Country Planning Association, 1962); Edgar M. Hoover and Raymond Vernon, *Anatomy of a Metropolis* (Cambridge: Harvard University Press, 1959); Jean Remy, *Charleroi et son Agglomération* (Bruxelles: Centre de Recherches Socio-réligieuses, n.d.); *Soviet Geography*, 3 (1962); Peter Scholler, "Wachstum und Wandlung japanischer Stadtregionen," *Die Erde*, 93 (1962), pp. 202–234.

47. See John Barron Mays, "Cultural Conformity in Urban Areas: An Introduction to the Crown Street Study in Liverpool," *Sociological Review*, 6 (1958), pp. 95–108; Ruth Glass, *Newcomers* (London: George Allen and Unwin, 1960); Otis Dudley Duncan and Stanley Lieberson, "Ethnic Segregation and Assimilation," *American Journal of Sociology*, 64 (1959), pp. 364–374; Albert J. Mayer and Thomas F. Hoult, *Race and Residence in Detroit* (Detroit: Institute for Urban Studies, Wayne State University, 1962).

48. See *The Paper Metropolis, op. cit.;* Hoover and Vernon, *op. cit.*

49. Some of the effects of the proliferation of tertiary industries have been suggested by Jean Gottmann in *Megalopolis* (New York: Twentieth Century Fund, 1961).

50. The extreme segregation in South African cities is a "test case" for a number of ecological propositions about industrial cities; see Leo Kuper et al., *Durban: A Study in Racial Ecology* (New York: Columbia University Press, 1958).

51. Harvey W. Zorbaugh, *The Gold Coast and the Slum* (Chicago: University of Chicago Press, 1929).

52. William F. Whyte, *Street Corner Society* (Chicago: University of Chicago Press, 1943); Herbert Gans, *The Urban Villagers* (New York: Free Press of Glencoe, 1962); Michael Young and Peter Willmott, *Family and Kinship in East London* (New York: Free Press of Glencoe, 1957).

53. Ned Polsky, "The Village Beat Scene: Summer 1960," *Dissent*, 8 (1961), pp. 339–359.

54. See Allen Kassof, "Now the Angry Young Ivans," *New York Times Magazine*, November 19, 1961, pp. 22 et passim.

55. See Claude S. Phillips, Jr., "Class Stratification in Soviet Russia: A Bibliography Survey of Recent Literature," *Michigan Academy of Science, Arts, and Letters*, 42 (1956), pp. 195–216. The divergent views concerning social class in American cities can be perceived by comparing the

writings of W. Lloyd Warner, Leonard Reissman, David Riesman, C. Wright Mills, Harold E. Lasswell, Talcott Parsons, Bernard Barber, and Robert J. Lampman, among others.

56. Cf. Alex Inkeles, "Social Stratification and Mobility in the Soviet Union: 1940–1950," *American Sociological Review*, 15 (1950), pp. 465–479; and Alex Inkeles and Raymond A. Bauer, *The Soviet Citizen* (Cambridge: Harvard University Press, 1959). It appears that Inkeles' views regarding the Soviet class system changed during the 1950's, largely because of a shift in reference points.

57. Irving B. Kravis, "International Differences in the Distribution of Income," *Review of Economics and Statistics*, 42 (1960), pp. 408–416; and Jean Fourastié, *The Causes of Wealth*, trans. and ed. by Theodore Caplow (New York: Free Press of Glencoe, 1960).

58. Seymour M. Lipset and Reinhard Bendix, *Social Mobility in Industrial Society* (Berkeley: University of California Press, 1959).

59. These issues are being raised largely by writers outside the mainstream of academia—for example, Peter Irons, "The Cybernation Revolution," *Progressive*, 29 (1965), pp. 18–21.

60. Alex Inkeles and Peter H. Rossi, "National Comparisons of Occupational Prestige," *American Journal of Sociology*, 61 (1956), pp. 329–339; Melvin M. Tumin (with Arnold S. Feldman), *Social Class and Social Change in Puerto Rico* (Princeton: Princeton University Press, 1961), pp. 425ff. See also J. Clyde Mitchell and A. L. Epstein, "Occupational Prestige and Social Status Among Urban Africans in Northern Rhodesia," *Africa*, 29 (1959), pp. 22–40.

61. For a first-rate essay on contradictory tendencies in the Soviet Union's class structure, see George Z. F. Bereday, "Class Tensions in Soviet Education," in George Z. F. Bereday and Jaan Pennar (Eds.), *The Politics of Soviet Education* (New York: Praeger, 1960), pp. 57–88.

62. C. Wright Mills seems to have feared industrial-urban development in the United States while apparently favoring its expansion in other societies. See his *The Power Elite* (New York: Oxford University Press, 1956).

63. See the special issue of *Daedalus* (Winter 1962) and *The Annals* (November 1961), both of which deal with youth in the United States and in other societies. See also William R. Vizzard, "Taiyozoku: A Youth Problem in Japan," *Sociologus*, 9 (1959), pp. 162–178; and Mark G. Field, "Alcoholism, Crime, and Delinquency in Soviet Society," *Social Problems*, 3 (1955), pp. 100–109.

64. See Rene König, "Family and Authority: The German Father in 1955," *Sociological Review*, 5 (1957), pp. 107–127; Paul Chombart de Lauwe et al., *Famille et Habitation*, II (Paris: Centre National de la Recherche Scientifique, 1960); Kent Geiger, "The Family and Social Change," in Cyril E. Black (Ed.), *The Transformation of Russian Society* (Cambridge: Harvard University Press, 1960), pp. 447–458. Italy also has been moving toward the "industrial model." See Franco Archibugi, "Recent Trends in Women's Work in Italy," *International Labour Review*, 81 (1960), pp. 285–318. But Italy and Japan have witnessed considerable resistance to the "emancipation" of women. See Yoshiharu Scott Matsumoto, *Contemporary Japan*, Transactions of the American Philosophical Society, Vol. 50, Part 1 (Philadelphia, 1960), pp. 17–33.

The patterns of female participation in the labor force in large cities are complex; see Andrew Collver and Eleanor Langlois, "The Female Labor Force in Metropolitan Areas: An International Comparison," *Economic Development and Cultural Change*, 10 (1962), pp. 367–385. Understanding the nature of the preindustrial city helps one interpret these statistical data, which indicate that various underdeveloped countries have more women in the labor force than do industrial orders. Actually, women in the preindustrial city's lower class have typically worked outside the home to help feed the family, and this pattern persists in transitional cities. In the preindustrial setting only upper-class women have been able to afford the luxury of extensive leisure time.

65. See Elizabeth Bott, *Family and Social Network* (London: Tavistock Publications, 1957).

66. See Max and Tobia Frankel, "New Soviet Plan—Feminine Females," *New York Times Magazine*, December 6, 1959, pp. 30 et passim; Vera Bacal, "The Latest Fashion News—from Moscow," *New York Times Magazine*, November 20, 1960, pp. 16 et passim. These and similar data indicate the nature of this trend in Soviet cities.

67. Peter Townsend, *The Family Life of Old People* (New York: Free Press of Glencoe, 1957); Young and Willmott, *op. cit.* ,

68. See J. B. Cullingworth, "Some Implications of Overspill: The Worsley Social Survey," *Sociological Review*, 8 (1960), pp. 77–96; Cullingworth indicates that the patterns delineated by Townsend and Young and Willmott change as people move to the suburbs. Moreover, Cullingworth believes that there is an untenable hidden assumption in the work of Young and Willmott, i.e., that the poor are basically happy. We believe that he is correct.

69. William J. Goode, *World Revolution and Family Patterns* (New York: Free Press of Glencoe, 1963), p. 76. This is a very important volume for students of industrial urbanization. Unfortunately, Goode's analysis is compromised by his failure to clearly delineate the familial structure of preindustrial societies.

70. See Daniel R. Miller and Guy E. Swanson, *The Changing American Parent* (New York: Wiley, 1958); Dennison Nash and Peter Berger, "The Child, the Family, and the Religious Revival in Suburbia," *Journal for the Scientific Study of Religion*, 2 (1962), pp. 85–93; Erwin K. Scheuch, "Family Cohesion in Leisure Time," *Sociological Review*, 8 (1960), pp. 37–61; Marvin B. Sussman and Lee Burchinal, "Kin Family Network: Unheralded Structure in Current Conceptualizations of Family Functioning," *Marriage and Family Living*, 24 (1962), pp. 231–240.

71. Fourastié, *op. cit.*

72. See Sanford Irwen Labovitz, "Regional Analysis of the United States," unpublished M.A. thesis, University of Texas, 1962.

73. Stanley Udy, Jr., *Organization of Work: A Comparative Analysis of Production among Non-Industrial Peoples* (New Haven: HRAF Press, 1959).

74. Mason Haire, Edwin E. Ghiselli, and Lyman W. Porter, "Cultural Patterns in the Role of the Manager," *Industrial Relations*, 2 (1963), pp. 95–117; David Granick, *The Red Executive* (Garden City: Doubleday, 1960); Frederick Harbison and Charles A. Myers, *Management in the*

Industrial World (New York: McGraw-Hill, 1959); J. E. Humblet, "A Comparative Study of Management in Three European Countries: Preliminary Findings," *Sociological Review*, 9 (1961), pp. 351–360.

75. For the emergence of some of these mediator roles in the Soviet Union, see Emily Clark Brown, "Interests and Rights of Soviet Industrial Workers and the Resolution of Conflicts," *Industrial and Labor Relations Review*, 16 (1963), pp. 254–278.

76. Marshall I. Goldman, "Product Differentiation and Advertising: Some Lessons from Soviet Experience," *Journal of Political Economy*, 68 (1960), pp. 346–357.

77. This issue has been raised in a somewhat different manner by Michael Polanyi, "Towards a Theory of Conspicuous Production," *Soviet Survey* (October–December 1960), pp. 90–99. The comments on Polanyi's article by Devons, Grossman, Jasny, Nove, Seton, and Wiles raise issues that have been ignored by urban sociologists concerned with such problems as "the hierarchy of cities."

78. Lipset, *op. cit.*; J. J. Spengler, "Economic Development: Political Preconditions and Political Consequences," *Journal of Politics*, 22 (1960), pp. 387–416.

79. Kerr et al., *op. cit.*

80. The impact of the expert even on the local community should not be underestimated. The pattern of local government seems to change once scientifically oriented experts are introduced into the formal structure.

81. Some of the inherent contradictions that plague a democratic order have been outlined in Bernard Berelson, Paul F. Lazarsfeld, and William N. McPhee, *Voting* (Chicago: University of Chicago Press, 1954), pp. 313–323.

82. The support for Hitler came from those who were marginal or outside the mainstream of the industrial-urban process. See Rudolf Heberle, *Social Movements* (New York: Appleton-Century-Crofts, 1951), pp. 222–236. On the other hand, the structure of the industrial-urban order, and the nonideological character of the middle class, leaves this system vulnerable to extremist movements. This may account for the passivity of the middle class in Germany and their rationalizations for the actions of the Nazis. See Raul Hilberg, *The Destruction of the European Jews* (Chicago: Quadrangle Books, 1961).

83. Among the writers who believe that some "democratization" is under way in the Soviet Union are Ulman, Djilas, Deutscher, and Bell. See Isaac Deutscher, *Russia in Transition*, rev. ed. (New York: Grove Press, 1960); Daniel Bell, "Russia's Eroding Ideology," *New Leader*, 46 (1963), pp. 18–23. Various data bear out this growing flexibility in the system: "Youth Paper Opens a 'Public Opinion Institute,'" *Current Digest of the Soviet Press*, 12 (1960), pp. 24–29; Patricia Blake, "Russia: The Scientific Elite," *Reporter*, 20 (November 14, 1957), pp. 17–22; Paul Jacobs, "The Boys on Gorki Street," *Reporter*, 23 (July 7, 1960), pp. 35–38. For an opposing view see Z. K. Brzezinski, *Ideology and Power in Soviet Politics* (New York: Praeger, 1962). It is significant that Brzezinski ignores science and the scientific method, as well as the technological revolution.

84. Among others, Galbraith, Riesman, Parsons, and Kornhauser think in these terms. See William Kornhauser, *Politics of Mass Society* (New York:

Free Press of Glencoe, 1959); Talcott Parsons, *Structure and Process in Modern Societies* (New York: Free Press of Glencoe, 1960), especially Chap. 6.

85. Henry C. Hart, "Urban Politics in Bombay," *Economic Weekly*, 12 (1960), pp. 983–988.

86. Hilberg, *op. cit.*

87. Some American sociologists have dealt with limited aspects of this issue. See Sidney M. Willhelm, *Urban Zoning and Land-Use Theory* (New York: Free Press of Glencoe, 1962), and Robert Dubin (Ed.), *Human Relations in Administration*, 2nd ed. (Englewood Cliffs, N. J.: Prentice-Hall, 1961). Although the Marxists have historically denied the existence of an individual-group dilemma, some, like the Pole Adam Schaff, have recently reconsidered the matter; see " 'Socialist Ethics' Studied by Poles," *New York Times*, April 30, 1961, p. 19.

88. See George Ginsburgs, "Objective Truth and the Judicial Process in Post-Stalinist Soviet Jurisprudence," *American Journal of Comparative Law*, 10 (1961), pp. 53–75; Harold J. Berman, "The Struggle of Soviet Jurists Against a Return of Stalinist Terror," *Slavic Review*, 22 (1963), pp. 314–320. For a discussion of the impact of scientific thought upon American legal norms, see William M. Evan, "Value Conflicts in the Law of Evidence," *American Behavioral Scientist*, 6 (1960), pp. 23–26, and James R. Richardson, *Modern Scientific Evidence* (Cincinnati: Anderson, 1961).

89. Letters to the editor in Soviet newspapers serve as one device for pressuring lower-level bureaucrats into adhering to the norms of universalism and efficiency.

90. One reason for the traditional intellectual's opposition to industrial urbanization is his loss of the ability to "predict" and "control" the future. This was the basis of his authority and power in the preindustrial city.

91. Frederic Dewhurst et al., *Europe's Needs and Resources* (New York: Twentieth Century Fund, 1961), Chap. 10; George Louis Payne, *Britain's Scientific and Technological Manpower* (Stanford: Stanford University Press, 1960). Cf. Nicholas DeWitt, *Education and Professional Employment in the U. S. S. R.* (Washington: National Science Foundation, 1961).

92. Dewhurst, *op. cit.*, Chap. 25.

93. C. P. Snow, *Science and Government* (New York: New American Library, 1962); see also *Science, An Interview by Donald McDonald with Hans Bethe* (Santa Barbara: Center for the Study of Democratic Institutions, 1962). Another facet of this problem is discussed by Wallace S. Sayre, "Scientists and American Science Policy," in Bernard Barber and Walter Hirsch (Eds.), *The Sociology of Science* (New York: Free Press of Glencoe, 1962). The book edited by Barber and Hirsch also provides us with data on the ideology of scientific enterprise.

94. See the special issue of *Daedalus* (Summer 1960) on "The Russian Intelligentsia," especially the essay by Burg.

95. For data on variations among societies, see "Les attitudes réligieuses de la jeunesse," *Sondages*, 21 (1959), p. 21. On variations within societies, see David Moberg, *The Church as a Social Institution* (Englewood Cliffs, N. J.: Prentice-Hall, 1962), Chap. 15, and Antonio Donini, "Practica y Actitudes Religiosas (Parte II)," *Sociologia Religiosa*, 8 (1962), pp. 9–172. One of the most significant differences between industrial and preindustrial

cities is the church attendance patterns of men and of women. In industrial centers women are the more avid church-goers, whereas in preindustrial cities women's religious activities have been "home centered" and the men have been the mainstays of the church.

96. Seymour Topping, "Rise in Religion Worrying Soviets," *New York Times,* February 12, 1961, p. 14; Seymour Topping, "Soviet Whittling at the Roots of 20 Churches in Leningrad," *New York Times,* April 2, 1961, p. 18.

97. For a discussion of the contradictory evidence, see William Petersen, "Religious Statistics in the United States," *Journal for the Scientific Study of Religion,* 1 (1962), pp. 164–178. One of the main reasons for our assumption that there has been a decline of religious commitment is the growing "tolerance" of different religious faiths for one another.

98. For an analysis of the influence of religion in a highly industrialized city, see Gerhard Lenski, *The Religious Factor,* rev. ed. (Garden City: Doubleday, 1963).

99. Thomas Luckmann, "On Religion in Modern Society: Individual Consciousness, World View, Institution," *Journal for the Scientific Study of Religion,* 2 (1963), pp. 147–162.

100. Some of these sectarian groups serve as socializing agencies for members of the lower socioeconomic strata, helping them adapt to and become assimilated into the urban environment. It is significant that in the U. S. S. R. the most active sects in the urban centers have been those catering to the lower class. See Walter Kolarz, *Religion in the Soviet Union* (New York: St. Martin's Press, 1961), Chap. 9.

101. We need also to investigate the persistence of magic even in supposedly "rational" spheres of urban life. See Neil Ulman, "Some Investors Turn to Stars for Answer to Market's Riddles," *Wall Street Journal,* April 16, 1963, p. 1 et passim.

102. Walter Laqueur and Leopold Labedz (Eds.), *The Future of Communist Society* (New York: Praeger, 1962), especially the "Introduction."

103. This view seems implicit in Herbert Blumer, "Early Industrialization and the Laboring Class," *The Sociological Quarterly,* 1 (1960), pp. 5–14.

104. James Abegglen, *The Japanese Factory System* (New York: Free Press of Glencoe, 1958). Odaka includes William A. Lockwood, Solomon B. Levine, Frederick Harbison, and Charles A. Myers in this school of thought as well; see K. Odaka, "Traditionalism and Democracy in Japanese Industry," a paper delivered at the Fifth World Congress of Sociology, Washington, D. C., September 1962.

105. Peter F. Drucker, "The Baffled Young Men of Japan," *Harper's,* 222 (1961), pp. 65–74.

106. Odaka, *op. cit.* Odaka argues that American social scientists who have imputed "positive functions" to the traditional social structure have served to bolster the conservative cause in Japan.

107. Dore, *op. cit.*

108. Marshall E. Dimock, "Management in the USSR—Comparisons to the United States," *Public Administration Review,* 20 (1960), pp. 139–147.

109. For example, William Petersen, "The Soviet Subject Viewed as Citizen," *Antioch Review* (Spring 1960), pp. 101–111.

110. Some of the methodological and theoretical issues that inhere in comparisons of industrial-urban societies, especially the economies of the Soviet Union and the United States, are set forth by various writers in "Comparisons of the United States and Soviet Economies," Joint Economic Committee, Congress of the United States (Washington, D. C.: Government Printing Office, 1960). Also see the essay by Alex Inkeles, and Sorokin's rebuttal, in P. J. Allen (Ed.), *Pitirim A. Sorokin in Review* (Durham: Duke University Press, 1963).

8

Political-Economic Aspects
of Urbanization in South
and Southeast Asia

Nathan Keyfitz

Purpose of This Chapter

This chapter follows well-established practice in considering the city
not in itself but in relation to a surrounding territory; it takes up in
particular the primate city and a hinterland which consists of the territory of a national state. The political-economic relationship between
city and national territory can logically fall under one of three categories: (1) There may be an uncontrolled market exchange of goods
between the city and its countryside, with economic domination in
the ecological sense. (2) The city may dominate the surrounding territory largely by force and organization, by legitimate power. (3) The
countryside may in effect tax the city through agricultural price supports or other devices. There seems to be some ground for the view that
(2) holds in preindustrial societies, and in them the flow of goods is
on balance toward the city, whereas (1) and (3) hold in later stages
when industry has outpaced agriculture. If this is true we may think
of the cities as first exerting force on the countryside, and then in turn
becoming the object of force, or at least of political pressure. When
cities grow as rapidly as they are growing in much of the underdeveloped world today, and when this growth is accompanied by a relative
inertia of industry, then the pressure which the cities have to place on
the remainder of their national territory in order to draw their food by
taxes, tariffs, exchange control, or other means, is likely to accentuate
the element of force in administration. This demographic fact may be
one of the components which account for the militarism that has arisen

in countries such as Burma which, in their culture and especially in their religion, one would have thought to be as far as possible from emphasis on force.[1]

There are two other tendencies which act along with the increasing population of the city to bring about strong central administrations. One is also demographic: it is the tendency of the countryside to fill up, to eat the grain or other foodstuff which, when population was smaller, it could provide as "surplus" to the city. The other depends on the seriousness with which economic development is taken: when the city elite is determined to develop at all costs, being possessed at the outset of no efficient manufacturing industry, its strategy is to sell abroad the products of the countryside in order to secure its first modern producers' goods. This exchange of food for capital goods occurred in instances of development as far apart as the United States and the U. S. S. R. It was unimportant only for Britain, which, being the first country to modernize, had to invent and construct its own capital.

Although we shall argue that demographic tendencies at the moment of attempted industrialization, along with the need of equipment for industrialization, require that the city in some way impose itself on the countryside, the question of the kind of regime through which it will accomplish this is left open. Whether it is to be a strong government elected by wide suffrage as in the United States, an encadrement of the country by a highly centralized political party which in effect elects itself as in the U. S. S. R., a paternalistic regime as in Japan, or a military dictatorship is an issue outside the scope of this chapter. Our object is to examine an ecological change associated with the growth of cities which has been common to countries that have been successful in developing, and which is found in incomplete form in those that are now in one phase or another of the initiation of development.

Also outside the scope of this chapter is any evaluation of the merits of the city as against the countryside, or any immediate policy suggestions on how development is to be attained. One must recognize that it is principally in the small fraction of the world's territory occupied by cities that the drama of history has been acted out; it is in them that the latest act of the drama, the attainment of economic development, will be decided. Only the developed city can grow to a large size without that exercise of power which has been the condition for concentrations of population beyond the size of market towns in most of the historical past. With the diminution in the amount of force required to maintain themselves comes a greater likelihood of stable democratic rule in the country of which the cities are part.

One can hope also that with high productivity and democracy the city will nurture a greater creativity in science and art, though the evidence of history on this point is ambiguous.

Volume and Density as Determinants of City Life

Cities have been studied in many kinds of framework. They have been seen as originating because the increasing volume of population over an area gives rise to points where "the social mass contracts more strongly than elsewhere";[2] at these points of urbanization there is developed, through the very fact of compression, "a continually maintained and increasing source of available energy," as a modern evolutionist[3] puts it. The effect of a steadily increasing volume and density of social beings in society is their increased differentiation which accompanies an ever finer division of labor.[4] Durkheim makes this point on the analogy of the plant and animal worlds, but he and others go far beyond this, and see in the same process the development of an unprecedented intensity of nervous stimulation,[5] and also a new kind of interiority.[6] These are considered to be explanations of how the industrial city comes into being. The existence of large and apparently static cities prevents us from accepting the thesis that simple pressure and competition, the result of increasing volume and density, will by themselves force a division of labor and hence industrial advance.[7]

The Ecological Approach

The most important empirical tradition of study considers the city in relation to a hinterland over which it exercises economic dominance;[8] in the competition among cities, and between city and countryside, the extent of dominance is determined principally by efficiency of production, and within the framework of the means of transport in use.[9] This dynamic approach has been submitted to statistical testing, which has given a substantial measure of empirical content to the notion of a dominant city and shows in detail how it

> controls many of the conditions of life of all the communities lying within a broad area surrounding it. This control arises from a higher than average degree of specialization in such functions as services and wholesaling, and from an ability to foster industrial development in its immediate vicinity by provision of favorable combinations of the factors of production. Other communities must accept these conditions of life by specializing in

other activities and by becoming dependent upon the central city for those goods and services which their residents require but which they cannot provide locally.[10]

Earlier, Mark Jefferson had anticipated this ecological perspective: "A million city cannot exist in isolation. It is a head office . . . of every important enterprise in its country, a heart in the national body. . . . Cities do not grow of themselves. Countrysides set them up to do tasks that must be performed in central places." [11] Here and elsewhere Jefferson plainly has in mind what we will follow Weber in calling the producer city—the one that earns its food by freely selling its produce to some hinterland. This requires, as we shall repeat again and again, a certain degree of efficiency in the city, an economic capacity that comes about principally with industrialization. Such efficiency is implied in models that go back as far as von Thünen, writing early in the nineteenth century. A recent and ambitious study using this approach is by O. D. Duncan and his collaborators who have prepared a detailed study of the functions of fifty major cities of the United States.[12]

Robert E. Park lists the different kinds or levels of dominance which are possible in human societies: "(1) the biotic, or ecological, (2) economic, (3) political, (4) cultural." [13] He gives as examples of ecological dominance the boll weevil, "moving out of its ancient habitat in the central Mexican plateau and into the virgin territory of the southern cotton plantations . . . not unlike the Boers of Cape Colony, South Africa, trekking out into the high veldt of the central South African plateau and filling it, within a period of one hundred years, with a population of their own descendants." [14] He contrasts this with dominance of a quite different kind: "In human society dominance not infrequently tends to become embodied in the persons of individuals, in a chief, king. . . ." [15]

The way a city fulfills a function in regard to a territory is not without effect on the internal arrangements within the city. For the economically developed society of the United States there has been observed a very elaborate internal structuring in terms of language, race, ". . . vocational interests, . . . intelligence, and personal ambition. . . . The physical or ecological organization of the community, in the long run, responds to and reflects the occupational and the cultural." [16] The laws whereby the relation of the city to its hinterland determines the spatial relations within the city are not easily discovered, but we shall assert at least that the latter are quite different between the city Park has in mind, which has typically drawn population to man its industry, and the city of the underdeveloped country, which has few industrial opportunities but is nonetheless swamped by migrants for whom the countryside provides no place.

These aspects of the concentrations of population called cities—occupational specialization, intensity of mental life, economic dominance of a territory, and internal spatial ordering—are general themes that run through this book. Reexamination of earlier hypotheses concerning cities, in the light of observations now available of five continents rather than just part of one continent, characterizes its several chapters. But the preceding brief account of the processes of economic dominance is enough for the purposes of this chapter. The question asked in this chapter is the more specific and limited one, posed neither by developed countries nor by those undeveloped ones that are sparsely populated in relation to their resources, but posed with great urgency in the crowded underdeveloped half of the world: what are the consequences for city growth and for national economic development of an increasing population? The problem concerns ecology in the fundamental, indeed primitive, sense of relating concentrations of population to the sources of their food: how will the city people eat as their numbers and the numbers of those in the countryside increase?

Food Supply in the Preindustrial City

Where the city depends for its sources of energy on men and animals, where there is little division of labor, where standardizations of goods and similar devices are lacking,[17] the products of the city have but a small margin of advantage over those of the countryside. The peasant can produce whatever the city can produce, sometimes more cheaply, and this fact limits the scope of free exchange and shifts the reference to force.

Writers on the origin of the city start with the question of efficiency in the countryside. Kingsley Davis speaks of the ox-drawn plow, the wheeled cart, and other innovations which enriched the technique of neolithic agriculture and transport and enabled these to produce the surplus that would permit "the concentration in one place of people who do not grow their own food."[18] "A precondition for the emergence and growth of cities is a level of agricultural production sufficiently high to release a substantial part of the population from agricultural labor, and to permit the concentration in cities of people engaged in nonagricultural enterprises formerly performed on the farm and in the villages."[19]

But this necessary condition was not sufficient; some kind of social organization was needed which would enable those in the city directly or indirectly to appropriate the part of the produce that would keep them alive. Production and trade would not achieve this: the productivity of the city was low, and most of what its artisans produced was for the use of its own upper classes. That its inhabitants had to receive food from the countryside—if there was to be a city at all— meant an asymmetry in the exchange of goods which somehow had to be balanced by an inverse asymmetry in the exchange of power. "Farmers were *persuaded* or *compelled* to wring from the soil a surplus above their own domestic requirements and this surplus was made available to support new economic classes not directly engaged in production of their own food." [20] To Lewis Mumford the city played a special part in stepping up power, accumulating and storing it in symbolic forms and transmitting it from generation to generation. He speaks both of physical power and of the imposition of common understandings which more effectively serves the same purpose. The two support each other: "The fact that understanding came to the aid of naked military and political power in general is what made it durable." [21]

The Surplus

Such considerations have been brought forward from time to time in discussions of the all-important agricultural surplus—is it primarily a technological or a social resultant? One view is that technology of production improved in neolithic times to the point where the peasant turned out more food than he and his family needed; this constituted a temptation to a ruler who appropriated it, or to a trader who gave something in exchange for it; the nonagricultural activities so nourished were the start of city life. This viewpoint seems to underlie much of the phraseology of Herskovits.[22] Thus he says that "nonliterate societies everywhere, producing more goods than the minimum required for the support of life, translate their economic surpluses into . . . social leisure." [23] This surplus for societies such as those of Polynesia "is facilitated by the favourable environmental conditions." [24] The notion has superficial reasonableness; how is it possible for anyone to steal, expropriate, or otherwise take food which does not yet exist? [25] Yet Polanyi,[26] Pearson,[27] Hauser,[28] and the present chapter argue just this; we oppose the assertion that the "surplus" created the institutions, including the cities, and say instead that the institutions created the surplus. More precisely, the building of cities is part of a process that includes instituting a surplus.

Pearson uses the distinction [29] among (1) reciprocity (of which gifts among family members are an example), (2) redistribution (taxes), and (3) exchange or sale and purchase.[30] Of economies held firmly in the reciprocities of kinship, neighborhood, and community, it is clear that prestige wealth represents a regular claim on the services and material resources of communities even on a very low level of subsistence. But surplus accumulation has also resulted from the power of arms to plunder and secure booty. "Corvée, boon days, tithes, censures, tax farming, auctions, markets by decree—these are some of the paraphernalia of surplus mobilization in redistributive economies. . . . Prestige institutions are not the result of surpluses appearing at certain stages of social development, but neither are cities, nor pyramids, nor markets, nor money, nor exploitation, nor civilization. . . . There are always and everywhere potential surpluses available. What counts is the institutional means for bringing them to life." [31]

There is a lack of exact data on the inputs and outputs of various types of agriculture on various kinds of land, but we may hazard some rough estimates based on current Asian yield statistics. With agricultural techniques still in use in the twentieth century and developed in the first millennium before Christ, the peasant can till and maintain the irrigation facilities for ten acres of land. On good soil he produces over 1500 pounds of grain per acre, say eight tons in all. If he and his family had one-third of eight tons they would be far better off than the average Indian family of today. Suppose we allow them three tons, and one ton for those other essential rural occupations concerned with transport and storage. In this situation one-half the food supply is available for use off the land, and thus one-half of the entire population could be in nonfood occupations, which is to say living in cities. But the proportion actually living in cities never rose to 5 per cent in classical times. Kingsley Davis speaks of 1 or 2 per cent as typical.[32] After what was probably a steady rise for five centuries through the Mogul and British periods, the Indian census of 1921 showed only 11.4 per cent urban.[33] The reason why performance in respect of city growth was so far below potential can only be that existing agricultural technology was not effectively used; the surplus is not "there" the moment it is technically possible but only after it has been institutionalized through taxes, trade, or other means. Before this the peasant does not grow all he can; what he grows he uses lavishly since he has no reason to save it.

The ways in which the surplus may be instituted are as varied as human societies. In India the simple power of a ruler, benevolent or tyrannical, to redistribute wealth was supplemented by customs of reciprocity such as are still exhibited in the village, where potter, barber, and watchman do their work as a matter of duty, and the farmer as a matter of duty provides them with a part of his harvest. The political power of the city came to be more highly organized in Mogul times than immediately before; there was more widespread use of money, and roads were built which helped to make power effective over longer distances. All this permitted the principal cities to increase their populations. Delhi and Agra introduced efficient taxing methods and expanded their crafts, military forces, and court followers. Craftsmen and courtiers lived directly off the taxes as functionaries and holders of various kinds of privileges, while a multitude of servants lived off them. Taxes were sometimes in kind, sometimes in cash; those in the form of grain were passed out directly to the ruler's following; those in the form of money could only be paid after the peasant had sold his product to a trader; the foodstuffs would pass through the hands of a series of other traders and ultimately be marketed in the city where they were presumably bought with the same money that had been collected in taxes. When the power of the ruler weakened and outlying provinces of an empire broke away, the capital city declined in population and provincial capitals grew; it might be possible to secure historical materials bearing on this hypothesis. The mechanism was perceived long ago by Ibn Khaldun who describes cycles in the expansion and contraction of empires of a period of one or two centuries, with corresponding fluctuations in the luxury and population of the cities which the imperial territory nourished.[34]

Surpluses Generated by Outside Conquerors

When the British came to India they systematized the Mogul administrative procedures with a minimum of technical change except in the field of transportation. It was essentially through organization and regularized tax collections that they created many new cities and expanded old ones; the whole system was reoriented to London through the founding of seaports and ultimately the construction of the Suez Canal. Later, Rangoon developed through a similar scheme of taxation, imposed more efficiently as a result of the Indian experience, and using the exceptionally fertile lands of the delta of the Irrawaddy. Again people were required to pay in taxes a fixed amount of money, which in practice meant a corresponding amount of rice. This was for each peasant a simple fraction (25 per cent [35]) of what the authorities considered the potential of his land. On the British system he was free to plant anything he wished, or to plant nothing at all, as long as he paid the tax; if he was not able to find the money for this, the land was sold to someone who could pay. Indian moneylenders contributed finance, and by high levies of interest, enforced under British law, they added to the surplus which was drawn to the cities, so generating a certain kind of development process along with a good deal of social disorganization.[36] The material result was striking: from cultivation mainly for subsistence up to about 1870, there was a rise to 720,000 tons of exports of paddy in 1872–1873, to two and one-half million tons by the end of the century, and to three and one-half million tons twenty years later. This was in addition to that part of the surplus which nourished Rangoon and other new cities.[37] Rangoon grew from an estimated 46,000 people in 1856 to 92,301 in the 1872 census, and up to 498,000 by 1941.[38]

It would be useful to study the circuits of colonial trade. One might start by tracing the rice of Burma from the paddy field to the consumer. Some of it went to Ceylon, to feed the labor on the up-country tea plantations; some went to Malaya, to be eaten by rubber workers. Since such customers, in considerable proportion Tamil indentured labor near the bottom of the colonial social scale, could hardly demand the best, Burma has been able to export its inferior rice and consume the higher grades at home. On the other hand, the tea which came out of Ceylon and north India and went to Britain was of the very highest quality; the inferior grades remained for local use. Burmese rice, along with that of the delta of the Mekong and the Menam, also provided food for the jute raisers of Bengal, the tin miners of Malaya, plantation workers producing sisal and palm oil in North Sumatra —as well as for the clerks, dock workers, runners, and sweepers who made up the rapidly growing populations of colonial Rangoon, Colombo, Singapore, and Batavia. The rice could be thought of as fuel, consumed internally by the colonial machine whose final exports to Europe were tea, rubber, jute, tin, and edible and nonedible oils. But this carries us away from the theme of the present chapter.

The levying of taxes in kind, called forced deliveries, as practiced by the Dutch in Indonesia, had a similar effect in respect to export products. Coffee sold in world markets bought the rice of Burma and the wheat of America, and maintained the cities of both Indonesia and Holland. Such instances, in which foreigners take sharp action to institute a surplus, make the process by which power generates cities especially obvious, if wholly out of accord with postcolonial moral ideals. But the process of development has everywhere been out of accord with moral ideals. We cite later the agricultural problems of the United States after the Civil War. The same complaints heard from Asian peasants—unfair taxes, exactions of moneylenders, extortion by middlemen, speculators, and transport companies—formed some of the main issues of American politics over the second half of the nineteenth century. Peasants are not induced to suffer willingly merely in the cause of economic development.

The exigencies of collecting the food, whatever the means used as long as force is their basis, bring about increased local concentrations of population, including cities of colonial type. From these the ruler's organization reaches to the surrounding countryside. On the other hand, the city that lives by manufacture and trade does not require land near by, or even on the same continent. With sufficiently effective economic institutions, the cities can live by export of their manufactures overseas, making their ecological base the land of other countries —though Wilbur R. Thompson shows that even on purely economic grounds a city draws advantage from a fertile hinterland surrounding it.[39]

City and National State in Relation to the Surplus

To put the matter briefly, as we have discussed it so far, we may distinguish three categories of ways in which the city can draw its supplies from the countryside:

1. Economic efficiency, especially available to the highly capitalized city of the developed country, drawing on various hinterlands for its several purposes, some of the territory from which it draws being on the other side of the globe under modern conditions of transport and modern organization of markets.

2. Combinations in various proportions of force, tradition, and other means of persuasion that depend in no way on the productive capacity of the city, classified by Polanyi as redistribution and reciprocity.

3. An intermediate case in which the efficiency of the city is sufficient that it can undersell the villages around and so relocate the manufacture of textiles, wood and metal products, etc., from them to it, but not such that it can compete in the world market. This is the city whose industry and hence population are supported by a hinterland around which it has used its power to raise a tariff against outside competition. The cities of developed and underdeveloped countries alike represent in some measure this case, which seems to form a considerable part of the *raison d'être* of the modern state.

The distinction which we are making here in terms of the flow of goods is to be found in the writing of Max Weber. Essential to all cities, in his system, is a marketplace in which goods are bought and sold among the citizens and between citizens and outsiders. Nonetheless, Weber speaks of the consumer and the producer city.[40] He con-

siders as consumer cities those that are the seat of a prince, of an association of warriors, of people living off rents or pensions, irrespective
of how the rights to these rents or pensions were secured. Producer
cities, on the other hand, contain "factories, manufactures, or home-
work industries supplying outside territories—thus representing the
modern type." [41] Somewhat intermediate is the city which provides a
utility of trade, an economic service, and where the goods traded come
essentially from outside it; this type has been common in all times and
places, sometimes as a seaport, sometimes as an island center at points
of break of bulk. Weber's consumer city claims its food from the surrounding country as taxes or rents; his producer city exchanges its
efficiently manufactured goods for food. The distinction is thus identical with that of the present chapter.

To bring Weber's distinction to the support of our study of the
underdeveloped world, we look at consumer cities as those concentrations of population where numbers of people exceed the ability to produce goods which can be exchanged with the outside world. (This
statement is quantifiable by making the unit of measurement of people
the quantity of cereals eaten by one person, and the production of manufactured goods expressed in terms of the cereals they will exchange
for in a free market.) In the circumstances where the first of these is
greater than the second, that is, inhabitants greater than production,
it is inescapable that the city will use any power it can mobilize to
press on its surrounding territory for supplies. The process of economic
development may be seen as one by which city production catches
up with and surpasses population growth, both expressed in cereal
units. This aspect of development is purely physical and ecological,
which is to say independent among other things of whether its framework is free enterprise or totalitarian rule.

It may help to show the significance of this direction of projecting
Weber's thought if we contrast it with that developed by his translator,
Don Martindale. Martindale emphasizes Weber's specification of the
city as able to defend itself militarily; now that "the modern city is no
longer a community with a firm military shell," the citizen is no longer
required to bear arms in its defense as he was in the European Middle
Ages, the city is not defensible against the state of which it is a part,
Martindale considers it to have ceased to exist as such. "The age of
the city seems to be at an end," he says. [42]

The argument of this chapter, on the contrary, is that the populations of primate cities along with the ambitions of their elites have
grown to such a point that they seek an ever firmer hold on a large and
definite territory. This territory will ideally provide security against

famine to the city as well as outlets for its developing industries. The modern state is as much as anything the institutional means by which the primate city wraps around itself, so to speak, a territory in which its food will be produced. For the city elite the nation is a means to power and survival; they are the first nationalists, creating the flags and other symbols of national unity. Nation building in the countries in the course of development includes the uniform spread of a common language, whose grammar and vocabulary—at least in their sophisticated forms—start from the cities and penetrate the countryside; the ability to read and write spreads in the same direction. Some encadrement of the countryside with local officials who will report to the central government is a feature of most developing countries. This was undertaken in France after the Revolution in the system of prefects in every department, with subprefects below them; the British in India had a similar sequence going down through Commissioners, Township Officers, and so on, to the village headman. The supreme example of recent times is that of the Communist Party in the U. S. S. R. The people who govern are the city elite; the ambitious countryman is not precluded from joining the elite, but he does so on the condition that he assimilate to city ways; he becomes a part of the national apparatus whose nerve center is the city.

The rural elite, the landholders, are widely regarded as the main foes of development. In the Russian industrialization debate of the 1920's which ended in the decision to undertake the heavy capitalization under Moscow control of the Five-Year Plans, Stalin seems to have won his point by arguing that although the country was progressing under the relatively liberal New Economic Policy, there was a danger if it continued that the rich peasants would get entirely out of hand.[43] We see today traditional rural allegiances everywhere under attack in the underdeveloped countries—those to caste as those to landlords. It is factually wrong to assert that the city is lost in the nation; it is rather that the nation is created by the city as a projection of itself over a territory. This primate city not only limits decentralization of functions to its countryside, it sometimes resents lesser cities as well, as has become explicit in the case of Colombo versus Galle in Ceylon.[44]

Apart from efforts to bridge differences through the strengthening of national symbols, countries do modify their very ecology in the interest of national unity. A country shaped like Burma, with its principal valleys funneling toward the south, permits the convenience of effective taxation of peasants even when they are in a state of insurrection. There is no physical means by which they can ship their surplus grain anywhere except through the government port of Rangoon. The Djakarta elite can well envy this situation, losing as it has in various periods a considerable part of the foreign exchange earned by smallholders' rubber which is shipped in small boats running illegally between Sumatra and Singapore. It is a part of nationalism no less in Canada than in Indonesia to fashion a transport system that allows the cities to have access to a national hinterland, and as far as possible discourages that hinterland from communicating with foreign cities. Whatever can be done to change the "shape" of countries, looked at in terms of minimizing the time of access from the capital to the various portions of its area by railways, shipping lines, and now air routes, strengthens the city alike in its economic and its political supremacy.

All cities do not have the physical possibility of making themselves secure and comfortable within a national territory. Some countries are too small, others too barren. The remarkable fact is that there is almost no country in which the city elite who make the development plans do not talk of self-sufficiency in food as a prime objective of policy, however irrational this may be from an economic viewpoint.[45]

Nonmaterial Items in the Urban-Rural Balance of Trade

The description of the city-countryside relation exclusively in terms of the actual movement of goods at a given point of time cannot explain the process by which countries pass out of the underdeveloped condition and into the developed one. A degree of complication of the view which is taken of the exchange process is required if we are to use it for understanding the process of change. We must recognize the possibility that the city uses the exactions it levies on the countryside in order to equip itself with capital.[46]

But first we consider several intangible items which enter the balance sheet. One is the services of the harbors through which exports are funneled and at which imports are unloaded; of the warehouses and railway stations through which goods and people pass; the banks that finance the clearing of jungle and the planting of a variety of crops whose period of maturing is as long as seven years or more in the case of rubber and coconuts. To these must be added administrative, health, educational, and other services, all managed from the city. These services are of importance in all phases of development; they presumably become more and more important as development proceeds, to judge from the increase in the proportion of the labor force devoted to such activities in the richer countries. And from the most backward princely seat up to a modern capital, a city incapable of manufacturing more efficiently than the peasants themselves can still organize the provision of law and order. One cannot assume that this is a free good which exists "naturally"; history in all ages shows how artificial a creation is peace and good government, as well as how necessary to all production. Peasants would certainly be willing to give up a portion of their crop to have secure enjoyment of the remainder; but in many parts of Asia the tax has amounted to one-half or two-thirds of the crop. We make no pretense of answering the question of just how much the peasants would find it worthwhile to give up for order—beyond what point they would rather face brigands than tax collectors. Nor do we try to say how much it costs to keep order; is it necessary to collect half the crop to maintain the army and the police, or would one-tenth do it? These are issues that depend on culture as well as ecology and have to be considered separately for each society.

Not only can the peasant be persuaded to give up part of his crop to support armies and police, education and health services, but he would rationally accept agricultural counseling from which he would benefit. In practice his willingness to give up part of the crop for all these and other purposes is increased by the sense that the urban rulers are legitimate, which is to say are entitled to carry out the collection and administration. This legitimacy is strengthened by religion in some places, and now by national symbols, just as in the past it was supported by the display of royal courts and the impressive style of life of landlords.

The City, the State, and Economic Development

But more than the current intangible services or the force of legitimacy, it is the prospect of industry that radically changes the situation of the underdeveloped country and makes any description of city-countryside relations in terms of the current exchange of goods seriously incomplete. If the city can somehow use the net balance of goods which it is at the moment causing the countryside to deliver as the means for capitalizing itself, then it has a realistic prospect of sooner or later coming into a relation with the countryside in which its domination will operate without force, through the exchange of goods of equal value. In the early phases agricultural products are needed not only to support people in the cities while they add the local component of capital in the form of factory buildings, but also, through their export abroad, to finance the purchase of machinery. Pakistan sells jute, India tea, Burma rice, Malaya rubber. The produce consumed in the cities or sold abroad may come from plantations, from peasant agriculture, from collective farms, but in general it must come without immediate full quid pro quo, for the cities, we assume, are not yet in a position to provide real savings. They must compel or induce agriculture to finance development—that is, to exchange for capital goods—unless they can secure capital goods from abroad without payment. And from this consideration arises a most important feature of foreign aid: insofar as it consists of food, and industrial equipment, both going to the cities, it may be expected—but only in those countries where there is a sufficiently ambitious urban elite—to get development under way with less political strain, and hence without the absolutism and suffering of communist countries.

Without gifts from abroad, the only actors in the development drama are the peasants in their countryside and the elite in its cities. The cities grow not in the degree in which they need factory hands, but in the much greater measure in which land is short in the countryside and at least some food is made available in the city. However miserable the situation of the marginal population of Calcutta, their numbers keep increasing; presumably the villages from which they come provide even fewer amenities than the Calcutta sidewalks. The increasing city population, whether productive or not, means increased pressure on the countryside to secure the means of keeping it alive. In exchange for food the city elite offer their peasant constituencies the promise of better things to come when development has occurred. Five-Year Plans are worked out which express this promise to those—whether in the countryside or the city—who for the moment have to deliver without receiving. They show in considerable concrete detail what the supplies of goods will be in the years to come, as well as how the resources of labor are to be deployed in order to secure this better condition. Stalin's first plan promised a substantial increase in consumer goods as well as in steel, though its performance was entirely in the latter.

There are important similarities in respect of development among Japan in the late nineteenth century, Germany, the U. S. S. R., India, and all other instances. In every case the crucial question is what is going on in the way of capital creation in the cities, more or less out of sight of the countryside, and certainly far beyond the ability of the peasants to judge. Even the experts cannot always discriminate between capital and income in relation to the national economy. Things are being built in the cities: football stadiums, private housing, factories, government offices. One would like to be able to say categorically that houses and stadiums are not really capital and that factories are, but the matter is not so simple. Factories may be grossly inefficient; they may be efficient but set to make the wrong things; the houses may or may not be used for the stimulation of labor, as genuine wage goods; they may or may not be assigned with relation to production. The experts are more aware than anyone else of the difficulty of saying which of the structures rising in the cities of the underdeveloped countries can properly be capitalized, and which on the other hand are bringing no closer the day when the city will be productive enough to enter into an equal exchange with its hinterland. Only in a completely free enterprise system, with capital accounting by firms which have to submit to genuine competition of other firms, has a satisfactory theoretical solution of this problem been given, and even this solution is subject to the difficulty of external economies.

One could imagine the process of development going on through the perfectly free issue of bonds and shares in the countryside which the peasants would buy with the food they sell, and which they could sell some years later when the city plants were in production to buy the produce of these plants. The development of France came about to some extent on this model. It is worth asking why such a model is far-fetched in relation to the crowded countrysides of the underdeveloped world today. The answer seems to be partly ecological and partly cultural. The pressure of day-to-day life on the peasant brings rates of interest in local loans for consumption that run to 50 per cent and more per annum. At these rates no city industrialist—private or governmental —could borrow and hope to attain solvency, no matter how quickly his plants came into efficient production; there is a limit to the returns on even the best of modern industrial methods. Hence the financing of development will continue to be by some combination of foreign aid and taxing of peasants. But taxes are associated with colonial regimes, and in the political democracy which has been introduced it is impossible to go before the electorate with proposals for taxation. Hence what is formally called taxation has diminished everywhere in the underdeveloped world. Sometimes this diminution has occurred by maintenance of a fixed amount of money taxes in the face of rising prices, supplemented by lack of firmness in tax administration. Since it is on the one hand essential to tax the peasantry and on the other hand impossible to admit that this is done, taxes have tended to take the form of exchange control, tariffs, differential price fixing, and other means of redistribution of real income.

The Formulation of the Physiocrats

The perspective of this chapter bears a resemblance to the thought of the early economists—Schumpeter [47] finds at least some of its elements successively in Petty, Cantillon, Quesnay, and Turgot. This is not surprising insofar as they also dealt with city-countryside relations in countries about to launch into development. Since industrial capital was small and its efficiency low, and there was no shortage of men, it seemed reasonable to assume that all productive power lay in land. In politics the physiocrats tended to take the side of the agricultural interest, and were opposed to the various protectionist measures by which a mercantilist king and court promoted industry and population. On the other hand they conceded that since any tax could only be paid by the produce of the land in the end, it would be well to eliminate the whole battery of taxes then in use and substitute for them the *impôt unique* on land,[48] that is, on Quesnay's *produit net* which was the same as Cantillon's *produit de la terre*.[49]

Although the situation of today's underdeveloped country (men in plenty, capital not yet in sight, and land the precious physical basis of the society) resembles the one that the physiocrats took as their model, the objective of the elite of the underdeveloped country is very different from that of the physiocrats and resembles more closely that of the mercantilists—the increase of domestic manufactures. However, the past 200 years have introduced at least two major changes—technical advance and the ideal of political democracy—and these permit us to drop the economic schools of the eighteenth century at this point.

Past Conflict in the Presently Developed Countries

THE UNITED STATES AND CANADA

There is a more pertinent item of western history and thought than the issue between physiocrats versus mercantilists to illuminate the conflict between town and countryside in countries entering upon development. The use of pressure on the countryside to extract a necessary surplus is a part of the history of North America. There the bitterness of political struggle seemed to reach its height at the point at which both agriculture and industry were growing fastest. In the United States this period occurred during the second half of the nineteenth century. But well before that the town and land interests had separated themselves out.

When the Constitutional Convention was called in Philadelphia in 1787, manufacturing went alongside other activities of city people—lending money at interest, often to farmers; the ownership of the public securities which had financed the War of Independence; the holding of western lands for speculation. These interests appear and reappear in Beard.[50] "Most of the members (of the Convention) came from towns, on or near the coast, that is, from the regions in which personalty was largely concentrated." [51] "Personalty" was the name given to the various economic holdings of townsmen, against the "realty" of farmers. Speculators and moneylenders played a major part in the drawing of farm produce to the cities from the earliest days of the Union.

During the time from the Civil War to the end of the century, midwestern farmers were in almost continuous agitation against the high rates charged by the railroads that brought their wheat and hogs to Chicago, and from there to the eastern seaboard, rates which they saw as simple profiteering. Their suspicions of the bribery of legislators were raised by the issue of free railway passes to public officials, and it was known that rebates were given to large (city) shippers. The "livestock ring" which manipulated prices in Chicago was the subject of widespread complaint which extended to middlemen in all fields.[52] Loan agents from the East pressed money on farmers which was hard enough to repay in the best of circumstances and doubly hard in a period of deflation which was assumed to be created by a banker-dominated government. And on the side of their expenditures the farmers were aroused by what they thought to be the monopoly pricing of the makers of farm machinery, sewing machines, and other patented goods.[53] The tariff on manufactured goods was a focus of American farm discontent; like the Burmese peasants of today, as we shall show, it was their immediate interest to buy freely in the cheapest markets and sell in the dearest, without hindrance of tariffs or exchange control.

> The Morrill tariff act of 1864, passed at the instance of the manufacturers, raised duties enormously and indiscriminately. When peace came, the tariff should have been drastically revised at once, but it was not touched until 1872 and then only slightly reduced. It cost the farmer heavily upon a hundred articles of constant use, from sugar upon his table and blankets upon his bed to the plowshare in his field.[54]

Direct taxes were a further means by which the farmers could be made worse off and the city people better off. The Civil War and the expenses of state government had to be covered; tax-free bonds, drawing interest at 6 per cent, were repaid in gold which commanded a premium.[55] The holders were city people, who presumably put their gains into industry, with a resulting rapid pace of growth.

Earle D. Ross repeats all this, and adds other respects in which there was injustice to the farmer—injustice which this chapter finds so useful for industrial growth:

In spite of all the advances in farming, the census of 1880 shows that the proportionate share of agriculture in the nation's income was becoming smaller. . . . The farmer was the exploitable victim of discriminatory utilities and of fraudulent salesmen and promoters. . . . The price of land increased disproportionately to the returns that could be obtained from its use. New farmers were seriously handicapped by the necessity of investing a large proportion of their funds in land . . .[56]

funds which they would have to repay out of subsequent crops.

Claims on behalf of the farmer by the Populists, in coalition with the Democratic Party under William J. Bryan, reached their peak in the campaign of 1896. "The heated, not to say hysterical, opposition of the industrial regions by all of the ingenious resources known to current political manipulation, augmented by those of the new business organization, was to be taken for granted." The party was defeated, largely through the inability of the farmers to hold together against the forces of "sound money." [57]

In Canada the agricultural and other export interests were more substantial than in the United States, and the free trade sentiment among them was strong. The resentment of farmers reached its peak when that in the United States was dying down. In 1902 the manufacturers began an energetic campaign to raise the tariff. "Only the vigorous opposition set up by the farmers of Ontario and the West checked the agitation for still higher duties. The new tariff of 1907 made many careful revisions upward as well as downward, but on the whole the existing level was retained." [58] Speaking of this period (1907–1908), O. J. McDiarmid said "pressure groups represented in the Canadian Manufacturers' Association were pitted against the Grange Movement in the West, and both gained in strength and political effectiveness. . . . Charges of combination and monopoly bred behind tariff walls were being made by agriculture and denied by the representatives of industry." [59]

Is it the object of these lines to draw up an indictment of urban usurers and speculators, and come to the defense of rural landholders, tenant farmers, and landless agricultural laborers who made up the great majority of the population of the United States at the time the Constitution was drawn up and through the nineteenth century? Quite the contrary: it is the thesis of this chapter that the agricultural surplus was increased by agricultural indebtedness, by taxes, and by sharp practices of city lenders and speculators. We separate our moral assessment of these means from their specific economic effect,

which was to cause the farmers to do what the early stages of industrialization absolutely required—produce a large uncompensated flow
of food to the cities. Some of this nourished the labor of the eastern
cities, some of it was sold in England, which had previously developed
industry to the point where it could export capital goods. Farmers paid
in one way or another both for domestic production of capital goods
and for the import of components from abroad. In real terms they were
the only portion of the community in a position to pay, until city
industry came to be more productive. One hundred years later the debt
was liquidated by agricultural support prices and other forms of subsidy paid to the few descendants of these pioneers who still remained
on their farms.

Another of the means by which the city drew produce from the
countryside in the developing countries of the nineteenth century
was the result of rural-urban migration. Farmers' sons who gave
up their portion of the land retained some rights to income from their
inheriting brothers. When a farmer sold his holding to a stranger and
went to the city with his family, his successor on the land would typically have to make mortgage payments into a city bank account. Such
payments arose out of the notion of property, always strong in the
American tradition. Remittances in the opposite direction—from the
son who has gone to the city toward the support of his parents and
brothers who remain on the farm, dictated by the sense of family
solidarity—occur to some extent in America, but to a much wider extent in India. There the typical migrant to the city will have moral
obligations in the countryside, and remittances are common.[60] In one
village described by Lewis, total outside income was calculated as
9050 rupees,[61] whereas the village tax revenue was 1397 rupees. These
figures alone, of course, do not measure the entire movement of payments, but they are enough to suggest which way the net balance
would fall. In this respect again, India fails to extract from the peasant
the surplus that American cities extracted.

JAPAN

The development of Japan was the work of a self-conscious elite
which aimed both at economic and extra-economic objectives. With
limited natural resources, an initial high density of population, and a
disinclination to borrow abroad, the problem of finance was especially
difficult. Land taxes had been heavy but irregular prior to the Meiji
Restoration. A land tax reform replaced the whole complex of feudal
dues by a tax payable in money on the value of the land, which
had recently been assessed for the purpose. The logic of a rigid tax

based on assessed productive value (rather than income or other more flexible criteria) appealed to the Meiji government as it had to British empire builders. A tax that was recognized by all as certain to come due, and whose nonpayment meant forfeiture of the land, constituted the basic incentive to produce. "For twenty-five years," says Lockwood, "this tax provided the national government with its chief source of revenue. Until 1882, indeed, it furnished over 80 per cent." [62] It seems that even as late as 1913 taxes on business income and property provided less than 15 per cent of the national tax collections. This theme of pressure on the peasants runs through Lockwood's book. (See pp. 9, 26, 35, 99, 285, 513, and 521.) Aside from it little was done to aid agriculture, for instance by helping the peasants to buy the plots they worked. All the evils of tenancy and usury prevailed on the Japanese countryside. The steady expansion both of cultivated area and of yield per acre could in part be attributed to an agricultural extension service, but measures along this line were skimpy. Lockwood considers that even the development of the empty lands of Hokkaido lagged for want of funds and of official interest (p. 556).

During the Meiji period the cities grew steadily. Communes of more than 10,000 population, which Taeuber [63] suggests constitutes a suitable definition of urban, were 22.9 per cent of the total population in 1888; in 1918 they were 31.9 per cent; in 1940 they were 49.9 per cent. The growth in absolute numbers over this half-century period was from five million people to 37 million. Insofar as much of the investment in the cities was carried out directly on government account, the relation between the agricultural surplus generated by the tax and the growth of the cities was particularly straightforward. By the First World War many of the industries initiated by government had been sold to private holders, and one can suppose that the elements of exchange between city and countryside began to be present. Tokyo doubled in population between 1920 and 1940,[64] as did the total of the six largest cities; presumably by this time they had created an economic base for themselves and depended much less on taxes. It was in the 1920's that discussion of social welfare began, that trade unions were permitted for the first time, and that real wages rose above a minimum subsistence level. Prior to that wages had been so low and working conditions so poor that despite poverty in the countryside employers had difficulty in getting and keeping the labor they needed. As in Europe the expansion of the cities was a function of the demand for labor within them, rather than of the lack of opportunities in rural areas.

As is inevitable in the change from household production to factory production, the financial difficulties of the peasants were accentuated by their elimination from the making of thread, textiles, and paper, as well as vegetable fuel oils which were replaced by kerosene. This undercutting of the sources of rural cash income forced the peasant into other activities which were more productive for the nation. Raw silk making constituted a source of supplementary income for two out of five farm families (Lockwood, p. 489); the silk could be exported to the United States whose industrial goods were badly needed for the equipping of Japanese factories. Villages were further helped by the remittances of their daughters who had gone to the city to work in textile factories, there to live in supervised dormitories. In addition some effort was made by government and industry to decentralize manufacturing to the countryside.

However necessary these changes were to the industrialization of Japan, they would not have taken place, certainly they would not have taken place so rapidly, if the countryside had had more power. But the peasantry was in no position to stand up against the dynamic bureaucrats of the Meiji regimes. And the landlords had been defeated or bought out after 1868. Like those of other countries undergoing industrialization, Japan's cities were not in the first phases able to offer consumer goods to farmers; they were still in building. But Japan's case was somewhat worse in the high proportion of the building which was plant for production of military goods, for instance, warships, which even in a distant future could hardly be offered to the peasantry as an inducement to sell its rice. One is inclined to say that Japan's military career imposed an additional burden on the city and rural population alike. Yet the dedication to national expansion also constituted a main part of the motivation to industrialize. Those attempting to provide a balanced explanation of Japan's growth would have to investigate two other factors which are rooted in her preceding culture and society: the widespread initiative which appeared as soon as opportunity showed, and what abstractly one might have thought would preclude this, the intense social discipline and universal sense of hierarchy.

ELSEWHERE

Lack of space here and of knowledge on the part of this writer prevent any further exposition of the methods used for the financing of the process of development. There are other instances, of which the U. S. S. R. perhaps would be the most interesting. Suffice it to say that the nature of the financing in question was far clearer in the minds of communist elites than it could be in any liberal or traditional society, and that whatever elements of ruse and force appear in the United States and Japanese cases are multiplied a hundredfold in the U. S. S. R.[65] None of these instances lends any encouragement to the view that industrialization is easy.

Social Organization as Creator of the Surplus

If we think of a given preindustrial level of technology, along with a given number of people on the land, as permitting a food surplus of given magnitude, then the role of power and the institutions through which power is expressed is to make that surplus actual. The surplus which in the given technical and social condition actually comes off the land determines the number of people who can live in cities within any closed region. This is a very different model from the one that is appropriate where industrial capital is used in the city and the city dominates through the attractiveness of the goods that it offers for sale. If this latter is appropriate to the fully developed market economy, then the former is applicable to the completely undeveloped one, whether modern or ancient. For either case we may think of the creating of institutions and the concentration of power, of which the existence of cities is a manifestation, as working against a kind of entropy which would disperse power to the village and leave no food for cities.

Certain forces of change which operate in the already crowded countrysides of a number of tropical countries seem to act as such a form of entropy. On the one side is a fact in the ecological order—the rapid increase of population—and on the other a fact in the social and psychological order—the trend to democracy and to what might be called short-run humanitarianism. The push of postcolonial institutional change combines with the increase of population to whittle down the surplus. Without pretending to be exhaustive we present three of the institutional means by which population growth in the countryside is encouraged in the countries which are now undeveloped, though no one plans them to that end and few even perceive that they have this effect. We refer to the virtual dropping of land taxes, the elimination of landlords, and the prevalence of work-sharing and crop-sharing practices.

Taxes in the New Countries

The levels of taxation in most of the countries of South Asia today are about the same as those of before the war in money terms, which means from one-quarter to one-fiftieth in goods. Indonesia showed less than 1 per cent of government revenue from land taxes; [66] India shows

6 per cent in 1950 and 7 per cent in 1958. One of the reasons why these percentages are low, in the explanations offered by administrators, is that the peasants are so poor. They are poor indeed, but not so much poorer than they were in colonial times. Taxes have always been a means, especially for the more skilled colonial administrations, of getting the peasant to produce more, some of which could be taken from him; they were not in general a means of taking part of his existing small income. This is made clear by their form: the peasant who owned land was required to turn over in taxes a certain fraction of the value of the crop that the land would produce if it was efficiently tilled. The one who owned no land was required, especially in Africa, to pay a head tax that he could secure only by working on a plantation or in a mine. In both cases the tax was taken seriously by the colonial authority: "The realization of the revenues was always a matter of violence. The ryots (village headman) of a group of villages would be gathered together; they would declare their complete inability to pay what was demanded of them: they would then be beaten, or stood in the burning sun with a heavy stone weighing down their heads." [67] The effectiveness of such methods in stepping up the production and transfer of foodstuffs was considered by administrators to be proportional to their severity. They brought land into use that was previously fallow, and provided an incentive to higher yields on land that was already in use.

Since independence, however, the increasing disinclination of the central power to use force has worked in the same direction as (1) the higher *level* of population, by which all readily accessible lands have been settled, and (2) the present rapid *growth* of population, by which increased yields through technical improvement find people to consume them as fast as they appear. In many places the peasant could not today be compelled to produce more by imposing a land revenue on him, for there is no more land on which he could work. The sound advice that the governments of the new countries reinstitute taxes goes unheeded for the reason, which becomes more valid every year, that with the land fully occupied the peasant could pay these taxes only by ejecting the relatives staying with him and selling the food which they now consume. There would be no loss of food as a result, since the taxed grain would be allocated through the market to the same people who are initially deprived of it, after they have moved to the city and taken productive jobs which paid them wages. But this classical form of the process of development appears too drastic to be applied intensively by a modern democratic regime.

Landlords

The tendency for the surplus to disappear is reinforced by the democratic and socialist antipathy to landlords, who are now being bought out—at least in their upper layers—through most of South and Southeast Asia. The exceptions are such out-of-the-way places as Nepal, and even these are showing signs of movement in the same direction. Landlords have neither any very deep-rooted traditional right to the produce of the soil, their claim in many places dating no further back than the colonial regime, nor any great role in the organization of production. Furthermore they tend to be unsympathetic to development and are likely to use their resources and power to frustrate it. They want to sell food abroad to buy the luxurious products of American industry, not the poor output of their own cities. But having said all this, we have to say also that their harshness and that of the stewards acted in the same direction as the harshness of the tax collector; whether their demands were for rice or for money, they resulted in food leaving the countryside and finding its way to the city. The peasant got little in return for his contribution. But insofar as the landlord, usually an absentee, lived in the capital city of his own country he supported retainers and city people to supply his personal needs. From a modern point of view such people are not very useful, and there would be little reason to bring them back even if this were politically possible. Depriving them of their rent forces them to seek industrial jobs. But the landlord's former take could well be recaptured in the interest of development, so that the new industrial city could be based on the same surplus as the preindustrial city in which the landlord lived. South Asian land reforms do sometimes substitute the state for the previous intermediary, but more commonly the peasant is given the right to buy his land in 4 or 10 or 20 annual instalments—in effect dismissing the landlord with a few years' notice. One can assume that the peasant can adduce the same argument for not paying rent to the state that he has for not paying taxes.

Sharing Practices

More field work is needed to find if ancient rural practices of hospitality, work-sharing, crop-sharing, and the giving of feasts, are extended and become more elaborate as population density increases; in what degree the sharing is the consequence of population increase as well as its cause. In what circumstances are men with hoes replacing water-buffalo-drawn plows in cultivation? What is the function of inefficient fragmentation of holdings in relation to rural sharing?

To what extent is the refusal to use even so simple an instrument as the scythe in harvesting the rice of Java based on the conscious wish to divide up the claim to the crop so that all villagers will have enough to eat and not lose their self-respect? My hypothesis is that there is an interaction between population growth and culture; that the low and even declining technical levels of agriculture are not a result of ignorance, but an at least half-conscious means of coping with the population problem. The means may be dysfunctional from the viewpoint of the national entity as a whole, but thoroughly functional in the short run for the countryside in its position vis-à-vis the city, with which we are here concerned.

Family Budgets in Varying Conditions of Development

It is well known (under the heading of Engel's law) that within a country the proportion of food in the budgets of families diminishes with increase of income. This inelasticity of the value of food consumed with changes of income arises from the inelasticity of the human stomach. It applies of course among countries, where degree of development is reflected in the proportion spent on food. We note for instance that the proportion was 85.3 per cent for Indian agricultural laborers in 1950–1951, and some 77.3 per cent in 1956–1957.[68] Both these figures seem high, especially if one takes account of the fact that the consumption of these families of the sample (461 rupees in 1950–1951 and 617 rupees in 1956–1957) was somewhat above the per capita income of India as a whole. Some budgets which I collected among poor families in a suburb of Rangoon in 1951 averaged 75 per cent food. Data on Japanese manual workers presented by Dore show 48.9 per cent of expenditures on food, but calculated without clothing and furniture.[69] Adding these into the denominator we lower the ratio of food to total to 44.6 per cent, which may be taken as representing a country that is not rich but is in process of rapid development. Proportions spent on food in an official French survey of 1951 run from 58 per cent for unskilled laborers down to 40 per cent for senior supervisors, as average monthly income rises from 11,760 francs to 27,600 francs.[70] For nine Canadian cities in 1957, the lowest family income group in which a substantial sample was secured was $2500–2999, which spent 30.4 per cent on food; the highest range was $6500–7500, with 20.5 per cent for food.[71] Above family incomes of $7500, which have now been attained on the average in most states of the United States, even the most demanding standards on the form in which nourishment is taken cannot push the percentage higher than 20 per cent.

A Matrix of Transfers of Goods

The cities described by the students of the American metropolitan community have large stocks of capital with which they can employ their people, and high enough efficiency in production that they are capable of entering successfully into competition not only with the nearby countryside and with other cities in their own country, but with the cities of other countries. Standards of living are high, and the greatest part of urban production is of goods that will be used by people in the same or other cities. Among countries there is bound to be a relation among (1) the proportion of the population living in cities, (2) the proportion of national production for which the cities are responsible, and (3) the proportion of consumption of people generally which consists of city goods. Because efficiency of production and standards of consumption differ between city and countryside in a given country, and because countries are not closed economic areas, 80 per cent of population living in the countryside may mean 70 per cent rather than 80 per cent of national production in the form of agricultural produce. In a highly developed country on the other hand, 10 per cent of the population of a country might be rural and engaged in agriculture, 12 per cent of national production might be food, and family budgets might average 20 per cent food. Food as it enters the family budget of the city person is much more than an agricultural product, including a substantial trade and service component. Budgets of city people include as "food" many items such as packaging, restaurant services, and so on, which for the purpose of the two-sector model should be counted as city production. Again, if it is really the rural-urban balance we are concerned with, we would have to take account of the agricultural component in nonfood items, such as the raw cotton contained in cotton fabrics, which in this chapter are also spoken of as "food." A number of writers have distinguished the economic effort of a city which supplies nonlocal demands—which they call "basic"—from that which caters to the needs of local inhabitants—which they call "nonbasic." [72, 73]

The calculation of the economic base of all the cities of a country taken together—which is the interest of this chapter—need not be more difficult than the calculation of the economic base of a single city. For the single city we are concerned with a balance of payments in which agricultural goods are imported while manufactured goods are both imported and exported; for the totality of cities in a closed area we think of the more simple exchange of manufactured goods (and services) against agricultural goods. One form of approximation is through labor force data, which have been fruitfully applied to this purpose for individual cities.[74] To apply this method between countries would be subject to some variations in the definition of agricultural labor force, but these need not be serious. Another form of approximation to the balance of trade of the cities taken collectively is via family budget data. By combining various kinds of data one might hope to overcome the shortcomings of each particular kind, at least in part.

One of the questions that would have to be taken up in the serious construction of a table of rural-urban transactions could be the movement of goods between cities. As the manufacturing sector becomes stronger, more and more specialization grows up in the cities within it, and there is more and more exchange of semimanufactured pieces. Subcontracting in the automobile industry is only an especially complex instance of a very common procedure. In addition the finished manufactured goods of one city are in considerable part destined for consumers in other cities. None of these movements of goods among cities is of concern for the thesis of this chapter. Aside from the fact that they constitute a smaller part of the undeveloped and the developing economies with which we are here mainly concerned than they do of the fully developed one, it is in any case the balance of cities in the aggregate against the countryside with which we have to deal.

There is no point here in going into the way in which the market not only determines which areas shall be the hinterland of the developed city, but creates specializations within that hinterland. Gottmann describes in some detail how the precious lands within Megalopolis, whose value depends more on their locality than on the fertility of their soils, are used to raise cows and chickens on feed that comes from the western plains (". . . these specialists, whether dairymen or poultrymen, are essentially manufacturers who buy a low-cost raw material in the form of feed grains and sell a high-priced product such as meat or milk"[75]); and how the farmer holds his lands for the biggest harvest of all—sale to the advancing city. Norton Ginsburg has shown how Shanghai created an agricultural area in its immediate neighborhood, bringing into use land which up to that time had been neglected. A certain amount of abstraction is forced upon us in the presentation of the present argument, an abstraction expressed by disregard both of intercity transactions within a country and of differentiation in the rural hinterland of the city or cities.

Efficiency of Production versus Physical Control of Sources of Food

The fully developed industrial city depends on no particular countryside to buy its products and furnish it with food; if there is a crop failure in the place of its usual supply, it can draw food from else-where. The fields of the world are its ecological base; it can draw their food with a security that is not available to the city that lacks efficient industry and services. The latter can have its base only in the area over which it has power. It is tied back to the base, normally the rural countryside of its own country. Its room for maneuvering, for meeting crises, is less in proportion as the standards of living in it and the territory on which it depends are already low.

The difference between 20 per cent and 80 per cent spent on food is important in theorizing about cities and the populations which they can contain. The Asian shoemaker cannot exchange his product with the shirtmaker, for this exchange covers only a small part of the budget of each; both are much more dependent on the product of the farmer than they are on each other. The policy consequence of this for the Asian government that wants to increase the population-hold-ing capacity of its cities without using mere power is clear: the pro-ductivity of the cities in goods that will exchange with the country-side is the decisive factor in determining the population the cities can economically sustain. The worst possible policy is to print money and put it in the hands of the city people, for then the city producers aim their goods at the city consumer in respect of style, advertising, and so on, and this has the effect of causing city industry to compete for a fixed total of possible sales, set by the total of food that comes into the city. The movement of the price level as a whole is less important for this purpose than the relative movement of food and other prices—as the marginal city manufacturers find when they have to shut down be-cause the prices they can get for their products do not suffice for them to pay their employees enough for sustenance. Along with the balance of payments between city and country the terms of trade as shown by prices of agricultural and manufactured goods demand study.

It will be argued that the discussion of the fate and prosperity of cities in terms of the food which they can secure, rather than of a balance of money payments, is something of a retrogression. Why not simply talk in the usual monetary aggregates of macroeconomics? The answer is that this retrogression in the manner of description, the re-version from a description in terms of money to one in terms of barter, is in the nature of the matter required as one moves from a developed to an undeveloped country. The developed country has to face the niggardliness of nature in respect of perhaps 20 per cent of its income, the undeveloped one in respect of 80 per cent. The projection of aggre-gate money incomes, absolute or per capita, always difficult, is espe-cially so if it conceals within it different trends in the agricultural and nonagricultural sectors.

The relating of cities to their food base today involves new elements. Consider the 27,000,000 people living in cities of 200,000 and over in 1961 in India.[76] We note that the total Indian supply of food grains consisted, for 1959–1960, of 71.8 million tons produced and about 4.5 million tons imported.[77] If we divide the total of these by the 430 million people who were living in the whole country at the time, we find (disregarding changes of stocks which can be assumed to be small) that the average consumption was 177 kilograms, which is to say roughly six people fed for a year per ton of grain. The largest part of the imports have been gifts from the United States under Public Law 480; in May 1960 an agreement was entered into by which 16 million tons of wheat and one million tons of rice were to be provided over the course of the following four years. Four and a quarter million tons of grain at six persons per ton means that 26 million persons are supported by the gift. The closeness of this figure to the total of the cities of over 200,000 population is worth noting, even though we cannot assert that it is exactly this grain which is feeding just those people, and we should make allowance for the fact that a ton of wheat nourishes fewer than a ton of rice. But with all allowances made, the ecological base of the largest Indian cities is in considerable part the wheat fields of the American west, and the means by which the wheat is drawn is neither trade nor political domination, but rather gifts paid for by the United States Treasury. Since the gifts are used to buy a surplus that came into existence in a fashion that is accidental in relation to the system of Indian cities and their problems, their degree of stability is correspondingly uncertain. Yet city populations are not only nourished but in a certain sense being created by them. The issues—of economics, of morality, and of international politics—which will be raised by any diminution of the gift in the future are fortunately beyond the scope of this discussion. We note only that issues will diminish in the degree in which economic development gets under way in India.

One could match the grain imports of Indonesia in the same way against the population of her large cities. In a poor year imports have been nearly one million tons, enough to supply about 6 million non-agriculturalists, which is equal to the population of the two largest cities.

Population Trends in Asian Cities

South Asia is the part of the world which best exhibits the interplay of population with restricted land in a fashion that constitutes the theme of this chapter. (Lack of data prevents us from saying very much about China.) In all countries of an area containing some 750,-000,000 people lying to the south and southeast of the Himalayas, urban population is increasing considerably faster than rural population. India was 11.4 per cent urban according to the census of 1921, 13.9 per cent in 1941, 17.3 per cent by 1951. In 1961 the preliminary figures show 17.9 per cent, still an increase though much less than that of the two preceding decades.[78] This sudden deceleration in the percentage growth of the cities of India may have the highest significance as evidence of an approach to a limit in urban-industrial growth. On the other hand it may be simply an artifact of the census—a change in the point at which the line was drawn between rural and urban. Delhi is an exception to the general rule; it grew from 1,384,000 in 1951 [79] to 2,344,000 in 1961,[80] which is very much more than the growth of India as a whole.

Estimates for the cities of Indonesia show very great increase from 1940; according to municipality reports, Greater Djakarta grew from 533,000 in the 1930 census to 2,081,000 in 1958; Bandung from 167,000 to 952,000; Surabaya from 342,000 to 1,135,000.[81] These triplings and quadruplings compare with about 50 per cent increase for the whole of Indonesia, and it is possible that these city estimates for 1958 are low. Rhoads Murphey publishes estimates for 1957 which are considerably higher except for Surabaya; he gives Djakarta 3,200,000; Djokjakarta 1,950,000 (a 15-fold increase from its 1930 census figure of 136,649).[82] He mentions that Saigon-Cholon increased from 498,000 in 1950 to an estimated 1,800,000 in 1956, largely owing to refugee immigration from Tonkin and disordered areas in the south. His figures presumably represent local opinion supplemented by such evidence as the Indonesian electoral registration of 1954.

Job Trends in Asian Cities

It is not easy to collate existing statistical data to ascertain the trend in the availability of industrial and commercial jobs. Is the number now greater in Asian cities than in Europe and America when those continents were in a corresponding stage of development? It seems that "at a time when the degree of urbanization was roughly the same in these (presently advanced) countries as in India now, the share of the labor force in manufacturing was substantially greater than in India in 1951." [83]

Does it make a difference that jobs in Asian cities tend to be service rather than manufacturing? Colin Clark describes how technical advance and the growth of cities moves people from primary (agricultural) into secondary (manufacturing) production, and how the further advance of cities moves them into tertiary (service) activities, and has interesting observations on efficiency in the three sectors.[84] Fourastié estimates that in the 1860's French primary industry turned out 58 per cent of the gross product, secondary industry 21 per cent, and tertiary industry 21 per cent; by 1961 primary was down to 14 per cent, secondary had risen to 41 per cent, and tertiary to 45 per cent.[85] Eric Lampard, with support from the economic historian A. G. B. Fisher, describes the process by which in the later stages of development tertiary activities come to absorb labor displaced by technical advance.[86] "If some such transfer of workers into the tertiary area had not occurred in the past, the worst prophecies of the early machine-breakers might have been fulfilled," he says of the presently developed countries. Granting the effect of such tertiary employment in quieting the claims of those who would otherwise be left out of the division of wealth, there remains the quite different problem of the economic health of the city as a whole, defined as dominance resting on export of useful goods to pay for the food needed by its growing population. Hence ideally one should leave out of the count of employment for our purpose domestic servants, most trishaw pushers, unnecessary peons in government offices, government staff doing unnecessary paper work. Statistics which make these distinctions are not ordinarily kept by either developed or underdeveloped governments. We thus observe that tertiary activities can be politically stabilizing at the same time as they are economically pointless. At the end of an argument to this general effect, Norton Ginsburg refers to the residual employment in the cities—despite the labor-intensive industry and the services of low productivity—and the political menace which it constitutes, especially in the absence of high productivity in the secondary sector and stable governmental institutions.[87]

Some evidence of the relationship is implied in the official discussion of manpower in India.[88] At the beginning of the Second Plan in 1956 there were 5.3 million unemployed, 8 million jobs were created (of which 6.5 million were outside agriculture), and the total of unemployed by 1961 was 9 million. The increase in the population able and willing to work during the Third Plan is estimated at about 17 million, and it is hoped that some 14 million jobs can be provided, of which 10.5 million are nonagricultural. Unfortunately no information is provided on the definitions of such difficult statistical concepts as "jobs" and "labor force," nor on the relation of these to city populations. In any case, the results of the 1961 census were not available to the Planning Commission at the time it made these estimates, and such figures from the census as have been released suggest a more rapid increase in the gap between jobs created on the one hand and persons available for employment on the other.

The crowded underdeveloped country suffers from the increase of population in its countryside, in that the agricultural surplus diminishes by the amount that the increment eats. Thus the country will experience greater difficulty both in feeding its cities and in exporting in order to pay for imports of capital goods. But it is equally a part of the thesis of this chapter that the country as a whole will suffer from the growth of its cities beyond their productive means, since the more people there are in the cities the more food will have to be brought in, and in the absence of new outside gifts the city will have to exercise more pressure on its peasants in order merely to keep its inhabitants alive. Which of these does more harm? The Japanese authorities of the Shogunate thought that people were less trouble in the country, and had laws—though not effectual ones—barring their movement to the city.[89] In England also there was some official attempt to check cityward movement in the eighteenth century, though it was much less effective than the enclosures which pushed people toward the city.

Is it possible to say in general whether increased population ought to be kept in the countryside or encouraged to go to the city? I do not believe that there is any single answer to this question that will apply to all crowded countries attempting to initiate development. For any particular country the answer would depend on estimates of marginal productivity, and marginal cost, of population in the city as compared with the countryside. It is conceivable that the national interest in development will not be automatically served by the currents of migration which spontaneously take place.

The Objective Conflict of Interest between City and Countryside during the Early Stages of Economic Development

Our argument, which sees the tension between countryside and city as constituting much of the dynamic of both politics and economics in preindustrial areas, requires that we investigate in what sense there is a conflict of interest between the two sectors, and after that to see if the conflict penetrates the individual consciousness of those concerned.

A conflict of interest can arise only in the face of a policy choice. Simplifying somewhat, the choice facing the underdeveloped country is whether to (a) step up taxes and savings for capital investment along with tariffs to protect infant industries, and have a strong central government plan and manage the process, or on the other hand (b) exercise a minimum of central effort and allow nature to take its course. In other words, whether or not to go ahead on the path which most of the governments of South Asia are trying to follow: rapid development in a nationalistic, protectionist, centralized, planned, socialist framework. One alternative to the presently expressed aims, would be a Gandhian decentralized society, in which cities would play a smaller role.

Whether there is a conflict of objective interest between the man of the city and the man of the countryside on this question will depend on the period of time considered. If we assume the economic theory underlying South Asian planning and grant that the measures taken are effective and will do what is expected of them—on which this chapter takes no stand—there is no doubt that average income over the next hundred years will be higher on the centralized development policy than on that of the rural idyll. But no one—in a peasant society or elsewhere—averages future income over a century to decide what his interest is. In the case of the peasant, the discount of the future is at a particularly high rate of interest, as one can see from the rates at which he is willing to borrow for consumption.

With the help of a few other assumptions we could work out a curve of future income on each of the two suppositions for each of the rural and urban sectors. The income per capita of the peasant under the static assumption would presumably remain constant over a period of time, and then decline as the population crisis came to a head and marginal lands had to be brought into use. The peasant's income under a program of development would start lower, and rise with a rapidity that depended among other things on the proportion of income that was invested during the first years, as well as the quality of management. The two curves would cross at a point of time that depends on these elements. One would also have to make some assumptions about the value of leisure, because people would certainly be required to work more on the development model than on the static one. We do not go into these matters, but merely suggest the rough shape of the two curves. (See Figure 1.)

That development requires sacrifice now can be seen clearly when we consider the position of the Burmese peasant. There are two acres of irrigated land per person in many parts of the delta; a person can eat well on the produce of half an acre. The rice he sells off the re-

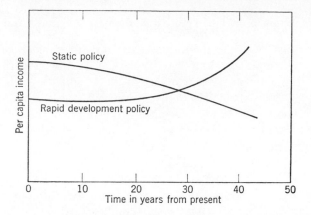

Figure 1. Prospective income of the peasant under two policies.

maining one and a half acres amounts to over a ton and will fetch over $100 in a free market. On such a calculation we arrive at a cash income, for a family of six persons, of well over $600 plus all the food they can eat. This amount will go far if one can buy clothing and bicycles and flashlights in the world market without the tariffs which are part of economic nationalism. But in the actual circumstances the peasant is required to sell his rice for Burmese currency at a rate that has been about $30 per ton during most of the period of independence. And the much smaller return can only be spent in the local market, buying imported goods on which high duties have to be paid, or local goods of lower quality protected by tariffs and exchange control. The peasant is called upon to forego imported goods in order to encourage and develop Burmese industry; this immediately benefits the city, and especially the city of Rangoon; it at first penalizes but will ultimately benefit the peasant. The point of intersection of the two curves would be at a different date for Burma than for India, because of differences in the population-land ratio and other elements. Under what circumstances is development in the interest of the peasantry of either country?

The answer depends on the rate at which one discounts the future. The peasant who discounts at 50 per cent per annum is not benefited by development; at 5 per cent he probably would be. Without trying to settle what is the realistic rate for this purpose, we repeat that in general the peasants must pay in the early stages of development; this applies even if the city elite who direct the process of development do so with absolute efficiency.

The Subjective Conflict of Interest between City and Countryside

I have shown that city dweller and peasant have opposed objective interests at least in the short run. These could only give rise to conflict if the protagonists become aware of them, which means the possibility that the peasant will actually go through the calculation I have presented. His ability to perceive alternatives and to make calculations increases by diffusion outward to him of city education and ways of thought. Even if the calculation of which policy is more advantageous to him is vague in his mind, he comes to feel resentment merely through observing the higher standard of living of some of the people in the city, which is irrational on his part because a difference in standard of living does not by itself prove a conflict of interest.

In fact, resentment on the part of peasants has determined Burmese politics ever since independence. Official declarations from the cities have blamed the resentment on mutual antipathies of minority groups and the activities of communists, which undoubtedly are real factors but could hardly have constituted such stubborn difficulties by themselves. The 1955 election results showed clearly that AFPFL support was in Rangoon, the opposition in the countryside.[90] If the communists were able to make converts it was because they could explain how wicked was Rangoon and the AFPFL elite associated with Rangoon. Behind the appeal of their assertions lies the difference between the domestic and the world price of rice.

On the social-psychological side, the urban elite in the new countries try to bridge the conflict of interest by creation of symbols of national unity. In this they have had some success, though once the issue is raised to the symbolic plane the elite has to struggle in all countries with a very considerable gap in culture that inhibits the creation of common symbols. The mutual suspicion of city and countryside has increased as a result of the colonial experience. Fanon tells us that the domestic intellectuals who are the successors of the imperial power in the capital cities of the new countries take over the foreigners' superior attitude to the rural masses.[91] "You never know how they will act," say the administrators, and, "You need a stick to get this country out of the Middle Ages." On their side the peasants are suspicious of the city man who "is dressed like a European, talking the language of the Europeans and working with them, appearing to the peasant as though he has abandoned the whole of what makes up the national patrimony. The people of the city are traitors who have sold out, who seemed to go along with the colonials and were ambitious to succeed in the colonial system." [92] And furthermore, the young men that they send down to the village, young and inexperienced but blessed with the authority of the central government, hope to run the village like a (rural) branch of an (urban) enterprise.[93]

The problem of "contact with the people" plays a part in Shils's analysis of the ambivalences of the Indian intellectual, the "people" being especially the rural masses.[94] Geertz speaks of the sophisticated city economically dependent upon the village, the rustic village culturally dependent upon the city, and the dual tradition which emerges from their confrontation as existing long before industrialization was thought of.[95] On this confrontation all development must necessarily be grafted; we have much too little information concerning the way in which the peasant, despising the city man for his rootlessness while he admires and fears him for his knowledge, modifies his viewpoint under the pressure of early industrialization. Hoselitz does not discuss the opposition of interest which I have stressed, but he does refer to the differences in economic level, political power, social status, culture, and world view.[96] In their need to make up for all these differences, "the cities of underdeveloped countries, above all their primate cities, [become] the centers of nationalist sentiment and political action." [97] Thus is repeated the phenomenon familiar in the West since the French Revolution: cities apply the most powerful symbols they can command to build a nation around themselves.

We are not arguing the inevitable necessity of the domination by the city of a hinterland in its own neighborhood, nor within a national boundary. The hinterland of London was for a long time—and is still— the plains of Canada, Australia, and the Argentine which produce its wheat, its beef, and its wool. In contrast to this classic instance, it is all the more worth noting the obsessive concern with self-sufficiency in food in the presently underdeveloped countries. There is a widespread unwillingness to trust international market processes which would provide a quite different kind of security. The attitudes of the urban elite are stimulated by their colonial experience to a reactive nationalism even fiercer than that of the colonial power which provoked them. In those that had larger surpluses for export, like the Argentine, the capital city seems bound to fill up to the point where it uses the entire surplus: one aspect of the meaning of Peronism and other forms of Argentine nationalism is that it stops that beef and wheat at the mouth of the Rio de la Plata and a smaller and smaller fraction of it goes beyond. Exports of beef were only 24 per cent of total slaughterings in 1958, against 34 per cent in 1937.[98]

Hypotheses for Further Study

The essential datum for study along the lines suggested by this chapter is the balance of payments, or balance of exchange of goods, between cities and countrysides within countries. The hypothesis is that an imbalance in the exchange of goods is made up by the exercise of power on the part of the city, and that the decline in the food surplus physically available in the countryside owing to the growth of its population, along with democratic ideals, attenuates the base which the cities had in colonial and precolonial times.

It would be possible to measure the degree of opposition between city and countryside which arises in the process, as well as the effectiveness with which national symbols are created. Content analysis of written and oral expression in the city and the countryside would show the differences in their orientation to the national state and to the several lines of policy proposed for its advancement. Correlation of these attitudes with the ecological facts of the preceding paragraph would presumably be possible.

One of the hypotheses which could be tested if measures of attitudes were available would be that the conflict between city and countryside is heightened in the degree in which urban population is concentrated in a single large city, moderated in the degree in which urban population is distributed among a number of cities in a position to compete economically with one another. India is a country in the last-named situation; Burma and Ceylon in the first.

In what degree is the decentralization of industry capable of being carried further, right into the countryside itself, and to what extent would this solve the problem presented in this chapter? Certainly there could be no tension of the kind described here if a thin layer of industry were spread over the whole of a country instead of being concentrated intensively in a few cities. Some attention has been given to the cost of industrializing in the dispersed fashion as against the concentrated, urbanized fashion, but no convincing general conclusion has been presented. Without dismissing the possibility altogether, one can say that the history of the presently industrialized countries does not give much encouragement to it. A sentiment in favor of an industrial growth which would be genuinely rural exists among a section of the Indian elite, but their efforts have not so far affected the growth of cities nor the proportion of total industry which these contain. The seed of development has always been sown at some one or a few points in a territory, selected by whatever accident of history, and these have exerted a pull on their territory, and so elicited development at other points. The best known statement of this spatial dimension of development is that of Perroux: "poles of development" are the indispensable initial concentrations of industrial and economic power.[99] Certainly it is in cities that modernizing elites have grown up; we refer again to Durkheim's moral density which stimulates specialization and the exercise of imagination. The great seaports of Asia and Europe have been the points at which innovations were created or imported from abroad.

It would seem that in the circumstances described in which population growth in each village climbs up on its food supply, there is at first a diminution in the purchasing power of the villagers for city goods, though they can still eat sufficiently, and later a shortage of food. One would like to know the effect of these respectively in driving people out of the village. For the whole of Java taken together, one has the impression that the application of new methods and varieties is increasing rice yields at about the same pace as the population is increasing, but this would hardly be uniformly so for the villages taken severally. In some of these at least sudden increases in the yield might occur. The effect of these on the migration of population and the surplus exported ought to be studied.

That the human overflow from the land has the possibility of going to the city is important for another reason unconnected with the thesis of this chapter. In India lower or service castes of the village have now been formally freed by national and provincial legislation in conformity with the universalist ideals that inspire the leadership of the Congress Party. Such legislation is not without effect in the villages, and is often referred to in disputes. But the small landholders who presently constitute the upper castes, their holdings diminished as a result of successive sub-dividing among heirs, itself a function of the growth of population, prefer not to have the services to which ancient custom entitled them; they would rather shave themselves, gather dung, make their own pottery and other articles. In dispensing with traditionally offered services they are more pleased to free the village caste servants as the law requires than the latter are to be freed. Some place in the city must be found to take up (1) at least enough of the landholders' sons to prevent further reduction of the plots, and (2) the members of the village service castes as quickly as they are freed from customary obligations. Otherwise the shortage of industrial jobs leads to social disorganization as the traditional mutual dependence of the castes is lessened.

However, from the viewpoint of development all of these problems are much less important than one which on the surface is more subtle, involving certain concepts developed by accountants. To state it requires that the city be looked at in analogy to a business concern, of which capital position is the most important attribute. Because of the difficulty of distinguishing between capital and current items in ordinary business accounting, it is not easy, even after four centuries of experience, for a single business concern to say where it really stands. Should it allow depreciation in real or money terms? Over what period should depreciation be spread? How should it be allocated to the several years of the period? How should costs be divided among products, especially relevant when some are capital and some consumer goods? Despite some distortion owing to ideological preconception, these issues are becoming as important to Soviet managers as to American.[100]

What is really asked is how the cities of Indonesia, or Burma, or Nepal stand if the activities going on within them are considered as placed on a balance sheet. The answer of the observer who tells us that buildings are being erected is of no more use than that of the observer who reports that the unemployed population is increasing. Such indications, concrete though they may appear, are vague in relation to the essential problem, which is the rate of capital construction, capital being valued not at cost but in terms of the future income it will generate. Invisible to the naked eye, the difference between people accumulating capital and dissipating it is vast in its consequences. The city in the early stages of economic development in effect borrows from the countryside; it demands the peasant's grain without being able to offer anything material in exchange. The loan will be liquidated if and when development takes place. Depending on how quickly it takes place, the peasant (or his children) will receive a higher or lower rate of effective interest on the food which he has loaned. If he is offered no repayment but asked to continue to make loans indefinitely, he will revolt, unless he is kept down by increasing application of force. A high value is set on present against future welfare by the peasant; he is impatient. His trust is a one-time contribution of capital.

The material side of this problem is one of the principal concerns of the careful work of Coale and Hoover [101] who handle it in accord with their view that the agricultural production of India will double during the next 25 years.[102] Given this increase of agricultural production, and also the industrial development and education which are now planned, modern economic attitudes will develop sufficiently that people will respond to differential price changes, and the coefficients of elasticity assumed by Coale and Hoover on the movement of consumption will materialize.

To the play of political forces that operate in the underdeveloped country between the rural and urban sectors, the growth of population in the countryside adds a pitiless ecological pressure. For those of us who see in the development-minded urban elites of the countries of South and Southeast Asia the only hope for the future of those countries, the issues which that elite now faces are serious indeed. The thinking of the underdeveloped world has had imprinted on it some entirely different notions according to which the chief conflict associated with industrialization is between industrial owners and their labor. The best minds of western Europe and America have come to see that owners, laborers, and peasants have a single common interest—the raising of national income per capita at a steady 5 per cent per year. It will be unfortunate if Europe's outdated antagonisms are transferred to Asia and permitted to impose themselves there so as to cover up the real issue. Put in one sentence, it is whether the urban sector can arrange a sufficiently rapid growth of production to permit repayment of the debt to the peasantry inevitably incurred in the early stages of development. The initial transfer of the food and the corresponding debt are capital transactions in the useful sense in which capital is defined by George C. Homans—"anything that allows (a society) to postpone action leading to some immediate reward in order to undertake others whose rewards, though potentially greater, are both uncertain and deferred." [103] And here as in many other junctures of human affairs, "the question remains whether the new arrangement will pay off before the capital runs out." [104]

NOTES

1. See John J. Johnson (Ed.), *The Role of the Military in Underdeveloped Countries* (Princeton: Princeton University Press, 1962).

2. Émile Durkheim, *De la division du travail social*, 7th ed. (Paris: Presses Universitaires de France, 1960), p. 239.

3. Teilhard de Chardin, *La place de l'homme dans la nature* (Paris: Union Générale d'Edition, 1956), p. 135.

4. Durkheim, *op. cit.*, p. 249.

5. Georg Simmel, "The Metropolis and Mental Life," in Paul K. Hatt and Albert J. Reiss (Eds.), *Cities and Society, The Revised Reader in Urban Sociology* (Glencoe, Ill.: Free Press, 1957), p. 635.

6. de Chardin, *op. cit.*, p. 137.

7. See Philip M. Hauser's Introduction to this book, where the explanation is given in terms of moral density, pp. 19–23.

8. N. S. B. Gras, *An Introduction to Economic History* (New York: Harper, 1922).

9. R. D. McKenzie, *The Metropolitan Community* (New York: McGraw-Hill, 1933).

10. Donald J. Bogue, *The Structure of the Metropolitan Community* (Ann Arbor: University of Michigan, 1950), p. 61.

11. "Distribution of the World's City Folks, A Study in Comparative Civilization," *Geographical Review*, 21 (July 1931), p. 453.

12. O. D. Duncan, W. R. Scott, Stanley Lieberson, Beverly Duncan, and H. H. Winsborough, *Metropolis and Region* (Baltimore: Johns Hopkins Press, 1960).

13. Robert E. Park, *Human Communities* (Glencoe, Ill.: Free Press, 1952), p. 163.

14. *Ibid.*, p. 150.

15. *Ibid.*, p. 162.

16. *Ibid.*, p. 170.

17. A situation perceptively described by Gideon Sjoberg, "The Preindustrial City," *American Journal of Sociology*, 60 (March 1955), and *The Preindustrial City: Past and Present* (Glencoe, Ill.: Free Press, 1960).

18. Kingsley Davis, "The Origin and Growth of Urbanization in the World," *American Journal of Sociology*, 60 (March 1955), p. 430.

19. National Resources Committee, *Our Cities: Their Role in the National Economy* (Washington, D. C.: U. S. Government Printing Office, 1937), p. 29. The same thought is expressed in Ralph L. Turner, *The Great Cultural Traditions*, Vol. I, *The Ancient Cities* (New York: McGraw-Hill, 1941), pp. 294ff.

20. V. Gordon Childe, *What Happened in History* (Harmondsworth, Eng.: Penguin Books, 1942).

21. Lewis Mumford, in *City Invincible*, an Oriental Institute Symposium (Chicago: University of Chicago Press, 1960), p. 9.

22. Melville J. Herskovits, "Population Size, Economic Surplus, and Social Leisure," Chap. 18 of *Economic Anthropology* (New York: Knopf, 1952), p. 395.

23. *Ibid.*, p. 412–413.

24. *Ibid.*, p. 405.

25. Marvin Harris, "The Economy Has No Surplus?" *American Anthropologist*, 61 (April 1959), p. 185.

26. Karl Polanyi in C. M. Arensberg and H. W. Pearson (Eds.), *Trade and Markets in the Early Empires* (Glencoe, Ill.: Free Press, 1957).

27. Harry W. Pearson, "The Economy Has No Surplus?," *ibid.*, p. 320.

28. Philip M. Hauser, *Population Perspectives* (New Brunswick, N. J.: Rutgers, 1960), p. 99.

29. Karl Polanyi, *The Great Transformation* (Boston: Beacon Press, 1945). See also Claude Lévi-Strauss, *Les structures élémentaires de la parenté* (Paris: Presses Universitaires de France, 1949), pp. 66 *et seq.*

30. Arensberg and Pearson, *Trade and Markets, op. cit.*, p. 336.

31. *Ibid.*, pp. 338–339.

32. Kingsley Davis, *op. cit.*, p. 432.

33. *India 1961* (Delhi: Ministry of Information and Broadcasting), p. 24.

34. "Idées sociologiques d'un philosophe arabe," in René Maunier, *Mélanges de sociologie nord-africaine* (Paris: Alcan, 1930), p. 18.

35. J. S. Furnivall, *Colonial Theory and Practice* (Cambridge, Eng.: Cambridge University Press, 1948), p. 34.

36. *Ibid.*

37. *Ibid.*, p. 85.

38. O. H. Spate and L. W. Trueblood, "Rangoon: A Study in Urban Geography," *Geographical Review*, 32 (1942), p. 57.

39. See Chapter 12 in this book.

40. Max Weber, *The City*, trans. by D. Martindale and G. Neuwirth (Glencoe, Ill.: Free Press, 1958), p. 68.

41. *Ibid.*, p. 69.

42. *Ibid.*, p. 62.

43. Alexander Erlich, *The Soviet Industrialization Debate, 1924–1928* (Cambridge: Harvard University Press, 1960).

44. International Bank for Reconstruction and Development, *The Economic Development of Ceylon* (Baltimore: Johns Hopkins Press, 1953), pp. 608–624. The recommendation of the experts that Galle be developed has never been taken up.

45. International Bank for Reconstruction and Development, *The Economic Development of Malaya* (Baltimore: Johns Hopkins Press, 1955), p. 73, says that "under the pressure for large and rapid increases in rice production the attention to cost-benefit relationships of individual rice projects has been quite inadequate," and that "we must reiterate our conclusion that rice self-sufficiency is not a practicable goal for the Federation, not only for physical and technical reasons but for economic and financial reasons as well." The desire for self-sufficiency constitutes an expression of the national elite's search for security.

46. The distinction in this and the following paragraphs between goods and services, as well as that which is even more important between income and accretions to capital, are due to my fellow members of the Committee on Urbanization, and especially to Wallace Sayre.

47. Joseph A. Schumpeter, *History of Economic Analysis* (Oxford, Eng.: Oxford University Press, 1954), p. 218.

48. *Ibid.*, p. 231.

49. *Ibid.*, p. 238.

50. Charles A. Beard, *An Economic Interpretation of the Constitution of the United States* (New York: Macmillan, 1913).

51. *Ibid.*, p. 149. See also pp. 53, 73, 265, 305–306, 310, 324.

52. Allan Nevins, *A History of American Life, 1863–1878* (New York: Macmillan, 1927).

53. *Ibid.*, p. 165.

54. *Ibid.*, p. 167.

55. *Ibid.*, p. 169.

56. "The Expansion of Agriculture," in Harold F. Williamson (Ed.), *The Growth of the American Economy*, 2nd ed. (Englewood Cliffs, N. J.: Prentice-Hall, 1951), p. 390.

57. *Ibid.*, pp. 396–397.

58. Oscar D. Skelton, *The Day of Sir Wilfrid Laurier*, Vol. 30 of *The Chronicles of Canada* (Toronto: Glasgow, Brook, 1916), pp. 236–237.

59. O. J. McDiarmid, *Commercial Policy in the Canadian Economy* (Cambridge: Harvard University Press, 1946), p. 243.

60. Oscar Lewis, *Village Life in Northern India* (Urbana: University of Illinois Press, 1958), p. 88.

61. *Ibid.*, p. 91.

62. William W. Lockwood, *The Economic Development of Japan* (Princeton, N. J.: Princeton University Press, 1954), p. 521.

63. Irene B. Taeuber, "Population and Labor Force in the Industrialization of Japan," in Simon Kuznets, Wilbert E. Moore, and Joseph J. Spengler (Eds.), *Economic Growth: Brazil, India, Japan* (Durham, N. C.: Duke University Press, 1955), p. 325.

64. Irene B. Taeuber, *The Population of Japan* (Princeton, N. J.: Princeton University Press, 1958).

65. David Mitrany, *Marx Against the Peasant: A Study in Social Dogmatism* (New York: Collier, 1961); also Alex Inkeles and Kent Geiger (Eds.), *Soviet Society, A Book of Readings* (Boston: Houghton Mifflin, 1961), especially Arcadius Kahan, "The Peasant and Soviet Agricultural Policy," pp. 349–360.

66. *Economic Survey of Asia and the Far East 1960* (Bangkok: ECAFE), p. 87.

67. J. Allan, T. W. Haig, and H. H. Dodwell, *Cambridge Shorter History of India*, Vol. 3 (Delhi: S. Chand, 1958), p. 500.

68. *India 1961*, p. 260.

69. R. P. Dore, *City Life in Japan* (London: Routledge and Kegan Paul, 1958), p. 403.

70. P. Chombart de Lauwe, *La vie quotidienne des familles ouvrières* (Paris: Centre National de la Recherche Scientifique, 1956), p. 156.

71. *Canada Year Book, 1961* (Ottawa: Queen's Printer, 1962), p. 985.

72. Mark Jefferson, *op. cit.*, p. 453.

73. John W. Alexander, "The Basic-Nonbasic Concept of Urban Economic Functions," *Economic Geography*, 30 (July 1954), pp. 246–261, reprinted in H. M. Mayer and C. F. Kohn (Eds.), *Readings in Urban Geography* (Chicago: University of Chicago Press, 1959), p. 87.

74. John M. Mattila and Wilbur R. Thompson, "The Measurement of the Metropolitan Area," *Land Economics*, 31 (August 1955), pp. 215–228, reprinted in Jack P. Gibbs, *Urban Research Methods* (Princeton, N. J.: Van Nostrand, 1961), p. 329.

75. Jean Gottmann, Chap. 6, "Megalopolitan Agriculture," *Megalopolis, The Urbanized Northeastern Seaboard of the United States* (New York: Twentieth Century Fund, 1961), p. 261.

76. *India 1961*, pp. 545–547.

77. *Ibid.*, pp. 246 and 248.

78. *Ibid.*, p. 24.

79. *Ibid.*, p. 25.

80. *Ibid.*, p. 547.

81. *Statistical Pocketbook of Indonesia.* (Djakarta: Biro Pusat Statistik, 1959).

82. Rhoads Murphey, "New Capitals in Asia," *Economic Development and Cultural Change*, 5 (April 1957), pp. 226–227.

83. Bert F. Hoselitz, "Urbanization: International Comparisons," in Roy

Turner (Ed.), *India's Urban Future* (Berkeley: University of California Press, 1961), p. 164.

84. Colin Clark, *The Conditions of Economic Progress,* 2nd ed. (London: Macmillan, 1951).

85. Jean Fourastié, *Le grand espoir du xxe siècle* (Paris: Gallimard, 1963), p. 103.

86. Eric Lampard, "The Growth of Cities in Economically Developed Countries," *Economic Development and Cultural Change,* 3 (January 1955), p. 100.

87. Norton S. Ginsburg, *Urbanization in Asia,* Macalester College (March 1959), p. 14 (mimeographed).

88. Government of India Planning Commission, *Third Five Year Plan* (Delhi: Government of India Printing Office, 1961), pp. 155–156.

89. G. C. Allen, *A Short Economic History of Modern Japan* (London: Allen and Unwin, 1946), pp. 19–20.

90. Hugh Tinker, *The Union of Burma,* 2nd ed. (Royal Institute of International Affairs and Oxford University Press, 1959).

91. Franz Fanon, *Les damnés de la terre* (Paris: François Maspero, 1961), p. 90.

92. *Ibid.,* p. 86.

93. *Ibid.,* p. 87.

94. Edward A. Shils, *The Intellectual between Tradition and Modernity: The Indian Situation* (The Hague: Mouton, 1961), p. 71 and *passim.*

95. Clifford Geertz, *The Religion of Java* (Glencoe, Ill.: Free Press, 1960), p. 227.

96. Bert F. Hoselitz, *Sociological Aspects of Economic Growth* (Glencoe, Ill.: Free Press, 1960), p. 225.

97. *Ibid.,* p. 229.

98. *Statesman's Year Book, 1961* (New York: Macmillan), p. 818.

99. François Perroux, *La coexistence pacifique,* Vol. 2 (Paris: Presses Universitaires de France, 1958).

100. Gregory Grossman (Ed.), *Value and Plan* (Berkeley: University of California Press, 1960), especially "Soviet Accounting and Economic Decisions" by R. W. Campbell and comment by Herbert S. Levine.

101. Ansley J. Coale and Edgar M. Hoover, *Population Growth and Economic Development in Low-Income Countries* (Princeton, N. J.: Princeton University Press, 1958), Chaps. 7–10.

102. *Ibid.,* pp. 110, 121, 124, 128, though they also say that "India will need, within the next three decades, to develop non-agricultural exports on a considerable scale in order to pay for importation of a fairly substantial part of the requirements for agricultural products" (p. 139).

103. George C. Homans, *Social Behavior: Its Elementary Forms* (New York: Harcourt, Brace and World, 1961), p. 386.

104. *Ibid.*

Urban Geography and "Non-Western" Areas [1]

Norton S. Ginsburg

As the discussion of Latin American urbanization in another section of this book indicates, there is a considerable urban geographical literature on cities outside North America and Western Europe. For the most part, such geographical studies traditionally have dealt either with the distribution of cities in countries or regions, frequently as an aspect of settlement distributions in general, or with the internal characteristics of the cities, in which morphology, sequent occupance, and urban genesis have loomed large. Since the middle 1930's, increasing attention has been given to studies of the relationships between cities and their hinterlands, to various associated aspects of nodality or centrality, and to comparative studies of morphology and function. In addition, fundamental questions are being raised concerning the nature of the urbanization process.

Specifically, as a result of a considerable literature on "non-Western" cities, there is reason to ask whether the urbanization process is unidimensional or multidimensional and whether it is culturally and areally, as well as temporally, differentiated. There is agreement, of course, that all cities bear certain resemblances to each other in both landscape and function, and that "systems" of cities have developed in all countries, evolving out of the socioeconomic conditions that characterize them. The controversial issue, one that intrigues geographer, sociologist, and historian alike, turns to a considerable degree on the relationships between value systems and social organization, on the one hand, and the development of city systems and various types of urban morphological patterns, on the other. It also involves levels of living and rates of economic development as they influence the nature

311

of cities in various societies and countries. In other words, if types of urban hierarchy or urban morphology are taken as "dependent variables," to what extent is "culture" as an "independent variable" significant in "explaining" the differentiation among them? Some light may be cast on some of these matters by a discussion of the urban geographical literature pertaining to certain major regions or countries, Africa briefly, and then southern and eastern Asia.

The Sub-Saharan African Case

The earlier urban geographical literature on Sub-Saharan Africa is exemplified by studies of individual cities such as Whittlesey's studies of Kano [2] or Jarrett's on Freetown,[3] in which the development of the town is examined historically, and attempts are made to deal with changing patterns of occupance as reflected in the changing urban landscape, or to use Smaile's phrase, "townscape." Such studies as these still make a major contribution to knowledge concerning urbanism in Africa, since they provide many basic data for purposes of general comparative morphological and functional study. Other studies, such as R. W. Steel's on Ashanti, have attempted to deal with the distribution of cities in various countries and relate it to their functions and size.[4]

Since the Second World War, greater concern with African city-hinterland relations and functional organization has been evidenced. The primary subjects for research have been the functions that a city performs for its hinterland and the effects different "sets" of functions have had on the creation of hinterlands and on modifying those hinterlands that developed when prior sets of functions predominated. The emphasis, in short, has been on the *process of urbanization,* broadly interpreted, and on the effects of modernization and political change upon urban functions, morphology, hinterlands, and city systems.

As an example of this perspective, Edwin Munger states: "Outgoing relationships . . . give an understanding of [city] functions and provide criteria by which the town can be distinguished functionally from others and by which changes in the functions of the town over various periods of time can be recognized." [5] He also asks: "To what extent do . . . varied geographic relationships [focusing on East African cities] coincide with existing political boundaries?" [6]

Similarly, growing preoccupation with culture contact, diffusion, and modernization is reflected in Larimore's assertion that:

> Urbanism has been introduced into East Africa by British colonialism. . . . The impact of British colonial and political activity

upon the subsistence polities of Busoga has reformed Busoga's patterns of spatial organization. The immigration of alien cultural groups to perform functions now necessary to Busoga's changing spatial organization has introduced cultural features of clustered settlement and Western urbanism to Busoga.[7]

Both Larimore and Munger deal with the hierarchical nature of spatial relationships in East Africa and with the role of the city as a center of change and as an organizer of area. Larimore especially observes the significance of racial segregation on urban morphology and the distribution of urban activities and functions.[8] Both also note the relationships between multi-ethnicism and urban structure. As is true in most studies of this sort, as well as others noted later, field work was essential to research, since adequate published data are not available, and the mapping of field data provided the bases for raising significant hypotheses.

Other studies have dealt especially with the demarcation of hinterlands, as well as with the functional transformations that underlie the growth of cities in Africa. Some have taken the rather traditional form of descriptive port and port-hinterland studies, such as those by Hance and his collaborators, which do not overtly test general propositions about port-hinterland relationships.[9] Others, perhaps more sophisticated but also based on field work, are exemplified by the work of Manshard on hinterland and "urban-field" delimitation in western Africa, using techniques developed by Green and Smailes in England and Godlund in Sweden.[10] Manshard provides an excellent bibliography in his study of West African towns, in which he discusses the hierarchy of settlement and functional differentiation of cities. Like Steel, he is concerned with the relevance of changing cultural and political conditions upon centers of exchange in West Africa, and he experiments with techniques of central-place study used elsewhere.

In addition, there are a few studies that discuss the areal aspects of urbanization over large parts of Africa, among which Harrison-Church's paper on West Africa provides a good example.[11]

Similarly, Hamdan presents a thoughtful appraisal of the characteristics of political capitals in Africa, in which he notes the exceptional role that so-called "colonial capitals" now play on the African scene, and the marked peripherality, relatively small size, and primacy that characterize all but a very few of the capitals of the African states. Implicit in his argument is the proposition that, with the exception of North Africa, and even to some extent there, the new African states, to a far greater extent than in Asia, are the consequences of colonialism and the products of new types of spatial economic, as well as political, systems, which have transformed the map of Africa in the past two centuries.[12]

A. K. Mabogunje expresses this theme explicitly in an as yet unpublished paper on Nigeria, a region in which a system of trading centers, albeit influenced by foreign, that is, Arab culture, preceded and laid the foundation for the existing distributional and functional pattern of cities. Mabogunje argues that "economic conditions call into being a system of cities. As such conditions undergo dramatic changes, the role of the cities is affected not uniformly but differentially," both in time and in space. He further concludes that cultural differences, even within countries, will lead to different urban functional patterns, and compares eastern with northern Nigeria as evidence, ingeniously using a sophisticated factor analysis of demographic data from the 1952 Census of Nigeria as his method. His statement of problem raises issues similar to, though more highly economically oriented than, those proposed at the beginning of this chapter, and perhaps even more relevant to the Asian case than to the overall African:

> What happens when on a system of cities developed under one set of market and transportation conditions a new, faster, more effective, more capacious transportation system is imposed; what happens when this is done in a rather selective manner as to the area served; what happens when the new spatial economic integration which is achieved by this new transportation system focusses the flow of commodities within the system to a few selected points, with a view to facilitating the export of these commodities . . . ; what is the nature of the adjustments that can be postulated as taking place within the system in consequence of this new development; and what effects would these adjustments have on the efficiency of the system and the growth of the country? [18]

As interpreted in these materials, urbanization in most of Sub-Saharan Africa seems to be, for the most part, a modern phenomenon. Most African cities have grown out of Western contact and arisen either *de novo* or from village or small-town origins, although it appears that in West Africa indigenous cities, or at least high-density population agglomerations, of considerable size existed prior to the period of European domination. Possibly for these reasons, none of the studies cited makes a special distinction between "preindustrial" and "industrial" cities, although several emphasize the distinction between "precolonial" and "colonial." This is in part because Sub-Saharan cities appear to be such recent phenomena, even "alien"; in part because industrialization was not, with few exceptions, a concomitant of African colonialism; in part, because ingredients associated with traditional patterns of settlement appear to have been incorporated directly into the growing new towns and form part of the integral contemporary townscape. With few exceptions, the "preindustrial-industrial" dichotomy appears, historically at least, to cast little light on the changing character of urban settlement in Sub-Saharan Africa. What appears to offer greater promise by far for further study is the impact of colonially derived administrative and transportation networks on the landscape and the consequence of areally differentiated economic development policies on urban structure, pattern, and hierarchy.

The Asiatic Triangle—Pakistan to Japan

Of perhaps even greater significance for the problem of "non-Western" urbanization is the great region of relatively dense settlement along the southern and eastern margins of Asia, not only because of the scale of the phenomenon there, but also because in these areas city-building and maintenance have stronger indigenous and historical roots. In fact, in countries like China, Japan, and India, most of the larger cities have their origins in sizable towns which have long had multifunctional characteristics. Since this is the case in most of the Asiatic Triangle, other than Southeast Asia proper, locational inertia and deeply rooted concepts of what urban living means have substantially affected the contemporary urban landscapes, and, with them, the areal arrangements of functions and occupance patterns in general.[14]

Certainly, Asian cities, other than those founded and/or developed by Europeans, and even those in many cases, display characteristics or morphology and functional organization that differ from those of the modern Western city. Some resemblance to the "preindustrial city" of the West lends credence to the proposition, as developed by Sjoberg, that many societies, given a certain degree of "urbanness," develop within them cities of a broadly "preindustrial type." On the other hand, the issue as to what sorts of cities are evolving from the older forms remains open. In fact, in Japan the larger and more modern cities display patterns that suggest both high inertial values and distinctive "non-Western" societal settings, which in turn may produce distinctive types of urban and metropolitan organization.

India

The morphology of the Indian city has been well described by Brush,[15] and his description is substantiated by at least two-score articles in the major Indian geographical periodicals dealing with townscapes.[16] Most Indian cities are the product of both indigenous and foreign traditions, but the melding of these traditions, with the partial exception of the great, European-developed port cities, has tended toward the creation of not one, but two cities, side by side, each with its own morphological and functional patterns, and rather poorly interrelated. Delhi-New Delhi is such an example. In such cases, dispersion of functions or of people from the older centers is proceeding slowly if at all, although dispersion from the "new towns" may be proceeding rapidly.

On the other hand, several of the larger cities of India are essentially foreign in origin. Nevertheless, even Bombay and Calcutta, for example, which are predominantly foreign creations, display only in highly modified form the hypothesized functional patterns of the Western city (for example, circular zones or sectors focusing on one central location, or a highly developed areal differentiation of functions). In fact, most are multinucleated, show only a modest development of a Central Business District, display little suburban development (and when they do, most socioeconomic characteristics of the suburbs differ from those in most Western cities), and in general either do not display the Western stellate pattern or display it in singularly embryonic form. In addition, most large Indian cities show the impress of British rule in the form of special districts for foreign residents, cantonments, housing estates for certain types of government employees, and the like. Furthermore, caste and ethnolinguistic differences serve to fragment even the relatively cosmopolitan and "postindustrial" cities into cells among which spatial interaction tends to be low. To some extent, these may be identified as "postindustrial" cities developing in predominantly "preindustrial" societies, and the slow rate of transformation from "pre-" to "postindustrial" forms might be associated with lags in economic development. Nevertheless, the significance of cultural values and social organization in determining this slow rate of change remains unclear.

The general literature on Indian cities is admirably reviewed by B. F. Hoselitz, who appends a substantial bibliography to his review article.[17] Hoselitz notes the various types of social surveys of individual cities which have been done under the auspices of the Programmes Committee of the Planning Commission, but he prefers the type of treatment given Banaras by Singh in his important prototypical work on that city.[18] In that study, Singh is concerned not only with the townscape, but also with the functional relations among the several land use subregions within the city and those between the city and its "umland" or immediate hinterland. A more recent and somewhat similar study, dependent again on field work, is that of V. A. Janaki and Z. A. Sayed on Padra, a pioneering attempt to deal with the internal and external patterns of a small Indian town, and to document the relevance of caste and religion to the morphology of such a town.[19]

Among the numerous studies of "urban fields" or "umlands," one of the more interesting is Reddy's on Hyderabad, which describes the evolution of vegetable marketing patterns; defines two vegetable hinterlands, one based on carts, the second on trucks; and observes the dominance of personal preference over distance and apparent convenience in the marketing structure.[20] An equally thoughtful study of Dacca also has identified key indices to the measurement of its "umland" and utilizes them to define it. The delimitation is tested by a formula based on nonagricultural employment in Dacca and other cities nearby.[21]

In addition, various attempts have been made to classify Indian cities according to their functions as measured by occupations and employment, of which Lal's method, an adaptation of the P. E. P.'s "location quotient" technique, is perhaps most useful.[22] Pakistan's cities also have been classified in similar ways by Kureshy and N. Ahmad.[23] On the other hand, V. L. S. Prakasa Rao, in his stimulating presidential address to the Council of Geographers (India), suggests a more sophisticated method of classification, which involves regression analysis and takes into account city-size differences.[24] Prakasa Rao also discusses methods for studying regional differences in the nature of the urban hierarchy and urban concentration and growth, including use of the centroid method and graphic correlations, which help identify relations between population concentrations, size of city, and occupation. These techniques have been employed by him and others in studies of Mysore State and South India which are just becoming available.[25]

N. R. Kar also has pioneered in applying contemporary methods of areal analysis to Calcutta and West Bengal and combining them with more traditional historical and taxonomic techniques. With regard to Calcutta, Kar concludes:

> Though the general trend of urban growth in Calcutta is in line with that of Western cities, its spatial character does not conform to the standard pattern or "norm" of urban and metropolitan growth . . . in the West. The smallness of the built-up areas, the absence of spread of . . . modern traffic nets over the Umland, the absence of a centrifugal drift of population into the fringe areas, and the low standard of suburbanization in the

peripheral zones are some of the features of Calcutta and other Indian cities, which often pose problems of a gigantic nature. . . .[26]

In the course of his study Kar also observes: "that the spatial distribution of population in Calcutta shows a concentric pattern. . . . This pattern is of methodological interest because it conforms to the usual . . . pattern found in most Western . . . cities"; [27] on the other hand, with regard to the central business district, he states: "The very small area of this zone, in comparison with any Western city of its magnitude, the gigantic volume of administrative, commercial, and other activities and services carried on daily in this area, and the comparatively little urban renewal, building activity, and vertical extension, are features of strong contrast with those of Western Metropolises." [28] He further emphasizes, *inter alia*, the "mono-functional" character of Calcutta's zones of occupance and the absence of large "neighborhoods . . . having a multi-functional character and acting as 'quasi-cities,' as in big American and European cities, [which] are totally absent in Calcutta"; [29] and, in recognizing the existence of an urban hierarchy in the Calcutta metropolitan region, he notes the "underdevelopment" of centralized services in the smaller towns in that hierarchy.[30] In another context, Mayfield has observed in the Punjab that Christaller's "space-preference" of the consumer is a culturally relative phenomenon which inevitably affects the size, location, and "service-mixes" of central places.[31]

Kar also has employed concepts developed by von Thünen, Lösch, Christaller, Platt, Carol, and Smailes to compare the urban hierarchy in West Bengal with that in parts of Germany and Britain, and to provide an introductory study of the process by which the urban pattern he calls "preindustrial," characterized by small regional service centers of approximately equal size, is transformed into an elaborate hierarchical structure with Calcutta primate, resulting from industrialization, locational specialization, and technological innovation. In this connection, he observes that although cities have been a part of Indian life for centuries, "there has hardly been a continuity of large-scale urban way of life in India since ancient [times], and 'urbanism,' as we see it in modern India, is of recent date, only about a century old." [32] This assertion is at variance with the commonly held argument that large-scale urbanization is part of India's continuous cultural tradition. It implies also (1) that the cities of Mogul India were in some ways alien to Indian society, and (2) that modern Indian urbanization is a process triggered by the Western impact on India.

The voluminous Indian urban geographical literature, stimulated by the contemporary enthusiasm for urban planning, is in part concerned with the morphology of landscape, but more important, with the application to the Indian city by a few competent practitioners of concepts developed in a Western context. In effect, this will mean stronger comparative studies and the modification of theories to fit different regional circumstances. Studies such as Kar's suggest major differences in both morphology and functional organization between Indian cities and models of spatial arrangements hypothesized for Western cities. The nature, causes, and longevity of these differences provide an admirable field for both theoretical and applied research. One can speculate that technology, levels of living, capital available for urban improvements, caste and ethnolinguistic and religious diversity, and other cultural concomitants are involved, but to what extent and for how long?

Clearly, here is support for raising once again perhaps the most important question in cross-cultural urban research: To what extent are basic differences in culture, even given the spread of "modern Western" technology and values, likely to give rise to different urbanization processes and the creation of cities as artifacts that differ from culture to culture? Or, to phrase the problem another way: What kinds of cities can be expected to evolve in different societies as these societies make their decisions to select, adopt, and modify those elements that characterize Western city-building, functions, and structure?

Japan

The same questions can be applied to urban development in Japan, but there are a number of significant differences that bear upon a comparison of the two. First, Japan is a highly developed country economically as compared with India, and its rate of economic growth also has been high, despite lapses, for the past eighty years or so. Second, the growth of Japan's cities has been largely an indigenous phenomenon, one not substantially stimulated by foreign enterprise, political or economic. (Sticklers may cite Kobe here and perhaps Yokohama as exceptions, but these do not substantially alter the generalization.) Third, Japan, even more than India, has long been a highly urbanized country, not so much in terms of the proportion of population living in sizable towns, but in terms of the role of the city in regional and national life and the awareness among rural dwellers of the existence and nature of an urban way of life. The "insular-cellular" ideal-type of social-areal organization so often applied to the

Sinitic world, including Japan, probably has less applicability there than in the Indic world.

Recognizing the importance of urban studies in Japanese geography, the Association of Japanese Geographers (*Nihon Chirigakkai*) established a Committee on Urban Studies in 1958. In 1959, this Committee, under the chairmanship of Professor Seiji Yamaga, published a report entitled *Research Materials on Urbanization* (*Toshika Kenkyū Shiryō*), much of which is devoted to a selected bibliography of materials on Japanese cities.[33] About 250 citations are given, all but a handful in Japanese, and only a dozen or so by non-Japanese. The organization of this bibliography is helpful in understanding the ways in which urban geographical studies are viewed by Japanese scholars themselves. The report is divided into five major sections, with a number of subsections:

Part   I. Theoretical Research on Urbanization
    a. General Theory
    b. History of Research and Research Methodology
Part   II. Empirical Research on Urbanization in General
Part III. Urban Research Focussing upon Special Topics
    a. Land Use and Agriculture
    b. Population
    c. Residences
    d. Transportation
    e. Commerce and Industry
    f. Cultural Facilities
    g. Land Values
    h. Other Indices (to Urbanization)
Part IV. Special Research Themes Related to Urbanization
    a. The Great City and the Overgrown City
    b. Satellite Cities and Belt Cities
    c. Urban Fields
    d. Urban Planning
Part   V. Other Literature

In this literature, every type of problem described by Professor Mayer in his chapter in this book is dealt with. Studies of land-use patterns, of urban structure and functions, of the spread of urbanized areas, of intrametropolitan structure, of economic base, and of the functional classification of cities are included. Special attention has been given to the ways in which the metropolis extends its influence into rural areas. From the Japanese point of view, urbanization is intimately associated with the absorption of long-established towns and villages, and studies directed toward understanding the changes in form and function that have taken place under such conditions are numerous.[84]

The A. J. G. report reflects the interest in general methodology of Japanese geographers, who have long been familiar with major organizational concepts in settlement geography, such as those of von Thünen and Christaller, but their problem has been to fit them into the Japanese scene for which the basic assumption of "an undifferentiated unoccupied plain" seems incongruous. A recent exemplary article by Professor Kiuchi discusses the necessity for cross-cultural studies, the differences between deductive and inductive approaches to urban studies, and, as an illustration, some structural differences between Japanese and European and American cities.[85] He suggests that many of the same forces are at work in all of these cases (for example, short-run centrifugal forces leading to the dispersion of urban functions and so-called "urban sprawl"), but he also observes that the historical and contemporary cultural and economic circumstances in different societies, such as the higher premium placed in Japan on certain types of relict structures or land uses, may be making for the long-term differentiation of urban structures among nations.

Although the Japanese methodological literature indicates understanding of its Western equivalent, there appears to be semantic difficulty among Japanese geographers in comprehending the meanings of terms such as "urbanization" and "urbanism" as they appear in the geographical and sociological literature in the United States.[86] They reject the definition of "urbanization," for example, as meaning simply a certain level of population density, and point out that in some areas urban densities and agglomerations of rural populations are as high as they are in cities.

In another provocative article, T. Ishimizu reviews recent methodological developments and observes that studies of urbanization as a process tend to fall into two major categories, the one concerned with landscape evolution and the other with functional dynamics. He espouses the second group as being potentially the more useful and productive and believes that functional analysis can be best pursued by the examination of "ecological processes."[87] Ishimizu also lists a number of problems which have been receiving particular attention from his colleagues. Under the heading "Types and Stages of Urbanization" he notes Takano's distinction between "premodern" and "modern" urbanization, Shimizu's "primary" to "quaternary" stages of industrialization, and the latter's emphasis on the necessity for dealing with consumption and not merely production indices to urbanization. He marks the distinctions made by Kiuchi and Shimizu between centrifugal and centripetal forces in the urbanization process, and he notes the distinction between "contiguous" and "discontinuous" (or "leap-frogging") urbanization, the latter of which has been associated by Yamaguchi, Hama, and Suzuki with contemporary urbanization, but which Kobayashi has identified in the Taishō period as well. Ishimizu also cites the contrasts between scale levels of urbanization as reflected in the urban hierarchy and contrasts a "metropolitan" scale with what might be termed "regional." In this, he concurs with Shimizu who, in the report just cited, graphs the various stages in each of two main urbanization streams—the "regional" and the "metropolitan." He emphasizes the unity of forces that change the character of the central areas of major cities and the suburbanization that goes on at their outskirts, and in so doing notes the relationships between changing land values and changing patterns of land uses and functional distributions. He then refers to the extensive literature on the changes in Japanese agriculture taking place along the urban-rural fringes of the larger cities, and concludes with Takano's and Shimizu's theses that modern urbanization in Japan is a function of a capitalistic and industrializing economic system, the elements of which interact with preindustrial elements to form urban artifacts enmeshed in systems with varying intensities of spatial interaction.

In contrast to the methodological literature, the empirical literature heavily emphasizes historical studies of urban development. The historical tradition is particularly strong in Japanese urban studies because Japan, among the Asian countries, has had so long a tradition of urbanism as a way of life, at least since the fifteenth century.[38] A wealth of historical data is available, and many Japanese geographers have had sound training in history as well, all this apart from the strong sense of cultural continuity that characterizes Japanese society and the academic subculture in particular.

There are numerous studies on the so-called "castle-town," or *jōkamachi,* which today forms the basic stratum of medium-sized cities in Japan and which accounts for thirty-four of Japan's forty-six prefectural capitals. These essentially regional capitals are almost always "diversified" cities in the various classifications of Japanese cities such as that of Y. Ogasawara, which apply to Japanese cities, with their excellent official data, taxonomic methods previously utilized in the West.[39] They form an indigenous underlayer to the overlayer of great cities and their industrial satellites, such as Tokyo and Osaka which, themselves castle towns, are more familiar to Western observers. The effects on Japanese urban morphology and structure as a result of these types of origins, as well as others such as temple and shrine towns and postroad stages, also occupy a fair proportion of the literature. One of the better known of such studies is in English,[40] but others, such as that of Matsumoto, are even more revealing of the role of inertia, as well as social change, in the structure of the modern Japanese city and in the creation within many of them of twin nodes, one of them associated with the old castle and its major gate, the other with the commercial quarter which developed after Meiji times.[41] In some cases, this morphological dualism developed even prior to the Restoration, however, as in Shizuoka and Yamaguchi cities.

This historical and evolutionary approach to Japanese city systems and internal morphology is by no means dominant, however, and other types of empirical studies with methodological implications illustrate the ways in which the historical theme is combined with the analysis of contemporary morphology and structural function.[42] More important, the great expansion of the urban population in Japan and the development of great cities to the point where these account for 64 per cent and 25 per cent (as included in the so-called "Densely Inhabited Districts" around the great cities) of the national population respectively, have occasioned an increasing number of studies concerned with the metropolitan region and its structure.[43] Many focus on the nature of the urban region and explicitly apply various familiar ideas of hierarchy, central-place functions, and spatial interaction to the Japanese scene.[44]

One of the more interesting and controversial of these appeared late in 1960 and attempted an analysis of the regional structure of Greater Tokyo (within forty kilometers of Tokyo Station), based upon a multiple-factor analysis of sixteen variables considered relevant to the metropolitanization process.[45] As a result of this analysis, three underlying trend complexes were identified: one associated with forces (Factor 1) termed general "urbanization," which exhibited a high concentration at the cores of the conurbation and along major lines of railroad transportation, and decreasing intensities with distance from them; a second factor called "residentialization"; and a third factor, "industrialization." Factors 2 and 3, significantly, showed no such spatial tendency, but, when mapped, were "clumped" in certain areas widely scattered over the metropolitan region. As a result, the metropolitan region was subdivided into nine composite subregions, each displaying different associations of these complexes and "mixes" of the sixteen variables selected.

Studies of urban fields and city-hinterland relationships, in general, using techniques similar to those employed elsewhere, also have been common. Several, including one in English, have emphasized the importance of topographic restraints upon theoretically derived patterns.[46] Others have dealt with problems of measuring accessibility as a necessary precondition to the determination of urban fields and influences, and still others have examined the changes in the trade areas of towns that have been undergoing absorption into the growing metropolitan areas.[47]

The literature also contains a variety of specialized studies on the internal organization of the large city. One of these analyses is of the location of manufacturing in the Greater Tokyo area.[48] The authors conclude that locational instability has been greatest with regard to some of the "heavier" industries which require increasing amounts of space as modernization is taking place, but that locational inertia in general is exceedingly high, especially in industries which follow the widespread Japanese industrial practice of farming out work to small companies which then return the processed raw materials to assembly plants about which they therefore cluster. This clustering, the authors argue, is characteristic of the areal distribution of Japanese industry in general and affects the structure of Japanese cities, large or small. Research also has focused on commuting, and the distribution of and explanation for contrasting nighttime and daytime population ratios.[49]

The distributions of service functions and business districts and their relationships to other urban characteristics have been studied as well. For example, Kitagawa has compared the business districts and retail functions of several cities in western Japan, particularly in terms of the relationships between size of shopping area and land values.[50] Using these variables as indicators, he arrives at a hierarchy of central functions within cities of different sizes that approximates for Japan Carol's ordering for European and American cities, although he notes the particular significance of wartime destruction of central areas in many cities in modifying the size, location, and complexity of their central areas. A related study of Sakai, now a suburb of Osaka but formerly a major commercial city, shows how wartime bombing destroyed the central business area, led to the development of a second business center, but was followed by the recreation of the old center and the present situation in which two core areas rather than one serve the city.[51] Preoccupation with land values as an important device for urban areal analysis is reflected also in a study of Tokyo in which the author observes the peaking of land values in an exceptionally large (by Western standards) central area, their continuation at a high level along major transport (that is, railway) arteries, and their falling off elsewhere with distance from the core zone.[52] Another study confirms a high relationship between central-area land values and size of city; [53] and a study of Sendai on the relationships between prices of retail goods and the areal differentiation of types of shopping streets or areas concludes that ubiquitous low-cost commodities are poorly related to specialized-function shopping areas, but luxury goods shops clearly cluster in functionally central locations.[54]

Other studies concerned with housing and residential distributions find the classic concentric zonation hypothesis interesting but wanting on a number of counts, even though concentricity of other sorts may be ascertained. Although studies of socioeconomic zonation are numerous in the sociological literature, ethnic or caste differentiation is of minor significance in a country which, despite the Eta and Koreans, is populated by a remarkably homogeneous cultural group.

Suburbanization in Japan, however, has proceeded at a rapid rate since the First World War and has been accelerated by the widespread destruction of the central portions of Japan's cities during the Second World War.[55] Unlike the Western situation, the spread of the city into rural areas has been associated with railways, not with highways and the increased use of the automobile, although the impact of the latter is beginning to be felt.[56] With few exceptions, suburban areas in Japan tend to be associated with lower-income groups, not with higher, and the penalty for being poor among Japanese urbanites means, on the one hand, living either in the shadow of a factory wall often on land subject to inundation from river flood or tidal wave,[57] or, on the other, traveling long distances to work.[58] Expansion of the larger metropolises generally has been in directions where drainage is better and conflict with paddy land is less.

Since 1955 or so, expansion also has been associated with the construction of public housing estates, or *danchi,* primarily for lower-middle or middle-class occupants,[59] and with the movement outward of certain kinds of space-demanding industries, which most often locate on the outskirts of sizable villages or satellite towns, some distance removed from the main built-up area of the conurbation. This "leap-frogging" phenomenon has yet to be fully explained, but it reflects partly the organization of Japanese industry, partly legal barriers to the easy conversion of wet-rice land to nonagricultural uses, and partly an agricultural revolution which has begun to release labor from agriculture for other tasks.[60]

The changing character of agriculture in the urban-rural fringe also has received much attention. Usually, but not always, land uses shift from paddy cultivation to even more intensive truck gardening for urban markets before land passes out of agricultural uses.[61] At the same time, part-time farm households or households only partly dependent on agricultural income near the larger cities have increased rapidly. In fact, nearly 70 per cent of *all* farm households in Japan obtain a substantial portion of their income from nonagricultural sources, chiefly employment in city shops, wholesale enterprises, and industries.[62] The rapid conversion of farmland to urban uses also has its effect on recreational activities and their spatial patterning, as apparently does size of city.[63]

Other exogenous factors than the proliferation of housing estates and the transformation of agriculture also are entering into the modification of the urban complex. One of these, which is centripetal in effect, is the heavy emphasis on tidewater land reclamation within or near the larger cities, almost all of which are located on coastal sites. As a result of what is an almost entirely government-controlled policy, virtually the entire shore of Tokyo Bay is expected to be in industrial land uses within the next ten years, and similar developments are taking place near Osaka. This means that the populations of Japan's two largest conurbations will be cut off from direct access to the sea. Even apart from the losses accruing to the destruction of fisheries, the noncommensurable costs resulting from the destruction of potential recreational areas will be high.[64]

Another factor, exogenous to intrametropolitan systems and centrifugal in nature, is the policy of governmental agencies both at the local and national levels to discourage the location of new industries in what are perhaps inappropriately termed the "over-grown cities." This policy is reinforced by the central government's "ten-year income-doubling" program which has as one of its major clauses the development of large industrial areas in designated potential "millionth" cities as far removed as reasonable from the larger conurbations.[65] How successful this policy will be remains uncertain, but it undoubtedly will contribute to the creation of an industrialized-urbanized belt extending from east of Tokyo, through the Nagoya and the Osaka regions, and the Inland Sea to northern Kyushu, where the new "millionth" city called Kita Kyushu (Northern Kyushu) has come into being (1962) as a result of the amalgamation of five previously administratively independent cities—Moji, Kokura, Tobata, Yawata, and Wakamatsu.[66]

As must be apparent by now, a long tradition of urbanism, postwar reconstruction, and an unparalleled expansion of the urban population since 1952, has stimulated an already intense interest in problems of urban planning. There are at least three journals concerned with urban studies and urban planning in general—*Toshi Mondai, Toshi Mondai Kenkyū,* and *Shisei*. In addition, almost every city of any size has a planning agency of some sort, and many have been studied with an intensity that has not yet been reached even in the United States, Britain, and Sweden.[67] Geographers' contributions to these volumes are substantial, and in the fall of 1960 the Association of Japanese Geographers and the Association of Human Geographers devoted their entire joint meeting to a conference on contemporary pressing planning problems.[68]

One of the extraordinary characteristics of the geographical literature on Japanese cities and urbanization has been the paucity of studies by non-Japanese. Most of the literature is in Japanese and, despite the English abstracts in the *Geographical Review of Japan*, it is generally not available to scholars without a knowledge of the Japanese language. Among publications in English and other European languages, however, there are the classic studies on cultural origins by R. B. Hall and G. T. Trewartha,[69] Schöller's excellent appraisals of recent metropolitan development,[70] studies of the urban fringe by Eyre and Thompson,[71] which focus more than not on agriculture, and examination of site conditions and urban locations by Kornhauser.[72]

On the other hand, Japanese scholars are well aware of the work being done elsewhere on cities, and their publications display, as already noted, a commendable familiarity with basic concepts concerning urban functional organization, the dynamics of urban morphological change, centrality and accessibility, cultural inertia and other influences on the urbanization process, and ecological relationships that in the United States tend to be of greater interest to sociologists than to geographers. While arguing for more comparative and cross-cultural studies, they refer back frequently to questions of the cultural relativity of the urbanization process. Out of their work are coming some stimulating applications of Western-derived concepts and techniques and possibly some important modifications, as well as confirmation, of theories concerning the functions, structure, and patterns of cities and urban systems.

China

The vast geographical literature on Japan's cities is in marked contrast to the paucity of the literature on Chinese cities, which contained within them an estimated 105 million persons in 1960.[73] Reference here is to the contemporary literature, since there is an as yet virtually untapped source of information concerning Chinese cities in the thousands of *hsien* (county) gazetteers (*hsien chih*) which provide information over the last millennium. One recent study on the *hsien* capital, which has utilized some of these materials, illustrates the significance in China of the designated administrative city as a focal point about which the rest of Chinese society traditionally has organized itself spatially.[74] To some extent, these *hsien* cities might be likened to the "castle towns" of Japan, but they differ from the Japanese model in that they were walled, they were far more numerous (about 1900 before 1950), they were separated out at an early period from more important provincial centers (less than fifty), and they were established by fiat of a highly centralized government, or series of governments, which for perhaps two and a half millennia was in the city-planning, or at least city-establishing, business. In fact, the present distribution of urban centers in China was quite well defined by the end of the Han Dynasty (A.D. 221), and later extensions of the distribution were to frontiers of settlement in the southwest, northwest, and northeast (Manchuria).

Thus, the *hsien* cities, and to a lesser degree the provincial capitals, have acted as the basic stratum of urban settlement, forming a close network (perhaps sixteen miles apart) of roughly comparable types of cities, functionally diversified, and underlying another stratum (somewhat similar again to the Japanese case) composed of treaty ports and great capitals or former capitals—for example, Pei-ching or Peking (northern capital) and Nan-ching or Nanking (southern capital). No systematic studies have as yet been made of the size and spacing of Chinese cities, or of the interrelationships that exist among various levels of what appears to be a clearly distinguishable hierarchy, although Chang associates the *hsien* capital with Christaller's *Kreisstadt*.[75]

It should be noted at this point that the treaty ports, including even Shanghai and T'ien-ching, were all based upon indigenous Chinese cities, usually *hsien* capitals, but their development after the middle of the nineteenth century was substantially as a result of foreign enterprise, despite their predominantly Chinese populations.[76] In this respect, the Chinese treaty port more nearly resembled the often heavily Chinese populated port cities of Southeast Asia than the Japanese port city, albeit also Western-influenced and externally trade-oriented.

One of the few important studies of the "treaty-port" stratum is that of Murphey on Shanghai, the largest and most important of the treaty ports.[77] Murphey's rather traditional historical-geographic study helps clarify the ecological processes which help explain the growth and functional organization of Shanghai, and it makes at least one contribution of far-reaching significance. In a chapter entitled "How the City Is Fed," Murphey demonstrates that, even as a city of some 3.25 million, Shanghai was fed not from abroad but by a hinterland less than 100 miles away, in which a traditional agriculture prevailed and where the transportation system consisted primarily of a network of canals and an enormous fleet of junks and sampans. This finding counters one of the major objections to the possibility of the development of millionth cities in China or elsewhere prior to the Industrial Revolution—that a native technology and a primitive transportation system were congenitally unable to support a city of that size.

Various aspects of the morphology and external relations of several Chinese cities have been explored by Ginsburg, Spencer, and others, each observing the dualism characteristic of the treaty port or of the industrial cities in Manchuria which were partly Japanese creations of the treaty-port type.[78] No strictly functional classification of Chinese cities exists, largely through lack of data, although Trewartha has attempted a classification by location on transportation routes,[79] and Ullman has attempted to classify the contemporary Chinese city according to size and function.[80]

In fact, much of the recent English-language literature on the Chinese city has dealt with the size and rate of growth of the urban population of the country, a kind of exercise in "demographic intelligence," which has given rise to some marked disagreements among experts. The difficulty, of course, lies in the fact that from the 1953 Census few data about cities were made public by the Chinese, and Russian sources of limited scope have had to be relied upon.[81] Moreover, very little systematic information concerning cities has come out of Communist China even apart from the census information. Contemporary Chinese-language sources in urban geography are virtually nonexistent. Geography in Communist China is following a Soviet pattern which places highest emphasis on physical geography and economic geography, the second of which focuses primarily on aspects of resource development and the delineation of "physico-economic" regions suitable for planning purposes.

The prewar Chinese geographical literature contains a number of studies of Chinese cities, but the majority of these are conservatively historical and descriptive, if somewhat analytical, and none are primarily methodological.[82] Nevertheless, from this literature a simple descriptive model of the "typical" Chinese city, other than foreign-developed treaty ports such as Shanghai, T'ien-ching, and Ch'ing-tao, or the very largest metropolises, can be assayed.

It began about 1000 years ago as a walled *hsien* capital, and developed a strong but small urban field and rather weak formal ties with other cities of similar size and function. Ties with provincial capitals and larger trading centers of *hsien*-capital origin often were rather close, however, and a clearly observable, though only loosely definable, urban hierarchy based on administrative and commercial functions existed. Internally, functional specialization was ill defined, except among administrative buildings, temples and their grounds, and all the rest of the built-up area. Density of the built-up intramural areas varied markedly. In some instances, buildings huddled eave to eave or shared common walls throughout; in others, there were sizable open spaces, many in cultivation. Typically, the urbanized area had spilled out through one or more of the main gates, forming a "market suburb" and lending to the urban landscape a dualism reminiscent of other Asian dualistic townscapes, but unlike most of them, not based on contrasts between "traditional" and "modern." Although generally an administrative center and "planned" for this purpose, the city was in fact rather markedly multifunctional and acted as residence for a landed gentry possessed of strong attachments to an urban way of life.[83]

To a considerable degree, the provincial city and the indigenous capitals followed a similar pattern, site conditions permitting, but there was a somewhat greater tendency toward specialization, especially in terms of streets devoted to the manufacture and sale of specialized types of products. There was virtually no separation of places of work and residence, and little areal distinction between manufacturing, wholesaling, and retailing activities. The city walls enclosed only part of the total built-up area, although in some instances (for example, Nan-ching), the wall enclosed large areas of cropland.

The recently founded or developed treaty ports and industrial towns were (or are) of two types. One of these, the more common, displays the ubiquitous dualism observed in Indian cities and those of Southeast Asia, as between an indigenous town, in the Chinese case, walled, and a new city, the latter often laid out in "planned" fashion. The former was usually small and densely populated (more so than smaller walled towns), with few streets cut through a maze of valleys, and "preindustrial" in personality. The latter contained Western-type buildings or Chinese shophouses (though taller than in the smaller towns), residential districts chiefly for foreigners or compradores, in which houses were set within spacious grounds or tall apartment buildings rose above the generally low roof level of the city; modern factories were located near the margins of the old town. Cities that fit this description to a greater or lesser degree include Shanghai, T'ien-ching, Han-k'ou, Mukden, Ch'ang-ch'un,[84] and, to a lesser degree, Canton. These differ substantially, however, as to the relative proportions of built-up area and population in old and new cities respectively, and as to the amount of change that has been imposed upon the old city (for example, little in Shanghai, despite its size; great in Ch'ang-ch'un where the Japanese created a new capital for Manchukuo).

The second type of city in this broad class is one almost wholly developed as a result of modern industrialization, but there are only a handful of these in China. Such a one would be An-shan in Manchuria, based upon mining and heavy industry, displaying many of the characteristics of a traditional Chinese city, but resembling in some respects also a British Midlands town. Somewhere between this type and the mixed type noted previously would be cases like that of Ch'ing-tao, in which virtually the entire existing city was constructed by the Germans after the razing of the old Chinese town, which included a new "Chinese" town laid out alongside the "Western" and disconcertingly Teutonic new town.[85]

Variants on these themes are found in T'ai-wan, for which there is a notable descriptive literature, chiefly in Chinese, but partly in English, about Taiwanese cities.[86] These are even more mixed than most, representing elements of earlier Chinese settlement, Japanese urban development and planning, and later postwar occupance by mainland Chinese.

The contemporary Chinese city bears the indelible imprint of its history, but its changing character is obscured by lack of information concerning urban development. One reads of great apartment blocks and administrative buildings going up on the outskirts of Peking; of new industrial towns, reminiscent of the Japanese towns in Manchuria, rising alongside traditional walled cities (for example, Pao-t'ou, site of one of the major heavy industrial developments in mainland China), but detailed studies are lacking.[87]

This is a pity, since China most likely could be the crucial test case for hypotheses concerning the multidimensional courses of urbanization. As the situs of more cities of size, in existence for a longer period than those of any other cultural region, China is blanketed by a long-established city system, poorly integrated as compared with Western countries, but much more highly integrated, through administrative ties, market hierarchies, and indigenous and modern transport facilities, than any country in Asia other than Japan, itself a Sinitic cultural variant. Here lies, perhaps, the greatest, if as yet inaccessible, frontier for urban research outside the Western world.

Southeast Asia

Urbanism appears to be alien to most societies of Southeast Asia. Where cities exist, they are associated with Chinese or Chinese enterprise, with Europeans or European activity, or with combinations of the two. There are virtually no exceptions to these categorical statements, despite the urbaneness (sic) of the Khmer and their architectural achievements at Angkor. In its nonindigenous character, urbanization in Southeast Asia bears a much closer resemblance to that in Africa or Latin America, for example, than it does to neighboring areas where Indic or Sinitic civilizations predominate. There is, of course, a history of Southeast Asia, but it is not, unlike that of China and Japan, an urban history. It was writ on a landscape almost wholly rural, by societies to which urbanism was a strange phenomenon.

In almost every country in Southeast Asia, with its 220 million people of which about 25 million live in cities, there are large cities, but every one of these is the product of a merging of European colonialism with Chinese urbanness (sic). Partial exceptions might be Hanoi, with a small minority of Chinese and several lesser towns in culturally Chinese Vietnam (for example, Hué); Rangoon, which was more Indian than Chinese until the Japanese occupation during the Pacific War; and Bangkok, which, strictly speaking, was never a center of colonialism, although it was and still is largely populated by Chinese.

In general, cities in Southeast Asia are relatively new creations, although they may have developed at focal points in existence before them. Most of them are ports. There is a poorly developed urban hierarchy, and primacy is common.[88] Thailand is perhaps the best and most extreme example of this phenomenon, and it also is characterized by the largest population size gap between the primate city (Bangkok) and the next stratum of settlement. Modifications of these propositions are most conspicuous in Malaya, where a communications network was relatively highly developed under British rule; they are less so but apparent in Indonesia, or more precisely on Java, where Dutch policies of local regionalism created towns or encouraged the enlargement of previously small native towns; and they appear also in the Philippines which were under the firm control of Western powers—Spain and the United States—for a longer period than any other country. As a corollary, the phenomenon of the "hill station," though found elsewhere, is particularly widespread in Southeast Asia.[89]

These circumstances are reflected in the nature of Southeast Asia's larger cities which tend to resemble the China treaty ports or India's larger cities. Most are easily divided into Western and non-Western zones. Most have some sort of recognizable central business district associated with foreign enterprise and display a high degree of ethnic segregation. In fact, much of the urban landscape in the cities of greatest Chinese population (for example, Singapore or Kuala Lumpur) is virtually indistinguishable from that in South China where the ubiquitous shophouse also prevails. Suburbanization is poorly developed on the whole, and commuting is relatively unimportant, although the cities are attracting increasing numbers of immigrants from rural areas who tend to bypass the smaller towns. Functional segregation is moderately developed, less so than in the West, and modern industry has tended to localize either in the port areas or on the outskirts of the urbanized areas. All of these generalizations must be qualified, of course, when applied to any one country or city. General discussions of them can be found in papers of Fryer, Ginsburg, and Murphey.[90]

For the most part, the urban geographical literature on Southeast Asia is scanty. Except for Malaya, little geographical research of quality is carried on in higher educational institutions within individual countries. The lack of comprehensive census data for most countries (Malaya has the best coverage) makes studies of the sort possible in Japan or even in India, impossible. Thus, many studies must either be field-oriented and covering relatively limited areas, or highly generalized and qualitative.[91]

For these reasons comprehensive studies of city systems in Southeast Asia are virtually nonexistent. One partial exception is Ullman's pioneering study of the Philippines, in which he establishes a hierarchy of cities based on size and functions, and compares it with theoretical hierarchies and those examined elsewhere.[92] He observes, however, both that the hierarchy is stunted and that it reflects the relative "stickiness" of Philippine society, as well as the insular character of the country. Even lower levels of spatial interaction and smaller trade areas might be expected in other countries in Southeast Asia, but data are not yet available to make comparative studies. A useful study by Hamzah on Malayan urban patterns casts some light on this problem, as does Withington's paper on Indonesian cities.[93]

Studies of urban morphology, at least for certain of the larger cities, are more common.[94] These tend to be descriptive and historical, but provide insights which point to some of the major problems that need further investigation. Hodder also has delved deeply into the matter of ethnic segregation in his historical study of Singapore,[95] and McIntyre has attempted to analyze the pattern of retailing in Manila.[96]

Interest in planning problems has generated some research into these cities, as in Singapore, Djakarta, and Bangkok, but generally results are not published or only superficially deal with fundamental aspects of spatial organization.[97] A number of nongeographical studies, however, are valuable in understanding the importance of ethnic and class segregation in determining the basic spatial patterns of cities, although few deal directly with this subject.[98]

The little evidence available nonetheless suggests that cities in Southeast Asia may come to resemble Western prototypes somewhat more rapidly than their equivalents in China and even in Japan and India. Without an urban tradition to fall back on, Western models are being followed to a greater or lesser degree, although this emulation appears to be restricted to the already large capital and port cities, and less in others. It is still true that even in the large Indonesian cities, the major form of land use is a *kampong*-type of residential area which physically is virtually indistinguishable except for densities from its rural equivalent. Nevertheless, the transformation of the largest cities from colonial to national capitals has meant an increasing concentration of Western-oriented cultural forms, including modern manufacturing, political-administrative offices, higher educational institutions, and mass communication facilities. In Malaya, for example, one finds government housing estates transforming the fringe areas and introducing, as in Japan, administratively derived occupance patterns which are not "natural"; and in Singapore in 1962 new flats were being provided at a rate of one unit every forty-five minutes, some of them well within the city where previously unsuitable land uses were converted (for example, the old airport at Kallang) or in the fringe areas which previously had been unattractive to people accustomed to think only of central areas as being desirable.[99] West of Kuala Lumpur, a continuous urban belt is in the making, extending from the swelling capital of the Federation of Malaya via the new University of Malaya campus and the wholly planned suburb (originally called a satellite) of Petaling Jaya, to the Selangor state capital of Klang, and an expanding Port Swettenham. Similar spectacular modifications of the urban fringe landscape are taking place in most countries in Southeast Asia, especially around Manila and Djakarta, but country differences in the scale and rate of change are predictable, at least roughly, in terms of the relative wealth of the countries concerned. The outcome of fundamentally political policies concerning urban development is unclear. Here again is a major research frontier, but one which, for the most part, is defined by the unpredictable parameters of political decision-making in politically unstable settings.

NOTES

1. This essay focuses on the urban geographical literature as it pertains to Asia and, to a lesser extent, Africa, thus reflecting the author's scholarly interests. It is intended to be in the nature of a selected annotated bibliography, with such commentary as is necessary to point out the significance of some of the contributions cited. No attempt has been made to include all the relevant geographical literature, and only occasional reference made to the wealth of materials by nongeographers.

2. D. W. Whittlesey, "Kano, a Sudanese Metropolis," *Geographical Review* (April 1937), pp. 177–199.

3. H. R. Jarrett, "Some Aspects of the Urban Geography of Freetown, Sierra Leone," *Geographical Review* (July 1956), pp. 334–354.

4. R. W. Steel, "The Towns of Ashanti," *Compte Rendus du Congres International de Geographie* (Lisbon, 1949), Tome IV, pp. 81–93; and his "The Geography of Urban Problems in Tropical Africa," International Geographical Union, *Abstracts of Papers* (Stockholm, 1960), pp. 276–277, in which Steel pleads for fresh approaches to types of cities presumably unique to the region.

5. E. S. Munger, *Relational Patterns of Kampala, Uganda,* Research Paper No. 21 (Chicago: University of Chicago, Department of Geography, 1951), p. 5.

6. *Ibid.,* p. 3.

7. Ann E. Larimore, *The Alien Town: Pattern of Settlement in Busoga, Uganda,* Research Paper No. 55 (Chicago: University of Chicago, Department of Geography, 1958), p. 6. To the extent that alien groups have provided a major impetus to urban growth, one might argue, however, that the East African case is more "Asian" than "Western."

8. For another sample study of these fundamental relationships, see H. C. Brookfield and M. A. Tatham, "The Distribution of Racial Groups in Durban," *Geographical Review* (January 1957), pp. 44–65. In this case, census-tract data were employed. The authors observe that ethnic pluralism in Durban extends even to the creation of two central business districts in that city. See also G. Hamdan, "The Growth and Functional Structure of Khartoum," *Geographical Review* (January 1960), pp. 21–40.

9. See, for example, W. A. Hance and I. S. van Dongen, "Dar Es Salaam, the Port and Tributary Area," *Annals,* Association of American Geographers (December 1958), pp. 419–435. The specialized character of most African port hinterlands is in striking contrast to those in more developed regions or in others, such as China, where overseas trade and highly complex civilizations have resulted in port-focused hinterlands characterized by great functional diversity. Also their "Beira, Mozambique, Gateway to Central Africa," *Annals,* Association of American Geographers (December 1957), pp. 307–335. In each of these the authors use commodity-flow data as the basis for determining the tributary area or hinterland of the port. In the Beira study they also distinguish between the port's "national" and "extra-national" hinterlands and examine the implications of this "dualism" on its future.

10. W. Manshard, "Die Stadt Kumasi (Ghana): Stadt und Umland in ihren funktionalen Beziehungen," *Erdkunde,* Vol. 15, No. 3 (1961), pp. 162–180. See also his "A Simple Teaching Model Explaining the Spatial Differentiation of Urban Functions," *Bulletin of the Ghana Geographical Association,* 1 (1960), pp. 21ff.; and his "Verstadterungsercheinungen in West Africa," *Sonderdruck aus Raumforschung and Raumordnung* (1961), Heft 1 (Berlin: Carl Heymanns Verlag, 1961). For references to the work of Green, Smailes, and Godlund, see the essays by Mayer and Berry in this volume.

11. R. J. Harrison-Church, "West African Urbanization: A Geographical View," *The Sociological Review,* 7, No. 1 (1959), pp. 15–28. Steel's second paper (1960) cited above also fits into this category.

12. G. Hamdan, "Capitals of the New Africa," *Economic Geography* (July 1964), pp. 239–253.

13. Akin L. Mabogunje, "Urbanization in Nigeria—A Constraint on Economic Development" (Unpublished paper, mimeographed. Available from the author at the Department of Geography, University of Ibadan, Ibadan. March 1964). See also his "The Residential Structure of Ibadan, Nigeria," *Geographical Review* (January 1962), and his "The Evolution and Analysis of the Retail Structure of Lagos, Nigeria," *Economic Geography* (October 1964), pp. 304–323.

14. Although, as Brush points out, some foreign-developed port cities (in India) "exhibit a remarkable blending of Indian and European urban traditions, producing a modified kind of European townscape in which Indo-British culture evolved and still continues to flourish." J. E. Brush in R. Turner (Ed.), *India's Urban Future* (Berkeley: University of California Press, 1962), p. 58.

15. J. E. Brush, "The Morphology of Indian Cities," Chap. 3 in R. Turner, *op. cit.,* pp. 57–70. This volume contains a number of valuable articles on Indian urbanization in general.

16. See, for example, O. H. K. Spate and E. Ahmad, "Five Cities of the Gangetic Plain," *Geographical Review* (April 1950), pp. 260–278; R. V. Joshi, "Urban Structure in Western India," *Geographical Review of India* (March 1956), pp. 7–19; A. K. Sen, "Techniques of Classifying the Functional Zones of a City," *Geographical Review of India* (March 1959), pp. 37–42; U. Singh, "The Cultural Zones of Allahabad," *National Geographical Journal of India* (June 1960), pp. 67–104; A. B. Tuvari, "The Urban Regions of Agra," *Agra University Journal of Research (Letters)* (January 1958), pp. 101–113; M. N. Nigam, "Evolution of Lucknow," *National Geographic Journal of India* (March 1960), pp. 30–46. Many such studies are strongly historical in nature, and, as Janaki has observed, some may be concerned with the identification of functional zones "to the extent of finding zones where they do not exist." See note 19 below.

17. B. F. Hoselitz, "The Cities of India and Their Problems," *Annals,* Association of American Geographers (June 1959), pp. 223–231. Reprinted with modifications in R. Turner (Ed.), *op. cit.,* pp. 425–443. Another useful bibliography which casts light on the type of literature considered important to at least one Indian urban geographer is found in A. Lal, "Review of Bibliography on Urban Geography," *National Geographical Journal of India* (September 1961), pp. 206–226.

18. R. L. Singh, *Banaras: A Study in Urban Geography* (Banaras: Nand Kishore, 1955).

19. V. A. Janaki and Z. A. Sayed, *The Geography of Padra Town,* M. Sayajiro University Geographical Series No. 1 (Baroda, 1962). A similar study, but on a less ambitious scale, is that of R. L. Singh and S. M. Singh, "Mungrabadshahpur: A Rurban Settlement in the Ganga-Ghaghara Doab West," *National Geographic Journal of India* (December 1960), pp. 199–206. Janaki and M. H. Ajwani also have produced an interesting study of the impact of urban influences on a nearby village: "Urban Influence and the Changing Face of a Gujarat Village," *Journal of the M. Sayajiro University of Baroda* (*Science*) (November 1961), pp. 59–87. Miss Janaki and M. C. Ghia argue, as does Mabogunje, that hinterlands vary over time with the introduction of improved and areally selective transportation facilities in their "The Tributary Area of Baroda," *Journal of the M. Sayajiro University of Baroda* (*Science*) (November 1962), pp. 81–99.

20. S. N. Reddy, "Vegetable Markets and Regional Relationships of Hyderabad City," *Geographical Review of India* (September 1961), pp. 24–40. On the last-named point, see Mayfield's article cited in note 31.

21. F. K. Khan and Mo. H. Khan, "Delimitation of Greater Dacca," *Oriental Geographer,* Vol. 5, No. 2 (1961), pp. 95–120. The formula is as follows: Dacca's proportional Range of Influence (as compared with city A) =

$$\frac{\text{Dacca's nonagricultural labor force} \times 100}{\text{DNALF} \times \text{City A's NALF}}$$

22. A. Lal, "Some Characteristics of Indian Cities of over 100,000 Inhabitants in 1951 with Special Reference to Their Occupational Structure and Functional Specialization" (Unpublished Ph.D. dissertation, Department of Geography, Indiana University, 1958); also, "Some Aspects of the Functional Classification of Cities and a Proposed Scheme for Classifying Indian Cities," *National Geographical Journal of India* (March 1959), pp. 12–24.

23. K. V. Kureshy, "Urban Development in West Pakistan" (unpublished Ph.D. dissertation, Department of Geography, University of London, 1957), pp. 271–278; and N. Ahmad, "The Urban Pattern in East Pakistan," *Oriental Geographer* (January 1957), pp. 37–39. A more refined typology, based on occupation data in the 1961 Census of Pakistan, has been developed by Q. S. Ahmad, Lecturer in Geography at University of Sind, Hyderabad. Q. S. Ahmad also used the statistical technique known as "nearest-neighbor analysis" in analyzing the distribution of cities in Pakistan, and presents a graphic model of the internal structure of these cities. Unfortunately, his study is not widely available. Q. S. Ahmad, "Urbanization in Pakistan" (unpublished Master's thesis, Department of Geography, University of Chicago, March 1963). Available on interlibrary loan.

24. V. L. S. Prakasa Rao, "Macro-urban Analysis: Geographers' Contribution," Presidential Address to the Council of Geographers (India), *Annual Proceedings* (Cuttack, 1962) (mimeographed).

25. V. L. S. Prakasa Rao and A. T. A. Learmonth, "Trends in Urbanization in Mysore State, India," an unpublished paper prepared for the 1960 Seminar on Urbanization in India, University of California. See also Maps 77–85 and 100–104 and accompanying texts in A. T. A. Lear-

month and L. S. Bhat, *Mysore State: An Atlas of Resources* (Calcutta: Indian Statistical Institute, 1960), Vol. I. On Map 81, "urbanism" is measured by an "index of concentration" based on the relations between population numbers and densities.

26. N. R. Kar, "Urban Characteristics of the City of Calcutta," *Indian Population Bulletin* (April 1960), p. 36.

27. *Ibid.*, p. 54, though socioeconomic characteristics may differ.

28. *Ibid.*, p. 55.

29. *Ibid.*, p. 57.

30. *Ibid.*, p. 65.

31. R. Mayfield, "The Range of a Good in the Indian Punjab," *Annals, Association of American Geographers* (March 1963), pp. 38–49.

32. N. S. Kar, "Urban Hierarchy and Central Functions around Calcutta, in Lower West Bengal, India, and Their Significance," in K. Norborg (Ed.), *Proceedings of the I.G.U. Symposium in Urban Geography, Lund, 1960, Lund Studies in Geography, Ser. B. Human Geography No. 24* (Lund: C. W. K. Gleerup, 1962). This volume contains 32 papers which form an admirable cross-section of contemporary urban geographic thought.

33. S. Yamaga et al., *Toshika Kenkyū Shiryō* (Tokyo: Nihon Chiri Gakkai, 1959). Since then, a member of the A. J. G. Committee has prepared an updated account of developments in Japanese geography which is based on and supplements this bibliographic report: S. Kiuchi, "Recent Developments in Japanese Urban Geography," *Annals*, Association of American Geographers (March 1963), pp. 93–102; and a volume by eighteen authors has just appeared in Japanese on the same topic: S. Kiuchi, S. Yamaga, K. Shimizu, and S. Inanaga (Eds.), *Nihon no Toshika* (*Urbanization in Japan*) (Tokyo: Kokon Shōin, 1964).

34. For example, see S. Yamaga, "The Urbanization of Kiyose, A Hospital Town in the Suburbs of Tokyo," *Chirigaku Hyōron* (*Geographical Review of Japan*) (January 1959), pp. 35–41; F. Suzuki, "The Functions of a Small City in a Metropolitan Area: A Case Study of Mobara, Chiba," *Geographical Review of Japan*, 33, No. 3 (1960), pp. 187–199; N. Kato, "A Geographical Study of Tajimi, A Satellite Town," *Chirigaku Hōkoku*, Aichi Gakugeidaigaku Chirigakkai (*Geographical Reports*, Geographical Society, Aichi Gakugei University) (May 1959), pp. 13–19. Each of these stresses the duality of pluralism of functions associated with older central places incorporated into a metropolitan system. Since many official cities have come into being in Japan since 1935, and especially between 1953 and 1956, numerous other studies examine their processes of urbanization and metropolitanization as part of a large metropolitan system. See also the series of articles on the changing character of Kasugai, a satellite in the Nagoya or Chūkyō metropolitan system founded in 1943, in *Chirigaku Hōkoku* (*Geographical Reports*, Geographical Society, Aichi University), No. 14 (1960) (entire volume). For an appraisal of the recent policy of administrative area reorganization, see H. Masami, *Shi-chō-son Ikino Kaihen no Kenkyū* (*The Administration of Cities-Towns-Villages: A Study of Areal Reorganization*) (Tokyo: Kokon Shōin, 1961). All references, unless otherwise specified, are in Japanese. Where available, English translations of titles that appear in the original volumes are used, but in some instances

they have been modified for clarity, in which cases the phrase "title modified" is inserted in the citation.

35. S. Kiuchi, "Problems of Comparative Urban Geography," in *Tsujimura, Taro Sensei Koki Kinen, Chirigaku Rombunshū (Geographical Essays: A Volume Commemorating the 70th Birthday of Professor Tsujimura)* (Tokyo, 1961), pp. 557–573. Kiuchi's standard work on cities, though now somewhat outdated, presents most clearly the catholic nature of Japanese geographers' approach to urban research: *Toshi Chirigaku Kenkyū (Studies in Urban Geography)* (Tokyo: Kokon Shōin, 1951; rev. ed., 1956).

36. One section of the Association of Japanese Geographers' report contains a discussion of the meanings of these terms, based in fact on questionnaires sent to various European and American urban geographers. Another discussion of the same problem appears in F. Takano, "A Typology of Urbanization and Definitions of Terms," *Geographical Review of Japan* (December 1959), pp. 629–642. Takano defines four types of urbanization as defined in terms of land uses and occupations: (1) a metropolitan type, (2) a regional center type, (3) a modern industrialization type, and (4) a traditional industrialization type, of which (1) and (3) are most significant in appraising the ways in which Japanese cities are developing today. See also T. Nakano's review of Kiuchi et al. (Eds.), *Nihon no Toshika* in the *Geographical Review of Japan* (May 1964), p. 255.

37. Teruo Ishimizu, "The Present Status of Urbanization Studies among Japanese Academic Geographers," *Geographical Review of Japan* (August 1962), pp. 362–373 (title modified).

38. One of the better examples of this approach is K. Kujioka's *Senshi Chiiki oyobi Toshiiki no Kenkyū: Chirigaku ni Okeru Chiiki Hensenshiteki Kenkyū no Tachiba (Prehistoric Regions and Urban Regions: Researches into Regional Evolution in Geography)* (Kyoto: Yanagihara, 1955). Part I includes an excellent introductory essay dealing with concepts in urban geography and ecology that are then applied to the development of urban systems in Japan as related to technological and social changes in the society. Some of his ideas are presented, in highly simplified form, in his "Feudal Traditions in the Forms and Zonal Structures of Japanese Cities," *Proceedings of the I. G. U. Regional Conference in Japan, 1957* (Tokyo: The Science Council of Japan, 1959), pp. 317–319. Interest in historical studies of continental cities also is high. See, for example, K. Yamori, "On the Distribution and Scale of Walled Towns during the Ri Dynasty," *Geographical Review of Japan* (August 1962), pp. 348–361 (title modified).

In general, Japanese urban geography should be viewed as part of a long-time interest in settlement geography. See Chap. 6, "Settlement Geography," in the *K. B. S. Bibliography of Standard Reference Books for Japanese Studies, with Descriptive Notes*, Vol. II, *Geography and Travel* (Tokyo: Kokusai Bunka Shinkokai, 1962) (in English).

39. Y. Ogasawara, "Industrial Population I, II," Plates 10 and 11 in K. Aki et al., *Nihon Keizai Chizu (Economic Atlas of Japan)* (Tokyo: Zenkokukyoikutosho, 1954). For translation of legends, see N. S. Ginsburg and J. D. Eyre (Eds.), *A Translation of The Map Legends in the Economic Atlas of Japan* (Chicago: Department of Geography, University of Chicago, 1959), pp. 22–26.

40. K. Tanabe, "The Development of Spatial Structure in Japanese Cities,

with regard to Castle Towns," *Science Reports of Tōhoku University, Seventh Series, Geography,* No. 8 (1959), pp. 88–105 (in English).

41. T. Matsumoto, "The Structure of Modern Castle Towns," *Geographical Review of Japan* (March 1962), pp. 97–112 (title modified); and "The Transformation of Modern Castle Towns," *ibid.* (May 1962), pp. 212–223 (title modified). Matsumoto relates the evolution of the castle town to its size and regional functions on the one hand and to Japan's changing social structure after the Meiji period on the other hand. See also his "Feudal Capitals and Their Changing Urban Structure in the Second Half of the 19th Century: The Cases of Yamaguchi and Shizuoka," *Geographical Review of Japan* (September 1960), pp. 473–482.

42. See T. Murata and S. Kiuchi (Eds.), *A Reconnaissance Geography of Tōkyō* (Tokyo: I. G. U. Regional Conference in Japan, 1957) (in English).

43. S. Muramatsu, "The Formation of the Hanshin Urban Region," *Toshi Mondai Kenkyū (Research on Municipal Problems)* (July 1959), pp. 52–65.

44. See F. Takano, "The City Region Network as the Structure of Area," *Proceedings of the I. G. U. Regional Conference in Japan* (1957), pp. 486–490; and his "Introduction to Research on the Urban Region," *Chirigaku Hōkoku (Geographical Reports,* Aichi Gakugei University), No. 13 (1959), pp. 1–17 and Nos. 15 and 16 (1960), pp. 18–24; and his "Study of the Regional Structure of Metropolitan Area Patterns: The Case of the Tōkai Region," *Geographical Review of Japan* (January 1963), pp. 57–67 (title modified), in which he develops an index of "urban power" based on commutation and shopping patterns.

45. K. Hattori, K. Kagaya, and S. Inanaga, "The Regional Structure of Tōkyō's Environs," *Geographical Review of Japan* (October 1960), pp. 495–514. This study, perhaps the first to use factor analysis for metropolitan subregional delimitation, utilizes a modification of Hagood's technique as described in *Social Forces,* Vol. 21 (1943), pp. 287–297, and is akin to (1) Berry's study "An Inductive Approach to the Regionalization of Economic Development," in N. S. Ginsburg, *Essays in Geography and Economic Development,* Research Paper No. 62 (Chicago: University of Chicago, Department of Geography, 1960); and (2) J. H. Thompson et al., "Toward a Geography of Economic Health: The Case of New York State," *Annals,* Association of American Geographers (March 1962), pp. 1–20. The study has been criticized chiefly on the grounds that the variables were arbitrarily selected and are not necessarily significant to understanding forces at work in functionally differentiating the Tokyo metropolitan region.

46. Y. Watanabe, "Types of Central Places in the Yokote Basin: Topographic Influences on Central-Place Distributions," *Science Reports of Tōhoku University, Seventh Series, Geography,* No. 8 (1959), pp. 68–87 (in English). Watanabe also is author of several papers which apply central-place theory to cities and areas in northeastern Japan. These also have been published in the *Science Reports of Tōhoku University, Seventh Series, Geography:* "The Urban Region of Sendai, A Study of Urban Concentric Zoning in Actual Pattern in Japan" (March 1953), pp. 30–52; "The Service Pattern of the Shinjo Basin" (March 1954), pp. 77–90; "The Central Hierarchy in Fukushima Prefecture" (March 1955), pp. 25–46; "Kitakami City: The Study of Functions of a 'Local' City in Japan" (March

1958), pp. 54–69. (All are in English.) The *Tōhoku Science Reports* include a number of other studies by Fujimoto, Tanabe et al., which also deal with central-place functions and distributions.

47. For examples, see S. Watanabe, "Accessibility Isopleths of a Local City and Their Relation to Its Service Hinterland," *Tōhoku Chiri*, Vol. 12, Nos. 3–4 (1959), pp. 43–48; K. Sawada, "Historical Changes in the Trade Areas of Towns on Tokyo's Northern Fringe," *Chirigaku Kenkyū Hōkoku* (*Geographical Research Reports,* Tōkyō Kyōiku University), 4 (1959), pp. 51–64, a comparison of data for 1932 and 1958 in which the trade areas of higher-order centers are found to be expanding at the expense of lower-order centers; K. Sawada, "Changes in the Trade Areas of Towns in the Tedori Fan Area of Ishikawa Prefecture," *Chirigaku Kenkyū Hōhoku,* 4 (1960), pp. 1–16, in which comparisons with an earlier study (1936) and based on purchases of cloth demonstrate the great expansion of Kanazawa's trade area at the expense of lower-order cities; and H. Kanazaki, "Nanao City's Spheres of Relationships," *Jimbun Chiri (Human Geography)* (April 1959), pp. 116–131, a study based on transportation services and the purchase of certain consumers' goods.

48. Y. Tsujimoto et al., "The Distribution of Industries in Tōkyō," *Geographical Review of Japan* (October 1962), pp. 477–504.

49. H. Hama, "Daytime and Nighttime Populations in the Tōkyō Metropolitan Area," *Toshi Mondai (Municipal Problems)* (December 1960), pp. 1361–1370.

50. K. Kitagawa, "The Differentiation and Development of Central Districts within Cities," *Geographical Review of Japan* (March 1962), pp. 130–148 (title modified).

51. K. Inoki, "Changes in Shopping Areas in War-Damaged Sakai," *Osaka Gakugei Daigaku Kiyō (Memoirs of the Osaka Gakugei University),* 7 (1959), pp. 124–138.

52. T. Wakita, "On Changes in Land Values and Their Geographical Consequences in Tōkyō," *Toshi Mondai (Municipal Problems)* (April 1960), pp. 447–459. The author based his study on current market values of land and not on assessed valuations, as other students of the subject apparently have done.

53. N. Sugimura, "The Size of Central Shopping Areas (Streets) and (Their Relation to) Size of City Populations and Major Services," *Geographical Review of Japan* (September 1958), pp. 548–555 (title modified).

54. K. Kawajima, "Commodity Prices and the Classifications of Shopping Areas (Streets)," *Geographical Review of Japan* (April 1960), pp. 232–237 (title modified). A related study is R. Fujimoto's "The Shopping Street: An Element of City Structure in North Japan," *Science Reports of the Tōhoku University, Seventh Series, Geography* (March 1953), pp. 19–29 (in English).

55. It is estimated that 40 per cent of the residential units in Osaka proper were destroyed during the war, and about a third of the city as a whole. See K. Inoki, *op. cit.*

56. It is interesting to note that in a typical Japanese metropolis, Nagoya, nearly 80 per cent of all automotive vehicles in 1960 were either *not* passenger automobiles or were owned by corporative groups (for example, taxis

and company cars), not individuals. This is precisely the reverse of the situation in the United States. An extensive literature on transportation problems is illustrated by Y. Kajimoto's "Urban Transport in Osaka and Its Environs," *Toshi Mondai Kenkyū* (*Research on Municipal Problems*) (November 1959), pp. 79–106.

57. The problem of land subsidence in large Japanese cities, with consequent flood hazards, is particularly acute, given the site characteristics of most of them, the increasing proportion of reclaimed land, and expanding withdrawals of groundwater for industrial uses. See Hakaru Takamura, "Chinka suru Deruta chitai: Nishi Ōsaka no Baai" ("Subsiding Delta Areas: The Case of Western Osaka"), *Shizen* (*Nature*) (July 1960), pp. 13–20.

58. "In Tōkyō, too, slums have been distributed near the city boundary [and] on marshy lands in industrial districts. The greater part of them are not in a deteriorated belt [near the central areas] as the slums in American cities are. They have migrated to [the] outer zones . . . with urban development." Murata and Kiuchi, *op. cit.*, p. 69.

59. Examples of studies of *danchi* are: T. Hara, "A Geographical Study of Housing Estates in Nagoya," *Chirigaku Hōkoku* (*Geographical Reports*, Aichi Gakugei University), No. 13 (1959), pp. 19–23, a study of the rates at which various types of services establish themselves in a new housing development; H. Mizuno, "Retail Trade in a Housing Estate," *Toshi Mondai Kenkyū* (*Research on Municipal Problems*) (September 1960), pp. 78–103, a study of the spatial structure of shopping in a middle to upper-middle class *danchi* on the outskirts of Nagoya.

60. See T. Ishimizu, "The Present Status . . . ," *op. cit.*

61. J. H. Thompson, "Urban Agriculture in Southern Japan," *Economic Geography* (July 1957), pp. 224–237. Of interest also in connection with commodity hinterland problems is J. D. Eyre, "Sources of Tokyo's Fresh Food Supply," *Geographical Review* (October 1959), pp. 455–476. Parenthetically, Eyre remarks, à propos the belief that radical changes are occurring in the Japanese urban diet:

> The diets of the wealthier . . . groups [in Tōkyō] include bread, Western vegetables and juices, salads, and other non-Japanese foods and food preparations in increasing number. Yet, the general pattern of Tōkyō food preference and consumption resembles that of smaller Japanese cities. Rice remains the basic bulk food around which smaller amounts of fish, noodles, vegetables . . . are added for taste, consistency, or nutritional value.

62. M. Saito, "Urbanization and the Increase in Part-time Farm Households in the Vicinities of Cities," *Geographical Review of Japan* (February 1962), pp. 77–88.

63. Y. Koike, "Recreation for Urbanites: Types and Patterns," *Geographical Review of Japan* (December 1960), pp. 615–625 (title modified).

64. For a stimulating and even revolutionary proposal to use shallow coastal waters for the redevelopment of a metropolitan area, see the K. Tange Team, *A Plan for Tokyo, 1960: Toward a Structural Reorganization* (Tokyo, 1961) (in English).

65. For a discussion of some of the urban planning implications of this

policy, see N. S. Ginsburg, "The Dispersed Metropolis: The Case of Okayama," *Toshi Mondai (Municipal Problems)* (June 1961), pp. 67–76.

66. The amalgamation question and its political ramifications form a major basis for controversy in planning and academic circles. The history of amalgamation in one highly urbanized area, Ōsaka Prefecture, is examined in K. Inoki, "Special Features and Problems of Amalgamation in Ōsaka Prefecture" (modified title), *Ōsaka Gakugei Daigaku Chirigakuho (Geographical Reports of the Ōsaka Gakugei University)*, No. 8 (1958), pp. 1–18.

67. As an English-language example, the reader is referred to *Basic Materials for the Comprehensive Development Plan of the Hanshin Metropolitan Region* (Osaka, 1960), Parts 1 and 2. These volumes were prepared for the use of a United Nation's Technical Assistance Mission to Japan, and unfortunately, only a limited English-language edition was published. A number of generalizations which appear in this chapter and are not otherwise documented are based in part on these materials.

68. See the program of the Autumn 1960 Okayama meetings of the two associations, subtitled "The Competition between Urban and Rural Land Uses," "Modern Cities and Transportation Routes," and "The Formation of Coastal Industrial Districts." A symposium on the "Regional City" at the Autumn 1962 meetings of the A. J. G. also dealt with some of these problems.

69. R. B. Hall, "The Cities of Japan: Notes on Distribution and Inherited Forms," *Annals*, Association of American Geographers (December 1934), pp. 175–200; G. T. Trewartha, "Japanese Cities: Distribution and Morphology," *Geographical* Review (July 1934), pp. 404–417.

70. P. Scholler, "Wachstum und Wandlung japanischer Stadtregionen," *Die Erde*, 93, No. 3 (1962), pp. 202–234; and his "Center-shifting and Center-mobility in Japanese Cities," in K. Norborg (Ed.), *op. cit.*

71. Thompson, *op. cit.* Thompson also has worked on patterns of industrial location, as in his "Manufacturing in the Kita Kyushu Industrial Zone of Japan," *Annals*, Association of American Geographers (December 1959), pp. 420–442.

72. D. H. Kornhauser, "Reflections on the Physical and Historical Roots of Modern Urbanization in Japan," Working Paper No. 10, New Jersey Seminar on Asian Studies (1962) (unpublished). See also his "Urbanization and Population Pressure in Japan," *Pacific Affairs* (September 1958), pp. 275–285.

73. Leo A. Orleans, "The Recent Growth of China's Urban Population," *Geographical Review* (January 1959), pp. 43–57. In the 1953 census, 77 million were listed as "urban," but the definition of "urban" has not been made public and apparently no uniform standard was used in previous estimates (p. 44). If Orleans' projection is correct, China has more people living in cities than any country except the U. S. A. and the U. S. S. R.

74. S. D. Chang, "Some Aspects of the Urban Geography of the Chinese Hsien Capitol," *Annals*, Association of American Geographers (March 1961), pp. 23–45. Chang also has published an illuminating essay on "Historical Trends in Chinese Urbanization," *ibid.* (June 1963), pp. 109–143. The distribution of the *hsien* capitals over the face of China is astonishingly even, especially when China's orographic diversity is taken into account. See map in Chang, "Some Aspects . . . ," p. 28. At sub-urban levels, a

similar network appears in the "village fairs" or markets (as in the North Indian *hat*), as described, for example, in J. Spencer's "The Szechwan Village Fair," *Economic Geography* (January 1940), pp. 48–58.

75. Chang, *ibid.*, pp. 42–43. See also Chap. 3 of A. Boyd, *Chinese Architecture and Town Planning 1500 B.C.–A.D. 1911* (Chicago: University of Chicago Press, 1962) for some brief comments on this question.

76. E. T. Williams, "Open Ports of China," *Geographical Review*, 9 (1920), pp. 306–334. In the year of publication there were 120 treaty ports in China, many of them inland commercial centers. A more elaborate discussion of the treaty port can be found in: "China, The Inspectorate-General of Customs," *Decennial Reports 1922–31* (Shanghai: The Inspectorate-General of Customs, 1933).

77. R. Murphey, *Shanghai: Key to Modern China* (Cambridge: Harvard University Press, 1954). A briefer description of Shanghai is J. E. Orchard's "Shanghai," *Geographical Review* (January 1936), pp. 1–31.

78. N. S. Ginsburg, "Ch'ang-ch'un," *Economic Geography* (October 1947), pp. 290–307; N. S. Ginsburg, "Ch'ing-tao," *Economic Geography* (July 1948), pp. 181–200; J. E. Spencer, "Changing Chungking: The Rebuilding of an Old Chinese City," *Geographical Review* (January 1939), pp. 46–60.

79. G. T. Trewartha, "Chinese Cities: Origins and Functions," *Annals*, Association of American Geographers (March 1952), pp. 69–93; and his "Chinese Cities: Numbers and Distribution," *ibid.* (December 1951), pp. 331–347.

80. M. B. Ullman, "Cities of Mainland China: 1953 and 1958," *International Population Reports*, Series P-95, No. 59 (Washington: Bureau of the Census, 1961). A map of city distributions according to size classes is included.

81. See *ibid.*; T. Shabad, "The Population of China's Cities," *Geographical Review* (January 1959), pp. 32–42; J. S. Aird, "The Size, Composition, and Growth of the Population of Mainland China," *International Population Statistics Reports*, Series P-90, No. 15 (Washington: Bureau of the Census, 1961); J. P. Emerson, "Manpower Absorption in the Non-Agricultural Branches of the Economy of Communist China," *China Quarterly* (July–September 1961), pp. 69–84; Irene B. Taeuber, "China's Population: An Approach to Research," *Items* (June 1964), pp. 13–19.

82. For example, see C. W. Wen, "Chukiang: A Study in Urban Geography," *Ti-li Hsüeh-pao* (*Journal of the Geographical Society of China*, now *Acta Geographica Sinica*) (January 1948), pp. 14–20; J. S. Shen and M. Y. Sun, "Chengtu: A Study in Urban Geography," *Ti-li Hsüeh-pao* (December 1947), pp. 14–30; and C. C. Wang and F. L. Cheng, "The Urban Geography of Paotou," *Ti-li Tsa-chih* (*Geographical Journal*) (March 1937), pp. 1–27. Wang and Cheng classified about 25 per cent of the land area of Pao-t'ou as a contiguous commercial area and an equal amount as cultivated land, although the city was walled and a key transportation center.

83. See H. T. Fei, *China's Gentry: Essays in Rural Urban Relations* (Chicago: University of Chicago Press, 1953), Chap. 5; and R. Murphey, "The City as a Center of Change: Western Europe and China," *Annals*, Association of American Geographers (December 1954), pp. 349–362.

84. Ginsburg, "Ch'ang-ch'un," *op. cit.*

85. Ginsburg, "Ch'ing-tao," *op. cit.*

86. See, for example, C. S. Chen, "Cities and Rural Towns of Taiwan," *Research Report No. 48* (Taipei: National Taiwan University, Institute of Agricultural Geography, 1953) (in Chinese and English); C. S. Chen, "The Port City of Keelung," *Research Report No. 83* (Taipei: National Taiwan University, Fu-min Institute of Economic Development, 1958) (in English); and T. H. Sun, "Population Growth and Movement in the T'ai-pei Basin: A Demogeographical Survey and Analysis," *Geography and Industries,* 6, No. 2 (November 1961), pp. 169–243 (in Chinese with English summary). Chen and his collaborators also have issued a series of descriptive monographs on other cities in Chinese.

87. J. F. Gellert, "Geographische Beobachtungen in Chineschen Grossstädten," *Geographische Berichte* (October 1962), pp. 142–152.

88. The "Primate City" concept was first introduced by Mark Jefferson in his "Law of the Primate City," *Geographical Review* (April 1939), pp. 226–232. Recently, Brian Berry has viewed primacy as part of a process of change in urban hierarchies, that is, related, *inter alia,* to economic development, in "City-Size Distributions and Economic Development," *Economic Development and Cultural Change,* Part I (July 1961), pp. 573–588. In general, primacy *in Asia* appears to be associated with low levels of living, a colonial heritage, relatively small size of county and population, and lack of an urban tradition. It may also, as Edward Ullman suggests, be associated with the port function, by which larger and wealthier overseas hinterlands are tied in with less extensive and poorer national hinterlands (e.g., Singapore as the entrepôt for the Malaysian world). In fact, the entrepôt function in particular may stimulate urban growth far beyond expectations based on size of contiguous hinterlands (e.g., Cebu).

89. J. E. Spencer and W. L. Thomas, "The Hill Stations and Summer Resorts of the Orient," *Geographical Review* (October 1948), pp. 637–651; also, W. A. Withington, "Upland Resorts and Tourism in Indonesia; Some Recent Trends," *Geographical Review* (July 1961), pp. 418–423.

90. D. W. Fryer, "The Million City in Southeast Asia," *Geographical Review* (October 1953), pp. 474–494; N. S. Ginsburg, "The Great City in Southeast Asia," *American Journal of Sociology* (March 1955), pp. 455–462; Rhoads Murphey, "New Capitals of Asia," *Economic Development and Cultural Change* (April 1957), pp. 216–243.

91. A discussion of data deficiencies and field work difficulties appears in R. J. W. Neville, "An Urban Study of Pontian Kechil, South-West Malaya," *Journal of Tropical Geography* (October 1962), pp. 32–56.

92. E. L. Ullman, "Trade Centers and Tributary Areas of the Philippines," *Geographical Review* (April 1960), pp. 203–218. The author notes (p. 205) that an "extensive descriptive table of trade centers and tributary areas is available in mimeographed form upon request to the *Geographical Review.*" A supplementary article, which attempts to better define the "real," as opposed to the "census," populations of some 29 cities is J. E. Spencer's "The Cities of the Philippines," *Journal of Geography* (September 1958), pp. 288–294.

93. Hamzah Sendut, "Patterns of Urbanization in Malaya," *Journal of Tropical Geography* (October 1962), pp. 114–129; W. A. Withington, "The

Kotapradja or 'King Cities' of Indonesia," *Pacific Viewpoint* (March 1963), pp. 87–91. Withington observes that the "rank-size rule" cannot be applied conveniently to Indonesian cities. He also tabulates and maps the proportions of city populations that were Chinese and other foreign in 1930 and 1957.

94. For example, see O. H. K. Spate and L. Trueblood, "Rangoon: A Study in Urban Geography," *Geographical Review* (January 1942), pp. 56–73; E. H. G. Dobby, "Singapore: Town and Country," *Geographical Review* (January 1940), pp. 84–109; H. J. Heeren, "Urbanization of Jakarta," *Ekonomie dan Kenangan Indonesia* (November 1955), pp. 696–736; W. A. Withington, "Medan: Primary Regional Metropolis of Sumatra," *Journal of Geography* (February 1962), pp. 59–67.

95. B. W. Hodder, "Racial Groupings of Singapore," *Malayan Journal of Tropical Geography* (October 1953), pp. 25–36.

96. W. E. McIntrye, "The Retail Pattern of Manila," *Geographical Review* (January 1955), pp. 66–80.

97. A useful paper, however, is J. M. Fraser's "Town Planning and Housing in Singapore," *Town Planning Review* (January 1953), pp. 5–25. Several other reports on Manila, Saigon, and Jakarta were prepared as working papers for the UN-UNESCO Regional Seminar held at the Indian Institute of Public Administration in New Delhi, December 14–21, 1960. U.N., *Public Administration Problems of New and Rapidly Growing Towns in Asia* (Bangkok, 1962) (62, II, H.1).

98. Among these are, Barrington Kaye, *Upper Nankin Street, Singapore* (Singapore: University of Malaya Press, 1960); Jacques Amyot, *The Chinese Community of Manila*, Research Series No. 2 (Chicago: Philippine Studies Program, University of Chicago, 1960); Donald Willmot, *The Chinese of Semarang* (Ithaca: Cornell University Press, 1960).

99. W. A. Hanna, "Malaysia, A Federation in Prospect; Part VIII: Billets for Ballots," *Southeast Asia Series*, 10, No. 12 (New York: American Universities Field Staff, 1962), pp. 1–2.

10

On the Spatial Structure of Cities
in the Two Americas *

Leo F. Schnore

Introduction

The Committee on Urbanization was initially asked "to review critically the extant assumptions and generalizations regarding the phenomenon of urbanization, its determinants, concomitants, and consequences, including their applicability cross-culturally and historically."
As a result, a great deal of the Committee's attention has been devoted
to problems of comparative research. In a research context, of course,
"comparative" need not mean "cross-cultural," for truly comparative
studies may be confined to a single culture. Of necessity, however,
much of the Committee's discussion of comparative research has been
highly abstract and general. This chapter narrows the focus to deal
with some of the more concrete and specific problems involved in such
research, for it is confined to a limited portion of the urban literature
in which the cross-cultural applicability of one generalization has been
questioned.

Sociologists have been as vocal as anyone else in calling for cross-
cultural studies of urban phenomena.[1] Nevertheless, the discipline of
sociology has contributed relatively little toward the establishment of
"laws" of urbanization (in the sense of cross-cultural regularities), and
some of us doubt that such laws are to be found. Still, the sociological
literature contains some scattered contributions that are directly relevant to the kind of critical review the Committee has taken as one of
its major responsibilities.

Surveying this sociological literature, in search of materials for such
a critical review, one quickly gains the impression that a rather large
amount of empirical effort has been devoted to *the internal spatial*

structure of cities. This topic is not a sociological specialism by any means; geographers, economists, and others share an interest in the physical distribution of population and land uses within the urban agglomeration. For this reason alone, the subject of spatial structure seemed particularly appropriate for review by a group with multi-disciplinary representation.

In any event, the basic materials initially consulted were drawn almost exclusively from the American sociological literature. A few contributions by social anthropologists were included at the outset, simply because they appeared in sociological journals, but sources in archaeology, anthropology, urban geography, and urban land economics were not systematically examined until the fundamental outlines of the problem had been established.

More important limitations on the scope of the inquiry were the following.

1. The study was confined to an examination of the *internal* spatial structure of cities; there was no attention accorded to such important topics as city location, rural-urban relationships, urban dominance over the hinterland, or intercity relationships, as in the concepts of the "urban hierarchy" or system of cities.

2. The study was exclusively limited to the Western Hemisphere, and it focused on the similarities and differences between cities of "Anglo" and Latin America.

Whatever their disadvantages, these deliberate limitations should serve to fasten attention on concrete issues, both methodological and theoretical.

Sociologists and the Study of Space

Within sociology, one school of thought—human ecology—has been traditionally concerned with the analysis of urban spatial structure. Space was the special object of attention in the "classical" ecological viewpoint that developed at the University of Chicago in the 1920's, an approach that is best represented by the work of Robert E. Park and Ernest W. Burgess and their students, R. D. McKenzie and James A. Quinn. To use McKenzie's formulation, "Human ecology deals with the spatial aspects of the symbiotic relations of human beings and human institutions." [2] Even the more recent versions of human ecology, wherein community structure is said to be the focus of attention, continue to place considerable emphasis on spatial patterns.[3]

Similarly, one sociologist's name has been particularly prominent in the literature dealing with urban spatial structure. We refer, of course, to Professor Burgess, whose "concentric zonal hypothesis" is the best known formulation of the problem if sheer number of references constitutes a reliable index. For purposes of discussion, we may assume some familiarity with the ecological viewpoint in general and with the Burgess hypothesis in particular. Nevertheless, it will be useful to review some of the main elements in the Burgess hypothesis, together with certain underlying assumptions, in order to point up the significance of the contrasts that have been observed in cities north and south of the Rio Grande.

The Burgess Hypothesis: An Exegesis and Critique

In December 1923 Professor Burgess delivered a paper entitled "The Growth of the City" at the annual meetings of the American Sociological Society.[4] In this brief paper he enunciated for the first time the major outlines of the concentric zonal hypothesis. Some five years later he restated the hypothesis at somewhat greater length, and we quote from this extended version in order to suggest the content of the various zones:

> Zone I: The Central Business District. At the center of the city as the focus of its commercial, social, and civic life is situated the Central Business District. The heart of this district is the downtown retail district with its department stores, its smart shops, its office buildings, its clubs, its banks, its hotels, its theatres, its museums, and its headquarters of economic, social, civic, and political life. Encircling this area of work and play is the less well-known Wholesale Business District with its "market," its warehouses, and storage buildings.
>
> Zone II: The Zone in Transition. Surrounding the Central Business District are areas of residential deterioration caused by the encroaching of business and industry from Zone I. This may therefore be called a Zone in Transition, with a factory district for its inner belt and an outer ring of retrogressing neighborhoods, of first-settlement immigrant colonies, of rooming-house districts, of homeless-men areas, of resorts of gambling, bootlegging, sexual vice, and of breeding-places of crime. In this area of physical deterioration and social disorganization our studies show the greatest concentration of cases of poverty, bad housing, juvenile delinquency, family disintegration, physical and mental disease. As families and individuals prosper, they escape from this

area into Zone III beyond, leaving behind as marooned a residuum of the defeated, leaderless, and helpless.

Zone III: The Zone of Independent Workingmen's Homes. This third broad urban ring is in Chicago, as well as in other northern industrial cities, largely constituted by neighborhoods of second immigrant settlement. Its residents are those who desire to live near but not too close to their work. In Chicago, it is a housing area neither of tenements, apartments, nor of single dwellings; its boundaries have been roughly determined by the plotting of the two-flat dwelling, generally of frame construction, with the owner living on the lower floor with a tenant on the other. While the father works in the factory, the son and daughter typically have jobs in the Loop, attend dance halls and motion pictures in the bright-light areas, and plan upon marriage to set up homes in Zone IV.

Zone IV: The Zone of Better Residences. Extending beyond the neighborhoods of second immigrant settlements, we come to the Zone of Better Residences in which the great middle-class of native-born Americans live, small business men, professional people, clerks, and salesmen. Once communities of single homes, they are becoming, in Chicago, apartment-house and residential-hotel areas. Within these areas at strategic points are found local business centers of such growing importance that they have been called "satellite Loops." The typical constellation of business and recreational units includes a bank, one or more United Cigar Stores, a drug store, a high-class restaurant, an automobile display row, and a so-called "wonder" motion-picture theater. With the addition of a dancing palace, a cabaret, and a smart hotel, the satellite Loop also becomes a "bright-light" area attracting a city-wide attendance. In this zone men are outnumbered by women, independence in voting is frequent, newspapers and books have wide circulation, and women are elected to the state legislature.

Zone V: The Commuters' Zone. Out beyond the areas of better residence is a ring of encircling small cities, towns, and hamlets, which, taken together, constitute the Commuters' Zone. These are also, in the main, dormitory suburbs, because the majority of men residing there spend the day at work in the Loop (Central Business District), returning only for the night. Thus the mother and the wife become the center of family life. If the Central Business District is predominantly a homeless-men's region; the rooming house district, the habitat of the emancipated family; the area of first-immigrant settlement, the natural soil of the patriarchal family transplanted from Europe; the Zone of Better Residences with its apartment houses and residential hotels, the favorable environment for the equalitarian family; then the Commuters' Zone is without question the domain of the matricentric family. The communities in this Commuters' Zone are probably the most highly segregated of any in the entire metropolitan region, including in their range the entire gamut from an incorporated village run in the interests of crime and vice, such as Burnham, to Lake Forest, with its wealth, culture, and public spirit.[5]

This five-zone scheme is the most familiar version of the Burgess hypothesis, although it should be noted that Burgess sometimes identified two additional zones lying beyond the built-up area of the city: "The sixth zone is constituted by the agricultural districts lying within the circle of commutation. . . . The seventh zone is the hinterland of the metropolis." [6]

Exegesis

1. The first point to be understood is that Burgess thought of his hypothesis as an "ideal" or "constructed" type; in his words, "All American cities which I have observed or studied approximate in greater or less degree this ideal construction; no one, however . . . perfectly exemplifies it." [7]

2. More important, the Burgess scheme must be seen as an attempt to deal with the reorganization of spatial relations that occurs with *growth* and radial expansion. The very title of his original essay—"The Growth of the City"—seems indicative of his intentions, but he was quite explicit on this point:

> The outstanding fact of modern society is the growth of great cities. . . . Almost as overt a process [as aggregation], that of *expansion*, has been investigated from a different and very practical point of view by groups interested in city planning, zoning, and regional surveys. Even more significant than the increasing density of urban population is its correlative tendency to overflow, and so to extend over wider areas, and to incorporate these areas into a larger communal life. This paper, therefore, will treat first of the expansion of the city, and then of the less-known processes of urban metabolism and mobility which are closely related to expansion.[8]

Further, Burgess observed that "the most evident process, looking at community growth ecologically, is that of radial expansion from the center." [9] Elsewhere, he asserted that "every community as it grows expands outward from its center." [10] And, in referring to the stylized map of Chicago that accompanied the first published statement of the hypothesis, he noted, "This chart represents an ideal construction of the tendencies of any town or city to expand radially from its central business district. . . . This chart brings out clearly the main fact of expansion, namely, the tendency of each inner zone to extend its area by the invasion of the next outer zone." [11] Thus it is clear that Burgess conceived his hypothesis as a "growth model," or a statement couched entirely in terms of *process,* and not as a static or cross-sectional representation of urban spatial structure.[12]

3. It is also important to note that Burgess recognized a number of *"distorting factors"* which may influence the concentric zonal arrangement. His most succinct enumeration of these factors is as follows:

> If radial extension were the only factor affecting the growth of American cities, every city in this country would exhibit a perfect exemplification of these five urban zones. But since other factors affect urban development [such as] situation, site, natural and artificial barriers, survival of an earlier use of a district, prevailing city plan and its system of transportation, many distortions and modifications of this pattern are actually found. Nevertheless, so universal and powerful is the force of expansion outward from the center that in every city these zones can be more or less clearly delimited.[13]

With reference to Chicago, he points out that "the lake front makes an important alteration in the pattern. In place of concentric circles are semicircles or belts. Other lake cities, like Cleveland and Detroit, exhibit this same variation." [14] More recently, Burgess has commented on these matters in greater detail.

> My name has been identified with a zonal theory of growth of the city as it would be interpreted graphically *if only one factor, namely, radial expansion, determined city growth.* The critics of this theory have been rather obtuse in not realizing that this theory is an ideal construction, and that in actual observation many factors other than radial expansion influence growth. . . . At no time in advancing this ideal construct of the effect of radial growth have I denied the existence of other possible factors which might also be regarded as ideal constructs. For example,

sectors, climatic conditions, types of street plan, barriers (hills, lakes, mountains, railroads) can each have an effect upon the formation of city structure.[15]

4. Finally, there is the matter of the *generality* of the hypothesis. In a passage quoted above, Burgess asserted that "so universal and powerful is the force of expansion outward from the center that in every city these zones can be more or less clearly delimited." This statement is somewhat misleading, for at other points Burgess makes it quite clear that he is speaking only of cities in the United States. For example,

> The studies that have given us this new knowledge of the city have come largely from relatively new approaches, those of economic and social history, urban economics, and human ecology. The materials of these studies tend to show that the city has a natural organization determined by the play of forces, economic and social, which with minor variations seem to be the same for all American cities.[16]

Assumptions

In addition to assuming a growing city, it is necessary to recognize that the Burgess hypothesis contains some additional implicit assumptions. The most important of these have been identified by Quinn.

1. First, Quinn notes that a certain degree of *heterogeneity* is assumed. In his view, the zonal pattern requires the presence of widely contrasting types of population within the city:

> (1) a large foreign population characterized by different degrees of assimilation, (2) members of different races, and (3) men and women who pursue different occupations, who enjoy different standards of living, and who control different volumes of purchasing power.[17]

It is doubtful that all of these elements need be present, but a certain degree of heterogeneity is obviously required in order for differentiated zones to appear. For example, social class gradations must actually exist if the residential population is to be sorted into bands occupied by different socioeconomic strata.

2. Quinn also observes that the hypothesis assumes a particular kind of *economic base*, that is, a mixed "commercial-industrial" city.[18] The land uses described as characteristic of the inner zones (central business district, warehouse and wholesale business district, industrial or

factory areas) make it clear that commerce and industry are assumed to be present.

3. Quinn has also commented on a range of *economic and cultural factors* that are assumed in the Burgess scheme. For example, Quinn believes that it assumes private ownership of property, economic competition, and the existence of specialized economic institutions occupying distinctive buildings and areas. With respect to transportation, "Burgess took for granted the operation of an efficient system of transportation, which enables the population of an urban agglomeration to utilize regularly and in person the specialized services of spatially separated institutions. . . . Burgess assumed, further, that transportation is equally easy, rapid, and cheap in every direction within the city." [19]

4. One might add that the Burgess hypothesis is based on certain assumptions concerning *the geometry of space*. It assumes a single center, and takes for granted the fact that physical area increases as the square of radial distance away from that point; space is thus in shortest supply near the center, and increasingly abundant as one moves toward the periphery. The hypothesis also implicitly requires an *economic* assumption concerning space. It is that the central areas are more highly valued, by virtue of (a) their short supply and (b) their greater accessibility to the area as a whole, which makes them subject to considerable demand. It is believed that competition for these highly valued sites will result. This competition is viewed as the mainspring of change in spatial structure, and it is assumed that a "sifting and sorting" of community units will ensue, with physical positions largely determined by economic ability to compete for space.

5. The Burgess hypothesis also seems to require certain assumptions regarding *occupancy patterns* on the part of the various socioeconomic strata making up the community. It seems to assume that the more favored classes will ordinarily preempt the newer and more desirable housing areas; with radial expansion, these areas typically have been located at the periphery in American cities. At the very least, the hypothesis assumes a high degree of locational freedom on the part of the wealthy, who may occupy practically any area, as compared with the lower classes, who are much more severely restricted with respect to residential choices.

Criticisms

It must be noted that the Burgess hypothesis has not gone without criticism. A number of the specific points at issue were reviewed by Quinn over twenty years ago, and it is not necessary to repeat all of them here.[20] Certain other objections have been raised since that time, however, and it will be worthwhile to consider some of the broad *types* of criticism that have been advanced, including both newer and older issues.

1. One line of criticism objects to the *zonal concept* itself. It has been most explicitly stated by Alihan, who examined data (presented by Burgess himself) on various "gradients" with distance from the center of Chicago:

> A relatively continuous progression or regression of rates is manifested along radial lines that cut the successive zones. In other words, the five zones, as presented by Burgess, cease to be sharply demarcated from each other, as they appear to be when described in terms of qualitative factors. . . . The standard zonal boundaries do not serve as demarcations in respect of the ecological or social phenomena they circumscribe, but are arbitrary divisions. They can be treated only as convenient methodological devices for the classification of data under smaller divisions than the total area included in a particular study. The zone can have significance only if it marks a distinction of gradients or between gradients. Otherwise, if the gradients are as continuous as the name implies, the zonal lines can be drawn indifferently at any radius from the center. Yet Burgess' description of the five zones clearly indicates that ecologists envisage these zones as distinct units, differentiated in terms of numerous factors.[21]

If one accepts the validity of gradients, then, zones cannot be distinguished as internally homogeneous land use categories.

2. Another closely related criticism that has been advanced has to do with this *zonal homogeneity*. The Burgess scheme, of course, posits five relatively homogeneous zones, although a number of different land uses (commercial, industrial, and residential) are said to characterize the first two zones, and the last zone is said to contain a wide variety of subcommunities, ranging from high to low in income. But other observers have detected considerable heterogeneity in the remaining zones as well. Criticisms on this point have been most explicitly presented by Davie, who conducted an intensive case study of New Haven, and by Hoyt, who surveyed residential rent patterns in a large number of cities, developing his well-known "sector theory." [22]

3. Closely related to the foregoing is the criticism based on the discovery of *discrepant land uses*. These are uses that are not predicted by the hypothesis, and they are best exemplified in the results of a case study of Boston presented by Firey. He found an upper-class resi-

dential area very near the commercial core of the city, and the highly valued land in the downtown area was also occupied by such "sacred sites" as Boston Common and various colonial burying-grounds.[23] Although these might be regarded as examples of the "survival of an earlier use of a district"—cited by Burgess as a distorting factor—they are clearly not stated as typical of the central zone in the Burgess theory itself.

4. Finally, there have been numerous criticisms concerning the *generality* of the hypothesis. As we have indicated, Burgess believed that the zonal pattern found expression in all American cities, though Quinn and others have narrowed the coverage to growing "commercial-industrial" cities of the United States.[24] The question here is one of "goodness of fit." Among the studies that have been conducted in this country, many have been interpreted by their authors as offering at least rough confirmation of the Burgess hypothesis.[25] On the other hand, several studies have been presented as refutations of the Burgess hypothesis.[26] The most recent inquiry—one that purports to offer the first systematic statistical comparison of the Burgess and Hoyt hypotheses— offers some support for both the zonal and sector hypotheses.[27]

If one moves beyond the borders of the United States, a number of additional studies can be examined. Even restricting attention to the American sociological literature, one can find an account of the "ecology" of at least one city in every major region of the world.[28] If one again employs a purely quantitative index, however, the greatest attention has been given to urban centers in Central and South America. As a consequence, we shall confine our attention to studies of Latin American cities, focusing on those portions that deal more or less directly with *the validity of the zonal hypothesis as a description of the residential distribution of social classes*. Although sharply circumscribed in coverage, this procedure should facilitate achieving our goal, for many of the methodological and theoretical issues would be the same, no matter where we started.

Seven Studies of Latin American Cities

Not only do we have the advantage of a larger number of concrete cases from Latin America, but we also have a single culture area that is commonly described as sharply contrasting with that of "Anglo" America. We shall begin with a review of seven studies that span three decades. Taken individually, they provide little more than descriptions of particular cities—descriptions that vary greatly in detail. Taken together and cumulatively, however, they represent at least an effort in the direction of comparative urban research, and they warrant our attention for that reason alone.[29]

All of these studies have a bearing—direct or indirect—on the cross-cultural applicability of the Burgess formulation, but one word of caution is in order. The nature of the materials to be reviewed obliges us to limit attention to only one phase of the Burgess hypothesis, that is, the portion that is concerned with *the distribution of various socioeconomic strata* between broad zones surrounding the core of the city. In general, we have noted that Burgess posited *a direct relationship between socioeconomic status and distance from the center*. In other words, the lower-status groups are said to be found nearest the center, the higher-status groups at the periphery. In the stylized map of Chicago that accompanied his original presentation, the existence of expensive residential hotels and apartment houses ("The Gold Coast") along the lake front indicated Burgess's awareness of an exception to this broad generalization, and other qualifications were explicitly stated in his later writings, but these may be more appropriately introduced in the sections that follow. Let us turn directly to the Latin American studies, first examining their descriptive findings, and then turning to certain methodological and theoretical considerations that these studies bring to the fore.

Hansen's Study, 1934

The first report on the "ecology" of a Latin American city was apparently Hansen's description of Merida, the site of Redfield's famous study of the folk culture of Yucatán. Hansen indicated that the spatial pattern in Merida had undergone striking changes in the course of population growth and organizational change. In brief, Hansen traced the broad outlines of a shift away from a "traditional pattern" that had been established during the colonial period. As he described it,

> The basic fact of the traditional pattern was the division between center and *barrios*. . . . The city was laid out around a central square. . . . This area of Spanish residence was the center. Some distance farther out, leaving room for the expansion of this center, areas were set aside on which the Indians might settle. These were the *barrios*. As the city grew, the center encroached upon the *barrios* and the Indians moved farther out.[30]

In Merida, according to Hansen, this traditional spatial arrangement persisted in all its essentials until about the turn of the present century, when "the center-*barrio* pattern began to break down rapidly." [31] Finally, and in contrast to the older spatial order—in which higher-status elements (the Spanish) inhabited the central area and lower-status groups (Indians) occupied the periphery—there ultimately emerged "an urban pattern approaching that of northern [American] cities." Thus "the center is characteristically a business district rather than a residential district of the aristocracy. . . . The wealthy occupy fashionable suburbs and there are certain streets to which the middle class drifts." [32]

All in all, the earlier relationship between social status and residential location with reference to the center tended to be *reversed* in the course of time, and to assume the "North American pattern" described by Burgess. The entire process was viewed by Hansen as a direct response to population growth and changes in social and economic organization, including the emergence of a "true" middle class. It is noteworthy that his interpretation was in general conformity with the "classical" ecological approach of Park and Burgess, for (in Hansen's words) "the basis of this sorting process is purely economic." [33]

Subsequent Studies, 1944–1954

Since Hansen's pioneering study, six other fairly detailed reports on individual Latin American cities have appeared in the American sociological journals. Taken together, these studies have produced remarkably similar empirical results. *All of these subsequent reports contain the main themes found in Hansen's original essay on Merida.* (1) All of the authors comment on the existence of the "traditional" or "colonial" pattern, in which higher-status groups tend to be found near the center. (2) In every case, however, this pattern is reported to be in one or another stage of "breakdown." (3) There is an apparent tendency for all of the cities—in Bolivia, Mexico, and Guatemala—to shift in the general direction of "the North American pattern."

Since this last point may be regarded as critical, it deserves some documentation. Such a shift is explicitly noted by Leonard in his discussion of La Paz.[34] Although the Hawthorns write that "the middle and upper class development of the suburbs has not proceeded as far as in the majority of Latin American cities," they report that it is definitely under way in Sucre.[35] Even in Oaxaca (a smaller provincial center in southern Mexico) Hayner indicates that there is some evidence that "suggests the beginning of an outward movement by the 'better' families." [36] As for Mexico City, Hayner observes that "the metropolis seems to be shifting toward a basic configuration similar to that of the cities of the United States." [37] In another article on Oaxaca, Hayner remarks in passing that "Guadalajara, second in size, with about 250,000 inhabitants, and Puebla, with 150,000, show changes similar to those in the capital but not so extreme." [38] A somewhat different perspective on Guadalajara's experience is provided by the Dotsons, writing ten years later; they report that the city "is growing rapidly and the breakdown of the classical pattern is far advanced. Yet here an essentially new ecological form . . . seems to be emerging —a form which is different from either the colonial pattern or that typical of North American cities." [39] Finally, Caplow also indicates that Guatemala City has departed considerably from the traditional pattern, and that it is moving toward the North American configuration.[40] Going further, he observes that 'if we arrange . . . the Middle American cities upon which some ecological data are available in order of size, it is at once apparent that the larger the community the further it has departed from the traditional colonial pattern, and this rough relationship appears to hold in some detail." [41]

So much for the major findings. Upon casual scrutiny, the evidence provided by these studies might seem to represent a rough cross-cultural verification of the zonal hypothesis; certainly these studies seem to suggest that there are forces at work in growing Latin American cities that are altering their shapes in the general direction of the Burgess model, at least with respect to the residential distribution of broad socioeconomic strata. Such inferences should not be drawn at this time, for reasons to be suggested in the following pages. For one thing, the various authors cited above do *not* present their material as confirmation of the zonal hypothesis. In fact, some of these articles have been rather critical of the "classical" ecological approach in general, and of the zonal hypothesis in particular. Among the articles reviewed here, those by Hayner, Leonard, and the Hawthorns do not contain such criticisms but the results of their studies have been taken by others (including Caplow and the Dotsons) as evidence that is contrary to "classical" ecological principles. It would be more profitable, however, to defer discussion of theoretical issues for the moment, in order to focus more explicitly upon methodological matters.

Methodological Considerations

First, these six studies have a number of broad methodological features in common; three of them should be noted at the outset.

1. As indicated, all six reports consist of *case studies of individual cities*. None of these studies examines a sample of cities, and only one of these writers appears to have studied more than one Latin American city; Hayner's reports on Mexico City and Oaxaca are presented as contrasting cases.

2. A number of these reports are based on what may be called

"byproduct" studies. Thus the report on Sucre by the Hawthorns grew out of a field study of stratification.[42] Caplow reports that his original intention was to study perceptions of class structure in Guatemala City, but that he was unable to carry it out.[43] Hayner's study of Mexico City was part of a broader investigation of the spatial distribution of crime.[44] Similarly, his study of Oaxaca was focused on patterns of historical change in the various social classes.[45] Again, the report on Guadalajara by the Dotsons seems to have developed out of a survey study of associational memberships.[46] Only Leonard fails to mention another study being carried on at the same time.

3. Although almost all of the reports contain one or more maps, there is *relatively little use made of statistical data,* other than census reports and estimates of city sizes. In some cases, such data were probably lacking altogether; in others, poor quality was probably a paramount consideration. In any event, detailed statistics are not shown in any of these articles. The only writers reporting on land values (Leonard on La Paz and Hayner on Mexico City and Oaxaca) indicate that they found the pattern observed in North American cities by Burgess and others, that is, land values declining with distance from the center. Caplow indicates that "such a study [of land values] was contemplated at the outset, but the resources of the investigator proved inadequate." [47] The Dotsons mention that they "obtained and plotted assessed land values for every block in the city." These data are not reported, however, for the Dotsons indicate that "marked disparities between these values and actual residential use showed this index to be untrustworthy for Guadalajara." They go on to note that "rapid expansion in recent years has brought with it a speculative fever, and *land values, as in the United States, tend to reflect distance from the commercial center* more closely than the nature of residential property." [48]

Theoretical Considerations

Another series of observations has to do with the *independent and dependent variables* that appear in the various analyses under review. This task is much more difficult. The reader of these reports must exercise a great deal of judgment—and indulge in some plain guesswork—in order to determine each author's views regarding the analytical status of broad "factors" or "variables" under discussion. A number of the presentations are extremely informal, descriptive, and discursive. However, we may identify the variables in a quasisystematic fashion for the purposes of our discussion.

THE DEPENDENT VARIABLE

None of these writers sets out to explain the total pattern of land uses. Although the amount of detail varies from study to study, each author discusses *changing patterns of residential distribution.* For this reason, we may take this phenomenon as the dependent variable that is common to all of the reports. As noted above, all of these reports emphasize a shift away from the traditional colonial pattern, but there are only passing references to land uses other than residential in most of them. (This narrow focus obviously prevents a full-scale "test" of the zonal hypothesis. Whatever the deficiencies of the original Burgess formulation, it was an attempt to deal with the total pattern of land uses in growing cities. To the extent that data on other than residential uses are omitted, these Latin American studies constitute only partial "tests" of the Burgess hypothesis. This is only one reason for reserving judgment on the question of the "cross-cultural validation" of the hypothesis, but it is an important reason.)

Another noteworthy feature of these reports, taken as a whole, is the *uneven coverage given to the factors that Burgess himself either* (a) *treated as "independent variables" or* (b) *assumed as "constant" for his purposes.* The materials to be presented here demonstrate that we do not yet have a real test of the hypothesis, even in its partial form.

INDEPENDENT VARIABLES

Above all else, the Burgess hypothesis was formulated as an ideal-typical description of *growing* cities. In addition, perusal of the original essay and examination of later statements by Burgess reveals that he placed special stress on local *topography* and *transportation* as important "distorting factors." Although all the reports under discussion give at least a few census figures or population estimates, and most of them devote at least brief passages to descriptions of the local terrain, there is very little information to be found in them concerning the availability of public and private means of transportation, costs, ease of movement in various directions, and so on. Thus only two out of three critical factors are given coverage that is anywhere near completeness.

CONSTANTS

"The "constants" are a bit more difficult to identify, mainly because of the informality with which Burgess presented his own hypothesis. As we have indicated, however, a number of factors—growth, heterogeneity, a certain type of economic base, and the like—are either explicitly or implicitly assumed. For our purposes, the assumption with respect to social classes is especially pertinent, for we have arbitrarily identified changing patterns of residential distribution on the part of social classes as the dependent variable that can be found in all of the Latin American studies under review. Further, we have pointed out that a "breakdown" and tendency toward reversal of the traditional colonial pattern is mentioned in every case. The higher strata, formerly concentrated near the central plaza, are said to be moving out, whereas the lower strata appear to be moving in; finally a middle class (or classes) must be occupying distinct areas of residence. The differentiation of social classes would thus appear to be a central concern.

In this light, however, the reports are all disappointing in some degree, in that they fail to provide a clear indication of the number of classes that might be recognized, the relative sizes of these classes, and (most importantly) changes therein. Hansen's 1934 report on Merida (which is cited by most of the later writers) gave a rather large role to the emergence of a middle class in effecting changes in residential patterns, but this potentially important lead was not followed. Better reports on these matters are given for the smallest centers (Oaxaca and Sucre), where the authors (Hayner and the Hawthorns) were primarily engaged in field studies dealing with certain historical aspects of stratification.

Closely connected is the question of the economic base. As noted, Quinn has asserted that the Burgess hypothesis assumes a mixed "commercial-industrial" city. Now in view of the relative recency of industrialization in Mexico, Bolivia, and Guatemala, at least a rough sketch of the economic base of each city, and changes therein, would be highly desirable. Again, however, the available reports on the Latin American cities are extremely uneven in their coverage. Perhaps the authors assume that their readers are sufficiently familiar with these places. In any event, most of these cities were exhibiting rather rapid growth during the periods in which they were under observation, and the possible relevance of changes in the economic base for changes in patterns of residential distribution makes it rather regrettable that fuller information is not provided.

Table 1 summarizes the presence or absence of information on these five broad factors—population growth, topography, transportation, class structure, and economic base. Whether treated as an independent variable or a "constant," each of these factors seems to be potentially relevant in determining patterns of residential distribution and changes in those patterns. Aside from the inconsistency of coverage, the most notable feature of this summary tabulation is clearly the relative ab-

TABLE 1. SUMMARY OF CHARACTERISTICS REPORTED FOR SELECTED LATIN AMERICAN CITIES

Authors* and Dates of Publication	City	Date and Source†	City Size	Average Annual Growth‡	Publication Contains Descriptions of:			
					Topography	Transportation	Class Structure	Economic Base
Hayner (1945)	Mexico City	1930c 1940c 1944e	1,029,068 1,448,422 1,699,955	3.38%	Yes	No	No	No
Dotson-Dotson (1954)	Guadalajara	1940c 1950e	229,200 378,400	4.91%	Yes	Brief references only	No	No
Leonard (1948)	La Paz	1928? 1942?	135,768 301,450	5.41%	Yes	Brief references only	No	No
Caplow (1949)	Guatemala City	1940c 1948e	186,000 230,000	2.64%	Yes	Brief references only	No	No
Hansen (1934)	Merida	1895c 1930c	50,000 85,148	1.48%	No §	Brief references only	Yes	Yes
Hawthorn-Hawthorn (1948)	Sucre	1930c 1942?	27,508 30,000	0.72%	Yes	No	Yes	Yes
Hayner (1944)	Oaxaca	1940c	29,306	Unknown	No §	Yes	Yes	No

* For full citations, see note 29 at the end of this chapter.
† Population data are those reported in the article; the sources are (e)stimates or (c)ensus reports.
‡ Implied average annual growth rates computed from the population figures reported in the article.
§ Both Merida and Oaxaca are located on level sites, the latter in a fairly large valley; this probably accounts for the lack of attention to topographic features.

sence of detailed information concerning the class structures, economic bases, and transportation systems of these cities.

The last theoretical consideration to be discussed may be regarded as crucial for our purposes, since it is central to any cross-cultural comparisons. In the course of restating his hypothesis, Burgess explicitly limited it to cities in the United States. To the extent that he did not attempt to apply it to urban areas in other parts of the world, he avoided *the problem of cultural differences*. Culture was thus implicitly assumed to be a constant, and variations in the spatial patterns that could be observed among United States cities were presumably to be explained in terms of variations in growth, topography, transportation, and so on—factors that complicate or distort the ideal-typical zonal arrangement.

As we have noted, Quinn has remarked that the hypothesis assumes a number of "economic and cultural factors," including private ownership and control of property and freedom of competition, and he has raised some interesting questions: "Would cultures without these characteristics tend to produce zones? If so, what ones? How do respective cultural factors tend to affect the spatial pattern of the city?" [49] Neither Quinn nor anyone else has attempted a systematic answer to these important questions. However, students of Latin American urbanization have given some attention to culture as an independent variable. It seems to be the judgment of some of the writers under review that differences between "Anglo" and Latin American culture really constitute the major explanation of the differences between the city patterns observed in the two Americas. Commenting on the differences between Guadalajara and North American cities, the Dotsons remark that "an answer may lie in the cultural values conditioning urban ecological processes north and south of the Rio Grande. . . . We suggest—although adequate proof is lacking—that upper- and middle-class Mexicans have a quite different view of urban life." [50] In a somewhat less cautious vein, Caplow asserts:

> The basic question raised by all ecological research, namely, what relation exists between the spatial community structure and the social organization associated with it, assumes additional interest in this case [Guatemala City] as soon as it can be demonstrated that growth under certain cultural conditions did not involve the ecological processes which the student of urban life in the United States takes for granted. [51]

Caplow's conclusions are worth reproducing in detail, since they contain the most explicit statement of the case for culture as a critical variable:

> The literature of urban geography and urban sociology has a tendency to project as universals those characteristics of urbanism with which European and American students are most familiar. Thus, since a large proportion of all urban research has concerned itself with Chicago, there was until recently a tendency to ascribe to all cities characteristics which now appear to be specific to Chicago and other communities closely resembling it in history and economic function.
>
> In the United States, almost all urban growth has been characterized by the rapid and uncontrolled expansion of the community and by unregulated competition for land. To a lesser extent this has been true also of modern Europe. It has not been true at all of Guatemala City. . . .
>
> In any event, the Middle American data strongly suggest that we have barely begun to describe and classify the possible varieties of urban organization and are therefore still unable to predict the complete range of alternatives open to increasingly urban societies like our own.[52]

Although it tends to overstate the case for "culture" as a relevant variable, this passage raises a serious question that requires close examination: *the extent to which it is possible to formulate "laws" of urbanization that hold for more than a single culture.* Before turning to this central issue, however, it is necessary to consider some additional materials on Latin American cities in order to determine whether or not our preliminary review—confined to the sociological literature —has yielded a seriously biased sample of cases.

Other Studies of Latin American Cities

In order to extend the range of our inquiry a large number of additional sources were examined. The search was initiated by consulting the bibliographies compiled on an annual basis in *The Handbook of Latin American Studies,* the "External Research" reports of the Department of State, *Population Index,* and the *Interamerican Bibliographical Review.* Other invaluable sources were the comprehensive bibliographies assembled by Guzman and Bazzanella.[53]

In all, over fifty additional studies were examined. It is literally impossible to summarize the detailed results of these investigations. They were conducted by representatives of a number of disciplines—geography, economics, sociology, anthropology, and archaeology—and the topical coverage varied considerably. Most of them were case studies of individual cities and towns. Some had no direct reference to spatial patterns.[54] In addition to monographs and articles, various planning papers and land use maps were examined. Finally, the geographic coverage turned out to be extremely uneven.[55] These materials were so diverse that we can only hope to accomplish two tasks: first, we can indicate the extent to which these additional materials *confirm or deny* the patterns observed in the seven studies that were initially reviewed; second, we can indicate some *additional problems or issues* that this broader search brought to our attention.

The Generality of the Patterns Previously Observed

The supplementary review made it abundantly clear that the seven highly selected sociological studies examined in the intial phase of this inquiry did not present a distorted picture of Latin American city structure. First of all, elements of the "traditional" plaza-centered pattern are almost perfectly ubiquitous in all but the newest cities of Latin America. Second, there is very frequent reference to changes in the direction of the "North American pattern"; although direct references to the Burgess zonal hypothesis are relatively rare, it is clear that a movement of the higher socioeconomic classes to *parts* of the periphery is under way in a very large number of the growing cities of Latin America. Third, it is clear that the increasing industrialization of many of these cities is playing an important role in reshaping their land use patterns. Finally, it is evident that an accretion of jerry-built peripheral slums still characterizes most of the larger cities of the region. Living conditions and levels of health and sanitation in these outlying slums are generally described as extremely low, and municipal officials seem powerless in their efforts to turn the tide.

As the end of this supplementary survey drew near, the writer encountered two works indicating that the major elements of the "traditional Latin American pattern" were far more general than he had originally supposed. The first source was the sweeping historical survey by Comhaire and Cahnman; consider, for example, the following passage concerning the spatial structure of European cities prior to the nineteenth century:

> In the European baroque town, everything is oriented around the palace. As in the middle ages the prestige-accented quarters

of the burghers were located around the market place because it was the focal point in the city, so had the baroque-age aristocracy its townhouses erected in the vicinity of the palace. In both instances the middle classes lived farther away from the center of town and the lower classes settled in the least desirable locations, for instance along the river banks, where sanitary conditions left much to be desired. On the outskirts were miserable hovels. For reasons that transcend the scope of this chapter this ecological pattern is reversed in contemporary cities.[56]

The second source was the massive comparative study by Sjoberg. His findings with respect to the "ecology" of preindustrial cities—past and present—were as follows:

> Concentrated in the city's "central" area (often coterminous with the physical center, but not necessarily so) are the most prominent governmental and religious edifices and usually the main market. . . .
>
> The preindustrial city's central area is notable also as the chief residence of the elite. . . . The disadvantaged members of the city fan out toward the periphery, with the very poorest and the outcastes living in the suburbs, the farthest removed from the center. Houses toward the city's fringes are small, flimsily constructed, often one-room, hovels into which whole families crowd. . . .[57]

Referring to archaeological, historical, and contemporary evidence from all of the major regions of the world, Sjoberg suggests that the available materials "all confirm the universality of this land use pattern in the non-industrial civilized world." [58] It would thus appear that the "traditional Latin American pattern"—one which has been identified as special to one culture area—is highly general to cities of a broad type, namely the preindustrial.

There are still controversial points at issue. Speaking of Pompeii, for example, Cahnman refers to "a general rule in urban ecology," as follows: "The upper classes tend to reside near the core of the city in times of insecurity but on the rim of the city in times of prosperity and peace." [59] Sjoberg has questioned this assertion.[60] At the same time, Sjoberg himself has called attention to the peripheral location of "the summer homes or ancillary dwellings of the elite" and to the fact that the center is "the best-protected sector of the city, often enclosed by a wall of its own, whereas residence on the periphery is hazardous in time of war or in the face of the recurrent banditry." [61]

Nevertheless, the available evidence points to a high degree of regularity in the residential distribution of broad social classes—a regularity that is all the more remarkable in view of the great cultural differences and wide diversity of environmental features on view in different times and places.

Some Additional Problems

The extended survey of the Latin American urban literature brought two additional issues to the fore. The first concerns *the role of conscious planning in the spatial structure of cities*. The principal reason for the emergence of this issue is the fact that many towns and cities of Latin America were founded by the Spanish during the colonial era. As Rippy has observed, "A conspicuous feature of Spanish colonization was the planting of towns and municipal institutions. Spaniards disliked the isolation of rural life and preferred to live in urban communities. There were some 200 towns in Spanish America by 1574 and perhaps 250 by 1600." [62] The significance of this historical development lies in the fact that towns were established in accordance with the famous Laws of the Indies.[63]

These laws prescribed a grid pattern centered upon a dominant plaza, and they defined with considerable clarity the proper location of public buildings, both religious and secular; they also recognized the connotations of prestige that attached to physical proximity to the central plaza and its important edifices.

Some writers have attached special significance to these laws. After reviewing the studies by Hansen, Gillin, Hayner, and the Hawthorns, Caplow asserted:

> An important element which none of these studies has stressed is the role of systematic and deliberate planning in the early period of urban growth. The rectangular street plan, the rational siting of churches and open spaces, the systematic subdivision of blocks, the sumptuary and technical regulation of construction, and the control of marketing, water supply, and commercial location are all elements that loom large in the early history of Guatemala and were presumably operative in Mexican communities as well.[64]

Two studies that are frequently cited in this connection are those by Stanislawski in Mexico and McBryde in Guatemala.[65] Commenting on their findings, Theodorson has said:

> [T]hroughout Spanish America there existed a traditional ecological pattern very different from that found in the United

States. That this pattern was not due, however, to any intrinsic features of the environmental setting of Spanish-American cities, but rather to a definite Spanish colonial policy, may be demonstrated by the differences between Spanish and Indian towns. McBryde, in a study of Guatemala, found that when a sizable number of Ladinos (of mixed Indian and Spanish descent, but considering themselves Spanish) is present, a settlement will take the form of a centralized town, while without many Ladinos an even larger Indian population aggregate will form only an agricultural settlement. . . . Stanislawski found a striking difference between Spanish and Indian towns. The Spanish towns follow the pattern described above. . . . We may conclude from the Spanish-American studies that those communities built by the Spanish in the New World were founded according to a definite conception of town planning and certain specific values.[66]

One would be more readily inclined to accept this judgment at face value if it were not rendered rather questionable by available archaeological and historical evidence. *The fact of the matter is that the "traditional Latin American pattern" could be observed in cities of the New World prior to the Spanish conquest.* Thus Rowe has described the spatial structure of one early Inca city as follows: "Cuzco . . . consisted of a central ceremonial area, inhabited only by nobles, priests, government officials and their servants, and a ring of small villages, separated from the center and from each other by open fields." [67] Violich states that the distance of one's habitation from the center depended on the degree of relationship to the Inca ruler.[68] Gibson has generalized further, claiming that among *both* the pre-Columbian Aztec and Maya civilizations, the elite "tended to live in the centers of the great cities." [69] Vaillant also has made it clear that Aztec cities were plaza-centered; for example, this was the form of Tenochtitlan, which became Mexico City.[70]

The existence of this pattern in pre-Conquest days can be inferred from more than archaeological evidence; it was also observed firsthand by travelers and missionaries. To quote Shook and Proskouriakoff:

> In building assemblages, in size, and in distribution, Meso-American settlements have great variety, but the fundamental unit of the town settlement, with its core of civic and religious buildings, is dominant in all periods and in all but the most remote and inaccessible localities. Landa's classic description of the town of Yucatán can be applied with only minor variations to most of the known archeological history within the area of high culture in Meso-America: "Before the Spaniards had con-

quered that country, the natives lived together in towns in a very civilized fashion . . . in the middle of the town were their temples with beautiful plazas, and all around the temples stood the houses of the lords and the priests, and then of the most important people. Thus came the houses of the richest and of those who were held in the highest estimation next to these, and at the outskirts of the town were the houses of the lower class." [71]

All of these materials, then, call into question the supposed importance of the Laws of the Indies in establishing the traditional pattern observed in Latin America. Some factors more powerful than "Iberian values" were apparently at work. The pattern was clearly in existence *before* the imposition of the laws, and the archaeological and historical evidence offers strong support for Sjoberg's claim that the residential distribution of social classes was essentially the same for all preindustrial cities. Whether or not "planning" was required must remain a moot question. Inca cities were apparently laid out in blocks by architects.[72] Given the strongly centralized character of their social and political systems, the cities of these early New World civilizations were very probably planned creations. In any event, the distinction should not consist of "planning" *versus* "no planning." Rather, the degree of centralization of authority appears to be the critical issue; even the chaotic jumble of nineteenth-century industrial cities was the product of "planning," but planning by individual entrepreneurs and householders, with locational decision-making decentralized in the extreme.[73]

An Evolutionary Sequence?

After completing a field survey of forty-five Brazilian cities and towns, ranging in size from less than 5000 to over a million, Carmin focused on the internal geographic structure of Anápolis, a regional capital of some 16,000 inhabitants. Commenting on the "traditional" Latin American residential pattern in evidence there, he contrasted it with the reverse pattern on view in the United States. At the same time, he called attention to the following fact:

[North] American cities do, however, show signs of the same situation having prevailed in the past when transportation was less adequate. Today many relict mansions can be found in or near American central business districts but they now serve as funeral homes, apartments, or apartments above with doctor, dentist, beauty shops, etc., below.[74]

This passage brings forcibly to mind an observation contained in the very first statement of the Burgess zonal hypothesis. Speaking of the "zone of transition," inhabited by members of the lowest strata, Burgess noted that "The present boundaries of the area of deterioration were not many years ago those of the zone now inhabited by independent wage-earners, and within the memories of thousands of Chicagoans contained the residences of the 'best families.'" [75] Consider the testimony of another leading student of city structure—Homer Hoyt. Two sets of maps showing "high-grade," "intermediate," and "low-grade" residential areas for Chicago in 1857, 1873, 1899, and 1930 reveal that the "high-grade" areas were very near the center in 1857 and that they shifted toward the periphery over the years. [76] Thus Chicago—the prototype of the concentric zonal scheme—is revealed to have undergone a radical structural change in the course of its growth.

Heberle offers the following account of developments in the American South:

> It seems to be characteristic for the older, smaller cities in the South that the homes of the socially prominent families were to be found just outside the central—and only—business district. . . . As the city grew and as wealth increased, the "old" families tended to move towards the periphery—following the general fashion of our age. . . . The old homes are then converted into rooming houses and "tourist homes." This in itself is nothing peculiar to the South. However, it so happens that in the kind of city under consideration, the poorer people usually lived at the edge of town. This was particularly the case with Negroes. It happens, therefore, quite frequently that white people infiltrate into suburban areas occupied by Negroes, buying their property or cancelling their leases. [77]

The possibility that the "traditional Latin American pattern" might have been typical of North American cities of an earlier era raises a fascinating question—*does the residential structure of the city evolve in a predictable direction?* Casual observation leads one to believe that "better" residential neighborhoods are found near the very center of small towns, even today, in every major region of the United States. Writing in the 1930's, Hoyt noted that "in small cities or cities of slow growth, the highest rental areas may occupy parts of sectors directly adjacent to the business center." [78] Could not this have been the typical North American pattern of an earlier era, prior to modern transportation developments, industrialization, and rapid population growth?

The problem of specifying temporal reference points is brought out clearly in a passage by the Dotsons, who have studied a number of Mexican cities and who have been extremely critical of the Burgess hypothesis:

> The discrepancies between his conception and reality (which are always considerable) undoubtedly are augmented by U. S. cities changing from the relatively compact type concentrated around the railroad, which served Burgess as an empirical model, to the dispersed form, broadly organized, which has been produced under the influence of the automobile. When as many empirical studies of the U. S. are accumulated as are available from other countries, it will be clearly seen that Burgess's conception, instead of having the degree of universality that he seemed to give it originally, actually fits only U. S. commercial and industrial cities, and—even more—fits these only in a limited period of their development.[79]

Despite its critical tone, this passage brings out the importance of local transportation, and suggests that cities in different technological epochs will display dissimilar spatial structures.

Assuming that a real reversal has taken place, could one account for the shift in residential pattern from one in which the elite occupy the center to one in which they abandon it for the periphery? At least three variables seem to be involved: (1) city growth, (2) local transportation technology, and (3) "social power," to use Sjoberg's terminology. If growth is accompanied by commercial and industrial development, there may well be new competitors for centrally located sites; in the face of this competition, residential areas may be abandoned to more intensive land uses. At the same time, the encroachment of business and factory uses, together with the traffic they generate, may render central areas undesirable for residence. For the elite to abandon the center, however, technological conditions must allow them to maintain relatively easy access to the center and its vital institutions. In the past, this was not the case, and still may not be the case. Speaking of Anápolis, Carmin has observed that "with no paved roads, and until recently almost no private automobiles, a residential site near the heart of town was and for the most part still is a prized location. Such a home site gives easy access to the shopping goods center, the churches and the places of entertainment (coffee houses, bars, etc.) as well as to the business establishments owned and operated by many of those who dwell in the Class A houses."[80]

Sjoberg points to the technological factor as crucial, but introduces an additional consideration:

How do we explain this [preindustrial] distribution of classes as between the central sector and the periphery? Throughout feudal cities, values operate defining residence in the historic center as most prestigeful, location on the periphery as least so. But reference to values alone can not account for the ecological differences between the traditional and the modern community. Far more pertinent is technology. For one thing, the feudal society's technology permits relatively little spatial mobility, thereby setting limits to the kinds of ecological arrangements that can obtain. People travel mostly on foot, occasionally on animal-back; only the privileged ride in the human- or animal-drawn vehicles, slow and uncomfortable though these may be by industrial standards.

Assuming that upper-class persons strive to maintain their prerogatives in the community and society (here social power enters as a factor in ecology), they must isolate themselves from the non-elite and be centrally located to ensure ready access to the headquarters of the governmental, religious, and educational organizations. The highly valued residence, then, is where fullest advantage may be taken of the city's strategic facilities; in turn these latter have come to be tightly bunched for the convenience of the elite—patterns that are readily revised with the introduction of rapid transit, telephones, and so on.[81]

In addition to easy access, however, the "prerogatives" enjoyed by those with social (and economic) power include the ability to maintain a particular location in the face of competing alternatives, and the ability to capture the newest and most desirable residential facilities. We have already observed that the Burgess hypothesis tends to assume something about the occupancy patterns of the upper classes, that is, that they will tend to occupy the newer areas. In the United States, such areas have been peripheral in location; in Latin America, they are increasingly so.

Hence we come to a kind of "commonsense" rationalization of the trends observable in both "Anglo" and Latin America. Given growth and expansion of the center, and given appropriate improvements in transportation and communication, the upper strata might be expected to shift from central to peripheral residence, and the lower classes might increasingly take up occupancy in the central area abandoned by the elite. Despite mounting land values occasioned by the competition of alternative (nonresidential) land uses, the lower strata may occupy valuable central land in tenements, subdivided dwellings originally intended for single families, and other high-density "slum" housing arrangements.

The evolutionary sequence that has been roughly sketched here is far from complete. For one thing, it requires more attention to what Burgess called "the survival of an earlier use of a district." More generally, it requires elaboration of the role of historical "residues," for example, the impact of a city's development in a particular transportation era. Casual observation suggests a whole series of differences between pre- and postautomobile cities in the United States—differences in street patterns, land uses, and residential densities. Unfortunately, historical data are difficult to obtain and to evaluate, and there is the vexing problem of attributing current significance to "survivals" from an earlier epoch.[82]

Finally, it should be noted that there is nothing in the preceding account that is intended to suggest that a fixed and immutable "stage" has been achieved in cities of the United States. Hauser has offered an extremely suggestive set of speculations concerning current and future developments:

> The combination of urban renewal in the inner zones of central cities and blight and urban sprawl in the suburbs is tending to disrupt the pattern of population distribution which has placed the higher income groups farthest out from the center of the city. Should these trends continue, the residential land use pattern in metropolitan areas would be turned inside out, with the newer and more desirable areas located in the rebuilt inner city zones as well as in the most distant parts of suburbia.[83]

What does emerge from this review is the possibility that (a) the Burgess concentric zonal scheme, wrongly regarded as indigenous to the United States, and (b) the preindustrial pattern, erroneously identified as unique to Latin America, are *both special cases more adequately subsumed under a more general theory of residential land uses in urban areas.* Unfortunately, such a theory does not exist at this time. We turn now, however, to a detailed consideration of some of the theoretical and methodological problems that must be solved before such a model will become possible.

Some Methodological and Theoretical Issues

For ease of reference, the following discussion is topically organized along the same lines as those followed in the foregoing review of the Latin American studies. The sharp separation between "methodological" and "theoretical" problems that is implied here is not entirely defensible, but this organization should allow us to deal with certain general questions of evidence and procedure without immediately getting involved in the merits and demerits of particular conceptual approaches—for example, the ecological. In other words, it should permit the elucidation of some of the more ubiquitous problems facing the comparative study of urbanization.

General Methodological Considerations

First of all, it should be clear that we are presently unable to formulate a specific set of methodological recommendations for cross-cultural research on urbanization. At this moment, there are no generally accepted "rules of comparative study" at our disposal. The comparative study of urbanization will probably have to depend on a methodological "evolution," with consciously developed prescriptions beginning to appear as deliberately comparative urban research designs are created.[84] Moreover, there is no good reason to believe that such rules —when and if they apear—will differ in any significant way from the methodological principles that guide research in other areas of social science. Nothing about "urbanization," however it may be operationally defined, requires distinctive treatment. Not only are there no special hazards in this area; there are reasons for believing that the phenomenon of urbanization is far less complex than many other subjects currently under investigation by social scientists.[85]

Among the social sciences, there are three disciplines that seem most likely to develop an explicit methodology of comparative research. They are demography, geography, and anthropology. The first two, of course, often display a descriptive bent that may inhibit the conscious formulation of such rules of inquiry; moreover, much of their comparative work seems to be carried out within the framework of an unarticulated set of broad methodological procedures. Measurement and other technical problems receive abundant attention, to be sure, but relatively little effort is directed toward the resolution of comparative questions per se. Perhaps anthropology is in the best position to provide a coherent statement on comparative methods. Questions of an appropriately broad order have preoccupied anthropologists since the days of the social evolutionists, and they continue to be debated with vigor.[86]

The Role of Case Studies

The utility of case studies in providing insight into a problem, and in permitting the trial formulation of hypotheses, is not to be questioned. This is no longer a matter for serious debate. The problems of *inference* that such studies entail, however, remain as vexing as ever.

Consider the problem involved in drawing conclusions from the results of two or more case studies. It is obviously difficult to use the work of different investigators, who typically employ dissimilar approaches and who encounter different problems in the field, as the basis for sound generalizations. There are obvious hazards in any attempt to synthesize the results of studies based on radically dissimilar approaches. (Some of the difficulties, in fact, are exemplified in this chapter, where only seven different studies are reviewed in detail.) At the same time, there are probably modest gains to be realized in "middle-range" syntheses, and obvious discrepancies in methods, gaps in the data, and divergences in approach should not discourage the effort.

A more serious question concerns the concept of the "negative case." There are those who assert that a single negative instance is sufficient to refute an hypothesis—at least if the hypothesis is formulated as a universal proposition. These same writers hold that an hypothesis phrased in the form of a statistical tendency cannot be so refuted. We are obviously incapable of devising "crucial experiments" at this time, given the difficulty that attends our attempts to control relevant variables. Conditions of near-perfect control might permit a single instance to be regarded as a decisive test of an hypothesis. But even a number of cases can be difficult to interpret. The best example is again to be found in the body of this chapter. As noted, the Latin American city studies cannot be regarded as evidence for *or* against the Burgess hypothesis, simply because the necessary controls are lacking and because so many relevant items of information are missing.

One argument against the use of case studies has to do with the investigator's perspective. There seems to be a tendency for the student of the single case to stress the unique and to lose sight of the general.[87] In this connection it is interesting to note that the single "test" of the residential portion of the Burgess hypothesis that has been conducted by means of a large sample of cities was Hoyt's well-known study. Although he rejected the Burgess view as an oversimplification of residential structure, his own work yielded a long list of generalizations, summed up in his "sector theory." [88] An examination of a range of cases may compel the researcher to see repetitive regularities. Still, we are able to find more in common among the Latin American cities than most of the original observers who examined them singly and in isolation; this may encourage the review and reanalysis of case studies by a number of researchers.

The Utility of "Byproduct" Studies

An investigator need not set out to test specific hypotheses with respect to urbanization in order to produce results of value to the student of urbanization. Data are where you find them. Moreover, one need not be a scientific investigator in order to develop valuable materials for scientific use. Just as historians have made good use of the accounts provided by explorers, adventurers, and missionaries, we might employ to good effect analogous materials on contemporary problems.

At the same time, the hazards of basing inferences upon "byproduct" studies are fairly obvious. Data gathered for entirely dissimilar purposes do not lend themselves to easy analysis. The difficulties are perfectly analogous to those attending "secondary analysis" of sample survey data, where the second investigator's inability to pursue and follow up leads that are developed is a serious inhibiting condition.

The Place of Statistical Data

It may be argued that there are special advantages in using quantitative data for the comparative study of urbanization. First of all, problems of comparability—of units and variables—are likely to be somewhat reduced; at the very least, the statistically oriented researcher is likely to be more sensitive to this question. Moreover, control techniques can be employed more readily in quantitative research designs. But there are disadvantages too. We are too often inclined to use powerful statistical techniques with inadequate data. In addition, some important questions are likely to be overlooked simply because quantitative data in a suitable form are not readily available. One special hazard is the tendency to "wait for better data" or to abandon a problem as not amenable to solution because the statistics are not perfect. Important questions that cannot be answered with census data (or comparable mass data) are likely to be overlooked or abandoned by the statistically oriented researcher.

Census data would appear to be especially appropriate for many comparative problems, including that of the spatial structure of cities. Yet it must be freely granted that we do not really know the limits of census data for such studies because such data have rarely been used in appropriate comparative designs. Even with more effort in this area, however, there will be obvious limits:

(1) Limits imposed by the number, definition, and categorization of *population characteristics*, all of which vary widely from one census system to another;

(2) Limits imposed by incomparable *areal units*; as an example, rather few census systems produce data for subcommunity units analogous to our "census tracts."

Culture from a Methodological Standpoint

As we have noted, the Latin American studies reviewed earlier have been interpreted as evidence of the critical importance of "culture" as a variable in the analysis of spatial structure. Now some aspects of culture are clearly more open to observation and measurement than others. To use a somewhat dated distinction, "material" technological elements are most amenable to observation and even counting, but problems of meaningful classification are no less severe than in the sphere of "nonmaterial" culture. Perhaps this question has the virtue of forcing one to define "culture" more carefully than in the usual case.

A radical interpretation of the cultural position would lead to the conclusion that students of urbanization in the United States may not be justified in ignoring cultural differences even when they are studying only their own cities. Similarly, one must ask himself whether or not a comparative study of urbanization could safely ignore cultural differences (a) if it were entirely confined to cities of Central and South America or (b) if it were limited to cities within a single Latin American nation. Quite obviously, one runs into the danger of pursuing "subcultures" in an almost infinite regress. Still, writers like Firey have been rather persuasive in arguing for the inclusion of certain *elements* of ideational culture—for example, values and sentiments—as independent variables in the analysis of urban spatial structure.[89]

General Theoretical Considerations

Within the field of sociology, it has been the human ecologists who have been primarily concerned with the problem of urban spatial structure. This holds whether their orientation has been "classical," "cultural," or "neoclassical."[90] There are other specialties and other disciplines concerned with urban spatial structure. Within economics, for example, "urban land economics" is a widely recognized field, although it has been moribund in recent years. Another perspective on problems of urban space is provided by "urban geography," a field marked by a great deal of creative activity over the past decade. These other disciplines provide alternative theoretical approaches that have not been explored in this chapter. In some instances, the parallels are striking; what is "invasion and succession" to the ecologist, for example, is "sequent occupance" to the geographer. Nevertheless, the divergences in approach and method are undeniable. Nothing that is said here should suggest that urban space is the private preserve of the human ecologist. We shall continue to stress the ecological approach because of the writer's greater familiarity with it, and in order to provide form and focus for the remainder of the discussion. Similarly, we shall continue to deal with theoretical issues in terms of "constants" and "independent" and "dependent" variables in order to sustain the emphases developed in earlier sections of this chapter. Finally, we shall continue to take the residential distribution of socioeconomic strata in urban space as the problem for explanation.

Specification of the Independent Variables

Any assessment of the factors that are most salient in the location of households must begin with an appreciation of the range of relevant variables. Moreover, the selection of variables hinges—at least in part—on the general mode of analysis that is contemplated. If one were an economist disposed to work within a "decision-unit" framework, for example, one might very well enumerate a list of variables that showed little overlap with the list produced by a human ecologist. An enormous range of variables has been mentioned by writers in the various disciplines concerned with urban space. Among these, we will specify only those that seem most critical from an ecological standpoint.

Elsewhere, the present writer has argued that the bulk of ecological effort has been devoted to an examination of the manifold interconnections between the various elements of the "ecological complex"—population, organization, environment, and technology.[91] Under these four principal rubrics, we may identify certain variable attributes of whole communities which may be expected to play a role in shaping the residential distribution of socioeconomic strata. Some of these variables have been mentioned in connection with the discussion of Latin American cities, whereas others have not been previously identified as relevant to the problem at hand.

Regarding the *environment*, the spatial distributions of population and land uses are obviously responsive to variations in topography and physical terrain. Thus differences in the physical environmental features of urban areas, even in the absence of other differences, will produce variations in spatial pattern. Burgess and others have mentioned these facts. In other words, the shape of every city will exhibit certain unique features directly attributable to the character of the physical sites that are occupied. (In view of this simple fact, repetitive regularities are more noteworthy than minor deviations in detail.) The Latin American materials offer examples of the many ways in which the physical environment may condition the spatial pattern of cities. Leonard, for example, points out that La Paz "occupies both sides of a deep ravine (quebrada) that, at its greatest depth, is approximately 1,300 feet below the level, high plain that surrounds it. . . . The rare physiography has inhibited the normal expectation pattern in its geographical growth." [92] With respect to Mexico City, Hayner points out that "until 1903 further expansion eastward was blocked by Lake Texcoco. At that time this lake was partially drained by a gigantic canal and tunnel project, but the establishment of new residential neighborhoods to the east was still discouraged by the alkaline character of the reclaimed soil." [93] The danger of earthquakes in Guatemala City was so great, according to Caplow, that "by expediency, as well as statute, buildings were until recently limited to one story, a limitation which automatically set restrictions on any rise in land values." [94]

With respect to *technology*, spatial distributions of population and land use are also subject to variations in accordance with the availability of means for overcoming the friction of space. Moreover, the overall orientation of intramural transport routes will be one of the prime determinants of the distribution of population and land uses, tending to set the general framework within which various activities are allocated to particular positions. The Latin American materials again offer some apt illustrations. In those few instances in which some attention is given to transport technology—as in the reports by Hayner on Oaxaca and Leonard on La Paz—the authors remark that the absence of rapid and inexpensive means of movement had a considerable role in maintaining the "traditional" Latin pattern of residential distribution. (Under such circumstances, the fact that higher-status groups tended to preempt the sites most accessible to the center may come as no surprise.) Sharp contrasts may be expected between areas in which the bulk of the population depends on walking and those in which rapid and inexpensive means of movement are utilized by the bulk of the population. Caplow notes that "the network of communication and transportation centralized in the capital is organized almost precisely as it was in 1889 although the specific means of transportation have changed," and he attributes some of Guatemala City's stability to this feature.[95]

The most succinct statement regarding the importance of transportation technology has been offered by Smith and McMahan:

> [O]ne who has visited South American cities can hardly have failed to notice that the worst slums frequently are on the very outskirts of the communities and that Rio de Janeiro's *favelas*, the miserable quarters in which a large share of the Negroes live, are spread over the hills which overlook the city. Such observations suggest that the availability and cost of transportation are basic factors in determining the ecological pattern of any city.
>
> The abundance of rapid, cheap, and convenient transportation, and especially the automobile, seems largely responsible for the fact that in [North] American cities generally the most undesirable residential districts are those nearest the center, whereas the most desirable are at the greatest distance from the downtown areas. On the other hand, in Buenos Aires, Santiago de Chile, Lima, and other such cities, where the automobile is still a luxury, residences of the least privileged classes are relegated to the more remote sections.[96]

Emphasis on transportation, however, should not obscure the possible relevance of other technological developments—for example, sources of power for industry, structural steel and concrete construction of "skyscrapers," the extension of power and sewage lines, and so on. Advances in the technology of communication are especially not to be ignored; they play a vital role in permitting the integration of functional units widely dispersed in space. All in all, the impact of technological change on the spacing of population and human activities is probably the most readily observed and widely appreciated of all the factors discussed here.

As for *population*, demographic factors also influence the spatial arrangements of localized aggregates. For one thing, communities of differing absolute size may be expected to reveal wide variations in physical pattern. This suggestion was advanced by Hoyt and Caplow. In addition, the spatial configuration of different areas will vary according to the rate of growth being experienced. Hoyt and Carmin mention this factor explicitly. Growth, in fact, is one of the key determinants of change in physical pattern; the latter cannot fail to respond to increments in population size. Although rapid population change makes for certain difficulties in the observation of spatial structure, the appropriate time perspective being difficult to establish, it can be safely asserted that demographic change is a critical variable with respect to the physical arrangement of land uses. Moreover, the "components" of population growth (for example, net migration versus natural increase) may exert an influence on spatial patterns; in general, growth via migration will probably be more conducive to change.

Size per se is perhaps not so critical as the organizational concomitants of size; larger populations, for example, are known to permit greater functional specialization, and small communities cannot be expected to exhibit the highly segregated patterns of specialized land uses that can only be expressed in larger aggregates. Growth, too, is of consequence to the extent that it requires alterations in the functional organization of the community; the creation of new service needs, the realignment of preexisting networks of exchange, and the introduction of new industries are examples of the kinds of functional concomitants of population growth that may introduce variations into the overall spatial distributions of localized aggregates.

With respect to population composition, variations in the make-up of local populations have implications for their spacing to the extent that they are indicative of functional differences between segments of the community. For example, variations in the racial and ethnic composition of populations (often the products of recent growth via migration) may be expected to influence the spatial layout only to the extent that the subpopulations are (and remain) distinct. Racial and ethnic minorities that are "socially" and occupationally assimilated into the community are residentially distributed in much the same fashion as the majority. Conversely, "occupational" segregation frequently is expressed in spatial terms as residential segregation.

Finally, *organization* must be taken into account. The Burgess hypothesis asserts that distinct functions and population groups will be physically segregated in space. The kind of segregation observable in modern American cities—areas of internally homogeneous land use and occupancy—would appear to depend on at least three factors, demographic, technological, and organizational. (1) Segregation requires a community *size* that is large enough to permit full representation of a wide array of functions; where only a few units are engaged in a particular function, their segregation in distinct areas cannot be expected. (2) Segregation assumes considerable *ease of movement* permitting exchanges between specialized parts; otherwise, units that are symbiotically linked (factories and households that supply their labor force requirements, commercial establishments and their supporting populations) must remain within close proximity.

(3) Segregation cannot exist without a considerable degree of *specialization and division of labor;* to choose only the most obvious example, a sharp bifurcation between industrial and residential areas does not appear where most manufacturing is conducted on a handicraft basis within the household.

All of the broad factors listed above—environment, technology, and population—affect the internal arrangement of cities by their joint effects upon organization. In short, all of the other variables in the "ecological complex" operate to affect spatial distributions by being mediated through functional organization. Thus variations in physical pattern are concomitants of structural variations. This view leads to the general proposition that different functional "types" of city will exhibit typical spatial patterns (within topographic limits), so that similarities in size, social structure, economic base, and transportation systems will yield commonalities in physical outline.

Let us summarize the foregoing discussion in outline form.

A. ENVIRONMENT

1. *Topography.* The local terrain constitutes a variable factor that must be recognized as important in affecting urban land uses. The presence or absence of bodies of water, and the entire configuration of the land surface, including its relief, pose physical conditions to which the urban spatial structure must be adapted. One matter that has not received emphasis is the sheer variability of local topography; given the extreme variety of physical settings in which cities have developed, one must be struck with the uniformities in spatial structure that have emerged. Every local environment is unique in some respect, or it contains a unique combination of physical features, and these must be responsible for some of the variations in spatial structure that can be observed.

B. TECHNOLOGY

1. *Transportation and Communication Facilities.* This is another factor that has received fairly widespread recognition in the literature dealing with the spatial structure of cities. Certainly Burgess was aware of the impact of radial transportation routes in "distorting" the concentric zonal pattern, and other writers have continued to accord it primacy. More detailed consideration of this factor requires recognition of local routes (their quality and physical layout) and short-distance carriers (for example, public versus private). The emergence of specialized residential versus employing areas (industrial and commercial) would appear to assume a reasonably efficient trans-

portation system; the appearance of commuting, and a physical separation between home and work place, might serve as indices of such a system's efficacy. This variable is clearly important with respect to the segregation discussed later, under the heading "Ecological Organization," and it should be seen as a critical variable with respect to the residential distribution of socioeconomic strata. Finally, we must recognize that an advanced communications technology also has a large role in permitting the spatial separation of interrelated functions without loss of contact that is on view in the contemporary metropolitan area. Although it may be less immediately relevant to the household, and less important than transportation in affecting the residential location of households, the communication system in use certainly warrants attention in the study of urban land use in general, for it helps to fashion the total community context within which such location occurs.

C. POPULATION

1. *Size.* A community must reach a certain size before we can expect any significant residential segregation of socioeconomic strata. Beyond that, we might anticipate some variation in the spatial ordering of these strata (for example, central versus peripheral location of the elite) according to size.

2. *Rate of Growth.* The city's rate of growth will influence its pattern of land uses in general and the distribution of socioeconomic strata in particular. It is worth mentioning again that the original Burgess essay was entitled "The Growth of the City," and our prior discussion should have made it clear that the concentric-zonal hypothesis is essentially a "growth model."

3. *Ethnic and Racial Composition.* Quinn has argued that the Burgess hypothesis assumes considerable racial and ethnic heterogeneity. Although this is not certain, the degree of population homogeneity may be a relevant factor, at least in those situations in which racial or ethnic segregation is practiced *independently of* segregation along socioeconomic lines. In any event, this variable should not be neglected in the absence of evidence concerning its role.

D. ORGANIZATION

1. *Economic Base.* As already noted, Quinn has asserted that the Burgess hypothesis assumes a mixed "commercial-industrial" city. This suggests that the economic base is a relevant variable. Certainly the presence or absence of industry on a substantial scale will influence the overall pattern of land uses, especially if separate factory districts

emerge, and residential distributions will be affected. The number and distribution of commercial establishments might also be expected to exert an influence on the residential pattern. Apart from a direct impact on land uses, there is also the indirect influence of variations in the economic base, for such variations produce differences in the number and composition of the city's socioeconomic strata. A city composed largely of low-wage industrial workers might be expected to exhibit a residential pattern substantially different from that of a prosperous trade center, a capital, or a university town. (This "social class" variable is discussed in more detail later.)

2. *Ecological Organization.* The term "ecological organization" is employed in the absence of a widely accepted and understood label for a neglected aspect of community life. It is designed to suggest an important variable—the extent to which an urban area is occupied by more or less isolated and self-contained *subsystems*. It refers to the everyday conduct of community life, and has to do with the frequency and kind of contact between members, in a gross "sociometric" sense. It has frequently been remarked by observant travelers that even large cities in backward countries tend to lack unity, consisting of whole clusters of contiguous quarters that remain relatively isolated from each other despite their proximity; they are frequently separated by walls and joined only by gates. This pattern of internal segregation, very often along lines of religion, language, and color, has been identified by Sjoberg as one of the most obvious spatial traits of the "pre-industrial city." [97] Such a pattern is a direct physical representation of the internal "segmentation" that Durkheim viewed as the hallmark of the undifferentiated social structure. Each of the quarters or districts may be more or less self-contained, in that the full round of life may be pursued within them; they may contain their own set of retail and service establishments, and most inhabitants may live and work within them, rarely leaving their confines. A whole series of such subsystems—or subcommunities—may be present, each very much like the next, and each relatively isolated from all its counterparts. The traditional *barrios* of Latin American cities serve as an example of these "transplanted villages" in the urban environment. For convenience, we may contrast such *cities composed of many communities* with the contemporary metropolitan areas of the United States—*communities composed of many cities*. Now it is obvious that technological features, including the forms of transportation and communication in use, will be critical conditioning factors, permitting easy contact and exchange or rendering it most difficult. Nevertheless, it appears worthwhile to treat the *organizational* element—the "social density" manifested within

the urban area—as a separate variable. The overall pattern of land uses, and the distribution of residences by social class, may be independently influenced by this variable characteristic of community organization.[98]

3. *Social Class Composition.* We have already alluded to the possible importance of the number of social classes and their relative sizes in our discussion of Latin American cities. In this case, we suggested, the emergence of a middle class would seem to be a matter of special interest; as Beals has observed, "In varying degrees the feudal base of Latin-American class structures still persists, but the usual description in polar or two-class terms is even more inadequate to describe the current situation than it was in colonial times." [99] We have also observed that class composition is not impervious to variations in the economic base. Nevertheless, the fact that our principal effort is directed toward explaining the residential distribution of the various social strata means that we should give separate attention to the numbers and relative sizes of the various classes as variable attributes of communities.

Culture as an Independent Variable

The foregoing outline makes it quite evident that certain elements or components of culture are omitted in our version of the ecological approach to urban spatial structure. Although technology and organization may be regarded as cultural elements *par excellence,* there is no attention accorded to "normative" or "ideational" components. In short, there is a decidedly "materialistic" emphasis or bias evident here. The possibility that space may be an object of sentiment, and that certain areas may become invested with "nonrational" values, are regarded as irrelevant in this approach. Similarly, the fact that residential location is motivated, or animated by ends or goals of a wide variety, is given no consideration. Finally, the fact that there are numerous institutional arrangements with respect to the use of land and the transmission of property introduces a variability that is not considered in ecological analysis. In some respects, all these factors are treated—if only implicitly—as "constants," or as exhibiting perfect covariation with the variables explicitly subjected to analysis. In any event, the neglect of such factors by ecologists has been the principal objection of writers in the "sociocultural" tradition. It must be frankly admitted that these controversial issues remain largely unresolved after two decades of debate. These omissions—regarded as sins by some writers—have been defended as virtues by others, if only on the basis of a kind of effort at theoretical parsimony. Moreover, the debate is likely to continue, for the issues are not the kind that can be readily resolved by means of empirical research, whether grand or modest in design.

It may be that the ecologist who ignores some of these cultural features is actually seeking something other than a full and complete description of urban spatial structure. Perhaps he is seeking a set of necessary but not sufficient conditions, or a series of rather abstract laws which admit of many minor variations in concrete historical instances. For example, there may be some highly general "functional prerequisites" affecting cities in all cultures, or some "universal functions" of cities that give rise to cross-cultural regularities in the use of space. One might suggest that certain mundane necessities—the provision of such things as water, sewage disposal, and circulation and movement in general—might be considered as vital functional requirements with important universal implications. Similarly, relatively high population density may be an "urban trait" that has fairly uniform consequences, no matter what the cultural milieu. In any event, the urban community should not be subject to any more cultural limitations than other commonly recognized sociological units, and there seems to be no intrinsic reason for expecting an inordinate amount of culturally induced variability in the use of space.

Theoretical Constants

Ogburn's favorite methodological dictum was to the effect that "a change cannot be explained by a constant." [100] The relevance of this methodological principle for the development of theories of urban spatial structure should be clear. An interpretation of changes in Latin American city structure in terms of "cultural values" requires some evidence for changes in values with respect to space; ideally, such changes in values must be independently observed and measured, and not inferred from actual changes in spatial structure per se, in order to avoid an intolerable circularity in the form of the argument.

If a factor can be shown to have exhibited literal constancy over time, it can be safely rejected as an explanation of observed change. This should apply to the study of urban spatial structure just as clearly as it does anywhere else. Moreover, the dictum has a cross-sectional corollary, for a perfectly ubiquitous element can hardly be employed to explain areal variation. A factor does not necessarily have to exhibit a literal absence of change over time in order to be regarded as a "constant," for the values on some variables may be treated as sufficiently similar to warrant their neglect. Most generally, a factor can be regarded as a constant under any one of the following conditions:

(1) if it maintains the same value through time;

(2) if it is perfectly ubiquitous in space;

(3) if it is shared by the two or more units under investigation in a comparative framework;

(4) if it has been "controlled" by statistical, experimental, or other means—including randomization, matching, or crossclassification.

The temptation to be avoided is the Weberian "mental experiment," wherein factors are eliminated from consideration by "thinking them away." To ignore a factor is not to control it.

Some Alternative Dependent Variables

Urban space is only one object of study. There are other variables that might be identified for purposes of systematic comparative analysis. The possibilities, of course, are almost endless, for we can create long lists of "questions needing answers." A review of the work of the Committee on Urbanization suggests that there is rather widespread and multidisciplinary interest in the following broad subjects: (a) rural-urban migration; (b) urban population composition; (c) vital rates in urban and rural areas; (d) levels and rates of urbanization at both national and regional levels; (e) typical urban functions and economic base analysis; (f) urban political organization; (g) the urban hierarchy, "primacy," and rank-size distributions; (h) urban history; (i) urban spatial structure; (j) industrial versus preindustrial cities; (k) "urbanism as a way of life."

Among these, two might be given strategic priority in a broad program of comparative research that would include cross-cultural studies. In view of the relative wealth of demographic data for cities around the world, *urban population composition* is a problem that deserves serious consideration in any realistic cross-cultural research program. The investigation of simple "biological" composition—including sex ratios and age distributions—should be the first order of business. However, a compositional view of population leads naturally into an interest in occupational and industrial make-up, so that functional classification and economic base analysis is facilitated.[101]

The second leading subject for comparative research is *urban spatial structure*. As we have indicated, this subject is of interest to a number of disciplines. Increasingly detailed census materials for cities, and for districts within them, are becoming available. More important, the city planning movement in such regions as Latin America is beginning to yield a wealth of data on urban land uses. Anderson has observed that

> very little comparative sociological nation-to-nation or region-to-region data on urbanism exist and that not much is being done about it, except in the demographical field. Cities can be studied profitably in terms of various other equally hard materials, much of which is obtainable.
>
> There is much good urban sociology, for example, in the study of land use, an ecological approach in which there is a widening interest, and which helps to lend meaning to statistics of urban population. A distinguished beginning has already been made in the United Nations' spot study of urban land policies.[102]

There are severe problems of comparability. Sjoberg and others have pointed out that many non-Western cities do not exhibit a high degree of spatial differentiation. Thus specialized industrial areas, for example, are not to be found in all the world's cities. A pattern of cottage industry, whether or not it is combined with the "putting-out" system, can be observed in many cities throughout the world. The very degree of spatial differentiation, however, is a variable of considerable interest. The development of effective land-use classifications for comparative study is being assiduously pursued by geographers, though easy solutions are not at hand. Nevertheless, the subject of urban spatial structure appears to be one deserving high priority in comparative urban research. The multidisciplinary interest in the topic, and the relative accessibility of relevant data argue strongly for emphasizing it. More important, the linkages between spatial structure and social and economic organization permit the pursuit of related inquiries that extend beyond the subject of space itself.[103]

NOTES

* The author was associated with the Urban Program instituted at the University of Wisconsin under the terms of a grant from the Ford Foundation, and his participation in the program facilitated the completion of this paper. At the same time, assistance from the Social Science Research Council, including an Auxiliary Research Award, permitted the collection and evaluation of certain fugitive materials pertaining to Latin American urbanization. These sources of aid are gratefully acknowledged.

1. Gideon Sjoberg, "Comparative Urban Sociology," in Robert K. Merton et al. (Eds.), *Sociology Today* (New York: Basic Books, 1959), pp. 334–359; Thomas O. Wilkinson, "Urban Structure and Industrialization," *American Sociological Review*, 25 (1960), pp. 356–363.

2. R. D. McKenzie, "Human Ecology," *Encyclopaedia of the Social Sciences* (New York: Macmillan, 1931), Vol. 5, p. 314.

3. See Amos H. Hawley, *Human Ecology: A Theory of Community Structure* (New York: Ronald Press, 1950).

4. Ernest W. Burgess, "The Growth of the City: An Introduction to a Research Project," *Publications of the American Sociological Society*, 18 (1924), pp. 85–97; reprinted in Robert E. Park, Ernest W. Burgess, and Roderick D. McKenzie, *The City* (Chicago: University of Chicago Press, 1925), pp. 47–62.

5. Ernest W. Burgess, "Urban Areas," in T. V. Smith and L. D. White (Eds.), *Chicago: An Experiment in Social Science Research* (Chicago: University of Chicago Press, 1929), pp. 114–123.

6. Ernest W. Burgess, "The New Community and Its Future," *Annals of the American Academy of Political and Social Science*, 149 (1930), pp. 161–162.

7. Ernest W. Burgess, "The Determination of Gradients in the Growth of the City," *Publications of the American Sociological Society*, 21 (1927), p. 178.

8. "The Growth of the City," in *The City, op. cit.*, p. 48.

9. "The Determination of Gradients in the Growth of the City," *op. cit.*, p. 178. These views are reminiscent of the treatment of "central" and "axial" growth outlined in Richard M. Hurd, *Principles of City Land Values* (New York: The Record and Guide, 1903).

10. Ernest W. Burgess, "Residential Segregation in American Cities," *Annals of the American Academy of Political and Social Science*, 140 (1928), p. 105.

11. "The Growth of the City," in *The City, op. cit.*, p. 50.

12. The general tendencies stressed by Burgess had been observed in London some twenty years earlier by Charles Booth et al., *Life and Labour of the People in London* (London: Macmillan, 1904), final vol. p. 205. Moreover, Booth pointed to a "centrifugal tendency," elsewhere designated as "the law of successive migration," wherein "the movement takes place gradually from ring to ring accompanied by a slow change of class." *Ibid.*, p. 183. Some years earlier, Friedrich Engels had discerned a zonation according to social class in Manchester. Based on observations made in 1842–1844, he published the following account in 1845:

> In the centre of Manchester there is a fairly large commercial district, which is about half a mile long and half a mile broad. This district is almost entirely given over to offices and warehouses. Nearly the whole of this district has no permanent residents and is deserted at night. . . . Around this commercial quarter there is a belt of built up areas on the average one and a half miles in width, which is occupied entirely by working-class dwellings. . . . Beyond this belt of working-class houses or dwellings lie the districts inhabited by the middle classes and the upper classes. The former are to be found in regularly laid out streets near the working-class districts. . . . The villas of the upper classes are surrounded by gardens and lie in the higher and remoter parts.

Friedrich Engels, *The Condition of the Working Class in England* (New York: Macmillan, 1958 ed.), pp. 54–55.

13. "Residential Segregation in American Cities," *op. cit.*, p. 108.

14. "The Determination of Gradients in the Growth of the City," *op. cit.*, p. 178.

15. Ernest W. Burgess, "The Ecology and Social Psychology of the City," in Donald J. Bogue (Ed.), *Needed Urban and Metropolitan Research* (Oxford, Ohio, and Chicago: Scripps Foundation for Research in Population Problems, Miami University, and Population Research and Training Center, University of Chicago, 1953), pp. 80–81.

16. "The New Community and Its Future," *op. cit.*, p. 161.

17. James A. Quinn, *Human Ecology* (New York: Prentice-Hall, 1950), pp. 120–121.

18. *Ibid.*, p. 121.

19. *Ibid.*, pp. 122–123.

20. James A. Quinn, "The Burgess Zonal Hypothesis and Its Critics," *American Sociological Review*, 5 (1940), pp. 210–218; see also James A. Quinn, *Human Ecology, op. cit.*, pp. 127–135.

21. Milla Aïssa Alihan, *Social Ecology: A Critical Analysis* (New York: Columbia University Press, 1938), pp. 224–225.

22. Maurice R. Davie, "The Pattern of Urban Growth," in George P. Murdock (Ed.), *Studies in the Science of Society* (New Haven: Yale University Press, 1937), pp. 133–161; Homer Hoyt, *The Structure and Growth of Residential Neighborhoods in American Cities* (Washington: Federal Housing Administration, 1939).

23. Walter Firey, *Land Use in Central Boston* (Cambridge: Harvard University Press, 1947); for a summary, see Walter Firey, "Sentiment and Symbolism as Ecological Variables," *American Sociological Review*, 10 (1945), pp. 140–148.

24. See Harvey W. Zorbaugh, "The Natural Areas of the City," in Ernest W. Burgess (Ed.), *The Urban Community* (Chicago: University of Chicago Press, 1926), p. 222.

25. For example, Elsa S. Longmoor and Erle F. Young, "Ecological Interrelationships of Juvenile Delinquency, Dependency, and Population Mobility: A Cartographic Analysis of Data from Long Beach, California," *American Journal of Sociology*, 41 (1936), pp. 598–610; Raymond V. Bowers, "Ecological Patterning of Rochester, New York," *American Sociological Review*, 4 (1939), pp. 180–189; E. Franklin Frazier, "Negro Harlem: An Ecological Study," *American Journal of Sociology*, 43 (1937), pp. 72–88.

26. These include the studies by Hoyt, Davie, and Firey, all cited above.

27. Theodore R. Anderson and Janice A. Egeland, "Spatial Aspects of Social Area Analysis," *American Sociological Review*, 26 (1961), pp. 392–398. See also Leo F. Schnore, "The Socio-economic Status of Cities and Suburbs," *American Sociological Review*, 28 (1963), pp. 76–85.

28. For example, Theodore Caplow, "Urban Structure in France," *American Sociological Review*, 17 (1952), pp. 544–549; Theodore Caplow, "Recent Research on the Ecology of Paris," *Midwest Sociologist*, 16 (1954), pp. 19–21; Paul F. Cressey, "Ecological Organization of Rangoon," *Sociology and Social Research*, 40 (1956), pp. 166–169; Peter Collison and John Mogey, "Residence and Social Class in Oxford," *American Journal of Sociology*, 64 (1959), pp. 599–605; Noel P. Gist, "The Ecology of Bangalore, India: An East-West Comparison," *Social Forces*, 35 (1957), pp. 356–365; Amos H. Hawley, "Some Observations on the Land Use Pattern in Manila,"

in his *Papers in Demography and Public Administration,* rev. ed. (Manila: Institute of Public Administration, University of the Philippines, 1954), pp. 68–82; Amos H. Hawley, "Land Value Patterns in Okayama, Japan, 1940 and 1952," *American Journal of Sociology,* 60 (1955), pp. 487–492. If one moves outside the strict confines of the sociological literature, many more cases can be assembled; see, for example, Homer Hoyt, "The Structure and Growth of American Cities Contrasted with the Structure and Growth of European Cities," *Urban Land,* 18 (1959), pp. 3–8; Kenichi Tanabe, "Development of Areal Structure of Japanese Cities in the Case of the Castle Town—As a Geographic Contribution to the Study of Urban Structure," *Science Reports,* Tohoku University (Seventh Series, Geography), March 1959, pp. 88–105; Y. Watanabe, "The Urban Region of Sendai," *Science Reports,* Tohoku University (Seventh Series, Geography), March 1953, pp. 30–52; F. L. Hauser, "The Ecological Pattern of Four European Cities and Two Theories of Urban Expansion," *Journal of the American Institute of Planners,* 17 (1951), pp. 111–129; Erdmann Doane Beynon, "Budapest: An Ecological Study," *Geographical Review,* 33 (1943), pp. 256–275; Sten de Geer, "Greater Stockholm: A Geographical Interpretation," *Geographical Review,* 35 (1945), pp. 74–97; W. William-Olsson, "Stockholm: Its Structure and Development," *Geographical Review,* 30 (1940), pp. 420–438; Julie Moscheles, "The Demographic, Social, and Economic Regions of Greater Prague," *Geographical Review,* 27 (1937), pp. 414–429; Robert E. Dickinson, *The West European City: A Geographical Interpretation* (London: Routledge and Kegan Paul, 1951). Again, the Burgess hypothesis does not receive unanimous endorsement or rejection.

29. The studies initially reviewed most intensively were the following, listed in the order of their appearance: Asael T. Hansen, "The Ecology of a Latin-American City," in Edward B. Reuter (Ed.), *Race and Culture Contacts* (New York: McGraw-Hill, 1934), pp. 124–152; Norman S. Hayner, "Oaxaca: City of Old Mexico," *Sociology and Social Research,* 29 (1944), pp. 87–95; Norman S. Hayner, "Mexico City: Its Growth and Configuration," *American Journal of Sociology,* 50 (1945), pp. 295–304; Olen E. Leonard, "La Paz, Bolivia: Its Population and Growth," *American Sociological Review,* 13 (1948), pp. 448–454; Harry B. Hawthorn and Audrey E. Hawthorn, "The Shape of a City: Some Observations on Sucre, Bolivia," *Sociology and Social Research,* 33 (1948), pp. 87–91; Theodore Caplow, "The Social Ecology of Guatemala City," *Social Forces,* 28 (1949), pp. 113–133; Floyd Dotson and Lillian Ota Dotson, "Ecological Trends in the City of Guadalajara, Mexico," *Social Forces,* 32 (1954), pp. 367–374. Other Latin American materials will be cited later at appropriate points, but these seven studies formed the core of our initial inquiry.

30. Hansen, *op. cit.,* p. 126.

31. *Ibid.,* p. 138.

32. *Ibid.,* p. 141.

33. *Ibid.,* p. 140.

34. Leonard, *op. cit.,* pp. 452–454.

35. Harry B. Hawthorn and Audrey E. Hawthorn, "Stratification in a Latin American City," *Social Forces,* 27 (1948), p. 23.

36. Norman S. Hayner, "Differential Social Change in a Mexican Town," *Social Forces,* 26 (1948), p. 383.

37. Hayner, "Mexico City . . . ," *op. cit.*, p. 295.

38. Hayner, "Oaxaca . . . ," *op. cit.*, p. 87.

39. Dotson and Dotson, *op. cit.*, p. 367.

40. Caplow, "The Social Ecology of Guatemala City," *op. cit.*, p. 132.

41. *Ibid.*

42. Hawthorn and Hawthorn, "Stratification in a Latin American City," *op. cit.*

43. Caplow, *op. cit.*, p. 132.

44. Norman S. Hayner, "Criminogenic Zones in Mexico City," *American Sociological Review*, 11 (1946), pp. 428–438.

45. Hayner, "Differential Social Change in a Mexican Town," *op. cit.*

46. Floyd Dotson, "A Note on Participation in Voluntary Associations in a Mexican City," *American Sociological Review*, 18 (1953), pp. 380–386.

47. Caplow, *op. cit.*, p. 132.

48. Dotson and Dotson, "Ecological Trends in the City of Guadalajara, Mexico," *op. cit.*, p. 368; italics added.

49. Quinn, *Human Ecology, op. cit.*, p. 123.

50. Dotson and Dotson, "Ecological Trends in the City of Guadalajara, Mexico," *op. cit.*, p. 373.

51. Caplow, *op. cit.*, p. 129.

52. *Ibid.*, pp. 132–133.

53. Louis E. Guzman, *An Annotated Bibliography of Publications on Urban Latin America* (Chicago: Department of Geography, University of Chicago, August 1952); W. Bazzanella, *Problemas de urbanização na America Latina: Fontes bibliográficas* (Rio de Janeiro: Centro Latino Americano Pesquisas em Ciencias Sociais, 1960).

54. See, for example, Raymond E. Crist, "The Personality of Popayán," *Rural Sociology*, 15 (1950), pp. 130–140.

55. In addition to land use maps and miscellaneous materials, over fifty published sources were consulted.

56. Jean Comhaire and Werner J. Cahnman, *How Cities Grew: The Historical Sociology of Cities* (Madison, N. J.: Florham Park Press, 1959), p. 40.

57. Gideon Sjoberg, *The Preindustrial City: Past and Present* (Glencoe, Ill.: Free Press, 1960), pp. 96–98.

58. *Ibid.*, p. 98.

59. Comhaire and Cahnman, *op. cit.*, p. 36.

60. Gideon Sjoberg, "The Development of Cities," *Economic Development and Cultural Change*, 9 (1960), p. 94.

61. Sjoberg, *The Preindustrial City, op. cit.*, pp. 98–99.

62. J. Fred Rippy, *Latin America: A Modern History* (Ann Arbor: University of Michigan Press, 1958), p. 64. See also George Kubler, "Mexican Urbanism in the 16th Century," *Art Bulletin*, 24 (1942), pp. 160–171.

63. Jose M. Bens Arrarte, "Inicio de urbanismo colonial en Hispano-América: Comentarios a las Leyes de Indias en lo referente a la fundación de ciudades," *Unión Interamericana del Caribe, Boletín*, 3 (1942), pp. 79–102; Dan Stanislawski, "Early Spanish Town Planning in the New World," *Geographical Review*, 37 (1947), pp. 95–105. The Spanish apparently imposed the same general pattern on the Philippines: "The most distinctive items in the whole settlement procedure were the organized and formal patterns that evolved. The plaza, the church, and the government buildings

were key units, with shops and the homes of leading families near the central area. Other families lived farther from the plaza and even at some distance." J. E. Spencer, *Land and People in the Philippines* (Berkeley: University of California Press, 1954), p. 141.

64. Caplow, *op. cit.*, p. 116.

65. Stanislawski, *op. cit.*; Felix W. McBryde, *Cultural and Historical Geography of Southwest Guatemala* (Washington: Smithsonian Institution, 1947), Institute of Social Anthropology, Publication No. 4.

66. George A. Theodorson (Ed.), *Studies in Human Ecology* (Evanston, Ill.: Row, Peterson, 1961), pp. 326–327.

67. John Howland Rowe, "The Inca Culture at the Time of the Spanish Conquest," in Julian H. Steward (Ed.), *Handbook of South American Indians* (Washington: Bureau of American Ethnology, 1946), Bureau of American Ethnology Bulletin 143, Vol. 2, p. 229.

68. Francis Violich, *Cities of Latin America* (New York: Reinhold, 1944), pp. 22–25.

69. John Charles Gibson, "A Study of the Relationship of Settlement and Socio-Cultural Patterns in Urban Spanish America" (unpublished M. A. thesis, Department of Sociology and Anthropology, University of North Carolina, 1953), p. 13.

70. George C. Vaillant, *The Aztecs of Mexico* (Harmondsworth, Middlesex: Penguin Books, 1950), Chap. 13.

71. Edwin M. Shook and Tatiana Proskouriakoff, "Settlement Patterns in Meso-America and the Sequence in the Guatemalan Highlands," in Gordon R. Willey (Ed.), *Prehistoric Settlement Patterns in the New World* (New York: Wenner-Gren Foundation for Anthropological Research, 1956), pp. 93–100. The reference is to the Franciscan Bishop, Diego de Landa, whose account of life in Yucatán was first published in 1566; see Alfred M. Tozzer, *Landa's Relación de las cosas de Yucatán* (Cambridge, Mass.: Papers of the Peabody Museum of American Archaeology and Ethnology, 1941).

72. Gibson, *op. cit.*, p. 21.

73. There is even difficulty in interpreting the significance of such a thing as the rectangular gridiron pattern. Comhaire and Cahnman have said that "Concerning street patterns, we need not restrict our attention to the North American continent in order to recognize the grid as the hallmark of secondary or colonial settlement. Almost all the cities of Spanish America are laid out that way." *Op. cit.*, p. 41. This identification of the grid with colonialism is perhaps too narrow, for a city with such a pattern was built at Kahun, some sixty miles south of Cairo in Egypt's Dynasty XII (*circa* 1900 B.C.) to house the workmen building a pyramid. Perhaps the grid should be associated with planned *new* towns, that is, those built *de novo*, from the ground up, rather than piecemeal. See Martin S. Briggs, "Town-Planning from the Ancient World to the Renaissance," in Charles Singer et al. (Eds.), *A History of Technology* (New York: Oxford University Press, 1957), Vol. II, pp. 269–299. Mohenjo-Daro, an Indian city dating from the third millennium B.C., also had a regular grid pattern; see Seton Lloyd, *Ruined Cities of Iraq*, 3rd ed. (Oxford: Oxford University Press, 1945). Despite a wealth of evidence for the existence of the rectangular street plan in the Western Hemisphere in pre-Columbian times, Stanislawski has asserted that this plan appeared nowhere in the New World prior to

the Spanish Conquest. Dan Stanislawski, "The Origin and Spread of the Grid-Pattern Town," *Geographical Review*, 46 (1946), pp. 105–120.

74. Robert L. Carmin, *Anápolis, Brazil* (Chicago: Department of Geography, University of Chicago, 1953), p. 69.

75. "The Growth of the City," in *The City, op. cit.*, pp. 50–51.

76. Homer Hoyt, *The Structure and Growth of Residential Neighborhoods in American Cities, op. cit.*, Fig. 29, p. 83, and Fig. 31, p. 166. This shift is described in detail in Homer Hoyt, *One Hundred Years of Land Values in Chicago* (Chicago: University of Chicago Press, 1933), Chap. 6.

77. Rudolf Heberle, "Social Consequences of the Industrialization of Southern Cities," *Social Forces*, 27 (1948), pp. 34–35.

78. Hoyt, *The Structure and Growth of Residential Neighborhoods in American Cities, op. cit.*, p. 76.

79. Dotson and Dotson, "La estructura ecologica de las ciudades mexicanas," *op. cit.*, pp. 43–45; our translation.

80. Carmin, *op. cit.*, p. 67. The differences between Latin American and U. S. cities are truly striking when local transportation is examined. The Federal District of Mexico City—one of the largest and most modern metropolises south of the Rio Grande—had 35 automobiles per thousand population in 1950; in the same year, Los Angeles County had 363 per thousand, and there were 152 per thousand in New York City, where dependence on public transit is very heavy. Petesch, *op. cit.*, p. 84. Associated with these differences are variations in population density; Mexico City's density was around 40,000 per square mile in 1950, whereas the three most densely settled cities in the U. S. showed density ratios of 24,537 (New York City), 17,450 (Chicago), and 16,286 (Philadelphia).

81. Sjoberg, *The Preindustrial City, op. cit.*, pp. 98–99. One wonders whether or not values are so "readily revised" with technological change, whether they are independent of such change, and whether they lead or lag in the process.

82. Some of the comparative materials encountered in this study offer intriguing suggestions concerning the ultimate development of a theory of "incremental growth and residues." The Japanese castle town, for example, developed with the preindustrial pattern centered around the castle. With industrialization, however, a new concentric zonation, focused on the railroad and a nearby business district, was superimposed on the older configuration. See Tanabe, *op. cit.*, and Watanabe, *op. cit.* For the United States, a suggestive treatment of the "evolution" of residential areas that follows these lines is contained in Edgar M. Hoover and Raymond Vernon, *Anatomy of a Metropolis* (Cambridge: Harvard University Press, 1959), pp. 190–207.

83. Philip M. Hauser, *Population Perspectives* (New Brunswick, N. J.: Rutgers University Press, 1960), p. 115.

84. One of the rare attempts to develop a coherent set of principles for comparative research in sociology was undertaken in the Cross-cultural Methods Project at Cornell University. See Edward A. Suchman, *The Comparative Method in Social Research* (Ithaca: Department of Sociology, Cornell University, n.d.), hectographed.

85. For a useful bibliography that suggests the broad topical scope of

current comparative inquiries, see "Comparative Cross National Research," *International Social Science Bulletin*, 7 (1955), pp. 622–641.

86. Four extremely enlightening statements are to be found in Erwin H. Ackerknecht, "On the Comparative Method in Anthropology," in Robert F. Spencer (Ed.), *Method and Perspective in Anthropology* (Minneapolis: University of Minnesota Press, 1954), pp. 117–125; Fred Eggan, "Social Anthropology and the Method of Controlled Comparison," *American Anthropologist*, 56 (1954), pp. 743–763; Oscar Lewis, "Comparisons in Cultural Anthropology," in *Yearbook of Anthropology—1955* (New York: Wenner-Gren Foundation for Anthropological Research, 1955), pp. 259–292; Gideon Sjoberg, "The Comparative Method in the Social Sciences," *Philosophy of Science*, 22 (1955), pp. 106–117.

87. Sjoberg discusses an example of this tendency in his critique of Leopold Rosenmayr, "Anotaciones sobre el Fenómeno de la 'Urbanización Allende de la Ciudad,'" *Revista Mexicana de Sociologia*, 20 (1958), pp. 737–738. According to Sjoberg, Rosenmayr argues that "the traditionally high prestige accorded residence in or near Vienna's historic nucleus is responsible for the low incidence of suburbanization, although he falsely considers this a peculiarly Viennese phenomenon. Like most urban sociologists, these writers have not perceived the generality of their findings, each being content to immerse himself in the culture or society that is his specialty." Sjoberg, *The Preindustrial City, op. cit.*, p. 98.

88. Although Hoyt says that "it is clearly apparent that the concentric circle theory of city structure is defective," he goes on to say that "it may be urged, however, that the concentric circle theory relates to an ideal pattern of city structure, and that if the rent areas of a city were fitted into a theoretical framework of concentric circles, a general tendency toward an upward gradation of rents from the center to the periphery of a city might be observed." Hoyt, *The Structure and Growth of Residential Neighborhoods in American Cities, op. cit.*, p. 76. More recently, Hoyt has claimed that the "sector" pattern is coming to typify cities throughout Latin America, despite its absence in the colonial cities of the past.

> The pattern of the old colonial cities south of the border established by the Spanish and Portuguese was characterized by the square city block approximately 400 x 400 feet with the outside walls of the dwellings built to the street line concealing patios, gardens and interior dwellings. In this type of development, as in Pompeii, the quality of the home and its elegance or poverty were not revealed to the passerby in the street. Houses of interior magnificence with spacious gardens were often built side by side with modest dwellings, an intermingling of rich and poor residents in the same block and no particular separation into neighborhoods in accordance with the sector theory. However, in recent times the newer growth of Latin American residential areas has been in the form of free standing houses and in these modern settlements the sector theory usually holds good; that is, the higher income groups live in one sector or on one side of the city and the poorer families in another sector.

Homer Hoyt, "The Residential and Retail Patterns of Leading Latin American Cities," *Land Economics*, 39 (1963), p. 449. See also Homer Hoyt,

"Recent Distortions of the Classical Models of Urban Structure," *Land Economics*, 40 (1964), pp. 199–212. Another recent objection to the Burgess hypothesis has been entered by Morse:

> In a Latin American city rural migrants and, in general, the proletariat are not customarily crowded into a blighted area at the urban core, as in the schema devised for the North American city by the sociologist E. W. Burgess; but they are scattered, often in makeshift dwellings, in peripheral or interstitial zones. The Latin American city center with its spacious plaza was traditionally the residence area for the wealthy and was the point of concentration for urban services and utilities. The quickening of commercial activity in this center may displace well-to-do residents without necessarily creating "contaminated" and overcrowded belts of social disorganization. The poor are often not attracted into transitional zones by cheap rents; they tend to move out to unused land as the city expands, erecting their own shacks. The downtown area becomes converted for commercial uses or for compact and modern middle- and upper-income residences.

Richard M. Morse, "Latin American Cities: Aspects of Function and Structure," *Comparative Studies in Society and History*, 4 (1962), p. 485.

89. Walter Firey, *Land Use in Central Boston, op. cit.*

90. Although they are not too helpful, these terms have come into widespread usage in recent years. The "classical" view is that enunciated by Park, Burgess, and McKenzie—members of the "Chicago School." Those like Firey, who criticize this view, and who advocate paying attention to values, sentiments, etc., are labeled "sociocultural" or "cultural" ecologists. Both Quinn and Hawley have been treated as "neo-orthodox" or "neo-classicists," which suggests that the category is not perfectly homogeneous. For a discussion of these supposed "schools of thought," see George A. Theodorson, *op. cit.*

91. See Leo F. Schnore, "Social Morphology and Human Ecology," *American Journal of Sociology*, 63 (1958), pp. 620–634; Otis Dudley Duncan and Leo F. Schnore, "Cultural, Behavioral, and Ecological Perspectives in the Study of Social Organization," *American Journal of Sociology*, 65 (1959), pp. 132–146; Leo F. Schnore, "The Myth of Human Ecology," *Sociological Inquiry*, 31 (1961), pp. 128–139. See also Otis Dudley Duncan, "Population Distribution and Community Structure," *Cold Spring Harbor Symposia on Quantitative Biology*, 22 (1957), pp. 357–371; Otis Dudley Duncan, "Human Ecology and Population Studies," in Philip M. Hauser and Otis Dudley Duncan (Eds.), *The Study of Population* (Chicago: University of Chicago Press, 1959), pp. 678–716; Otis Dudley Duncan, "From Social System to Ecosystem," *Sociological Inquiry*, 31 (1961), pp. 140–149.

92. Leonard, *op. cit.*, pp. 448, 452.

93. Hayner, "Mexico City . . . ," *op. cit.*, p. 298.

94. Caplow, *op. cit.*, p. 130.

95. *Ibid.*, p. 131.

96. T. Lynn Smith and C. A. McMahan, *The Sociology of Urban Life* (New York: Dryden Press, 1951), p. 346. See also Philip M. Hauser (Ed.), *Urbanization in Latin America* (Paris: UNESCO, 1961), *passim*.

97. Gideon Sjoberg, *The Preindustrial City, op. cit.,* pp. 91–92. See also Svend Riemer, "Functional Housing in the Middle Ages," *Transactions of the Wisconsin Academy of Sciences, Arts, and Letters,* 2 (1951), pp. 77–91.

98. The planning literature is replete with discussions regarding the place of the "neighborhood" in the contemporary city. In some respects, planners are advocating a deliberate re-creation of subcommunities that are as self-sufficient as possible. For an extreme version, see the discussions of the *microdistrict*—a residential compound supplied with schools and trade and service establishments—in *The Soviet Review,* 2 (1961), pp. 28–40.

99. Ralph L. Beals, "Social Stratification in Latin America," *American Journal of Sociology,* 58 (1953), pp. 329–330. Speaking of the last thirty years of Latin American history, Rippy has identified three critical trends: rapid population increase, urban growth, and expansion of the middle class. Rippy, *op. cit.,* pp. 402–403.

100. W. F. Ogburn, *Social Change,* 2nd ed. (New York: Viking Press, 1950), especially "Social Evolution Reconsidered," pp. 369–393.

101. See, for example, Surinder K. Mehta, "A Comparative Analysis of the Industrial Structure of the Urban Labor Force of Burma and the United States," *Economic Development and Cultural Change,* 9 (1961), pp. 164–179; Andrew Collver and Eleanor Langlois, "The Female Labor Force in Metropolitan Areas: An International Comparison," *Economic Development and Cultural Change,* 10 (1962), pp. 367–385.

102. Nels Anderson, "Urbanism and Urbanization," *American Journal of Sociology,* 65 (1959), p. 70. Anderson refers to United Nations Secretariat, *Urban Land Policies* (New York: United Nations, 1952).

103. This chapter was originally prepared during the academic year 1960–1961, and it has not been thoroughly revised to take account of more recent developments in urban research in the two Americas. Some of the more important and relevant contributions are cited in Charles Wagley (Ed.), *Social Science Research on Latin America* (New York: Columbia University Press, 1964) and in Leo F. Schnore, *The Urban Scene: Human Ecology and Demography* (New York: Free Press of Glencoe, 1965).

PART THREE

Selected Research Problems

Each of the four chapters in this part is devoted to the consideration of specific research areas or problems. They represent the current interests of the authors, who with one exception (Brian J. L. Berry) served as members of the Committee on Urbanization; they are not intended to select problems on a comprehensive basis or to establish priorities in research.

The first chapter in Part 3, Chapter 11, by Brian J. L. Berry, is an account of "Research Frontiers in Urban Geography." It deals with some of the more advanced theories and techniques of research that have come to be known as "regional science," which makes extensive use of mathematical models and electronic computers. The major substantive topics considered by the geographic frontiersmen have been: (1) systems of cities; (2) correlates of city size and urbanization, including models of city-size distributions; (3) relations between urban patterns and transportation systems; (4) the spatial structure of land uses within cities; and (5) simulation models as the means of conducting "laboratory experiments" in urban areas.

Chapter 12, "Urban Economic Growth and Development in a National System of Cities," by Wilbur R. Thompson, focuses on a problem in "macroeconomics," the aggregate performance of the urban area as a whole rather than the internal arrangement of its parts. The city is viewed as a local labor market—a cluster of work places surrounded by workers' homes. Stressing economic growth, the chapter deals with such questions as the determinants and consequences of the level, distribution, and stability of local income and employment. At the same time, the city is seen as a dependent, vulnerable subeconomy, interlocked in a broad national system of cities—a subeconomy whose fate rests only partly in its own hands.

Chapter 13, "The Folk-Urban Ideal Types," is made up of two parts. Part A, by Oscar Lewis, offers "Further Observations on the Folk-Urban Continuum and Urbanization with Special Reference to Mexico City." In this essay Lewis contributes to a growing field of study in anthropology. Earlier anthropological interest in cities was focused primarily upon the origin and growth of cities. Within the past thirty years, beginning with Hansen's study of Merida (as part of the Redfield study of Yucatán), anthropologists have begun to study population sectors within contemporary cities. Lewis's study of Tipoztecan families in Mexico City was one of the first of this new type of study. In this statement Lewis returns to some of the themes first developed in his restudy of Tepoztlan, the Mexican village that served as the basis of Redfield's thinking about the folk-urban continuum. He suggests that "we may learn more about the processes of change by studying relatively short-run sequential modifications in particular aspects of institutions in both the so-called folk and urban societies than by global comparisons between folk and urban." He concludes that in place of the latter we need "a large number of subtypes based upon better defined variables and perhaps the addition of new ones."

Part B, by Philip M. Hauser, is in a similar vein. Entitled "Observations on the Urban-Folk and Urban-Rural Dichotomies as Forms of Western Ethnocentrism," it is an essay (originally written in 1955) that criticizes the manner in which these concepts have been received and used by the social science community. His central theme is that these ideal-type constructs have been widely accepted more as research findings than as instruments designed to further research. The inapplicability of the folk-urban and rural-urban typologies to the underdeveloped areas is indicated and the need for more empirical investigation is urged.

The final chapter in Part 3 and in the book is by Eric E. Lampard. Under the rubric "Historical Aspects of Urbanization," Chapter 14 presents a study of societal differentiation or division of labor within a framework of human ecology. Primordial urbanization is viewed as a process of collective adaptation which first enabled populations in half a dozen areas of the Old and New Worlds to organize and utilize a productive "surplus," or social saving. By means of definitive urban organization, populations formed into more productive social systems in a growing variety of physical and social environments. At no time before the industrial revolution of the eighteenth century, however, did any population achieve the capacity to support more than a small fraction of its total numbers in the urban centers. Throughout most of its six-thousand-year history, the process of urbanization was checked by its dependence on a relatively undifferentiated agrarian base. Only when populations had achieved the technological capacity to convert and the organizational capacity to control high per capita levels of inanimate heat-energy did an urbanized society become possible.

It must be emphasized that the research problems to which references are made in these chapters are highly selected. They clearly do not represent a rounded or comprehensive attempt to map out the many areas of research that beckon the student of urbanization.

11

Research Frontiers in Urban Geography

Brian J. L. Berry

Urban geography also has its "young men on new frontiers." The research of a growing group of these men appears, at first glance, to be markedly different from that of other urban geographers in the recent past. Differences, however, occur in the ways in which research is undertaken rather than in basic objectives and concepts. Substantive foci of urban geography remain unchanged. Research on the "frontier" simply has greater theoretical orientation and shows increased reliance on quantitative analysis and modern digital computers.

The "new frontier" is a decade old at the most. It is found primarily in American and Swedish urban geography, and there exist few signs of penetration elsewhere.[1] In this short time no dramatic contributions have been made. Most new studies have been preoccupied with testing existing concepts and theories. Clarification and reformulation of such concepts and theories have been the keynotes, although with some attempts at extension.

Since the past decade has been dominated by rapid technical advance throughout the social sciences, it is not surprising that geography has been caught up in the quantitative maelstrom. Incisive mathematical and statistical methods have been introduced to the discipline, along with improved theory-building devices,[2] but use of these devices has been limited by the availability of simple, concise, precisely stated concepts. Hence, the main concern of most recent theoretically oriented quantitative work has been to begin putting the conceptual house in order.

Among the major substantive topics considered by the frontiersmen have been: (1) systems of cities; (2) correlates of city size and urbanization, and models of city-size distributions; (3) relations between urban patterns and transportation systems; (4) the spatial structure of land uses within cities; and (5) simulation models as the means of conducting urban "laboratory experiments." In the following pages we shall review the work that falls under each of the foregoing headings, and examine in detail any new departures or particularly interesting contributions that have been made.

Systems of Cities

The argument underlying work with systems of cities may be summarized in the following way:

1. We live in a specialized society in which economic activities are performed at those locations that provide the greatest competitive advantage and in which an efficient transportation system facilitates exchange between the various specialized interdependent parts.

2. Of the specialized economic activities, some require considerable area (agriculture, for example), whereas others are more efficiently performed in limited local concentrations.

3. The locally concentrated activities, which provide the basic support for cities, may be classified into those that are oriented to raw material, those that are located at points intermediate between raw materials and markets, involved in intermediate and final processing and transformation of raw materials, and those that are market-oriented. Activities oriented to raw material are dominantly primary and secondary, and display marked differences from place to place depending on the developed resource endowment of those places. Activities in intermediate locations are usually secondary and are found most frequently at some favorable spot on a transport system, such as an assembly point, a gateway, a break-of-bulk point, or a port. Market-oriented activities may be secondary (for example, when there is a weight gain involved in the final processing of raw materials or of intermediates prior to delivery) but are dominantly tertiary, concerned with direct service of consuming populations. Since the consuming population of a country like the United States (whatever the specialized activity that provides the basic economic support) consumes an essentially similar basket of goods wherever it may be, market-oriented activities repeat themselves in many places. Their spatial patterns and the size of locational concentrations are therefore a function of (a) the efficiency with which they can supply the universally similar demands and (b) the spatial distribution of the demands.

4. The three orientations of locally concentrated activities give rise to three principles of urban location: cities as the sites of specialized

economic activities, cities as the expression of breaks in transportation, and cities as central places. All three principles, or some combination of them, may operate in any particular city.

Differences among cities as the expression of breaks in transportation on the one hand, and the relations of urban location and transport networks on the other, should be distinguished. All specialized economic activities are influenced in their choice of location by, and many have their locational patterns prescribed by, transport costs and the nature of transport networks. Some activities may locate at intermediate points on transport networks when there is a break of bulk or when processing-in-transit privileges are granted; this, however, is not the same as the interlocking relationships of transportation and specialization, which are basic to understanding all three principles of urban location.[3]

Explicit mention has been made only of economic activities, but cities are also centers of political and social life, of education and the arts. These other functions may be analyzed with varying degrees of adequacy under the rubric of market orientation, using central-place principles, although certain kinds of recreational functions involve orientation to raw materials.[4]

Cities as Central Places

Most recent work dealing with systems of cities has involved re-examination and elaboration of central-place principles. Many of the implications of central-place theory as it has been generalized from Christaller have been verified, and certain obscurities of the original theoretical statement have been clarified by a series of comparative studies.[5]

Evidence has been provided, for example, that a central-place hierarchy is indeed present in many parts of the world: by Berry and Garrison in the northwestern United States, Godlund in Sweden, Carol in Switzerland and the Karroo, Mayfield in the Punjab, Kar around Calcutta, and by Green and Philbrick in the United Kingdom and the American Midwest, among others.[6] In addition to providing this evidence relating to a hierarchy of centers, these studies have also revealed a hierarchy of trade areas. Many of these studies have been traditional in conception and execution. Applications of new methods are to be found, however, in the statistical analyses of Godlund, Berry and Garrison, and Mayfield.

New departures have been provided by Thomas, Nystuen, and Dacey. Thomas placed Christaller's concept of "centers of the same population size-class" within a stochastic framework.[7] Thus he was able to provide a critical test of the hypothesis that size classes have associated with them "typical" distances by which centers of the same class are separated, and that as size increases, so does distance. He found that the hypothesis was verified only in part, although distance-size relations were shown to have been extremely stable through time in Iowa.

Nystuen has helped clarify why trade areas for particular kinds of goods vary in size between higher- and lower-order central places, basing his analysis on considerations of utility derived from consumer shopping trips of different kinds.[8] Dacey generalized nearest-neighbor methods of analyzing the spacing of central places.[9] Nystuen and Dacey also applied the mathematical theory of graphs to the analysis of nodal regions centering on higher-order centers, and to problems of the rank or status of central places.[10] The methods they introduced involve expression of linear graphs in terms of matrices, and the inversion of these matrices to obtain indexes of association.

There have been several attempts to restate and generalize the theory. One attempt was by Berry and Garrison, who sought to express the essential concepts of central-place theory in a form free of the limiting assumptions that lead to a hexagonal spatial geometry.[11] Morrill tried to generalize ideas of trade areas using notions of spatial price equilibrium.[12] Bunge has used set theory and topology in his attempts to show that certain restrictive geometric assumptions are unnecessary.[13] The economist Beckmann has stated the traditional theory in a more concise form.[14] These studies indicate the feasibility of developing a general central-place theory. A further step toward such a general theory was recently taken with the development of a model [15] that describes many of the features of central-place systems in the aggregate and incorporates systematic links between the aggregate relations and the more traditional picture of a steplike central-place hierarchy that may be found in more local (elemental) studies.[16]

Parts of the aggregative model are as follows:

DEFINITIONS

P_c = population of the central place
P_{ex} = population of the tributary area
D_m = maximum distance consumers travel to a central place of a given size
A = area of trade area
C = number of central functions performed by a center
Q = gross population density
E = number of establishments located in a center

IDENTITIES

$$P_t = P_c + P_{ex} \tag{1.1}$$

$$A = f(D_m) \tag{1.2}$$

$$P_{ex} = AQ_{ex} = f(D_m)Q_{ex} \tag{1.3}$$

$$P_t = AQ_t = f(D_m)Q_t \tag{1.4}$$

STRUCTURAL EQUATIONS [17]

$$\log P_c = a_1 + b_1 C \tag{2.1}$$

$$\log D_m = a_4 + b_4 C \tag{2.2}$$

IMPLICATIONS FROM 1.1–2.2

$$\log P_{ex} = \log Q_{ex} + \log \{f[\log^{-1}(a_4 + b_4 c)]\} \tag{3.1}$$

$$\log A = \log \left\{ f\left[\log^{-1}\left(a_4 - \frac{b_4 a_1}{b_1}\right) P_c^{b_4/b_1}\right]\right\} \tag{3.2}$$

$$\log P_t = \log Q_t + \log \left\{f\left[\log^{-1}\left(a_4 - \frac{b_4 a_1}{b_1}\right) P_c^{b_4/b_1}\right]\right\} \tag{3.3}$$

The implications 3.1–3.3 have been verified empirically.[18] Fits to both structural equations and implications have coefficients of determination exceeding 0.84 in seven different study areas.

Although continuous functional relationships are described by the model, the comparative studies also show that, if small areas are studied, then the observable patterns are those of the classical steplike hierarchy of central places, nested trade areas, and predictable consumer travel behavior.

A set of inequalities applied in conjunction with 3.2 and 3.3 provides the link between these elemental patterns and the aggregative findings, which at first glance might seem to be at odds:

VILLAGES

$$\log A < 10.4 - 2.67 \log P \tag{4.1}$$

TOWNS

$$\log A < 9.3 - 2.067 \log P \tag{4.2}$$

CITIES

$$\log A < 22.25 - 4.75 \log P \tag{4.3}$$

From these, the maximum trade area of centers of any rank may be obtained, after equations 3.2 and 3.3 have provided overall relationships between areas and populations served at given gross densities.[19]

A final conclusion of the comparative studies was that the aggregative model and the attendant inequalities are applicable not simply to systems of urban centers, but *also to systems of business centers within cities*. The same basic relationships repeat themselves, with inequalities 4.1–4.3 referring to streetcorner, neighborhood, and community centers, respectively. Note that all the inequalities have negative signs on the righthand side. This means that as population densities fall, centers of a given level in the hierarchy become smaller and simpler. Centers of the same size under different density conditions thus are *not* centers of the same relative importance to their immediate environs, a fact that should be kept in mind in subsequent comparative studies.

Specialized-Function Cities

Studies dealing with cities as the sites of specialized economic activities have been fewer and less well coordinated than recent central-place studies. Many classifications of cities continue to be based on economic activities.[20] Residuals from population-tertiary function regressions have been used to identify the contributions of specialized functions to the economic base of small towns.[21]

The only attempts to use any systematic framework of concepts in a study of specialization have been made by Webb and Pred.[22] Webb described the role of economic integration and interdependence in a specialized society, and then attempted to construct an index to reveal the degree of specialization of functions of any urban complex. Pred studied the changing external relations of cities during periods of industrial revolution from a theoretical viewpoint, emphasizing the interrelations of changing scale of industry, transport improvements, and migration patterns.

These studies show that more and better theory is needed in this field. Specialized functions need to be viewed in terms of national economies and even international economic systems, if reasonable interpretations of the character and distribution of specialized-function cities are to be developed. Work along these lines undoubtedly will be stimulated by the coordination of methods of regional analysis and the codification of basic location theory in two recent volumes of Walter Isard,[23] whose *Methods of Regional Analysis* introduces urban complex analysis, which seems to be a step in the right direction.

Cities and Transport Networks

The traditional study of the city performing functions at intermediate transport locations has almost vanished (except for port studies).[24] It has been replaced by studies of the relations of systems of cities and entire transport networks. This change is a result of the recognition of the mutual interdependence between economic specialization and transportation, and the fact that transportation is therefore basic to an understanding of all cities. Only a few replacement studies have been made, however, and these fall into two categories: (1) the studies of inter- and intra-urban transportation systems, by far the most abundant, discussed in a separate section later; and (2) "network effect" investigations, of which only one, by Garrison,[25] has yet been sent to the publisher. Garrison attempts to measure the accessibility of urban places to entire transport networks using the mathematical theory of graphs and matrix algebra. Most of the mathematics is too complex to review here, but it is worth noting that the attempt was quite successful; several meaningful measures of connectivity and accessibility were derived.

Related to the network-type investigations is the idea of systems analysis. Very recently, concepts of systems analysis were used in Ajo's investigation [26] of the interdependent spheres of influence and focal role of cities in Finland. Extremely good fits to his equations were derived, and a general set of system equations presented. As in Garrison's introductory use of the theory of graphs, it appears that ideas drawn from systems analysis open up promising lines of research that merit further investigation, although, once again, the mathematical formulation is too detailed to review here.

Other Features of the Spatial Distribution of Cities

Another kind of study that has undergone technical, if not much theoretical, transformation during the past five years is that of the spatial distribution of urban characteristics. Traditionally, studies of this kind have taken several related characteristics of cities, and then followed these steps: (1) map each distribution (perhaps the study involved the United States); (2) compare the maps and try to create a new map of regions within which the several characteristics display uniformity; (3) describe and try to explain the pattern of uniformity and the similarities and differences among regions.

Derivation of regions often is useful both for pedagogic purposes and to serve specific research undertakings, provided that it is done properly. In the foregoing studies, however, regions were derived because the techniques that facilitate study of the concomitant variations of many variables were not known, and it was therefore easier to work with regional averages. Now that urban geographers are acquiring greater familiarity with such techniques as multiple-regression and principal-components analysis, these types of studies are undergoing substantial change.

Two related studies will serve as illustrations of the new departures, one by Hartman and Hook on the distribution of substandard housing in the United States [27] and the other by Fuchs on intra-urban variations of residential quality in the United States.[28]

Hartman and Hook began with a conventional description of the distribution of substandardness (measured as a per cent of total housing, using U. S. Census of Housing data), attempted a regional division of the United States based on this single criterion, and then examined the deviants from regional averages using standard deviations. They then explained the spatial distribution of substandardness without making use of the regional division, calculating correlation coefficients to facilitate formulation of six hypotheses that could be tested using simple regression analysis. They concluded that substandardness could be explained in terms of median family income, overcrowding, and proportion of nonwhite families, but not by proportion of renter families, unemployment, or employment in manufacturing. One conclusion of their analysis was that certain regional subdivisions of the country are important in determining the relative role of the explanatory variables, and that a covariance framework based on some realistic regional division of the country would markedly improve predictions derivable from their model, as would use of multiple rather than simple regression analysis.

Some of these suggestions were adopted by Fuchs in his analysis of intra-urban variations in residential quality. First, he described the intra-urban variations using coefficients of variation of housing costs, computed for each of 209 cities in the United States (163 central cities, the rest noncentral). He then described the spatial pattern and attempted to derive regions. To explain variations in the coefficients of variation he adopted a multiple regression framework and concluded that the following independent variables were significant: (a) per cent of families with less than two thousand dollars income, and (b) per cent of dwelling units owner-occupied. The spatial distribution of residuals from the regression was examined to look for further explanatory variables, and again it was suggested that analysis within a regional frame would increase the explanatory power of the model (in the case above $R^2 = 0.67$). Findings were shown to be applicable to central cities, but not to noncentral cities.

Where do studies such as these lead? Unfortunately, in the absence of a theoretical framework dealing with the regional distribution of various phenomena in an area such as the United States, each is an entity unto itself. Therefore, each repeats the procedures of previous studies, although hopefully each succeeding study at least improves technically on its immediate predecessor.

The question is whether the United States can be divided into a theoretically significant regional pattern that is meaningful for urban studies of this kind and that will provide a framework for integrating repetitive studies of the distribution of phenomena in American cities. Perhaps it can be, and if so we should certainly be looking for this pattern. A useful starting place might be the ideas expressed by Edward Ullman in a recent essay, "Geographic Theory and Underdeveloped Areas." [29]

Correlates of City Size and Urbanization

The frontier has also touched on regularities in city-size distributions and on the correlates of city size and degree of urbanization.

City-Size Regularities

The rank-size rule, proposed by Zipf as a description of observed distributions of city sizes, has been examined in detail in articles by Stewart, Berry and Garrison, Beckmann, and Thomas.[30] The rule specifies that

$$P_r = P_1 r^{-x}$$

where r is the number of cities greater than or equal to size P_r (the rank of the city of size P_r), P_1 is a constant, and x is an exponent. In the United States, Zipf observed that P_1 was approximately the population of New York and x equaled 1, so that the rth ranking city has a population $1/r$ that of New York. He argued that "principles of least effort" were sufficient to account for the emergence and persistence of such a regularity.

Stewart questioned whether Zipf's regularity in fact exists, arguing that sound logical foundations for it cannot be found. He suggested that the empirical reality is, in fact, an S-shaped distribution. On the other hand, after reviewing the empirical evidence, Berry and Garrison concluded that Zipf's rank-size regularities do exist in many countries. They then proceeded to examine the various proposed logical bases for the regularity. Zipf's argument they found to be inconsistent, and those of Rashevsky and Christaller consistent only in special cases. Following Simon,[31] they concluded that a Yule distribution, a general frequency function to which rank-size regularities conform, provides a satisfactory explanation for the emergence of such regularities.

The Yule distribution has a frequency function of the form

$$f(i) = ai^{-c}b^i$$

which yields the steady state of a stochastic growth process. Assumptions underlying the stochastic growth process are that probabilities of percentage growth of cities are independent of their size, and that there is a steady rate of addition of cities to the system at that lower threshold size which cities must satisfy to qualify as members of the system. The result is a dynamic equilibrium in which the overall pattern remains constant while urban populations are expanding. Stochastic growth may be interpreted as growth that is the product of so many forces and decisions acting in so many ways that it appears to be a random process, except that the larger the city, the greater its chance of growth. Individual cities may vary in population within the pattern, but as the system expands the shape of the distribution describing the pattern remains the same.

Beckmann, in an independent contribution, came to the same conclusions as Berry and Garrison. He found that rank-size regularities showed consistency with Christaller only in special cases, whereas the Zipf rule could be shown more readily to be the result of allometric (that is, stochastic) growth processes.

Thomas, following proposals of Berry and Garrison, showed that the Zipf distribution could just as well be considered lognormal as Yule. Shapes of the lognormal and Yule distributions are very much alike. The only difference in their underlying assumptions is that the lognormal is generated by a stochastic process in a closed system of cities, whereas the Yule assumes a steady rate of addition of cities to the system. He also found, however, that in Iowa city-size distributions were log-lognormal. Working theoretically, he found that this distribution resulted when, in a closed lognormal system, growth was a random *power* of size. At the empirical level, he found that the city-size distribution pattern of Iowa remained relatively constant from 1900 to 1950. At each decennial census the pattern was log-lognormal, and no succeeding census had a significantly greater skewness than its immediate predecessor.

Which distribution provides the more satisfactory description, and via its assumptions, explanation of city-size patterns—the Yule, lognormal, or the log-lognormal? The log-lognormal is relevant when growth is a random power of size, whereas the Yule and log-normal are applicable when probabilities of growth are simply proportional to city size. If the number of cities in the system is relatively stable, then the lognormal applies, whereas if the system is expanding, the Yule distribution is most applicable.

It is clear that great strides have been made during the last few years insofar as our understanding of city-size distribution is concerned. Not only is there ample evidence that certain regularities exist, but alternative theories have been sifted, and an explanation via stochastic growth processes has been accepted. Alternative stochastic models have been provided to satisfy different underlying conditions. Moreover, these models are the same models that have been shown to be applicable in many other equilibrium situations in the biological sciences and in the other social sciences.[32]

Correlates of City Size

In contrast, work by geographers with correlates of city size has been highly empirical and has not led to improved theory. Two examples of such work are by Stewart and Warntz,[33] and Ullman and Dacey.[34]

Stewart and Warntz studied relations between the areas of cities and their populations in both the United States and the United Kingdom, and argue that in both cases, dating back at least to 1890, there has been a consistent relationship such that area equals three-fourths the power of population. The power of the model is not given. These studies by Stewart and Warntz have recently been the subject of considerable debate and controversy within geography. Some of the reasons include lack of faith in macroscopic "social physics" and the reluctance of most members of the discipline to accept the asserted universal validity and utility of gravity and potential models. Gradual provision of more viable and informative models of spatial interaction appears to be justifying the resistance to social physics evidenced by other geographers.

Ullman and Dacey developed the "minimum requirements approach" to basic-nonbasic analysis, and found consistent relationships between size of city and the minimum percentage of employment in various categories. Their methods have been severely criticized, however, even though the regularities they found were apparent enough. What was questioned was (a) whether they were actually dealing with basic-nonbasic analysis, and (b) whether basic-nonbasic analysis was very useful, especially since Isard has provided a more viable alternative in the form of interregional input-output analysis. (Basic-nonbasic anlysis is essentially framed as a two-region, two-sector input-output analysis, with relations within the exogenous sectors and regions ignored.)[35]

Urbanization, City-Size Distributions, and Economic Development

In recent investigations Berry and Ginsburg have been able to throw light on the complex interrelationships between urbanization, type of city-size distribution, and economic development.[36] The investigations began with the collection of some forty-eight proposed indices to economic development of countries. The dimensions of economic development underlying these indices were then derived using principal components methods.[37] One of the indices was of degree of urbanization (per cent of population in cities of 20,000 and more). This index fell into a basic pattern that differentiated countries according to income, industrialization, specialization and trade, and so on. Since this basic pattern was then interpreted to be the basic pattern of differentiation of countries according to level of economic development, the relationship between urbanization and economic development was established.

Berry then took cumulative-frequency distributions of city sizes in thirty-eight countries and classified them according to whether they were lognormal (rank-size), primate, or some stage intermediate between rank-size and primate. The lognormal case was used because of the ease of plotting cumulative frequencies on lognormal probability paper and testing for linearity. Basing his argument on a variety of recent studies, he hypothesized that the progression from primate to rank-size city-size distribution is a function of the level of economic development of countries. This hypothesis was tested and rejected. Many lesser-developed countries have lognormal city-size distributions, whereas advanced countries may have primate distributions. An alternative model was then formulated based on the assumption that a lognormal distribution indicates a steady state, or condition of entropy, whereas a primate distribution may indicate a simpler, patterned structure. Progression from the primate to the lognormal stage is reached when the urban society is old and complex and has been influenced by large numbers of forces in many ways, such that the patterning effects of any one of these forces are lost. Evidence to support this hypothesis was found in the fact that the advanced countries with primate distributions usually were very small, which limited possible complexities entering into the urban scene, and the lesser developed countries with lognormal distributions were generally very large and with long histories of urbanization, which increased the possibility of the urban pattern being affected by many forces.

More work is obviously needed on these matters, but it is clear that some interesting avenues have been opened by these explorations, and at least one model is available to provide a frame of reference. An interesting avenue would be to undertake similar analyses of the internal structure of countries, after completing analyses of differences in the economic development of regions within these countries, to see if the same generalizations emerge.[38]

Studies of Relations between Urban Patterns and Transport Networks

Several studies now completed by urban geographers relate urban patterns and transportation systems, and evaluate the economic and social effects of changes in transport facilities both within cities and in systems of cities.[39] These studies are already contributing to policy-making at the federal level, for they have been the first studies to produce empirical evidence that unexploited scale economies exist in the space economy to be tapped by transportation improvements.[40]

The better studies work in a consistent theoretical framework, usually of location theory, which provides them with the necessary hypotheses about interdependencies between transport systems and economic patterns. They then record the economic patterns and identify such aspects of the interdependencies as they can. This sets the stage for an evaluation of the effects of a transport improvement on the patterns, by examining changes in the identified aspects of interdependency.

Two findings have repeated themselves throughout the studies: (1) the main effect of transport improvements on the system of cities is to increase the competitive advantage of larger centers versus smaller centers; and (2) the principal effect on the internal pattern of cities is to facilitate sprawl on the one hand and specialization on the other. We surmised these relationships before, but they have some interesting facets.

For example, the main impact of transportation improvements on a system of central places is to set off a chain of centralization tendencies such that the higher-order centers gain at the expense of the lower-order, and the lowest-order centers decline. Centralization is thus accompanied by an upward movement of functions and a reshuffling of trade areas.

Ullman has succinctly described the impact of transport improvements on the internal patterns of cities: "As urban transport improves, cities not only can expand in area, but urban sites within a city can specialize more in what they can do best because of inherent local advantages and less because of strategic location." [41] Berry has provided some information about this process in urban business.[42]

Thus Adam Smith's dictum that "degree of specialization is directly related to the size of the market" appears to be basic to an understanding of one set of trends affecting our cities—trends related to the constant improvement of means of transportation and communication. Location theory, via comparative statics, already has much to say about these trends and their effects and implications, but the time is coming when we will be able to incorporate such consistent relationships into dynamic spatial models.

The Spatial Structure of Land Uses within Cities

One way of stating the argument lying behind recent studies of the internal structure of cities is: cities are supported by "basic" activities whose locations are determined exogenously to the city by comparative advantage in regional, national, and international economic systems. Such "basic" activities universally include a central business district, the focus not only of the city but also of its tributary region. Various specialized activities will also be present, such as steel-making in Chicago, aircraft production in Seattle, or meat-packing in Omaha. Locations of the basic activities, plus a transport system, provide the skeletal features of the urban pattern.

This pattern is filled out by the residences of workers in the "basic" activities and is given a dynamic quality by the daily ebb and flow of commuters and, from beyond the city's limits, of goods and customers to and from the sites of the basic activities. Further patterning is provided by the orientation of business services to the "basic" activities and by tertiary activities to the consuming workers and their families. Shopping trips create yet another ebb and flow. Major changes result from socioeconomic differentiation of urban neighborhoods and their relations to the urban site. Then appear all the "second-round" effects: locations of the residences of workers in the "nonbasic" activities, additional commuting, more demands for tertiary activities, and so forth, in an increasingly complex chain of multiplier effects.

Specification of the precise form of these patterns and their underlying functional relationships has been the objective of the work dealing with the internal structure of cities. Of course, there have also been many exercises in definition, notably those dealing with the central business district. Examples include attempts to derive indices for standard definition of CBD boundaries,[43] for separating the CBD into component parts such as its "core" and "frame," [44] and for categorizing the specialized functional areas within it.[45] Since these definitional matters have already been dealt with in detail in Chapter 3 by H. M. Mayer, we will confine the discussion here to attempts at clarifying relationships among residential patterns, business locations, and accessibility.

The Residential Pattern

One group of studies has dealt with the residential pattern of cities. Marble, for example, has tested a series of concepts relating to residential site selection, including multiple nuclei and concentric zonation, and found them wanting.[46] He postulated that residential site selection, as measured by land values, was a function of residence location with respect to the CBD and to various other business centers within the city. A random sample of fifty blocks was taken in Spokane, Washington. Using multiple-regression analysis, he found that land values were not significantly related to distance from the CBD or from any one of a variety of other kinds of retail business centers. Thus the study gave little support to the concepts of concentric zonation and multiple nuclei. In fact, the only significant spatial variable to emerge was distance from arterial highways, suggesting the role of accessibility in producing "starfish" urban patterns.

Since there were inadequacies in the data used and because multi-collinearities may have affected the results of the analysis, Marble went on to fit more complex models using data derived from a sample of seventy-one blocks in Cedar Rapids, Iowa. Again, the tests were of the efficacy of concepts of concentric zonation and multiple nuclei in predicting residential land values, with place of work added, although the number of business center referents was reduced. The hypotheses were again rejected.

If there are multiple nuclei or concentric zonations of residential patterns in urban areas, one would also expect relationships between transport inputs at urban residential sites and the location of households, for basic to urban land-use theory is the idea of substitutive relations between rents and transport costs. Marble had data in the form of monthly travel diaries for a sample of eighty-nine families in Cedar Rapids, which enabled him to proceed from this other point of view.

Three separate multiple-regression analyses were made, with the dependent variables representing three different measures of transport inputs to the household: total number of hours spent away from home; number of trips made in a specified period; and total distance traveled. Addition of socioeconomic variables to the analysis enabled him to evaluate the relative roles of both spatial and other variables in determining the level of transport inputs of the household and, by extension, the level of rents. Similarly, the journey-to-work was added as an explanatory variable, to add yet another facet to ideas of multiple nuclei.

In every analysis except one, only socioeconomic variables proved to be significantly related to the level of transport inputs of the households. The exception was that total distance traveled bore a negative exponential relationship to distance from the CBD.

Related results have been provided more recently by Knos.[47] In studies of Topeka, Kansas, he found land values to be a function of location with respect to the city center, to the main traffic artery of the city, and of location within what he called "sectors of relative growth" in the city. The latter sectors were defined as regions within the city having similar histories of growth and development, and they correspond somewhat to the "socioeconomic regions of the city." A relatively powerful model describing the land-value pattern of Topeka was developed.

Similarly, in a study of the Chicago metropolitan area, de Vise suggested recently that the combination of zonal, sector, and socioeconomic types of organization was such that if the metropolitan area were subdivided into a series of sectors and zones, suburbs located within the resulting subareas would have relatively uniform social and economic structures.[48]

Thomas throws some additional light on de Vise's work in a study of population growth within the same study area.[49] His hypothesis was that the population growth of an outlying city is a function of size of population of the outlying city, density of population of that city, cost of housing, birth-death differential, age of the city, quality of schools, number of persons engaged in manufacturing, accessibility to the central city, and amount of vacant land. For the urbanized area of Chicago as a whole, only population densities and birth-death differentials were significant, and only 36 per cent of the variations in population growth were explained. However, by fitting the model separately for the northern, western, and southern radial sectors of the urbanized area, 80, 22, and 60 per cent explanations were achieved, respectively. Thus, at least in the northern and southern sectors, some consistent generalizations were produced, and a covariance analysis showed that sectoral differences should certainly be taken into account in any analysis of changing residential patterns. This latter finding is compatible, of course, with Hoyt's sector thesis of urban growth.

These findings imply that the concept of multiple-business nuclei is of no help in analysis of the level of transport inputs of the urban household, of urban rent levels, and of residential site selection. This is compatible with central-place theory, because the tertiary pattern is dependent on that of residences, rather than the other way around.

In fact, the only significant relationships to emerge in the several studies just described were between transport inputs and socioeconomic variables, except for the association of total distance traveled and distance of the residence from the central business district in Marble's studies, and land values, distance from the city center, transport arteries, and sectoral location in the works of Knos, de Vise, and Thomas. The importance of ecological theories of the residential pattern of cities, such as those developed by Duncan or Shevky, thus looms larger, and this is why geographers must take second place to urban sociologists in studies of the residential patterning of cities. The one consistently significant spatial variable indicates negative exponential zonal arrangements of land values, travel behavior, and land use about the central business district, in ways that are compatible with Burgess's and Colby's notions. More important, however, the available evidence emphasizes that we should not be sanguine about our knowledge of the residential pattern of cities. It has lent little support to the idea of a multinuclear organization of residential land uses, at least insofar as tertiary business nuclei are concerned. A real need remains for carefully designed work that will codify, in a series of comprehensive comparative studies, what in fact does exist insofar as the residential pattern of cities is concerned.[50]

Population Densities

The negative exponential decline of phenomena with increasing distance from the city center is nowhere more apparent than in urban population densities. Regardless of time or place, this is the pattern to be found; in some four hundred cases examined so far there are no exceptions.[51] Here, therefore, is one finding of great generality.

Recent additional explorations confirm that the rate of negative exponential decline bears regular relationships to city size, and that changes in rate through time vary significantly between "Western" and "non-Western" societies.[52] The larger the city, the less the rate of decline; small cities are thus more "compact" than larger. As Western cities grow through time, the rate of decline diminishes, but it remains constant in "preindustrial" or "non-Western" cities. Reasons lie in the differing socioeconomic patterns of Western and preindustrial cities: in the West the poor live at the center on expensive land, and the rich at the periphery on cheaper land; in non-Western cities the converse is true—the least mobile, poorest groups live at the periphery. Despite transport improvements, non-Western cities, therefore, lack the large number of highly mobile suburbanites who continually push the city's circumference outward and reduce the density gradient.

The Commercial Pattern

Considerable attention also has been focused on patterns of retail and service business within cities.[53] Results of these studies are more encouraging than those of studies of the residential pattern.

First, they show that central-place theory is applicable to the study of the internal business structure of the city. Clearly, the idea of a hierarchy of business centers, with spacing related to trade-area delineations and to density of population, provides a meaningful description and is useful in an analysis of the pattern of streetcorner, neighborhood, community, regional, and central business districts within cities. Smaller urban centers such as towns have only outlying streetcorner and neighborhood business centers, because their central business districts are essentially of community order, whereas cities like Chicago have business centers of all five orders. Similarly, the aggregative model and attendant inequalities outlined earlier are also applicable within the built-up urban area.

Second, the studies show that central-place theory has limitations in studying internal business structure. It cannot explain the distribution of localized facilities within cities, such as automobile row, but can only indicate the level of urban center at which such localized developments will enter the urban business pattern. Similarly, in its conventional form the theory cannot explain ribbon developments of either of the two kinds identified—highway-service ribbons or urban arterial ribbons consisting of strings of equipment, supply, and repair establishments. As in the localized patterns, existing theory explains the level of urban center at which these features enter the business complex, but it does not explain the pattern within each center.

The uses and limitations of central-place theory as a theory of internal business structure both have been demonstrated by a considerable body of empirical research. This research has led to the identification of the major functional and spatial components of the intra-urban pattern of tertiary activities. Typical analytic methods included correlation-cluster analysis and principal-components analysis.[54] Usually, the empirical investigations have used the measurement of groups of spatially associated business types as a point of departure. The following groups have been recognized:

1. the hierarchy of nucleated business centers
2. urban arterial business districts of the supplies-repair types
3. highway-service districts
4. localized developments such as "automobile row"

The state at which each component and subcomponent of the nucleated group enters as towns grow in size also has been identified. But, as Otis Dudley Duncan points out, these studies have not accounted for the increased differentiation that develops within any business type as city size increases (for example, the greater specialization of various kinds of automobile repair establishments in cities of increasing size).[55] This is but one of the many avenues yet to be explored or at present under investigation, which should lead to a more general theory of the location of tertiary activities.

One such avenue is being explored by Nystuen.[56] He points out that inclusion of the frequency of demand and such characteristics of consumer travel as the linkages of retail and service establishments on the same shopping trips may well help in the development of a more general theory. He has made a first attempt to reformulate theory in this context, and has developed an interesting simulation model in which he is able to predict the number of trips to other stores on trips beginning with a given business type, and the kinds of businesses that will be visited on these trips. Similarly, Marble is working on a clarification of principles associated with highway-service location. He hopes that the result of his work will be a predictive model using computer-simulation techniques, made possible by the clarification of demand characteristics and the locational responses of highway-service facilities.[57] In another study, Curry suggests that a completely new approach to central-place studies of the internal business structure of cities is required, and he attempts to provide the new approach in a probabilistic formulation of locational choice, using poisson series.[58]

Berry, in more recent studies, has been able to isolate the proportion of the spatial pattern of each of 150 business types that may be accounted for by (a) the size of business centers; (b) regular, repetitive patterns of spatial association of business types; and (c) random "noise." These studies have also shown that the same basic system of relationships lies beneath the hierarchy of business centers within cities and the hierarchy of urban centers.[59]

Simulation Models

As yet, dynamic spatial models that predict given results in terms of explanatory variables do not exist. Hence some geographers are turning to Monte Carlo simulation models to provide methods of analyzing developing patterns of land uses within cities and developing systems of cities.[60]

Simulation is not a new idea. The geologist who uses a sandpile to show how fluvial erosion works is using a simulation model. His problem is less complicated, in a sense, than that of the urban research worker, however, for many of the forces operating to shape urban patterns are not known, or are subject to a high "noise level." Thus an urban simulation model has to deal in probabilistic terms, by specifying the probabilities of given events taking place at certain locations in a given time period. It has the same idea as the geologist's model, however, because for the first time it provides the investigator with a means for studying the development of a city in a laboratory framework, observing what would happen to the urban growth process under different assumptions and conditions, and operating under alternative restraints.

Let us take the case of a simulation model of the internal pattern of cities, which works as follows.[61] In time period one we have a set of locations in front of us. We have decided by other means how much the urban population will grow in this time period. This growth may be translated into a demand for a certain number of houses. Where will the new houses be located? Each location is assigned a probability of being occupied. Then, using a set of random numbers, the houses are allocated to locations. (In technical terms, we have allocated houses using Monte Carlo methods.) The resulting pattern of houses enables probabilities to be assigned to sites for the allocation of the required number of new shopping centers, schools, parks, and so forth. When all land uses have been allocated in time period one, the process is repeated in time period two, with probabilities at locations being influenced by the pattern resulting from allocation in the first time period, and so on to time period n. Now we can start all over again, and repeat the whole process a number of times. When we have a large enough sample of simulations, each showing one of the ways in which the city might develop, we can estimate the average growth pattern and the expected variability.

Of course, the process can also be repeated using many different assumptions as to how much the city will grow and what restrictions upon the growth process will be applicable. The value of this to the policy-maker is obvious, but the person concerned with developing dynamic spatial models also will benefit, for simulation provides insights into the nature of the growth process under a variety of conditions, and the probability framework allows for the uncertainty in human behavior.

The same kind of model can be applied to such topics as the development of a central-place pattern through time. Morrill has worked on this problem. He hopes to be able to compare the results of his simulations with the excellent Swedish historical data relating to the growth of their system of cities.[62] Similarly, Garrison will soon publish examples of simulations of the emerging pattern of land uses at intersections on the new system of federal interstate highways.

A restriction must be noted. Very large-scale simulations are not yet feasible because of the limited internal-storage capacity of existing computers, for to simulate an urban pattern a vast memory section is required to record probabilities for all locations. As computers grow larger, more realistic simulations will become feasible, however, and we would expect the same valuable result as have accrued in studies of migration and the diffusion of innovation waves.[63]

Retrospect and Prospect

Thus urban geography, during the last several years, has been characterized by rapid technical advance. Perhaps most significant is the fact that many workers have learned the advantages—and also a few disadvantages—of the new techniques, and in turn have discovered the need for more and better theory and concepts. Progress has been made as part of this learning process in other ways, however. We can cite the work in the central-place field as applied both to the internal patterns of cities and to systems of cities, the clarification of the logical arguments lying behind studies of internal structure and systems of cities, and the theoretical work dealing with city-size distributions, as substantive advances. New lines of research have also been opened dealing with the relations of city-size distributions and economic development, in the field of dynamic spatial models using computer simulation, and in the use of the mathematical theory of graphs or concepts of systems analysis to study the relations of systems of cities and transport and communication networks.

If priorities for research in the next few years can be specified, in light of this review of recent work, among them will be these:

1. Development of a general central-place theory applicable both to the internal business structure of cities and to systems of cities, and further exploration of spatial systems and network problems.

2. Integration of ideas concerning specialized-function cities with concepts relating to the spatial structure of entire economic systems, using location theory and advanced methods of regional analysis. Related to this, we need further exploration of the feasibility of deriving an "urban regionalization" of cities and a multivariate classification of cities in the United States. This would facilitate the integration of

the many studies of the geographical distribution of urban characteristics in a theoretically meaningful manner. The regionalization and
classification should be related to the spatial structure of the economy
of the United States and differences in level of economic development
from place to place.

3. Development of an adequate theory to deal with correlates of
city size, and additional studies of problems of different kinds of city-
size distributions, their relations to relative economic development,
and of changing city-size distribution patterns through time.

4. Codification and theoretical integration of concepts dealing with
the internal structure, especially the residential pattern, of cities.

5. The development of a general urban simulator.

NOTES

1. The reader will note, however, parallel developments in the fields of
urban sociology and *human ecology*, exemplified by the work of Otis Dudley
and Beverly Duncan; in *land economics,* as exemplified by Richard F. Muth
and Lowdon Wingo, Jr.; and in *regional science, by* Benjamin H. Stevens
and Gerald A. P. Carrothers.

2. One example drawn from another facet of geography is William L.
Garrison and Duane F. Marble, "The Spatial Structure of Agricultural Activities," *Annals,* The Association of American Geographers, 47 (1957), pp.
137–144. In this case formal logic is applied to prove the theorem that for
every location there exists some optimum combination of intensity of use,
type of land use, and group of markets.

3. See the review of pertinent work in Brian J. L. Berry, "Recent Studies
Concerning the Role of Transportation in the Space-Economy," *Annals,* The
Association of American Geographers, 49 (1959), pp. 328–342.

4. The administrative-political principle is one of Walter Christaller's
three principles of central-place organization. See his *Das Grundgerüst der
raümlichen Ordnung in Europa* (Frankfurt: Frankfurter Geographische
Hefte, 1950), and Brian J. L. Berry and Allen Pred, *Central Place Studies:
A Bibliography of Theory and Applications* (Philadelphia: Regional Science
Research Institute, 1961).

5. For a general review of the theory and empirical studies, see Berry and
Pred, *op. cit.* Also Otis Dudley Duncan et al., *Metropolis and Region* (Baltimore: Johns Hopkins University Press, 1960), for a review by nongeographers. The most recent series of systematic comparative studies is by
Berry et al., *Comparative Studies of Central Place Systems* (final report,
U. S. Office of Naval Research, Contract NONR 2121-18, 1961), and by
Berry and H. Gardiner Barnum, "Aggregate Relations and Elemental Components of Central Place Systems," *Journal of Regional Science,* 4 (1964),
pp. 35–68.

6. H. Carol, "Industrie und Siedlungsplanung," *Plan* (1951), pp. 191–
209; "Das Agrargeographische Betrachtungssystem: Ein Beitrag zur Land-

schaftkundlichen Methodik dargelegt am Beispiel der in Südafrika," *Geographica Helvetica*, 1 (1952), pp. 16–67. Sven Godlund, *The Function and Growth of Bus Traffic within the Sphere of Urban Influence*, Lund Studies in Geography, Series B, No. 18, 1956. A. K. Philbrick, "Principles of Areal Functional Organization in Regional Human Geography," *Economic Geography*, 33 (1957), pp. 299–336; A. K. Philbrick, "Areal Functional Organization in Regional Human Geography," *Papers and Proceedings*, Regional Science Association, 3 (1957), pp. 87–98. Brian J. L. Berry and William L. Garrison, "The Functional Bases of the Central Place Hierarchy," *Economic Geography*, 34 (1958), pp. 145–154; Brian J. L. Berry and William L. Garrison, "A Note on Central Place Theory and the Range of a Good," *Economic Geography*, 34 (1958), pp. 304–311. F. H. W. Green "Community of Interest Areas: Notes on the Hierarchy of Central Places and their Hinterlands," *Economic Geography*, 34 (1958), pp. 210–222. R. Mayfield, "A Central Place Hierarchy in Northern India," *Quantitative Geography* (Northwestern Studies in Geography, 1965); R. Mayfield, "Conformations of Retail and Service Activities," *Proceedings of the I.G.U. Symposium in Urban Geography*, Lund Studies in Geography, Series B, No. 24, 1962, pp. 77–90; N. R. Kar, "Urban Hierarchy and Central Functions around the City of Calcutta, India, and Its Significance," *Proceedings of the I.G.U. Symposium, op. cit.*, pp. 253–274; Edward J. Taaffe, "The Urban Hierarchy: An Air Passenger Definition," *Economic Geography*, 38 (1962), pp. 1–14; D. E. Snyder, "Commercial Passenger Linkages and the Metropolitan Nodality of Montevideo," *Economic Geography*, 38 (1962), pp. 95–112. For discussions of the related concept of a "dispersed city" or "truncated hierarchy," see Ian Burton, "Retail Trade in a Dispersed City," *Transactions*, Illinois Academy of Science, 52 (1959), pp. 145–150; Howard A. Stafford, "The Dispersed City," *The Professional Geographer*, 14 (1962), pp. 8–10; Ian Burton, "A Restatement of the Dispersed City Hypothesis," *Annals*, The Association of American Geographers, 53 (1963).

7. E. N. Thomas, "Toward an Expanded Central Place Model," forthcoming in *The Geographical Review;* "The Stability of Distance-Population Size Relationships for Iowa Towns from 1900–1950," *Proceedings of the I.G.U. Symposium, op. cit.*, pp. 13–30; "Some Comments on the Functional Bases for Small Iowa Towns," *Iowa Business Digest* (Winter 1960), pp. 10–16; "The Spatial Behavior of a Dispersed Non-farm Population," *Papers and Proceedings*, Regional Science Association, 8 (1962), pp. 107–133; "The Comparative Spatial Behavior of Two Dispersed Populations," *Journal of Regional Science*, 4 (1964).

8. John D. Nystuen, "A Simulation Model of Intraurban Travel," *Quantitative Geography* (Northwestern Studies in Geography, 1965).

9. Michael F. Dacey, "Analysis of Central Place Patterns by a Nearest Neighbor Method," *Proceedings of the I.G.U. Symposium, op. cit.*, pp. 55–76. A more recent application is Leslie J. King, "A Quantitative Expression of the Pattern of Urban Settlements in Selected Areas of the United States," *Tijdschrift voor Economische en Sociale Geografie*, 53 (1962), pp. 1–7.

10. John D. Nystuen and Michael F. Dacey, "A Graph Theory Interpretation of Nodal Regions," *Papers and Proceedings*, Regional Science Association, 7 (1961), pp. 29–42; "The Rank of Cities in Regional Association,"

forthcoming in *Proceedings* of the first western meetings of the Regional Science Association, Las Vegas.

11. Brian J. L. Berry and William L. Garrison, "Recent Developments of Central Place Theory," *Papers and Proceedings,* Regional Science Association, 4 (1958), pp. 107–120.

12. R. L. Morrill, Part V of Garrison et al., *Studies of Highway Development and Geographic Change* (Seattle: University of Washington Press, 1959).

13. W. Bunge, *Theoretical Geography,* Lund Studies in Geography, Series B, No. 25, 1962.

14. Martin J. Beckmann, "City Hierarchies and the Distribution of City Size," *Economic Development and Cultural Change,* 6 (1958), pp. 243–248.

15. *Comparative Studies, op. cit.*

16. Berry and Barnum, *op. cit.,* present these findings in detail.

17. For the larger set of structural equations, see *ibid.*

18. *Ibid.*

19. *Ibid.,* for examples.

20. Howard J. Nelson, "A Service Classification of American Cities," *Economic Geography,* 31 (1955), pp. 189–210, presents one somewhat unsatisfactory effort. A more sophisticated attempt to obtain relatively uniform economic groups of towns is provided by Robert H. T. Smith in his *Commodity Movements in Southern New South Wales* (Canberra: Department of Geography, Australian National University, 1962). Undoubtedly the most outstanding contribution in this general field is the multivariate classification of British towns completed in the Center for Urban Studies of University College, London. See the book by C. A. Moser and Wolf Scott, *British Towns, a Statistical Study of Their Economic and Social Differences* (Edinburgh: Oliver and Boyd, 1961).

21. Brian J. L. Berry, "The Impact of Expanding Metropolitan Communities upon the Central Place Hierarchy," *Annals,* The Association of American Geographers, 50 (1960), pp. 112–116; E. N. Thomas, *Maps of Residuals from Regressions* (Department of Geography, State University of Iowa, Publications in Geography No. 2, 1960).

22. J. W. Webb, "Basic Concepts in the Analysis of Small Urban Centers in Minnesota," *Annals,* The Association of American Geographers, 49 (1959), pp. 55–72. Allen Pred, *External Relations of Cities During "Industrial Revolution"* (University of Chicago, Department of Geography, Research Paper No. 76, 1962).

23. Walter Isard, *Methods of Regional Analysis* (Cambridge: M.I.T. Press, 1960), and his *Location and Space-Economy* (Cambridge: M.I.T. Press, 1956).

24. For example, Baruch Boxer, *Ocean Shipping in the Evolution of Hong Kong* (University of Chicago, Department of Geography, Research Paper No. 72, 1961).

25. William L. Garrison, "Connectivity of the Interstate Highway System," *Papers and Proceedings,* Regional Science Association, 6 (1960), pp. 121–138. See Sven Godlund, *The Function and Growth of Bus Traffic, op. cit.,* which also contains a few relevant comments.

26. Reino Ajo, "An Approach to Demographical Systems Analysis," *Economic Geography*, 38 (1962), pp. 359–371.

27. G. W. Hartman and J. C. Hook, "Substandard Housing in the United States, A Quantitative Analysis," *Economic Geography*, 32 (1956), pp. 95–114.

28. R. J. Fuchs, "Intraurban Variations of Residential Quality," *Economic Geography*, 36 (1960), pp. 313–325.

29. In Norton S. Ginsburg (Ed.), *Essays on Geography and Economic Development* (University of Chicago, Department of Geography, Research Paper No. 62, 1960), pp. 26–32.

30. Charles T. Stewart, "The Size and Spacing of Cities," *The Geographical Review*, 48 (1958), pp. 222–245; Brian J. L. Berry and William L. Garrison, "Alternate Explanations of Urban Rank-Size Relationships," *Annals*, The Association of American Geographers, 48 (1958), pp. 83–91; E. N. Thomas, "Additional Comments on Population-Size Relationships for Sets of Cities," *Quantitative Geography, op. cit.*; Martin J. Beckmann, "City Hierarchies and the Distribution of City Size," *op. cit.*; Michael F. Dacey, "A Note on the Yule (Rank-Size) Distribution," working paper, Wharton School, Philadelphia, 1962.

31. See also M. G. Kendall, "Natural Law in the Social Sciences," *Journal of the Royal Statistical Society*, Series A (General), 124 (1961), pp. 1–19.

32. As first suggested by George K. Zipf, later by Herbert A. Simon, and most recently by M. G. Kendall in his presidential address to the Royal Statistical Society, *op. cit.*

33. John Q. Stewart and William Warntz, "Physics of Population Distribution," *Journal of Regional Science*, 1 (1958), pp. 99–123. See also Ronald R. Boyce and Dilip K. Pal, "Changing Urban Densities," *Annals*, The Association of American Geographers, 52 (1962), p. 321.

34. Edward L. Ullman and Michael F. Dacey, "The Minimum Requirements Approach to the Urban Economic Base," *Papers and Proceedings*, Regional Science Association, 6 (1960), pp. 175–194.

35. Walter Isard, *Methods of Regional Analysis, op. cit.*, especially the sections dealing with interregional input-output analysis.

36. Norton S. Ginsburg, *Atlas of Economic Development* (Chicago: University of Chicago Press, 1961), pp. 34–37 and Sect. 8; and Brian J. L. Berry, "City Size Distributions and Economic Development," *Economic Development and Cultural Change*, 9 (1961), pp. 573–588.

37. Brian J. L. Berry, "An Inductive Approach to the Regionalization of Economic Development," in Norton S. Ginsburg (Ed.), *Essays on Geography and Economic Development, op. cit.*, pp. 78–107.

38. Studies of Malaya, Mexico, and Pakistan completed by students in the Department of Geography, University of Chicago, appear to bear out Berry's generalizations insofar as the internal patterns of countries are concerned. Furthermore, a recent application of his model to Israel shows that the model works through time as well as cross-sectionally; see Gwen Bell, "Change in City Size Distribution in Israel," *Ekistics*, 13 (1962), p. 103.

39. William L. Garrison and M. E. Marts, *Influence of Highway Improvements on Urban Land: A Graphic Summary* (Seattle: Highway Economic Studies, University of Washington, 1958); Brian J. L. Berry, "Recent Studies Concerning the Role of Transportation in the Space Economy," *An-*

nals, The Association of American Geographers, 49 (1959), pp. 328–342; William L. Garrison and M. E. Marts, *Geographic Impact of Highway Improvement* (Seattle: Highway Economic Studies, University of Washington, 1958); William L. Garrison et al., *Studies of Highway Development and Geographic Change* (Seattle: University of Washington Press, 1959); Brian J. L. Berry and William L. Garrison, "Cities and Freeways," *Landscape* (May 1961); John R. Borchert, *Belt-Line Industrial Commercial Development* (Minneapolis: Highway Studies, University of Minnesota, 1960).

40. See the evaluation of these works in the Final Reports of the Highway Cost Allocation Studies, transmitted to the Congress by the Secretary of Commerce, and published in House Documents 54 and 72, 87th Congress, 1st Session, 1961.

41. Edward L. Ullman, "The Expansion of Urban Areas" (mimeographed notes in connection with the Meramec Basin Research Project, Washington University, St. Louis, 1960). This is, of course, consistent with Edgar S. Dunn's generalization of von Thünen's theories of land use.

42. Brian J. L. Berry, "The Impact of Expanding Metropolitan Communities upon the Central Place Hierarchy," *op. cit.*

43. Raymond E. Murphy and J. E. Vance, "Delimiting the CBD," *Economic Geography,* 30 (1954), pp. 189–222; P. Scott, "The Australian CBD," *Economic Geography,* 35 (1959), pp. 290–314; D. Hywel Davies, "Boundary Study as a Tool in CBD Analysis: An Interpretation of Certain Aspects of Cape Town's Central Business District," *Economic Geography,* 35 (1959), pp. 322–345.

44. E. M. Horwood and R. R. Boyce, *Studies of the Central Business District and Urban Freeway Development* (Seattle: University of Washington Press, 1959); D. Hywel Davies, "The Hard Core of Cape Town's Central Business District: An Attempt at Delimitation," *Economic Geography,* 36 (1960), pp. 53–69.

45. P. Scott, *op. cit.;* C. E. Browning, *The Structure of the Mexico City Central Business District* (Xerox copy available from University Microfilms, Ann Arbor, Michigan, 1958). Also see the pertinent comments in Duane F. Marble and C. D. Durden in "The Role of Theory in CBD Planning," *Journal of the American Institute of Planners,* 27 (1961), pp. 10–16. The same ideas have been used recently in less developed parts of the world, for example by Harm de Blij, "The Functional Structure and Central Business District of Lourenco Marques, Mocambique," *Economic Geography,* 38 (1962), pp. 56–77.

46. Duane F. Marble in W. L. Garrison et al., *Studies of Highway Development and Geographic Change, op. cit.* See also his *Transport Inputs at Urban Residential Sites* (Xerox copy available from University Microfilms, Ann Arbor, Michigan, 1959).

47. Duane S. Knos, *Distribution of Land Values in Topeka, Kansas* (Lawrence: Center for Research in Business, 1962).

48. P. de Vise, *A Social Geography of Metropolitan Chicago* (Chicago: Northwestern Illinois Metropolitan Area Planning Commission, 1960). A companion volume dealing with the City of Chicago itself is in preparation.

49. E. N. Thomas, "Areal Associations Between Population Growth and Selected Factors in the Chicago Urbanized Area," *Economic Geography,* 36 (1960), pp. 158–170.

50. Some beginnings along these lines have been made. Otis Dudley and Beverly Duncan recently published the results of a study indicating that the internal residential structure of cities reflects the industry composition of their economic base and the locational determinants of the basic industries. They argue that "any adequate theory of urban residential structure must reckon with both the locational pattern of industrial activity and the socio-economic differentiation of residential areas which comes about through general city growth." See "The Measurement of Intra-City Locational and Residential Patterns," *Journal of Regional Science,* 2 (1960), pp. 37–54. Also of interest is J. E. Vance, Jr., "Labor-Shed, Employment Field, and Dynamic Analysis in Urban Geography," *Economic Geography,* 36 (1960), pp. 189–220. More recently, Beverly Duncan has completed a study of "Variables in Urban Morphology," in Ernest W. Burgess and Donald J. Bogue (Eds.), *Contributions to Urban Sociology* (Chicago: University of Chicago Press, 1964), pp. 17–30. This study represents the most careful evaluation of the internal residential and socioeconomic patterns of cities completed to date.

51. The original contributions in this field were by the economists Clark and Sherratt. See Colin Clark, "Urban Population Densities," *Journal of the Royal Statistical Society,* 114 (1951), pp. 110–116, and G. G. Sherratt, "A Model for General Urban Growth," in *Management Sciences: Models and Techniques,* Vol. 2 (New York: Pergamon Press, 1960). See also H. K. Weiss, "The Distribution of Urban Population and an Application to a Servicing Problem," *Operations Research,* 9 (1961), pp. 860–874; Richard F. Muth, "The Spatial Structure of the Housing Market," *Papers and Proceedings,* Regional Science Association, 6 (1961), pp. 207–220.

52. Brian J. L. Berry, James W. Simmons, and Robert J. Tennant, "Urban Population Densities: Structure and Change," *The Geographical Review,* 53 (1963), pp. 389–405.

53. See the extensive list in Berry and Pred, *Central Place Studies: A Bibliography of Theory and Applications, op. cit.;* and, in particular, William L. Garrison et al., *Studies of Highway Development and Geographic Change, op. cit.,* Part II; Brian J. L. Berry, "Ribbon Developments in the Urban Business Pattern," *Annals,* The Association of American Geographers, 49 (1959), pp. 145–155; H. Carol, "The Hierarchy of Business Centers within the City," *Annals,* The Association of American Geographers, 50 (1960), pp. 419–438. For an attempt to generalize the theory in this light, see Brian J. L. Berry and William L. Garrison, "Recent Developments of Central Place Theory," *Papers and Proceedings,* Regional Science Association, 4 (1958), pp. 107–120. A study of London also has recently become available: W. I. Carruthers, "Service Centres in Greater London," *Town Planning Review,* 33 (1962), pp. 5–31.

54. Berry and Pred, *op. cit.,* and Berry et al., *Comparative Studies of Central Place Systems* (Final Report, Project NONR 2121-18, NR 389-126, Geography Branch, U. S. Office of Naval Research, 1962).

55. Otis Dudley Duncan, "Service Industries and the Urban Hierarchy," *Papers and Proceedings,* Regional Science Association, 5 (1959), pp. 105–120.

56. Part IV of Garrison et al., *Studies of Highway Development and Geographic Change, op. cit.;* also his *Geographical Analysis of Consumer*

Movement (Xerox copy available from University Microfilms, Ann Arbor, Michigan, 1959); and "A Simulation Model of Intraurban Travel," *Quantitative Geography, op. cit.* In the latter article he develops the various postulates, theorems, and lemmas of the theory of shopping centers and travel behavior.

57. Duane F. Marble, "A Model for the Location of Highway-Oriented Retail Business," paper presented at the Lund Symposium on Problems of Urban Geography, Lund, Sweden, 1960, in connection with the XIXth International Geographical Congress.

58. L. Curry, "The Geography of Service Centres within Towns: The Elements of an Operational Approach," *Proceedings of the I.G.U. Symposium, op. cit.,* pp. 31–54.

59. *Comparative Studies . . . , op. cit.*

60. William L. Garrison, "Toward a Simulation Model of Urban Growth and Development," paper presented at the Lund Symposium on Problems of Urban Geography; R. L. Morrill, "Simulation of Central Place Patterns over Time," pp. 91–108 and 109–120 respectively of *Proceedings of the I.G.U. Symposium.* See also John D. Nystuen's use of similar methods in "A Simulation Model of Intraurban Travel," *Quantitative Geography, op. cit.;* and Edward J. Taaffe and B. J. Garner, *A Geographic Consideration of the Journey-to-Work to Peripheral Employment Centers,* Transportation Center, Northwestern University, 1963.

61. Here we follow Garrison's presentation closely.

62. A volume reporting on these studies will be published in 1965 in the Lund Studies in Geography.

63. T. Hagerstrand, *The Propagation of Innovation Waves,* Lund Studies in Geography, No. 4, 1952: "Migration and Area," in D. Hannerberg, T. Hagerstrand, B. Odeving (Eds.), *Migration in Sweden,* Lund Studies in Geography, No. 13, 1957; and the larger volume of studies available in Swedish in *Innovationsforloppet ur Korologisk Synpunkt* (Lund: Department of Geography, University of Lund, 1953).

12

Urban Economic Growth and Development in a National System of Cities *

Wilbur R. Thompson

Economics is the last of the social sciences to recognize the city as an important unit for classification and analysis. Much of the thin literature on urban economics has been written, in fact, by noneconomists, specifically urban geographers, urban sociologists, human ecologists, and city and regional planners. A number of outstanding economists have skirted the edge of the city in their location theory, most notably the work of Lösch,[1] Hoover,[2] and Isard,[3] wherein conventional (microeconomic equilibrium) theory was extended to rationalize the place of a city in the national system of cities, and occasionally one has approached the city from the vantage point of history, such as Lampard.[4] But, all in all, only a handful of economists from the mainstream of economic thought have moved into the heart of the city and accepted urban economics as a major and abiding professional preoccupation, in the manner of Perloff, Fitch, Hirsch, Hoover, and Tiebout, to cite the principal exceptions. More often a contribution is made in passing, as in the New York studies of Haig[5] and Vernon.[6]

This is not to disparage the major contribution to our understanding of cities made by a small group of fine urban land economists who concentrated their efforts on the narrower forces influencing housing and urban land values. But this group, Fisher, Hoyt, Ratcliff, and Weimer,[7] to cite but a few leading names, is not really in the inner circles of the economics fraternity. Witness the fact that most of these men were or are associated with Schools of Business and Commerce, not Departments of Economics. Finally, and most damning of all, the first text in urban economics has yet to be published.

431

Even though the literature on urban economics is relatively thin, the legitimate subject matter is most extensive, ranging from the rise and fall of cities to the changing function of the central business district. To keep this paper within manageable bounds and readable proportions, the author has somewhat arbitrarily chosen to emphasize the aggregate performance of the urban area as a whole (macroeconomics) rather than the internal arrangement of its parts. That is, the city is seen here as a local labor market—a cluster of work places surrounded by workers' homes to a distance roughly equal to a barely acceptable daily journey to work. And it is as a primary unit of employment and income generation that the economist most easily establishes rapport with the urban area as a fundamental unit of economic analysis, commensurate with the time-honored "industry."

Within the self-imposed bounds of urban income and employment analysis, a further choice was made to focus mainly on economic growth, weaving into the analysis other macroeconomic questions, such as the determinants of the level, distribution, and stability of local income and employment, only to the extent that they are significantly affected by local growth patterns or, in turn, feed back on and induce further growth or decline. Although the viewpoint is sometimes provincial, from within the local economy looking outward, the city is also seen as a dependent, vulnerable subeconomy, interlocked in a broad system of cities. Relative change and hierarchical position are even more stressed than is the urban area's absolute change and position. Perhaps the most distinctive contribution of the economist *qua economist* to our understanding of the city is his conception of an urban area as a subnational economy whose fate rests only partly in its own hands.

But to limit the subject matter to urban economic growth and development is akin to scaling down one's objective to encompass only one-half of the infinite, so other arbitrary boundaries must be self-imposed. A third constraint is that the growth analysis will be confined to the North American experience, in keeping with the author's limited experience. Ordinarily so limited a sample from the world of cities might be highly objectionable, especially in a book such as this, but the saving grace may be that much of the world is moving toward an industrial pattern approximating that of North America and is probably also moving toward some of the same urban patterns and problems discussed later in this chapter. Even though very substantial modifications must be made to take account of very persistent cultural differences, the analysis to follow may still have some rough predictive value for the less industrialized parts of Europe and Latin America, and with greater modification even for Asia and Africa.

The state of the art—the received doctrine—in the field of urban growth economics consists largely of a number of variations on the "export-base" theory of small-area growth and development. Brief, informal references will be made to this literature, in the normal course of pursuit of the main theme. This chapter, however, will not undertake to trace through, in a formal way, the history of urban economic thought or even of that part directly relevant to this chapter, largely because that literature was written by noneconomists out of their interests, from the base of their distinctive skills and for their special purposes—in the face of default on the part of economists. To criticize this work on criteria drawn from the orthodoxy of economics would take on a kind of academic preciousness. The better course would be to begin, constructively, with the distinctive interests and skills of the economist.

When we turn from urban growth theory to the legacy of thought on the ramifications and implications of urban growth, the harvest is no richer. On the nature and cause of interurban differentials in levels of living, we have only the tenuously relevant, *interstate* income analyses of Hanna [8] and Perloff.[9] The emphasis in the existing literature on interstate comparisons of income levels to the virtually complete neglect of interurban analyses, despite the clear superiority of the urban area over the state as a meaningful small-area economy, can be explained simply on the grounds of the relative availability of data. We have rather firm *annual* estimates of state personal income extending back to 1929, but only *Decennial Census of Population* urban income figures for two years, 1950 and 1960. Because the findings of these interstate income analyses are heavily influenced by wide variations in urban-rural proportions between states, their conclusions are not directly transferable to our questions. An exception is the work of Hanna and Mansfield, cited later in a substantive context, which relates city size and income level, a scholarly empirical work which suffers, however, for lack of theoretical content.

On the question of the nature and cause of interpersonal income inequality within urban areas—local labor markets—almost no work has been done, except that which may lie hidden in fugitive materials. We know not whether some urban areas are just a little or much more egalitarian than others, much less why?

In the matter of regional business fluctuations we have a solid piece of comparative work at the state level by Borts,[10] which is, again, only roughly translatable into our context. On the local level we have had some pioneering work by Glenn E. McLaughlin in 1930, covering the 1920's, in which local cycles were found to be related more to degree of specialization in durable goods than to industrial specialization per se. Rodgers, a geographer, also tried to trace through the implications of local industrial diversification on various economic characteristics of cities, including cyclical stability. Although his work was quite imaginative, incisiveness was lost for lack of formulation of testable hypotheses prior to marshalling the data.[11] In probably the most ambitious study to date, Neff and Weifenbach [12] analyzed the business cycles in six cities during the Great Depression of the 1930's, but this very careful study has grown cold over the years; it examined the local reaction to a national business cycle experience which will probably never again be repeated in intensity or duration in this country. The lack of urban cycle studies is attributable to the lack of data even more so than in the case of urban income level analyses, for one needs quarterly data to do sound business cycle work and even annual data is scarce at the local level.

Finally, it should be made quite explicit that the decision to concentrate on urban growth and development and related macroeconomic phenomena has its "opportunity cost." Whatever contribution might have been made by developing the other mainstream of economic thought, price and allocation theory, as it applies to urban problems, is sacrificed. More specifically, urban land use patterns and problems can be seen as extensions of price theory. Slum crowding, "urban sprawl," and the changing function of "downtown" are, in part, problems in microeconomics. Again, the battle between the automobile and mass transit for the dominant role in urban movement can be seen, in part, as a problem in relative prices—license fees, bus fares, expressway tolls, property taxes on commuter railroad rights-of-way, gasoline taxes, and so forth—prices that should reflect not just private but also social costs of urban movement. Although the Vernon-Hoover chapter in this book provides a stimulating introduction to the subject, a comprehensive treatment of urban economic efficiency must largely be left for another time and place. This is done fully realizing that urban economic growth and development also impinges on local efficiency and that the latter, by influencing comparative costs of production and residential amenities, has important feedback effects which modify local growth potential.

The Urban Growth Process: An Impressionistic Overview

Following the reasoning we have set forth, let us not begin by picking critically at the simplistic export-base logic on which practically the whole economic rationale of the city has been founded. In brief, the export-base hypothesis is that cities live by selling products or services to the outside world, gaining thereby the wherewithal with which they pay for indispensable imports, and by extension that the cities rise and fall with the growth and decline of their export industries. Instead, a much broader and more eclectic approach is favored, even at the risk of being less rigorous and even intuitive and impressionistic at times. In due course, we will return to the export-base logic, recast in a less heroic growth role, and examine and evaluate it free from extreme pretensions.

The Many Lines of Linkage

An intuitive appreciation of the rich mosaic of urban growth forces can be gained by working through a much oversimplified presentation of the lines of linkage between a hypothetical urban area and the outside world, as outlined in Figure 1. We arbitrarily break into the pattern of urban economic development by beginning with the three local meat-packing (export) plants (1) which have been drawn together, in horizontal agglomeration, by the external economies of a large local pool of specialized and skilled labor (2), created by their own *combined* demand. Because they have clustered together, these three plants have attracted a common supplier, a plant manufacturing meat-cutting tools (3), and this vertical agglomeration has added to local exports, indirectly, by increasing the proportion of the meat products sales dollar that remains within the area (that is, local value added is now a higher proportion of sales).

Local slaughtering produces hides as a byproduct and this encourages shoe firms (4) to locate nearby to save transportation costs on their chief raw material; this is "joint supply" with a spatial dimension. The agglomeration of shoe plants may be reinforced by the fact that shoes are subject to comparative shopping by wholesalers and retailers and an out-of-the-way shoe plant is at a severe disadvantage. All of this greatly increases the demand for local business services (5), such as transportation, financial and marketing services, and thereby improves their quality and variety and lowers their cost.

As local business services become more varied and improve in quality, they steadily replace similar services (6) previously imported from larger, more highly developed neighboring cities. Although the net effect is for the local economy to become ever more self-sufficient in business services, the growing complexity of the local economy may bring a need to import at least a modest amount of new, more esoteric business services (for example, specialized financial and commercial services related to importing foreign steels for the meat-cutting-tool

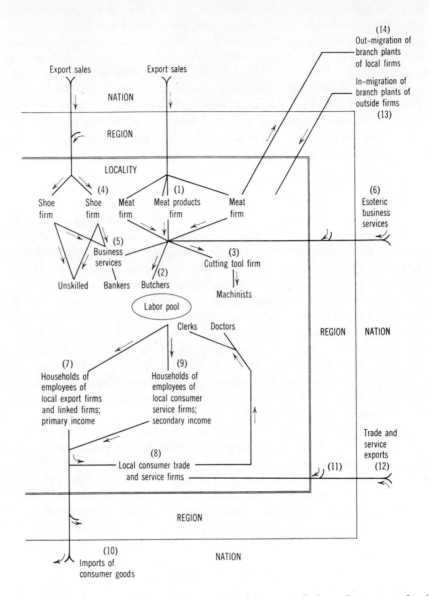

Figure 1. Schematic outline of the principal lines of linkage between a local economy and the outside world.

firm). Simultaneously, the addition of successive firms augments local payrolls and personal income of local households (7) which, in turn, enriches the consumer service sector (8); as successive consumer spending mounts, the variety store gives way to the department store and then the "custom shoppe" and the "salon" are added.

Consumer expenditures rise faster than export industry payrolls as the multiplier effect takes hold and employees of the local service facilities (9) take incomes earned by servicing the households of employees of the export industries and the linked business service and cutting-tool firms, and spend them for other locally produced goods and services. Parallel to the pattern developing in the local business service sector, as the local consumer service sector matures, imports of consumer goods and services (10) will decrease, in relative terms, although the absolute amount of consumer imports will probably increase as the local economy grows in size (more households to demand imports) and complexity (for example, "road shows" now stop to play the town).

Our hypothetical urban area is now moving up in rank in the hierarchy of cities. As it becomes first a provincial and then a regional capital its rising status will be explicitly recognized by an industrial structure which changes to reflect its new role: an exporter of services. A true metropolis—"mother city"—reaches out and renders the more specialized and skill-demanding administrative, financial, legal, educational, recreational, medical, and governmental services to its satellites. The first step, usually, is to export a growing range of services to nearby cities of the next smaller size (11), which in turn merchandise a somewhat abridged line of services to the next lower level of cities. With growth, however, the metropolis may extend its reach to embrace the whole nation or a very large portion of it (12) for a much narrower group of services: New York with finance, corporate administration, entertainment, and others; Chicago with nearly as broad a group; Miami, recreation and amusement; Washington, government and tourist services; Boston, education and research.

Even local manufacturing tends to become more diversified and self-sufficient as the growing local market attracts the branch plants of outside firms (13), while the branch plants of the growing local firms are spun off in complementary fashion to the large and growing metropolitan areas elsewhere (14). Piece by piece, additional business and consumer services and manufacturing operations are added to the local economy as the growing local market affords ever more economies of scale and cuts the cost of local production to the point at which the remaining cost disadvantage vis-à-vis the bigger and/or more efficient operations elsewhere is less than the transportation costs from each of them.

Finally, the metropolis, with its universities, museums, libraries, and research laboratories becomes one big, spatially integrated "coffee house," however functionally compartmentalized it must be in this age of specialization, where bright minds out of diverse cultures clash and strike sparks that ignite the fires of new products and processes—new export industries. We have now come full circle to where we began, or better, we have entered upon an endless and self-regenerative growth cycle.[13]

The Stages of Urban Growth

Can these many pieces of the urban-regional growth puzzle be grouped and arranged in time sequence, that is, in "stages of growth"? We might identify, first, the Stage of Export Specialization in which the local economy is the lengthened shadow of a single dominant industry or even a single firm. This initial stage gives way with growth and size to the Stage of the Export Complex in which local production broadens to other products and/or deepens by extending forward or backward in the stages of production, by adding local suppliers and/or customers of intermediate products. Next, the Stage of Economic Maturation (Service Sector Puberty) follows in which the principal expansion of local activity is in the direction of replacing imports with new "own use" production; the local economy fills out in range and quality of both business and consumer services. Fourth, the Stage of Regional Metropolis is reached when the local economy becomes a node connecting and controlling neighboring cities, once rivals and now satellites, and the *export of services* becomes a major economic function.

One more common phase is the Stage of Technical-Professional Virtuosity; national eminence in some specialized skill or economic function is achieved. This stage may succeed or precede the status of regional metropolis: Detroit was a national center of automotive design and engineering long before it became a regional metropolis, if indeed it is one now. Boston's acknowledged eminence in education and, more recently, research and development followed its role as the capital of New England. San Francisco is a national culture center, perhaps second only to New York, quite apart from its co-captaincy with Los Angeles of the West Coast region.

These purported "stages" of urban growth are, of course, highly impressionistic generalizations and deserve a hearing only as the most tentative hypotheses from which careful empirical work might be begun. Moreover, these growth sketches leave much too strong a feeling of the inevitability of growth and development—onward and upward forever. What are some of the dampening and restraining forces that surely must exist? We see all about us evidence of local economic stagnation and decay and even demise.

Failure of Momentum between Stages in Growth

Suppose the original growth stimulus—the economic environment at genesis—did not generate a sufficiently strong impulse to lift the economy to a level at which derivative growth forces could take over. For example, the local harbor and connecting waterways may not have been so superior or the local ore deposit may not have been rich enough, given the current ore prices and the remoteness of the mine and so forth, to create a town large enough or a technology advanced enough to build an attractive labor force. Without this latter attraction, the local economy never drew the manufacturing plants which would have moved the local economy into the second stage of export diversification and into a state of general industrial enrichment, before the preferred mode of transportation changed or the vein of ore gave out. Or, if the local mining economy did manage to add a few manufacturing firms, and limp through the second stage of growth, not enough of an industrial complex was created to develop the local market to a point where a strong surge of local service industry formation developed, replacing imports with local production. Thus the growth of the local economy may hesitate and stagnate between any of these stages if the momentum at the end of a phase is not strong enough to carry the economy to the point at which the mechanism or process of the next stage is activated.

An insufficiency of momentum may be relative rather than absolute in relevant magnitude, especially with reference to the fourth stage, metropolis formation. Typically, one city will rise from a group of rivals to become the "mother city" of the group. Whichever city gets the jump on the others and achieves early economic dominance usually finds that success breeds success as external economies of service industry agglomeration pave the way for progressive, cumulative *coups*.[14] The wholesale trade center for the group may become the financial center and the latter gain may commonly lead to administrative dominance and subsequent legal eminence and so forth. This sequence is not just sketchy, it is purely illustrative because historical and/or statistical-empirical work on this facet of urban growth dynamics is exceedingly scarce.[15]

Promotion up through the hierarchy of cities is, then, partly a matter of the right timing, usually an early lead amply fortified with local leadership. Surely, a lagging city can forge ahead to dominance through some exceptionally fortunate circumstance, such as being the chance host to a firm which is destined to become *the* individual "success story" of *the* growth industry of the era (for example, Ford Motor Company and Detroit) or through the discovery of great natural wealth (for example, Houston). Ordinarily, however, success breeds success and the rich get richer, at least in the urban growth process.

"Challenge and Response": A Tale of Three Cities

If the rich always did get richer (and the poor poorer) in inter-regional competition, long-range urban forecasting would be much easier than it actually is. But victories can bring complacency and defeats can be challenges. We might postulate a crisis theory of human behavior in regional economic development; a community rises to the occasion in a variation on the theme of "challenge and response" —Toynbee in microcosm.

When urban growth slackens or stalls—when the rate of growth of new jobs falls below the rate of natural increase in the local labor force—heavy, chronic unemployment creates local crises, personal, social, and governmental. Out-migration, the economist's solution, is often sluggish, especially in an era of ever more pervasive home ownership, tighter job seniority, and broadening unemployment compensation. Millions for unemployment compensation, but not one cent for relocation expenses. In depressed areas, sagging tax collections and soaring welfare costs upset municipal budgets and force politicians and public administrators to strain for more imaginative and incisive area industrial development programs.

Agonizing reappraisals are made of local business taxes, relative to competing urban areas, and the efficacy of tax concessions, subsidies in the form of rent-free use of vacant buildings and other industrial lures are reviewed. Comparative transportation facilities, wage rates, utility rates, and other leading plant location factors will also come in for close scrutiny during these trying times. If necessity is the mother of social invention too, the probability of imaginative and effective local action, both public and private, designed to improve the local business climate and nurture new industrial growth will be significantly increased in time of local stagnation.[16]

Perhaps, on close inspection, the recent economic histories of Boston, Pittsburgh, and Detroit would exhibit substantial evidence of a challenge-and-response developmental syndrome. Boston was the first of the three to experience economic stagnation and was a declining economy prior to the outbreak of the Second World War. But shortly after the end of the war, building on a base of superior higher educational facilities, that area spawned a complex of research and development work and manufacturing activity in research and development-oriented industries (for example, electronics and instruments) almost overnight, greatly softening the blow of losing the textile and shoe industries to the South. How much of this new work was generated by increased organized efforts at industrial development and how much was due to the pure chance (?) location of Harvard University and Massachusetts Institute of Technology in the area is debatable—if not unfathomable. But local awareness of a need to rebuild a faltering economy on a new industrial base is evidenced by the mere number of economic studies and reports on the area that poured forth in the prewar and early postwar period.[17]

Contrast the case of Boston with that of Pittsburgh, an economy which boomed during the war and briefly in its aftermath as it worked to supply the backlog demand for steel. Hit hard by the first postwar recession in 1949, for the next half-dozen years Pittsburgh stagnated as local leadership went through a period of intellectual and emotional readjustment, apparently culminating in a clear understanding that this urban area could either stagnate as a steel city or hunt for some broader industrial rationale on which to found its resurgence.

The striking rebirth of Pittsburgh—smoke abatement, physical renewal in the Golden Triangle, and the sponsorship of a highly sophisticated economic development study in cooperation with the local universities [18]—gives every evidence of being just as spectacular as the Boston rebirth, at least when considered in the light of the fact that the image and prospects of a steel city are decidedly inferior to those of a center of culture, in a time of education and affluence.

Consider now the third city, Detroit, an area which rode through the first two postwar recessions (1949, 1954) relatively unscathed on a huge backlog demand for automobiles. Not until 1955, much later than the other two cities, did automobile manufacturing employment in Detroit reach its peak. For almost five years thereafter, as manufacturing employment sagged lower and lower, the local industrial pundits misread warning signs of structural transformation in the local economy as if they signaled only a temporary cycle trough. About 1960, the *chronic* nature of the crushing level of unemployment, left in the wake of an automobile industry that had matured, decentralized, automated, and demilitarized (in the new missile age), all in an indigestibly short period of time, began to percolate through to the opinion molders in the local economy. True, the first serious stirrings had begun about two years before, with an epic state tax study [19] and a few small-budget industrial development analyses,[20] but serious efforts at organizing industrial development investment funds, industrial parks, and the like lagged the *trend turning point* in local manufacturing employment by five or six years.

On careful quantification, we might find that the challenge of an employment crisis elicits its response in a resurgence of local economic leadership with various lags of roughly predictable length, under various sets of circumstances. For example, in the cases of these three industrially mature cities, about a half-dozen years elapsed between the beginning of steady deterioration and widespread appreciation of the structural character of the local malady. Public and private counteraction, in magnitude commensurate with the gravity of the challenge, lagged by another half-dozen years. And industrial reconversion may take a decade or so. Thus, overall, as much as two decades may elapse between shifts from one economic base to a substantially new one. Of course, this is the very kind of knowledge that once revealed might effect changes in the pattern because of that knowledge, and hopefully would shorten the period of response.

The Urban Size Ratchet

If the challenge of economic adversity does indeed beget the response of revitalized community leadership and individual creativity, how can we explain the many abandoned towns and depressed areas that plague us and find their counterparts in booming Europe? [21] The coal towns of Pennsylvania, West Virginia, and Kentucky have been "challenged" by chronic unemployment for decades now with little evidence or prospect of significant "response"; the smaller urban places in Nebraska, the Dakotas, and Montana—the wheat belt—have been declining for decades and give every indication of continuing to do so.

But these illustrations are all of the smaller urban areas; clearly a scale factor is at work. Witness the difficulty one experiences in trying to cite the case of an urban area of over half-a-million population which has suffered an absolute decline in population. Perhaps some critical size exists, short of which growth is not inevitable and even the very existence of the place is not assured, but beyond which, while the growth rate may slacken at times even to zero, absolute contraction is highly unlikely. In sum, at some range of urban scale, set by the degree of isolation of the urban place, the nature of its hinterland, the level of industrial development in the country, and various cultural factors, a growth mechanism, similar to a ratchet, comes into being, locking in past growth and preventing contraction.

A number of possible rationalizations of the purported urban-size ratchet could be adduced. One argument would be that with growth and size comes industrial diversification, and even a random blending of young, mature, and decadent industries tends to produce local growth rates, which deviate only slightly from the national average rate or the rate applicable to some broad, surrounding region (for example, New England, the Southwest). Slow rates of decline provide the large urban area time in which to react to adversity—a period of grace. (The relationship between urban size, industry mix, and stable growth is developed more fully in a later section.)

A second possible basis for irreversible urban growth after some threshold size has been achieved is simply power politics. With a larger population comes greater electoral power at both the state and national levels and with reference to both executive and legislative bodies. True, political power may increase less than proportionately with population increase, as in malapportioned state legislatures and in the U. S. Senate, but increase it does and significantly. Thus, to the extent that federal and state financial aids and public works projects can revive faltering urban economies, the bigger urban areas are in a position to press harder for government support.

Third, somewhat related, is the fact that tremendous amounts of fixed capital have been sunk in social and private overhead in the very large urban area—streets, sewers, schools, water mains, electric power lines, stores and housing—so that even if the area's (export) productive facilities are worn out or technically obsolete, public service and utility costs are so low that it would be very uneconomic to abandon so much immobile capital. No nation is so affluent that it can afford to throw away a major city.

Fourth, a larger and larger proportion of industrial activity is consumer-oriented rather than tied to its sources of supply, and the larger urban areas amass potential customers. A large local economy becomes almost self-justifying as a product market alone. New industries, born elsewhere, eventually reach a stage of development at which they are likely to establish branch plants in this large local market, sustaining local growth.

Finally, a large urban area is more likely to give birth to new industries at critical points in its life cycle than is a small urban area—an industrial birth which rescues it from the brink of stagnation or decline. Although a large place may not produce more new ideas per thousand population per year than a small place—and some evidence will be cited later to suggest greater industrial creativity in larger places—a surer and steadier supply of invention, innovation, and promotion is to be expected in larger places. A simple illustration might help here. Suppose that an entrepreneurial genius occurs only once in every ten thousand births; then a fifty-thousand-population urban area with, say, one thousand births per year will produce this key person only once every ten years, on the average. This area may not have a new industrial savior ready at the time of critical need, whereas the five-hundred-thousand-population urban area, spawning a genius a year, almost certainly will. Gifted persons born in smaller places tend, moreover, to migrate to bigger cities. Sheer size may stabilize the supply of the key human resources necessary to economic growth and development.

In sum, if the growth of an urban area persists long enough to raise the area to some critical size (a quarter of a million population?),[22] structural characteristics, such as industrial diversification, political power, huge fixed investments, a rich local market, and a steady supply of industrial leadership, may almost ensure its continued growth and fully ensure against absolute decline—effect irreversible aggregate growth.

Urban Management as the Scarce Factor in Urban Growth

Absolute size may also operate to stifle growth as cities experience, after a certain critical level, increasing cost of public services due to density, congestion, bureaucracy, and so forth. The principal diseconomy of scale may well turn out to be managerial efficiency, with a high variability between areas. The impression that management may be the limiting factor in urban scale is partly inferential by analogy from orthodox economic thought and partly intuitive.

In search of a theoretical constraint on firm size, without which neither competition nor the self-regulating price system itself could be preserved, economists long ago found that they were forced to rely primarily on the limited expansibility of the managerial factor. The supply of land, labor, and capital did not seem to pose serious constraints on firm size. Apart from the managerial limitation, economists could rationalize firm-size limits only by turning to imperfect competition and invoking a "downward sloping demand curve"—the inability of a firm to sell an endless amount of a given product at a constant price.[23] Although the firm might continue to grow even here by adding new product lines, multiproduct operations pose even greater managerial demands. Sooner or later, management would come to be the principal limitation or scarce factor.

The managerial factor may also be the critical limitation on city size. As the city grows in total population, density of population, and physical extent, a point may be reached at which the unit cost of public services begins to rise or the quality of the service begins to fall appreciably. Local export firms, with their costs of production rising, find themselves disadvantaged in interregional competition for shares of the national market; manufacturing firms must move their trucks through congested streets to cramped loading docks, while paying higher property taxes for the less efficient urban public services. The city size at which increasing public service costs first turn sharply upward varies, of course, with the current level of urban technology.

The parallel to the multiproduct firm is the highly interrelated set of local public services that must be integrated or coordinated to preserve the efficiency of the city, seen now as a huge factory with its streets, power lines, and pipes as the assembly lines, and its complex of legal, financial, and technical services as a magnified version of the "front office." If we believe that success in business is closely tied to the efficiency and creativity of the firm's management, is it not equally likely that the efficiency of the local public economy will vary widely from place to place according to the quality of urban management? Just as efficient management of the General Motors Corporation can push back the point at which net diseconomies of scale take effect, so public service inefficiency and rising unit costs can be postponed considerably, even if not indefinitely, by able and experienced local public legislators and administrators.

But the recruitment of talented people to serve as public officials, the development of a science of local public administration, and the professionalization of urban management is not enough. The organizational and institutional framework within which they function is paramount. Even the most able urban managers may not be able to provide efficient government in a politically fragmented, uncoordinated urban area. Ultimately, then, diseconomies of scale in public services and quasipublic services, such as water supply, sewage disposal, electricity, gas, and transportation, may constrain the size of the city. But only if technological progress, political innovation, and administrative ingenuity do not keep pace, and they have up to now.

Urban Growth Analysis: The Demand Side

One of the simplest and most useful analytical frameworks within which to view the urban economy is the highly popular "export-base" construct, an analytical rationalization of the urban economy first set forth explicitly in 1928 in Robert M. Haig's classic study of the New York region and more recently integrated into the mainstream of economic theory in the work of Charles Tiebout.[24] The urban area is depicted as an "open" economy, heavily dependent on external trade, quite like the small, industrially advanced nation in the world market, only more so. Both Switzerland and Denver must export or die. A small metropolitan area (fifty to one hundred thousand population) may devote as much as one-half of its economic activity to producing goods for sale outside its borders, greatly surpassing even the most trade-oriented small nation in this regard.[25] With the proceeds of its "export" sales, complementary goods are purchased from outside ("imported"), roughly equivalent in dollar amount to the value of the area exports.

Applicability of the Export-Base Logic

Thus the export sector is cast in the key role as the active instrument of change, the point of contact between the national and the local economies, and national forces are presumed to be more powerful and more autonomous than local forces. A typical characterization of the urban growth process, at least as it has evolved in the literature of regional geography and city planning, is that a given number of export workers "supports" a given number of local service workers.[26] This has given rise to a long and sometimes bitter dispute over who "supports" whom. The export-base logician argues that if the export jobs were to disappear, the local service jobs would also be lost—the very town would vanish—but if, instead, some part of the local service work were lost, say, through business failures, replacement service business would spring up automatically.

But this is not wholly convincing because one might also argue that replacement export firms could also be reborn on the base of a viable local service sector, if the reason for that industry being in that place still existed. Going behind local services per se, an urban economy based on natural or persistent economic advantages (for example, a good port and railhead, a pleasant climate and topography, the homes of skilled workers who resist migration) may give birth to wholly new export industries to replace lost ones with only modest labor pains. The defenders of the virtue of the local service sector, led by Blumenthal,[27] rising to the challenge, have even argued that it is really the local service sector which is "basic" and enduring, and that this latter sector supports the chameleon-like export sector which is founded on transitory manufacturing firms—taking a very long view.

In short, a severed export appendage of the urban corporate body can, *in time*, be regenerated by a viable and efficient local service sector.

The phrase "in time" is critical. In the analysis of local business cycles the export-base logic is employed, quite legitimately, under the reasonable assumption that the industrial composition of the export sector of an urban economy is highly unlikely to experience any substantial amount of structural alteration in the short space of time within which business cycles take place. Not only the same industries but even the precise firms will probably remain intact. The local service industries, moreover, are probably not going to alter the competitive position of the local economy in any major way through increases or decreases in the cost or quality or availability of services rendered. Therefore, in analyses which extend over periods of time so short that the industrial *structure*—both export and local service —is largely fixed in kind and quality, the primacy of the demand for export products in effecting change seems clear and incontestable.

When the time dimension is extended, however, circularity sets in. The demand for local services *is derived* indirectly from the external demands for the export products of the area and directly from the local spending of payrolls and profits generated by that export production. In that sense the export sector is primary. On the other hand, local services are important costs of export production and the efficiency of the local service sector is critical to export firms. An abiding electric utility and commercial bank that successively serve the firms and employees of, first, a wagon-maker and then an unsuccessful automobile firm and then a railroad car firm and so on, have strong claims to be counted "basic" in the local economy. But in order to avoid flagrant bias in the argument, we should note that the area exporter could well have been the same steel plant, year after year.

We observe the opening of an iron mine in Minnesota (export industry) stimulating the growth of a whole town (with its complex of derivative local service industries); alternatively, we observe the existence of a farm service center in Iowa with an efficient and pleasing local service sector (for example, schools, utilities, shopping centers) attracting a manufacturing plant (exporter) which, of course, generates more local services. In a growth context, this is a chicken-and-egg problem which, if treated at the level of gross generality, can become a fool's game. When treated in a specific context, such as the emphasis on external demand and the export-base in local business cycle analysis, selective emphasis can be both proper and incisive.

Urban Economic Projection as Demand Analysis

Still, the complexity of urban-regional growth does not completely vitiate the value of the simplistic export-base logic. One important element in any long-range growth prognosis is a projection of the demand for the area's current mix of export products—the lengthened shadow of the sales charts of a handful of key industries.

One can begin an analysis of the trends in demand for an area's leading exports with a standard economic concept: income elasticity of demand, the ratio of the per cent change in spending on a good to the per cent change in disposable income. A 10 per cent increase in income might increase cigarette sales by only 2 per cent—an income inelastic good—whereas sales of fashion dresses might increase by 20 per cent—an income elastic good. We are interested here in identifying which are the "inferior" goods from which the consumer turns as his living standard rises secularly (for example, grits and rice, bus and rail transportation), and which are the "superior" goods to which he turns in response to a steadily rising income (for example, beef and wine, automobile and air transportation).[28] Time is clearly on the side of the urban areas that are producing goods for which the long-run income elasticity of demand is greater than unity, the "luxury" goods, and the reverse. And this is obviously an operational concept, although precise measurement is difficult.

Next, changes in tastes—autonomous changes now, not changes in consumption patterns in response to higher income through diverse income elasticities of demand—have always been an important source of change, perhaps now more than ever before. Despite isolated instances of extreme and self-conscious individualism (for example, "beatniks"), the prevailing opinion seems to be that we are moving toward a mass culture, with our society pursuing security and finding it in increasingly close conformity. The image here is nationwide television networks and Madison Avenue. And by coupling uniform consumption patterns to a high and rising per capita income, an ever greater share of which is "discretionary income," the danger is that capricious shifts in consumption spending may come to dominate the pattern of economic activity.

"Discretionary spending" could come to ebb and flow in massive tides as fads and fashions dictate: from big cars and small boats to small cars and big boats. Manufacturing plants selling in national markets may increasingly find themselves alternately awash with demand, then left stranded on the beach. Even whole industries may rise and fall over very short time periods. The small, remote urban economy exporting a single product, probably even a single brand, would run the greatest risks, especially if it is a "luxury" good. Small one-industry towns, long subject to the risk of great cyclical instability, may no longer be a viable *long-run* form of socioeconomic organization in the Age of Affluence.[29]

The Economic Viability of the Small Urban Area

Other disadvantages of the small urban area in today's fierce competition for industry can be cited. Highly automated factory and office operations will assemble labor forces too small to support a community,[30] especially in light of the growing range of goods and services that are considered necessary. Not only "bright lights and action" but also good museums, technical libraries, and community colleges are urban "necessities" today and they cross the threshold of economical operation at relatively large population sizes. Only the clustering of many automated operations will provide the necessary supporting population. Further, more and more industries are clustering into mutually supporting complexes, based on input-output linkages, complementary labor demands, technological interactions, and so forth. Linked, individual firms cannot enter or leave their present location easily or unilaterally; therefore, an urban area finds it more difficult to attract interdependent firms. In sum, bigger, tighter-knit industrial complexes imply larger and fewer manufacturing centers.

The economic uncertainty and instability of the small urban area will tend to be reflected in higher labor costs—either compensatory higher wage rates for high-grade labor or the need to depend on lower-grade labor—and other competitive disadvantages, such the alternating periods of capital shortages (congestion) and idle capital (heavy overhead costs) which accompanies heavy fluctuations in economic activity. All in all, when we add together (*a*) the precariousness of specialization in discretionary goods in the affluent society to (*b*) the difficulty of supporting a community on the base of a "worker-less" plant to (*c*) the trend toward more integrated industrial complexes, it is difficult to be sanguine about the economic prospects of small towns or even small cities.

Although the small one-industry town would seem to be highly vulnerable, even obsolete, in a country which has achieved an advanced stage of economic development, an interesting and perhaps highly significant exception may exist. A number of small and medium-size urban areas, connected by good highways and/or other transportation facilities, may form a loose network of interrelated labor markets. With widespread ownership of automobiles (or a good bus system) and with expressways permitting average speeds up to fifty miles an hour between home and work place, such a network could extend radially for 25 to 30 miles around one of the larger urban places or embrace a square 50 miles on a side and still be tied into a single, integrated local labor market. A half-a-dozen towns of, say, 25,000 population with two or three main industries each plus a dozen small one- or two-industry towns of half that size add up to a three-hundred-thousand population, extended local labor market, built on the moderately broad base of a couple of dozen industries. This federated local economy may achieve the minimum size necessary to activate the urban size ratchet effect already mentioned, preserving the *collective* existence of these smaller urban places.

The case for the federated local labor market can be made more programmatically. A number of small nearby towns could join with a few medium-size places to develop a coordinated employment service that would ensure an expeditious marshalling and efficient allocation of the full areawide labor supply. In addition, area industrial development efforts designed to attract new firms could be coordinated, even to the point of developing common research and industrial parks at central points. Some evidence of this pattern can be seen in North Carolina, a state filled with small and medium-size urban areas, where a research and development complex is being created in the Chapel Hill-Durham-Raleigh triangle, fifteen to thirty miles on a side and enclosing about a quarter of a million people.[31]

The long-range viability of the smaller urban areas can be assured, however, only if one other ingredient is added to the recipe. The current generation of young adults will probably not be satisfied with rural or small town life, since they are an urban generation. The pictured loose federation of towns, however, could support a rather wide range of consumer services and urban amenities if they joined forces. Differentiation of urban function could be accentuated far beyond that which has naturally evolved. The smaller urban places could become analogous to the dormitory suburbs of the large metropolitan area, with their central business districts becoming regional shopping centers. The largest or most centrally located town could become the central business district—downtown—for the whole network of urban places, with travel times not significantly greater than those that now exist in the typical million population metropolitan areas.

The fate of whole regions, the West North Central wheat belt and the Appalachian Mountain area for example, may rest on the ability of conurbations of smaller urban places to emulate the spatial-functional form of the large metropolitan areas. Although local jealousies and capital gains and losses in real property are not to be taken lightly, the depth of the local crises that attend inaction may prompt bold measures. Both public and private investments could be planned strategically. Instead of a half-a-dozen small, bare community halls sprinkled across the area, one generous size, acoustically pleasing auditorium could be built where good music could be heard. Instead of a half-a-dozen two-year community colleges staffed as extensions of the local high schools, a full-fledged, four-year college of high standards could be supported. Again, museums, athletic teams, complete medical facilities, and other accouterments of modern urban life could be supported collectively. As these federated places grew and prospered the interstices, of course, would begin to fill in, moving the area closer to the large metropolitan area form. But alert action in land planning and zoning could preserve open spaces in a pattern superior to those found in most large urban areas. The federated urban area could become even more livable in some ways.[32]

The political difficulties of achieving the federated urban area are substantial and should not be waved aside, but the constituent political entities are the creations of and subject to the state. Without predicting that it will move into this vacuum, the state could implement, at will, the spatial-functional form suggested here, and the alternatives seem bleak.

Urban Growth Analysis: The Supply Side

Although a demand orientation has been the more fashionable for the past decade, the existence of a supply side to urban-regional economic development has long been recognized, even antedating the demand (export-base) model. A supply orientation is implicit in the typical "inventory" of local resources with which many area development studies begin—and too often end. A supply approach need not be naive for it holds a greater potential for unraveling the pattern and determinants of urban *growth* than does the relatively *static* export-base logic.

We might generalize to the effect that the longer the time period under consideration, the greater the relative importance of supply—local resource endowment and industrial culture. The recent New York study, for example, highlighted the fact that the New York metropolitan area grew by incubating new functions, nurturing them, and finally spinning them off to other sections of the country, all the while regenerating this cycle. The flour mills, foundries, meat-packing plants, textile mills, and tanneries of the post-Civil War period drifted away from New York, their place taken by less transport-sensitive products, such as garments, cigars, and office work. Currently, New York is losing the manufacturing end of many of its most traditional specialties, as garment sewing slips away to low-wage eastern Pennsylvania leaving only the selling function behind, and as printing splits away from immobile publishing. But New York's growth never seems to falter as the new growth industries are much more than proportionately regenerated in its rich industrial culture.[33]

Again, Perloff and associates found "no positive correlation between the proportion of workers in 'growth industries' and the relative rates of increases in total economic activity among the many states." [34] A number of possible explanations come to mind: growth industries are (a) quantitatively dwarfed by other activity, or (b) they are based on new products that are most likely to be invented and/or innovated in mature (slow-growing) industrial areas either out of superior know-how or (c) out of desperation, as suggested earlier in the challenge-and-response argument. In any event, the industry-mix approach—a demand-side technique that ignores new industry—can only provide a partial basis for a long-run growth theory.[35] We turn, therefore, to a brief survey of the supply side of urban growth, conventionally enough with the economist's classic four factors of production: land, labor, capital, and entrepreneurship.

Labor

The historical pattern of industrial development in an urban area may greatly influence its future pattern of growth, and inherited traits may be especially noteworthy with reference to the local labor force. A farm market town on the verge of its industrial baptism can look to only the most routine kinds of manufacturing operations—a work-shoe factory, a textile mill, a food-processing plant. Ordinarily, the local labor market will progress systematically from apprenticeship to journeyman status. Moreover, as skill levels rise, so do wage rates, and the higher local standard of living may automatically evoke a middle-class morality that further spurs growth. Personal achievement—"success"—is not only reasonably attainable now, it is highly emphasized and the financial means are at hand with which the principal instrument toward that end—education—can be applied. Further, personal saving and capital formation become a basic cultural trait, opening the way to small business entrepreneurship.

Seldom, however, is an appreciation of this process accompanied by a sense of the time dimension of the industrial acculturation process.

Do the steps upward in labor skill span a decade or generation? What is the principal mechanism of skill transmission: through the industrial base and personal contact (from father to son) or through earnings and improved public services (from productivity to income to tax base to good schools)?

But "what is past is prologue" may cut both ways. If a strong and aggressive local union presses for wage rate increases in excess of the rate of increase in local labor productivity, and if the local employer is confident that he can easily pass along the increase in labor costs (plus his mark-up), because his competitors are few and collusive (oligopoly), and similarly circumstanced (nationwide union), the union is likely to find their employer quite accommodating, with only token resistance for the sake of appearance. But a day of retribution arrives when the local economy, affluent beyond its expectation or merit, must face the task of gaining additional employment.

Even if the local export oligopolist survives forever, it is highly unlikely that this firm will add continually to *local* operations, as the typical pattern is for a growing firm to move to multiplant operations and to disperse its plants to minimize transportation costs. But the natural increase in local population and labor force alone demands expanding employment, and because technological advances ("automation") will probably *reduce* employment in the local plant appreciably, new firms must be acquired and they will probably have to be recruited almost entirely from industries new to the area. But high local wage rates would tend to put most of the low-wage, nondurable goods industries out of reach, as long as large pools of cheap labor exist elsewhere, and high wage rates *relative to local skills* dim the prospects of getting even new durable goods industries. Probably a significant part of the current stagnation and structural unemployment of the Detroit and Pittsburgh areas is traceable to wage rate increases that outran skill and productivity gains during the long, lush war and early postwar periods. Painful wage rate adjustments under the pressure of protracted unemployment may be an integral part of the industrial redevelopment of the heavy-industry towns.[36]

But the local industrial legacy influences the local labor market in ways other than through labor skills and wage rates—in labor mobility, for example. A growing preference among new entrants to the labor force—the "younger generation"—for the broad welfare fringe benefits and the prestige of employment in a large corporation is becoming evident. Personnel placement and job recruiting studies have demonstrated that "name" corporations do, in fact, find recruiting easier,[37] as retirement and stock purchase plans attract the young men and glamorous buildings in exciting central locations attract the young women.[38] The security-glamor effects must be separated from the fact that the big corporation also has the added advantage of recruiting with a full-time, professional personnel staff.

Not only does firm size aid in the augmentation of the local labor force, thereby widening and deepening the selection of human resources available at that location, but the large corporation may also facilitate a more orderly contraction of the local economy under adverse business conditions. Big firms are usually multiproduct operations and are spatially dispersed; when demand or supply conditions change, the requisite adjustments in their labor force can often be swiftly and smoothly accomplished within the protective shell of the corporate family. A worker may be shifted from a failing to an expanding line of production within the same plant, assuming the skill level is about the same, or he may be transferred without job change to a distant plant serving a region growing more rapidly than the nearby region, although often not without strong "persuasion." That the new jobs of a firm will be offered first to their own displaced workers seems ever more certain as the courts continually expand their interpretation of jobs as property rights,[39] and as the unions win fringe benefits covering this same contingency. In sum, big multiproduct firms probably increase the mobility of labor both in and out of their local labor markets, and thereby both enrich the local supply of labor, and also reduce frictional and structural unemployment in the area. This would seem to be a testable hypothesis.

Finally, *unbalanced* local labor demands have supply repercussions which may stimulate local growth. If the local industries hire only males, this creates a shortage of jobs for women and, though temporarily depressing to average family income, the surplus pool of female labor tends to attract industries with complementary labor demands. Hoover cites the classic examples of silk mills being drawn to the Pennsylvania coal towns, and shoe and textile industries to the New England port towns.[40] Clearly, this argument carries more force in a full employment economy than in one with widespread unemployment. Moreover, the long experience of Cincinnati, Pittsburgh, and other places with unbalanced labor demands has shown that righting the balance may be greatly delayed—commercial and financial secretarial work does not flow readily into isolated places or factory towns. Urban growth analysis has much to glean from studies-in-depth of local labor markets.[41]

Entrepreneurship

No one denies that entrepreneurship—inventiveness, promotional artistry, organizational genius, venturesomeness, and so forth—lies at the very heart of industrial development, yet we hurriedly pay our formal respects to this critical factor and then move on in embarrassed haste to surer, more easily charted ground. But this is a mistake; we cannot act so cavalierly toward the entrepreneur, least of all in growth analysis, even if we might excuse such action in, say, cyclical analysis, where the time period is much shorter.

A number of naive but intriguing hypotheses on the role of entrepreneurship in urban-regional growth literally cry out for even the loosest testing, so that we may then strike more sophisticated reformulations. For example, Chinitz [42] offers one hypothesis that emphasizes risk-taking:

> My feeling is that you do not breed as many entrepreneurs per capita in families allied with steel as you do in families allied with apparel, using these two industries for illustrative purposes only. The son of a salaried executive is less likely to be sensitive to opportunities wholly unrelated to his father's field than the son of an independent entrepreneur. True, the entrepreneur's son is more likely to think of taking over his father's business. My guess is, however, that the tradition of risk-bearing is, on the whole, a more potent influence in broadening one's perspective.

A complementary hypothesis offered here is that there are recurring "cycles" of local entrepreneurial vigor; this is another kind of "challenge and response," at the local level and on a more personal basis. A dynamic entrepreneurial group—even a single outstanding figure—arises in a particular area, perhaps because of mere chance, and this group generates rapid industrial development in that locality. Commercial success and the resultant rise of large local firms produces an environment characterized by complex managerial routines, and administrative talents become both the critical local need and the *sine qua non* of local industrial leadership. The rough and unorthodox inventor-innovator-promoter type is pushed into the background as "scientific management" takes over. The new gods are efficiency, stability, and industrial statesmanship.

As the new industry matures, the local giants begin the almost inevitable regional decentralization, as branch plants are spun off into major product markets to minimize transportation costs. This leads inevitably to a slowing rate of *local* employment growth in this industry, and a concomitant growth in local unemployment, as population and labor force grow faster than job opportunities. With local stagnation the dominant concern, necessity literally becomes the mother of invention, as a frantic search is conducted for unexploited old opportunities and renewed emphasis is placed on the concoction of new products and processes. Efficiency pales alongside creativity or promotional artistry; the inventor is king again and the unorthodox is welcomed, almost uncritically.

As a corollary to this set of propositions, we might also hypothesize that inventor-innovators tend to bunch in time and space; dynamic persons create an atmosphere that attracts more of the same, to share the fraternity of protest against the old and excitement in the new. The barroom of the old Pontchartrain Hotel in Detroit is reputed to have been a hothouse of early automotive technology in the early years of this century. Later the burgeoning automobile industry attracted financial wizards (for example William Durant who put General Motors together) and finally that host of apt managers who see any rapidly expanding, and therefore mildly chaotic, industry as an escalator to rapid promotion.[43]

The parallel between the challenge-and-response and long-cycle hypotheses at the community level, outlined earlier in this chapter, and at the firm level, at issue here, may even be extended to suggest the possibility of some direct linkages between them. For example, the stellar local firm(s) may well catch the brightest young men of the community in its web of glamor, power, and financial security; local public service may have to make do with lesser talent. Both for this reason and because of sheer corporate power, the local legislative and public administrative bodies may be dominated by local big business. In such an event, one would expect the business values to prevail in the community and be reflected in a relatively *efficient* local public economy. But an imaginative and, consequently, unorthodox local political leadership would hardly be expected, and might not even be tolerated. Thus as the local corporate giant decentralizes and precipitates a local employment crisis, a political revolution may well be a prerequisite to effective community response. That is, political innovators may be—must be—spawned to complement the economic ones generated in the private sector.

We have hypothesized that the presence of the giant manufacturing firm turns a local economy into a town full of "organization men," temporarily breaking the tradition of individual enterprise, at least in manufacturing, and dampening creative effort. This is offered as a research hypothesis, not a value judgment. The hypothesis might have been formulated otherwise. For example, giant firms, with their market power and administered prices, are much more likely to have the funds necessary to support a large research and development program. Oligopolists, moreover, have the feeling of permanence to give them the extended time horizons that justify more roundabout research and that permit more deferred payoffs—basic research leading to radical breakthroughs.

True, some students of research and development have expressed strong reservations about the capability, or at least the likelihood, of large corporations to perform significant creative work, despite their longevity and wealth.[44] They have argued that truly creative work almost invariably disturbs production schedules until the "bugs" are worked out, imposes large redesign and retooling costs, and challenges the conventional wisdom laid down by the senior members of management—an attack on older ideas may be construed as an attack on older and wiser heads. Moreover, with their current line of products highly competitive with newer products, by sheer force of market control if nothing else (for example, saturation advertising, exclusive dealerships, and omnipresent service organizations), oligopolists can often suppress or soften the necessity that mothers invention.

But even granting all this—and that would be too generous—if it is local leadership in the formation of new industries that is at issue, and not contributions to scientific progress per se, the advantage may lie with the local economy that serves the oligopolist who, however much he may bide his time in *invention,* retains a fine sense of timing in *market innovation.* In short, the glistening, well-equipped laboratories of the giant firm may be quite conventional in research and development but still spawn greater aggregate local growth than an equivalent amount of small business, simply because it is better able to commercialize its own research as well as that of the "alley workshop inventor." [45] Still, an intuitive presumption in favor of the giant firm does not necessarily favor the host local economy because its innovations may be launched elsewhere in branch plants, whereas the smaller firm is more likely to innovate at home. Clearly, we need empirical work here.

How does one go about measuring entrepreneurship, especially interregional differentials in that elusive quality? Attempts have been made to express the propensity to invent in both input and output terms. The most notable surrogates are (the input of) expenditures and/or manpower by business on research and development, and (the output of) patents issued. We can cite no comparative regional analyses, or even isolated case studies, of inventiveness using expenditure data, probably largely owing to the absence of regional breakdowns on the national aggregate expenditure data, and we can cite only one using manpower data.[46] Except for one early incidental use of patent data at the state level by Ullman,[47] the only regional analyses with this latter index that can be reported are two experimental efforts made by the author. First, and with limited success, an attempt was made to introduce patent grants to local residents in selected patent classes (for example, "metal working") as an independent variable into employment growth-estimating equations for associated census industry groups (for example, "fabricated metal products"), as part of a broad-gauge, cross-sectional, multiple-regression analysis of 1947–1954 state growth.[48] Second, this same patent data was later disaggregated and reclassified by the metropolitan area of residence of the patentee. This latter effort succeeded in identifying patentees (and presumably inventors) as city-dwellers, rather than rural tinkerers.[49]

> The best estimate is now this: the approximately 57 per cent of the population who resided in standard metropolitan areas (in 1945) or within 25 miles of the central city of such an area received (in 1947–48) approximately 90 per cent of the patents granted in sixteen selected patent classes covering chemistry, metal, machinery and engine products and processes.

This study did not succeed in identifying any significant relationship between either city size or industry mix and the rate of inventiveness of the local population, or the lack of any such relationship, owing mainly to various statistical difficulties discussed at length in the paper. But progress was made toward preparing the patent variable for subsequent inclusion in some broader analytical framework of urban regional-growth analysis.

A second facet of entrepreneurship, the ease of entry of new blood into the top echelon of management, might be estimated by working with the length of time spent in grade at the various intermediate levels by those who eventually rose to the top, in a given firm or, more damning, elsewhere. Intellectual nepotism might be assessed by the degree of concentration of background and training among the top management—a preponderance of lawyers, for example. The willingness to accept new managerial technology might be related to such measurable indexes as investment in electronic data-processing facilities (edited for ostentatious display and other extraneously motivated purchases) and to the proportion of the junior executive group exposed to postgraduate university work in management science (for example, game theory, operations research, and other quantitative innovations in business school curriculums which have occurred since the present management graduated). Whether or not this advanced training was pursued on company time or with the company paying tuition fees might also be quite relevant.

Certainly, these concepts are difficult to quantify; moreover, the underlying functional relationships are almost certainly multivariate rather than single variate, and curvilinear rather than linear (for example, top-level management turnover should not be too high or too low). But if promotion within the firm has any substantial quantitative foundation, interfirm (interregional) comparative analysis is feasible. Besides, if one rules out every facet of growth that is difficult to count or weigh with precision—inventiveness, managerial skill, the productivity of the labor force, the supply of risk capital, and so on—nothing but second-rate determinants will be left. Growth analysis will remain purely deductive and in roughly the same stage as business-cycle analysis in the 1920's, when a distinguished professor was distinguished by having his very own business-cycle theory.

Capital

Capital more than any other of the four coordinate factors of production is highly mobile, spatially, so much so that a local capital market may not really exist to any significant extent.[50] The fact of a national capital market would probably make for greater regional-growth differentials than would be probable in a set of semiautonomous local capital markets because there would be little or no spatial friction to prevent unlimited amounts of the full national supply of savings from flowing to any given region. In sharp contrast, labor and entrepreneurship move much more sluggishly, and the friction of migration dampens the growth of the most buoyant areas and retards contraction and collapse of disadvantaged areas. Is there a local capital market of any consequence? Or are interest rates everywhere the same and risk capital everywhere equally available?

The very large, nationally known corporation does operate largely in a national capital market. Its financial needs are such that the urban areas in which it is located could hardly be the dominant sources of funds without precariously concentrating the investment portfolios of local individuals and financial institutions. Besides, commercial banks are prohibited by law from lending to a single borrower sums greater than a specified per cent of their net worth—generally about 10 per cent.[51] Moreover, the larger, well-known corporation probably finds that its credit does not suffer appreciably with distance from its physical operations. In short, we may be able to disregard the very large borrowers for our present purposes—disregard them on the demand side, at least.

The very small firms, especially the prospective new entrants into business, are usually known only locally (and personally) and can secure outside capital only on the most adverse terms. To them the capital market is predominantly a local market. And we would be surprised if careful study of the medium-size firms did not place them firmly in the middle of this spectrum. What is not deductively obvious, however, is whether distance makes much difference after the boundaries of the home area have been passed. That is, can a medium-size business in Akron borrow on as good terms in St. Louis as in nearby Cleveland?

When we turn from the users of funds to the sources of funds, we find that it is not so easy to dismiss some sectors to concentrate on others. We must run the gamut from individuals to the largest commercial banks. The widely publicized, purported shortage of risk capital suggests the importance of individual investors, specifically those willing and able to make equity investments. We may care, then, whether or not a given local economy has more or less than its share of wealthy residents. Although the total amount that this group is willing to invest in any given firm may be trivial compared to the needs of a very large corporate business, resident wealth might easily marshal enough capital to build a veritable hothouse for the growth of small firms. Through general and limited partnerships and subscriptions to small local stock offerings, the wealthy residents of an area may serve as financiers and patrons to local inventors and innovators.

How common—statistically frequent and probable—is the occurrence of an urban area wherein a small wealthy group could appreciably affect the local supply of risk capital? Are these wealthy groups more inclined toward area industrial development or toward retarding local industrialization and urbanization—keeping the area pleasantly rural for residential amenities? These two questions may well be closely interrelated: the smaller urban areas are probably both the places where resident wealth is a more significant component of the local capital supply and where the residential amenity factor may be critical. Which way it goes depends on whether the locality will be deemed by the local rich to be a more pleasant place to live if it remains small and bucolic or grows large and exciting.

Finally, are the local rich venturesome, as those in Houston have often been characterized (caricaturized?), or are they inclined toward graceful living, as is often reputed to be the case for most of the Deep

South and some of the more idyllic places, such as Denver? [52] At issue here is the kind of capital that is most critical to growth and the source that is most distinctively local. The question is basically one of quantitative significance and therefore demands an empirically based answer.

Although the importance of equity capital is universally recognized, the critical role of commercial banks and other suppliers of working capital loans is not so thoroughly appreciated, especially in the case of new and growing businesses. In the early stages of its life cycle, a firm economizes on fixed capital by leasing its plant (an old vacant store or loft spaces in a rundown section of the city) [53] and subcontracts much of its fabricating and subassembling to economize on machinery. Often the young firm is sorely pressed for working capital to pay wages and buy supplies and to extend credit to customers, and short-term borrowing of working capital can be very expensive for small, unknown firms.[54] The point is that the speed and ease with which new and small firms can gain access to the larger and lower-cost sources of short-term credit, commercial banks for the most part, is perhaps just as important to local growth as the more dramatic supply of risk capital.[55]

The receptivity of commercial bankers to the needs of smaller, riskier business depends, in part, on alternative opportunities. If local bankers can keep fully supplied with prime commercial paper—that is, if they can lend entirely to only the business of the bigger and safer local firms—they can minimize administrative costs and maximize safety by ignoring the needs of small business. This may be most likely to occur during periods of rapid local growth, when the local market is a lenders' market. Conversely, when local growth has slowed, excess reserves (unused lending power) pile up and the local commercial banks may begin to take an interest in the more marginal borrowers in the area. At this point, one is tempted to infer that commercial banks, as suppliers of local working capital, act as governors in local economic development by slowing rapid growth and stimulating slow growth. But this sounds much too good to be true and it is much too early in the conceptual stage of so complex a subject to take any purely deductive proposition very seriously.

We argued earlier that a legacy of aging oligopolies might dampen local venturesomeness and even prevent potential entrepreneurs from being "born," as the giant corporations recruit the most talented local graduates. We hypothesize here that aging oligopolies might also, indirectly, lay a heavy hand on local financial practices. Chinitz,[56] reflecting on the state of the stagnant Pittsburgh economy, has suggested:

When banks cater to competitively organized industry, they are more likely to accept the insurance principle of making money, not on each customer, but on the average customer. If you have U. S. Steel and Westinghouse on your rolls, you do not have to learn to make money on the insurance principle.

The willingness of Detroit bankers to back the fledgling automobile industry has been cited as an important factor in the rise of that industry in that area.[57] Eastern bankers were reportedly much more reluctant to support the struggling young eastern automobile firms. Has this characteristic of Detroit bankers endured, or did they also become conservative with success and affluence? Returning to a point made in the previous reflection on entrepreneurship, perhaps there are "long cycles" of local venturesomeness and conservativeness in financing. Are Detroit bankers becoming more inclined toward risk-taking now that the automobile industry has matured and growth must be sought elsewhere—among small firms with radical new products and processes?

One final caveat, lest the unwary be misled by irrelevant relative magnitudes. Since big business accounts for a very large part of total activity and since big business raises new capital largely out of retained earnings and from security sales in a national capital market, one might too quickly conclude that local capital supplies to small business are dust in the balance. But a handful of these small businesses of today are destined to become the industrial giants of tomorrow. Thus the availability of local capital to small business today may be a major determinant of the rate of area growth a decade hence —the tail does come to wag the dog.

Land

The economist's "land"—natural resources in the broadest sense—would seem to be the least likely candidate among the four classical factors of production to be instrumental in *urban* economic development. Because the economics of natural resources does seem on first thought to be nearly synonymous with rural economics, we might do well to begin by considering the relevance of the rural hinterland of a city to the economic development of that city. The quality of the soils, mineral deposits, and forest resources determine the productivity and income of the surrounding farms, mines, and lumbering operations, and the owners and employees of these facilities are the customers of the trade and service establishments of the central city of the area. Thus the quality and quantity of nearby rural natural resources are important economic factors in urban growth to the degree that the urban economy is a service exporter. Although rural-area market towns are typically the smaller urban places, even very large cities may depend *indirectly* on rural prosperity by functioning as service centers to middle-size cities that serve as service centers to the smaller ones that serve the rural areas directly. The Chicago economy is undoubtedly quite sensitive to changes in the prosperity of the corn-and-hog economy of the Middle West, albeit indirectly.

Further, rural areas are not only important immediate customers of urban areas, they are also suppliers to the cities. A given city may be disadvantaged in interurban competition for industry and share of the national market if the sites of extractive activity to and from which it has a spatial-transportation advantage are experiencing depleting supplies and rising costs relative to the raw material-producing areas closer to its manufacturing rivals. Turning from business to households, New York and Buffalo lose ground relative to Chicago and Milwaukee as preferred residential areas when dairying costs in New York state rise relative to similar costs in Wisconsin. Blending the two concepts together, natural-resources developments which favor the Middle West over the East also favor Chicago over New York by enriching the customers of Chicago's service industries—a money income effect—and by lowering food prices in Chicago—a real income effect.

Turning now to urban land proper, flat terrain promotes urban efficiency by reducing street construction and maintenance costs and by smoothing and speeding traffic flow. Flat land also lowers housing costs by simplifying grading operations and by facilitating mass-production building. But hills provide more pleasing housing sites.[58] If, therefore, the upper-income groups make the basic industrial location decisions that apply at the interurban level, and if they are guided in these business decisions to some appreciable degree by the personal considerations of residential amenities, the hilly, scenic areas might be favored in aggregate growth, or at least suffer a lesser disadvantage than physical efficiency considerations alone would dictate.

Natural-resource endowments other than topography and economic considerations other than construction costs bear heavily on urban growth prospects. What is the net effect on population growth of Los Angeles' sunshine and ocean frontage on the one hand and its smog and water shortage on the other? How does one weigh the rivers of the Washington, D. C., area, rivers which create both traffic congestion and recreational opportunities, with bridges easing the former and pollution burdening the latter?

Practically everyone writing today on industrial location and regional growth hastens to point out the growing role of the natural features that make for pleasant living, especially climate.[59] With rising productivity, every year more of us can afford the luxuries of living where climates are pleasant, scenery attractive, and outdoor recreation facilities convenient—and if the most pleasant sites are not also the most efficient ones we do pay a price in foregone production and money income to live there. In addition, that part of our increased productivity which we take in shorter hours of work also operates to move us toward the sites of greatest amenities, as greater leisure may become merely prolonged idleness and weigh heavily unless the beauty of the environment is enhanced. Exaggerating to illustrate, it may be cheaper to move our cities than to build mountains and seashore.

To further ensure that the inclusion of "land" as a fourth factor and full partner in this supply approach to urban growth is not regarded as strictly academic, an impressionistic model of the location of economic activity in an age of research and development is offered. Suppose automation reduces the force of the labor factor in industrial location by reducing the amount of direct labor input and unionization continues to spread its influence, equalizing wages everywhere, especially for key skilled labor. Suppose differentials in capital supply come to be of only minor importance as omnipresent giant enterprise creates a national capital market. Entrepreneurship could then become the critical location factor, if inventors and promoters do bunch in time and space as hypothesized earlier. But what is more footloose, in aggregate, than an entrepreneurial complex; there is no obvious reason why an exciting and fruitful inventive-innovative environment might not be developed in a pleasant place to live rather than a less pleasant one. Inventors and scholars and promoters are human too—at least their wives are. What could be more logical than for these intellectual-industrial centers to be consciously implanted in places that offer natural beauty and outdoor recreation? The case for Palo Alto and Santa Monica, California, as centers of research and development does not need extended arguments; it is hard to argue with success. Perhaps only cities offering superb consumer capital (for example, museums, libraries, theaters, and so forth), such as New York and Boston can hold their own in competition for research and development activity with such garden spots.

The Welfare Implications of Urban Growth and City Size

Although economists shy away from the term "goals," they would probably agree almost unanimously on three basic measures by which the "performance" of an economy—national or local—might be rated: the level of per capita income, the equitableness of the distribution of that income, and the stability of the flow of income over time. Having discussed at some length the processes and patterns of urban economic growth and development, we might now turn to examine the consequences of urban growth. Because growth leads inevitably to greater size, we extend the scope of our analyses to cover the effects of both the *process of growth* and its direct consequence, *city size,* on the stability, level, and distribution of income, in that order.

Growth, Size, and Cyclical Stability

One feels intuitively that a rapid rate of aggregate growth in an urban area should foster local cyclical stability, if for no other reason than that growth would swamp the local cycle. This hypothesis gains stature if it is linked to the conviction that the national depression is a relic of the past, in this age of mild recessions. The verification of this impression is complicated, however, by a subtle measurement problem. Although the cycle in a rapidly growing local economy may be rather large when measured around the trend (with trend removed), a cycle trough that is barely lower than the preceding prosperity peak is a "depression" in only a very special sense of the word. The concrete manifestation of such a "depression" is probably a reduced rate of in-migration of labor, with local employment holding steady.

This peculiarity of cycle pattern can only occur in a context of very rapid growth—the rate of *secular growth* must equal the rate of *cyclical decline,* a situation highly unlikely at the national level but literally true in both Los Angeles and San Diego in the 1953–1954 recession.[60] Regardless of the formal numerical interpretation that one might derive from what is ordinarily a sensible measure of cyclical instability at the national level, local cycle troughs do not feel like depressions to anywhere near the same extent in a rapidly growing small-area economy—and they are not.

The deductive presumption favoring a systematic functional relationship between urban *growth* and economic stability seems at first to lack any counterpart in urban *size* and stability, working through, say, some functional relationship between city size and industrial structure. Clearly, increased city size brings greater industrial diversification, but does diversification bring cyclical stability?

In sharp contrast to the classic strategy for dealing with *seasonal* instability by pairing complementary "seasonals"—the proverbial coal-and-ice business—cyclical stability poses a much more difficult planning problem. The cycle peaks and troughs of the various industries are not randomly distributed in time, but they are quite similar in timing. (Otherwise, of course, there could not be an aggregate business cycle.) At best, then, a given urban economy is restricted to choosing between industries with greater or lesser cycles. Industrial diversification, moreover, becomes an averaging process which betters or worsens the cyclical stability of the local economy, depending on whether the cycle amplitudes of existing local industry are greater or less, respectively, than those of the industries to be added. To rephrase, industrial diversification leads toward a cycle pattern approximating that of the national economy—an improvement for Milwaukee (machinery) and Pittsburgh (steel), but not for Washington, D. C. (federal public service) and Durham, North Carolina (cigarettes).

The tentative hypothesis, then, is that large urban economies tend to have diversified industrial structures and, therefore, tend to replicate the national degree of cyclical instability; the smaller urban economies exhibit a much greater range of cyclical instability by virtue of their heavier specialization, in both the more unstable and the more stable industries. The expected relationship between city size and cyclical stability, assuming that size randomizes the local industry mix, is shown schematically in Figure 2.[61]

Growth Stability, Migration, and Capital Budgeting

Trends are not straight lines, we only draw them that way. If we knew the true trend, we might measure "growth instability" by the

Figure 2. Schematic presentation of hypothesized relationship between city size and local cyclical instability.

number of major changes in the rate and/or direction of growth; or, more pragmatically, by the frequency with which we need to revise our linear projections. (Illustratively, we might quantify growth instability over a given time period by the degree of the polynomial trend equation which best fits the data, degrees of freedom considered.) This is not to deny the difficulty of separating trend from cycle, to say nothing of the paucity of data. But when one recalls the huge amounts of local public investment almost irrevocably committed over very long amortization periods in schools, streets, and sewers (that is, the inflexibility of urban capital supplies) and that trend shifts persist much longer and are more likely to induce major amounts of in- and out-migration than cycle movements (that is, the variability of urban capital demands), the need to understand and anticipate growth waves is at least as great as similar skill with local cycles. This is certainly so at the local level, especially in the context of physical planning.

Again, city size is of interest. Industry growth trends, like seasonal but unlike cyclical patterns, are probably randomly distributed in time. A narrowly specialized urban economy may be dominated by industries that are secularly young or mature or decadent. Accordingly, industrial specialization offers both the prize of maximum growth and poses the threat of local stagnation and decay, depending on time and the "luck of the draw." Or, if a given urban society has a clear and strong aversion to risk, it may, at least conceptually, compound an industry mix of complementary growth trends. Even random industrial diversification becomes a form of long-range hedging; the more heterogeneous the industry mix, the more stable the industrial growth rate. Deductively we would expect: (a) the larger the urban economy, the more diversified its industry mix, the more stable its growth; (b) the larger the urban area, the more it resembles the national economy in both growth rate and growth stability. Of interest to urban planners and administrators is the corollary that "nationalizing" the local growth pattern renders it more predictable.

The relationship between the *rate of aggregate growth* and *growth instability* is quite different. A very rapid rate of growth—fast enough to swamp the local reflection of the national business cycle—may sweep a local economy smoothly upward for a decade or so, through perhaps two or three "minor cycles" in national business activity. But rapid rates of growth are very hard to maintain; usually they are built on the stage of most rapid growth of a single industry—the increasing-rate-of-increase phase of a logistic curve, for example. Now growth in one industry may well develop the industrial base that spawns another, but the probability is that the new growth will not germinate at a rate that will exactly match the declining primary growth rate. In short, there are transitional pauses—periods in which gains are consolidated—in even the most vibrant local industrial areas. A tentative hypothesis is that a rapid rate of aggregate growth tends to create growth instability. In sum, large size may bring growth stability but achieving that size rapidly may be temporarily destabilizing.

Growth, Size, and the Level of Money Income

Most economists would refuse to accept aggregate growth per se as a legitimate social goal, preferring instead to identify "growth" with economic progress only if expressed as a rising level of per capita income.[62] Most appropriately, therefore, we turn to the question of the relationship between aggregate growth, size, and the standard of living.

Although traditional economics has had more to say on the association between growth and the level of income in a region than almost any other topic broached in this paper, the analyses have almost invariably reversed the direction of causation over that which most concerns us here. That is, areas with relatively high wage rates and per capita incomes are seen as attracting workers and population from areas of lower wage rates and income. (This assumes that the relatively high wage rates reflect a tight local labor market and are not "equalizing wage differentials" due, for example, to a high cost of living in that community, as in New York City and Fairbanks, Alaska.) Again, location theory has stressed the fact that high wages create a rich local market and may draw market-oriented industries, and a number of empirical studies have shown that market-oriented industries are a very large and growing part of all industry.[63] But little can be cited on the effect of growth on the level of local money income.

Nor have economists, with a few notable exceptions, shown any substantial or prolonged interest in the relationship between city size and the level of local income. Still, city-size considerations are so central to city planning, and the economist's contribution to the city planner's question sufficiently important, that the economist may well have a moral obligation here to render a crossdisciplinary service. Even a handful of moderately firm numbers here would aid immeasurably in cleaning up a lot of loose generalization on central city "sprawl" versus "new town" colonization, and on suburbs versus satellite cities and so forth.[64] It is fashionable among planners to lament their lack of control over city size and spatial form, but their work lacks convincing evidence of what should be done if such power ever were to be conferred. Specifically, can metropolitan growth be checked with greenbelts and satellite cities without significant loss of productivity and income? Could we all move to small cities, as Mumford suggests,[65] with economic impunity?

A few attempts have been made to correlate urban income differentials with city size, based on loosely argued and largely implicit hypotheses having to do with bigger cities assembling populations of higher economic productivity—the younger adults, the talented, the educated, the ambitious—and/or creating superior working environments. The principal empirical offering from economists on city size and income level are the Hanna-Mansfield studies which suggest a modest but statistically significant tendency for income level to rise by about 25 per cent from the lowest of eight city-size classes to the highest.[66]

A number of demographic trends are at work, moreover, which bid well to alter the nature and significance of interurban variations in the level of income, and to make obsolete most of our meager knowledge about them. Under current trends, population growth will agglomerate preponderantly in the larger cities and their environs, and the very large urban areas probably tend to be even more homogeneous in income level than the smaller ones. The argument supporting this assertion is parallel to the one advanced to explain the schematic scatter diagram (Figure 2) used to relate cyclical stability to city size, and the pattern might well be very similar too. Just as small cities tend to specialize in either (not both) the stable or unstable industries, so, too, small cities tend to host *either* the high-paying *or* the low-paying ones. And just as size brings a mixture of stable and unstable industries, so, too, it surely blends high- and low-paying industries into a bland average wage rate.

Certainly, it is quite possible that the large city does create an environment especially favorable to production or especially attractive to the more gifted and venturesome individuals, as is tenuously suggested by the early empirical returns. We can easily accommodate such a possibility by tilting the regression line of a city size-income level diagram (not shown) so that it slopes upward and to the right without damaging in the slightest the argument that interurban *variation* in per capita income decreases with increased city size. Simply said, the hypothesis is that large cities have highly diversified industrial structures and randomized income sources that, perforce, resemble each other, and, as we develop into a nation of very large city-states, we may come to experience surprisingly little interregional (interurban) variation in per capita income.[67]

One implication of such a trend is that the role of the federal authority in urban affairs may come to be less that of an agent of regional redistribution of income (for example, the farm program) and more that of an agent of urban efficiency and of the interregional redistribution of population and industry in accordance with new national objectives.

From Money to Real Income:
Interregional Variations in the Cost of Living

As little as we do know about interurban variation in money income, we know even less about the relative cost of living in different cities. And surely we cannot rationally choose between big and small cities, individually or collectively, without some reasonably firm basis on which to translate money income differentials into real income differentials by adjusting for variation in local price levels. We may at this point extend the export-base logic from growth to efficiency. If the export sector is the breadwinner of the city, the local service sector is its housekeeper, bearing primary responsibility for the efficiency of the city as a consuming unit. High wages earned at the local factory may be deflated by a decrepit, mismanaged bus system, an inefficiently small (high-cost–high-price) municipal water plant, and/or a collusive and rigidly conventional retail trade industry. The absence of data on the relative cost of living in different cities is a glaring and deplorable statistical gap.

The efficiency of the local service sector is probably a function of (a) the location of the urban area, both its absolute position with reference to natural resources and capital facilities (for example, the productivity of its agricultural hinterland, proximity to water and rail transportation) and its relative position in the national system of cities; (b) the current rate of growth the area is experiencing (for example, a high rate of population in-migration causes congestion, shortages, and other inefficiencies and a declining area must support costly excess capital); and (c) the size of the urban area, in both population and area. An isolated city is forced to become relatively self-sufficient (or do without) at inordinately low levels of output in many goods and services, especially in services because of the extremely high costs of transporting services. A comparison of living costs between, say, isolated Spokane, Washington, and South Bend, Indiana, nestled in the heartland of the Middle West, would be most instructive on the cost of enforced self-sufficiency.

Increasing local self-sufficiency is, of course, most often attained gracefully and economically through growth and large size, as the growing local market pulls one activity after another across the threshold of economic local production. And as the local market continues to grow, each of these new local activities gains whatever additional economies of scale occur at outputs beyond that output at which the activity could first be profitably introduced locally, and so production cost gains may be added on to the savings in transportation costs.[68] But the real obstacle in quantifying the change in consumer welfare lies not in measuring the cost of a given market basket of goods and services available in two different cities, but rather in assessing the value of having a greater selection from which to choose in the larger city, that is, in assessing the "cost" of not being able to buy a given good or service in a smaller place. (Can one determine the price of attending an opera in Scranton, Pennsylvania, by adding in the cost of transportation to New York, including lost time and possibly food and lodging en route?) Thus the esoteric services of the big city provide the principal measurement problem, and this is not trivial because it is precisely these services that are the attraction of the metropolis.

Without trying to be comprehensive in the handling of the relationship between urban size and the local cost of living, let it be noted in passing that the size of an urban area also affects urban efficiency, through competition, but in an ambivalent way. A large, local market spawns a large number of competitors (for example, more department stores, banks, homebuilders) tending thereby to lower costs, squeeze profit margins, stimulate innovation, and otherwise improve the consumer's position in the private sector of the local economy. Let the images here be the "discount house," an artifact of the big city, and the single ("list price") appliance dealer in the small town.

But the population expansion also spills across the central city limits, politically fragmenting natural public service districts and raising the cost and/or lowering the quality of public services. Either the public service costs may be higher and service quality poorer in *absolute measure* (for example, uncoordinated police systems, mismatched transportation networks) or, at the very least, potential *economies* may be lost that could have been achieved under political consolidation. For example, central city water and sewage disposal plants, although larger than in many politically unified smaller urban areas, and perhaps somewhat more efficient, would not reach output levels or attain the internal economies of size they could have if the central city system were to service the full metropolitan area. (Suburbanites might still, of course, choose to forego the cost advantages of political consolidation, that is, trade them for various political, philosophical, or psychological gains associated with very small, personalized local government.) [69] Paradoxically, then, greater urban size serves to break up "local monopolies," both the inefficient ones in the private sector and the efficient ones of the public sector, effecting gains from increased competition in the former and the loss of internal and external economies of scale in the latter.

But then there are diseconomies of scale, too. Land values and their reflection in housing rents rise very rapidly with urban size—as much as one-third the price of a home is land value in the New York metropolitan area, whereas land might account for only one-tenth or less of the combined land and house value in a small town. Again, the cost of commuting to work, including tension and fatigue, in the very large urban area need not be labored, especially when compared to the advantages of walking to work in a small urban place. And the cost of outdoor recreation may range from practically nothing to its virtual unavailability with increasing urban size—here again is the difficult task of comparing the price of a service to the "cost" of doing without it, reversed in favor of the small urban place.

But we have in hand much more than just an empirical problem; there is a subjective facet to cost-of-living comparisons which is at least as critical in quantification as specification of the objective price indexes. Even if we knew the price of each good and service both in some isolated small town and in some part of the Atlantic Coast "megalopolis"—even if we had all the "price relatives"—we could construct a composite price index which would synthesize and summarize this bewildering mass of information only if we knew what "weights" to use. That is, the weight we attach to the "fact" that opera is cheaper in the big city and to the fact that outdoor recreation is cheaper in the small urban place must reflect the frequency with which the consumer chooses the two activities—the relative quantities consumed.[70]

Clearly the same set of price relatives might show that a low-income family, with only a grade-school education and only recently removed from rural surroundings, might find the cost of living lower in a small town, given their preference for picnicking and fishing and their heavy expenditures on rent and transportation. Conversely, the upper-income, educated, confirmed urbanite would apply a wholly different set of weights to these same price relatives and would choose the big city at the same or even a lower money income to attain the highest real income—satisfaction. Fortunately, we do not need to quantify individual taste patterns ("preference maps"). We need only provide the major price relatives—the price of housing, transportation, food, recreation, and so forth—in various places, and then trust the individual to do his own weighting, multiplying and summing to make his own location decision.

But suppose that city size influences the level of money and real income largely in the range from small to medium-size cities, and suppose that two-thirds of our population will soon reside in urban areas of one-half million and over.[71] Then the critical residential choice would come to be not in which urban area to live, but rather whether to choose the core area, inner ring, suburbia, or exurbia? Abstracting from the very real and pressing social problem of racial discrimination in housing,[72] the householder presumably selects the home site, from those he can afford, which maximizes his family's utility. Perhaps we will come to need *intra*-urban consumer price indexes even more.

The modern, large metropolitan area offers its inhabitants variety ranging from "cliff-dwelling" at the edge of a vibrant downtown to garden patches under near-rural conditions at the urban fringe, virtually matching within one urban area the variety of many separate cities.[73] And when we recall that this very substantial range of residential choice is coupled with the opportunity to choose from a wide selection of jobs without having to change one's residence, then a strong case can be made that freedom of choice has been extended by the development of the very large metropolitan area. And extended choice can be associated with an increase in individual and social welfare with fewer reservations than almost any other alternative goal that we might pursue.

Growth, Size, and Income Inequality

Rapid urban growth serves to reduce impoverishing cyclical and structural unemployment in a number of ways. The point was made earlier that, in a booming local economy, a local cycle trough may be no more than a brief pause in the secular growth of employment, rather than a period of heavy unemployment. Again, "hard-core" unemployment, which otherwise would crystallize when structural shifts in taste patterns and technology close up business firms and close out various occupations, yields to the powerful solvent of replacement job opportunities in the local growth industries. Changing jobs, happily, does not also entail changing place of residence. In a booming local labor market, moreover, the less-skilled workers are upgraded to high-wage work especially rapidly, almost under forced draft. Thus the weight of evidence from the labor market seems to be preponderantly on the side of linking rapid aggregate growth with income equality and stagnation with income inequality.

The only cause for some hesitancy in tentatively associating rapid growth with income equality is the side effect that rapid (employment) growth attracts the rural poor—persons lacking both assets and urban-industrial skills. A reservoir of near-indigent families abides in the urban hinterland (for example, underemployed farmers on marginal land, itinerant laborers in stagnant small towns), eager to enter the big city, awaiting only some sign of a tightening in the major local labor market. This tends to perpetuate the existence of a sizable group with a very low income and to retard the trend toward greater equality stemming from growth as an unemployment-reducing force. But migration is sluggish, so this is not cause enough to reverse the impression that vigorous growth brings greater income equality, only that in-migration is a partial offset in an open economy.

But growth leads to large size and we would expect the larger urban area to exhibit greater interpersonal variation in income for a number of reasons. On the supply side, large cities tend to attract the most gifted and ambitious individuals and accentuate these greater differences in natural ability by offering the best professional and technical education. Thus with their human resources ranging from the most talented and aggressive to the most marginal rural-farm migrant, not to mention sizable populations of students, social rebels, skid-row derelicts, and other very low-income groups, a compelling deductive argument that labor-income inequality increases with city size can be built up solely from the supply side.

The demand side is, moreover, deductively complementary. The large city is more likely to be the home office of the "name" corporation with its "executive suite" and research laboratory, and all the ancillary business services that call for the highest professional skills (for example, corporation lawyers and financial counselors). In sharp contrast, the smaller city seems more often to be built on manufacturing industry and routine mass-production activities in particular, with the concomitant narrow range of skills and with wage rates further compressed by the egalitarian influence of the labor union.[74] Again, the large city is probably, much more proportionately, the home of the very rich, as a very large income would be redundant in a small place with its narrow range of consumer goods.

All this combines to suggest the hypothesis that as the small rural service center acquires factories and grows in size it probably also becomes a more egalitarian society, but, with further growth and true metropolis standing, ever more esoteric services are exported over ever greater distances (for example, administrative, legal, financial), turning the income distribution back again toward greater inequality by expanding both the opportunity to express personal talents and to manipulate private property.

Growth, Size, and Income Redistribution

Rapid growth, with its attendant in-migration of the rural poor, and large urban size, with its attendant political fragmentation, combine to intensify another form of income inequality, intergovernmental inequality. The rural in-migrants usually settle in the core of the central city for the simple reason that this area contains the oldest (generally, the shabbiest) housing in the area and is especially an area of concentration of furnished rooms and rental housing that most fits the needs of migrants. And, if the in-migrants are nonwhite, the core area may be the only area open to them. Since these people are new to urban living they often have not yet acquired an urban culture, even in such simple and mundane matters as the proper disposal of waste matter, and it is not surprising that their arrival tends to set off a wavelike motion of residential displacements, with each income class pushing outward and upward to better housing, holding their place in line as it were.[75]

Although the growth may not change the basic concentric spatial pattern, in which income and wealth vary directly with distance from the central city, the fact that political boundaries are usually fixed, especially those of the landlocked central city, means that rapid growth can impoverish the central city. To oversimplify, by the time the central city houses only one-half of the population of the local labor market (metropolitan area), it will have the poorest one-half, and with continued growth the poorest one-third, and so forth.

Not only does urban growth tend to spill over the political boundaries of the central city and dichotomize the regional population, with the poor concentrated in the central city, but further income segregation occurs in the suburbs as the middle- and upper-income classes separate into little homogeneous residential enclaves that become hardened and formalized by political boundaries. In general, the greater the number of political subdivisions in a metropolitan area, the greater the differentials in median income among subdivisions. This follows, if for no other reason, from the simple fact that a small land area can be filled with the houses of just the rich or the middle class or the poor, whereas a large subdivision must of necessity mix classes to some degree to exhaust its land area. Thus a high degree of political fragmentation implies a high degree of variation in income level among local political entities. Expressed more starkly and pragmatically, political fragmentation divorces tax base from public service needs.

This separation of local public service needs and fiscal capacity is especially critical when we recall that urban living involves the "need" for greater income redistribution than rural living. Urban life is much more complex and (impersonally) interrelated than rural life; residential proximity to the poor increases the threat of the poor to the rich (for example, public health and safety) and through awareness increases their compassion or sense of guilt for the lot of the poor (for example, expands private and public welfare programs) and offends esthetic senses (for example, the "city beautiful" foundation of slum clearance and urban renewal). Political fragmentation of metropolitan-area labor markets in an era of rapid technological change, heavy job dislocations, and critical problems in mass education are luxuries we probably cannot afford.

Residential Segregation by Income and Human Resource Development

The distinctive residential and political spatial patterns formed as an urban area grows to large size not only hamper the redistribution of income through local public services, they also operate to hobble further economic development, both local and national. Even though residential segregation by income class may be practiced no more strictly in large urban areas than in small ones, sheer size itself may create a difference in kind.

In a large urban area the slum section may be so extensive that the slum child may almost never transcend it—may almost never participate in or even witness bourgeois socioeconomic phenomena. By contrast, the slum child in the small town regularly attends school and at least occasionally plays with the children of the middle- and upper-income classes. Some of the cultural advantages of a superior home environment, therefore, may be acquired indirectly by the slum child as he is exposed to experiences which may both implant higher aspirations and, by providing good examples, show the way. Conant [76] has written persuasively on the value of the small town comprehensive high school as an instrument of democracy, and it is emphasized here as a tool of human resource development.

At home, the less productive members of the labor force—the parents of the slum child—might receive more sympathetic and sophisticated treatment if they were not so spatially isolated from the social, economic, and political leaders of the community. This unfamiliarity leads to a lack of interest in their plight as well as to a stereotyped image of their characteristics. Certainly, one cannot blithely assume that residential proximity of the rich and poor would set in motion inexorable forces leading toward human conservation and personal development, merely by exposing a presumably sensitive and sensible upper-income class to the plight and potentialities of their more unfortunate "neighbors." The rich and poor already live side by side in East Manhattan and along the Chicago Gold Coast with slight salutary effect.

Still, one can induce some inferential support for the existence of an "awareness effect." Our urban renewal program has a decided physical bias—we renew buildings to renew people, rather than the reverse—probably at least partly because the *sight* of slums offends the esthetic sense of the upper classes as they commute past them between their suburban homes and central-city work places.[77] A more intimate exposure to urban poverty would reveal the even uglier cases of malnutrition and tuberculosis hidden inside, or, less dramatically, just the almost invariably lower level of general health.[78] Our urban renewal programs might then be coupled with a new set of welfare programs that strike at the basic problems of human rehabilitation and personal economic development, replacing current programs that merely spread cosmetic salves on these sores and soothe guilty consciences. The road to lasting slum clearance probably should begin with the physical and mental health of the slum dwellers, proceed to education, productivity, and income and end with grace and beauty.

When the leaders of an affluent nation such as ours call for greater economic growth surely they must mean the expansion and extension of opportunities for creative expression and personal achievement, and not merely some undifferentiated increase in gross national product—not just a bigger pile of automobiles and refrigerators. So as long as the more marginal members of the labor force remain "out of sight and out of mind" and as long as slum children can encounter only other slum children no matter in what direction they reach out, human *resources* are being wasted and human *beings* treated shabbily. Thus the very large metropolitan areas we have created, economically, socially, and politically fragmented as never before, would seem to have at least one facet that could be a major obstacle to achieving a rapid rate of local and, therefore, national economic development. Have we, too, built a "wall" seriously hampering social interaction and human progress in our rapidly growing and proliferating giant metropolises?

We have now turned from the effects of growth back to the determinants of growth; we have come full circle.

The Pattern: Reprise

This discussion of the socioeconomic implications of urban growth and size is sufficiently slippery and tortuous to warrant a brief recapitulation of the central theses and the basic assumptions. Assuming that the rural areas and the small towns of the nation will continue to empty out and that the largest metropolitan areas will continue to host the majority of the migrants, an urban pattern is foreseen in which roughly two-thirds of the population of the United States will reside in a couple of dozen huge metropolitan areas of over a million population within a decade or two.

Although these metropolises may not enjoy greater cycle stability than smaller places—an average industry mix brings an average cycle —the business cycle has yielded steadily to federal monetary and fiscal remedies, so that the instability problem that will most plague urban areas in the future will be that of shifting growth trends—the chaos of too rapid growth or the poverty of stagnation. And large urban size does promote *growth stability* through industrial diversification, mixing random blends of industries in various stages of growth—the young, mature, and decadent.

Again, large size and random industrial diversification also brings a varied mix of industries, occupations, and population groups: high- and low-paying industries, skilled and unskilled work, and breadwinners and dependents. Accordingly, we would expect the average money income to become very similar in Baltimore, Chicago, Atlanta, and Los Angeles, and, with our population largely residing in such major metropolitan areas, interregional income redistribution would not seem to be nearly as critical in the future as in the past—as in the transitional context of interregional income transfers from urbanized Connecticut to rural-farm Georgia.

Even though all of the large metropolitan areas may have roughly the same average income, very substantial differences in real income (satisfaction) will be experienced by any given household at various residential sites within any given area. The major family residential decision, then, will be less which major urban area to choose to inhabit—they will all provide everything—and more in which part of any one of them to site the home—core, inner ring, suburbia, exurbia —given the family income and taste pattern.

None of this implies that the interpersonal distribution of income will become a lesser problem with time (in fact, this author would argue the reverse), only that the national range of interpersonal income inequality will tend to be replicated in each of these large metropolitan areas, almost in full; Baltimore, Chicago, Atlanta, and Los Angeles will each have their share of the rich and the poor.[79] The major politicoeconomic implication is that if our metropolitan areas remain politically fragmented, they will find it increasingly difficult to handle the provision of even the more traditional public services (for example, public safety and transportation) and almost impossible to perform responsibly on welfare needs, as tax base is divorced from public service needs and decision-making is decentralized without coordination.

Finally, the major socioeconomic implication drawn is that the longstanding practice of residential segregation by income class is transformed by sheer size from the relatively innocent act of pursuing personal living amenities into a major impediment to social interaction among classes and to the development of human resources. In an age of rapid and even forced technological change—at a time when the brightest of us are exhorted and handsomely financed to accelerate efforts that displace the dullest of us from accustomed work—it could prove to be disastrous to lose contact between classes, from both an economic and ideological point of view.

In sum, the principal domestic issues of the next couple of decades will probably originate within these new giant city-states and require treatment within that context.

NOTES

* This paper has been drawn from the author's book-length manuscript entitled *A Preface to Urban Economics: Toward a Conceptual Framework for Study and Research,* sponsored by the Committee on Urban Economics of Resources for the Future (Washington, D. C.: August 1963, lithographed). The first three sections are a slightly abridged version of Chapter 1 on growth, and the fourth is a heavily abridged version of growth-related material in the remaining four chapters in the first half of the manuscript.

1. August Lösch, *The Economics of Location* (New Haven, 1954).
2. Edgar M. Hoover, *Location of Economic Activity* (New York, 1948).
3. Walter Isard, *Location and Space-Economy* (New York, 1956) and other work cited below.
4. Eric E. Lampard, "The History of Cities in Economically Advanced Areas," *Economic Development and Cultural Change,* 3 (1955), pp. 81–136.
5. See note 24.

6. Raymond Vernon, *Metropolis 1985* (Cambridge, 1960), the summary volume of a nine-volume study.

7. Three of the leading works in the field are Arthur M. Weimer and Homer Hoyt, *Principles of Real Estate* (New York, 1939, 1948, 1954), Richard U. Ratcliff, *Urban Land Economics* (New York, 1949), Ernest M. Fisher and Robert M. Fisher, *Urban Real Estate* (New York, 1954).

8. Frank A. Hanna, *State Income Differentials* (Durham, 1959).

9. Harvey S. Perloff, Edgar S. Dunn, Eric E. Lampard and Richard F. Muth, *Regions, Resources and Economic Growth* (Baltimore, 1960).

10. George H. Borts, *Regional Cycles of Manufacturing Employment in the United States,* Occasional Paper 73, National Bureau of Economic Research, 1959.

11. See note 61.

12. Philip Neff and Annette Weifenbach, *Business Cycles in Selected Industrial Areas* (Berkeley, 1949).

13. This summary and loose synthesis of the complex of forces underlying urban-regional economic growth and development draws liberally, of course, from innumerable sources, and only an unabridged history of doctrine in this field of thought would suffice to assign credits of authorship. The most comprehensive review of this literature and the most exhaustive bibliography published to date (or likely to be published for some time to come) is in Walter Isard et al., *Methods of Regional Analysis: An Introduction to Regional Science* (New York, 1960).

Eric Lampard has provided us with an excellent historical example of one of the many patterns in which urban growth can unfold, in his incisive description of Manchester, England, in the nineteenth century.

> The earliest factories in textile districts using water-wheels were commonly situated outside of the urban center, but "they had to be near a town . . . to be close to a market, both for buying and selling purposes. Labour was needed, not only for the actual work in the factory, but also for the subsidiary domestic industry [hand weavers]." . . . Manufacturing capitalists were then [in the 1820's] obliged to install the improved power loom and "to integrate the spinning, weaving, and finishing branches in single establishments employing from 300 to over 1,000 hands."
>
> More significant, from the standpoint of our general theory of urbanization, was the tendency for other concerns to congregate around the cotton manufacture . . . foundries were casting wheels and pipes for steam engines and shafts, while tin-platers, braziers and harness makers were putting out the parts for spinning frames . . . [and more indirectly linked] . . . railways, building, brewing, chemicals, coal supply and numerous wholesale trades. . . . The Bank of England felt obliged to come to town in the late twenties and several joint stock companies got underway. . . .
>
> From the mid-18th century cotton merchants and manufactures . . . offered attractive rewards for practical inventions. The "Manchester Literary and Philosophical Society" debated the application of science to the industrial arts. . . . These same business leaders gave a new meaning to the word "freedom" . . . "whereby trade has

been kept open to strangers of every description, who contribute to its improvement by their ingenuity." . . . Manchester society was open for achievement. The early industrialists had mostly risen from the ranks of skilled craftsmen. . . .

In short, one thing led to another. Lampard, *op. cit.*, pp. 105–108.

14. For example, in the historic rivalry between Chicago and St. Louis for supremacy in the Middle West and as a gateway to the West, natural factors, such as the Mississippi River, as a north-south transportation facility and as an east-west barrier, and social factors, such as a river-minded leadership group in St. Louis and the disruptive effect of the Civil War on the border-state hinterland of St. Louis, all combined to edge Chicago past St. Louis. Cumulative forces in growth then widened the gap. See Lewis F. Thomas, "Decline of St. Louis as Midwest Metropolis," *Economic Geography*, 25 (1949), pp. 118–127, for a brief account, or Wyatt Winton Belcher, *The Economic Rivalry between St. Louis and Chicago, 1850–1880* (New York, 1947) for a more extended treatment.

15. A number of static, cross-sectional studies have been made which classify cities according to their principal economic function—manufacturing, wholesale trade center, transportation center, seat of government, and so forth. But dynamic analyses that take a city through a sequence of functions with sufficient analytical rigor to permit generalization are still to be done or lie hidden in fugitive materials. On the classification of U. S. cities according to economic function, see Chauncy D. Harris, "A Functional Classification of Cities in the United States," *Geographical Review*, 33 (1943), pp. 86–99, and Howard J. Nelson, "A Service Classification of American Cities," *Economic Geography*, 31 (1955), pp. 189–210, both reprinted in Harold Mayer and Clyde F. Kohn (Eds.), *Readings in Urban Geography* (Chicago, 1959); Gunnar Alexandersson, *The Industrial Structure of American Cities* (Stockholm, 1956); and Otis Dudley Duncan, W. Richard Scott, Stanley Lieberson, Beverly Duncan, and Hal H. Winsborough, *Metropolis and Region* (Baltimore, 1960).

16. Perloff and associates found a low *negative* correlation between the location of growth industries and the local growth rate. Perloff et al., *op. cit.*, p. 68. Perhaps this is due to the tendency for invention, innovation, and promotion to come more than proportionately out of the industrially mature regions, a point they themselves make later in their work. This more than proportionate incubation of new industries in the older industrial areas may originate in their greater technological sophistication, and then again it may originate in purposeful desperation as local entrepreneurs rise to the challenge of heavy local unemployment and business losses.

17. Culminating in *The New England Economy*, A Report to the President by the Committee on New England Economy of the Council of Economic Advisors (Washington, 1951).

18. The final report of the Pittsburgh area study, jointly financed by the Commonwealth of Pennsylvania and the Ford Foundation as a successor to the New York Metropolitan Area Regional Study and directed by Edgar M. Hoover, was recently published in three volumes: *Region in Transition, Portrait of a Region,* and *Region with a Future* (Pittsburgh, 1963).

19. *Michigan Tax Study, Staff Papers,* Legislative Committee, House of Representatives, Lansing, Michigan, 1958. This is one of the two best analyses of state and local finance extant, including academic efforts; the other is the earlier *Report of the Governor's Minnesota Tax Study, 1956.* The latter, which goes beyond the usual coverage of such studies to include an excellent analysis of regional economic growth factors, was also initiated in response to a local "crisis" of slower-than-average economic growth.

20. For example, William Haber, Eugene C. McKean, and Harold C. Taylor, *The Michigan Economy: Its Potentials and Its Problems* (Kalamazoo, 1959)', and Paul W. McCracken (Ed.), *Taxes and Economic Growth in Michigan* (Kalamazoo, 1960).

21. See *Distressed Areas in a Growing Economy,* A Statement of National Policy by the Research and Policy Committee of the Committee for Economic Development (New York, June 1961), and current unpublished memoranda on area redevelopment circulated by the Manpower and Social Affairs Committee of the Organization for Economic Co-operation and Development (Paris). The former is directed to United States depressed-area problems and the latter to the European counterparts.

22. Of the 212 Standard Metropolitan Statistical Areas, only seven experienced population losses between 1950 and 1960: Texarkana (92,000 population), Altoona (137,000), Wheeling (190,000), Scranton (235,000), Johnstown (280,000), Wilkes-Barre-Hazleton (347,000), and Jersey City (611,000). If Jersey City, N. J., is regarded as one of the central cities of the consolidated New York-Northeastern New Jersey metropolitan area, and it is alternatively classified that way in the Census, then we find no absolute declines in the one-half-million-and-over class and only two cases in the one-quarter to one-half million population class. U. S. Bureau of the Census, *Statistical Abstract of the United States: 1961* (Washington, D. C., 1961), Table 10.

23. See the chapter on "monopolistic competition" in any standard economics textbook. This idea dates back to the brilliant article by Piero Sraffa, "The Laws of Returns under Competitive Conditions," *The Economic Journal,* 36 (1926), reprinted in George J. Stigler and Kenneth E. Boulding (Eds.), *Readings in Price Theory* (Chicago, 1952), especially pp. 189ff.

24. Robert M. Haig, *Major Economic Factors in Metropolitan Growth and Arrangement,* Vol. I, *Regional Survey of New York and Environs* (New York, 1928). The economic base or export-base logic of urban-regional growth has a long history of conceptual development traced through most thoroughly in the first of a series of articles by Richard B. Andrews, "Mechanics of the Urban Economic Base: Historical Development of the Base Concept," *Land Economics,* 29 (1953), pp. 161–167. The full series of ten articles together with eleven others are reprinted in Ralph W. Pfouts (Ed.), *The Techniques of Urban Economic Analysis* (West Trenton, N. J., 1960). Economic base theory was developed more rigorously in two articles by Charles M. Tiebout, "The Urban Economic Base Reconsidered" and "The Community Income Multiplier: A Case Study," pp. 280–289, also reprinted in *Readings in Urban Geography, op. cit.,* pp. 105–109 and pp. 342–358, respectively, and reaches its height of elegance in Tiebout's work, *The*

Community Economic Base Study, Supplementary Paper No. 16, Committee for Economic Development (New York, December 1962).

25. Exports may account for a full one-half of local economic activity in urban areas with as many as a quarter of a million people, in cases of heavy industrial specialization. For example, the Flint, Michigan, "urbanized area," with a total population of 278,000 and an employed labor force of 100,000, had over 51,000 workers in manufacturing of which close to 50,000 were producing motor vehicles or related intermediate products. Almost all of the automobile output, one-half of total local activity, is sold outside the Flint area. Derived from the U. S. Bureau of the Census, *U. S. Census of Population: 1960, General Social and Economic Characteristics, Michigan* (Washington, D. C., 1962), Tables 32 and 75.

26. With repeated handling, and the occasional intervention of economists, the export-to-service ratio became more sophisticated. An appreciation of the way in which it changes (decreases) with larger city size is most clearly conveyed in Irving Morrissett, "The Economic Structure of American Cities," *Papers and Proceedings of the Regional Science Association,* 4 (1958), pp. 239–256.

27. See especially, Hans Blumenfeld, "The Economic Base of the Metropolis," *Journal of the American Institute of Planners,* 21 (1955), pp. 114–132, reprinted in Pfouts, *op. cit.,* pp. 230–277.

28. One must take care to distinguish between the deliberative reaction of buyers to the slow steady increases in per capita income which come with economic development and the quick, first response of buyers to sudden (cyclical) fluctuations in their income. The distinction is a major one. In cycle analysis the durability of the good—the ease of postponing the replacement of an aging automobile or refrigerator—is the single most critical factor in determining income elasticity of demand, but in growth analysis the durability-postponability characteristic is of little interest. The time period spanned by a growth study is much too long to reflect the transitory postponements and accelerated purchases of durable goods that are part of the buyers' business-cycle strategy. Compare the treatment of income elasticity of demand in any standard text on business cycles or national income with its treatment in any standard text on price theory. For example, Robert M. Biggs, *National-Income Analysis and Forecasting* (New York, 1956), pp. 319–320, and Richard H. Leftwich, *The Price System and Resource Allocation* (New York, 1961), pp. 83–86.

29. John Kenneth Galbraith in *The Affluent Society* (Boston, 1958) introduced the first systematic analysis of the economics of affluence; however, he laid siege to orthodox economic theory, and questioned the central concept of *unlimited* human wants as an *inexhaustible* spur to greater production. Here, however, we are concerned less with the rationality or morality of artificially stimulating wants (for example, advertising, promoting materialistic social values) and more with the destabilizing effect of affluence—a large and growing proportion of income spent for goods that satisfy weakly felt wants.

30. See Aaron Fleisher, "The Influence of Technology on Urban Forms," *Daedalus* (Winter 1961), p. 55, for bare mention of this provocative point.

31. Malcolm Ross, "North Carolina, Dixie Dynamo," *The National Geo-*

graphic (February 1963), especially pp. 141–149. Ross writes, "Visit the State capital, Raleigh, and the first thing you hear about is the Research Triangle." The Triangle connects the State College of Agriculture and Engineering at Raleigh, Duke University at Durham, and the University of North Carolina at Chapel Hill, and encloses the Textile Research Center and other industrial laboratories.

32. The concept of a city region can be traced back, of course, to Christaller and Lösch and, in a more limited sense, back to Von Thünen. And geographers have been doing empirical work on city regions for years; see, for example, Robert E. Dickinson, *City, Region and Regionalism* (London, 1947). Again, Karl Fox has been developing a nationwide system of "functional economic areas," which integrate the Census standard metropolitan areas and Bogue's "state economic areas" into a single comprehensive system of city regions that exhaust the land area. See Karl A. Fox, *Economic Models for Area Development Research*, Workshop on Area Development, Stillwater, Oklahoma, May 8–9, 1963 (mimeographed), or "The Study of Interactions between Agriculture and the Non-farm Economy; Local, Regional and National," *Journal of Farm Economics*, 44 (1962), pp. 1–34, for an earlier published account.

But the community of interest between city and hinterland in these works is based on their economic complementarity and the resulting trade (for example, rural food products for city professional services). What is offered here is quite different. Namely, that a cluster of small cities with more or less parallel industrial structures may find their community of interest in combining to achieve economies (and qualities) of scale in public investment and other kinds of social overhead. Small, vulnerable, one-industry towns, facing stagnation or even extinction, form a "region" for developmental purposes. For a source of additional material on these matters, see F. Stuart Chapin, Jr., and Shirley F. Weiss (Eds.), *Urban Growth Dynamics* (New York, 1962), a treatment of the Piedmont Industrial Crescent of North and South Carolina.

33. Raymond Vernon, *Metropolis 1985, op. cit.*, pp. 35ff. This historical evidence of New York's vitality as an industrial innovator-promoter is later supplemented with a more analytical exposition attributing New York's growth over the past three decades to its absolute and comparative advantage in the "external-economy industries" (pp. 61–62). Large metropolitan areas, in general, must and can depend on relatively tight-knit industrial complexes for their growth, and on the related group of industries that draw broadly on a well-developed social overhead, ranging from private consultants to public libraries.

34. See note 16.

35. The New York study moves from historical description to a statistical analysis of industrial change over the past thirty years. The area is characterized as having had an industry mix relatively rich in the fast-growing industries but whose "promise was not realized" as these industries grew locally at rates slower than their national counterparts. Although this is a statistically valid explanation of the region's slower-than-average total growth, a more revealing formulation might be to see the area as one that grows, despite the fact that it steadily loses share (spins off) in almost every activity it undertakes, by constantly creating some new *raison d'etre*.

If, indeed, New York is the birthplace of new ideas and new industries, much more than proportionately, and it did not experience a declining market share of these industries as they matured, the New York area would come to embrace most of the nation's economic activity and population. The great value of the New York study is precisely that it demonstrates that giant metropolises grow by serving an entrepreneurial rather than a caretaker function. This message does come through but only obliquely, probably partly because the historical work showing the long-run industrial sequences and the short-run, industry-mix analyses were performed by different persons. Raymond Vernon, *op. cit.*, Chap. 3.

36. Absolute reductions in the local wage rate are rare, especially under trade unionism, but the reluctant acceptance of wage increases of less than average amount is quite common and even wage freezes at the current level for a year or two are accepted even under unionism in emergency cases. Thus local wage deflation ordinarily takes the form of a *relative* decrease, as local wages stand still or lag behind national increases.

37. Henry C. Thole, *Shortages of Skilled Manpower: Implications for Kalamazoo Businessmen* (Kalamazoo, 1958), especially pp. 26–39.

38. In a slightly different context, Hoover and Vernon observe that "the young woman's preference for a job in the central business district today . . . is based . . . on the increased opportunities for after-hours recreation, lunch-hour shopping (or window shopping), and the greater opportunities for husband-hunting." Edgar M. Hoover and Raymond Vernon, *Anatomy of a Metropolis* (Cambridge, 1959), p. 102.

39. On the Fall 1961 docket of the United States Supreme Court were two cases turning on the question of whether employees of a firm that has relocated its operations have seniority rights to jobs at the new site. One case was filed by Teamster Union Local 852 against the Glidden Company (paints and chemicals) for damages to workers at the old Elmhurst, N. Y., plant who were not offered jobs at the new Bethlehem, Pa., site. In the second case, five employees of the Gemmer Manufacturing Co. of Detroit, Mich. (steering gears) were suing the company for agreeing to hire only local workers at the new Lebanon, Tenn., site, in return for a $2.4 million plant construction loan extended by the community. In both cases, the lower court had ruled in favor of the employees. Reported in *The Evening Star*, Washington, D. C., August 30, 1961, p. B-9.

40. Hoover, *op. cit.*, pp. 118–119.

41. This is not to say that the literature of labor economics is especially rich in materials that relate the labor supply to economic growth. Much more can be found on this subject in the literature on economic development, and probably at least as much has been written by sociologists as economists. The student wishing to pursue this subject might do well to begin with the journal *Economic Development and Cultural Change* and other such sources.

42. Benjamin Chinitz, "Contrasts in Agglomeration: New York and Pittsburgh," *American Economic Review*, 51 (1961), pp. 284–285.

43. See Lawrence Seltzer, *A Financial History of the American Automobile Industry* (Boston, 1928), especially Chap. 4, "The General Motors Corporation." Seltzer writes: "William C. Durant was a vigorous promoter and salesman rather than an operating executive; and the career of the

General Motors Combination, until very recent years, has largely reflected his personality. His temperament and his unbound confidence in the automobile industry led him to seek rapid growth . . . he was ready to expand by acquisition," pp. 223–224.

44. See, for example, John Jewkes, David Sawers, and Richard Stillerman, *The Sources of Invention* (New York, 1958).

45. One can do little better than refer the reader to the imperishable work of Joseph A. Schumpeter; see especially Chap. 7, "The Process of Creative Destruction" in *Capitalism, Socialism and Democracy* (New York, 1942).

46. George Perazich, *Growth of Scientific Research in Selected Industries, 1945–60*, Report to the National Science Foundation by Galaxy Incorporated (Washington, D. C., October 14, 1957, mimeographed).

47. Edward L. Ullman, "Regional Development and the Geography of Concentration," *Papers and Proceedings of the Regional Science Association*, 4 (1958), pp. 189–191.

48. Patents granted in an aggregate of five chemistry classes did join with plant and equipment expenditures as the two independent variables in the best employment-estimating equation for "chemicals and allied products," fitted to the 1947–1954 data, a period of very rapid growth. Although the chemical industry equation exhibited one of the lowest multiple-correlation coefficients—was one of the poorer fits—the patent variable was sufficiently promising in each of the seven industries in which it was tried to warrant further work with this index. Patent grants, for example, were much more promising than many of the old perennials in area industrial-development analysis, such as the relative level of state and local taxes. Wilbur R. Thompson and John M. Mattila, *An Econometric Model of Postwar State Industrial Development* (Detroit, 1959), pp. 6, 11–12, 18, 23–25, 43, 63–64.

49. Wilbur R. Thompson, "Locational Differences in Inventive Effort and Their Determinants," *The Rate and Direction of Inventive Activity, Economic and Social Factors*, A Conference of the Universities-National Bureau Committee for Economic Research and the Committee on Economic Growth of the Social Science Research Council (Princeton, 1962), p. 259.

50. Edgar M. Hoover offered some time ago that "Capital funds for new investment, however, are highly mobile and show relatively small geographic differentials in price. Interest rates exhibit a tendency to vary with distance from major financial centers but are rarely a significant factor of location within any one country." *The Location of Economic Activity, op. cit.*, p. 70. Hoover cites the empirical work of August Lösch, *The Economics of Location, op. cit.*, pp. 461, 505. Interestingly, later works have ignored regional aspects of the capital market. Neither the most comprehensive general reference work on location theory, Isard, *op. cit.*, nor that on regional growth, Perloff et al., *op. cit.*, include "interest" in their very detailed subject indexes.

51. Harry G. Guthmann and Herbert E. Dougall, *Corporate Financial Policy*, 3rd ed. (Englewood Cliffs, N. J., 1955), Chap. 20, especially p. 423.

52. J. Schaefer, "Denver: The Mountain Metropolis," *Holiday* (September 1961), pp. 56–69.

53. Edgar M. Hoover and Raymond Vernon, *op. cit.*, pp. 49–55.

54. A small business that is forced to sell or borrow on its accounts receivable at a discount of face value, to get cash sooner than the normal business sequence would provide, will have to pay interest rates of 12 per cent and over, in most places and at most times. Passing up trade discounts allowed for prompt payment of its own bills is usually even more expensive; for example, one of the more common trade terms ("2/10, net 30") is convertible into an annual interest rate equivalent to about 36 per cent. See Guthmann and Dougall, *op. cit.*, p. 441.

55. For a most dramatic case of the critical character of working capital in the early years of a new small business, see J. Keith Butters and John Lintner, *Effects of Federal Taxes on Growing Enterprises* (Division of Research, Graduate School of Business Administration, Harvard University, Boston, 1945), Chap. 12, "Lithomat Corporation."

56. Chinitz, *op. cit.*, p. 286.

57. Lawrence H. Seltzer, *op. cit.*, pp. 29–30. The author quotes Roy D. Chapin, a man identified with the automobile industry in its early years, as telling him in a personal interview that "the banks here played an important part. There was a great deal of prejudice in other parts of the country on the part of bankers, particularly in the east. They lacked the business sense that was needed. The Detroit bankers had it and were not afraid of our sight drafts."

58. Homer Hoyt long ago called attention to the tendency for the upper-income groups to choose the high ground for residential sites, "The Pattern of Movement of Residential Rental Neighborhoods," *The Structure and Growth of Residential Neighborhoods in American Cities* (Washington: Federal Housing Administration, 1939), reprinted in *Readings in Urban Geography, op. cit.*, p. 504.

59. The best-known work here is Edward L. Ullman, "Amenities as a Factor in Regional Growth," *The Geographical Review*, 44 (1954), pp. 119–132.

60. In the 1954 national recession, local manufacturing employment fell by about 3 per cent nationally, but actually increased by 0.7 per cent and 1.8 per cent in the Los Angeles and San Diego metropolitan areas, respectively. These were local "slumps" only when compared to their phenomenal manufacturing employment growth rates of 7.1 and 11.6 per cent, respectively, as measured from a linear logarithmic trend line fitted to annual data for the period 1947–1960. These estimates were derived from an empirical study of local cycles currently being conducted by John M. Mattila and the author, sponsored by CUE-RFF, drawing on data from the various *Censuses and Surveys of Manufactures*.

61. McLaughlin found no statistically significant correlation between local "industrial concentration" (percentage of value added by manufacture in the five largest local industries) and cyclical decreases in value added in manufacturing in the 1919 and 1921 recessions. Glenn E. McLaughlin, "Industrial Diversification in American Cities," *Quarterly Journal of Economics*, 45 (1930), pp. 131–149, especially pp. 148–149. Rodgers also tested the relationship between degree of manufacturing diversification and cyclical variation for twelve urban areas in Pennsylvania over the period 1925 to 1950. The coefficient of linear correlation was .22, not significant. Although both McLaughlin and Rodgers were forced to use very rough

measures of cyclical variation and industrial diversification and their findings should be treated as preliminary, they do confirm our *a priori* expectation. Allan Rodgers, "Some Aspects of Industrial Diversification in the United States," *Economic Geography*, 33 (1957), pp. 16–30, especially p. 27.

62. See Kenneth E. Boulding, *Principles of Economic Policy* (Englewood Cliffs, N. J., 1958), pp. 21–27, for a much broader-gauge treatment than usual which still retains output per man-hour and its cousin, income per capita, as the proper measures of economic progress.

63. Harvey S. Perloff and Lowdon Wingo, Jr., "Natural Resource Endowment and Regional Economic Growth," *Natural Resources and Economic Growth*, Papers presented at a conference held at Ann Arbor, Michigan, April 7–9, 1960, under joint sponsorship of Resources for the Future, Inc., and Committee on Economic Growth of the Social Science Research Council (Washington, D. C.: Resources for the Future, Inc., 1961), pp. 203–204, and Wilbur R. Thompson and John M. Mattila, *An Econometric Model . . .*, *op. cit.*, Table 10, p. 51, and Table 12, p. 68, and John M. Mattila and Wilbur R. Thompson, "The Role of the Product Market in State Industrial Development," *Papers and Proceedings of the Regional Science Association*, 1960, pp. 87–96.

64. A number of city planning axioms are much less inviolable than their promulgation implies. The notion of "urban sprawl" as a devastating phenomenon of the auto age has been so widely popularized that documentation is made to seem superfluous, but some appreciation of the implicit assumptions on which it is precariously balanced and of the case *for* sprawl can be gained from the highly challenging article by Jack Lessinger, "The Case for Scatteration," *Journal of the American Institute of Planners*, 28 (1962), pp. 159–169. Lessinger argues that the open spaces left scattered about as residential subdividers leap-frog across the urban-rural fringe ensure against having vast tracts of uniform-age houses that deteriorate at the same time, creating future slums. He also argues that open spaces ensure land-use flexibility for adjustment to change—for example, easements for superhighways.

65. Lewis Mumford, *The City in History* (New York, 1961). Mumford looks approvingly on England's New Towns—"relatively self-contained, balanced communities, with a sound industrial base—amply demonstrated" (p. 557)—but a later observer argues that "we shall have to revise our ideas about their [New Towns] most appropriate size; there is nothing to suggest that a population of 80,000 to 100,000 is necessarily ideal and experiments should begin with new communities twice or three times that size." Gerald Manners, "The Crisis of Regional Planning," *Westminster Bank Review* (August 1962), p. 20.

66. Edwin Mansfield, "City Size and Income, 1949," *Regional Income: Studies in Income and Wealth*, Vol. 21 (Princeton, 1957) and Frank A. Hanna, *op. cit.*

67. The fifteen largest urban areas in the United States (excluding Washington, D. C.) exhibit increasingly similar income levels. The coefficient of variation (the standard deviation divided by the arithmetic mean) of median family incomes in these fifteen Standard Metropolitan Statistical

Areas fell sharply from .069 in 1950 to .057 in 1960. Derived from the *U. S. Censuses of Population, 1950 and 1960*.

68. The literature on the size of the local market and the range of available goods, and on the "threshold" concept is relatively large and well developed. See P. S. Florence, "Economic Efficiency in the Metropolis," *The Metropolis in Modern Life* (Garden City, N. Y., 1955) and Duncan et al., *op. cit.*, Chaps. 3 and 4.

69. See Robert C. Wood, *Metropolis Against Itself* (New York, 1959).

70. See any standard economics statistics textbook on price-index construction, especially the "weighted average of price relatives" or the "weighted aggregate" indexes; for example, Frederick C. Mills, *Statistical Methods*, 3rd ed. (New York, 1955), pp. 448–454.

71. In 1960 approximately 81 million of the 180 million population of the United States (45 per cent) resided in "Standard Metropolitan Statistical Areas" of over one-half million population.

72. For example, the Negro population in the Detroit area has been described as more residentially segregated in 1960 than in 1950, 1940, or 1930. See Albert J. Mayer and Thomas F. Hoult, *Race and Residence in Detroit* (Urban Research Laboratory, Institute for Urban Studies, Wayne State University, August 1962). Or, in a broader context, the Advisory Commission on Intergovernmental Relations also found that "population is tending to be increasingly distributed within metropolitan areas along economic and racial lines," *Government Structure, Organization, and Planning in Metropolitan Areas* (Washington, D. C., 1961), p. 7.

73. See Charles M. Tiebout, "A Pure Theory of Local Expenditures," *Journal of Political Economy*, 64 (1956), pp. 416–424, for a defense and rationalization of political fragmentation as a means of extending the range of choice in residential and community environmental arrangements.

74. Intermediate-size cities are often highly specialized in manufacturing for far-flung markets, with 40 to 50 per cent of total employment in manufacturing quite common. The very largest urban areas, however, typically have less than one-third of their employment in manufacturing, ranging from San Francisco's 21.0 per cent to Detroit's 40.7 per cent. *U. S. Census of Population, 1960, General Social and Economic Characteristics, U. S. Summary*, Table 142.

75. See Leo F. Schnore, "On the Spatial Structure of Cities in the Two Americas," Chapter 10 in this book, for an interpretation of Ernest W. Burgess's concentric zone theory in a growth context, similar to its use here.

76. James B. Conant, *Slums and Suburbs* (New York, 1961), p. 4.

77. "While there is a great variety in our city slums, most of them have one thing in common: they are eating away at the heart of the cities, especially their downtown areas. The slums would, in fact, be much easier for the cities to endure if they were off in the fringe areas." Daniel Seligman, "The Enduring Slums," *The Exploding Metropolis*, The Editors of Fortune (Garden City, N. Y., 1957), p. 100. Perhaps we are fortunate that the poor are not tucked away in outlying slums, easily forgotten, until they erupt volcanically, as is true in many Latin American cities. Still, our new depressed expressways bid fair to hide even core-area slums from the suburban commuters.

78. In a "secondary analysis" of civil-defense survey data from eleven

large cities compiled by the Survey Research Center of the University of Michigan, Schnore and Cowhig found the "perceived" (self-rated) health of an individual varied directly with socioeconomic status for both the 35–49 and 50 and over age groups. The per cent of persons who reported only fair or poor health was well over twice as great in the under-$3000 family income group as in the over-$5000 group. Even greater variation was associated with educational level. Although the analysis was pursued under the implicit hypothesis that poverty leads to poor health, the authors pointed out that a reverse causation may be just as defensible: "poor health—whether real or imagined—might so inhibit the individual's activities as to prevent the acquisition of further education and contribute to lower family income." Leo F. Schnore and James D. Cowhig, "Some Correlates of Reported Health in Metropolitan Centers," *Social Problems*, 7 (1959–1960), Table 3 and p. 225.

The rejoinder that our slum-clearance programs are designed to improve the healthfulness of the environment would be more convincing if the slum dwellers so dislocated were relocated back in the new housing units, rather than left to shift for themselves in a way that usually leads to overcrowding in nearby neighborhoods and the formation of new slums.

79. The fifteen largest urban areas in the United States (excluding Washington, D. C.) exhibit increasingly similar degrees of income inequality. The interquartile deviation in family income $(Q_3 - Q_1)/(Q_1 + Q_3)$ was computed for each of the fifteen metropolitan areas for 1950 and 1960. The coefficient of variation of these deviations fell sharply from .076 in 1950 to .065 in 1960. Thus, even though interpersonal inequality within these areas changed little (decreased by less than 3 per cent), the interarea variation in inequality fell by almost one-fifth. Derived from the *U. S. Censuses of Population, 1950 and 1960*.

13

The Folk-Urban Ideal Types

A. FURTHER OBSERVATIONS ON THE FOLK-URBAN CONTINUUM AND URBANIZATION WITH SPECIAL REFERENCE TO MEXICO CITY

Oscar Lewis

My interest in studies of urbanism and the urbanization process in Mexico City has been a direct outgrowth of my earlier study of Tepoztlan. In that work I suggested that the folk-urban continuum was an inadequate theoretical model for the study of culture change and that it needed drastic revision.[1] Later, in my follow-up study of Tepoztecans who had migrated to Mexico City, I found evidence which strengthened this conviction, this time viewing the problem from the urban pole.[2]

Each of the terms folk, rural, and urban encompasses a wide range of phenomena with multiple variables which have to be carefully sorted out, ordered, dissected, and perhaps redefined if we are to establish meaningful, causal relationships among them. Each of these terms implies relatively high-level abstractions intended for the characterization of whole societies or large segments thereof. Although such characterizations are attractive because of their simplicity and may be useful in distinguishing gross stages or types in societal evolution, they confuse issues in the study of short-run changes, and their heuristic value as research tools has never been proven.

Hauser has put this criticism admirably. He writes,

> There is evidence, by no means conclusive as yet, that both parts of these dichotomies [i.e., folk-urban and rural-urban] represent confounded variables and, in fact, complex systems of variables which have yet to be unscrambled. The dichotomizations per-

haps represent all too hasty efforts to synthesize and integrate what little knowledge has been acquired in empirical research. The widespread acceptance of these ideal-type constructs as generalizations, without benefit of adequate research, well illustrates the dangers of catchy neologisms which often get confused with knowledge.[3]

In his elaboration of the folk-urban continuum, Redfield sought to achieve greater sophistication than earlier societal typologies by utilizing traits or variables that were of a general, more abstract nature. For example, whereas Hobhouse, Wheeler, and Ginsburg distinguished among food-gathering, hunting and fishing, agricultural, and pastoral economies, and sought to establish their social and juridical correlates, Redfield's definition of the folk society as an ideal type never specified a type of technology or economy beyond stating that it was simple, subsistence motivated, without money, familial, and so on.

In his later work Redfield showed some important but subtle changes in his thinking which have not been given sufficient emphasis by his followers and disciples, many of whom suffer from fixation or culture lag. Here I should like to mention two such changes. First, he seemed to be less sanguine about the possibility of deriving sound general propositions concerning social and cultural change and gave more stress to descriptive integration, "understanding," and the element of art in the social sciences. Compare, for example, his *Folk Culture of Yucatán* with *The Village That Chose Progress*. In the former, he was still optimistic about finding regularities in culture change. In the latter, he gave us a brilliant description of changes in Chan Kom but made no attempt to relate these changes to the theoretical framework of the folk-urban continuum.

A second change is to be seen in *The Primitive World and Its Transformations,* where he no longer conceives of the folk society exclusively as an ideal type. Rather, he treats it as a type of real society. In this book Redfield takes a frank neo-evolutionary stance, identifying the folk society with the preagricultural or preneolithic period and with the tribal (and I would add pretribal) level. In an effort to find common elements he paints with a big brush, lumping together all the peoples of the world prior to the neolithic, irrespective of whether they were food-gatherers, fishers or hunters, whether they had rich or poor resources, whether they were starving or produced some surplus. In the very nature of the case, this approach glosses over the more refined archeological distinctions, between the Lower and Upper

Paleolithic, each with subdivisions based upon new technologies and inventions.

True, we have little evidence about societal types for the prehistoric periods. However, a theoretical scheme must somehow take into account many levels and types of societal development prior to the rise of cities. Otherwise, there are unexplained and sudden breaks in the postulated evolutionary sequence from folk to urban. Indeed, if one had to choose between evolutionary schemes, there is still a good deal to be said in favor of Morgan's *Ancient Society* despite its many factual errors and crude technological determinism. Fortunately, we have other and more sophisticated alternatives, such as the multilinear evolution of Julian Steward and the recent work of Irving Goldman.[4]

The identification of the folk society with the preneolithic seems to me to invalidate or, at least, to raise serious questions about Redfield's work in *The Folk Cultures of Yucatán*, since all of the Yucatán communities were agricultural peasant societies, which, by his own definition, are part societies subject in varying degree to urban influences. Even his most "folk-life" community of Quintana Roo was producing hennequin for the world market!

Similarly, some of my own criticism of his Tepoztlan work, as well as Sol Tax's criticism based on the Guatemalan studies, would seem to be beside the point since both Tax and I were dealing with communities which had left the folk stage (if they were ever in it) for at least a few thousand years. To this extent, Ralph Beals' comment that Tepoztlan was not a crucial case for evaluating the transition from folk to peasant to urban has considerable merit, because Tepoztlan was already a well-advanced peasant society in pre-Hispanic days. But by the same token, I know of no other contemporary community study in Meso-America which would serve this purpose any better. Actually, Redfield had assumed a survival of folk, that is, paleolithic, elements in Tepoztlan, a period for which we have no evidence in that village.

The traditional contrast between societies based on kinship versus those based on nonkinship or contract is not only inaccurate but of so broad and general a nature as to be of little help in the analysis of the process of change. To say of a society that it is organized on a kinship basis does not tell us enough for purposes of comparative analysis. It may be a nuclear family system as among the Shoshone Indians, a lineage system as in Tikopia, or a clan system as among the Zuni Indians. We still have a lot to learn about the more modest problem of how and under what conditions in a given society, a simple nuclear, bilateral system turns into a unilateral clan system, and the social, economic, and psychological concomitants thereof. As a general proposition I would like to suggest that we may learn more about the processes of change by studying relatively short-run sequential modifications in particular aspects of institutions in both the so-called folk and urban societies, than by global comparisons between folk and urban.

Preurban and preindustrial societies have been capable of developing class stratification, elaborate priesthoods, status rivalry, and many other phenomena that are implicitly and unilaterally attributed to the growth of cities, according to the folk-urban conception of social change. Tonga, the Maori, and native Hawaii are good examples of this. Even among a fishing and hunting people like the Kwakiutl Indians, we find class stratification, slavery, and war. The Kwakiutl case illustrates the importance of including natural resources as a significant variable in evolutionary schemes. I find no such variable in the folk-urban continuum.

In place of, or in addition to, the handy designations, folk society, peasant society, urban society, we need a large number of subtypes based on better defined variables and perhaps the addition of new ones.[5] Hauser's observations on the western ethnocentrism implicit in the folk-urban and rural-urban dichotomies is well taken. Redfield's firsthand research experience in Mexican communities, which were essentially endogamous, tended to confirm his preconception of the folk society as "inward-looking." The thinking of Simmel, Tönnies, Durkheim, and others, which influenced Redfield, was also based on experience with the endogamous peasant communities of Europe. Had these men done field work with the Nuer of Africa, with the Australian aborigines, or with the north Indian peasants, it is quite possible that Redfield's ideal-type model of the folk society might have been somewhat different.

Before turning to an examination of some of the assumptions of the Simmel-Wirth-Redfield axis regarding urbanism, I would like to present in brief some of my own research findings in Mexico which can serve as a starting point for the discussion. The relevant findings of my first Mexico City study of 1951 can be summarized as follows: (1) Peasants in Mexico City adapted to city life with far greater ease than one would have expected judging from comparable studies in the United States and from folk-urban theory. (2) Family life remained quite stable and extended family ties increased rather than decreased. (3) Religious life became more Catholic and disciplined, indicating the reverse of the anticipated secularization process. (4) The system of *compadrazgo* continued to be strong, albeit with some modifications. (5) The use of village remedies and beliefs persisted.

In the light of these findings I wrote at the time, ". . . this study provides evidence that urbanization is not a single, unitary, universally similar process but assumes different forms and meanings, depending upon the prevailing historic, economic, social, and cultural conditions." [6]

Because of the unusual nature of my findings, I decided to test them in 1956–1957 against a much wider sample of non-Tepoztecan city families. I selected two lower-class housing settlements or *vecindades*, both located in the same neighborhood within a few blocks of the Tepito market and only a short walk from the central square of Mexico City. In contrast with the Tepoztecan city families who represented a wide range of socioeconomic levels and were scattered in twenty-two *colonias* throughout the city, my new sample was limited to two settlements whose residents came from twenty-four of the thirty-two states and territories of the Mexican nation. [7]

On the whole, my research findings tended to support those of the earlier study. The findings suggested that the lower-class residents of Mexico City showed much less of the personal anonymity and isolation of the individual which had been postulated by Wirth as characteristic of urbanism as a way of life. The *vecindad* and the neighborhood tended to break up the city into small communities that acted as cohesive and personalizing factors. I found that many people spent most of their lives within a single *colonia* or district, and even when there were frequent changes of residence, they were usually within a restricted geographical area determined by low rentals. Lifetime friendships and daily face-to-face relations with the same people were common, and resembled a village situation. Most marriages also occurred within the *colonia* or adjoining *colonias*. Again, I found that extended family ties were quite strong, as measured by visiting, especially in times of emergency, and that a relatively high proportion of the residents of the *vecindades* were related by kinship and *compadrazgo* ties.

In spite of the cult of *machismo* and the overall cultural emphasis upon male superiority and dominance, I found a strong tendency toward matricentered families, in which the mother played a crucial role in parent-child relations even after the children were married. In genealogical studies I found that most people recalled a much larger number of relatives on the mother's side than on the father's side.

I also found that the *vecindad* acted as a shock absorber for the rural migrants to the city because of the similarity between its culture and that of rural communities. Both shared many of the traits which I have elsewhere designated as "the culture of poverty." Indeed, I found no sharp differences in family structure, diet, dress, and belief systems of the *vecindad* tenants according to their rural-urban origins. The use of herbs for curing, the raising of animals, the belief in sorcery, and spiritualism, the celebration of the Day of the Dead, illiteracy and low level of education, political apathy and cynicism about government, and the very limited membership and participation in both formal and informal associations, were just as common among persons who had been in the city for over thirty years as among recent arrivals. Indeed, I found that *vecindad* residents of peasant background who came from small landholding families showed more middle-class aspirations in their desire for a higher standard of living, home ownership, and education for their children than did city born residents of the lower-income group.

These findings suggest the need for a reexamination of some aspects of urban theory and for modifications which would help explain the findings from Mexico City and other cities in underdeveloped countries, as well as those from Chicago.

Wirth defines a city as "a relatively large, dense, and permanent settlement of socially heterogeneous individuals." By "socially heterogeneous" he had in mind primarily distinctive ethnic groups rather than class differences. Wirth defines urbanism as the mode of life of people who live in cities or who are subject to their influence. Because Wirth thinks of the city as a whole, as a community (and here, I believe, is one of his errors), he assumes that all people who live in cities are affected by this experience in profound and similar ways, namely, the weakening of kinship bonds, family life, and neighborliness, and the development of impersonality, superficiality, anonymity, and transitoriness in personal relations. For Wirth the process of urbanization is essentially a process of disorganization.[8]

This approach leads to some difficulties. For one thing, as Sjoberg has pointed out, ". . . their interpretations [i.e. those of Park, Wirth and Redfield] involving ecology have not articulated well with their efforts to explain social activities."[9] Wirth himself showed some of the contradictory aspects of city life without relating them to his theory of urbanism. He writes of the city as the historic center of progress, of learning, of higher standards of living, and all that is hopeful for the future of mankind, but he also points to the city as the locus of slums, poverty, crime, and disorganization. According to Wirth's theory both the carriers of knowledge and progress (the elite and the intellectuals) and the ignorant slum dwellers have a similar urban personality, since presumably they share in the postulated urban anonymity and so on.

It is in the evaluation of the personality of the urban dweller that urban theory has gone furthest afield. It leaps from the analysis of the social system to conjecture about individual personality; it is based not on solid psychological theory but on personal values, analogies, and outmoded physiopsychological concepts. Some of the description of the modern urbanite reads like another version of the fall of man. The delineation of the urbanite as blasé, indifferent, calculating, utilitarian, and rational (presumably as a defensive reaction to preserve his nervous system from the excessive shocks and stimuli of city life), suffering from anonymity and anomie, being more conscious and intellectual than his country brother yet feeling less deeply, remain mere statements of faith.[10]

Besides the lack of an adequate personality theory, it seems to me that some of the difficulty stems from the attempt to make individual psychological deductions from conditions prevailing in the city as a whole. The city is not the proper unit of comparison or discussion for the study of social life because the variables of number, density, and heterogeneity as used by Wirth are not the crucial determinants of social life or of personality.[11] There are many intervening variables. Social life is not a mass phenomenon. It occurs for the most part in small groups, within the family, within households, within neighborhoods, within the church, formal and informal groups, and so on.

Any generalizations about the nature of social life in the city must be based on careful studies of these smaller universes rather than on a priori statements about the city as a whole. Similarly, generalizations about urban personality must be based on careful personality studies. The delineation of social areas within cities and a careful analysis of their characteristics would take us a long way beyond the overgeneralized formulations of "urbanism as a way of life."

Basic to this Simmel-Wirth-Redfield approach are the supposed consequences of the predominance of primary relations in small rural communities versus the predominance of secondary relations in large cities. It seems to me that the psychological and social consequences of primary versus secondary relations have been misunderstood and exaggerated for both the country and the city. I know of no experimental or other good evidence to indicate that exposure to large numbers of people per se makes for anxiety and nervous strain or that the existence of secondary relations diminishes the strength and importance of primary ones. Primary group relations are just as important psychologically for city people as they are for country people, and sometimes they are more satisfying and of a more profound nature. And although the sheer number of secondary relations in the city is much greater than in the country, these relations can also be said to be secondary in the sense that their psychological consequences are minor.

The number of profound warm and understanding human relationships or attachments is probably limited in any society, rural or urban, modern or backward. Such attachments are not necessarily or exclusively a function of frequency of contact and fewness of numbers. They are influenced by cultural traditions which may demand reserve, a mind-your-own-business attitude, a distrust of neighbors, fear of sorcery and gossip, and the absence of a psychology of introspection.

George Foster's recent comparative analysis of the quality of interpersonal relations in small peasant societies, based on anthropological monographs, shows that they are characterized by distrust, suspicion, envy, violence, reserve, and withdrawal.[12] His paper confirms my earlier findings on Tepoztlan.

In some villages, peasants can live out their lives without any deep knowledge or understanding of the people whom they "know" in face-to-face relationships. By contrast, in modern Western cities, there may be more give and take about one's private, intimate life at a single "sophisticated" cocktail party than would occur in years in a peasant village. I suspect there are deeper, more mature human relationships among sympathetic, highly educated, cosmopolitan individuals who have chosen each other in friendship, than are possible among sorcery-ridden, superstitious, ignorant peasants, who are daily thrown together because of kinship or residential proximity.

It is a common assumption in social science literature that the process of urbanization for both tribal and peasant peoples is accompanied by a change in the structure of the family, from an extended to a nuclear family. It is assumed that the rural family is extended and the urban, nuclear. It must be pointed out that not even all primitive or preliterate people are characterized by a preponderance of the extended family as the residential unit. The Eskimo is a good example. Among peasantry, also, one finds a wide range of conditions in this regard. In most highland Mexican villages the nuclear family predominates as the residence unit. Very often and without any evidence, this fact is interpreted as a symptom of change from an earlier condition. In India, one finds a remarkable difference in family composition by castes within a single village. For example, in Rampur village in the state of Delhi, the Jats and Brahmans, both of whom own and work the land, have large, extended families, whereas the lower-caste Sweepers and Leatherworkers have small nuclear families.

I suggest that we must distinguish much more carefully between the existence of the extended family as a residence unit and as a social group. In Mexico the extended family is important as a social group in both rural and urban areas where the nuclear family predominates as the residence unit. In Mexico the persistence of extended family bonds seems compatible with urban life and increased industrialization. Moreover, the *compadre* system, with its extension of adoptive kinship ties, is operative, though in somewhat distinctive ways, on all class levels. I suspect that increased communication facilities in Mexico, especially the telephone and the car, may strengthen rather than weaken extended family ties.

One of the most distinctive characteristics of cities, whether in the industrial or preindustrial age, is that they provide, at least potentially, a wider range of alternatives for individuals in most aspects of living than is provided by the nonurban areas of the given nation or total society at a given time. Urbanism and urbanization involve the availability of a wide range of services and alternatives in terms of types of work, housing, food, clothing, educational facilities, medical facilities, modes of travel, voluntary organizations, types of people, and so on.

If we were to accept these criteria as definitive traits we could then develop indices of the degree of urbanization of different sectors of the population within cities. For example, if the population of any subsector of a city had fewer alternatives in types of clothing, foods, and so on, either because of traditional ethnic sanctions or lack of economic resources, we could designate this population sector as showing a lower degree of urbanization then some other sector. This does not apply to the city alone; the scale of urbanization can also be applied to villages, towns, and to their respective populations.

As I see it, therefore, there are two sides to the urbanization coin: one, the amount and variety of services and the like to be found in any city, and two, the extent to which different sectors of the city residents can partake of these services. From this distinction it follows that two cities may show the same urbanization index in terms of the number and variety of services per capita but may be very different in terms of the degree of urbanization (cosmopolitanism) of the various sectors of its inhabitants.

It also follows that there are many ways of life which coexist within a single city. This is particularly evident in the underdeveloped countries where class or caste differences are sharp. In Mexico City, for example, there are approximately a million and a half people who live in one-room *vecindades* or in primitive *jacales,* with little opportunity to partake of the great variety of housing facilities available for the tourists and the native bourgeoisie. Most of this large mass still have a low level of education and literacy, do not belong to labor unions, do not participate in the benefits of the social security system, make very little use of the city's museums, art galleries, banks, hospitals, department stores, concerts, airports, and so on. These people live in cities, indeed, a considerable portion were born in the city, but they are not highly urbanized. From this point of view, then, the poor in all cities of the world are less urbanized, that is, less cosmopolitan, than the wealthy.

The "culture of poverty" is a provincial, locally oriented culture, both in the city and in the country. In Mexico it is characterized by a relatively higher death rate, a higher proportion of the population in the younger age groups (less than 15 years), a higher proportion of gainfully employed in the total population, including child labor and working women. Some of these indices for poor *colonias* (districts) of Mexico City are much higher than for rural Mexico as a whole.

On another level the "culture of poverty" in Mexico, cutting across the rural and the urban, is characterized by the absence of food reserves in the home, the pattern of frequent buying of small quantities of food many times a day as the need occurs, borrowing money from money lenders at usurious interest rates, the pawning of goods, spontaneous informal credit devices among neighbors, the use of secondhand clothing and furniture, particularly in the city which has the largest secondhand market in Mexico, a higher incidence of free unions or consensual marriages, a strong present-time orientation, and a higher proportion of pre-Hispanic folk beliefs and practices.

In the preoccupation with the study of rural-urban differences, there has been a tendency to overlook or neglect basic similarities of people everywhere. In a recent paper Bruner [13] has illustrated this point for Indonesia where he found that the urban and rural Toba Batak are essentially part of a single social and economic ceremonial system.

Mexico-India contrasts also illustrate his point. In Mexico, Catholicism gives a similar stamp to many aspects of life in both rural and urban areas. The nucleated settlement pattern of most Mexican villages with the central church and plaza and the barrio-subdivisions, each in turn with its respective chapel, makes for a distinctive design which is in marked contrast to the north Indian villages where Hinduism and the caste system have made for a much more segmented and heterogeneously organized type of settlement pattern. It is my impression that a similar contrast is to be seen in some of the cities of these two countries and I believe this merits further study. Taking another example from India, we find that the way of life of the urban and rural lower castes, such as Washermen and Sweepers, have much more in common with each other than with the higher caste Brahmans in their respective urban and rural contexts.

Although I agree that number, density, permanence of settlement and heterogeneity of population is a workable definition of a city, I believe we need an additional, more elementary set of variables, with a narrower focus, to explain what goes on within cities. The sheer physical conditions of living have a considerable influence on social life, and I would include, among the variables, such factors as stability of residence, the settlement pattern, types of housing, the number of rooms to a family, and property concepts.

A type of housing settlement like the *vecindad*, which brings people into daily face-to-face contact, in which people do most of their work in a common patio, share a common toilet and a common wash-stand, encourages intensive interaction, not all of which is necessarily friendly. It makes little difference whether this housing and settlement pattern is in the city or the country, indeed whether it occurs among the tribal peoples of Borneo or the Iroquois Indians. In all cases it produces intense interaction, problems of privacy, quarrels among children, and among their parents.

Stability of residence too has many similar social consequences wherever it occurs. As I have already shown, in Mexico City the *vecindades* make for a kind of community life which has greater re-semblance to our stereotyped notions of village life than to Wirth's description of urbanism. Stability of residence may result from a wide variety of factors, both in rural and urban areas. Nor can we as-sume that it is a necessary concomitant of nonurban societies; witness the nomadism of the Plains Indians or of agricultural workers in parts of the Caribbean.

Certain aspects of the division of labor stand up well as an elemen-tary narrow-focus variable. When the family is the unit of production and the home and the work place are one, certain similar consequences follow for family life, both in the country and the city. I have in mind similarities in family life of small artisans in Mexico City and rural villages. In both, husband and wife spend most of the day together, children are early recruited into useful work, and there is much inter-action among family members. Thus, in terms of the amount of time husbands spend away from home, there is much more similarity between a peasant and a factory worker than between either of these and an artisan.

What we need in comparative urban studies as well as in rural-urban comparisons, within a single culture and crossculturally, are carefully controlled, narrow-focus comparisons of subunits. Here I shall list what seem to me to be priorities in research, with special reference to the underdeveloped countries.

1. The delineation of distinctive regions within cities in terms of their demographic, ecological, economic, and social characteristics with the objective of developing measures of urbanization for distinctive population sectors as well as for the city as a whole.

2. Crosscultural studies of comparable population sectors within cities. For example, we might compare lower-class areas in cities of Japan, India, England, and Mexico, utilizing a common research methodology, so that we could check the role of distinctive cultural factors on comparable urban sectors.

3. Comparisons of the economic, social, and psychological aspects of an equal number of families with the same full-time nonagricultural occupations in a village and in the city within a single country. One objective would be to test the influence of the rural versus the urban milieu and the many theories associated with the presumed differences between them.

4. Studies of the socioeconomic and psychological consequences of the introduction of factories in villages and towns in predominantly peasant countries. A crucial methodological point in such studies would be to select communities prior to the introduction of the factory so that we could have a solid baseline against which changes can be measured. One of the weakness of practically all studies to date is that they have had to reconstruct the prefactory conditions of the community. For example, the otherwise excellent study of a Guatemalan community by Manning Nash had to reconstruct the village culture as it was seventy years before, when the factory was first introduced.

5. Most studies of the influence of factories have dealt with light industries such as textiles or rayons. It would be good to have studies on the effects of heavy industries such as steel or mining, or chemical plants which demand more skilled labor and continuous operation.

6. Intensive case studies of individuals and families who have moved from tribal communities to urban centers, focusing on the problems of adjustment and the process of acculturation. In terms of

method, it would be important to select families from communities which have been carefully studied.

7. Similar studies should be done for peasants and plantation workers who move to the city. The objective of studying subjects from different backgrounds is to learn what differences, if any, this will have upon the urbanization process. I suspect that the greater disorganization reported by Joseph A. Kahl in his review of African materials as compared to Mexican data can be explained by the fact that the African studies reported on tribal peoples moving to the city whereas in Mexico we are dealing with peasants. On purely theoretical grounds I would expect that culture shock would be greater for tribal peoples.

B. OBSERVATIONS ON THE URBAN-FOLK AND URBAN-RURAL DICHOTOMIES AS FORMS OF WESTERN ETHNOCENTRISM

Philip M. Hauser

That relatively permanently settled large-population agglomerations make a difference in the way of life has been recognized perhaps for as long as there have been large cities. In the Hebrew literature, for example, the prophets discussed the effects of urbanization, and they explained such phenomena as corruption, personal disorganization, and other evidences of social and personal pathology as products of the urban environment.[1] In much of the nineteenth-century literature, including material that may be regarded as prolegomena for the emergence of sociology, systematic efforts were made to explain the differences between urban and preurban behavior.[2] For example, in 1861, Maine in his *Ancient Society* differentiated between organization based on kinship in which position was fixed by "status" and that based on territory in which position was manifest in "contract." Tönnies, in his *Gemeinschaft und Gesellschaft,* published in 1887, set forth his well-known dichotomization of community and society with considerable elaboration of their differential characteristics. Durkheim, in his *Division of Labor* and other works, differentiated between the "mechanical" and "organic" society and discussed with great insight, in his consideration of "social morphology," the significance of "volume," "mass," and "density" in the social order.

In the more recent past Sumner in his discussion of folk society, Goldenweiser in his description of primitive societies, and Becker in his elaboration of the "sacred society" have added to the literature which focuses largely on the characteristics of "folk society." [3] Redfield brought much of the earlier observations to a head in a series of works highlighted by his article in "The Folk Society." [4]

Paralleling the literature focusing largely on the characteristics of the folk society, there were other series of writings that noted the difference between the "urban" and "rural" social orders in Western societies. This literature included, of course, a treatment of the urban-rural dichotomy by the United States Bureau of the Census, and such considerations as set forth by Williams in 1925, Park and Burgess in 1925 and 1926, and Ogburn in 1937.[5] Wirth perhaps provided the most systematic statement of the personal and social effects of the city in his now classical article "Urbanism as a Way of Life" published in 1938.[6]

Differentiation between the folk and urban society and the urban and rural social orders became so widely diffused in the literature of sociology and anthropology, in the literature of general education, and in the general lay literature, as well, that they were accepted as generalizations resulting from sociological and anthropological research. Yet the fact is that most of the scholars who contributed to the emergence of these concepts regarded them not as generalizations based on research but, rather, as "ideal-type constructs."

The wide acceptance of these constructs as products of research, however, together with the increasing recognition of students that there were many departures in reality from the ideal-type constructs, led to a literature of criticism especially during the past two decades. Among the critics were Tax in 1939 and 1941; Wirth in 1951; Oscar Lewis in 1951; William Kolb in 1954; Dudley Duncan and Albert Reiss in 1956; and with the rising choruses of voices this writer in 1955 and 1957.[7]

This chapter is an attempt to focus, more explicitly than has been done so far, on the details of the ideal-type constructs in relation to the characteristics of metropolitan areas in Asia. The analysis up to this point is based primarily, on the one hand, on a summary of the literature and, on the other, on impressions of the writer gleaned from residence in a number of cities in Asia over a period of about two years. The primary purpose of the paper is to call for more rigorous inquiry into the matter. Such research could lead among other things to a reformulation of these ideal-type constructs, which have been in the literature now for a number of decades.

The Constructs

Redfield in his construction of the "folk" ideal type made quite explicit the method which he pursued and the purpose of the construct.

> The construction of the type depends indeed upon special knowledge of tribal and peasant groups. The ideal folk society could be defined through assembling in the imagination, the characters which are logically opposite those which are to be found in the modern city. . . . The complete procedure requires us to gain acquaintance with many folk societies in many parts of the world, and to set down in words general enough to describe most of them those characteristics which they have in common with each other and which the modern city does not have.[8]

The rationale behind the ideal-type construct was also explicitly stated by Redfield: "As the type is constructed real societies may be arranged in order of the degree of resemblance to it. The conception develops that any one real society is more or less folk." [9]

The characteristics of the folk society as set forth by Redfield may be listed as follows: small; isolated; nonliterate; homogeneous; strong sense of group solidarity; simple technology; simple division of labor; economically independent; possessing "culture," that is, an organization of conventional understandings; behavior strongly patterned on a conventional basis—traditional, spontaneous, uncritical; informal status; no systematic knowledge—no books; behavior is personal; society is familial; society is sacred; mentality is essentially personal and emotional (not abstract or categoric); animism and anthropomorphism manifest; no market, no money, no concept of "gain."

Redfield was quick to acknowledge that the ideal-type constructs are not to be found in the real world. He asserted, for example, that "the societies of the world do not arrange themselves in the same order with regard to the degree to which they realize all of the characteristics of the ideal folk society." [10] And he went on to say, "On the other hand there is so marked a tendency for some of these characteristics to occur together with others that the interrelations among them must be in no small part that of interdependent variables." [11]

The "urban" ideal type is the opposite of the "folk" ideal type. In his treatment of "urbanism as a way of life," Wirth not only stated the characteristics of the "urban" ideal-type construct but linked them with the characteristics of the urban society which he designated as: large population; density; heterogeneity; and permanance. According to Wirth,

The central problem to the sociologist of the city is to discover the forms of social action and organization that typically emerge in relatively permanent, compact settlements of large numbers of heterogeneous individuals. We must also infer that urbanism will assume its most characteristic and extreme form in the measure in which the conditions with which it is congruent are present.[12]

The specific characteristics of the "urban" social order as elaborated by Wirth will be enumerated in detail later in relation to the presence or absence of such characteristics in the metropolis in the economically less developed areas, such as in Asia.

The Criticism

In his discussion of Guatemala, Tax saw in that society a folk order that departed from the characteristics of the ideal-type construct. A stable society can be small, unsophisticated, homogeneous in beliefs and practices "with relationships impersonal, with formal institutions dictating the acts of individuals, and the family organization weak, with life secularized, and with individuals acting more from economic or other personal advantage than from any deep conviction or thought of the social good." Tax was quoted by Redfield in his article (p. 308). Redfield also took note of Tax's criticism: "A primitive world view, that is a disposition to treat nature personally, to regard attributes as entities, and to make 'symbolic' rather than causal connections coexists with a tendency for relations between man and man to be impersonal, commercial, and secular as they tend to be in the urban society." [13]

Wirth was quite explicit about the limitations of the ideal-type construct as empirical generalizations. In a fragment published posthumously in 1956, although first uttered in 1951, he stated:

To set up ideal typical polar concepts as I have done, and many others before me have done, does not prove that city and country are fundamentally and necessarily different. It does not justify mistaking the hypothetical characteristics attributed to the urban and rural modes of life for established facts, as has so often been done. Rather it suggests certain hypotheses to be tested in the light of empirical evidence which we must assiduously gather. Unfortunately this evidence has not been accumulated in such a fashion as to test critically any major hypothesis that has been proposed.[14]

I submit that Wirth's observation in 1951 is as applicable today as it was then.

Without question the most detailed and documented criticism of the ideal-type folk-urban construct and its use is found in the works of Oscar Lewis. In his *Life in a Mexican Village,* in 1951, he first makes the following general basic methodological point:

> Still other differences, such as those summarized in the pre-ceding pages, must be attributed to the most part to differ-ences in theoretical orientation and methodology, which in turn influence the selection and coverage of facts and the way in which these facts were organized. In rereading Redfield's study in the light of my own work in the village, it seems to me that the concept of the folk-culture and folk-urban continuum was Redfield's organizing principle in the research. Perhaps this helps to explain his emphasis on the formal and ritualistic aspects of life rather than the every day life of the people and their problems, on evidence of homogeneity rather than heterogeneity and the range of custom, on the weight of tradition rather than deviation and innovation, on unity and integration rather than tensions and conflict.[15]

Lewis goes on to indicate that this is probably what led Beals in his review of Lewis to comment on what he regards as "the hereti-cal suggestions" that "to insist that field studies must have a theoreti-cal hypothesis is perhaps a dangerous procedure." [16] This observation might well be compared with Francis Bacon's injunction against "anticipating nature." Lewis also notes, however, that Beals in one sense comes to Redfield's defense in suggesting that due to proximity to urban centers Tepoztlan was not a good example of a folk society. Thus he shifts his criticism of Redfield in pointing to Redfield's failure to place Tepoztlan in any historical or geographic context, as a "con-trol" in his construction of the folk ideal type.

Lewis in his analysis then proceeds with a presentation of six other criticisms of the folk-urban dichotomy. They consist of:

1. focus on the city as a source of change;
2. the notion that change can come from increasing heterogeneity of culture elements in a nonurban society;

3. the erroneous treatment of criteria of folk society as interdependent variables—that is, they might better be treated as independent (Tax's earlier observations are supported by Lewis's study);

4. the folk-urban typology obscures "one of the most significant findings of modern cultural anthropology," that is, the wide range of ways of life and value systems among primitive peoples; it also tends to obscure urban differences;

5. has serious limitations in guiding research because of "highly selective implications of categories and narrow focus";

6. value judgments underlie the dichotomy in Redfield. Redfield, like Rousseau, envisioned "noble savages," a point of view that is documented, says Lewis, in a number of Redfield's writings.

All in all, from a reading of Lewis on the dichotomy, there is implied in his work, if not a complete junking, a drastic revision of it.

William L. Kolb in "The Social Structure and Functions of Cities," attacks the urban end of the dichotomy to complement Lewis's attack on the folk end.[17] Kolb does so, however, through the vehicle of disagreements with ecologists, following the Firey line, and the use of the Parsonian pattern variable schema which adds little to the issue. Kolb states, "size and density of cities will not by themselves or assisted by heterogeneity create the primacy of secondary relations, isolation and loneliness. Only when there is extreme stress on universalism and achievement accompanied by other features of industrialization, can these demographic factors produce such social characteristics." [18]

Kolb in general and in somewhat extreme fashion argues that generalizations about the urban mostly derive from Park and his students' work on the Chicago of the 1920's. The ideal-type construct is not based on universal observation then; it tends more to be a unique description of a given city in a given time and place. In this respect he undoubtedly misreads Park, as Hughes indicates,[19] but there is something to his observation that generalizations based on the study of Chicago have not been subjected to the kind of test consistent with the imagery of science.

Duncan and Reiss in their *Social Characteristics of Urban and Rural Communities,* a monograph based on the 1950 Census, not only indicate that the urban-rural dichotomy might better have been stated as a continuum, but also that the continuum itself does not hold when reality is examined.[20] Various characteristics of populations ordered by city size from the very largest metropolises to the rural-farm population reveal quite a variety of patterns in relationship, that is, the relationship is not necessarily linear. The deviations from the dichotomization of the urban and rural documented in a volume such as Duncan and Reiss's may be regarded as evidence of the departure of reality from the ideal-type construct. Along with other evidence, it also points to the need for modification of the construct itself.

Finally, as a brief note prior to the elaboration of my own thinking on the matter, I should state that the folk-urban and urban-rural dichotomies, although they had troubled me earlier in connection with observations in the city in the United States itself, struck me as especially inadequate after my exposure to Asian cities and also to South American cities, especially since 1951. My personal observations convinced me that the dichotomizations in the literature in the form of the folk-urban and urban-rural ideal-type constructs were on the whole inapplicable to the metropolis of the less-developed area, and that more refined constructs were probably desirable for the furthering of research in this general field.

Although my major quarrel with the folk-urban and urban-rural dichotomies lies with the way in which they have seeped into the literature and have become accepted as generalizations based on research, rather than their utility as ideal-type constructs, I have come to feel that even in the latter role they perhaps may have outlived their usefulness. In view of this, it is perhaps a little sad that a tendency is evident to defend the constructs, as such. I regard this situation as sad because any ideal-type construct has its defense in its utility. If it fails to be as useful as it might be then the time has come for its modification.

Redfield in his article "The Folk Society" in 1947 recognized Tax's criticism, as I have already indicated. He acknowledges, "So it may appear that under certain conditions a literate and, indeed, at least partly urbanized society may be both highly commercial and sacred—as witness, also, the Jews—while under certain other conditions an otherwise folklike people may become individualistic, commercial and perhaps secular." [21] He does say, "It is, of course, the determination of the limiting conditions that is important," [22] but he does not follow through, either with an indication of the limiting conditions or the modification of the dichotomy.

In a more recent article, "The Cultural Role of Cities" with Singer, the folk society and the city are further considered with no reference to the work of the critics. The folk society concept is presented as in the past as an "imagined combination of societal elements." [23] The city is visualized "as that community in which orthogenetic and heterogenetic transformations of the folk society have most fully occurred."

> The former has brought about the Great Tradition and its special intellectual class, administrative officers and rule closely derived from the moral and religious life of the local culture, and advanced economic institutions, also obedient to these local cultural controls. The heterogenetic transformations have accomplished the freeing of the intellectual, esthetic, economic and political life from the local moral norms, and have developed on the one hand an individuated expediential motivation, and on the other, a revolutionary, nativistic, humanistic, or ecumenical viewpoint, now directed toward reform, progress and designed change.[24]

Cities are then classified by type as orthogenetic or heterogenetic. Without further pursuing the implications of these neologisms and the questions they raise, it may be noted, for the moment, that folk society is now differentiated from the two types of cities which are set up.

The "transformations of folk societies" is then considered in two forms—"primary" and "secondary" urbanization. Cities are more closely integrated with the country in the primary phase of urbanization, the city flowing from the Great Tradition. The Great Tradition and the Little Tradition, in primary urbanization, are held together as it were—for in primary urbanization literature the intelligentsia and the cosmopolitan are prominent. In secondary urbanization, in contrast, integration depends more on symbiotic relations, on the rate of technological development, and on the scope and intensity of contact with other cultures. The Redfield-Singer analysis builds on the folk-urban dichotomy and is in large measure, then, dependent on the folk ideal-type construct. To the extent that that construct does not correspond to reality, it follows that the additional edifices also are defective.

Redfield and Singer do note exceptions to the expected folk-urban dichotomy. "In societies where social change is slow, and there has developed an adjustment of mutual usefulness and peaceful residence side by side of groups culturally different but not too different, the culturally complex society may be relatively stable. But where urban development is great such conditions are apt to be unstable." [25] On the whole, however, the Redfield-Singer discussion presents an extension of the older dichotomizations rather than a modification based on continued research and commentaries of the critics.

Application of the Ideal-Type Constructs to the Metropolis in the Economically Less-Advanced Area

As a preliminary to the type of research and analysis by means of which the ideal-type constructs, both the folk-urban and the urban-rural dichotomizations, could be subjected to the test of empirical research, there follows a detailed listing of the characteristics of the urban social order as set forth by Wirth, in relation to the characteristics of the urban society, that is, size, density, and heterogeneity, respectively. For each of these items, a judgment is indicated in column 2 on whether the characteristic is, in fact, observable in the urban society in Asian cities in which the writer has lived (primarily Rangoon, but including Bangkok, Djakarta, and Calcutta).

Urban Condition	Expected Characteristic	Actual Characteristic (Presence of characteristic in urban areas of less developed countries)
Size	1. Atomization (Simmel)	No
	2. Schizoid character	No
	3. Segmental roles	Some
	4. Secondary contacts	Some
	5. Superficiality	Some
	6. Anonymity	Some
	7. Sophistication	No
	8. Rationality	No
	9. Loses spontaneous self-expression	Mainly no
	10. Utilitarian contact	Some
	11. Pecuniary nexus	Some
	12. Interdependence—specialization	Some, but very limited
	13. Mass media of communication	Mainly no
Density	1. Differentiation and specialization	Mainly no
	2. Shift in media through which we orient ourselves to urban milieu and fellow man, that is the emphasis on vision world of artifacts, etc. (Simmel)	Very little

Urban Condition	Expected Characteristic	Actual Characteristic (Presence of characteristic in urban areas of less developed countries)
	3. Place of work separated from place of residence	Some, but limited
	4. Glaring contrasts Poverty and riches Squalor and splendor Ignorance and intelligence	Some
	5. Patterning of city ecologically— the Burgess hypothesis	Yes and no
	6. Secularization of life	No
	7. Competition, aggrandizement, and mutual exploitation	Yes and no
	8. Clock and traffic signals as symbols	No
	9. Loneliness	Yes and no
	10. Friction, irritation, frustration	Some
Heterogeneity	1. Breaks caste lines, complicating class structure	No
	2. Instability and insecurity of individual	Yes and no
	3. Sophistication and cosmopolitanism	Mainly no
	4. No single group has undivided allegiance	No
	5. Turnover in group membership rapid	Mainly no
	6. Personality segments corresponding to group memberships	Mainly no
	7. Place of residence, employment, income, interests fluctuate	Mainly no
	8. Not a home owner	No
	9. Mass behavior fluid and unpredictable	No
	10. Depersonalization	Yes and no
	11. Money economy	Yes and no
	12. Mass media communication operate as leveling influences	Mainly no

If we turn next to a consideration of the characteristics of folk society set forth by Redfield, and look for their presence or absence in the large urban area in the economically less-advanced areas in the world, a similar table may be prepared.

Expected Characteristic	Actual Characteristic (Presence in urban areas in less developed countries)
Social unit is:	
1. Small	Yes
2. Isolated social world	Yes and no
3. Nonliterate order	Yes
4. Homogeneous groups	Yes
5. Strong group solidarity	Yes
6. Simple technology	Yes
7. Simple division of labor	Yes
8. Economically independent	Yes and no
9. "Culture"—the organization of conventional understanding	Yes
10. Behavior strongly patterned conventional	Yes and no
11. Status	Yes
12. No systematic knowledge	Yes
13. Behavior personal	Yes
14. Society familial	Yes and no
15. Society sacred	Yes
16. Mentality personal and emotional	Yes
17. No market	Yes and no

It is hardly necessary to reiterate that the responses indicating the "actual" in relation to the "expected" are not responses grounded in empirical research. *They are based largely on the limited experience and impressions of the writer.* They are not presented, therefore, as definitive answers to the questions raised, but rather as approximations or hypotheses that merit further investigation for their validation or rejection.

Concluding Observation

The folk-urban and the urban-rural dichotomies may be regarded as ideal-type constructs which are the products of Western writers. These ideal-type constructs have not been used in accordance with Weber's injunctions on the use of ideal-type constructs.[26] Even in the literature of social science as well as that in general education, there has been a relatively blind acceptance of the ideal-type constructs as generalizations based on research rather than as tools to be utilized in research. Investigators have been more impressed with their findings of conformance than motivated to look for deviations from the constructs. Moreover, fundamental logical errors have been committed in the utilization of these constructs in the drawing of diachronic conclusion from synchronic observations. That is, the concepts have also been used in a neo-evolutionary way on the assumption that the "folk" and the "urban" actually represented different stages in the development of societies.[27]

There is evidence, by no means conclusive as yet, that both parts of these dichotomies represent confounded variables and, in fact, complex systems of variables which have yet to be unscrambled. The dichotomizations perhaps represent all too hasty efforts to synthesize and integrate what little knowledge has been acquired in empirical research. The widespread acceptance of these ideal-type constructs as generalizations, without benefit of adequate research, well illustrates the dangers of catchy neologisms which often get confused with knowledge. In some respects, these ideal-type constructs represent an admixture of nineteenth-century speculative efforts to achieve global generalization, and twentieth-century concern with the integration of knowledge for general education purposes, as a result of which integration is often achieved of that which is not yet known.

It is hoped that the materials which have been presented will help to highlight the need for next steps in the evaluation of these ideal-type constructs. Obviously, what is necessary are well-designed empirical researches in which deviations from the constructs are noted in greater detail and with greater precision than are now available. Such research would better illuminate the nature of diverse social orders and, in the process, perhaps lead to the construction of ideal typology more useful than that which is now available as prolegomena to empirically based generalizations.

NOTES

Part A

1. Oscar Lewis, *Life in a Mexican Village: Tepoztlan Restudied* (Urbana, Ill.: University of Illinois Press, 1951).

2. There has been a growing literature of criticism of the folk-urban and rural-urban dichotomies by urban sociologists. See, for example, Theodore Caplow, "The Social Ecology of Guatemala City," *Social Forces*, 28 (De-

cember 1949); Philip M. Hauser, "Observations on the Urban-Folk and Urban-Rural Dichotomies as Forms of Western Ethnocentrism," Part B of this chapter; William L. Kolb, "The Social Structure and Function of Cities," *Economic Development and Culture Change* (October 1954); O. D. Duncan and Albert J. Reiss, Jr., *Social Characteristics of Urban and Rural Communities, 1950* (New York: Wiley, 1956), Part 4; Gideon Sjoberg, "Comparative Urban Sociology," *Sociology Today* (New York: Basic Books, 1959), pp. 334–359. Horace Miner has attempted to defend the Redfield position in what seems to me to be a rather apologetic article. A careful reading will show that he accepts most of the criticism although he swallows hard. See his "The Folk-Urban Continuum" in Paul K. Hatt and Albert J. Reiss, Jr. (Eds.), *Cities and Society* (Glencoe, Ill.: The Free Press, 1957), pp. 22–34.

3. Hauser, *op. cit.*, p. 514.

4. Julian H. Steward. *Theory of Culture Change* (Urbana, Ill.: University of Illinois Press, 1955); Irving Goldman, "Status Rivalry and Cultural Evolution in Polynesia," *American Anthropologist*, 57, No. 4 (August 1955), pp. 680–697; Irving Goldman, "Cultural Evolution in Polynesia: A Reply to Criticism," *Journal of the Polynesian Society*, 66, No. 2 (June 1957), pp. 156–164; Irving Goldman, "The Evolution of Status Systems in Polynesia," in A. F. C. Wallace (Ed.), *Men and Cultures* (Philadelphia, 1960), pp. 255–260.

5. I have made this point in an earlier paper "Peasant Culture In India and Mexico," in McKim Marriott (Ed.), *Village India, American Anthropologist*, Vol. 57, No. 3, Part 2. Memoir No. 83, June 1955: "For both applied and theoretical anthropology we need typologies of peasantry for the major culture areas of the world. . . . Moreover, within each area we need more refined subclassifications. Only after such studies are available will we be in a position to formulate broad generalizations about the dynamics of peasant culture as a whole." P. 165.

6. Oscar Lewis, "Urbanization Without Breakdown: A Case Study," in *The Scientific Monthly*, 75, No. 1 (July 1952). In this article I have suggested a number of specific Mexican conditions which might explain the special findings. More recently, Joseph A. Kahl has restated and elaborated upon some of these points in his article "Some Social Concomitants of Industrialization and Urbanization: A Research Review," *Human Organization*, 18 (Summer 1959), pp. 53–74.

7. Oscar Lewis, "The Culture of the Vecindad In Mexico City: Two Case Studies," *Actas del III Congreso Internacional de Americanistas*, Tomo I, San Jose, Costa Rica, 1959, pp. 387–402.

8. Louis Wirth, "Urbanism As A Way of Life," *American Journal of Sociology*, 44 (July 1938), pp. 1–24.

9. Sjoberg, *op. cit.*, p. 340.

10. Wirth, "Urbanism As A Way of Life," in *Community Life and Social Policy* (Chicago: University of Chicago Press, 1956), pp. 119–120.

11. Sjoberg has correctly criticized the logic of comparison inherent in the writings of Redfield and Wirth on folk-urban theory on the ground that they were comparing a whole society with a part society. Here my criticism is that Wirth treated the city as a whole society for purposes of social relations and personality.

12. George Foster, "The Personality of the Peasant," paper read at the

58th Annual Meeting of the American Anthropological Association, Mexico City, 1959.

13. Edward M. Bruner, "Urbanization and Culture Change: Indonesia," paper read at the 58th Annual Meeting of the American Anthropological Association in Mexico City, December 28, 1959.

Part B

1. Joyce O. Hertzler, *Social Thought of the Ancient Civilizations* (New York: McGraw-Hill, 1936), pp. 298ff.

2. Henry Maine, *Ancient Law* (London: J. Murray, 1961); Ferdinand Tönnies, *Gemeinschaft und Gesellschaft* (1st ed., 1887), trans. and ed. Charles P. Loomis as *Fundamental Concepts of Sociology* (New York: American Book Co., 1940); *Emile Durkheim on the Division of Labor in Society*, trans. George Simpson (New York: Macmillan, 1933).

3. William Graham Sumner, *Folkways* (Boston: Ginn, 1907); A. A. Goldenweiser, *Early Civilization* (New York: Knopf, 1922); Howard Becker and Harry Elmer Barnes, *Social Thought from Lore to Science* (Washington, D. C.: Harren Press, 1952), Chap. 1.

4. Robert Redfield, *Tepoztlan, A Mexican Village* (Chicago: University of Chicago Press, 1930). See also his: "The Folk Society and Culture," Louis Wirth (Ed.), *Eleven Twenty-Six* (Chicago: University of Chicago Press, 1940), pp. 39–50; *The Folk Culture of Yucatán* (Chicago: University of Chicago Press, 1941); "The Folk Society," *American Journal of Sociology*, 41 (January 1947), pp. 293–308; (with Milton Singer), "The Cultural Role of Cities," *Economic Development and Cultural Change*, 3 (October 1954), pp. 53–73; *The Primitive World and Its Transformations* (Ithaca, N. Y.: Cornell University Press, 1953).

5. James Mickel Williams, *Our Rural Heritage* (New York: Knopf, 1925); Robert E. Park, Ernest W. Burgess, and R. D. McKenzie, *The City* (Chicago: University of Chicago Press, 1925); Ernest W. Burgess (Ed.), *The Urban Community* (Chicago: University of Chicago Press, 1926); William F. Ogburn, *Social Characteristics of Cities* (Chicago: The International City Manager's Assn., 1937).

6. Reprinted in Wirth's posthumous *Community Life and Social Policy* (Chicago: University of Chicago Press, 1956), pp. 110–132.

7. Sol Tax, "Culture and Civilization in Guatemalan Societies," *Scientific Monthly*, 48 (May 1939). Also his "World View and Social Relations in Guatemala," *American Anthropologist*, 43, No. 1 (January–March 1941), pp. 27–42. Louis Wirth, "Rural-Urban Differences," in *Community Life and Social Policy* (Chicago: University of Chicago Press, 1956). Oscar Lewis, *Life in a Mexican Village: Tepoztlan Restudied* (Urbana, Ill.: University of Illinois Press, 1951). William Kolb, "The Social Structure and Function of Cities," *Economic Development and Cultural Change*, 3, No. 1 (October 1954), pp. 30–46. O. D. Duncan and Albert J. Reiss, Jr., *Social Characteristics of Urban and Rural Communities, 1950* (New York: Wiley, 1956). This paper was originally written in 1955 for the Institute of Social Research at the University of Chicago. See also Philip M. Hauser (Ed.), *Urbanization in Asia and the Far East* (Calcutta: UNESCO, 1957), p. 195.

8. Redfield, "The Folk Society," *op. cit.*, p. 294.

9. *Ibid.*

10. *Ibid.*, p. 306.

11. *Ibid.*

12. Wirth, *op. cit.*, p. 117.

13. Redfield, *op. cit.*, p. 308.

14. Wirth, *op. cit.*, pp. 173–174.

15. Lewis, *op. cit.*, pp. 431–432.

16. Ralph L. Beals, book review of Oscar Lewis, *Life in a Mexican Village: Tepoztlan Restudied* (Urbana, Ill.: University of Illinois Press, 1951), *American Sociological Review*, 16, No. 6 (December 1951), pp. 895–896.

17. Kolb, *op. cit.*, pp. 30ff.

18. *Ibid.*, p. 44.

19. Everett Hughes, "Robert E. Park's Views on Urban Society: A Comment on William L. Kolb's Paper," *Economic Development and Cultural Change*, 3 (October 1954), pp. 47–49.

20. Duncan and Reiss, *op. cit.*, Chap. 2.

21. Redfield, "The Folk Society,"*op. cit.*, p. 308.

22. *Ibid.*

23. Redfield and Singer, *op. cit.*, p. 58.

24. *Ibid.*

25. *Ibid.*, p. 69.

26. Max Weber, *The Theory of Social and Economic Organization*, trans. A. M. Henderson and Talcott Parsons (New York: Oxford University Press, 1947), pp. 11ff.

27. For example, Robert Redfield, in *The Primitive World* . . . , *op. cit.*

14

Historical Aspects of Urbanization

Eric E. Lampard

The presence of cities presupposes a more or less attendant societal process of urbanization. The relation of urbanization to cities may indeed be construed, for present purposes, as one of "cause" and "effect." Thus, while urbanization itself has never constituted a distinctive field of historical research, it is possible to gain some general notion of its incidence and form from the large and mostly unorganized body of writings on cities. From this literature one may derive an impression of the level of urbanization that obtains in a given area and also a sense of whether that level is rising, falling, or holding stable. Variations in the incidence of urbanization, as indicated by changes in the numbers and sizes of cities, for example, are at once a matter of intrinsic interest and a proximate index of other change. This chapter is concerned with other change, however, only insofar as it is reflected in the *organization* and *incidence* of urbanization.[1]

Even these limited agenda impose an obligation to descend from the mandarin heights to the tedious business of terms. Broadly speaking, three conceptions of urbanization have currency in the social sciences: the behavioral, the structural, and the demographic. (1) The first conceives of urbanization as an adjustment of personal behavior in the sense that it focuses on the conduct of individuals. Certain patterns of behavior or thought, regardless of social environment and locale, are said to be "urban." Hence the process of urbanization is one experienced by individuals over time. This approach has the special merit of not restricting urbanism to the city's physical milieu and is one favored by many students of culture and the arts. (2) The structural concept ignores the patterned behavior of individual persons and fastens on the patterned activities of whole populations. The process of urbanization is typically said to involve the

519

movement of people out of agricultural communities into other and generally larger nonagricultural communities. This conception gives primary recognition to the differential ordering of occupations or industries within a given territorial space. The structural approach has many applications in the social sciences and is the framework for virtually all economic models concerned with development. (3) The demographic approach again focuses on space but it largely ignores individual behavior and the structure of occupations. In its most succinct form it postulates that urbanization is a process of population concentration. Only two variables are recognized: population and space. Hence the connection between urbanization and, say, a certain occupational structure or personality trait is not prejudged.[2] This approach is one commonly adopted by students of population and human ecology.

Each of these approaches is suited to a different range of analytical questions and each poses its own peculiar difficulties of definition and measurement. None is wholly acceptable to the general purposes and practices of historians. Behavioral and structural concepts are largely matters of definition; their categories are often composed of highly equivocal variables and subject to much the same empirical weakness as index numbers applied over extended periods of time. Historians are wise to suspect this "type" thinking which often tends to distort experience by creating resemblances and suppressing differences. Even the austere demographic concept leaves something to be desired since such attributes as size and density may be very dubious indicators of urbanization in many historical and cultural contexts. But it is precisely the exclusive simplicity of the concept rather than its refinement that enhances its utility for exploratory research. It discriminates among processes which, although associated with population concentration, may in fact have counter effects upon it; thus the structural concomitants of urbanization at any time are not to be ignored, "they are simply to be distinguished from it."[3]

The concern in this chapter is with the historical incidence and organization of urbanization. By "incidence" is meant the range of occurrence of the phenomenon or the extent of its effect. "Organization" means the way in which the phenomenon forms a social system such that its components achieve regular and reciprocal interaction. Since the data regarding the historical occurrence of urbanization limit the investigator to determining, more or less, the numbers and sizes of cities at any time, the demographic approach is especially suited to the study of incidence. Organization, on the other hand, involves a consideration of the patterning of interactions in a population, hence the narrow demographic approach is less helpful than an avowedly structural approach. Where sufficient data are available it is possible to combine the two, although, likely as not, whatever is gained thereby in realism is partly offset by heightened ambiguity.

Under a demographic formulation, cities are viewed as points of population concentration; they are the product or outcome of urbanization. Thus urbanization is a societal process that necessarily precedes and accompanies the formation of cities. There is no reason why urbanization in an area may not be focused on a single city. If urbanization is sustained the city will grow, but there will be no necessity for its growth to outstrip the growth of total population. If the number of points of concentration does grow as well as their size and if, as is the case in certain parts of the modern world, a majority of population does come to live in cities, these aspects of urbanization are not to be explained by the process, for they define the process. Other conditions must apply.

For cities to increase in number and size, therefore, there must be not merely population and space, but relevant capacities as well. These capacities are essentially attributes of the population. What a population does in and with its environment depends in large part on the material means at its disposal and the form of social organization it adopts, that is, upon *adaptation*. Hence the actual number and sizes of population concentrations at any time are largely determined by the technological capacity of the population. The existence of natural resources is a further condition, but the utilization or "availability" of such resources is again a function of the technological and organizational capacities of the population. To see this point, one simply has to compare the contrasting responses of aboriginal Americans and European colonists to their North American environments. Broadly speaking, the larger and more differentiated the technological repertory, the greater and more diverse the potential resource inventory. Thus technologies and resources are alike components of the population's achieved capacity for adaptation.

Urbanization itself may be regarded as the organizational component of a population's achieved capacity for adaptation. It is a way of ordering a population to attain a certain level of subsistence and security in a given environment. The technological component is always a direct constituent of social organization but it is distinct from it. Technology is the *sine qua non* of urbanization, as of every other form of community organization, but it is "not the exclusive property of the city; it operates in every province and pocket of society." [4] Thus the demographic approach not only defines the process of urbanization with absolute parsimony but, by the addition of one "cultural" variable, technology, it elucidates the role of a fourth "social" variable, organization. Together the four variables—population, technology, organization, and environment—may explain the prevailing pattern of urbanization, indicate how that pattern emerged in the past, and adumbrate what its immediate future shape may be. By means of this *human ecological* framework, the task of explaining the process of urbanization over time—of identifying its determinants—becomes more amenable to solution.[5] The demographic concept of urbanization, in short, is not as constricting as it first might have appeared; its scope allows inquiry into many facets of social change, and its root in population preserves a vital interest in the attributes and conditions of human beings living in organized communities.[6]

Human populations have been forming into "cities" for almost seven thousand years. For much of that time, however, urban settlements were scarcely recognizable and when, little more than five thousand years ago, they first became definitive, they were still confined, under apparently restrictive conditions of environment, to a few widely separated areas on the earth's surface. At no time did the urban centers themselves contain more than a small fraction of the total population in an area; perhaps they held as much as 15 to 20 per cent on a restricted local basis, but no more than 5 per cent on any larger regional scale. After several thousand years of such relatively stable levels of urbanization, the past two or three centuries have witnessed an unprecedented increase in both rates and levels of urbanizaton with repercussions and ramifications that mark the changes of the period *c*. A.D. 1750–1850 as one of the crucial disjunctions in the history of

TABLE 1. ESTIMATES OF WORLD POPULATION, 8000 B.C.–A.D. 1960
(millions)

Date	B.C.			A.D.				
	8000	4000	40	1650	1750	1800	1900	1960
Number	5.3	86.5	133.0	545	728	906	1,608	2,995

Sources: B.C. estimates: E. S. Deevey, Jr., "The Human Population," *Scientific American* (September 1960).
1650, 1750: W. M. Wilcox (Ed.), *International Migrations*, 2 (1931), pp. 33–84. A. M. Carr-Saunders, *World Population*, 1936, p. 42.
1800, 1900: Kingsley Davis and Hilda Hertz Golden, cited by P. M. Hauser (Ed.), *Urbanization in Asia and the Far East* (UNESCO, 1957), pp. 55–60.
1960: United Nations *Demographic Yearbook*, 1961, p. 120.

human society. Whatever constraints had hitherto checked or moderated the growth and redistribution of population were suddenly relaxed. The emergence of rapidly urbanizing societies, with well over 50 per cent of their burgeoning populations resident in cities, represents one of the most far-reaching changes in human capacities for social organization since the "agricultural" and "urban revolutions" some six to ten thousand years ago. (See Tables 1 and 2.)

This chapter treats this transformation from the standpoint of urban incidence and organization. Within a framework of human ecology, it explores the history of urbanization in two phases:

1. *Primordial urbanization:* the first achievement of incipient urban organization as an *additional* and more *productive* mode of collective adaptation to physical and social environment.

2. *Definitive urbanization:* the culmination of primordial tendencies in the additional and *alternative* form of social organization: the definitive city. By means of its capacity to generate, store, and utilize social saving, the definitive city artifact is capable of transplanting itself from out of its native uterine environments.

In a later study, definitive urbanization will be treated with special reference to the marked changes in incidence and organization (in rates and levels of urbanization) before and after *c.* A.D. 1700. These changes are to be subsumed in two further categories:

3. *Classic urbanization:* when various constraints and circumstances combine to moderate the growth of population and cities, as it were, through "systemic" or built-in social checks and balances.[7]

4. *Industrial urbanization:* when prevailing constraints and conditions are relaxed through the final achievement of technological and organizational capacities for unprecedented population concentration. By means of its unique capacity to convert and control high *per capita* levels of *inanimate* heat-energy, the industrial-urban city establishes itself outside its native uterine setting in still wider ranges of social and physical environment.

High mortality notwithstanding, the constraints which arrested growth of population and urbanization under classic conditions were imposed less by the environment than by limited capacities of the population. It is possible that, even before the secular decline in mortality *c.* A.D. 1850, industrial urbanization had allowed sizable gains in human fertility. Once a population had accumulated technological means and requisite organization, urban concentration gathered greater momentum than the population increase itself.

TABLE 2. WORLD POPULATION AND WORLD URBAN POPULATION, 1800–1960

Year	World Population (millions)	Population in Cities 5000 and Over (millions)	Per Cent in Cities 5000 and Over	Per Cent in Cities 100,000 and Over
1800	906	27.2	3.0	1.7
1850	1,171	74.9	6.4	2.3
1900	1,608	218.7	13.6	5.5
1950	2,400	716.7	29.8	13.1
1960	2,995	948.4	31.6	20.1

Sources: 1800–1950: Kingsley Davis and Hilda Hertz Golden, see Table 1.
1960: U.N. Demographic Yearbook, 1962, Tables 9, 10.

Although classic central place and market orientation continued to exert their nodal and hierarchical sway on the overall pattern of the industrial-urban system, there was a greater tendency for economic site advantages to determine the locus of city growth and to impart a more asymmetric distribution of specialized kinds of activities within the system. At all events, in terms of urban incidence and organization, the divergent capacities exhibited before and after 1700 A.D. were essentially technological in character. It is technological capacity in the broad sense, operating through related organizational capability, that at once redefines environment and gives form and focus to related movements of the population.

Primordial Urbanization: Toward a More Productive Mode of Collective Adaptation

Knowledge of men's earliest approaches toward urban life has recently been enlarged by the expansion of archeological research and the introduction of new research methods. With the multiplication of sites and application of natural-science techniques, it becomes possible to follow the history of human society from the late Pleistocene period (after 15,000 B.C.) up through the beginnings of urbanization. Comparative study of primordial urbanization for the first time allows some consideration of what Robert J. Braidwood and Gordon R. Willey have termed "the varieties of cultural build-ups" leading to the thresholds of urban civilization.[8] Examination of the still very incomplete record of eleven Old World and seven New World areas reveals that each passed through a variety of progressions from loose-knit systems of food collecting to more or less effective food production and that all but two of them had reached at least the point of incipient urbanization before Columbus linked the two worlds into one. Not only were there significant variations among the areas in climate, topography, vegetation, crops, and animals, but in dependence on irrigation, in the emergence of cult and ceremonial centers, in social stratification, and in size and density of settlements as well. But everywhere the progression followed a prolonged uncertain process from the first cultivation of wild cereals and herding of wild animals to the level of wholly sedentary, year-round, village farming communities, such as Jarmo (c. 6750 B.C.) in Iraqi Kurdistan or the Mesa de Guaje sequence in Mexican Tamaulipas (c. 1500 B.C.).[9]

Definitive urbanization was finally achieved in the "fertile crescent" of southwest Asia by the fourth millennium B.C., in the Indus valley and Huangho basin from the third to the second millennia B.C., in Mesoamerica very late in the first millennium B.C., in the Central Andes, northern Europe, and possibly in sub-Saharan Africa during the first millennium A.D. Some elements necessary to effective food production had already been "diffused" from these areas before the transition to definitive urbanization was fully realized. Propagation of plant or animal husbandry to new environments was, by standards of archeological time, a move of remarkable suddenness. Yet the techniques of cultivation had to be adapted to the new environments no less than the plants or animals themselves. Successful adaptation to the forest lands of northern Europe and America, for example, depended on the extensive development of cutting and burning techniques. Obstacles to propagation posed by the physical environment, moreover, were often heightened by the apparent indifference of a population which was already well adjusted to an intensified food collecting way of life (including, say, hunting or fishing together with supplemental agriculture). Instances of "abortive" propagation can be found in Baltic Europe, eastern aboriginal North America, and in the forest region of Siberia.[10]

The successful transference of agricultural, ceramic, or metallurgical elements, on the other hand, does not necessarily stimulate urbanization, nor does it detract from the indigenous character of any urbanization subsequently achieved in the area. The agricultural repertory of the Central Andean area (which already included maize and root crops) was augmented after 1400 B.C. by an improved strain of Mesoamerican maize, but six or seven centuries more were required "before full village agriculture could be said to have resulted from cultural or social changes set in motion by this innovation." Improved strains of maize were also transmitted to a so-called Intermediate area—between the Mesoamerican and Central Andean areas of New World civilization—where they were duly incorporated in an effective seed agriculture. Thereupon this agriculture "stagnated" for well over a thousand years, although the populations concerned evidently knew of great civilizations flourishing both north and south in environments only slightly less inhospitable than those of the Intermediate area itself.[11] Did the coming of Europeans eventually arrest primordial urbanization in the area or did factors such as "the scarcity of irrigation, the relative simplicity of social stratification and religion, the lack of specialization by occupation, and the apparent paucity of large-scale trading" prevent the indigenous populations from surmounting their own village level of attainment? [12] Answers to these questions are not now available, but the questions serve to indicate the kinds of hypotheses that occur to experienced anthropologists working with a well-defined problem in a wide variety of physical and temporal contexts. The hypotheses, moreover, appear to stress the potential signifiance of *social organization* rather than such cultural "imperatives" as technology or the "necessities" of environment.

That urbanization is a social as well as a cultural process is implied by the kinds of abstract criteria—deducible from archeological data—that constitute definitive evidence of cities. Some ten of these criteria, formulated by V. Gordon Childe, indicate a compact settlement with at least 4000–5000 inhabitants, including full-time craftsmen and artists, an effective capital "surplus" based on agriculture, augmented by "foreign" trade; with monumental public architecture, writing or other script system; calendrical or mathematical sciences; social stratification; and political hierarchy. Concrete instances of early cities, of course, vary as much as "the plans of their temples, the signs of their scripts and their artistic conventions," but the urban criteria are, nevertheless, objective in the sense that they can be inferred with high probability, and in a wholly detached way, from material remains.[13] Just how many of the criteria need be present before a large village or other settlement must be adjudged a city is a matter for specialists to determine. Some students of Mesoamerica, for example, have suggested that the dispersed populations of great centers in the Maya lowlands are not "urban" in a strict sense, other sociopolitical attributes notwithstanding. A distinguished Egyptologist has referred to his own area down through the close of the New Kingdom, c. 1100 B.C., as a "civilization without cities." [14]

None of these exceptions or gaps in the record, however, diminishes the potential relevance of social organization as an independent variable. This point has been made most succinctly by Robert M. Adams in his consideration of the immediate origins of cities during the fourth millennium B.C. in Mesopotamia: "The rise of cities . . . was pre-eminently a social process, an expression more of changes in man's interaction with his fellows than in his interaction with his environment." The novelty of the city consisted in "a whole series of new institutions and the vastly greater size and complexity of the social unit, rather than basic innovations in subsistence." [15] Ultimately every high civilization, with the possible exception of the Mayan, attains the level of urbanization, and in most the primordial process begins early.

Primordial urbanization required both the technological achievement of food production and the social organization of village agriculture. These achievements underlie most documented cases of sedentary populations with high densities. On such foundations some populations developed an array of cultural correlates which included monumental buildings, forms of writing, and great arts. These, in turn, were associated with social innovations such as "foreign" trade, rudimentary specialization, and a religio-political hierarchy. But if this unfolding was necessary to the subsequent climax of urbanization, the achievement of particular items did not assure the entire sequence or even an acceleration of changes in an inevitable direction. The build-up toward urbanization remained essentially a contingent process. In the state of present knowledge, therefore, the student of historical urbanization must inch forward with descriptive statements of possible occurrences in comparative contexts rather than formulate precisely testable hypotheses of universal relevance.

In light of the Childe criteria and pertinent archeological data, the "problem" of urbanization can be restated in terms of human ecology. The community structure or *oikumene* at any time is conceived as a balance between a population aggregate and its environment, mediated by technology and social organization. Where contact with other peoples is involved, their presence is subsumed under environment, social as well as physical. Both technology and organization are attributes of the population. Technology may be regarded as a cultural variable and organization as a social variable, the one through which a population aggregate takes on its "systemic" aspect. Organization is also the crucial ecological variable since, in its absence, regularities of interaction are reduced, technology is not applied, and the aggregate disintegrates. The antonym of "systemic" is "chaotic," describing a situation in which, so to speak, "everything depends on everything else." A chaotic society, therefore, is almost a contradiction in terms.[16]

Restatement of the "problem" in terms of the human ecosystem takes the following form. Further *differentiation* of functions within a population and its territory results in more specialized components; in the *integration* of such parts into a coherent "system" of interdependence, the level and form of urban organization is achieved.

In spite of differences of terminology and emphasis, the analyses of anthropologically-minded archeologists often coincide with those of human ecologists. Kwang-chih Chang, for example, concludes his consideration of the appearance of Yin-Shang civilization during the course of the second millennium B.C. as follows:

> It is only now that, equipped with a good deal more data, we can begin to consider some of the major premises afresh and adopt a holistic, configurational, and functional approach that a new and probably truer picture has emerged . . . the structural covariations and efficient causes are being stressed in terms of social mechanism and cultural pattern.[17]

Similarly, Gordon R. Willey suggests that regional variations within a relatively confined area of Mesoamerica or Peru "might have been a crucial circumstance in the development of cultivated plants and the subsequent achievement of village agriculture." The assumption is, of course, that prolonged interstimulation within a "naturally" differentiated area created a system of symbiosis, one in which specializing subcultures did not overwhelm each other. The further query is posed whether regional variation could have fostered later developments, namely urbanization, "in a more strictly cultural rather than a cultural-botanical sphere?" Willey concludes that "regional intercommunication and interstimulation . . . promoted cultural growth." Thus, at a point when the threshold of definitive urbanization was reached, no single region of Peru or Mesoamerica exerted dominance over the others, although great interregional art styles, Chavín and Olmec, and possibly attendant religions, prevailed in their respective areas. Only after the threshold was crossed did the regionalism of subcultures break down before "what appeared to be the beginnings of attempts at area-wide empires."[18]

Southwest Asia furnishes another instance of intra-areal symbiosis but with the complication of a territorial shift from the earliest village-farming sites "in the environmentally varied hill flanks . . . [to] the generally uniform semiarid alluvial plain of southern Mesopotamia." Nevertheless, the relative physical uniformity of land between the two great rivers did not preclude what Braidwood calls the "interchange of both things and ideas" with neighboring areas. Although the yields of available archeological sites in southern Mesopotamia and Susiana (contiguous Iranian Khuzestan) reveal "curious differences" from their counterparts in Mesopotamia proper, the sites of the northern Iraqi piedmont and the hill flanks of the Iranian Zagros do reveal archeological traces from Ubaidian times on "of a generalized commonalty of understandings and traditions." [19] The riverine core of the alluvial southland had already become a focus of areal inter-action and, certain regional differences notwithstanding, manifested a characteristic interregional distribution of artifacts and art forms comparable to that noted by Willey for Preclassic Mesoamerica and Peru.

The conclusion or protohypothesis toward which these comparisons point may now be stated in brief and oversimplified form. Whether from indigenous forerunners or external contacts, *primordial urbanization most likely emerged in areas that contained diverse but closely juxtaposed subenvironments or cultures which, through social interaction, were symbiotically exploited.*

Where traces of incipient urban organization are not found, it may be hypothesized that intra-areal stimulus was lacking. Explanations may then be sought in the character of physical and/or social environments. Areas of intense aridity, cold, or other climatic extreme would not be likely to provide a suitable milieu for sedentary cultivation and food production in the first place. Where rainfall, drainage, soils, and temperature were not prohibitive, Braidwood and Willey suggest that the condition of sufficiently articulated subenvironments might not be met. Certainly, vast reaches of jungle, forest, savannah, or steppe, although not so inhospitable to human population or techno-logical adaptation as desert or tundra, would offer inadequate intra-areal variety of terrain and climate to afford sustained interaction and symbiotic specialization. Indeed, where grass- and woodlands offered extensive navigable water systems, as in northern Europe, southern Siberia, eastern North America, or tropical Amazonia, Africa, and Asia, the very facility and habit of migratory movement might have fostered a condition of "endemic warfare" among peoples of broadly similar culture and comparable strength. Such a "state of nature" might have involved "a drain on manpower, interests, and energies" that constituted "an effective deterrent to the development of civilization." The capital surplus was not dissipated, it was simply never achieved. Finally, the possibility of an abundant livelihood in fertile enclaves, isolated by desert or ocean, proffered an environ-ment "too favorable" to the persistence of inherited ways of food col-lecting to warrant sustained interaction and differentiation.[20]

The tendencies of primordial urbanization become definitive when relations among the partly differentiated subenvironments are *integrated* at an areal level. Symbiotic interaction has meanwhile evoked destabilizing experiences that raise the social horizons of village farming people above their existing bounds and afford intimations of a larger comity. Sooner or later repeated transactions in goods, persons, and ideas adumbrate and reinforce a pattern of reorganization within the area in question. Increasing contact and exchange articulate a pattern that leads eventually to a more formalized interdependence and *pari passu* an enlarged social product. Thus the projection of village farming life through differentiation results not simply in a larger village but in its virtual transformation; organization is compounded and the settlement at the node takes on the character of a "city."

The achievement of such "systemic" attributes as larger numbers, greater sustenance, and the sharing of artifacts and ideas, requires closer coordination of activities and hence the institution of more specialized control functions that can define new boundaries and heighten organization. By these means, the larger population acquires greater survival value for its members (the assurance of food, mates, and defense) and enhances its capacity for survival through division of labor and transitive ("more round about") methods of production. At the same time, the population reduces potential frictions among its members by establishing the claims of families or other primary groupings to territorial resources and by determining an order of priority among competing claims. These latter attributes of the new order are "political"; they imply the exercise of power by elements within the population and underline the crucial relationship between differentiation and stratification.

Although the differentiated parts of an urbanizing system are interdependent, some parts—to adapt George Orwell—are "more interdependent" than others. The subordination of some functions to others proceeds with reference to social controls that mediate vital relationships of a population to its environments, namely, the provision of *sustenance* and *security*. Under village organization, farming and fighting remained largely undifferentiated functions; division of labor was principally according to age and sex of population members. In the case of slaves, status was also involved. But in larger population areas under conditions of urbanization, functions are increasingly differentiated and the maintenance of systemic cohesion becomes the specialized task of governance. By virtue of their operations, control functions determine the conditions under which other more or less specialized functions are carried on; the latter "expect" control functions to assure them, directly or indirectly, whatever is necessary for their specialized role performance. The distribution of power is thus skewed with reference to certain *strategic* functions and the social structure of the urbanizing population is hierarchical.[21]

In the course of instituting this pattern of interdependence, the focus of energies and emotions becomes fixed. The outlying population orders its life and activities around the center which, in turn, encompasses the diversity of its bounded hinterland. Where the central focus of energies differs from that of the emotions, social cohesion may be harder to implement. Nevertheless, in the concentration of people and differentiated activities at a center, the primordial process of urbanization approaches its climax and the city has emerged on the historical scene.

The archeological record, of course, provides no warrant for such a nice formulation of urbanism. A social transformation of the sort just sketched is a hypothetical figment derived from the study of population in a framework of human ecology. Yet, in regard to organization, nothing essential to it is incompatible with evidence from the field.

Over long passages of time the village farming way of life stabilized itself internally and was reproduced across wide areas of Eurasia and Africa. A stable, year-round settlement of stone-using people with both plant and animal domesticates existed in east-central Mesopotamia at Jarmo during the first quarter of the seventh millennium B.C. Some twenty-five well-constructed rectilinear dwellings were present, although residents still obtained some part of their sustenance from collected foods; pottery did not appear until quite late in the phase. Amounts of obsidian at the site indicate far-ranging contacts, the closest natural source being in the vicinity of Lake Van in Anatolia. A few recent Carbon 14 determinations in the Jarmo area indicate the presence of still older settlements.[22]

A more spectacular, roughly contemporary settlement has been uncovered at the Jericho oasis in the Jordan valley. This "Jericho" had circular brick buildings and was circumscribed by a high thick wall, flanked on the inner side by a tall tower which contained an inner staircase. In important respects this settlement was developing along lines different from the Jarmo people; effective food production has not yet been ascertained at the site although domesticated wheats and barleys were prevalent at the time throughout "the hilly zone of the entire Middle East." One distinguished authority, Jean Perrot, appears convinced that there is no firm evidence of primary food production on the Mediterranean littoral much before the close of the fifth millennium.[23] On the other hand, village farming settlements were fully matured across the interior of Southwest Asia by the middle of the sixth millennium B.C.

In the course of the next thousand years certain of these agricultural villages on the alluvial plain of southern Mesopotamia greatly increased in size and were decisively changed in structure. Their wheat, barley, and livestock were now supplemented by dates and fish; wood and reeds furnished construction materials in place of stone. Hard-fired clay was adapted for tools. These achievements culminated in organized city-states, such as Eridu and Ur, containing tens of thousands of inhabitants, elaborate religious, military, and political organization, social stratification, a scribal class, an advanced technology including metallurgy, and extensive trading contacts.

Definitive Urbanization: The Capacity for Nodal Organization

From an archeological standpoint, the quickening of definitive urbanization in several parts of the world is more evidently associated with spiritual nourishment than with gross physical subsistence. In a number of culture areas the key feature of the change is ideological and social rather than economic. In the Southwest Asian, the first phase is marked during the Ubaidian period, c. 4000 B.C., by a sequence of temple buildings at Eridu which are distinct from the free-standing shrines that are typical of village settlements to the north. By the close of this period, before 3000 B.C., walled city-states have emerged. In the ensuing Early Dynastic period, still larger cult chambers were surrounded by a complex of store houses, workshops, and other buildings, constituting perhaps the first "full" cities. From Protoliterate seals and stone carvings it is clear that an occupationally specialized priesthood had appeared and engaged in liturgical activities. From temple ration or "wage" lists, it is no less apparent that priests were also the "managers" of a redistributive type of social economy.[24]

The second phase in the transition was marked by the rise of monumental palaces and what appears, on the basis of later mythology, to have been an almost explicit political tradition. Further differentiation of power in the institution of dynastic rule and the paramountcy of the palace was associated with the accentuation of class differences, made strikingly evident in the contrast of simple and relatively uniform graves of the Ubaidian period and the lavishly ornamented and richly furnished tombs of royalty and other persons at Ur in the latter part of the Early Dynastic. During the first half of the third millennium B.C., kingship itself had taken on more of a hardened military aura, with specialized production of weapons, impressment of labor on defense works, and the maintenance of bodies of armed retainers.

The two phases of definitive urbanization in Mesopotamia were both the achievements of social organization. Technological, economic, even demographic features of the change seem dependent on patterns of organization: (1) religio-political, representing internal restraints, and (2) military-political, reflecting external constraints. To be sure, the appearance of cities on the alluvial plain also reflected the greater fertility and more diverse resource inventory of the riverine setting (at least until late in the third millennium) but by Ubaidian times, if not earlier, natural endowment was less the "gift" of nature than a function of human resourcefulness and adaptive behavior.[25] In short, Childe's celebrated "surplus," like the definitive city itself, was a societal product.

The techniques of husbandry themselves do not appear to have been greatly altered by the shift to the plain. Similarly, the incremental product was not inherent in the physical environment, nor even in the increased labor input required by rudimentary irrigation; it had to be realized and appropriated by social behavior. Hence the older view that both the achievement and the form of urban civilization in the oriental city-state were founded upon the establishment and maintenance of large-scale water works is neither necessary in ecological theory nor supported by the archeological record. A similar conclusion concerning irrigation also holds for Mesoamerica and the Indus valley.

The more elaborate hydraulic systems of remote antiquity postdate the achievement of definitive urbanization. Quite limited flood-control works sufficed in Ubaidian times to insure adequate springtime pasture along the meandering water courses. Large-scale irrigation systems were not forthcoming in the more urbanized parts of Sumer, says Robert M. Adams, until after "the process of political integration into territorial states was well under way." Farther north in Akkad, "the onset of large-scale irrigation occurred even later." But if controlled irrigation does not account for the origins of centralized bureaucracy, it is nonetheless related to agricultural advance, increasing stratification, and to hierarchical organization of the population along functional lines.[26]

The fuller exploitation of arable techniques and the integral husbanding of larger cattle herds under critical natural conditions imposed a more regularized sequence and synchronizing of seasonal tasks. A more certain conduct of the growing array of sustenance activities, carried on simultaneously and serially, required the introduction of a more specialized managerial component. Dependence of larger ruminants upon supplementary feeding during parched summers or after postharvest grazing, the wider use of the ox- or ass-drawn plow, alike prompted an extension of communal control. Meanwhile irrigation works on almost any scale involved differential access to tracts of most productive ("scarce") land and, in outcome, the institution of a new order of land management. Thus archeologists have noted the adoption of regular shaped fields and their subdivision into smaller, possibly family-sized, units displacing the earlier resort to shifting areas apportioned among extended kin groups.[27] In addition to the division of work space, some formal division of work-time (beyond the seasonal routines) would also be necessary in order to implement transitive input-output relations—among cultivators, herdsmen, sailors, fishermen, navvies, plowmakers, shipwrights, and so on—to the extent that functions were differentiated and returns to their performance varied. The organization of population in occupationally defined classes foreshadowed a new order of man management and, in the upshot, a new society.

The hub of the emerging order was evidently the "temple city." At some point, denizens of the temple came to mediate men's secular relations with the physical and social environment as well as their transcendental involvements in the cosmos. But whereas the association of nature and cosmos long antedated the first city-states, the validation of a social-territorial order by sacral authority would have marked a significant step toward a more *exclusive* definition of the population and its boundaries and hence toward closure of the system. The identification of ethos and order would have heightened the degree of working cohesion among the population and would have contributed to a necessary sense of "community" or psychological differentiation from others.[28] That the realization and appropriation of the "surplus" were functions that accrued to the priestcraft discloses the extent to which the temple was, already in Protoliterate times, the cynosure of deferential feeling and itself the source of true condescension. That the ramification of social controls was centered in the temple may also account for the rapid growth and diversification of the ceremonial node, although the exact moment and precise occasion for this unfolding have not yet been determined.

Much the same historical obscurity shrouds the emergence of specialized "kingship." It is only in the Mesopotamian Early Dynastic period (after 3000 B.C.) that monumental palaces and royal tombs appear in the archeological record—only a few centuries after the expansion of the temple complex. Whether this apparent articulation of political authority arose primarily from internal or external considerations cannot be ascertained but the weight of later mythologic tradition points to a general heightening of insecurity in the social environment and the profound impact of organization for war.[29] The construction of great walls and battlements by impressed labor, together with the maintenance of specialized armies, evidently involved a reallocation of the surplus among different parts of the population with increasing reference to key defense functions. Specialization of the political role away from the temple hierarchy did not diminish the priestly function but it did entail some restructuring of control and a more overt reliance on secular force.

The novel attribute of kingship as a form of political authority was its permanence; its special service was to ensure continuity. Whereas the improvisation of leadership by "representative" bodies in times of crisis may have sufficed to cope with internal upheaval or intermittent conflict with neighboring peoples, some continuing organization was necessary in periods of expansion or of prolonged assault by populations from outside the alluvial south. In such dire circumstances successful war leaders were able to transform their temporary office into a dynastic succession ruling over a number of cities: for example, the early kingdom of Kish in Akkad or the League of Kingir centered on Nippur. The resulting establishment was one in which the ceremonial association of the military and the religious endowed public authority with legitimacy. Needless to add, the unfolding of monarchical institutions involved an acceleration of social differences and greater social distance among the various parts of the population in the urbanized area. By the time this transformation to monarchy was complete the city-states and leagues were reaching out with their garrisons toward the north.[30] During the last quarter of the third millennium the Akkadian empire under Sargon and that of the Third Dynasty of Ur were attempts at areawide political systems.

During the early third millennium B.C. well over a dozen sizable population concentrations appeared on the semiarid alluvial plains of Sumer-Akkad. The three or four largest centers ranged from 12,000–24,000 inhabitants and the greatest of these was Ur. These concentrations—perhaps the first fruit of the urbanization process anywhere in the world—took the form of a closely built-up, heavily fortified nucleus surrounded by dependent estates and villages whose residents worked in the irrigated fields and outlying grazing lands. Some of these estates originated as land grants to royal officers and their management was in the hands of dependent clients after the older pattern of temple estates. The integral functions performed by the nucleus—chiefly provision of authority, security, and sustenance—served to integrate the system of interdependence among the differentiated parts of the population and its territory. The nodal "urban" component of the system often covered an area of more than 250 acres within the walls. At the close of the Early Dynastic period, *c.* 2400 B.C., Uruk, one of the very largest centers, enclosed an area in excess of 1100 acres containing up to 50,000 inhabitants.[31]

Definitive urbanization was achieved more or less independently between 4000 B.C. and A.D. 1000 in half a dozen widely separated areas in the Eastern and Western hemispheres.[32] The variety of cultural experiences already manifest in the primordial phase was carried over and intensified in the definitive historical achievements. The course of early urbanization outside southern Mesopotamia does not repeat the sequence, let alone the pattern, of ancient Sumer. Thus the archeotypological definition of "urban revolution" advanced by V. Gordon Childe, mostly in the light of Southwest Asian experience, does not bear much comparative archeological or historical analysis.

The size of excavated urban sites in southern Mesopotamia, for example, appears much larger than the typical center of ancient Egypt, at least down to the New Kingdom *c.* 1500 B.C. Differentiation in Egypt seems to have been integrated through a few comparatively small court centers of god-kings. In terms of area, population, and number, therefore, Nile valley centers differed from their roughly contemporary counterparts in the Tigris-Euphrates valleys. Rates and levels of urbanization were evidently lower in Egypt than in Mesopotamia because physical and social environments were probably less conducive to city building. The comparatively regular cycle of the Nile's flow greatly simplified the "problem" of water management and at the same time facilitated navigation and communications. This comparatively "effortless" unity of the lower Nile over five or six hundred miles of its course, together with relative isolation from other city-states and nomadic peoples, may help account for the different size and structural aspect of early Egyptian centers. Egypt had attained an almost legendary political-ecological unity at a very early date and may not have experienced a city-state phase comparable to Proto-literate and Early Dynastic Mesopotamia. The effect of this situation is underlined by the absence of massive fortifications of the kind enclosing Mesopotamian nodes, although in most other respects the availability of stone in the Nile valley made for a more impressive and enduring monumental architecture. Perhaps the most provocative formulation of this historical contrast is that of John A. Wilson when he affirms that "for three thousand years until the founding of Alex-andria, ancient Egypt was a major civilization without a single major city." [33]

This contrast between Egyptian and Mesopotamian nuclei persisted despite an interlude of intense cultural contact by land and sea c. 3000 B.C. Sumerian influence is detected in early Egyptian art forms, and cuneiform writing may well have accelerated or otherwise stimu-lated independent writing in Egypt, albeit along very different hiero-glyphic lines. The potter's wheel and techniques of mud brick con-struction may also have come into the Nile valley with the same provenance. Clearly, the mere fact of contact does not lead neces-sarily to the displacement of a native "lower" cultural form by an external "higher" form. The reception of particular elements—artifacts, techniques, or concepts—in no way reduces the indigenous character of the definitive urban achievement in an area. In one important respect, however, the experience of Egypt and Mesopotamia is alike: in both areas the vast majority of the populations remained resident in village agricultural settlements.

Diversity characterizes the end product of definitive urbanization in all its known contexts. The more complete the archeological records become, the harder it is to insist on any single set of sociological at-tributes or attendant conditions as definitive. Writing, for example, which many scholars deem necessary for communications and scien-tific progress and which Childe included among his criteria, did not exist in early cities of the Central Andes. It remained relatively crude even in the large Mesoamerican centers where certain lines of formal scientific calculation registered notable advance. Alpine copper mining villages, on the other hand, developed a sophisticated understanding of metallurgical chemistry without the achievement of writing. (Miners of the Urnen period, however, eventually did devise a system of rough signs.) In Mesoamerica, on the other hand, little general technological progress is noticeable either before or during the definitive urban phase. The Indus valley cities, which served as the controlling nuclei of a large political-economic symbiosis with subordinate farming pop-ulations, were likewise technologically undistinguished and do not seem to have realized the full potential of "bronze age" metallurgical and toolmaking techniques, nothwithstanding contacts with Sumer from c. 2500 B.C. Furthermore, neither Mesoamerican nor Indus valley settlements were enclosed by great defense works and, unlike Sumer, armaments and warlike motifs were absent from their high art styles. Both Mohenjo-daro and Harappa were laid out on a regular geo-metric or chessboard plan, with uniformly designed areas for granaries, workshops, and housing, quite unlike the irregularly patterned buildings and streets of Mesopotamian centers. Even the more formally built-up temple and palace precincts of Sumerian cities show little resemblance to the elevated citadels that loomed over the western edge of the Indus capitals.[34]

China, like the distant Americas, stands apart from the great arc of urbanization that reached from the lower Nile in the west across the Mesopotamian heartland to the Indus valley and Gangetic plain in the east. The agricultural development of third millennium China alone represented a distinctive combination of a grain culture from Southwest Asia with a rice culture derived from monsoon Asia. A garden husbandry of the hoe and spade variety, coupled with artificial irrigation and drainage, resulted in a pattern of agricultural settlement markedly different from the extensive arable cultivation of Southwest Asia. Nevertheless, the Yin Shang centers of the Huangho basin, in spite of their unusual plan, were definitive "bronze age" urban. The last and most eastern of their capitals toward the middle of the second millennium, Anyang, was laid out in a large rectangular pattern significantly reminiscent of a chariot encampment. Anyang took the form of an extensive grouping of almost contiguous handicraft-farming hamlets sharing a specialized ceremonial and administrative core, Hsiao-t'un. A comparable earlier Yin Shang settlement at Chengchow, also in northern Honan, centered on an earth-walled nucleus of somewhat smaller dimensions.

In view of the military prowess of its ruling charioteer aristocracy, it is surprising that military themes are not featured in the highly conventionalized Shang art. One explanation is that the forms of this work are derived perhaps from the still older wood carving traditions of preurban Lungshan or Yangshao levels. A peculiar feature of Yin Shang urbanization was its ideographic script, quite unlike the forms of writing that evolved in Sumer or Egypt. Another interesting point, in light of the dictum that Chinese civilization was spread by the plow and not by the sword, is the fact that plows have not been found in China before the fourth century B.C., or late in the Chou dynasty. If, nevertheless, the buffalo was domesticated and the wooden plow adapted to animal traction before the close of Yin Shang, the dependence of Chinese villagers and townsfolk on animal power or livestock products was always much less than in Southwest Asia, North Africa, or Europe.[35]

Thus definitive urbanization is neither a universal nor a uniform process of society. Where urban centers have emerged, they have not conformed to any one spatial or structural pattern. The great variety of urbanizing experiences underlines the fact that population concentration is everywhere an *adaptive* process. Each urban tradition, like each city, represents a continuing accommodation of general societal tendencies to particular sets of demographic and environmental exigencies. In this manner each takes on its "unique" identity. The study of definitive urbanization, therefore, leads not to some universal definition of "the city"—that is the lexicographer's problem —but rather to a closer analysis of the sequence of social interactions that gives rise to such variegated manifestations in time and space.

As the primordial tendencies to urbanization are reinforced by further interaction, some hitherto dispersed and relatively undifferentiated roles become more articulated. Functions mediating the fundamental relationships to nature and to social environment are most likely affected, in particular the integral functions having to do with transcendence and war. Ritual mediation with nature and other modes of collective self-consciousness help assure the production and distribution of the life-enhancing surplus. These habits of interaction stimulate still more complex symbolic and esthetic expressions which serve to heighten the territorial and cultural solidarity of the larger population-area. It is still a moot point whether the boundaries of nascent urban systems coincide with ethnolinguistic divisions; there is clear evidence that a common symbolic language may come to provide a matrix of given understandings even better than a vernacular spoken language. The controlling sanctions of religious ideology also have important political implications and there are doubtless other situations in which a political definition of consensus was as pronounced as the religious. As intercourse with external populations increases, and as extramural connections contribute to the surplus, specialized military and political functions loom larger on the scene. Palaces, storehouses, craft shops, residences, roadways, waterworks, citadels, and tombs proliferate in or about the temple precincts, and in some localities almost the entire agglomeration is circumvallated. Henceforward such definitively "urban" settlements constitute an additional and *alternative* form of collective adaptation, an innovation in ways of living.

This type of social artifact could eventually be transplanted outside its native riverine settings and rooted—with lower incidence to be sure—in areas watered exclusively by rainfall or nourished only by contact and communications. By means of appropriate technologies and complex organization, certain populations had developed collective capacities to build and maintain urban settlements in a wider range of physical and social environments.

Crystallization of the urban process took the form of the concentration of integral functions at a node. As a greater number and variety of differentiated units and parts became centered, the point of their concentration was endowed with sets of strategic functions and itself became a differentiated part. Its role can be characterized as a cumulative specialization in services essential to the maintenance of a larger whole. The city is, in this sense, *a multifaceted central place,* a focus of generalized nodality.

The notion that cities are not only apart from, but opposed to, the life and livelihood of the country is unfounded in ecological theory. At their most "unmutual," urban-rural relations are always reciprocal. When exploiting landlords raise rural rents or when terms of trade turn against farm produce, the urban-rural relation is still one of interdependence. Through performance of its nodal functions, the center gives definition and structure to outlying parts. Without focus and direction, sedentary life outside the city would stultify or relapse into folkish independence, a comparatively uniform order of subsistence unrelieved by the stimulus of difference.[36]

This is not to identify nodal relations exclusively with the city. A measure of nodality is implicit in most social organizations: in families, clans, villages, corporations, courts, armies, cults, and so on. Many interactions are ordered around nodes other than cities. Complex societies have maintained a certain focus and direction without benefit of a multifaceted central place. Religious emotions have centered on groves and shrines. Political power has radiated from a chieftain's encampment, an itinerant court, or a country manor. Military force can be exerted from such different headquarters as castles, stockades, or the inaccessible strongholds created by nature. The communications necessary to these and other activities may be transmitted or received through way stations, periodic fairs, breaks in transportation routes, or through chance meetings of strangers on main traveled roads. Indeed all interrelations may be viewed simply as networks of channels and nodes, and all societies as overlaid networks with varying potentials. The distinctive attribute of an urban center is its *general* nodality for some larger system; the crucial requisite is the accretion of several strategic functions, not the presence of any particular one.

As a form of collective adaptation, nevertheless, a city meets both universal human and parochial cultural needs. The biological side of human nature finds primary expression in the need for sustenance, the social in the need for order, and the cultural side in the need for communication. Already in the microcosm of the family, human beings meet further needs for reproduction and meaning. Variations on such universal themes, along with those of a cultural nature, can be found in larger communal systems from the local to the most general. In one sense a city is a model of the larger society projected on an interrupted scale: the relations of its components are well represented, even their shapes are preserved, but area has been drastically reduced. Not surprisingly, the node in some cultures is regarded as a paradigm of the universe, an *imago mundi*.[37] The degree of generality represented in a city, therefore, will vary with the properties of particular environments and cultures. Broadly speaking, the larger and more diverse the population area, the more ramiform and complex its integrating nodes. During the last century three or four great cities have come to be regarded as *Weltstädte;* over the millennia there have always been centers in one or another part of the world presuming to the title.

The Social-Structural Dimension: Classic and Industrial Urbanization

Thus far the concentration of integral functions has been treated as the spatial or *horizontal* differentiation of a center from its surrounding parts. A theoretical corollary and measurable concomitant of the same process, however, is the *vertical* or social-structural differentiation of a center. From the standpoint of social change, the vertical dimension is more likely to be decisive than the horizontal one, although the interrelation of the two is inextricably involved.

The evidence of archeology and the logic of human ecology both indicate that urbanization involves increasing vertical stratification, closely tied to controls over land use and raw material supplies. Somewhat paradoxically, however, this tendency leads to a growing "dominance" of nodal functions over those carried on in peripheral parts. The reciprocity of differentiated roles leads not to an equality of relationships, still less to a superordinate ranking of "producers" over mere "consumers," but to the dependence of all parties on the system and its integral hub. Dominance is an attribute of those specialized individuals or units which, formally or informally, determine the conditions under which other specialized individuals and units will perform.[38] It is a centripetal or centralizing restraint exerted by units which perform the strategic "systemic" functions.

The social consequences of vertical differentiation can scarcely be exaggerated. Awareness of the divergence of power and status inherent in relations of functional interdependence fosters a sense of affiliation or identification among individuals and units which are differentiated along similar lines. Theirs is the sustentive sense of "being in the same boat," of sharing an identity, of eating at the same table. Such feelings of solidarity are a powerful counterweight to the sense of dependence that individuals and units feel in regard to those with whom they are functionally interdependent. Individuals and units who relate by affiliation or identification constitute *categoric* groups composed of members who perform the same function, have similar occupations, or other attributes in common: for example, members of the same sex, age category, caste, or ethnic group. Sometimes the tie may be no more than a common enthusiasm or animus. Such commensal feelings, whether based on objective or subjective factors, are potentially a disruptive threat to the functional or *corporate* integration of the system. Much education is necessary to ensure the uninterrupted performance by members of categoric groups of their functional corporate roles. But where commensal interests and feelings are transient or can be successfully reconciled to the discharge of corporate functions, greater cohesion is woven into the social fabric.

Definitive urbanization was the organization and appropriation of an agricultural surplus. The capacity to realize and invest the net social saving was the primary achievement of the first cities; it involved prolonged and many-sided operations beyond the capabilities of other known forms of sedentary adaptation. Hamlets and villages could neither store nor protect a large and varied social product. Thus the realization and control of the saving—whether instituted by bureaucratic, military, commercial, or fiduciary means—became the strategic function that established the framework within which other routinized roles would be performed. Herein lies the explanation of why decisions emanating from the center had such a profound dominance over the population area as a whole. The integration of an urban system yields economies and diseconomies of scale; but, by the conventions of redistributive accounting, the same organization will determine which units and individuals receive the "benefits" and which bear the "costs."

Justified by the liturgical authority of priestcraft, enlarged and defended by the combative force of captains and kings, the mobilization of a net social product at the center constituted an unprecedented concentration of energy potential on a minute territorial base. This *implosion* of energies, to adopt Lewis Mumford's term, was henceforth subject only to the limits of control techniques, at the disposal of decision-making groups lodged in the node.[39] Their demands gradually shaped the composition of the social product and their purposes governed the allocation and utilization of the crucial net.

The tendency for innovations to occur in or, more likely, gravitate toward the city milieu is no less understandable. Innovations are cultural events but their application in everyday life is contingent on *social* selection and review. Command over social savings, therefore, made of the city a locus for innovation as well as the guardian of tradition. As the pool of the system's specialized skills and cultivated intelligence, as the depository of its surplus and the storehouse of knowledge, the node became the primary consumer of differentiated goods and services and, in this way, a creator of new values. Members of the city population could most readily appreciate the adaptive potential and dysfunctional possibilities of novelty in prospect. To the extent that a novelty augments the social product, by whatever custom of reckoning, an innovator's expectation to share in the fruit of his creativity could be with greatest certainty fulfilled. Yet once again there is no necessity about the propensity for innovation. The greater receptivity of the city is merely a heightened probability. In this regard there are striking differences among cities and among cultures.

There are differences within the universe of cities no less than among persons in a population. But, whereas an individual person is a physical organism made up of differentiated parts and interdependent members that have never had a truly independent existence, a population of "like" organisms, such as an army, a business, or a city, is composed of members that are independently mobile and generally replaceable. Hence any extended analogy between persons and organizations, their "biographies" and "personalities," is a literary convention, a metaphor. People are organisms and cities are organizations. The fact that organizations in operation present certain mechanistic or systemic aspects is again no reason for regarding an organization as a mere machine. Members of an organized population can be replaced by reproduction or adoption. An organization of organisms, in this sense, unlike the organisms themselves, has no inherent limit on its growth or longevity. When organized, such a population acquires the distinctive capacity for division of labor. Limits on the size, durability, and accomplishments of an organized population, therefore, are wholly circumstantial. The limits of an organized population, in short, are ecological.[40]

In much the same way and for many of the same reasons that individuals and families are organized into functional units, and units into populations of the kind called "cities," cities and their dependent settlements may be organized into larger aggregations—leagues, nations, empires, and so on. It is surely significant that there is no one category of a nonpolitical nature to apply to such larger populations. The term "economy," for example, refers to only one narrow aspect of their larger interaction. They might be called "systems of cities" provided it is understood that the systems include settlements other than urban nodes. The term "larger community" is also a possibility but resort to the word "community" heightens the ambiguity and almost begs the question. From the standpoint of human ecology, relations among the units of supra-urban systems, regardless of nomenclature, are broadly analogous to those outlined above for components of urban and sub-urban systems. For purposes of adaptation, the larger no less than the smaller systems require boundaries and integration and these are alike a function of control.

Boundaries for systems of cities may be organized in various ways but, historically, the most common line is the one drawn by an effective political authority. Although further transactions across intersystem lines are both possible and advantageous, they occur at the discretion of the political control.[41] Historically, a system of interdependence is often created by military conquest and whether the resulting symbiosis is productive or merely predatory will depend on the character and motivation of the conquerors. The force exerted from a capital may range from the most indirect and subtle persuasion to outright coercion. At one historical pole is the direct impingement of primate organization, at the other a more relaxed and round-about influence of centers and subcenters in hierarchical array.

By extension, the entire globe might be regarded as a supra-urban system. Yet no integral control has emerged to surmount the physical, commercial, cultural, psychological, not to mention political, frictions that impede world organization. Though natural world boundaries are given, integration even for such limited purposes as trade or communications has not gone far beyond the level of voluntary cooperation or the informal relations of market exchange. The world remains populated, therefore, by systems of cities aggregated as political power systems for intersystem dealings; commensalistic feelings prevail over corporate feelings or, in other words, a sense of global commensalism does not yet obtain. World population is organized as a congeries of part-systems, not as a system of parts. This does not preclude many productive interchanges for particular purposes but it rules out exchanges that could effectively reinforce corporate responses to a point where they would be transformed into a categoric identity. Perhaps modern communications which, in the form of "hot lines" and ICBM's, allow for spatial separation without loss of contact may at last furnish the technological capacities to motivate a process of primordial organization toward "world community."

Short of this consummation, definitive urbanization has taken the form of subglobal systems of cities. Each city comprises an historical cluster of more or less differentiated units integrated via transitive input-output relations with one another and units located elsewhere. Most centers, therefore, present a "mix" of activities and, in the course of urbanization, the mix will change. Although part of a functional mix may have relevance for the system as a whole, the larger part will probably be preoccupied by regional or wholly local concerns. Aside from the case of a mere dependent tributary, what one city has to traffic with another is contingent on specialization, the degree of which will turn on its capacity to maintain a comparative advantage over potentially alternative sites in production of some good or service in general demand.

Before the industrial revolution of the eighteenth century A.D. relatively few cities could achieve a site specialty beyond that which arose from some immediate natural endowment or topographical feature. Hence competition among cities within the same system was highly restricted. Occasionally some peripheral point, a treaty port or port of entry *vis-à-vis* other systems, might also achieve a certain site advantage. But the most ubiquitous form of specialization for a city was at all times in its historically definitive role as a *general central place*. The larger a system's population area, the more numerous the central places it would require. Only the largest, wealthiest, and most "central" agglomeration would normally serve the entire system with the whole range of highly specialized goods and services, whereas the least specialized items were available locally throughout the system on the basis of comparative accessibility or competition.

The incidence and organization of these low-order centers are broadly determined by their nodality for a complementary area whose bounds are set by the comparative accessibility of like centers offering similar goods and services. Theoretically, there will be a different boundary for each item offered but, historically, the convenience and economy of a single center in a locality rules out a multicentered provision of goods of the same low order. The principle of comparative accessibility also governs the arrangement of higher-order foci, except that the latter are "pulled" by major traffic flows toward the main lines of communications emanating from the center of highest accessibility. This ultimate focus is usually the center of politico-religious and secular administration, the integral node for the entire system; its complementary population area is broadly congruent with that of the system as a whole. Thus evolves the essentially symmetrical hierarchy of "classic" urban organization.[42] Such a symbiosis, even without benefit from industrialism, can enlarge the system product and thereby heighten the security of the whole.

The label "classic" adumbrates important structural features of nonindustrial urbanization. Under classic conditions, the process of population concentration produces a coherent patterning of settlements, the proportions and balance of which do not alter much over considerable periods of time. Classic components, moreover, exhibit comparatively stable relationships of interdependence in ascending order of nodality: hamlets, villages, towns, metropolis or capital. Such a pattern is doubly "classic" insofar as its principles of organization and resultant order endure in diverse situations without ever presenting a visible uniformity of style or outlook. Differences of environment and culture would appear, therefore, to have a profound bearing on the actual incidence and organization of classic centers in various parts of the world.

This notably "static" order of classic urban systems—from antiquity through the medieval efflorescences of China, Europe, and Africa into early modern times—was rooted in the constraints of a largely *undifferentiated* agrarian base. Apart from relatively minor flows of interregional trade and tribute, productive activity remained local and unspecialized. Under such conditions, most centrifugal movements of non-nomadic populations had to do with the extension of agrarian settlements and centripetal movements with their integration into an expanding system. Historic examples of these processes are: the development of intensive rice culture in the Yangtze valley and its integration, via canals and coastal waters, into the ancient north China system; the *Ostsiedlung* into the trans-Elbian lands under the Christian knights; the occupation and settlement of lands in the Americas by Europeans in the sixteenth and seventeenth centuries A.D. Increased exchanges among physically diverse regions had much the same effect on centripetal movement as the colonization of new land but in neither case would large numbers of people become urbanized.[43] An upward (or downward) shift of a few percentage points in the typically low levels of classic urbanization would, therefore, reflect a gain (or loss) of system nodality that is wholly disproportionate to the numbers of people actually moving into (or out of) cities. Such weak pulses work, nevertheless, as multipliers to component interactions that raise or lower the degree of articulation prevailing in a system and affect the size and composition of social product accordingly.

Returns to scale and low overhead are sharply reduced when, for reasons of inner dysfunction or exogenous pressure, a system experiences loss of contact among its components which costly bureaucratic or military adaptations are unable to restore. Under conditions of rising uncertainty, constituents are thrown back on their parochial resources and the system dissolves into lesser parts, characterized by lower nodality and smaller major centers. Similarly, reduction of exigent demands and recovery from paralysis enhances the potential for more specialized exchange and reintegration into larger systems. Whether this division of labor is implemented via autonomous ports and city-states or by the controlling hand of empire, neither the levels of urbanization nor the structural form of settlements will be significantly changed. Nor, it only remains to add, need the material consumption of the masses contribute much to the enlarged social product. Yet, for all the appearance of stasis, the rise and fall of nodality implicit in the neap tides of classic urbanization constitutes a useful indicator of secular movements in society and economy.

This is not to imply that industrial urbanization altogether lacks pattern and symmetries, only that balance and proportion are not the hallmarks of its style. During its rapid unfolding since the introduction of fuel-burning machines, industrial urbanization has revealed itself to be a cumulative process with rising incidence and more differentiated structures. It is an unstable process, moreover, which has constraints but no apparent limits—short of the entire population. The few large cities and scores of small towns have given way before an *incessant urbanization*, with not merely 10, 15, or even 20 per cent of population resident in cities but 50, 60, or 80 per cent and more in some instances. The singularity of the industrial-urban movement seems to reside in the following features:

1. that in this form urbanization had a critical role in sustaining both the economic and the population upsurge;
2. that in the more industrially advanced nations urban increase and population increase have become virtually coterminous;
3. that population increase and, more recently, urban increase have gathered momentum on a global scale. (See Table 3.)

The past two centuries have also witnessed the most massive and sustained growth in production of inanimate energy and in the productivity of resources supply. Unfortunately, the areas of most rapid population-urban increase and productivity of resources supply no longer coincide. But, meanwhile, a further point has emerged: throughout most of its six-thousand-year history, definitive urbanization pro-

TABLE 3.   SHARES OF REGIONAL POPULATIONS IN LARGE CITIES,
100,000 AND OVER, 1800–1960

1800		1850		1900		1950		1960	
Europe a	3.0	Europe	5.8	Oceania	21.7	Oceania	39.2	N. Amer.	60.2
WORLD	1.7	N. Amer.	5.5	N. Amer.	18.5	N. Amer.	29.0	Oceania	43.3
Asia	1.6	WORLD	2.3	Europe	14.5	Europe	21.1	Europe	33.0
Russia b	1.4	Russia	1.8	S. Amer.	5.7	U.S.S.R.	18.5	S. Amer.	24.1
S. Amer.c	0.4	Asia	1.7	WORLD	5.5	S. Amer.	16.5	U.S.S.R.	23.9
Africa	0.3	S. Amer.	1.5	Russia	4.2	WORLD	13.1	WORLD	20.1
N. Amer.d	...	Africa	0.2	Asia	2.1	Asia	7.5	Asia	12.3
Oceania e	...	Oceania	...	Africa	1.1	Africa	5.2	Africa	8.1

a Europe, excluding Russian Empire-U.S.S.R.
b Russian Empire-U.S.S.R.
c Western Hemisphere, excluding U.S.A. and Canada.
d Continental U.S.A. and Canada.
e Chiefly Australasia and Hawaiian Islands.
Sources: Retabulations and minor adjustments by author of Kingsley Davis and
Hilda Hertz Golden, see Table 1, and Homer Hoyt, Urban Land Institute–Technical Bulletin No. 43 (1962).

ceeded not in the swelling and apparently irreversible flood of the past
two centuries, but in an irregular *alternation* of advancing and reced-
ing tides extending over millennia.

Finally, location of functional units within a system—classic or
industrial—registers the balance of net advantage available to themselves and to the system. The striking of the balance turns on the
capacities of units—governmental and religious agencies, families,
enterprises, and so on—first to perceive and then to find their "optimal"
locus under conditions of performance laid down by system dominants.
There is little evidence before the sixteenth century A.D. to suggest,
the growth of medieval capitalism notwithstanding, that many units
were rational maximizing agencies in the strictly economic sense or
to indicate that location decisions were precisely governed by an
exact pricing calculus of "costs" and "benefits." Even in Europe dou-
ble-entry bookkeeping was not widely applied. Karl Polanyi has in-
sisted that no sets of institutional market behavior in a modern sense
existed anywhere much before 500 B.C.[44] Nonetheless, any persistent
effort to reduce frictions of distance, to maintain continuity of interactions, and to achieve an elemental social system, would tend to
produce a rough ordering of activities and units along the lines of
central-place hierarchy, even without the additional fillip of rational

price accounting. The fundamental distribution of populations in their environments is, we have argued, ecological, not economic. Hence the prevailing concentration or scatter of units and unit clusters, the character and degree of nodality, are closely affected by the available technology and organization.

More specifically, the patterning of cities and their systems is intimately bound up with technologies of transport and communications. To be sure, change may originate with any of the four major ecological variables, but their effects will always be registered in organization. Sooner or later, disturbances in the pattern are accommodated either by heightened nodality, relaxation, or breakdown. More extensive relations of interdependence, for example, may be instituted through chains of relatively autonomous intermediaries, feudal hierarchies, or corporate bureaucracies, to mention only the most common, and each of these modes is adaptable to a variety of tasks and conditions. Each, in turn, involves a different degree of dominance. But the progressive differentiation of communications and information processing from physical transport media in modern times has been crucial since it permits the organization of systems of increasing complexity and nodality.[45] Instant communication allows greater spatial separation without loss of contact. It thereby affords a reach of ubiquity to dominant centers and control functions which quite transcends older notions of physical accessibility. A system of cities may now be conceived as approximating a complex of well-defined networks integrated via nodes which have greater or lesser powers to interpose coded sets of "permits" or "denials." Through a feedback of experience the control codes are made subject to review and the system to renewal.

Conclusions

The historical incidence and organization of urbanization can be broadly understood in this framework of human ecological variables. Although there are doubtless other and more rewarding approaches to particular segments and fragments of urban history, the ecological framework promises to be a fruitful way of treating long-run phenomena of urbanization and social change. Its terms are applicable to both micro- and macro-problems. The study of urbanization as a societal process of population concentration, leaving the explanations for the numbers and sizes of cities to the interplay of technology and organization on particular environments, makes a more manageable problem of a highly complex and significant phenomenon in the history of society. Out of the changing relations of cities to their physical and social environments, to adapt Oscar Handlin's language, stem some of the central problems for a history of society:

1. the differential organization of social space,
2. the creation of a social order within a population,
3. the adjustment to a reorganization of social environment by the human personality.

If the historical study of cities is ever to surmount what Sylvia Thrupp calls its tendency to lean "either to extreme particularity of detail or to an unconvincing generality" (surely not a defect of urban history alone), it may be by exploring such "large questions of a common and comparative nature" within a framework of human ecology.[46]

A full historical study of urbanization that treats behavioral as well as structural and demographic aspects of the subject will certainly involve closer cooperation with specialists in many branches of social and behavioral science. The contributions of humanists and experts in the architectural and visual aspects of city life will furnish additional and indispensable perspectives on the field.[47] Historians are not likely to attain either the formal sophistication of economists and demographers in their more defined frames of inquiry or the universal style and relevance of philosophers and poets. Nevertheless, there will always be a story to tell and, in the last analysis, it will remain the high obligation of the historian, whether dealing with one city or many, to try to tell the story whole.

NOTES

1. The present chapter is part of a larger historical investigation of urbanization and industrial opportunity. It was supported in part by a grant from the Research Committee of the Graduate School, University of Wisconsin.

2. For a more extended discussion, see Eric E. Lampard, "Urbanization and Social Change: On Broadening the Scope and Relevance of Urban History," in Oscar Handlin and John Burchard (Eds.), *The Historian and the City* (Cambridge, Mass., 1963). This volume will be cited hereinafter as *HATC*.

3. This conception of urbanization was first advanced by Hope Tisdale, "The Process of Urbanization," *Social Forces*, 20 (1942), pp. 311–316. See also Eric E. Lampard, "American Historians and the Study of Urbanization," *American Historical Review*, 67 (1961), pp. 49–61.

4. Tisdale, *loc. cit., et passim.*

5. These four broad factors have been identified as "the ecological complex" by some writers in the field. For the first statement, see Otis Dudley

Duncan, "Population Distribution and Community Structure," *Cold Spring Harbor Symposia on Quantitative Biology*, 22 (1957), pp. 357–371. Another use may be found in Leo F. Schnore, "Social Morphology and Human Ecology," *American Journal of Sociology*, 63 (1958), pp. 620–634. For a perfunctory critique, see Sidney M. Willhelm, "The Concept of the 'Ecological Complex': A Critique," *American Journal of Economics and Sociology*, 23 (1964), pp. 241–248. Also, Leonard Reissman, *The Urban Process: Cities in Industrial Societies* (New York, 1964), pp. 111–121.

6. On human ecology today, see Otis Dudley Duncan, "Social Organization and the Ecosystem," in Robert E. L. Faris (Ed.), *Handbook of Modern Sociology* (Chicago, 1964), pp. 36–82. Also, P. B. Medawar, *The Future of Man* (New York, 1960).

7. The author acknowledges the suggestion of the term "classic" by his colleague Rondo Cameron. It is used here in the sense of pre- or nonindustrial urbanization.

8. Robert J. Braidwood and Gordon R. Willey (Eds.), *Courses Toward Urban Life: Archeological Considerations of Some Cultural Alternates* (Chicago, 1962), pp. vi–viii. This symposium volume cited hereinafter as *CTUL*. The section on primordial urbanization draws heavily on contributions and references in this volume. The present author must acknowledge at this point what will soon be apparent, the vice of trespassing outside his field of study. In extenuation, he can only say that (1) the intrinsic importance of the materials and methods of study have exercised an irresistible attraction, and (2) citations are given more as bibliographic references than as "authorities" for the views expressed herein. The author has also tried to preserve a distance from the substantive materials and issues; these are better left to the specialists.

9. R. J. Braidwood and Bruce Howe, "Southwestern Asia beyond the Lands of the Mediterranean Littoral," *CTUL*, pp. 134–140; G. R. Willey, "Mesoamerica," *ibid.*, pp. 91–94. But see A. J. Arkell, "Khartoum's Part in the Development of the Neolithic," *Kush*, 5 (1957), pp. 8–12.

10. Braidwood and Willey conclude that some 2750 years were required for effective food production to "move" the 2000 miles from Syro-Cilicia to the Rhine Delta (*c*. 7000–4250 B.C.) and roughly 2250 years to move the 2000 odd miles from the vicinity of present-day Mexico City to Pittsburgh, Pa. (*c*. 1500 B.C. to A.D. 700), *CTUL*, pp. 330–358. Also, Carl-Axel Moberg, "Northern Europe," *ibid.*, pp. 309–324; Joseph R. Caldwell, "Eastern North America," *ibid.*, pp. 288–307; A. P. Okladnikov, "The Temperate Zone of Continental Asia," *ibid.*, pp. 267–286.

11. Donald Collier, "The Central Andes," *CTUL*, 165–174; Irving Rouse, "The Intermediate Area, Amazonia, and the Caribbean Area," *ibid.*, pp. 34–57.

12. Rouse, *op. cit.*, pp. 56–57.

13. V. Gordon Childe, "The Urban Revolution," *Town Planning Review*, 21 (1950), pp. 3–17.

14. Willey, *op. cit.*, pp. 97–98. John A. Wilson, "Egypt through the New Kingdom: Civilization without Cities," in Carl H. Kraeling and R. M. Adams (Eds.), *City Invincible: Urbanization and Cultural Development in the Ancient Near East* (Chicago, 1960), pp. 124–136. Cited hereinafter as CI.

15. Robert M. Adams, "The Origin of Cities," *Scientific American* (September 1960).

16. R. A. Johnson et al., "Systems Theory and Management," *Management Science*, 10 (1964), pp. 367–384. Otis D. Duncan and Leo F. Schnore, "Cultural, Behavioral, and Ecological Perspectives in the Study of Social Organization," *American Journal of Sociology*, 65 (1959), pp. 139–146. Amos H. Hawley, *Human Ecology: A Theory of Community Structure* (New York, 1950), pp. 29–31.

17. Kwang-chih Chang, "China," *CTUL*, p. 190.

18. Braidwood and Willey, *op. cit.*, pp. 354–355, cite W. T. Sanders, unpublished doctoral dissertation, Harvard University, 1957.

19. *Ibid.*, pp. 355–356.

20. *Ibid.* Candidates for the "too favorable" environments are the relatively variegated areas of northwest Africa and California. Also, A. L. Kroeber, *Cultural and Natural Areas of Native North America* (University of California Publications in American Archeology and Ethnology, Vol. 38, 1939), pp. 148–149.

21. Terms used in this section have been freely adopted from the writings of Amos H. Hawley and Talcott Parsons.

22. Braidwood and Howe, *loc. cit.*

23. Jean Perrot, "Palestine–Syria–Cilicia," *CTUL*, pp. 147–162. Also, Kathleen M. Kenyon, "Some Observations on the Beginnings of Settlement in the Near East," *Journal of the Royal Anthropological Institute Great Britain and Ireland*, 89 (1959), pp. 35–43. W. F. Albright speaks of "hundreds, if not thousands, of such installations . . . from Pakistan to Thessaly" c. 7000–5000 B.C., *CI*, p. 72. He agrees with Braidwood that such primordial centers are not "urban."

24. Adams, "The Origin of Cities," *loc. cit.* Also, *idem*, "Early Civilizations, Subsistence and Environment," *CI*, pp. 269–292.

25. Adams, "The Origin of Cities," *loc. cit.* Also, *idem*, "Factors Influencing the Rise of Civilization in the Alluvium: Illustrated by Mesopotamia," *CI*, pp. 24–34. Thorkild Jacobsen, "Mesopotamia up to the Assyrian Period, Political Institutions, Literature, and Religion," *ibid.*, pp. 62–70.

26. Adams, "Factors Influencing the Rise of Civilization," *CI*, p. 27. Also, Braidwood and Willey, *loc. cit.*, pp. 357–358.

27. Adams, "Factors Influencing the Rise of Civilization," *CI*, pp. 28–30.

28. Adam Falkenstein, "La cité-temple sumérienne," *Journal of World History*, 1 (1954), pp. 784–814. Mircea Eliade, "Structures and Changes in the History of Religion," *CI*, pp. 351–356, speaks of the "solidarity between man and plant life." Jacobsen, "Mesopotamia up to the Assyrian Period," *ibid.*, p. 67, suggests that "only social differentiation—first makes possible some grasp of the distance, the *majestas*, of the divine."

29. Jacobsen, "Mesopotamia up to the Assyrian Period," *CI*, pp. 63–66. *Idem*, "Early Political Development in Mesopotamia," *Zeitschrift für Assyriologie*, 52 (1957). During the third millennium B.C. an alternative and, in some respects, inimical mode of collective adaptation formed upon the grasslands of central Asia: the nomadic encampment, based upon a complex of domesticated animals. For the impact of nomadic encroachments on the sedentary-agricultural, trading centers, see Stuart Piggott, "The Role

of the City in Ancient Civilizations," in R. M. Fisher (Ed.), *The Metropolis in Modern Life* (Garden City, N. Y., 1955), pp. 5–17.

30. *Ibid.* The monarch embodied in his person "a variety of functions, some old and some new." The King's monopoly of force made him judge and legislator; occasionally he played the role of "reformer" with the issuance of elaborate law codes. The palace eventually took charge of major irrigation works.

31. Adams, "Origin of Cities," *loc. cit.*, and Henri Frankfort, "Town Planning in Ancient Mesopotamia," *Town Planning Review*, 21 (1950), pp. 99–115. Also, Guillaume Cardascia, "Les Villes de Mésopotamie," *La Ville*, Part II, "Institutions économiques et sociales," pp. 51–61, *Recueils de la Société Jean Bodin*, 7 (1955). Cited hereinafter as *La V. II.*

32. Every continent achieved the level of primordial urbanization, with the apparent exception of Australasia.

33. Wilson, "Egypt through the New Kingdom," *CI*, pp. 124–135, indicates that the physical areas of Egypt's shifting capitals are not comparable, say, with Nippur or Babylon. Jacques Pirenne, "Les Villes dans l'Ancienne Egypte," *La V. II*, pp. 29–47, never questions the urbanity of Egyptian centers but agrees with Wilson on one major point, namely, that the autonomy and initiative of the towns was greater in periods of "feudal" or weak central government. It would be interesting to know how the structure of family life was affected in such periods: for example, did the position of women deteriorate?

34. Ignace J. Gelb, *CI*, p. 55, affirms that "writing is of such importance that civilization cannot exist without it and . . . that writing cannot exist except in a civilization." G. R. Willey, *CI*, p. 157, remains skeptical about writing in view of Maya achievement but he concedes that the Maya had "civilization without the formal container of the city." On the Urnen miners, see Richard Pittioni, "Southern Middle Europe and Southeastern Europe," *CTUL*, p. 224, which provides a trenchant examination of Childe's criteria of "urban culture." Sourindranath Roy, "The Social and Economical Problems of Urban India," *La V. II*, pp. 233–271.

35. Kwang-chih Chang, "China," *CTUL*, pp. 177–191. Also Cheng Te-k'un, *Archeology in China*, I: *Prehistoric China* (Cambridge, 1959); II: *Shang China* (Cambridge, 1960).

36. On the concept of the city in Mesopotamia, A. L. Oppenheim says: "the city is the institutionalization of the desire for continuity" and the city "was always accepted as the basic institution for civilized living," *CI*, pp. 79–81. More generally on the role of the city, see Gideon Sjoberg, *The Preindustrial City: Past and Present* (Glencoe, Ill., 1960), pp. 25–49.

37. Paul Wheatley, "What the Greatness of a City Is Said to Be," *Pacific Viewpoint*, 4 (1963), pp. 163–188. Also, Leonard Woolley, "The Urbanization of Society," *Journal of World History*, 4 (1957).

38. For a fuller explanation of terms such as *dominance, categoric* and *corporate* groups, see Amos H. Hawley, *Human Ecology, passim.*

39. Lewis Mumford, "The Natural History of Urbanization," *Man's Role in Changing the Face of the Earth* (Chicago, 1956), pp. 382–398. *Idem, The City in History, Its Origins, Its Transformations and Its Prospects* (New York, 1961), proclaims the ascendancy of structural organization over human requirements and leads Mumford to assert, in effect, the inhumanity of

all social systems. His viewpoint seems rooted in an as yet undemonstrated notion of the libidinal wholesomeness of preurban village life and the unhistorical notion that warfare is the invention of the city. Mumford's uncritical fondness for the *polis* and the medieval commune, along with his polemic against the "insensate" industrial city, give this more recent work the character of metahistory.

40. This conception of "population" follows that of A. H. Hawley, "Population and Social System: An Essay in Human Ecology," processed, n.d.

41. On the creation of effective social, economic, and political space, see John Friedmann, "Integration of the Social System: An Approach to the Study of Economic Growth," *Diogenes* (Spring 1961), pp. 75–97.

42. Eric E. Lampard, "The History of Cities in the Economically Advanced Areas," *Economic Development and Cultural Change*, 3 (1955), pp. 90–104. Also, Walter Christaller, "Die Hierarchie der Städte," Lund Studies in Geography, Ser. B, *Human Geography*, 24 (Lund, 1962), pp. 3–11.

43. Lao Kan, "Population and Geography in the Two Han Dynasties," and Chüan Han Sheng, "Production and Distribution of Rice in Southern Sung," *Chinese Social History, Translation of Select Studies*, by E. Tu Zen Sun and John De Francis (Washington, D. C., 1956), pp. 83–101, 222–232; Richard M. Morse, "Latin American Cities: Aspects of Function and Structure," *Comparative Studies in Society and History*, 4 (1962), pp. 473–493.

44. Karl Polanyi, "On the Comparative Treatment of Economic Institutions in Antiquity with Illustrations from Athens, Mycenae, and Alalakh," *CI*, pp. 329–350. Also, Polanyi et al., *Trade and Market in the Early Empires: Economies in History and Theory* (Glencoe, Ill., 1957).

45. Colin Cherry, *On Human Communication: A Review, A Survey, and A Criticism* (Cambridge, Mass., 1957), pp. 19–29. Also Richard L. Meier, *A Communications Theory of Urban Growth* (Cambridge, Mass., 1962). The conception of cities as "systems" is founded on the assumption of observable regularities in collective behavior. In isolation such a system will tend to its most probable state or equilibrium; deviations from regularity will be counteracted by "self-correcting" feedback and hence continuity of behavior restored. A somewhat more realistic model allows for cumulative change; in Maruyama's terms, for "morphogenesis" as well as "morphostasis." In this model, feedback may sometimes lead to the *amplification* of departures and hence progressive modification of behavior patterns: M. Maruyama, "The Second Cybernetics: Deviation Amplifying Mutual Causal Processes," *American Scientist*, 51 (1963), pp. 164–179.

46. Oscar Handlin, "The Modern City as a Field of Historical Study," *HATC*, p. 3; Sylvia Thrupp, "The Creativity of Cities," *Comparative Studies in Society and History*, 4 (1961), p. 53.

47. Asa Briggs, "Historians and the Study of Cities," George Judah Cohen Memorial Lecture, University of Sydney, 1960, pp. 3–24; Eino Jutikkala, "The Borderland: Urban History and Urban Sociology," *Scandinavian Economic History Review*, 4 (1958), pp. 191–195. Also introductory remarks by Werner Conze and Wolfgang Köllmann to the latter's *Sozialgeschichte der Stadt Barmen im neunzehnten Jahrhundert* (Tübingen, 1960), pp. v–xv.